IDAHO'S 200 Cities

The East

Learning about Idaho and each of its 200 incorporated cities –
Their Past – Their Present – and Their Future

Volume 3 of 3

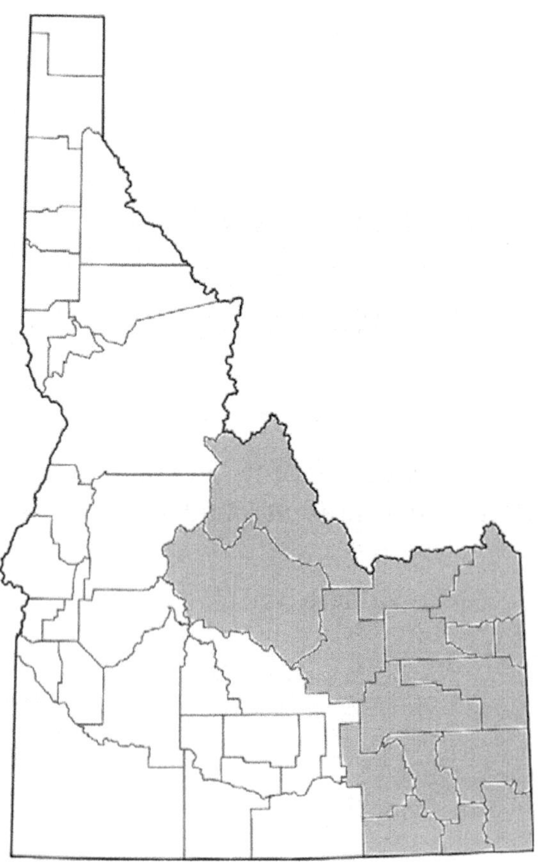

IDAHO'S 200 CITIES

The East

Volume 3 of 3

Their Past – Their Present
– and Their Future

Edited by Hal Bunderson

A Project of
The Association of Idaho Cities

Ridenbaugh Press
Carlton, Oregon
2017

IDAHO'S 200 CITIES: THE EAST

For more information, contact Ridenbaugh Press, P.O. Box 834, Carlton OR 97111.
Printed and bound in the United States of America.
First edition October 2017
10 9 8 7 6 5 4 3 2 1

Library of Congress Cataloging in Publication Data

Association of Idaho Cities.

History – Idaho – cities

Bibliography

1. History. 2. Idaho.

I. Association of Idaho Cities. II. Title.

ISBN-13 978-0-945648-43-7 (softbound)

For more information, or to order more copies of this book, contact:

Ridenbaugh Press
P.O. Box 834, Carlton OR 97111
Phone (503) 852-0010
www.ridenbaugh.com
stapilus@ridenbaugh.com

The Association of Idaho Cities has produced Idaho's 200 Cities for the three-fold purpose of:

- Fostering goodwill, knowledge and understanding of each of Idaho's three Regions and 200 Incorporated Cities
- Helping Idahoans, in fact and at heart, learn of our shared rich heritage
- Promoting economic development and strategic planning in Idaho and in each of its 200 incorporated cities and 44 counties

Proceeds from the sale of Idaho's 200 Cities will finance the not-for-profit purposes of The Association of Idaho Cities.

The Association of Idaho Cities thanks all of the volunteers and staff – too numerous to list – for their contributions to this work.

Table of Contents

Foreword

Idaho's 200 Cities is a six-volume book project that tells the story of Idaho through the history and development of its communities. Three of the books cover history and background about the three north, southwest and east regions of the state; three additional volumes consist of trivia questions and answers.

The project was conceived in 2004 by former Idaho State Senator Hal Bunderson of Meridian who served seven terms in the Idaho Senate and chaired the Senate Local Government & Taxation Committee. During his service in the Legislature, Bunderson was a passionate advocate for local government. He believed policymakers would benefit from a resource that would help them better understand Idaho's communities and their history, opportunities and challenges.

Bunderson presented his novel idea at an Association of Idaho Cities annual conference, generously offering to volunteer his time and expenses to complete this ambitious work if AIC and the cities would do their part. The conference delegates responded with a standing ovation, and the AIC Board unanimously approved the project. Bunderson's late wife, Mary Kay, joined him in his commitment. As Executive Director of AIC, I invited four experts to form a Blue-Ribbon panel of reviewers and editors to read each pre-final draft chapter approved by Senator Bunderson and offer comment:

- Bob Fick, longtime Associated Press Correspondent and Administrative Support Manager for the Idaho Department of Labor;
- Keith Petersen, formerly Idaho State Historian and Associate Director of the Idaho State Historical Society;
- Martin Peterson, former State Budget Director, Executive Director of the Association of Idaho Cities, and Special Assistant to the President of the University of Idaho; and
- Dr. James Weatherby, former Executive Director of the Association of Idaho Cities and Director of the Public Policy Center at Boise State University.

GayDawn Oyler, AIC Administrative Assistant, was designated to manage and control the work on each of the 203 chapters and trivia. In addition to her normal workload, she monitored and managed the progress on hundreds of draft manuscripts and communication between the cities and volunteers, and between Senator Bunderson and the Blue-Ribbon Panel.

As soon as the Board approved the project, Bunderson and AIC staff set about designing the book format and structure as a template for writing the city chapters. The Blue Ribbon Panel and the AIC Board approved the format. Mayors appointed city staff and citizens to help in providing original research and writing their city's chapter using the standard chapter format. Bunderson then led the effort of compiling, editing and writing where necessary, each of the city chapters. He also wrote the regional chapters and trivia books.

Over 100 people contributed several thousand hours of research, writing, proofing and editing for this project. AIC is grateful for the excellent work of these many volunteers. The purposes of this project are five-fold.

1. Promote Economic Development: The books provide valuable information for people considering moving their residence or business to or within Idaho. In a short period of time, people can learn the essential information about a city: its population, elevation, climate, geology, amenities and attractions, economy and major industries, education, health care, transportation, and utilities and services. They can also learn about the history of each city, including the pre-incorporation years, incorporation, turning points and Vision for 2050.

2. Support Long-Term Planning: AIC encourages long-range planning by cities with input from their business leaders and citizens. Over 70 percent of Idaho residents live in incorporated cities and the vast majority of Idaho's jobs and economic activity are located in cities. Idaho's wellbeing depends in large measure on the health and vitality of its cities, which is grounded in long term land use and strategic plans adopted at the local level.

3. Encourage Statewide Unity: Technology has revolutionized the way we live. The geographic, demographic and cultural barriers of the past are losing their significance. The diverse communities of Idaho have much more in common than many people realize. Understanding our shared histories and vision helps us recognize that life is better when we work together for the common good.

4. Education: These volumes are intended to provide a fun, easy way to learn highlights of Idaho history—the warts and the roses. The trivia may also be used to add interest to school history classes, as well as parties and family reunions.

5. Vision for the Future: These volumes offer a projection of what each city may look like in 2050. Going forward, it may assist city officials and candidates for public office with a better opportunity to contemplate, articulate and communicate their vision for their city or political jurisdiction.

While special care has been taken to ensure sound research and accuracy, there may still be errors. AIC invites public comment and additional trivia (with documentation) that may be considered for subsequent editions.

Proceeds from the sale of the books, net of production and publishing costs, will finance nonprofit purposes of the Association of Idaho Cities.

This book project is affectionately dedicated to Senator Hal Bunderson and his wife, Mary Kay. Senator Bunderson's dedicated service to the State of Idaho and its communities is best reflected in these words by Henry Wadsworth Longfellow:

"The heights by great men reached and kept
Were not attained by sudden flight,
But they, while their companions slept,
Were toiling upward in the night."

Ken Harward
AIC Executive Director (1998-2014)

Idaho's Cities: The Basics

Idaho's 200 cities display a wealth of diversity that reflects the social, economic, geographic and political diversity of our state. Despite these differences, Idaho cities have much in common. All look to the Idaho Constitution and state laws governing the creation, form, powers and limitations of city governments. Similarly, all municipal corporations, regardless of population size, operate under the same laws and are referred to as "cities."

About the Association of Idaho Cities

The Association of Idaho Cities (AIC) was founded in 1947 and is a nonpartisan, nonprofit corporation owned, organized and operated by Idaho's city governments. The association's mission is to promote excellence in, and advocate for, city governance, community leadership, and services to citizens to strengthen Idaho cities. AIC provides vital training, technical assistance and advocacy for Idaho's 200 incorporated cities. The organization is governed by a Board of Directors of city elected officials representing seven geographical districts.

Cities by the Numbers

- Idaho has 200 incorporated cities.
- Cities range in population from 218,281 in Boise to a low of 3 in Warm River, a tiny resort community in Fremont County (2016 U.S. Census estimates).
- There are 1,084 elected city mayors and councilors serving their communities.
- 70% of Idahoans choose to live within cities, a percentage that has been steadily increasing over the years.
- To keep Idaho communities safe there are currently 1,300 police officers, 2,700 career fire fighters, and 7,300 volunteer fire fighters responding to emergency service calls.
- Cities are responsible for 2,600 centerline miles of streets and 267 bridges.
- Cities have invested $1 billion in wastewater treatment facilities and treat over 5.84 billion gallons of wastewater each year.
- Cities have invested $475 million in drinking water treatment and delivery facilities.
- Idaho public libraries have 4.3 million print materials in circulation and nearly 1,600 public access Internet terminals.
- Idaho cities have invested $40 million in swimming pools, $90 million in parks and playground equipment, and $35 million in ballparks, tennis courts and skate parks.
- There are over 5,000 acres of city parks and open space, and over 150 miles of developed greenbelts and pathways.

Pre-Statehood

Before Idaho achieved statehood in 1890, the Territorial Legislature granted city charters to three cities: Boise, Lewiston and Bellevue. These charters covered the form of government, powers and responsibilities, taxes and revenue, indebtedness, elections, and the city's ability to grow through annexation.

Lewiston and Boise abandoned their territorial charters in the 1960s when voters approved transitioning the cities to operate under state law.

Bellevue still retains its city charter, which has several distinctive elements relative to other Idaho cities. Members of the city governing body are called aldermen instead of councilors, and the mayor and aldermen are elected to two-year terms (elected officials in cities operating under state law generally serve four-year terms). The Legislature must approve any changes to Bellevue's charter.

Incorporation of New Cities

Any community with a population of 125 or more qualified electors can file a petition for incorporation with the County Commissioners in the County in which it is located. The petition must be signed by 60% of the qualified electors of the proposed city, and must include the name and boundaries of the proposed city. The County Commissioners then have guidelines to follow, including calculating the distance between the petitioning community and any other already incorporated cities in the area, before granting the incorporation request. If the request is granted, a copy of the Articles of Incorporation and the approval are filed with the Secretary of State's Office.

Classification of Cities, Recodification of the Municipal Code

Before 1967, Idaho law provided for three classifications of cities—first class cities, second class cities and villages—with the classifications based on population. Within these three classes of cities, the law provided for four different forms of government: mayor-council, council-manager, commission and village.

Cities in each class operated under different provisions of law concerning the structure, powers and duties of city government, and these laws were amended many times over several decades. The need to modernize and simplify municipal government laws led to a recodification of the municipal code, which was passed by the Idaho Legislature in 1967.

Under the new municipal code, all city classes were abolished and the forms of government were reduced to two: the mayor-council and council-manager. All cities, from the largest in population to the smallest, would operate under the same laws and be called "cities," (except for charter cities). The recodified municipal code was much more streamlined, considerably shorter in length and easier for people to understand.

Forms of City Government

The mayor-council form of government is established by Idaho law as the default form of city government, with a mayor and either four or six councilors. The term of office for mayors and councilors is normally four-years; however, there are occasionally two-year council terms that occur when a vacancy arises in the first two years of the four-year term.

Elections for city mayors and councilors are held in November of odd-numbered years.

At local option, cities may adopt the council-manager form of government, with a five or seven-member council and a professional city manager serving at the pleasure of the council. Currently, only the cities of Lewiston, McCall and Twin Falls operate under the council-manager form of city government.

In council-manager cities, the mayor is selected by the council from among its members at the first meeting in January following a general city election for a two-year term. The mayor's primary role is in chairing council meetings, and the mayor is entitled to vote on all matters before the council, but exercises no tie-breaking or veto power.

The city manager is responsible for overseeing the administration of the city, ensuring that city laws and policies are faithfully executed, appointing department heads, advising the council of the city's financial condition, preparing and submitting a tentative budget for the upcoming fiscal year, and other duties as prescribed by the council.

Roles and Responsibilities

In cities operating under the mayor-council form of government, the mayor is the chief executive and administrative official of the city and has the following powers and responsibilities:

- Breaking tie votes of the council;
- Serving as the presiding officer at council meetings;
- May veto ordinances passed by the council, subject to council override by a majority of the full council;
- Ensuring that city and state laws are enforced;
- Supervising city employees; and
- Performing marriage ceremonies.

The city council is the legislative governing body for the city and has the following powers and responsibilities:

- Adopting local laws (ordinances),
- Determining what services will be provided by the city and the fees for these services,
- Adopting the city budget,
- Setting the city's property tax levy, and
- Receiving financial reports from the city treasurer.

Powers of City Government

Article XII, Section 1 of the Idaho Constitution charges the Idaho Legislature with responsibility to "provide by general laws for the incorporation, organization and classification of the cities and towns, in proportion to the population, which laws may be altered, amended, or repealed by the general laws."

Most of the laws governing cities are found in Title 50 of Idaho Code, titled

Municipal Corporations, which defines:

- Forms of city government;
- How to incorporate new cities and disincorporate cities that no longer need to function;
- The process for enlarging the city through annexing adjacent land;
- Roles and responsibilities of the mayor, council, and other city officials;
- How to pass local laws (ordinances);
- City budgeting and finances; and
- Use of urban renewal and tax increment financing to address urban blight and promote economic development.

Cities exercise two distinctly different types of powers: governmental powers and proprietary powers.

- **Governmental Powers:** The most prominent is the police power, which vests cities with authority to pass laws to protect the public health, safety and welfare, provided the laws do not conflict with state or federal law. The police power is derived from Article XII, Section 2 of the Idaho Constitution. Other governmental powers include the powers of taxation, eminent domain and annexation and are derived from laws enacted by the Idaho Legislature.
- **Proprietary Powers:** Cities are empowered to provide certain business-type services for the benefit of citizens and businesses in the city, such as water and sewer service, solid waste collection, street maintenance, parks, airports, etc. Cities derive their proprietary powers from laws enacted by the Idaho Legislature.

How Do Cities Relate to Other Units of Government?

In our federal system of government, the federal government is supreme and cities must comply with federal law and the United States Constitution.

The situation is similar at the state level: the Idaho Legislature and the Idaho Constitution is supreme to all local governments in Idaho and the Legislature exercises considerable control over local governments through policymaking.

Cities are unique among local governments because they are created by their citizens to provide needed services for the community, and cities exercise both governmental and proprietary powers.

In contrast, counties are created by the State of Idaho to perform a mix of state mandated and discretionary functions.

- Counties are empowered by Article XII, Section 2 of the Idaho Constitution to adopt ordinances to protect public health, safety and welfare. County ordinances only apply to the unincorporated territory of the county—cities have police power authority within city limits.
- Counties serve as an arm of the state in administering the property tax system, courts, law enforcement, jails, disaster planning and preparedness, and elections at the local level.
- Other state mandated county services include: indigent medical care,

public defenders for indigent criminal defendants, juvenile corrections, planning and zoning, roads and bridges, landfills, and weed control.

- County discretionary functions include: airports, ambulance service, hospitals, parks and recreation, fairs, agricultural extension, and historical societies and museums.

Special districts—highway, cemetery, water/sewer, recreation, library, etc.—are formed by citizen petition to provide necessary and desired services in a specific geographic area and have no regulatory authority.

Cities' Roles in Economic Development

Cities are the engine of Idaho's economy and city officials work in partnership with the Idaho Department of Commerce to attract and retain businesses. The infrastructure cities provide—water, sewer, streets, and stormwater drainage—is an essential factor for businesses deciding where to locate.

Over 40 Idaho communities have urban renewal agencies, which finance infrastructure to make sites ready for new businesses, as well as revitalize deteriorating downtown areas.

An urban renewal plan is adopted by the city council that identifies the work that needs to be done in an area and the funding sources that will pay for the projects. Most urban renewal projects are financed through tax increment financing, which dedicates property tax revenue from development within the area to urban renewal projects.

One of the most powerful economic development incentives in Idaho is the Tax Reimbursement Incentive (TRI), which offers a tax credit of up to 30% on income, payroll and sales taxes for up to 15 years. The incentive is available for a broad range of industries, including aerospace, agriculture, food processing and high-tech, and it is open to existing businesses looking to expand and businesses new to Idaho.

To be eligible for the incentive, the business must:

- Create at least 20 new jobs in rural areas, or at least 50 new jobs in urban areas;
- New jobs must be full-time (30 hours or more) and pay equal to or greater than the average county wage;
- The community must provide a meaningful match, which can be met through in-kind work done by city employees or through the capital investment property tax exemption;
- The company must prove its stability and a significant economic impact to the community and state; and
- The company must provide that the incentive is a critical factor in its decision to locate or expand.

Another economic development incentive often used with the TRI is the capital investment property tax exemption. Businesses that invest a certain amount in new non-retail commercial or industrial facilities can receive a full or partial exemption of property taxes on the new facility and equipment for up to five years. The county commissioners determine the minimum level of capital investment, which must be at least $500,000.

The TRI and capital investment property tax exemption have a proven track record of success in attracting and retaining businesses.

Amy's Kitchen, the nation's leading maker of organic and non-GMO convenience food, purchased the 500,000-square foot facility in Pocatello formerly operated by Heinz. Amy's currently employs approximately 400 employees. When the project is fully staffed over 15 years, the economic impact to the state of Idaho is expected to include new capital investment of $76 million, new total wages of $342 million and new direct state tax revenue of $30 million. Amy's Kitchen received a 26% TRI credit over 15 years and a 75% property tax exemption for capital investment over five years.

Quest Aircraft expanded its existing facility in Sandpoint, adding 75,000 square feet to its production facility that builds KODIAK turboprop airplanes for backcountry and personal use. By the end of the 12-year project term, it is anticipated that there will be 187 new jobs, capital investment of $5.4 million, project wages of $75.8 million and new direct state tax revenue of $4.5 million. Quest received a 25% TRI credit over 12 years. Quest was also granted a 75% property tax exemption for its investment in buildings and structural components, and its exemption for equipment and machinery was 100% in the first two years, 75% in the third year and 50% for the fourth and fifth years.

Cities' Responsibilities in Planning and Zoning

Idahoans are fortunate to enjoy a quality of life that is envied by the rest of the country. Each year, thousands of new residents come to Idaho seeking a new way of life. This growth enhances our economy through housing construction and enlarges the local tax base; however, it also results in increased citizen demands for services and infrastructure, and can lead to development that may threaten the qualities that make our communities so special.

The growth and development of our communities is guided by the planning and land use policies of city and county governments. Under the Idaho Local Land Use Planning Act, every city and county is required to adopt a comprehensive plan, a zoning ordinance, a subdivision ordinance and area of city impact ordinances. These policies are the essential tools for growth management, allowing local officials to direct future development and protect the unique features of their community.

- Comprehensive Plan: The foundational document used to guide the growth and development of a city or county. The planning process emphasizes citizen involvement and a careful study of the social, economic, and environmental characteristics of the planning area. The result is a document that represents the community's consensus about where residential, commercial, and industrial growth should occur; ensures that public services and infrastructure are developed in the most cost-efficient way; and protects quality of life for residents.
- Zoning Ordinance: Historically zoning was used to protect residential areas from incompatible industrial uses like rendering plants. Today, zoning is used to regulate development in floodplains and on hillsides,

conserve valuable agricultural land and open space, protect drinking water sources and preserve historic neighborhoods. Zoning exists to provide a regulatory framework to implement the vision defined in the comprehensive plan. The zoning ordinance consists of two main components: the zoning map and the text of the ordinance. The zoning map shows how the city or county is divided into zoning districts. The text of the ordinance defines the zoning districts, which generally fit within the broad categories of residential, commercial, industrial and agricultural, and defines the types of land uses that are permitted, conditionally permitted and prohibited in these districts. Each zoning district also has standards for lot size, lot coverage, building height, number of stories and setbacks.

- Subdivision Ordinance: The original purpose of subdivision regulations was to provide a simple, secure method of conveying land by requiring property to be surveyed and mapped before the owner could divide and sell the land. While subdivision regulations continue to provide a secure method of conveying land, they also ensure that land is developed consistent with the comprehensive plan and that facilities and infrastructure are constructed to serve the new development that meet minimum standards of health and safety.
- Area of Impact Ordinance: The area of city impact is the region surrounding a city that will eventually develop and be annexed into the city. The area of city impact serves two main purposes: it defines the area for city growth and establishes the land use regulations governing the urban fringe area. The area of city impact is established by negotiation between city and county officials. These negotiations result in two ordinances: an ordinance establishing the area of city impact map; and an ordinance setting forth the comprehensive plan, zoning and subdivision regulations that will apply in the area of city impact (city, county or some combination of both). Both ordinances must be approved by the city council and the county commissioners.

The Region

This chapter profiles significant historical matters that either apply to Eastern Idaho as a whole, multiple cities within the region or conditions and events that influenced the character, culture and heritage of Idaho and the region.

Distinctive Geographic and Geological Features

Eastern Idaho has some of the most imposing and beautiful geographic and geological contrasts in the state and the nation.

The northwest part of the region – Custer and Lemhi Counties – has a combined land area of 5.2 million acres and a population of just 12,000. Salmon is the region's northernmost city. The Salmon River, the River of No Return – so called because early supply boats could only make one-way trips – flows through both counties.

The 425-mile-long Salmon River drops over 7,000 feet from its headwaters about 15 miles northwest of Sun Valley to its confluence with the Snake River, about 40 miles south of Lewiston. It is the longest free-flowing river in the contiguous United States. Lewiston, located 465 miles from the coast, is Idaho's seaport to the Pacific Ocean.

The Frank Church-River of No Return Wilderness is mostly in Northern Idaho but also comes into western Custer County. The Continental Divide and Montana form Lemhi County's eastern border. Idaho's tallest mountain, 12,662-foot Borah Peak, is about 30 miles southeast of Challis. The fabulous Sawtooth and White Cloud Mountain Ranges, the Sawtooth National Recreation Area and Redfish Lake are located in southwestern Custer County near Stanley.

Yellowstone National Park, which extends two miles into Idaho, and the Grand Targhee Mountains in Wyoming are in the region's northeastern corner.

West of Yellowstone is the forested Island Park Caldera, one of the largest calderas in the world. South of the caldera is the famous Henry's Fork of the Snake River trout fishery; the 11,000-acre Harriman State Park; the beautiful Mesa Falls; and the St. Anthony Sand Dunes, rising to 365 feet – a height greater than the dunes in Death Valley, California.

To the south is the Upper Snake River Plain, the eastern part of an ancient 400-mile-long and up to a 70-mile-wide depression shaped like a crescent. Cut by the river, the plain spans Southern Idaho from Wyoming to Oregon.

The Upper Snake River Plain covers several hundred thousand acres of fertile farmland, vast tracts of sagebrush-covered desert and ancient lava flows that include the Craters of the Moon National Monument and dormant volcano cone buttes that pierce the high-desert sky.

Most of the Snake River Plain lies atop the Snake River Aquifer – one of the largest aquifers in the world. Farmers and city officials have drilled hundreds of wells into the aquifer to irrigate farms and provide domestic water for cities. Most of the wells extend over 1,000 feet below the surface. (*See The Snake River and Snake River Aquifer below.*)

South of the Snake River Plain, the forested mountains and sagebrush-covered foothills of the Caribou-Targhee National Forest surround rural communities in fertile mountain valleys with streams, lakes and reservoirs.

The stunningly blue, six-mile-wide and 16-mile-long Bear Lake – half in Utah – is in the southeastern corner of the region near the city of St. Charles.

Seventeen miles west of Malad, just over the Pleasantview Hills, is the 47,000-acre Curlew National Grassland. Fifty miles further west in Southwestern Idaho is the City of Rocks National Reserve, the remains of a prehistoric batholith that eroded, leaving massive granite rock outcroppings that resemble cathedrals, towers, domes, walls and weird shapes that rise to 600 feet and was a rest stop for California Trail pioneers – a trail that began near Soda Springs in Eastern Idaho as it cut off from the Oregon Trail.

The geologic features that include prehistoric Lake Bonneville, the Snake River and Snake River Aquifer and the volcanic activity of millennia ago have shaped the development of both Eastern and Southwestern Idaho. In Northern Idaho, the prehistoric Lake Bonneville flood cut the Snake River Canyon gorge, which forms part of the border between Idaho and Oregon and Washington and extends through Hells Canyon – the deepest canyon in North America, at one point nearly 8,000 feet from the top to the river below – before reaching Lewiston.

Prehistoric Lake Bonneville. South of Downey is the geologically significant Red Rock Pass. For millennia, Lake Bonneville covered most of Southern Idaho, northern Utah and parts of Nevada. The lake had a similar surface area but was deeper than Lake Michigan. The Great Salt Lake and other low-lying lakes in Utah are remnants of this prehistoric freshwater lake.

The Red Rock Pass ridge formed a natural dam at the lake's lowest elevation. About 14,500 years ago, the lake overtopped the dam, eroding an outlet at Red Rock Pass that dropped Lake Bonneville around 300 feet to a new shoreline near Provo, Utah. The breach caused a one-time flood of immense proportions that reached a top speed of 60 miles per hour and lasted about eight weeks.

The floodwaters generally followed the natural drainage of the Snake River to the Columbia River and the Pacific Ocean. When the water reached Portneuf Narrows, 45 miles northwest of Red Rock Pass, geologists estimate the discharge at approximately 15,000 cubic feet per second, cresting through the geologically lower Portneuf Narrows – a few miles east of what is now Pocatello – at between 300 and 400 feet.

The flood tumbled house-size boulders for hundreds of miles, leaving massive deposits of sands, soils, rocks and gravel. The tall boulders of Massacre Rocks State Park near American Falls were deposits from this great flood. In the Hagerman Valley, about 150 miles downstream from Red Rock Pass, the flood left "melon gravel," boulders ranging in size from watermelons to a compact car.

It also cut deep gorges and canyons along the Snake River drainage. There are now several hydroelectric and irrigation storage dams on the river. However, Shoshone Falls near Twin Falls – sometimes called the Niagara Falls of the West –

and Hells Canyon, just west of Riggins in Northern Idaho and which is deeper than the Grand Canyon in Arizona, are examples of Snake River gorges that remain largely as they were following that great flood.

The Snake River and Snake River Aquifer. The Snake River is the lifeblood of the Eastern and Southwestern Idaho economies. The river originates near the Continental Divide in Yellowstone National Park in northwestern Wyoming. It enters Idaho about 60 miles southeast of Idaho Falls and runs 1,056 miles across southern Idaho and north to Lewiston where it flows another 150 miles west before joining the Columbia River near Kennewick, Washington. The Snake River falls from an elevation of 9,840 feet at its headwaters in Wyoming to 340 feet at its confluence with the Columbia River.

Boulders in Massacre Rocks State Park deposited by the Lake Bonneville flood 14,500 years ago.

The Snake River Plain encompasses 20,000 square miles – 12.8 million acres. The soil, not covered with prehistoric lava flows, is very fertile due to accumulations of volcanic dust, sand and clay particles deposited over millennia. When irrigation water is delivered to this high-desert land, it "blossoms." The volcanic soils and climate are ideal for producing Idaho's "Famous Potatoes" and many other field and row crops.

Deep below the plain is a huge aquifer of porous basalt rock. The Snake River and Aquifer irrigate about 3.8 million acres in Idaho. About two-thirds of this water comes directly from the river while the other third is pumped from the aquifer.

Twenty-five hydroelectric and irrigation storage dams cross the main stem of the Snake River, producing over 1,200 megawatts of electrical power annually.

One of these dams – Milner Dam in Southwestern Idaho between Burley and Twin Falls – often diverts substantially all of the water in the Snake River at that point for irrigation. Except for a small required minimum flow, the river nearly dries up. However, a few miles downriver, millions of gallons of cold crystal-clear water fed by the Snake River Aquifer burst from the eastern walls and springs in the narrow valley of the Snake River Canyon near Twin Falls and Hagerman, replenishing the river.

Many Idaho cities owe their origins and existences to the irrigation water and hydroelectric energy of the Snake River.

Craters of the Moon National Monument and Preserve. The 53,545-acre Craters of the Moon National Monument, 18 miles southwest of Arco, is part of the 750,000-acre Craters of the Moon National Monument and Preserve. Most of the preserve is in Southwestern Idaho.

The preserve includes the 60-mile-long and up to 5-mile-wide Great Rift National Natural Landmark. The rift is the site of over 60 lava flows, 25 cinder cones and eight eruptive vents, which produced the area's massive lava field. These eruptions included flows of molten rock, some erupting and oozing out from fractures in the earth's surface and flowing up to 45 miles from the vents.

The volcanic activity began over 15,000 years ago. The most recent eruption likely took place around 100 AD. Volcanic eruptions produced accumulations of dust, sand and clay particles that became the fertile soils of the Snake River Plain.

In 1924 President Calvin Coolidge created Craters of the Moon National Monument. The Great Rift became a national landmark in 1962. Because of the area's moon-like appearance, America's Apollo 14 moon astronauts – members of the third manned lunar landing mission charged with detailed exploration – trained on the lava beds on August 25, 1969, learning how to identify the type of high-value rock specimens they would later select to bring back from their walk on the moon.

Lewis and Clark

Meriwether Lewis and William Clark, leaders of a small military expedition named the Corps of Discovery, were the first non-Indians to enter what is now Idaho. President Thomas Jefferson and Congress authorized the expedition to map a route across the northern part of the nation's Louisiana Purchase and then west to the Pacific Ocean to find "the most direct and practicable water communication across this continent" and establish a U.S. presence on the land that, at the time, was also claimed by England. (*See Federal Lands – Private Ownership and Preservation Laws below.*)

They started from their base camp near the mouth of the Wood River in Illinois, located across the Missouri River from St. Louis, in May 1804. After traveling up the Missouri River for over a thousand miles, they spent their first winter near a Mandan Indian encampment in what is now North Dakota.

That spring the party divided. Lewis and Clark dispatched a few men to take their accumulated journals, maps, sketches and specimens of newly discovered plant, animal and bird life to President Jefferson.

The main party that moved west consisted of 33 people including Clark's black slave, York; the French interpreter, Charbonneau; his young Shoshone Indian wife, Sacajawea; and their infant son. Among other things, Lewis believed traveling with a woman and child would be an outward sign of their peaceful intentions.

The expedition first entered what is now Idaho from the east in August 1805, coming over Lemhi Pass about 20 miles southeast of what is now Salmon in Eastern Idaho. There they met a tribe of Shoshone Indians, coincidentally led by Sacajawea's brother Cameahwait.

Four years earlier, a Hidatsa Indian raiding party had kidnapped Sacajawea. Charbonneau won Sacajawea and another young girl gambling with members of the raiding party and took Sacajawea as his wife.

The meeting with her brother was a happy and emotional event for Sacajawea. Largely due to her influence, Lewis and Clark traded for horses, gained valuable information about the next phase of their journey and enlisted an Indian guide they named Old Toby.

They found there was no navigable stream over Idaho's mountains and the downstream Salmon River was impassable. Based on a reconnaissance expedition by Clark and Cameahwait's description of the country and river ahead, Lewis wrote, "vast mountains of rock eternally covered with snow ... Perpendicular and even jutting rocks so closely hemned (sic) in the river that there was no possibility of passing along the shore ... the whole surface of the river was beat into perfect foam as far as the eye could reach."

Old Toby said they could cross the mountains over a Nez Perce trail further north. He led the expedition more than 100 miles into what is now Montana and then along the eastern side of the Bitterroot Mountains before re-entering Idaho at Lolo Pass. (*See Northern Idaho, The Region, Lewis and Clark for a history of their Idaho crossings*.)

American Indians

Scholar Sven Liljeblad has estimated that when Lewis and Clark passed through Idaho in 1805, the numbers of American Indians living within the present boundaries of the state varied from 6,000 to 10,000. The Pend d'Oreille, or Kalispel, could have numbered about 300; the Coeur d'Alene 700; Kutenai 200 or more; and about 3,000 Nez Perce. These were distinct tribes that existed peacefully together. Liljeblad estimated that there were about 3,000 Shoshone-Bannock. Some Northern Piute could also have been living within the state's boundaries.

Statue of Sacajawea at the Sacajawea Cultural, Educational, and Interpretive Center in Salmon. Sculptor: Agnes Vincen "Rusty" Talbot. Photo courtesy of Cheryl Jones.

Eastern Idaho Tribes. Tribes of Shoshone, Bannock and Paiute Indians were the principal inhabitants of Eastern Idaho when the first trappers came into the region. The Nez Perce also came into the northern part of the region along with the Blackfoot who also came into the eastern part of the region as did the Gros Ventre for seasonal encampments.

The Indians rejected the United States government's claim to the land and resented the increasing numbers of trappers; gold prospectors; and wagon trains of Oregon, California and other pioneers coming into their historic hunting grounds and killing the wild game – a matter that provoked hostilities from both sides, often leading to deadly skirmishes. (*See Federal Lands – Private Ownership and Preservation Laws below*.)

The majority of the early settlers in Eastern Idaho were members of The Church of Jesus Christ of Latter-day Saints (Church) – also known as Mormons, Latter-day Saints or LDS. (*See Pioneer Settlements below*.)

Church leaders taught that it was better to feed the Indians than fight them and sought permission from Indian leaders before settling an area. However, as the settlements expanded many Indians were still resentful of the steady conversion of their ancestral lands into cultivated farms with herds of livestock grazing on the native grasses in competition with big game. Even though the Indians could receive food supplies at the settlements' central locations, relations between the settlers and the Indians were often tenuous and sometimes contentious.

The mid-1800s was characterized by harsh conflict between the federal government and the Indians. Federal treaties with the Indians were often broken promises. By 1878 overwhelming U.S. military force finally put down the last significant Indian resistance in Idaho Territory and forced survivors onto reservations.

Bear River Massacre. In the early 1860s a complex set of circumstances, prejudices and events occurring in the broader region would, on January 29, 1863, come to a head resulting in a terrible battle wherein the U.S. Army attacked a large band of Northern Shoshone Indians encamped several miles north of Franklin. Later called the Bear River Massacre, it was one of the bloodiest killings of Indians in U.S. history.

Problems had been brewing for decades as Western settlement – which included killing the wild animals; domestic livestock devouring the native grasses and plants on which the Indians depended for food, clothing and shelter; and converting the grasslands into farms – pushed the Indians out of their historic hunter/gatherer way of life. Utah Superintendent of Indian Affairs, James Duane Doty, the only Indian agent from "Fort Laramie to California," wrote to his superiors on July 30, 1862, "To say they are "destitute" but feeble describes their situation." He warned of all-out war by the Indians on travelers and settlers if Congress did not appropriate adequate funds to feed and clothe them to maintain their goodwill.

Bear River Massacre Monument, erected by the Daughters of the Utah Pioneers.

Doty recommended the Indians be placed on a reservation so that they could "cease to be beggars and could learn to be herdsmen," a dramatic cultural-changing prospect that was abhorrent to the traditionally nomadic bands of Indians.

At that time, settlers – members of the Church of Jesus Christ of Latter-day Saints – were expanding into Cache Valley. Church leader Brigham Young counseled that it was better to feed the Indians than fight them. Settlers generally sought to befriend the Indians and provide food and supplies when requested even when they had limited quantities for themselves. In 1860 Church leaders received approval from Shoshone tribal leader Chief Kettemere to establish settlements in the northern end of Cache Valley.

This policy of co-existence worked reasonably well for most of the Indians and settlers, but not all Indians agreed with Chief Kettemere. Already angry about the large numbers of prospectors and travelers coming into the region and ensuing conflicts, they took their resentment out on the settlers and continued to raid outlying farms and rustle livestock. The settlers formed local militias they called Minute Men that could come on short notice to protect against Indian raids.

In 1862 prospectors discovered gold at Grasshopper Creek in what is now western Montana. This was the beginnings of a gold rush that would bring many determined people onto the traditional lands of the Shoshone. The Oregon and California Trails, started in 1841, passed less than 50 miles north of Franklin through what are now Soda Springs and Lava Hot Springs.

Federal officials, embroiled in the Civil War, directed Colonel Patrick E. Connor to take his California Volunteers to establish a military fort in the Great Salt Lake Valley. His command included the territories of Utah and Nevada and Southern Idaho. The fort was to principally protect the overland mail, immigrants headed West, settlers and the ever increasing number of gold prospectors.

Dr. Brigham D. Madsen, in his book The Shoshoni Frontier and the Bear River Massacre, wrote that when Connor left California for Utah he had 850 men and "faced discipline (and desertion) problems within his command of freebooting Volunteers," who were soured by their orders to fight Indians as opposed to finding military glory in the war against the Confederate States.

By the time Conner had established Camp Douglas in the foothills overlooking Salt Lake City on October 20, 1862, his troops had already responded to Indian conflicts, including the death of about 12 immigrants on the Humboldt River – wherein they were under orders to "destroy every male Indian whom you encounter in the vicinity of the late massacre ... in no instance will you molest women and children." During that general time period, there were reports of several other immigrant killings in the region, including the August 1862 Indian attack on Oregon Trail immigrants at what is now Massacre Rocks State Park west of American Falls.

On January 6, 1863, a band of Indians attacked a small party of miners headed to Salt Lake City. They raided the wagons, drove off the livestock and killed one of the men. When one of the miners, William Bivens, arrived in Salt Lake City, he signed an affidavit before Chief Justice John F. Kenny describing the murder. Kenny issued a warrant for the arrest of Chiefs Bear Hunter, Sanpitch and Sagwitch – leaders of Northwestern Shoshone Indian bands – and ordered the territorial marshal to seek assistance from Connor in arresting the chiefs.

In January 1863 Conner received intelligence about the three chiefs' winter encampment on the Bear River several miles north of Franklin along with a report – a gross overstatement – of the number of warriors and their fortifications. In reality there were probably around 450 Indians in the village including less than 200 warriors. Chief Pocatello and members of his band had visited the camp earlier but left the previous day.

Conner was not interested in arresting the chiefs. He planned a full-scale attack and warned his troops against shooting women and children. Fearing the Indians would find out about his planned attack and escape, he announced his troops were going to escort wagon trains coming from Cache Valley. Leaving on January 22, a company of 69 infantry and 15 supply wagons that carried drivers and two howitzers would become stuck in the snow 6 miles from the battle and never be used, avoiding greater carnage. Two days later, Conner left with four cavalry companies – 220 men – often moving at night to avoid detection.

When the infantry and wagons entered Franklin at 5 p.m. on February 28, three Indians boys were in the town picking up nine bushels of wheat to take to their village, authorized by Church Bishop Preston Thomas. The settler helping them had only loaded six bushels on their pack horses when the boys saw the soldiers approaching. They quickly left without the remaining three bushels, acknowledging to the settler that there might be a fight. Chief Bear Hunter was also in Franklin trading for supplies. He saw the infantry, but since he did not see Conner and the four cavalry companies that arrived at midnight and did not know Conner's intent, he was apparently not alarmed.

As dawn broke on the morning of January 29, the Indians awoke to see the soldiers looking down on them from the bluffs. Relying on the natural protections of dense willow forests that would become the scene of hand-to-hand fighting where the soldier's pistols were a distinct advantage; up to 200-foot-high bluffs edging the floodplain; and fortifications they had made from willows, the chiefs rallied their warriors to defend the village.

Conner's first attack was repulsed with several soldiers killed. He then directed flanking maneuvers that allowed his men to overrun the outgunned Indians. Women and children were often killed or wounded in the crossfire. When the Indian women found the troops were not shooting at them, many stood up with their children and bravely walked out of the line of fire.

As the battle ended, some of the unscrupulous members of Connor's troops – technically following orders to not shoot women and children – went through the village killing the wounded and committing unspeakable atrocities.

When the carnage was over, and although reports vary significantly, Dr. Madsen concluded that around 250 Indians were killed, including women and children. Twenty-four soldiers lost their lives. About 160 women and children were spared, allowed to take food and trek north to find their people. Several Indian warriors, including Chief Sagwitch, escaped.

Franklin residents opened their homes to the wounded on both sides and to children orphaned or needing assistance. Two days later, the settlers assembled 18 horse-drawn sleds and transported the dead and wounded soldiers back to Camp Douglas. Conner was promoted to brigadier general.

The military named the conflict the "Battle of Bear River." Non-military historians call it the "Bear River Massacre."

The site, four miles north of Preston, is marked by a stone monument erected by the Daughters of Utah Pioneers. It was designated a National Historic Landmark in 1990. The Western Shoshone Indians acquired property at the site in 2008 and plan to build a memorial.

Fort Connor. In late 1863 General Connor established a military post at Soda Springs named Fort Connor. The fort only operated for about two years, but it was the location where certain bands of Shoshone Indians were compelled to sign a peace treaty. Around that time, Indians at Fort Bridger, Wyoming; Box Elder, Utah; and Fort Boise, Idaho, also signed peace treaties.

In 1868 the Shoshone and Bannock Indians signed the Fort Bridger Treaty which created the Fort Hall Indian Reservation. Under the terms of the treaty, the Shoshone-Bannock Indians agreed to live on the reservation, and the U.S. Government agreed to provide food and supplies to supplement the loss of their traditional hunter/gatherer food sources.

Most of the Indians affected by these treaties, as well as certain other Indians, were moved or given military escort, many under harsh conditions, to the Fort Hall Indian Reservation.

The Bannock War – 1878 – Idaho's Last Indian War. After the Indians moved to the Fort Hall Reservation, the federal government failed to provide the provisions promised in the treaties it had made with them. Needing food, the Indians continued their summer migrations into the Camas Prairie near what is now Fairfield to gather Camas Lilly bulbs for winter food storage and to hunt wild game.

However, cattlemen were already moving their herds to graze on the Camas Prairie. Some brought hogs that foraged for food, digging up the Camas bulbs with their snouts.

The Indians were incensed that the settlers were destroying their traditional food sources and the U.S. Government was not fulfilling its promises. In May 1878 about 200 Bannock warriors left the Fort Hall Reservation, attacked the settlers at Glenn's Ferry, skirmished with the miners at Silver City in Southwestern Idaho and continued on into Oregon, attacking white settlements, killing settlers, taking provisions and destroying property along the way.

Over the next 16 months, a voluntary militia and the U.S. Cavalry pursued the remainder of these and other Indians back into Idaho, concluding the campaign by capturing the remaining renegades who sought to join a Shoshone band called the Sheepeater in the Salmon River Mountains. Surviving Indians were escorted to designated reservations. Collectively termed the Bannock War, these conflicts were Idaho's last Indian war.

Lemhi Shoshone teepees, about 2 miles north of Salmon City. Courtesy Lemhi County Historical Museum.

Following the war, the defeated Shoshone-Bannock Indians ceded the southern part of the reservation to the federal government, including land as far south as McCammon.

Dawes Severalty Act. In an attempt to assimilate Indians into the white mainstream and open reservation land for settlement, Congress passed the General Allotment Act of 1887 or Dawes Severalty Act.

The act gave the head of each Indian family 160 acres, each single person over 18 years 80 acres and each orphaned child 40 acres. Any lands not allotted became "surplus" and were made available for non-Indian settlement.

Indians who did not want to farm could either sell or lease their land. This policy encouraged large-scale settlement by non-Indians on former reservation lands. This created checkerboard ownership throughout the nation's reservations.

At the signing of the Fort Bridger Treaty which created the Fort Hall Indian Reservation in 1868, the Fort Hall Reservation comprised 1.8 million acres. Within a few decades, subsequent federal actions, Indian land sales and the effects of the Dawes Severalty Act, the reservation had been reduced to 544,000 acres.

In 1934 Congress replaced the Dawes Severalty Act with the Indian Reorganization Act, which placed surplus land that had not been settled by non-Indians into tribal (reservation) trusts.

Today's Reservations. There is one Indian reservation in Eastern Idaho, one in Southwestern Idaho that extends into Nevada and two reservations and one tribal land grant in Northern Idaho. Each tribe now has or has planned gaming casinos and resorts on its reservation and is involved in natural resource conservation efforts and other economic development activities.

Most members of the Shoshone and Bannock Tribes live on Eastern Idaho's Fort Hall Indian Reservation near Pocatello. The 2000 U.S. Census reported 4,019 of the reservation residents were tribal members.

Other members of the Shoshone and Paiute Tribes live on the 289,820-acre Duck Valley Reservation in Southwestern Idaho. That reservation straddles the Idaho/Nevada border with about half of the reservation land in Owyhee County. Most of the reservation's Indian population of around 1,200 resides on the Nevada side of the line. The tribe recently advanced plans to build a casino in Nevada near the Idaho border.

The 2000 Census reported the Nez Perce population in Idaho of 1,962. Their reservation lies west and south of Lewiston and encompasses about 770,000 acres.

With a 2000 population of 858, the Coeur d'Alene Reservation lies south of the city of Coeur d'Alene and comprises about 345,000 acres.

The Kootenai Tribal land is near Bonners Ferry overlooking the Kootenai River. It comprises 12.5 acres provided to the tribe in a 1975 federal land grant settlement of a conflict – the tribe had declared a peaceful but highly publicized war against the United States seeking just compensation. The 2000 Census reported the reservation had a population of 110.

Early Trappers/Explorers

In 1810 Andrew Henry of the Missouri Fur Company led a beaver fur trapping expedition into Eastern Idaho. He built a fort of several log cabins near what is now St. Anthony on the west side of the Henry's Fork of the Snake River. He named the post Fort Henry and stayed the winter.

Even though trapping was excellent, Henry was unprepared for the harsh winter.

He stayed at the fort, but the big game animals his men relied on for food had migrated south to lower and warmer elevations. The next spring he and his starving men, who subsisted largely on beaver meat, abandoned the fort and returned to Missouri with 40 packs of beaver pelts.

In 1811 Wilson Price Hunt led an expedition of trappers working for John Astor's Pacific Fur Trading Company – 62 men, one woman and two children. French-Canadian members of Hunt's party are responsible for naming the Teton Mountain range "Trois Tetons," three teats. In October, the party stayed in the Fort Henry cabins before leaving their horses, a decision they would later regret, and setting off by canoe on the Snake River to find Fort Astoria on the Pacific coast at the mouth of the Columbia River.

Hunt's party ably navigated the Snake River through Eastern Idaho, but, when they got to Southwestern Idaho, they found the river too treacherous. They lost one of their men, some canoes and part of their equipment to the rapids and waterfalls. Scouting ahead and finding the river too treacherous to proceed by canoe, they stashed their gear and completed their expedition on foot. (*See Southwestern Idaho, The Region, Early Trappers/Explorers.*)

Pierre's Hole; Teton peaks in the background.

Over the next three decades, other trappers came into Eastern Idaho, but not without risk. In 1823 Finan McDonald was leading a Hudson's Bay Company expedition of 29 trappers through the Lemhi Valley when they were attacked by a band of about 75 Blackfoot warriors. The experienced trappers out maneuvered the Indians, killing or seriously wounding 68 while losing six men. For several years, this decisive battle had a limiting effect on further Indian conflicts.

In 1823 Antoine Godin's French fur traders came into the Lost River Country near Arco. They tried to follow a river, the Big Lost River, from the mountains across the desert to the Snake River. However, when the river reached the lava formations of the Snake River Plain and the Snake River Aquifer, it sank into oblivion. They named the stream the Lost River.

In 1824 Peter Skene Ogden, an employee of the Hudson's Bay Company, led a successful beaver trapping expedition to the Snake River country. During this trip, one of Ogden's French trappers named Portneuf lost his life to hostile Indians while working a tributary to the Snake River near what is now Pocatello. Ogden named the stream the Portneuf River after his departed colleague. The name survived and would also become the name of the river valley and eastern mountain range.

Around that time, fur-trading companies began the rendezvous system of trading, wherein they brought food, horses, guns, iron goods, trade beads, whiskey, tobacco and supplies to a prearranged location. Several hundred of the region's mountain men, trappers and Indians would converge at that location with their winter's harvest of furs and handiwork to trade.

One "rendezvous" location was in the Teton Basin near what is now Driggs at the western foot of the magnificent Teton Peaks. The traders named the location Pierre's Hole after "Old Pierre" Tevanitagon, an Iroquois Indian working for the Hudson's Bay Company.

The 1832 rendezvous turned deadly when about 100 departing fur trappers and some of their Indian allies encountered several hundred men, women and children of the Gros Ventre Tribe, sometimes known as Blackfoot. The Indians were traveling about eight miles south of Pierre's Hole near what is now Victor when two of the Indians traveling with the trappers killed a Gros Ventre chief, who had come to parley. A fierce battle ensued with many deaths on both sides. The battle ended when the Gros Ventre band escaped quietly into the night.

Two years later, Nathaniel Wyeth built a trading post on the east bank of the Snake River, now part of the Fort Hall Indian Reservation. He named the post Fort Hall after Henry Hall, the Bostonian who financed his enterprise. The British Hudson's Bay Company purchased the fort in 1838, operated it as a trading post and flew the Union Jack over the fort until the Treaty of 1846, when the U.S. and England fixed most of the dividing line between Canada and the U.S. at the 49th parallel. Three years later, the U.S. Army set up a military post near Fort Hall. Today, one of Pocatello's Ross Park amenities, next to the city zoo, is a replica of the original Fort Hall.

French emigrant Benjamin L.E. de Bonneville took leave from the army in 1830 to lead 110 men and 20 wagons West. For the next three years, he and his men trapped beaver along many of the rivers and streams of Eastern and Southwestern Idaho. The author, Washington Irving, made Bonneville famous with his 1837 book The Adventures of Captain Bonneville. Settlers later honored Bonneville by naming a county and a prehistoric inland lake after him. (*See Prehistoric Lake Bonneville above.*)

One of the last full-time trappers in the region was Richard "Beaver Dick" Leigh. His Indian wife and children died in 1876 from smallpox. Their graves are in Beaver Dick Park west of Rexburg.

Early Christian Missionaries

Several Christian missionaries of different denominations passed through but never stopped to establish missions in Eastern Idaho. Those that passed through were headed to Northern Idaho, Washington or Oregon.

In 1834 Methodist Missionaries Jason and Daniel Lee conducted a church service at Fort Hall – the first church service conducted in Idaho. They then traveled hundreds of miles northwest to the Willamette Valley, then part of the huge Northwest region that included what is now Idaho and was called Oregon Country.

Two years later, Presbyterian missionaries Henry H. and Elisa Spalding – who started a mission with the Nez Perce in Northern Idaho, now the Nez Perce

National Historical Park-Spalding Site – joined a party of trappers and passed through Soda Springs and Fort Hall.

In 1841 Roman Catholic missionary Father Pierre De Smet was a member of the first overland migration of Oregon Pioneers. The party passed through Fort Hall before part of the group turned southwest to California, and the rest of the party turned northwest to Oregon. De Smet was instrumental in establishing missions in the Northwest, including the Old Mission at Cataldo – the oldest standing building in Idaho, a National Historic Landmark and part of Idaho's Old Mission State Park. (*See Northern Idaho, The Region, Early Christian Missionaries.*)

The Church of Jesus Christ of Latter-day Saints established the only Christian mission in Eastern Idaho in May 1855 when Brigham Young, leader of the Church, asked 27 missionaries to build roads as they settled among the "buffalo-hunting Flathead, Bannack and Shoshone Indians." They were to befriend the Indians and teach them Christianity and the advantages of modern civilization including building permanent houses, growing crops and living peaceably. Within two years, the mission grew to about 100 settlers. (*See Pioneer Settlements below.*)

Young hoped that the missionaries would have stopped somewhere around what is now Blackfoot, where they would be closer to the main body of the Church. However, they traveled over 150 miles north of Blackfoot to about 20 miles southeast of what is now Salmon. There the Shoshone, Bannock and Nez Perce Indians had summer encampments to catch salmon during their annual spawning runs.

The missionaries approached the leaders of each band, explained their purpose and received permission to stay. However, unlike many missionaries who established their mission with a single tribe, these missionaries put themselves in the untenable position of befriending members of three tribes who distrusted and sometimes raided and fought each other.

The missionaries named their post "Fort Limhi" in honor of King Limhi, a prominent Book of Mormon figure. The name was later mispronounced and misspelled Lemhi. They built a fort and cabins, dug a well, diverted water for an irrigation system, plowed and leveled the ground and planted grain and other crops that they shared with the Indians of each tribe as they came to the fort seeking assistance.

The mission's future looked bright until December 1857 when jealousies and a complex set of motives and relationships between Indians, trappers and missionaries clashed. It started with the Bannocks and Shoshones rustling Nez Perce horses. The missionaries, unaware of the theft, gave food to the marauding Bannock and Shoshone Indians when they stopped at the fort.

Nez Perce warriors in pursuit of the horse thieves later stopped at the fort and received food and shelter for the night. The Bannocks and Shoshones wanted to raid the Nez Perce again. However, when they saw the missionaries befriending the Nez Perce, they accused the missionaries of favoritism and, over the next several days, rustled the missionaries' livestock – eventually stealing 235 head of cattle and killing two missionaries.

A few days later, Shoshone tribal leaders came to the fort seeking peace and eventually bringing back 36 head of cattle, asserting that the Bannocks had kept the rest.

However, it was too late. The missionaries had already sent word of the attacks to Brigham Young, who sent a large militia with wagons to close the mission and escort the missionaries and their families back to Utah. The departing missionaries donated the fort and a thousand bushels of wheat to Indian converts at the fort, many of whom wept to see the missionaries leave.

Despite the short tenure of Fort Limhi, the missionaries created a lasting legacy. The misspelled Lemhi became the name of a river, a valley, a county, a mountain range and the pass over the Continental Divide that Lewis and Clark crossed when they first entered Idaho. One Indian Tribe – the Agai-Dika – called themselves "Lemhi Shoshone" to differentiate themselves from the Shoshone at Fort Hall.

Oregon and California Trails

When Oregon and California immigrants began their treks West in 1841, their early route entered Eastern Idaho about 15 miles southeast of Montpelier and proceeded northwest to Soda Springs, then on to Fort Hall. The National Oregon-California Trail Center in Montpelier is an interpretative center located on the site of the original trail.

Soda Springs, named "Beer Springs" by early explorers because of its carbonated spring water that had the effervescence of beer, was a prominent layover for Oregon and California Trail pioneers. Today, the city of Soda Springs has parks that offer free-flowing fountains of artesian carbonated waters. The Soda Springs Oregon Trail Country Club has preserved the nearby trail's original wagon ruts.

Oregon Trail ruts near Soda Springs.

Fredrick W. Lander, using federal funds, blazed another trail in 1849 – the Lander Road-California Trail. This road went over South Pass, Wyoming; entered Idaho about 40 miles northeast of Montpelier; and proceeded almost due west to Fort Hall. This shorter route soon became preferred by most travelers. From Fort Hall, both the Oregon and California routes generally followed the south side of the Snake River into Southwestern Idaho to a point near Raft River where the trails divided. Those headed to California left the main trail and headed south to the City of Rocks in Southwestern Idaho and then continued southwest through Nevada to California.

Fort Hall was a welcomed supply station for Oregon and California Trail immigrants until 1849, when Benoni Hudspeth founded a California Trail cutoff starting near Soda Springs which proceeded southwest to the City of Rocks, reducing the trip by 25 miles. James F. Wilkens, an 1849 California Trail immigrant, gave the unusual geologic area its "City of Rocks" name and many of the over 200,000 travelers passing through between 1843 and 1869 left axel grease inscriptions that are still visible on the towering granite pillars. Wagon ruts and journal accounts also mark their passing through this stunningly unusual land.

The pioneers taking the Hudspeth Cutoff bypassed Fort Hall. They traveled over 30 miles to the south through what is now Lava Hot Springs where they enjoyed a refreshing washing and bathing stop at the hot mineral springs that Indians and many travelers believed had therapeutic attributes. By 1855 with traffic through Fort Hall largely drying up and the beaver trapped out, the fort closed. Fort Hall was designated a National Landmark on October 15, 1966.

Oregon-California Trail immigrants also passed through what is now Massacre Rocks State Park located west of American Falls. It is a 1,000-acre park bordering the Snake River whose principal features are numerous up to house-size smooth boulders that were rolled, polished and deposited 14,500 years ago during the Great Lake Bonneville Flood.

Oregon-California Trail immigrants marked their passage with axel grease on the boulders. The park is the site where five immigrants died in an Indian ambush on October 9, 1862. The next day, some of the survivors pursued the Indians, losing four more men in a brief battle. The number of Indian casualties is not known. (*See Distinctive Geographic and Geological Features, Prehistoric Lake Bonneville above.*)

Pioneer Settlements

Many pioneers traveled via covered wagon, such as the one to the left.

The early settlements of southern Idaho and northern Utah have several common roots. The first settlers in Utah and many of the first settlers in Eastern Idaho were members of The Church of Jesus Christ of Latter-day Saints – also known as Mormons, Latter-day Saints or LDS. The nickname “Mormons” stems from their belief that the Book of Mormon, Another Testament of Jesus Christ is a record of certain ancient inhabitants of the American continents and a canon of sacred scripture that is a companion to the Holy Bible and two other books that contain certain revelations, translations and narrations – The Doctrine and Covenants and The Pearl of Great Price. (*See Politics, Polygamy and Civil Rights below.*)

Many of the settlements initiated by Church leaders had a consistent grid pattern – 10-acre city blocks laid out on a north-south axis separated by 132-foot-wide streets. Irrigation water diverted from streams often flowed down small ditches that ran at the edge of the streets to provide irrigation water for residential gardens and orchards.

People began settling in Utah in 1847 when several thousand members of the Church, fleeing mob persecution in Illinois, formed wagon trains and handcart companies and traveled over what is called the Mormon Trail, headed to the Great Basin where they hoped to live in peace in a desert land that no one wanted. During the next several decades, these pioneers were joined by thousands more converts emigrating from Canada, Europe and the Eastern United States.

Church leaders directed many of these pioneers to settle in arable locations throughout the Great Basin, including Southern Idaho. In some cases, they called proven leaders – the Church operates with an unpaid lay ministry – from among the ranks of its local members to lead groups of immigrants to settle specified areas such as Bear Lake and the Upper Snake River Plain. On the other hand, other Idaho cities, such as Franklin in northern Cache Valley, developed by natural, self-directed migration to available land. (*See Federal Lands – Private Ownership and Preservation Laws below.*)

In the early "frontier" years with limited involvement from the territorial government and no municipal structure, it was convenient for the settlers to look to Church leaders to handle ecclesiastical matters as well as to play a role in meeting community, school and welfare needs. Church doctrine admonishes members to pay 10 percent of their increase to the Church. In early settlement years, tithing payments often took the form of goods and labor. The Church authorized a tithing house, a central bank for commodities to match donations with needs. Using an organized barter system, some families donated goods, and others provided labor on community projects and, in return, received credits toward withdrawal of food and goods from the tithing house. This barter system provided for the welfare of the poor and, along with general tithing labor, supported construction of needed community infrastructure.

Bear Lake. In 1862 Brigham Young sent a surveyor to explore the Bear Lake Valley for potential settlement. Upon receiving a favorable report, Young negotiated with the chiefs of local bands of Shoshone and Bannock Indians about settlement.

They agreed that Church immigrants could settle around the northern part of the lake but not the southern. The southern meadows were a traditional Shoshone gathering place.

On August 23, 1863, Young asked for an advance party of 50 men from Cache Valley to follow Charles C. Rich and build a wagon road across the mountains from Franklin to the valley on the northern end of Bear Lake, a distance of about 46 miles, building houses and animal shelters for those who would spend the winter. The following month, the advance party, along with settlers who would stay the winter, built 20 aspen-log cabins and animal shelters; harvested meadow hay as feed for their animals during the winter; and founded Paris, the first community in the valley.

The pioneers endured the first winter by producing the play William Tell with music provided by settlers who could play the violin. Some of the men donated one day in 10, tithing labor, to make a weekly trip to Cache Valley with the mail.

The following spring, 700 additional settlers joined the original pioneers with more to follow. Under Rich's direction, in addition to Paris, the settlers started several new communities including what are now the cities of Bloomington, Georgetown, Montpelier and St. Charles.

Upper Snake River Plain. Construction workers on the Utah and Northern Railway line from Utah to the Montana gold fields – prospectors first discovered gold in Montana in 1862 – returned to their Utah homes between 1879 and 1881. They gave glowing assessments of the settlement potential of the Upper Snake River Plain. (*See Mining, The Gold Road – Precursor to Settlement of Eastern Idaho below.*)

In 1882 Church leaders asked 54-year-old Thomas E. Ricks to be an ecclesiastical leader – bishop – of the settlers headed for the Rexburg area. Ricks, a Kentuckian, had joined the Church in 1844, crossed the Great Plains to Salt Lake City in 1848 and was a proven leader.

Ricks led a party of settlers to what is now the site of Rexburg in January 1883. The land, located between two large rivers with a smaller one close by, was ideal. Game was plentiful, the soil fertile, grass for their animals abundant and there was plenty of water for irrigation.

Two months later, Andrew S. Anderson, on assignment from Church leaders, arrived to survey the new town. The settlers first wanted to name their town "Ricksburg" after their leader. Perhaps due to Ricks' modesty, they agreed to name the town Rexburg on the assertion Rex was the German stem word for Ricks.

As settlers kept coming, the district under Ricks' ecclesiastical jurisdiction – called the Bannock Ward – spread across the Upper Snake River Plain with several new towns. Later, the railroad provided the basis for starting or expanding other towns. Bishop Ricks assisted people in the new communities in many ways – providing advice, building town sites, arranging for surveys, organizing settlers to build diversion dams and irrigation canals and establishing equitable water rights.

Church records listed 815 members living in the Bannock Ward by December 1883. A year later, the number had increased to 1,420. As the number of Bannock Ward members grew, Church leaders created additional wards (congregations) in each community and called lay bishops to preside over each. Most of these communities would later become incorporated cities. The geographical area of the Bannock Ward became a stake – the name given to a geographical area that includes several ward and branch congregations – with Ricks as stake president. This continued until the increased number of members and congregations warranted further division, creating additional stakes.

Cache Valley. Cache Valley, a 50-mile-long and up to 20-mile-wide mountain meadow, crosses the Idaho/Utah border with the northern third in Idaho. Settlement of the southern part of the Cache Valley – Utah Territory – generally began in 1850 and moved progressively north. Franklin, Idaho's oldest town, was founded in 1860. Many settlers thought they were still in Utah Territory until the federal government surveyed the 42nd parallel in 1872. (*See Idaho/Utah Boundary Resolution below.*)

Four years later, Ezra T. Benson, a member of the Church's Quorum of Twelve Apostles, directed a party of seven men to select and plat townsites north of Franklin. They established the towns of Clifton, Dayton, Oxford, Preston and Weston.

Fighting the Jackrabbit Menace. Farming during the early years had many perils. In addition to the vagaries of the weather and crop-eating insects, one of the most menacing was hordes of jackrabbits. These large hares lived in underground burrows and came out from the vast tracts of sagebrush-covered land by the thousands at night to feed on range grass and farm crops.

The jackrabbit populations tended to increase and subside in cycles lasting several years. Often when populations became excessive, the rabbits contracted tularemia and died off. Humans could also contract the dreaded disease from insect and tick bites or by handling the rabbits.

When the jackrabbit population surged, they threatened farmers and ranchers with economic ruin. The rabbits would devour both growing crops and stacked hay.

The settlers resorted to the best option they had – drives to capture and slaughter the jackrabbits. They built a series of two net-wire fence lines hundreds of yards long in the shape of "Vs" with pens where the fence lines converged. People would spread out across the mouth of the V and walk forward beating the sagebrush. Thousands of jackrabbits ran ahead into the fenced enclosures at the base of the V and were exterminated.

In the 1980s animal rights and other groups brought national media attention to the clubbing aspect of the drives with little consideration of rational suggestions of how Western farmers could better fight the jackrabbit menace. In recent decades, populations of the big hares have not increased to the epidemic proportions of the past.

Idaho Territory

One of the bills debated in Congress creating Idaho Territory had a provision, passed by the House of Representatives on February 12, 1863, that named the developing boomtown of Idaho City as the territorial capital. However, that bill failed, and on March 4, 1863, President Abraham Lincoln signed the Organic Act, creating the Idaho Territory and appointing William H. Wallace as territorial governor. The law left it up to the territorial governor to name the temporary capital and the Legislature to name the permanent capital city. (*See Territorial Capitals – Lewiston and Boise below.*)

At that time, the territory included all of what is now Idaho and western Montana and Wyoming and had four counties. The Legislature consisted of a seven-member "Council" and an 11-member House of Representatives. Indian reservations were treaty lands and not part of federal territory.

"One of the most intriguing mysteries of Idaho history is the origin and meaning of the name Idaho," wrote historian Merle W. Wells. It was one of the names the Pikes Peak miners suggested as the name of their new territory – eventually named Colorado – after they found Congress would reject their first choice of Jefferson because of its opposition to naming territories after former U.S. presidents.

Promoters of the new territory asserted that Idaho was an Indian name meaning Gem of the Mountains. The U.S. Senate Committee on Territories was favorably disposed toward naming the territory Idaho until they discovered that Idaho was not an Indian word. They then chose Colorado, the next prominent name under consideration.

However, the name "Idaho" did not lose its appeal and was used to name geographical locations in Colorado and the Northwest. When Idaho Territory was created in 1863, the name "Idaho" beat out "Montana" as the name of the new territory. Once named, leaders of the new Idaho Territory soon adopted the previously asserted meaning of the word, "Gem of the Mountains," as it ably described the state's physical beauty and mineralization and, later, applied the "Gem State" nickname. (*See Gem State below.*)

Territorial Capitals – Lewiston and Boise. Governor Wallace declared the boomtown of Lewiston as the temporary territorial capital and called the first legislative session to begin December 7, 1863. Lewiston was a fresh-water port that received steamers coming up the Snake River from the Columbia River and the Pacific Ocean and was the most accessible town in the territory. It was the trailhead for thousands of prospectors heading to the gold fields in Pierce, 75 miles east of Lewiston. (*See Northern Idaho, The Region, Gold Mining.*)

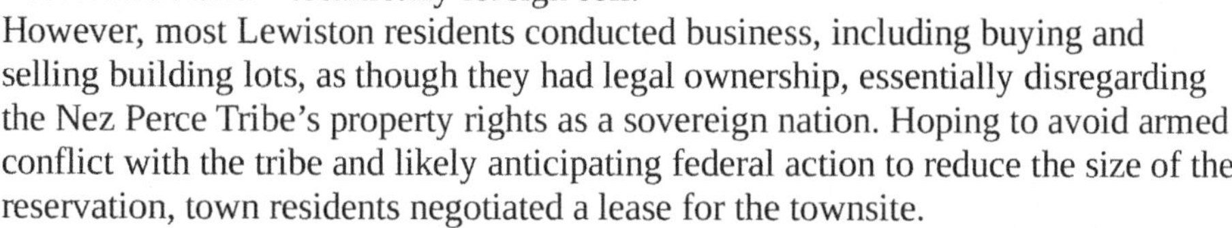

Before the session started, Wallace was elected as the territorial delegate to the U.S. Congress. He resigned as governor and on December 6, 1863, left for Washington, D.C., leaving Territorial Secretary William B. Daniels to serve as acting governor and to give the first governor's address to the Legislature. President Lincoln appointed Caleb Lyon as Wallace's successor. However, Lyon did not arrive until the next August.

Lewiston was legally on Nez Perce Reservation land – technically foreign soil. However, most Lewiston residents conducted business, including buying and selling building lots, as though they had legal ownership, essentially disregarding the Nez Perce Tribe's property rights as a sovereign nation. Hoping to avoid armed conflict with the tribe and likely anticipating federal action to reduce the size of the reservation, town residents negotiated a lease for the townsite.

On June 9, 1863, the Bureau of Indian Affairs reached an agreement with about half of the Nez Perce Nation to reduce the size of the reservation established under the Treaty of 1855. The Nez Perce bands that refused to sign the highly controversial treaty included those led by Chief Joseph's father and, later, Chief Joseph himself – an omission that would lead to war. (*See Northern Idaho, The Region, American Indians – Nez Perce War.*)

The 1863 treaty moved the reservation boundary to the east of Lewiston making the town legally part of Idaho Territory. However, Congress did not ratify the treaty until April 20, 1867, thus delaying the treaty's legal effective date. Most settlers disregarded that technicality and proceeded with their affairs as though the 1863 treaty was in effect.

By that time, the Pierce goldfields were playing out and most miners were moving to the gold discoveries in such places as Elk City, Florence and the Boise Basin. By the fall of 1863 Lewiston's population had declined to 414.

In contrast, the Boise Basin gold rush was reaching its peak. Over 16,000 prospectors, miners and settlers had converged on the basin and started several boomtowns. At that time, Boise Basin was second only to Portland as the most populous area in the Northwest. With political power shifting to the Boise Basin and the governor not yet in Lewiston, the 1863 Legislature deferred naming the permanent territorial capital until the next session.

The second session of the Territorial Legislature convened in Lewiston on November 14, 1864, and on December 7 passed landmark legislation, signed by Governor Lyon, that created Ada County and made the 17-month-old "Boise City" a charter city, the Ada County seat of government and Idaho's permanent territorial capital.

Even though the Legislature incorporated the town, Boise had no city government. The new law specified that for the incorporation to be final, the town's citizens had to approve the charter in a city election. Most Boise City residents felt the town had too much government oversight already – territory and county – and did not need any more.

Before the matter was resolved, it would take over three years and considerable effort including several elections; a new charter from the Legislature, January 11, 1866, which allowed appointment versus election of the first city officials; and the realization by community leaders that the owners of city lots could not get clear title to their property without a functioning city government. On November 18, 1867, pragmatic members of the community took charge and carried out the requirements of the 1866 charter by appointing Boise's first mayor and city council. (*See Southwestern Idaho, The Region, Idaho Territory, Territorial Capitals – Lewiston and Boise*.)

Loss of the territorial capital to Boise outraged the citizens of Lewiston and Northern Idaho who filed suit, alleging the law was invalid because the Legislature met six weeks before its official term of office began.

Lewiston Probate Judge John G. Berry sided with the plaintiffs and issued an injunction against moving the Great Territorial Seal of Idaho (Seal) and the territorial archives from Lewiston and summoned Governor Lyon to appear in court and answer the charges.

Under the guise of a duck hunting trip, Lyon crossed the river into Washington Territory where he could not be arrested and forced to appear in court. The sheriff carried out the balance of the court order by locking the Seal and archives in the Lewiston Jail.

In Lyon's absence, newly appointed Territorial Secretary Clinton DeWitt Smith became acting governor. On March 2, 1865, Smith requested the federal troops stationed nearby to retrieve the Seal and artifacts and rendezvous with him outside the city.

Six weeks later, Smith entered Boise with the Seal and archives. However, that did not end the dispute. Lewiston officials appealed the matter to the territorial district judge, who sustained the ruling of the lower court.

Smith appealed the case to the newly created Idaho Territorial Supreme Court in Boise. On June 14, 1866, the Supreme Court overturned the district court, in effect ruling that Boise was indeed Idaho's permanent territorial capital.

Fred T. Dubois.

Change in Idaho Territorial Boundaries, 1863 to 1890, Suffrage and Statehood. Between the time Congress made Idaho a territory in 1863 and a state in 1890, it modified Idaho's territorial boundaries three times. These changes reduced the size of Idaho to just over a fourth of its original size, from 325,000 square miles to 84,439 square miles of land and water area, about 54 million acres.

In 1887 Congress attempted to change Idaho's territorial boundaries a fourth time by approving a bill that split off the Panhandle from Idaho Territory, adding it to Washington Territory. At the same time, certain Nevada politicians had designs on making Southern Idaho part of Nevada. Citizens of Lewiston, chagrined about their loss of the territorial capital to Boise, greeted the news with a brass band and community celebration. Four days later, however, they learned that Idaho Territorial Governor Edward A. Stevenson and Congressional Delegate Fred T. Dubois had persuaded President Grover Cleveland to pocket-veto the bill. That veto put an end to further modification of Idaho's territorial boundaries. Idaho Territory was now ready to become a state.

Fred T. Dubois was one of Idaho's more colorful politicians. Illinois born, he came to Idaho Territory and served as U.S. Marshal from 1882 to 1886. He was an arch antagonist to any man that ran afoul of anti-polygamy laws. (*See Suffrage below.*) Leonard J. Arrington, in his *History of Idaho* wrote, " ... the Dubois juries convicted anyone on a polygamy charge, regardless of evidence."

Dubois was a highly regarded and gifted politician, representing Idaho for fifteen years in Washington, D.C. He is the only Idaho politician who has been elected to the U.S. Congress by two parties and served with three. He was elected as a Republican as Territorial Delegate from 1887 to 1890 and to the U.S. Senate from 1891 to 1897. He served for the Silver Republican Party in the U.S. Senate in 1901 – the Silver Republicans broke with the Republican Party which supported the Gold Standard. Before the year was out, Dubois announced he would complete the balance of his six-year term as a Democrat. Although he tried, he was not re-elected.

Governor Stevenson vetoed a bill making Eagle Rock – now Idaho Falls – the location for Idaho's land grant college in 1887. Two years later, in an attempt to appease the Northern Idaho faction, the 1889 Territorial Legislature passed the "olive branch" law locating the state's land grant college, now the University of Idaho, in Moscow. (*See Federal Lands – Private Ownership and Preservation Laws – 1862 Morrill Land Grant Law below.*)

Idaho's State Constitutional Convention convened on July 4, 1889. On November 5 of that year, 12,126 or 66 percent of the 18,408 citizens voting approved the constitution. The 1890 census reported Idaho's population at 88,548.

Because of Idaho's restrictive suffrage laws in effect at the time, only a minority of the adult population were allowed to vote. Although now repealed, Idaho territorial laws that carried over into statehood withheld the basic civil rights of voting, holding public office and serving on juries from people who, if their voice and vote were not silenced, could have changed the political landscape then dominated by elected officials of the Republican Party.

The largest body of adult citizens denied suffrage rights were women.

Suffrage rights were also denied to bigamists or polygamists, a felony, or essentially marriages marked by a formal ceremony and family structure and to monogamist men who were members of an organization that taught the acceptability of bigamy, polygamy and celestial (eternal) marriage as a doctrinal rite. The law included a required test oath to identify these men. However, the law did not extend to men involved in either informal co-habitation arrangements or extramarital affairs or multiple premarital relationships common in society – non-practicing monogamists.

Since most known or suspected polygamists and bigamists were either in prison, in court or had an arrest warrant issued because of their alleged felonious actions, they had, for all practical purposes, already lost their suffrage rights. Any additional laws denying those rights were redundant as it related to them.

Therefore, the primary objective of the law was to disenfranchise monogamous men who were members of an organization that taught the acceptability of bigamy, polygamy or celestial marriage. Under these provisions of the law, any suspected members of such an organization were, under penalty of perjury, required to take a complex test oath of over 200 words before they could exercise their civil rights. If they signed the test oath, they were essentially disavowing any relationship with the suspected organization and were allowed to vote. If they were subsequently found to be a member of the organization, they were subject to arrest and prison. Any suspected organization members who refused to sign the test oath were denied their suffrage rights.

While the law did not name the organization, the only known entity in Idaho that fit the definition of that law was The Church of Jesus Christ of Latter-day Saints. (*See Pioneer Settlements above.*) At that time, the Church approved of polygamy under limited conditions – as in ancient Israel – and taught that under certain circumstances the marriage covenant can be binding eternally (celestial marriage). Members of the faith comprised about a fourth of Idaho's population, of which only a small fraction practiced polygamy, but they were perceived by leading politicos to support the Democratic Party and vote as a block. Accordingly, Republican politicians crafted the law so as to disenfranchise this large block of voters – adult male Church members who did not practice polygamy and would not disavow their faith. (*See Politics, Polygamy and Civil Rights below.*)

In many local elections in southern Idaho, the test oath resulted in a huge shift of political power away from the majority to a minority of citizens with all the potential mischief such undemocratic actions could produce. (*See Eastern Idaho, The Region, Politics, Polygamy and Civil Rights.*)

Also denied suffrage rights were people of Mongolian descent, aimed at disenfranchising Idaho's Chinese populations; American Indians who had not renounced tribal affiliation; adults under guardianship; and felons.

In November 1896 Idaho voters amended the state constitution to give women the right to vote. Idaho was the fourth territory/state to do so – behind Wyoming, 1869; Utah, 1870; and Colorado, 1893. The federal anti-polygamy Edmunds-Tucker Act of 1887 overturned Utah Territory's 1870 women's suffrage law. It was reinstated in Utah's constitution when it became a state in January 1896. Today, Idaho adult suffrage restrictions apply only to felons.

U.S. President Benjamin Harrison signed legislation making Idaho the 43rd state on July 3, 1890.

Gem State. Idaho's "Gem State" designation is a carryover from Colorado and Idaho territorial days when the U.S. Congress erroneously believed the name "Idaho" was an Indian name – no tribal language was specified – meaning Gem of the Mountains. (*See Idaho Territory preamble above.*)

What they could not know at the time was that Idaho indeed had numerous and diverse deposits of gems as well as prodigious ore bodies of precious and industrial metals and minerals in each region of the state.

Idaho gems include the rare Star Garnet found only in Northern Idaho and India, which the Legislature named the state gemstone in 1967 – the most prominent Idaho deposit of the Star Garnet is at Emerald Creek Garnet Area, a Unique Natural Feature 10 miles north of Bovill. Other gems include the distinctive Spencer Opal semi-precious stone mined near the city of Spencer in Eastern Idaho and quartz, agate, jasper, garnet and geodes found in many locations throughout the state.

Spencer opal.

Today, there are numerous publications directing collectors and rockhounds to where they can find old and new mineral deposits and how to beautify the gems, stones and crystals they find. Thousands of hobbyists as well as professionals make beautiful jewelry and art objects using cut and/or polished Idaho rocks, gemstones and precious metals. Many of these pieces of art are displayed and sold at gem and county fairs held around Idaho and other states as well as in jewelry stores.

By whatever measure – from its diverse natural beauty to mineralization – Idaho is indeed worthy of its designation "Gem of the Mountains."

Federal Lands

Federal land ownership generally began between 1781 and 1802 when original colonies ceded their western lands between the Appalachian Mountains and the Mississippi River to the new national government.

During the 1800s as the nation moved West, it acquired practical ownership of land previously claimed by France, the 1803 Louisiana Purchase; England, the Treaty of 1846 (*see below*); Mexico, the Treaty of 1848 (see below); and Russia, the Alaska purchase in 1867. Hawaii was annexed into the U.S. as a territory in 1898.

In substantially all cases, Congress, backed by its modern Army, did as other nations and gave limited consideration to the land claims of the Indian tribes, implementing what many termed the nation's Manifest Destiny. The land that Congress did not purchase from the Indians they took by treaty, conquest or passed law that laid claim to the land – actions that the primarily nomadic hunter/gatherer Indians were ill-equipped to prevent.

The total land and water surface area of the U.S. now approaches 2.4 billion acres of which nearly 2 billion is in the 48 contiguous states, 0.4 billion in Alaska and 4 million acres comprising the Hawaiian Islands.

Eventually the federal government would transfer ownership of all but about 30 percent of the federal land preserve to private interests and the states. Today, most of the land under federal jurisdiction is in the 11 contiguous Western states and Alaska. About 64 percent of Idaho is federal land.

Congress transferred land ownership by passing numerous laws designed to encourage settlement, promote timber harvests and metals and minerals extraction and provide land grants to the states to help fund public education and certain infrastructure.

One of the first methods Congress used to dispose of the nation's land was payment of debts in lieu of cash to soldiers – Bounty Land Warrants – first issued to Revolutionary War soldiers and, later, to soldiers fighting in the War of 1812. However, the federal government's principal method of disposing of the property from the nation's land and mineral preserve was to use grants or sell at low prices to private parties including farmers, ranchers, railroad companies and miners.

The following is a summary of the more significant laws affecting transfer of federal lands to private and state ownership that may have affected Idaho as well as laws providing for federal management of the remaining land in the nation's preserve.

To encourage settlement and establish an American presence in the West, Congress passed the Preemption Act of 1841, which sanctioned squatters' rights and allowed a person to claim up to 160 acres – a quarter of a 640-acre section or one square mile – of unsurveyed federal land and later pay a small fee per acre to the federal government for clear title.

In 1843 non-Indian settlers in Oregon Country's Willamette Valley, mostly U.S. citizens, drafted a constitution for a provisional government that included a provision allowing settlers to claim up to 640 acres of land at no charge. Many of the early Oregon Trail immigrants who began their overland treks in 1841 were motivated by the prospect of this free land in the lush Willamette Valley.

The Treaty of 1846 with England established the boundary between the two countries at the 49th parallel. Congress created Oregon Territory, land between the 49th parallel on the north and the 42nd parallel on the south, on August 14, 1848. The new territory included what are now Oregon, Washington, Idaho and western Montana and Wyoming.

Mexico gave up its land claim south of the 42nd parallel when it lost the war with the U.S. and signed the February 2, 1848, Treaty of Guadalupe Hidalgo. (*See Idaho/Utah Boundary Resolution below.*)

Two years later Congress passed the Donation Land Claim Act of 1850, the forerunner to the Homestead Act. It nullified provisional land grants; created the Office of Surveyor General of Public Lands to provide deeds to property; and granted 320 acres to a white male, or a white male who was 50 percent Indian, over 18 years of age who had resided on the property on or before December 1, 1850, and, if married, an additional 320 acres deeded to his wife – essentially grandfathering many elements of the provisional government's law. Recipients had to improve the property and live on it for four consecutive years from the time they first settled. This law influenced many marriages.

Male claimants who located on property between December 1, 1850, and December 1, 1853, received 160 acres of land, 320 acres for married couples. In 1854 Congress extended the law for two more years. Thereafter, people could purchase up to 320 acres for $1.25 an acre. Subsequently the price was increased and the number of allowable acres decreased. Publication of these liberal land grant laws further spurred the flow of Oregon Trail immigrants crossing Southern Idaho, headed to the Willamette Valley and other locations throughout the West.

The Homestead Act of 1862 superseded the Donation Land Claim Act and provided transfer of 160 acres to a settler, conditional on them improving the property and living on the land for five years. This law was used extensively in Idaho.

Early settlers claimed water rights by diverting irrigation water under the "Doctrine of Prior Appropriation – first in time-first in right." Later, water rights were administered by the laws of each state as opposed to federal law. In Idaho, these laws were codified in Idaho's Constitution which was approved by the territorial voters on November 5, 1899.

The 1862 Morrill Land Grant Act provided state grants of 30,000 acres for each member of the state's Congressional delegation – Senate and House – for the purpose of providing a source of funds for a state college that taught agriculture, engineering and military tactics. The University of Idaho is Idaho's land grant "college."

The Pacific Railways Acts of 1862, 1863 and 1864 provided massive land grants, including mineral rights and issuance of government bonds to railroad companies to encourage them to build the first transcontinental railroad – which was completed at Promontory Summit, Utah, in 1869 – and many other railroad lines that would be built throughout the West. Many in Congress expected this land to be sold off in smaller parcels to promote agriculture, harvest of natural resources and building townships. This was done in many cases; however, railroads needing more cash to finance their enterprises sold much of their forested land grants in large blocks to lumber manufacturing companies and investors. (*See Forest Products below.*)

The General Mining Laws of 1866 and 1872 generally codified the self-rule methodologies prospectors and miners previously used to govern development of mining districts.

The Timber Culture Act of 1873 allowed homesteaders an additional 160 acres if they planted trees on 40 of those acres. The law's sponsors thought it would have the greatest use in the settlement of the Great Plains. The law had many problems, and Congress repealed it in 1891.

The Desert Land Act of 1877 generally granted farmers ownership of up to 640 acres of arid federal land if they brought it under cultivation and irrigation within three years. This law was of limited use in Northern Idaho but in the mid-twentieth century was actively used in the arid areas of Southern Idaho.

The Timber and Stone Act of 1878 – that was intended to facilitate logging and mining – allowed wooded and other lands unfit for farming to be sold in parcels of 160 acres for $2.50 per acre to those who certified they were buying the land for their own use. This law was principally used in Oregon, Washington, California and Nevada and was heavily abused. It had the practical effect of greatly expanding ownership of forested and mineral lands to large timber companies and syndicates who bought the land through nominal owners. It was repealed in 1891.

In 1905 Congress passed a livestock grazing law under which the federal government sold grazing permits on Forest Reserve land as a means of managing livestock access. In 1934 Congress passed the Taylor Grazing Act, further clarifying federal grazing law on all public lands. The 1976 Federal Land Policy Management Act and the 1978 Public Rangelands Improvement Act provided, among other things, that grazing fees were to be based on market values. Matters relating to livestock grazing on public lands continue to be controversial.

Concurrent with statehood in 1890 and under other federal laws, Idaho received federal grants of about 3.6 million acres to finance public education, the penitentiary and public buildings. Subsequent sales have reduced Idaho's Endowment Trust Lands to approximately 2.5 million surface acres and 3 million mineral acres – all managed by the Department of Lands with oversight from the State Board of Land Commissioners, a five-member board of state-wide elected officeholders chaired by the governor.

At the turn of the twentieth century, Congress passed two other laws that had limited use in Northern Idaho but played crucial roles in the reclamation of Southern Idaho's arid lands, turning sagebrush-covered deserts into agricultural oases – the Carey Act in 1894 and the Newlands Reclamation Act in 1902. In Idaho, the Carey Act had its greatest impact in the Magic Valley. The Reclamation Act that authorized creation of the U.S. Reclamation Service – now the Bureau of Reclamation – built irrigation storage, flood control and hydroelectric dams throughout Southern Idaho. (*See Southwestern Idaho, The Region, Agriculture and*

Irrigation and below.)

Generally starting with the federal land management laws – the Taylor Grazing Act of 1934 and the Federal Land Policy and Management Act in 1976 – the national policy of retaining ownership of the nation's remaining land preserve was established. Legal challenges by "state's rights" advocates seeking management or control of federal lands within a state's borders have proven unsuccessful. (*See Mining and Forest Products – Leading Causes for Loss of Economic Dominance below.*)

Agriculture and Irrigation

Up through most of the twentieth century, agriculture-based businesses have been the principal employers that underpinned Eastern Idaho's economy. Irrigation, agricultural research (University of Idaho), food processing plants and railroad transportation helped turn the region's early pioneer farms into some of the most productive in the state.

Lorenzo Firth homestead1894, Firth.

Most of the pioneers who settled the Upper Snake River Plain emigrated from Utah where they had firsthand knowledge of state-of-the-art irrigation practices developed over the previous three decades of settling the arid Intermountain West.

Upon arriving, pioneers almost immediately began to divert water from rivers and streams and build gravity-flow irrigation canals and ditches. Once they designed and surveyed the course of a canal, workers dug the water conveyances with picks, crowbars, shovels, occasional blasting powder and horse-drawn Fresno scrapers.

Generally, pioneers benefiting from a particular flow of irrigation water formed irrigation districts and worked together building diversion dams and digging and maintaining the irrigation canals and ditches delivering water to their fields.

The "Doctrine of Prior Appropriation, first in time-first in right," was the general basis for administering water rights in the territory for beneficial uses, sometimes called the "Colorado Doctrine." It was incorporated into Idaho's constitution.

In order to provide sustainable flows of irrigation water throughout the growing season, the Bureau of Reclamation later interceded to promote or build large dams and reservoirs, provide hydroelectric energy and integrate and improve existing irrigation canal systems. (*See Federal Lands – Private Ownership and Preservation Laws above.*)

Some of the greatest benefits of irrigation and research by the University of Idaho Department of Agriculture included greatly improved crop yield, rotation and diversification. Farmers were able to rotate fields of potatoes, sugar beets and corn that required more water with their standby crops of wheat, barley and hay. Some cities became inextricably linked to a particular farm crop. Sugar City was so named because of the sugar factory that once dominated its economy. Blackfoot is known as the "Potato Capitol of the World."

The desolate desert landscape around Basalt before irrigation.

After irrigation, agriculture flourished, a field near Rockland.

Carey Act Projects. Under the Carey Act, the federal government would cede each Western state up to one million acres of federal land that was brought under irrigation. Each state was required to create a regulatory commission, which in Idaho was the State Land Board. Under this law, private investors built the dams and canals, platted townsites and sold water rights. The state sold the land. The law allowed farmers to purchase parcels of up to 160 acres.

Between 1905 and 1914 Idaho completed 23 Carey Act projects that irrigated 850,000 acres and attracted over $100 million of out-of-state investment along with about 50,000 people who settled the area.

The largest Carey Act project was the 1905 Milner Dam on the Snake River in Southwestern Idaho whose South Side project irrigated 244,000 acres by gravity flow and founded the cities of Buhl, Kimberly, Filer and Hansen; and the North Side project would pump water into storage reservoirs that would ultimately irrigate 185,000 acres and established the cities of Eden, Jerome, Hazelton and Wendell.

One notable project in Eastern Idaho was the first Carey Act project in Idaho – the 1895 Aberdeen-Springfield Canal project where farmers diverted 1,250 second feet of Snake River water from nearly 50 miles upriver near Firth to the fertile but arid high-desert farms around Aberdeen. The second notable project was a 6,000-acre project near the unincorporated town of Marysville, east of Ashton – which, after 15 years of delays and cost overruns, was completed in 1914. The 1889 American Falls and Power County project, designed to irrigate 60,000 acres, did not have adequate water until the American Falls Dam was completed in 1927.

Bureau of Reclamation – Minidoka Project. The Bureau of Reclamation's Minidoka Project was one of the agency's most complex irrigation systems. The hydroelectric Minidoka Dam, located 35 miles upriver from Milner Dam near Acequia, included the integration of Eastern Idaho's American Falls Reservoir in 1927 and Palisades Reservoir in 1957 as well as Jackson Lake in Wyoming.

Sheep ranching near Iona.

It brought 116,000 acres of Southwestern Idaho land under cultivation and created the cities of Acequia, Heyburn, Paul and Rupert as well as Lake Walcott State Park and the Minidoka National Wildlife Refuge.

Cattle ranching near Island Park.

Livestock. Partially attracted by high meat prices paid in the mining districts but primarily motivated by free grazing on vast tracts of public lands, ranchers brought herds of cattle to Idaho and eastern Oregon in the 1860s from such locations as Nebraska, Texas, California and western Oregon. The ranchers then formed cattle drives of their grass-fattened cattle to the stockyards at Cheyenne, Wyoming, where they were shipped to Omaha, Kansas City and Chicago. Leonard J. Arrington, in his book, History of Idaho wrote, "Eastern Idaho (which includes parts of Southwestern Idaho as defined herein) was almost one big cattle ranch in the 1870s and early 1880s."

After the Oregon Short Line Railroad completed its line between Granger, Wyoming, and Huntington, Oregon, in 1884 creating another transcontinental railroad, sheep ranchers began bringing their flocks to Idaho. Scottish, Basque and other immigrants herded flocks ranging in size from 2,000 to 3,000 head. Many grazed in the mountains and wintered on the more temperate high-desert Snake River Plain. Idaho Falls, Soda Springs and St. Anthony were important lamb and wool-shipping centers in Eastern Idaho. Mountain Home and Ketchum were large centers in Idaho's Southwestern region.

With cattlemen and woolgrowers competing for the same public grazing lands in the 1880s until the turn of the century, conflicts ensued. In Southwestern Idaho the conflict became deadly. The Oakley Cemetery bears witness to that violence. There lie the remains of three men murdered in two separate incidents while herding sheep. Their alleged cattlemen assailants were charged but never convicted. (*See Southwestern Idaho, The Region, Livestock.*)

In 1905 Congress passed a livestock grazing law under which the federal government sold grazing permits as a means of managing access to public lands. In 1934 Congress passed the Taylor Grazing Act, further clarifying federal grazing law. (*See Federal Lands – Private Ownership and Preservation Laws above.*)

By the time the United States entered World War I in 1917, over two and a half million head of sheep were in Southwestern and Eastern Idaho. Because of market factors, today's sheep herds are a fraction of that number. However, each October the cities in the Wood River Valley commemorate their heritage of large sheep drives with the "Trailing of the Sheep Festival." One of the events of the three-day festival is approximately 1,500 sheep being driven from Bellevue through Hailey and Ketchum to Sun Valley.

While the demand for lamb and wool fiber has declined dramatically, the cattle industry has flourished. Large herds of cattle still graze on public lands. The high desert of the lower Snake River Plain is now home to large dairies and feedlot operations. The sale of dairy and meat products is now over three times greater than potatoes for which Idaho is "famous." Idaho is now the third largest dairy producer in the nation.

Mining

Many of Idaho's first settlements were established or grew because of the discovery of gold and other minerals. The 1862 discovery of gold in western Montana had the greatest impact on the settlement of Eastern Idaho because it was on a principal transportation route to the Montana gold mines – a wagon road, called the "Gold Road," from Utah through Eastern Idaho to what is now Montana. It was later replaced by the railroad. From March 4, 1863, to May 26, 1864, when Congress created Montana Territory, western Montana was part of Idaho Territory. Communities developed around the many stagecoach stations and, later, train stops along the route.

The cities of Salmon, Clayton, Challis and Mackay were mining boomtowns or supply stations serving miners working their remote claims in the mountains. The discovery of phosphate near Soda Springs and Pocatello had a major effect on the economy and growth of those communities.

The Gold Road – Precursor to Settlement of Eastern Idaho. Over 200 miles of the Gold Road ran through Eastern Idaho. It passed through Franklin, Pocatello and Blackfoot; crossed the Snake River at Eagle Rock, now Idaho Falls; then turned north generally following what is now Interstate 15 over Monida Pass into Montana.

The stage stops along the road often became communities where passengers and freighters found a variety of services including livery stables, blacksmiths, merchandise stores, hotels and rooming houses and saloons.

By the early 1880s the Utah and Northern Railroad substantially replaced the historic Gold Road and facilitated further settlement and development of Eastern Idaho's agriculture, food processing and other industries.

Salmon Area – Gold, Silver, Cobalt and More. In July 1866 prospectors discovered gold in the mountains above the confluence of the Salmon and Lemhi Rivers. By the spring of 1867 about 2,000 fortune seekers invaded the area. Merchants built the city of Salmon as a supply base for the remote mines located in the western mountains.

As the gold played out, prospectors made successive discoveries that included tungsten, silver, tin, copper and cobalt. Each discovery revived Salmon's mining economy to well after World War II. Even though it was also subject to economic swings in the market, agriculture remained a stabilizing force in the local economy.

Greater Challis: Yankee Fork, Bayhorse and Clayton. Prospectors discovered gold in 1876 on the Yankee Fork River in the mountains about 30 miles southwest of Challis. Large deposits of silver were discovered in the Bayhorse area, 10 miles southwest of Challis a year later. Most freight came to the mines from Corrine, Utah, over the Gold Road through Franklin to Blackfoot then north to the supply center of Challis, where it was loaded on pack animals and transported to the miners. In 1879 a freighter/entrepreneur obtained a charter from the Idaho Territorial Legislature and completed construction of a toll road from Challis to the mining boomtowns of Custer and Bonanza. Gold mining continued until 1911. In 1933 the federal Civilian Conservation Corps reconstructed the historic toll road.

In 1940 Eastern financiers, estimating that there was still $11 million of unrecovered placer gold in the Yankee Fork Valley, built a 112-foot-long, 54-foot-wide and 64-foot-high gold dredge that floated across self-created shallow ponds. The dredge scooped up and reprocessed the gold-bearing gravels, sands and soils on the valley floor through its enormous sluice, leaving thousands of four-to-eight-foot-high tailing piles behind the dredge. Dredging continued until 1952.

Volunteers dedicated to preserving the history of the Yankee Fork now manage the abandoned Yankee Fork Dredge and the ghost town of Custer, which today are part of Land of the Yankee Fork State Park that also includes the Custer Motorway, Challis Bison Jump and the old mining towns of Bonanza and Bayhorse. Today, the primary access to the historic mining area is a paved forest road north from Idaho Highway 75 at Sunbeam.

Mackay – Copper, Lead and More. Prospectors discovered copper-lead ore – which also contained significant amounts of zinc, silver and gold – west of Mackay in the White Knob Mountains in 1879. The richest discoveries were on Mackay's Mine Hill. The mine area, called the Alder Creek Mining District, straddled the main stagecoach and freight wagon road connecting Blackfoot with Challis and the Salmon River mining camps and extended to the mines about 20 miles west across the mountains in the Copper Basin.

At the turn of the century, the Mine Hill properties were acquired by the White Knob Mining Company whose principal investor was John Mackay one of the owners of the Nevada Comstock Lode mines. By 1901 the company had the mine's infrastructure in place. It included a concentrator, a smelter, a 12-mile railway system to transport ore from the mines, a spring gravity-fed water system and company housing. The Oregon Short Line Railroad constructed a spur line from Blackfoot to the smelter.

When mine operations closed around 1950, Mine Hill had produced large quantities of precious and industrial metals. (*See Historical Mine Production and Ranking below.*) The mine is now a tourist attraction.

Soda Springs and Pocatello – Phosphate. Today, phosphate mining is one of Idaho's most significant mining activities. Most of the state's phosphate deposits are in Eastern Idaho near Soda Springs. Mining companies generally removed the phosphate deposits by using open-pit mining techniques wherein after the ore was removed, they replaced the topsoil, planted native grasses, shrubs and trees and moved on to recover the ore in other locations. All but perhaps three of nearly 30 phosphate mines, including a large mine near Pocatello on the Fort Hall Indian Reservation, are now closed. The Environmental Protection Agency has declared several of the old mines Superfund sites because the naturally occurring selenium found in the ore has leached into surface and ground waters.

The mines that remain open produce phosphate for fertilizers and elemental phosphorus used in the manufacture of a wide variety of products such as soft drinks, toothpaste, baking and leavening agents, water treatment chemicals, insecticides and herbicides.

Historical Mine Production and Ranking. Mining is one of Idaho's three historic signature industries that include forest products and agriculture. Northern Idaho's Coeur d'Alene Mining District, the Silver Valley, is recognized as the largest silver-producing mining district in the United States and is likely one of the three most productive in the world. Northern Idaho mines produced 1.2 billion troy ounces (tr. oz.) of silver as well as 16.7 billion lbs. of lead, 6.6 billion lbs. of Zinc, 415 million lbs. of copper and 2.7 million tr.oz. of gold. (*See Northern Idaho, The Region, Silver Valley Mines – Historical Mine Production and Ranking.*)

Nevada, the self-proclaimed "Silver State," has produced less silver than Idaho. Nevada's total historic silver production through 2000 is substantially less than Idaho's total silver production of 1.3 billion tr. oz. The silver production of 190 million tr. oz. from Nevada's famous Comstock Lode is also less than the 360 million tr. oz. produced by Idaho's Sunshine Mine in the Silver Valley. If the right to claim the designation "The Silver State" was based on silver yield by state, Idaho would be the champion going away.

Eastern Idaho's four prominent historic mining areas are Salmon; the greater Challis area of Yankee Fork, Bayhorse, Clayton and Ima Mine; Mackay; and the phosphate mines near Pocatello and Soda Springs.

The tungsten-molybdenum Ima Mine has 21 patented mining claims located about 15 miles east of Challis near the unincorporated town of Patterson. Before the Ima tungsten mining operations closed in 1957, the mine was one of the nation's leading sources of tungsten. Today, mine owners are mining for molybdenum.

Based on 2009 wage records, there were 962 metal mining jobs in Idaho with a payroll of $66 million and 1,012 non-metal mining jobs with a payroll of $45 million.

In recent years, the price of precious and industrial metals has increased dramatically. This condition is causing a resurgence of mining, particularly in Northern Idaho. Ore concentrates are now shipped out of state for smelting and refining. In Eastern Idaho phosphate mining is still the most significant.

In addition, limestone deposits near Inkom are being processed to make Portland cement. For many years in the mid-1900s, limestone used in the manufacture of sugar was shipped from the mines at Victor to sugar factories in the upper Snake River Plain.

Forest Products

There are presently relatively few sawmills operating in Eastern Idaho. Historically, however, sawmills and the harvest of timber from national forests have played important roles in the development of many of the region's cities and agricultural settlements. Changes in federal law and policy have had, and continue to have, significant effects on the region's forest products businesses and national forests.

When Henry and Eliza Spalding started Idaho's first sawmill on the Clearwater River in 1836 while on their mission to the Nez Perce Indians, magnificent virgin forests, including trees hundreds of years old, covered many parts of Idaho. Forests of Western White Pine – Idaho's state tree, which could exceed 8 feet in diameter at the base and a height of over 200 feet – were common in Northern Idaho. The largest white pine in the world now stands at 219 feet near the city of Elk River. Over the last century, most of those giants have been cut to help satisfy the lumber needs of a growing nation. Others have been ravaged by fire. (*See Great Fire of 1910 below.*) Magnificent forests still cover Northern Idaho and parts of Southwestern and Eastern Idaho, but they are generally trees of younger growth.

Big tree in Bloomington Canyon in 1955.

The first sawmills were generally started to meet local market needs, often agricultural-based settlements or mine owners needing to provide timbers to shore up mineshafts and lumber for buildings at the mines and the burgeoning boomtowns they created. Later, railroads facilitated growth of forest products companies by providing service to communities built up around sawmills and transporting lumber to distant markets.

Timberlands and Sawmills. For more than a century after becoming a nation, Congress passed laws transferring ownership of public lands to private interests to pay obligations, encourage settlement, build railroads, harvest the nation's timber and mineral wealth, harness water for beneficial uses and grant land to states to fund public schools and infrastructure. (*See Federal Lands, Private Ownership and Preservation Laws above.*)

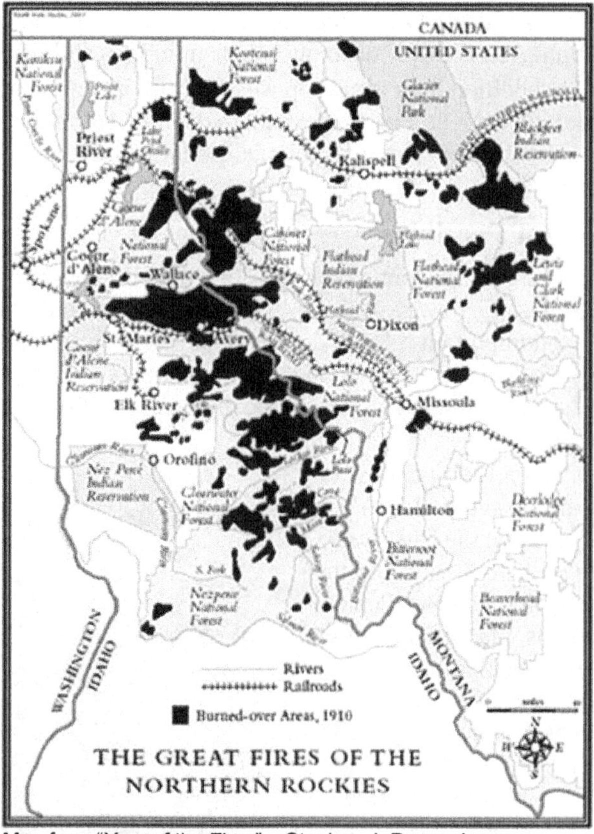

Map from "Year of the Fires" – Stephen J. Payne. Image courtesy of the Wallace District Mining Museum and the U.S. Forest Service.

Beginning in the late 1800s railroads began extending into timber and other regions and, in the case of timberlands, selling their land grants and providing transportation services to numerous new sawmills that were harvesting timber off federal and private lands. Farmers and ranchers often purchased cleared forestlands and began agricultural operations. Towns grew up around each significant commercial venture.

In 1891 Congress passed the Forest Reserve Act that allowed the President of the United States to set aside specific areas of public forestlands "to improve and protect the forest ... securing favorable conditions for water flows, and to furnish a continuous supply of timber for the use and the necessities of citizens of the United States." At that time, President Benjamin Harrison placed 13 million acres into the reserve. Succeeding presidents increased the reserve's size. In 1905 Congress placed management of the forest reserves under an agency in the U.S. Department of Agriculture – now known as the National Forest System. The U.S. Forest Service now administers 191 million acres.

By 1900 forestlands in the Great Lakes states were becoming depleted and lumbermen began looking elsewhere to set up sawmills. Railroads had received and were receiving massive federal land grants as an inducement to provide rail service throughout the region.

Although not a railroad man, Fredrick Weyerhaeuser was one of the largest ultimate beneficiaries of federal forested land grants to the railroads. Already a successful lumber industrialist, buying timberlands, companies and sawmills and harvesting the merchantable timber from Wisconsin and Minnesota forests, Weyerhaeuser set his eye on the Pacific Northwest.

Weyerhaeuser resided in St. Paul, Minnesota, and was neighbors to Jim Hill, head of the Northern Pacific Railroad which received its first federal railroad grants in 1864 that, over the next several years, would exceed 47 million acres for building railroads across the Northern United States. The two men served on each other's boards. One evening Weyerhaeuser learned that Hill had to redeem bonds and was short of cash. On January 3, 1900, Hill sold Weyerhaeuser's syndicate of investors 900,000 acres of timberland in Washington for $5.4 million.

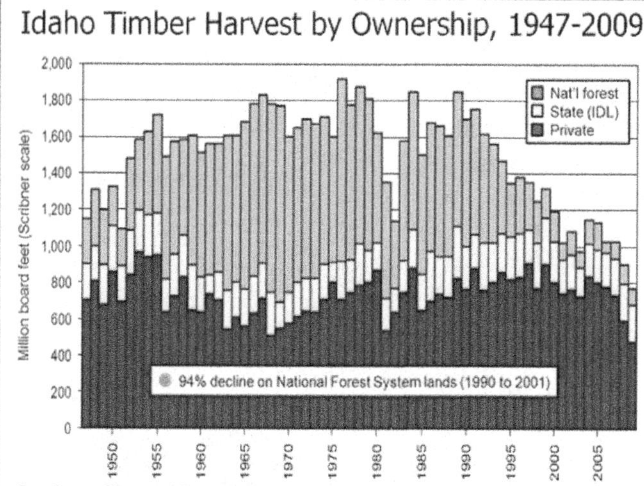

Idaho Timber Harvest by Ownership, 1947-2010 (million board feet, Scribner scale). Source: Idaho's Forest Products Industry Current Conditions and 2011 Forecast.

This transaction was one of the first of many ownership transfers of railroad grant timberland to Weyerhaeuser and other lumber industrialists. Later, Weyerhaeuser would form a company to hold certain of his Idaho timberlands, some of which were sold to a predecessor of Boise Cascade Corporation – now consisting of its successors, the privately owned Boise Cascade Holdings L.L.C. and the publically traded and affiliated Boise, Inc., which acquired Boise Cascade's Paper Group operations in 2008. Both companies are headquartered in Boise. Neither company owns timberlands.

Weyerhaeuser, along with John H. Humbird and other Midwestern sawmill owner-operators and investors went on to purchase other large tracts of railroad grant and other timberland in Washington, Oregon and Idaho that had not been designated as national forest reserves and built sawmills at optimum locations.

Idaho has one pulp and paper mill, the Lewiston facility of Clearwater Paper Corporation, headquartered in Spokane, Washington, a 2008 spinoff from Potlatch Corporation. The company owns vast tracts of timberlands in Idaho. At its Lewiston facility, the company manufactures lumber, bleached paperboard, pulp and consumer tissue products. (*See Northern Idaho, the city chapters of Lewiston and Potlatch.*)

Great Fire of 1910. For two terrifying days – August 20 and 21, 1910 – following a summer of drought and high temperatures, a cold front came through bringing fierce winds that whipped smaller fires into raging infernos with flames leaping hundreds of feet high and clouds of smoke rising high into the atmosphere. These conflagrations generated their own blowtorch winds, blowing embers great distances, jumping from tree crown to tree crown and igniting other fires in a hopscotch fashion and ravaging Northern Idaho and western Montana.

The fire killed 85 men, mostly firefighters, destroyed several communities in Idaho and Montana and charred others, including much of what is now Wallace – in total burning 3 million acres. Although estimates vary widely on the equivalent board feet destroyed, historian Stephen Payne, in his book Year of the Fires: The Story of the Great Fires of 1910, said, "The Forest Service settled on a figure of six billion board feet, about twice the entire national output and that in a year of record production." The conflagration was so large some credited it with blowing ash halfway around the world. The fire, sometimes termed the Big Burn or the Big Blowup, is the largest fire in U.S. history – greatly influencing future federal forest-management policies.

Fire Aftermath – Changing Forest Management Practices. The Great Fire was a catalyst that persuaded Congress to pass the Weeks Act of 1911, named for John W. Weeks of Massachusetts. The act authorized the federal government to buy private lands within the watersheds of navigable streams and include such lands in the national forest system. While the law was initially used to buy lands in the East, it was also applied in the West. One of the major provisions of the act was legislating emergency fire fighting funds for aggressive wildfire suppression.

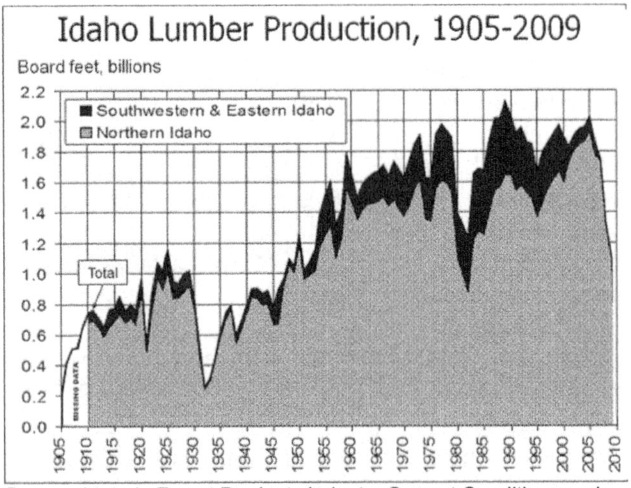

Idaho Lumber Production, 1905-2009

Source: Idaho's Forest Products Industry Current Conditions and 2011 Forecast.

In 1935 the Forest Service adopted the firefighting goal termed the "10 a.m. policy" – all newly detected forest fires were to be put out by 10 o' clock the next morning. The practice of parachuting firefighters near hard-to-reach fires – now termed Hotshot Crews – began in 1940. The familiar Smokey Bear advertising character and his slogan, "Only you can prevent forest fires," began in 1944.

These aggressive fire suppression programs had the desired effect of reducing forest fires but there were adverse consequences as well. Dr. Jay O' Laughlin,

University of Idaho, Forestry and Policy Analysis, said, "Remove fire from the system and over time fuels will accumulate, making the next fire more difficult to control."

The conclusion of World War II started a nationwide housing boom. Providing lumber to build millions of homes for the families of soldiers returning from the war – many going back to school under the G.I. Bill before entering the workforce – was a federal priority. The Forest Service helped satisfy this demand by opening the national forests to increased timber harvests. In just over a decade, the timber harvest from federal lands in Northern Idaho had more than doubled – a high level of timber harvest that would continue for over two decades – all facilitated by improved heavy tractors, equipment and trucks and the 1950s invention of the single-person hand-held gasoline chain saw.

Table 2--Idaho timber harvest (MMBF, Scribner) by county, selected years (sources: Keegan and others 1982, 1988, 1992, 1997, Morgan and others 2004).

County	1979		1985		1990		1995		2001		2006	
	MMBF Scribner	Percent of Total	MMBF Scribner	Percent of Total	MMBF Scribner	Percent of Total	MMBF Scribner	Percent of Total	MMBF Scribner	Percent of Total	MMBF Scribner	Percent of Total
					Northern Idaho							
Clearwater	544	29.0	335	21.0	267	16.0	234	17.0	182	18.0	174	15.6
Shoshone	206	11.0	217	14.0	183	11.0	194	14.0	172	17.0	200	17.8
Idaho	190	10.0	156	10.0	174	10.0	113	8.0	65	6.0	66	5.8
Bonner	142	8.0	175	11.0	197	12.0	139	10.0	124	12.0	93	8.3
Benewah	100	5.0	94	6.0	152	9.0	117	9.0	129	13.0	144	12.9
Boundary	94	5.0	80	5.0	86	5.0	69	5.0	57	6.0	53	4.8
Kootenai	65	4.0	80	5.0	152	9.0	114	8.0	81	8.0	100	8.9
Latah	57	3.0	89	6.0	84	5.0	96	7.0	70	7.0	125	11.2
Nez Perce	8	0.0	12	1.0	17	1.0	8	1.0	4	0.0	10	0.9
Lewis	4	0.0	13	1.0	20	1.0	17	1.0	14	1.0	12	1.1
Northern Idaho	**1,410**	**76.0**	**1,254**	**79.0**	**1,332**	**79.0**	**1,100**	**80.0**	**899**	**89.0**	**976**	**87.1**
					Southern Idaho							
Valley	107	6.0	88	6.0	52	3.0	67	5.0	39	4.0	65	5.8
Boise	84	4.0	67	4.0	127	8.0	93	7.0	20	2.0	25	2.2
Adams	52	3.0	66	4.0	87	5.0	28	2.0	25	2.0	30	2.7
Washington	4	b	9	1.0	4	b	6	b	-	b	c	b
Elmore	25	1.0	14	1.0	5	b	38	3.0	7	1.0	c	b
Other Counties	20	1.0	3	b	6	b	11	1.0	1	b	6	0.5
Southwestern Idaho	**292**	**16.0**	**247**	**16.0**	**281**	**17.0**	**242**	**18.0**	**91**	**9.0**	**126**	**11.3**
Fremont	76	4.0	43	3.0	20	1.0	2	b	3	b	1	0.1
Lemhi	34	2.0	11	1.0	16	1.0	6	b	1	b	1	0.1
Clark	10	1.0	10	1.0	16	1.0	-	b	1	b	6	0.6
Caribou	4	b	10	1.0	3	b	5	b	5	b	4	0.3
Other Counties	24	1.0	19	1.0	24	1.0	15	1.0	7	1.0	7	0.6
Southeastern Idaho	**148**	**8.0**	**93**	**6.0**	**79**	**5.0**	**27**	**2.0**	**17**	**2.0**	**19**	**1.7**
Southern Idaho	**440**	**24.0**	**340**	**21.0**	**360**	**21.0**	**269**	**20.0**	**108**	**11.0**	**145**	**12.9**
Idaho Total	**1850**	**100.0**	**1594**	**100.0**	**1692**	**100.0**	**1,370**	**100.0**	**1,007**	**100.0**	**1,121**	**100.0**

[a] Percentage detail may not sum to 100% due to rounding

[b] Less than 0.05 percent

[c] Less than 1 MMBF

At this time, the commercial practice of clear-cutting, generally defined as the removal of all stems in a specified area whether the stems were viable for merchantable timber or not, became a common but highly controversial practice of timber harvest – a practice that would continue for more than two decades. Opponents, asserting the practice was tantamount to deforestation and the destruction of natural wildlife habitat, used photos of large clear-cuts to influence public opinion in favor of their preservationist cause.

In 1965 certain federal agencies combined resources to form the National Interagency Coordination Center and National Interagency Fire Center located in Boise. There are now eight participating federal agencies. The center in Boise coordinates resources to fight fires that may occur in any of the 11 geographical areas, called Geographical Area Coordination Centers, headquartered at a city in each of 11 designated areas of the United States, including Alaska.

Beginning in the 1970s Congress passed several laws affecting the protection of the environment, ecosystems, species and riparian areas and access to federal lands for the purpose of mining and harvesting timber. (*See Mining and Forest Products – Leading Causes for Loss of Economic Dominance below*.)

By 1992 there were numerous lawsuits and court injunctions in the Pacific Northwest involving the protection of endangered species and their habitat, including future timber harvests in "old growth" forests. From that time on, as shown in the following chart, timber harvest from federal lands began to fall precipitously.

In Eastern Idaho the loss of access to federal lands decimated the industry. In 1979 Eastern Idaho sawmills produced 8 percent of Idaho's total timber harvest but by 2006 it had dropped to 1.7 percent, a decline of nearly 80 percent. (*See Idaho Timber Harvest [MMBF, Scribner] by county [and region] below.*)

The next major change in federal forest management law came with passage of the Healthy Forest Restoration Act of 2003. Under the act, federal agencies were required to work collaboratively with other stakeholders to reduce the risk of large destructive wild fires by thinning dense tree-stands, undergrowth and brush in forested areas; creating fire breaks; improving firefighting practices and insect control – infestations of the pine beetle have killed millions of acres of forests in the West; and requiring communities in affected areas to develop wildfire protection plans. The law also directs the courts to consider the risk of forest fires in deciding cases that could delay thinning projects. Opponents to the law generally asserted that the law could lead to a return to the open commercial harvest of larger trees of the past with limited positive effect in reducing fire hazards.

Today, the Forest Service employs a mix of fire-fighting policies and tactics including prescribed burning – intentionally set fires designed to achieve specified outcomes – and being slow to intervene in fires started by natural causes such as lightning (natural burns).

Dr. O'Laughlin said that during 2000 to 2009, the average number of acres burned each year exceeded 6 million, more than double the average of the preceding two decades.

Opponents to the federal burn practices assert they waste good timber, and if the Forest Service employed the mixed-use methodologies used on private and state-owned forestlands, forest fires could be better controlled, habitat preserved and more jobs created.

On August 7, 2007, The Idaho Statesman reported that in the heavy wildfire year of 2003 one private forestland owner of 180,000 acres experienced burns of only 100 acres, contrasted with the burn of 708,000 acres of federal forestlands in Idaho.

Forest Service managers assert their ability to fight wild fires is constrained for multiple reasons including lack of funds, road access and their priority to protect homes that are increasingly being built in forested areas. In addition, Dr. O' Laughlin said, "Forest Service management practices today are designed primarily to modify ecological conditions rather than provide timber supplies. In contrast to federal policies, private and state-owned forestlands are generally managed for a mix of uses that includes timber production ... "

Today, 36 percent of Idaho's 54 million acres is owned by private, state or local government entities. Federal agencies are responsible for managing the balance of the land – U.S. Forest Service 39 percent, the Bureau of Land Management 21 percent and other federal agencies 4 percent.

Idaho's Lumber Production History. Researchers at the University of Idaho have estimated that Idaho's statewide lumber production grew from 1.5 million board feet (bf) in 1870 to nearly 1.2 billion in 1925 before falling to around 200 million during the Great Depression of the 1930s. Following the Depression, production rebounded as shown in the chart below, reaching over 1.2 billion bf in 1950.

By the mid-1950s there were over 300 sawmills in Idaho. Within five decades, all of the mills had closed except for 35. However, as shown in the chart above, the remaining mills were producing about the same quantity as the 300 mills were producing decades earlier. Of the 35 remaining mills, 14 each had annual production of generally greater than 50 million board feet of lumber prior to the global economic decline of 2007. These mills operate using state-of-the-art computer process control systems including lasers, scanners, mechanized log and lumber handling systems and improved saw-blade, edger and trimmer technologies that use substantially fewer, albeit more highly skilled, workers.

As the chart illustrates, the global economic decline that began in 2007 has had a significant adverse effect on lumber production in Idaho as it has in the industry as a whole. However, as illustrated in previous economic cycles, production will resume as the economy improves.

Idaho Timber Harvest by Region. As illustrated in the table below, in 2006 about 87 percent of Idaho's timber harvest came from Northern Idaho, 11 percent from Southwestern Idaho and 1.7 percent from Eastern Idaho.

The underlying basis for calculating timber harvest in the chart below is different than that used to calculate Idaho timber harvest and lumber production used in the table above – largely due to formula inconsistencies in handling the declining size of logs being milled. Dr. O'Laughlin said that many of Idaho's sawmills began to re-tool during the 1980s to handle smaller diameter logs. By 2003 nearly 60 percent of all logs processed in Idaho were less than 10 inches small-end diameter, and some mills were processing logs less than 6 inches small-end diameter.

The U.S. Census Bureau has also reported Idaho lumber production at amounts different than that shown herein. No attempt has been made to reconcile differences as the information disclosed herein is based on methodologies that are generally accepted in the industry to reasonably calculate timber and lumber harvests. The calculations do not include timber used for paper manufacturing and unprocessed logs sold to foreign countries.

Loss of Economic Dominance

The production of dimensional lumber and silver, lead and zinc ingots were Idaho's largest manufacturing businesses and dominated the economy of Northern Idaho and many cities across the state for nearly a century. In Southwestern and Eastern Idaho, these industries were less pervasive as agriculture was then dominant, but they still had a profound economic effect – placer gold and other mining activities were dominant in many communities until the mines played out.

Although totally different in operation, raw material, end product and environmental impact of processing, these two natural resource-based industries were subject to many of the same federal laws and regulations including, during recent decades, the almost total loss of access to federal lands.

The following provides leading causes for the decline in economic influence of the mining and wood products industries in Idaho as well as the nation.

Until around 1970 Congressional actions toward natural resource-based industries were very accommodating. Motivated by a desire to connect the continent with railroad transportation, settle the West and obtain timber and minerals needed for the nation's rapidly growing economy, Congress gave railroad companies over 100 million acres of land grants, including mineral rights that they could sell to help finance the construction of railroads. However, the largest numbers of federal land grants – totaling the most acreage – were to farmers, ranchers and states. (*See Federal Lands – Private Ownership and Preservation Laws above.*)

The federal priority was to encourage private businesses to produce the timber and minerals needed for the nation's rapidly growing economy. There was limited governmental oversight. Business practices generally focused on profitability as opposed to environmental impact and safety of workers until the 1970s.

The use of public lands for mining was, to a great extent, open to all who wished to file mining claims. Claims with proven ore bodies could become patented or deeded to the claim owner. Most of today's mining activity is on patented land.

The use of public forests was largely unregulated until around 1905 when President Theodore Roosevelt, often described as a conservationist who generally supported sustainable harvest and multiple-use concepts of forest management, helped create the United States Forest Service.

Beginning in 1907 Roosevelt used his executive authority to create scores of national forests, primarily in the Western states. In Idaho, he created 15 – many of which, due to changes in forest management practices and policies, have been combined or consolidated. Idaho's original national forests were the Caribou, Challis, Salmon, Clearwater, Coeur d'Alene, Pend d' Oreille, Weiser, Nez Perce, Idaho, Payette, Boise, Sawtooth, Lemhi, Targhee and Bitterroot.

U.S. Senator Weldon Heyburn from Wallace favored open use and opposed Roosevelt's conservation initiatives to protect and manage public lands for public recreation and commercial purposes. On the other side of the debate were the preservationists such as John Muir, founder of the Sierra Club, who wanted to maintain pristine natural environments by banning all development.

In the latter half of the twentieth century many people across the nation became concerned about the declining quality of air in cities and industrial areas as well as ground and surface water quality, wildlife habitat and the general lack of care government agencies had given to the nation's public lands, environment and worker safety. This motivated Congress to enact laws more closely in accord with preservationist ideology for the management of public lands and the commercial use of natural resources.

In 1970 Congress created the Environmental Protection Agency (EPA), the Occupational Safety and Health Administration (OSHA) and the National Institute for Occupational Safety and Health (NIOSH). A few years later, the federal Mine Safety and Health Administration (MSHA); the Federal Water Pollution Control Act, also known as the Clean Water Act (CWA); and the Endangered Species Act of 1973 (ESA) – successor to the Endangered Species Preservation Act of 1966, laws protecting specific animal species and their habitat – were also enacted.

Idaho created what is now the Department of Environmental Quality and divided Idaho's counties into seven regions, creating health districts in each. These state agencies, in cooperation with federal agencies, have legal oversight of certain environmental matters.

Targhee National Forest.

All federal and state agencies and the regulations they promulgated established minimum environmental protection and health and safety standards and practices, including those affecting worker safety and the discharge or emission of pollutants into the air as well as total maximum daily loads (TMDL), as required by the CWA, of pollutants in surface water and groundwater contamination. Compliance with these laws required major changes in the operating processes and practices of business.

Certain business activities on public lands were further restricted as environmental groups used these laws to challenge the adequacy of the environmental studies and approvals, especially the National Environmental Policy Act of 1970 and its requirement for a "hard look" at environmental impacts of any significant action involving federal lands or resources before decisions are made.

The National Forest Management Act of 1976 required comprehensive long-range planning. Many private and federal activities became tied up in the courts with appeals and calls for incorporating new science extending project decisions for years. These lawsuits influenced federal policy and played a significant role in delaying or preventing access to federal lands for mining and timber harvest purposes. Such delays had the practical effect of stopping any business activity working on a return-on-investment timetable.

Decades of aggressive fire suppression and, later, timber harvest restrictions have exacerbated deadfall buildup on the forest floor with the consequence of potentially more severe and exceptionally hot forest fires that destroy merchantable timber and modify wildlife habitat.

Mining and wood products were also adversely affected when Congress acted in 1964 and again in 1980 to protect 4 million acres of Idaho national forests as components of the National Wilderness Preservation System, precluding mining and timber operations as provided by the Wilderness Act of 1964. In 2009 Congress also set aside 517,000 acres of Owyhee County in Southwestern Idaho as wilderness. This wilderness has limited amounts of merchantable timber and few mining properties.

At the time the wilderness laws were enacted, there were many relatively small parcels of private land in wilderness areas. The laws grandfathered private property rights, allowing people as well as commercial outfitters and guides to use wilderness areas for recreation, hunting and fishing. Private interests, including stock ownership membership resorts, still own parcels of land in the wilderness. Their members and clients, many of whom are hunters, fly in on small aircraft or helicopters to their backcountry airstrips or float in on the rivers or ride horses into their wilderness properties that often have horse stables and modern, fully-furnished cabins and lodges with small hydroelectric systems providing electricity and satellite. (*See National Wilderness Areas below.*)

Federal law changes, with attendant increased operating cost requirements to comply with the law, were only some of the reasons natural resource businesses were not successful. Competitive global market factors, competition from businesses in less or unregulated countries and cost of replacing outdated plants challenged the ability of natural resource-based businesses to achieve profitable operations – forcing many to close.

Many mines, particularly gold mines, closed because the mines simply played out. However, as new metal-recovery technologies became available, old mines were often reopened and even the mine tailings were reprocessed to extract the metals that the old processes failed to remove.

With the closure of mines and sawmills, rural school districts, counties and cities that relied on revenues from timber sales and mine production, as well as property taxes from the local businesses, sustained major budget reductions. Congressional appropriations to make up the revenue shortfall have been inadequate.

During this time, federal agencies also began requiring owners of properties where their industrial activity had damaged the environment to pay the cost of cleaning up the hazardous waste – called Superfund sites. The ore-processing component of the mining industry was the principal activity affected by these actions. Many companies opted to go out of business, leaving the government – taxpayers – to pay the remaining clean-up costs. (*See Northern Idaho, The Region,*

Silver Valley Mines – Superfund and Aftermath.)

Compared to mining, wood products businesses caused significantly less damage to the environment. Albeit staying compliant with TMDL regulations requires care to prevent erosion into surface waters caused by road cutting and maintenance and timber harvesting. Compliance with ESA laws to protect rare plants and animals and habitat or endangered species is often problematic for timber harvesting. Although not prohibited by law, the historic practice of clear-cutting remains controversial. Both mining and wood products industries were directly affected by federal health and safety laws.

By the end of the twentieth century, logging and mining on federal lands had almost ceased. Albeit, the Forest Service still conducts timber harvests – generally for ecological purposes. Responding to lawsuits, courts have often blocked removing merchantable timber damaged in forest fires and beetle infestations. However, in February 2011 the Forest Service released new rules intended to aid in consensus building and give the Forest Service more flexibility in ecosystem restoration and logging. Mining continues but generally on patented mining claims – concentrated ores are generally shipped out of state for smelting and refining.

Technological innovation has changed how mining and wood products businesses operate. These once labor-intensive businesses now have much higher productivity with significantly fewer employees, albeit the average educational requirements, skill level and wage of today's natural resource employees have increased substantially. The Idaho Department of Labor published projections of Idaho's total fourth quarter 2010 employment for natural resources businesses – mining, forestry and logging – at 3,251 and wood product manufacturing at 4,526 with average wages of $54,250 and $36,193, respectively. This compared to the state's total employment of 661,334 with an average wage of $34,332.

While lumber manufacturing remains the core business of the wood products industry, changes in the size of logs processed and new technologies and niche businesses that have emerged over the past few decades are changing the industry and, in some cases, broadening the variety of products produced from wood. In addition to expansion of small-log sawmills, there are businesses that press wood mill waste such as sawdust and chips into compressed wood pellets and logs for heating in pellet stoves and fireplaces or to be sold to paper mills. Bark is processed through large rotating screens producing various sizes of bark used as ground cover in decorative residential and commercial landscapes. Idaho businesses manufacture log homes, wood moldings, laminated beams and trusses and other specialty or niche products.

At the same time, businesses producing and selling competing products – such as steel studs and trusses, extruded plastic moldings and framing, dimensional lumber made from plastic or lumber made from wood fiber combined with resins – are slowly increasing their market share.

Railroads

Following completion of the first transcontinental railroad in 1869 in northern Utah, entrepreneurs began a narrow-gauge rail line north to handle the heavy transportation business between Utah and the Montana gold mines. In May 1874 the first rail line to enter Idaho reached Franklin. For the next few years, financial and other problems stopped construction. Scores of wagons came daily to the Franklin railroad terminus to deliver and pick up freight and passengers traveling the Gold Road to Montana.

Entrepreneurs formed the Utah and Northern Railway Company in 1878 to acquire the assets of the previous railroad and build a narrow-gauge line north to Helena, Montana. The railroad reached Pocatello in 1878; Eagle Rock, now Idaho Falls, in 1879; and into Montana in 1880. The line established train depots along the way, spawning towns such as Arimo and Dubois. The railroad established its Idaho headquarters and maintenance shops at Eagle Rock, swelling the town's population to around 2,000.

Many of the construction workers on the rail line were from northern Utah. Following completion of the Montana railroad, many of these workers spread the word in northern Utah about the favorable settlement potential of Eastern Idaho. (*See Pioneer Settlements – Upper Snake River Plain above.*)

Railroad in Montpelier.

The Oregon Short Line Railroad began building a line in 1881 that started at Granger, Wyoming, and angled northwest through Pocatello, Shoshone and Caldwell before connecting with the rail line in Huntington, Oregon. Completed November 17, 1884, the line provided the link between the commercial centers of Omaha, Nebraska, and Portland, Oregon, creating another transcontinental railroad.

Fierce windstorms in 1886 destroyed the Utah and Northern Railway Co. roundhouse and facilities at Eagle Rock. Since railroad officials had already concluded that Pocatello would make a better headquarters location, they decided to rebuild in Pocatello. As a result, railroad worker families and businesses that relied on the railroad – about 80 percent of Eagle Rock's population – moved to Pocatello, an event that caused Eagle Rock community leaders to reinvent themselves, including changing the name of their town to Idaho Falls.

The railroad converted its narrow-gauge line to standard gauge and a few years later the Oregon Short Line and the Utah Northern Railway merged into the affiliated Union Pacific Railroad, and Pocatello became a regional terminal.

Idaho/Utah Boundary Resolution

The boundary line between Idaho and Utah, the 42nd parallel, dates back to the Transcontinental Treaty of 1819, also known as the Adams-Onis Treaty, between the United States and Spain. The treaty, among other things, established the 42nd parallel as the boundary separating the two countries' land claims across the Rocky Mountains to the Pacific. Following the Mexican revolution of 1822, Mexico succeeded to Spain's position. Following the U.S. war with Mexico in 1848, Mexico released these land claims to the U.S. The Treaty of 1846 between the U.S. and England established the boundary between those countries at the 49th parallel – Idaho's northern border.

However, it was not until 1872 that the federal government surveyed the 42nd parallel. Prior to that time, most of the northern Cache Valley and Bear Lake settlers managed their affairs as though they were part of Utah Territory. The survey changed all of that, showing that they were really in Idaho Territory. These settlers now had to travel 300 miles to the territorial capital in Boise instead of the much shorter distance to Salt Lake City.

Looking out over Franklin, Idaho's oldest city.

The survey also had other significant effects. It caused restatement of the Idaho Territory's official 1870 population, increasing it 19 percent, from 14,999 to 17,804. The town of Franklin, located one mile north of the surveyed territorial border and founded in 1860, became Idaho's oldest city. The survey also divided Bear Lake almost evenly between the two territories.

Politics, Polygamy and Civil Rights

Politically, the last two decades of the nineteenth century were troubling for leaders and many members of the Church of Jesus Christ of Latter-day Saints, also known as Mormons, Latter-day Saints and LDS. (*See Pioneer Settlements above.*) At that time, the Church approved the practice of plural marriage (polygamy) under limited conditions – as in ancient Israel – and taught that under certain circumstances the marriage covenant can be binding eternally (celestial or eternal marriage).

The U.S. Congress in 1882 passed the Edmunds Act declaring polygamy a felony in the territories – not in the states. This act was augmented by the Edmunds-Tucker Act of 1887.

In Idaho Territory, many politicians perceived that Southern Idaho's rapidly growing population of Church members posed a threat to their political power base. In the 1880s most members of the Church in Idaho supported the Democratic Party and were perceived by politicos to vote as a block. Republicans controlled the governor's office and the Legislature. Many Republicans worried that, if Church members did vote as a block, they would lose their political power to the Democrats.

Those seeking to limit the Church's political influence saw polygamy as its Achilles heel. While obviously tolerant of informal, family-destabilizing sexual arrangements and relationships – informal co-habitation agreements including extramarital affairs and multiple premarital relationships common in society (non-practicing monogamists) – these politicians nevertheless expressed public outrage at the Church's approval of plural marriage essentially marked by a formal ceremony and family structure. They successfully used polygamy as a lightning rod to inflame political and public opinion against the Church and its members. (*See Idaho Territory, Change in Idaho Territorial Boundaries 1864 to 1890, Suffrage and Statehood above.*)

These territorial legislators passed anti-polygamy and test oath laws in 1885 that carried over into statehood, essentially denying suffrage to any suspected bigamist or polygamist, already a felony, or any monogamist man who was a member of an organization that taught the acceptability of bigamy, polygamy and celestial (eternal) marriage as a doctrinal rite. They could not vote, hold public office or serve on juries. To identify these men, the law required any suspected "offender" to take a complex, over 200-word test oath.

While the law spoke in general terms, not naming organizations, the only known organization in Idaho that fit the definition of the law was the Church of Jesus Christ of Latter-day Saints whose members comprised about a fourth of Idaho's population and of which only a small fraction practiced polygamy. Republican politicians targeted the law to disenfranchise this large block of voters, adult male monogamous Church members who would not disavow their faith, who they believed would vote for their political opponents.

Only adult men suspected of being members of the Church were required to take the test oath. Women already had no suffrage rights under Idaho law. If a man signed, he essentially disavowed his faith but was allowed to vote. If he was subsequently found to be a member, he was subject to arrest and prison. Any who refused to sign the test oath were denied their suffrage rights.

These anti-polygamy laws were aggressively enforced and, as a result, "Idaho's territorial prison (that had a maximum population of 603 inmates) overflowed with men convicted of a polygamy charge." John Codman, a summer resident in Soda Springs wrote in the National Democrat on September 18, 1890, of the " ... painful scene which justly arouses indignation ... old men ... dragged to prison for no other cause than an occasional visit, in open daylight, or taking a meal ... (to) the house of a plural wife."

In many Southern Idaho local elections, the test oath resulted in a huge shift of political power from the majority to a minority of citizens with all the potential mischief such undemocratic actions could produce.

Idaho became a state on July 3, 1890. Wilford Woodruff, President of the Church of Jesus Christ of Latter-day Saints, issued a "Manifesto" on October 6, 1890, prohibiting the further practice of plural marriage by Church members.

On February 1, 1895, the Idaho Legislature repealed the test oath laws and many members of the Church became Republicans.

Invention of Television

Philo T. Farnsworth invented television in Rigby, at age 14.

At a time when prominent scientists from around the globe were trying to develop technologies to transmit live images over the airwaves, the unlikely boy genius Philo T. Farnsworth at Rigby High School laid the technical groundwork for patents that established him as the inventor of television.

In 1920 at age 14, Farnsworth worked out the principle of the "image dissector television camera" and wrote the mathematical formula on the school's chemistry class blackboard. Farnsworth's chemistry teacher wrote the formula down and produced the "prior art" evidence in a patent case that Radio Corporation of America, now known as RCA, brought against Farnsworth. In 1935 the patent court ruled in Farnsworth's favor, establishing him as the inventor of television.

Over his career, Farnsworth produced hundreds of patents and lived in several cities. While many cities have markers commemorating his stay, Rigby commemorates its native son with the "Farnsworth TV & Pioneer Museum" which houses some of Farnsworth's original memorabilia.

Idaho National Laboratory

Idaho National Laboratory.

The U.S. Department of Energy's Idaho National Laboratory (INL) is one of the nation's 10 national laboratories. INL's 570,000-acre site between Idaho Falls and Arco is the nation's largest laboratory site.

With over 7,000 scientists, technicians and support personnel, the INL is Eastern Idaho's largest employer and provides additional employment by outsourcing work to Idaho universities and businesses.

There are two primary sites. The research, development and construction site is located in the desert 35 miles west of Idaho Falls. The general offices and the Science and Technology Campus are located in Idaho Falls.

INL is the nation's premier nuclear research facility. Its charge includes research, design and development of the next generation nuclear power plant and an enhanced portfolio of non-nuclear fuels, biological and renewable energy, hydropower, fuel reforming and related alternative and renewable energy research needed for the nation's energy and security programs.

The facility opened in 1949 as the National Reactor Testing Station for prototype research and development of nuclear reactors. Over the years, INL produced 52 primarily first-of-a-kind reactors, most of which are now decommissioned.

Beginning in the 1940s the U.S. Navy had a presence on the site, later developing its first nuclear propulsion systems for submarines. Over the next few decades, 40,000 sailors assigned to nuclear submarines were trained at the site.

On December 20, 1951, Experimental Breeder Reactor Number 1 (EBR-1) produced electricity that lit four light bulbs. On July 17, 1955, it supplied the world's first nuclear-generated electricity for commercial purposes when it powered the lights in the nearby city of Arco for two hours. EBR-1 is now a Registered National Historic Landmark and, during the summer, is open to the public.

The 890 square miles reserved for INL are home to 269 species of wild mammals, birds and reptiles and more than 400 species of plants. It is the nation's second largest national environmental research park.

In the early years, disposal of nuclear waste was particularly problematic. Current technology has corrected for those problems, and the old waste is being cleaned up. Management of nuclear waste continues to be a matter of national concern.

In order to remove any doubt about Idaho's strong support for INL activities, the Idaho Legislature unanimously passed a joint memorial to President George W. Bush, Secretary of Energy Samuel Bodman and Congress in 2006 supporting continued and expanded work at the site.

Teton Dam Disaster

Teton Dam breaking on June 5, 1976.

In 1976 the U.S. Bureau of Reclamation was nearing completion of the Teton Dam, a 300-foot-high, 3,100-foot-long structure backing up the Teton River for irrigation and flood control. The reservoir had been filling from the spring runoff and the level of the water was at 175 feet.

Early on June 5 fractures in the volcanic rock canyon encasing the reservoir began releasing increasingly large flows of water from behind the inadequately-designed earthen dam. Before the morning was over the dam breached, releasing 80 billion gallons of water down the valley.

The flood created one of Idaho's largest disasters, affecting the greatest number of citizens and prompting the most significant outpouring of volunteer support in the state's history.

Floodwaters covered over 300 square miles of mostly farmland before dissipating three days later 100 miles southwest in the backwaters of the American Falls Reservoir. The flood killed 11 people and 18,000 head of livestock. About 25,000 people fled their homes. The flood largely swept away the community of Sugar City as well as seriously damaging or destroying parts of several other communities including Rexburg, Salem, Roberts, Shelley, Firth and Blackfoot.

After the flood, private and government agencies and volunteers converged to provide humanitarian relief and help with the clean up. The largest of the private volunteer organizations was the Church of Jesus Christ of Latter-day Saints. The majority of the victims were members of the Church. Local Church leaders coordinated with governmental relief agencies to provide over 50,000 volunteer laborers, some coming from hundreds of miles away for days and weeks at a time. They brought tools, food and supplies with some providing heavy construction equipment.

The Church converted the facilities of Ricks College in Rexburg – now Brigham Young University-Idaho – and other area church buildings for temporary shelters and food preparation and serving centers.

Local restaurants and food chains, volunteers from other church denominations, businesses and individuals gave substantial time and resources to help the victims.

The total coordinated clean-up effort took three months. The federal government took responsibility for the dam's failure and paid damages. Most of the affected property owners chose to stay and rebuild their homes, businesses and lives. The city of Rexburg commemorates the disaster with its Teton Flood Museum located in the historic Tabernacle Civic Center.

Famous Potatoes

Many factors led to the development of Idaho's potato business. They include Luther Burbank's work in developing the Russet Burbank potato variety in 1873 and research into potato diseases and promoting the use of certified seed and commercial fertilizers by the University of Idaho's agricultural experiment station in Aberdeen.

A truck load of potatoes.

With the advent of World War II, the U.S. military placed

massive orders for dried potatoes with the J.R. Simplot Company. Simplot and, later on, other potato processors skinned, diced and dried potatoes on screens passed through gas fueled drying ovens, filling 5-gallon cans and putting them in wooden crates for shipment by rail. The product was nutritious, but it had an unappetizing brown-gray color and pasty texture. (*See Southwestern Idaho, The Region, World War II – Jack Simplot, Food Processing and Frozen French Fried Potatoes.*)

From those origins came a host of excellent processed potato products. The volcanic soils, irrigation and weather of Eastern Idaho produced potatoes – principally Russet Burbanks – of exceptional quality.

Today, Idaho produces nearly 30 percent of the nation's potatoes. In 2006 the U.S. Department of Agriculture reported Idaho's gross receipts from potatoes at $648 million, making potatoes Idaho's third largest agricultural commodity behind dairy at $1.3 billion and cattle at just over $1 billion.

Every fall, the City of Shelley sponsors "Spud Days" with parades, potato-eating contests and other events. Researchers at Aberdeen have developed new varieties of potatoes to meet changes in consumer demand. Blackfoot is the home of the "Idaho Potato Expo," a spud-shaped building that honors all things potato.

Since 1948 the Legislature has passed laws approving some form of potato industry advertising on automobile license plates. In 1957 the Legislature approved the "Famous Potatoes" slogan that now appears across the bottom of Idaho's standard issue plates.

National Wilderness Areas

All or part of four national wilderness areas are in Eastern Idaho. The 2.4 million acre Frank Church-River of No Return Wilderness is Idaho's largest wilderness and lies mostly in Northern Idaho with the southeastern part extending into Custer and Lemhi Counties in Eastern Idaho and the southwestern part in Valley County in Southwestern Idaho. (*See Northern Idaho and Southwestern Idaho: The Region, National Wilderness Areas.*)

The 217,000-acre Sawtooth Wilderness encompassing much of the fabulous Sawtooth Mountain Range is near Stanley.

The 43,000-acre Craters of the Moon Wilderness, is near Arco and abuts the Craters of the Moon National Monument and Preserve.

The 276,000-acre Boulder-White Clouds Wilderness is near Stanley and consists of three units – the Jim McClure-Jerry Peak (117,000 acres), White Clouds (91,000 acres) and Hemingway-Boulders (68,000 acres). This wilderness comprises a major portion of the Boulder-White Cloud Mountains and was signed into law on August 7, 2015.

The eastern border of Eastern Idaho also abuts two wilderness areas in Wyoming that are generally accessed through Idaho – the 124,000-acre Jedediah Smith Wilderness on the western slope of the Grand Teton Mountains near Driggs and the 11,000-acre Winegar Hole Wilderness east of Ashton. The Caribou-Targhee National Forest and conservation groups have proposed that Congress increase the size of the Winegar Hole Wilderness to include 2,000 acres in Idaho.

Idaho's U.S. Senator Frank Church, who served from 1957 to 1981, is generally recognized as one of the major influencers in creating and passing the Wilderness Act of 1964 (floor sponsor in the Senate) and establishment of a viable process for designating wilderness areas in the future. He would later co-sponsor other wilderness legislation including The Wild and Scenic Rivers Act of 1968, The Eastern Wilderness Areas Act of 1974 and The Endangered American Wilderness Act of 1978.

Apple orchard.

The effort to develop and pass the Boulder-White Clouds Wilderness law was led by Idaho's U.S. Congressman Mike Simpson – an effort that took him more than a decade and a half – with the support of Idaho U.S. Senator Jim Risch in the Senate.

Institutions of Higher Learning

The region's principal institutions of higher education are Idaho State University in Pocatello and the private Brigham Young University-Idaho operated by The Church of Jesus Christ of Latter-day Saints in Rexburg. Eastern Idaho Technical College and University Place, a campus where Idaho State University and the University of Idaho collaborate in providing degree programs, are both in Idaho Falls.

Brigham Young University-Idaho

Branches of other universities and colleges and Internet-based institutions also provide degree and certificate programs.

The Economic Base – Historically and Today

Historically, agriculture and mining underpinned Eastern Idaho's economy. Today, technological innovation and consolidation have changed the once labor-intensive production agriculture and food processing businesses into more productive operations using a fraction of the previous labor force. Except for phosphate, most mining activity in the region has ceased.

Today, technology, education, health care, retail and food processing businesses provide most of Eastern Idaho's jobs. Many of these jobs require a substantially more educated workforce. INL is the region's largest employer. Other major employers include elementary and secondary schools, institutions of higher learning, regional hospitals, food processing operations and retail shopping centers.

Idaho State University.

BANNOCK COUNTY

- Arimo
- Chubbuck
- Downey
- Inkom
- Lava Hot Springs
- McCammon
- Pocatello (*County Seat*)

Flag Day in Arimo, 2008.

Arimo

Statistical Data

Population: 356 *
Elevation: 4,736 feet
Precipitation: 10 inches **
Average Snowfall: 18 inches **
County: Bannock

Temperature Range – Fahrenheit: **
Spring: 26 to 67
Summer: 45 to 86
Fall: 24 to 75
Winter: 16 to 37
* U.S. Census Bureau Estimates July 2015
**Historical averages

The high-desert city of Arimo is situated near the center of Marsh Valley, 40 miles north of the Idaho/Utah border.

The Caribou National Forest frames the valley. The Portneuf Mountain Range is on the east, and the Bannock Mountain Range lies to the west.

Arimo residents have the "better of two worlds." They live in a peaceful, rural environment yet only 29 miles from Pocatello and the excellent shopping, employment and higher education opportunities offered there.

Pre-Incorporation Years

In the early 1860s following discovery of gold in western Montana, Marsh Valley became a thoroughfare for thousands of prospectors, freighters and fortune seekers.

Freight wagons and stagecoaches ran from Ogden, Utah; across the Snake River at Eagle Rock, now Idaho Falls; across the continental divide at Monida Pass; to the gold fields near Virginia City, Butte and Garrison, Montana. Western Montana was part of the Idaho Territory until the Montana Territory was created on May 26, 1864.

They called the route the "Gold Road." Between the late 1860s and early 1870s, about half of the supplies for the Montana goldfields came over the 466-mile stretch of road between Ogden and Garrison. (*See The Region, Mining – The Gold Road – Precursor to Settlement of Eastern Idaho*.)

Hauling freight to the mines was often more profitable than prospecting. The demand for food and goods delivered to the miners was so high that freighters could sell their cargo for several times more than they paid for it.

The stagecoach stations were spaced about a day's journey apart to provide passengers and freight wagon crews a safe place to get food and rest for the night.

Faster moving stagecoaches hauled passengers and mail. Freight wagons, whose cargo and chassis could weigh up to 12 tons, moved much slower. Two or three of these freight wagons were often connected one behind the other and pulled with several teams of mules or oxen.

As a rule of thumb, animals had to pull a load equivalent to their weight – hence the origin of the term "pull your own weight." Replicas of these wagons are featured at the "Wagon Days Festival" each Labor Day in Ketchum.

One freighter, "Fast Freight Bill," hauled salt from Corrine, Utah, to Virginia City. When he passed through Marsh Valley, he sold saltlicks to the ranchers for their livestock.

At the time, Marsh Valley was part of Oneida County – a county as large as the states of Maryland and Delaware combined and named after Lake Oneida in New York.

In 1868 a man named Ruddy built his home and a stagecoach station, Ruddy Station, next to the Gold Road at the mouth of Garden Creek two miles west of what is now Arimo. At the same time, settlers began coming to the area, filing their homestead claims, building canals and diverting water for irrigation from the nearby creeks, springs and rivers. (*See The Region, Federal Lands – Private Ownership and Preservation Laws*.)

Arimo, circa 1879, then called Oneida. The *Union Pacific Magazine*, August 1926.

Marsh Valley has many springs and artesian wells. Settlers used some wells for irrigation, but most irrigation water came from the Portneuf River, a river that several decades earlier yielded numerous beaver pelts. (*See The Region, Early Trappers/Explorers*.)

The early settlers built the canals and diverted Portneuf River water at great personal sacrifice. Many could not afford shoes and worked barefoot. The going wage for laborers was 25 cents a day.

A town began to grow up around Ruddy Station. As the community grew, it took on the name of Oneida.

Many settlers built their first houses out of logs hauled down from the mountains. The roofs were made of poles and branches covered with sod.

In 1869 railroad interests completed the transcontinental railroad at Promontory, Utah. Five years later, an independent railroad company built a line from Ogden to Franklin, Idaho. Following a succession of business failures and mergers, the Utah and Northern Railroad Company (UNR) emerged – owned primarily by certain principals of the Union Pacific Railroad. Congress granted the company a railroad right-of-way north of Franklin to Helena, Montana.

Marker at site of original Oneida Train Depot.

In 1878 the UNR built a narrow gauge line that generally followed the Gold Road. The track was three inches high and set approximately 3 – feet apart – much easier and less expensive to build than the wider and heavier standard-gauge railroad. The narrow-gauge was used successfully for several years before being replaced by the standard-gauge that became the national standard. (*See The Region, Railroads*.)

The railroad built a depot at Oneida, further promoting growth of the town. The town soon boasted a post office, two blacksmith shops, three hotels, a bakery, mercantile stores and many saloons and dance halls. The population swelled to 2,000.

Oneida was a rough and somewhat lawless town. John William Stinger, one of the early residents, cooked for a "work-train." His father, John Henry, operated bakeries in Oneida and Pocatello. They witnessed some of the lawlessness and said that gambling and drunkenness were prevalent.

Faro and roulette were favorite gambling games. When the stakes got high, gamblers piled bags of gold dust and silver on the table. Gunfights and thefts were common. Sometimes men would shoot through the kitchen walls to hurry the cooks. At times they threw dishes and cooking utensils at each other.

In 1878 the railroad, which was then partly owned by the Oregon Short Line Railroad, began converting its narrow-gauge line to standard-gauge. A few years later, UNR merged into the Oregon Short Line and built a new standard-gauge line between Ogden and McCammon. The new line was more direct and shorter, bypassing Oneida about two miles to the east. (*See The Region, Railroads*.)

The Oneida railroad depot, along with the post office, moved next to the new railroad track, creating a name identification conflict between the two towns that would take a decade to correct.

Most businesses and many homeowners sold or moved their buildings. Some structures were jacked up, put on horse-drawn skids and dragged to the new site. Others arranged with the railroad before the old tracks were removed to haul their dismantled buildings on flat railcars to the new site where they were reassembled.

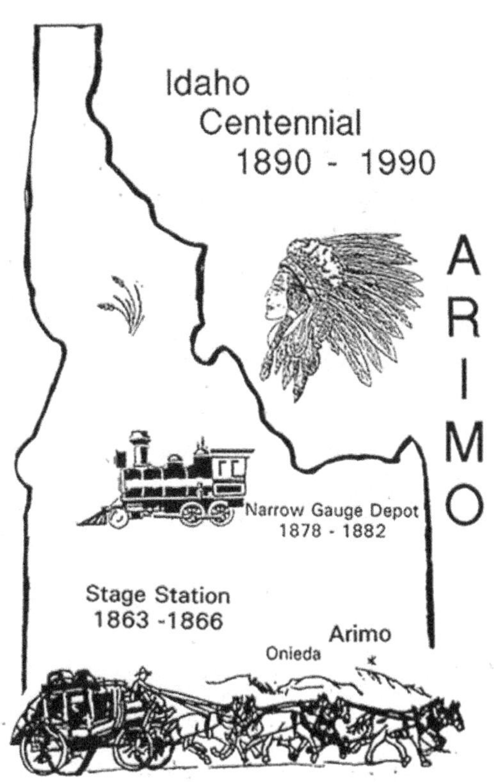

Arimo history book cover. Used with permission.

The Woodland Store was a saloon and hotel when it was in the old town. James Henderson purchased the building, moved it to its present location on Main Street and turned it into a mercantile store and post office. Henderson's store sold everything from ice blocks cut from a frozen pond and stored in an icehouse filled with sawdust to machinery, candy and shoelaces. Indians traveling between Fort Hall near Pocatello and Fort Washakie, Utah, often stopped at the store.

A marker built from the original train depot's foundation stone is the only evidence of the old rip-roaring railroad town of Oneida.

After the move to the new location, the town prospered. Four grain elevators and a lumber and coal business started and a one-room school opened.

With the railroad, the sheep industry flourished. The area was the winter home for 30 to 40 herds of sheep consisting of 3,000 to 4,000 head each. Every spring before being moved to higher elevations to graze, the sheep were sheered in local shearing sheds and the wool shipped to market. In the fall, the herds returned for winter range with a new crop of fat lambs. Oneida was the area shipping point for both wool and lambs. Each spring and fall vast herds of sheep trailed through the community. (*See The Region, Livestock.*)

In 1912 town leaders began formal action to change the name of the new community and separate it from the sordid reputation of the original Oneida village. They selected Arimo in honor of Chief Arimo of the Shoshone Indians who befriended early white settlers. On April 2, 1912, postal authorities confirmed the new name when they changed the name of the post office to Arimo. (*See The Region, American Indians.*)

Several months later, W.W. Woodland completed platting 640 acres as the Arimo town site. Woodland's plat included existing buildings and the donation of lots for the Arimo Cemetery and schools. On December 29, 1913, residents ceremoniously dedicated their new town of Arimo.

Incorporation

A decade later, on December 24, 1923, Arimo was incorporated as a village. On January 5, 1967, under a new state law, the village became an incorporated city.

Turning Points

Ruddy Station Although Ruddy Station was two miles west of what is now Arimo, it was the catalyst for creating the present-day town.

Arimo Cemetery.

Were it not for the commercial and residential infrastructure built up around Ruddy Station, the railroad bosses may not have chosen first the old and then the new town of Oneida to locate their depots and post office.

Railroad When the railroad arrived in 1878, it provided local service and was a major stimulus to the agricultural economy. In 1940 there were 16 businesses along Front Street, most of which owed their existence to the Arimo train depot and the commerce it brought.

Over time, motor vehicles and better roads gradually eroded the demand for train service. On November 29, 1968, Union Pacific closed the depot and ceased stopping at Arimo. Later it tore down the depot, stockyards and other facilities that previously supported the train stop.

The loss of the railroad was devastating to the city as retail businesses also closed their doors and ranchers and farmers came less frequently into town, relying solely on trucks to haul their livestock and crops to market.

Irrigation and Domestic Water. Irrigation significantly increased the productivity and profitability of the land previously dry farmed and greatly expanded the types of crops farmers could grow. In addition to growing wheat, barley and hay, irrigation and food-processing businesses allowed farmers to grow such crops as potatoes and sugar beets.

Some of the many free-flowing springs in Marsh Valley still provide domestic water for the city.

Electricity. Utah Power and Light Company brought electricity to Arimo in 1920. As a condition to receive the electric power, residents purchased appliances and stock in the company.

Marsh Valley School District. In 1955 voters from Arimo, Downey, McCammon, Lava Hot Springs and Inkom approved the consolidation of their school systems into a single school district, so they could provide better educational facilities and curriculum for their children at less cost.

Under the consolidation, the elementary schools stayed in or near each city and the Marsh Valley High School and Middle School were located in Arimo. This added many new stable jobs of mostly university-educated people, strengthened the city's economy and made Arimo more attractive to families.

The schools also added to the city's culture. In 2005 the school district built the Marsh Valley Performing Arts Center on the school's campus where students put on a variety of concerts and performances that are open to the public.

Arimo Today

Amenities and Attractions The city leases a large park in the center of town from the school. It is a center of athletic activity with a baseball diamond, lights for games at night, a pavilion and playground equipment.

The city is also developing a small park by the fire station for small gatherings and family activities.

Every July 4, the city celebrates Independence Day with a flag ceremony and parade followed by an afternoon of picnics and family-oriented activities.

The Hawkins Reservoir Recreation Management Area is eight miles west.

Economy and Major Employers The Marsh Valley School District with 255 employees is the city's largest employer. Arimo has a few retail stores that also provide employment.

Local farmers produce wheat, potatoes, cattle and milk. These commodities are trucked to other cities for sale or processing.

Education The Marsh Valley School District provides substantially all of the elementary and secondary education for five cities over a 1,100 square mile area. Pre-school through sixth grade students attend schools in or near their own communities. The older students attend school at the Marsh Valley High School and Middle School in Arimo. The closest institution of higher learning is 29 miles north at Idaho State University in Pocatello.

Health Care Health care and ambulance service are available at general medical clinics in Lava Hot Springs and Downey. The Bannock Regional Medical Center in Pocatello is the nearest full-service hospital.

Transportation Interstate 15 borders the western edge of the city. The closest airport for light private and charter aircraft is in Downey. The closest airport for commercial aircraft is Pocatello.

Utilities and Services Private companies provide electric, telephone and satellite services. The City provides domestic water. A volunteer fire department provides fire protection and the Bannock County Sheriff's Office provides law enforcement services. Residents and businesses are on individual septic systems.

Vision for 2050

For several decades, Arimo's population has held around 300. Except for the growth in the Marsh Valley schools and people choosing to live in Arimo and commute to work in Pocatello, the historical population trends will likely continue.

Existing infrastructure is adequate to sustain this population pattern and moderate growth.

In 2050 Arimo will continue to be a place where people believe rural living is best, a place for people of all ages who want to live clean, safe, tranquil lives.

Mayors

1923 Henry J. Nelson *
1927 O.E. Henderson *
1955 W.W. Winn *
1959 Leonard Howe *
1963 T.J. Smith *
1969 J.A. Primm
1973 Morris Woodland
1974 Wayne Lyman
1977 Modell Christiansen
1978 Steven Christensen
1988 Keith Anderson
1997 John Ackerman
2000 Jean Anderson
2006 Fred Winward
2010 Lionel Ware

* Village Chairman

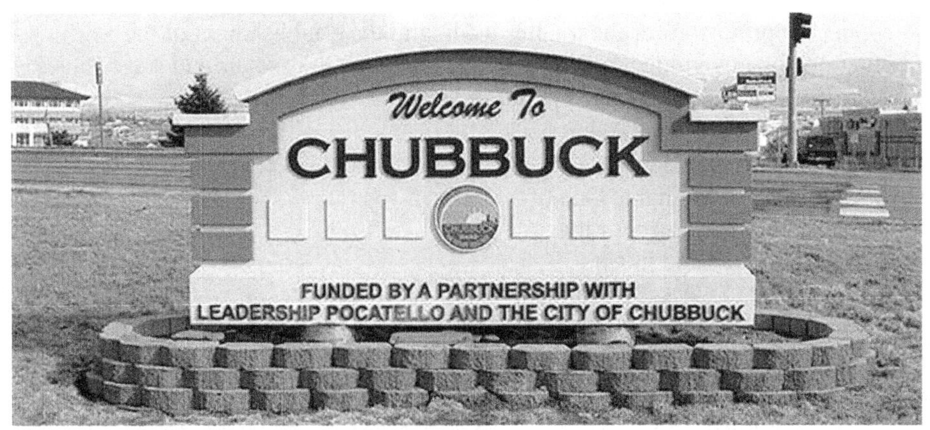

Chubbuck

Statistical Data

Population: 14,229 *
Elevation: 4,448 feet
Precipitation: 11 inches **
Average Snowfall:37 inches **
County: Bannock Winter: 13 to 38
Website: www.ci.chubbuck.id.us

Temperature Range – Fahrenheit: **
Spring: 25 to 66
Summer: 44 to 84
Fall: 22 to 74
* U.S. Census Bureau Estimate July 2015
**Historical averages

Chubbuck, originally a bedroom community for Pocatello, has grown from a population of 1,590 in 1960 to Idaho's 19th largest city.

Chubbuck's eastern border is defined by I-15, and its southern border abuts I-86 and the city of Pocatello. The 63-mile-long I-86 – the shortest east-west freeway in the nation – merges into I-15 at the city's southeastern corner. The Fort Hall Indian Reservation borders the city's area of impact on the north and west.

As Chubbuck has grown, the boundaries separating it and Pocatello have become transparent. The leaders of the two cities have used this close proximity to find ways, in cooperation with the County, to work in harmony for their common good. The business community has done the same, and the Greater Pocatello Chamber of Commerce serves both communities. The burgeoning retail development between the two cities allows shoppers to move between them as they shop from store to store.

Pre-Incorporation Years

The histories of Chubbuck and Pocatello are intertwined.

In 1867 following a series of military conflicts, the Fort Hall Indian Reservation was established. Various groups of American Indians, primarily from Shoshone tribes, agreed to live there. At that time, the reservation included the area now occupied by Chubbuck and Pocatello.

Under the provisions of the treaties leading to the establishment of the reservation, the government could construct telegraph lines, overland stage routes, stage stations and railroads on reservation land.

In 1860 prospectors found large quantities of placer gold in the streams of western Montana. One of the principal supply routes for the flood of prospectors and miners heading to Montana was through the Fort Hall Indian Reservation with a stage stop in Pocatello. The road – called the Gold Road – crossed the Snake River at Eagle Rock, now Idaho Falls, and entered Montana over the Continental Divide at Monida Pass.

Yellowstone and Chubbuck Roads.

In 1877 the Utah and Northern Railroad began building a rail line from Utah to the gold fields in Montana. The line generally followed the Gold Road through Pocatello and Eagle Rock. At that time, the railroad's roundhouse and maintenance facility were at Eagle Rock.

In November 1884 the Oregon Short Line completed a rail line from Granger, Wyoming, through Pocatello to Huntington, Oregon. Completion of this line resulted in connecting Portland, Oregon, and Omaha, Nebraska.

In 1886 a fierce windstorm caused significant damage to the railroad's Eagle Rock roundhouse. The railroad chose not to rebuild at Eagle Rock but rather to relocate to Pocatello. Many Eagle Rock residents followed the railroad to the Pocatello area. With the merge of the Utah and Northern into the Oregon Short Line in 1889, Pocatello became a regional railroad hub.

West Chubbuck and Hawthorne Roads.

In 1887 in an attempt to assimilate American Indians into the white mainstream, Congress passed the General Allotment Act, also known as the Dawes Severalty Act.

Under this Act, Native Americans received an acreage allotment of reservation land, generally 160 acres. Any lands not allotted became "surplus" and were made available for non-Indian settlement, primarily under the 1862 Homestead Act.

Indians who did not want to farm could either sell or lease their land. In many parts of the nation, this law encouraged large-scale settlement by non-Indians on previous reservation lands and created a checkerboard ownership pattern throughout the reservations. The Dawes Severalty Act and the Homestead Act allowed homesteaders to settle Chubbuck. By 1934 Congress repealed most of the Act's provisions.

Homesteaders began moving into Chubbuck after passage of the Dawes Severalty Act and the Homesteading Act. By 1916 the settlers in the area were successful in securing federal water rights to divert Snake River water into a complex system of irrigation canals and ditches.

Homesteading was arduous. Just providing a family's basic domestic water needs required a major effort. In the early years, homesteads did not have individual wells. Instead, they generally hauled their drinking water from rivers and streams in wooden barrels. They hauled their bath water from nearby irrigation ditches and, typically, had to let the ditch water stand overnight before using it so that the suspended soil in the water could settle to the bottom. Baths were often a Saturday night ritual. Beginning with the girls, the family's children often bathed in the same tub of water.

Each new well in the area became a matter of local news. As homesteaders dug wells, clean cool water became available and was shared with neighbors. In the early 1900s sugar beets became an important commodity in southern Idaho. Sugar companies constructed several sugar beet processing factories in the area.

Aerial view of Capell Park.

In the Pocatello area, each fall farmers would haul their sugar beets to a railroad siding in what is now Chubbuck. There, the sugar beets were loaded on rail cars and shipped to the processing plant in Paul. The train engineer in charge of the railroad siding was a man named Earl Chubbuck. The railroad stop soon became known as "Chubbuck's Siding."

Chubbuck Road became the main road through the community. For many years, sheepherders brought their sheep through town as they moved their herds between the summer grazing land in the eastern hills to the lambing and winter range several miles west.

Construction of U.S. Highway 91 between Utah and Montana began in 1925. The highway was a 24-foot-wide concrete road that passed through the Chubbuck area.

One of the first buildings in town was a dance hall called the Blue Moon. The first store was a general merchandise store located on the northwest corner of

Yellowstone and West Chubbuck Roads. The store attracted a large clientele. Local residents, farmers and Indians stopped and bartered for goods at the store. During the next decade, other hospitality and retail stores and a bank opened.

Chubbuck residents have a reputation for generosity and service. One shining example of this is Harry Hart, one of Chubbuck's leading citizens. Orson Talbot, his wife and physically handicapped daughter moved into the village in 1947. Talbot, a blacksmith, provided prompt turnaround service even if he had to work all night. The Talbots' daughter required constant care and Talbot or his wife had to be with her at all times. Hart would go by the Talbot home for a few hours once or twice a week and care for the child so the Talbots could get some relief. Hart later donated land to the City for its water tank farm.

War memorial at city hall.

Incorporation

In 1947 the Idaho Legislature passed a law governing the sale of liquor by the drink and the licensure of establishments offering those beverages. A provision of the law required businesses selling alcoholic beverages to be located within incorporated cities or villages.

At that time several bars, nightclubs and other hospitality businesses in the unincorporated Chubbuck community were selling liquor by the drink and had slot machines.In order to conform to the law, the proprietors of these establishments sought to incorporate a relatively small parcel of land around their businesses as a village. However, they did not have the minimum number of voters living within their designated boundaries. To overcome this barrier, they moved in trailer homes and otherwise recruited people to move within the boundaries of their new community.

Idaho Central Credit Union corporate office.

Residents in the greater Chubbuck area found out about the action and began circulating a village incorporation petition for a much larger area. They did not want Chubbuck to become a seamy "wide-open village."

On December 6, 1949, the Bannock County Commissioners approved the petition for the larger village. The local hospitality business proprietors challenged the commissioners ruling in court. The lower court ruled in favor of the hospitality businesses because they submitted their petition first. On appeal, the higher court

City Hall.

upheld the action of the county commissioners.

Turning Points

Railroad The 1886 decision by railroad officials to make Pocatello a rail hub led to establishing the economic base that led to the founding of Chubbuck.

Federal Land Reclamation Law The General Allotment Act of 1887 and the Homestead Act of 1862 played critical roles in the settlement of Chubbuck. The first opened up the land for non-Indian settlement, and the second induced settlers to turn the arid land to farms and ranches. The 1894 Carey Act and the 1902 Reclamation Act were critical to the widespread development of irrigation systems.

Aerial view of Chubbuck.

Idaho Alcohol Beverage Law Passage of the 1947 law limiting sale of liquor by the drink to businesses located in incorporated municipalities precipitated the drive to establish the incorporated village of Chubbuck. Without that law, the city of Chubbuck may have never developed.

Interstate 86 and 15 Construction of the Interstate freeways on the east and south of Chubbuck had a profound effect in defining the city and promoting its economy. The freeways established two of Chubbuck's boundaries and the increased traffic and freeway access encouraged development of a regional mall and retail shopping center.

Chubbuck Today

Amenities and Attractions The city has fourteen parks. Each park has walking paths. Parents particularly like the paths because they provide a safe place for their young children to ride their tricycles and wagons.

The city's largest park, Cotant Park, has seven baseball diamonds. The baseball complex has been used to host several Western Regional Little League Tournaments through the years.

The next largest park, the 17-acre Capell Park, has three softball diamonds. A privately owned and operated roller hockey facility is under construction at Capell Park.

Chubbuck has received the Tree City USA award.

The city has constructed a monument in front of City Hall on which is inscribed the names of each Chubbuck man and women who served in the U.S. armed forces.

Mystique.

One of the city's prized amenities is its close proximity to public lands and outstanding fishing and hunting.

A few miles due west of the city are the shores of the 65,000-acre American Falls Reservoir. The lake – created by the hydroelectric dam on the Snake River near the City of American Falls – has over 200 species of birds. The lake is a popular place for fishing, hunting, camping, boating and water skiing.

The Caribou National Forest begins a few miles southeast of the city. The forest provides opportunities for hiking, biking, fishing, hunting, ATV riding and snowmobiling. Additionally, downhill skiing is available at Pebble Creek Ski Resort, 25 miles southeast of the city. Its ski runs are in the Caribou Forest's Portneuf Mountain Range on the slopes of the 9,271-foot-high Mount Bonneville.

Approximately 40 miles north is the lower edge of the U.S. Department of Energy's Idaho National Laboratories (INL) 570,000-acre plant site and National Environmental Research Park. (*See Eastern Idaho, Idaho National Laboratories – Eastern Idaho's Largest Employer.*)

Economy and Major Employers The Pine Ridge Mall, constructed in 1980, was a catalyst for bringing other retail businesses along the I-86 corridor – such as Wal-Mart and Home Depot. Taken together, these retail businesses employ over 2,000.

Other major employers include Steel West, Inc, a steel fabricator; the Pocatello Railroad Credit Union; and Idaho Central Credit Union.

Education The Pocatello/Chubbuck School District provides most of the elementary and secondary education. Three elementary schools are located in the city. The city's middle and high school students attend school in Pocatello.

The closest institution of higher learning is Idaho State University in Pocatello.

Idaho Skin Institute.

Health Care The Portneuf Regional Medical center in Pocatello provides most of the city's health care needs. The Portneuf Valley Hospital and Rehabilitation Center, also located in Pocatello, is a skilled nursing facility.

Transportation Interstate 15 borders the city on the east. I-86 marks the city's southern boundary. U.S. Highway 91 – also named Yellowstone Highway – intersects the city.

Pocatello Regional Airport with its 9,056-foot-long runway lies nine miles west.

Rail service for freight is available in Pocatello.

Utilities and Services Private companies provide electricity, telephone, gas, cable and satellite services. Pocatello provides municipal wastewater treatment for Chubbuck under a contract between the Cities.

Chubbuck provides police and fire protection and domestic water service. The city's present water sources are capable of accommodating a population exceeding twice its present size.

Chubbuck has successfully used tax increment financing to pay for street, water and sewer system improvements as well as to develop city parks.

Vision for 2050

Over the past decade, Chubbuck's population has grown from two to three percent annually. Should those trends continue, by 2050 Chubbuck's population will more than double.

The unincorporated non-reservation lands to the north and west of the city and underutilized infill land within the city limits is adequate to accommodate this growth.

The city already has adequate water sources to accommodate future growth. It is working with Pocatello and Bannock County in establishing a Joint Powers Agreement to develop municipal wastewater systems adequate to accommodate the future growth of each community.

Regional cooperation is necessary to protect the integrity of our shared aquifer, provide stable and orderly growth patterns for each community and conserve tax dollars. As part of this process, the city has engaged an engineering firm to evaluate the feasibility of expanding sewer services to certain of its unincorporated areas.

Aerial view of Chubbuck.

By 2050 there should be interchanges built on I-15 at Siphon Road and on I-86 at Philbin Road with a 5-lane road providing a beltway access between the two. These interchanges will encourage both commercial and light industrial development as well as easy access to planned residential growth. It would also promote the steady progression of Chubbuck's "main street," Yellowstone Avenue, to the north with retail and office facilities.

The I-86 interchange at Yellowstone Avenue is a magnet for retail development in both Chubbuck and Pocatello. This growth in retail store development will continue. The new desired interchanges will attract similar growth.

Long before 2050 the Idaho Central Credit Union will have completed construction of its new office buildings and expansion of its Chubbuck headquarters.

The futures of Chubbuck and Pocatello are inextricably connected. The good working relationship between the two cities is essential for the common good of both communities. Both cities, as well as Bannock County, will continue to move forward in a cooperative effort.

By 2050 this cooperative effort will extend to other cities in the region.

Mayors

1949 J.O. Cotant *
1951 John Valenty *
1959 Larry David *
1964 D.T. Worsencroft *
1965 Willis Ward *
1967 R.C. Hillman *
1968 Boyd Twiggs
1968 Leslie Henry
1970 John O. Cotant
2006 Steven M. England
2014 Kevin England
* Village Chairman

Aerial view of Downey.

Downey

Statistical Data

Population: 617 *
Elevation: 4,854 feet
Precipitation: 12 inches **
Average Snowfall: 40 inches **
County: Bannock
Website: www.downeyidaho.com

Temperature Range – Fahrenheit: **
Spring: 30 to 70
Summer: 60 to 90
Fall: 40 to 80
Winter: 10 to 60
* U.S. Census Bureau Estimates July 2015
**Historical averages

Downey is a small high-desert farming community at the southern end of Marsh Valley, 40 miles south of Pocatello.

The Caribou National Forest nearly surrounds the valley. The Bannock Mountain Range is on the west and south, and the Portneuf Mountain Range lies to the north and east. The beautiful 9,200-foot Oxford Peak in the Bannock Mountains punctuates the city's southern skyline.

Its rural setting and traditional values have allowed Downey to be largely crime free. With Interstate 15 nearby, residents can live in a peaceful mountain valley and still take advantage of the amenities offered in larger communities located less than an hour away.

Pre-Incorporation Years

Around 1866 William Jackson and Cyrus Coffin built the first cabin in the area near Nine Mile Creek just a few miles north of what is now Downey. This building now stands under a covered roof in Downey City Park.

In 1878 the Utah and Northern Railroad – later the Oregon Short Line Railroad – built a line from Utah through Eastern Idaho to the Montana gold fields. (*See The Region, Mining, The Gold Road – Precursor to Settlement of Eastern Idaho.*)

Railroad depot at Downey.

By 1879 several homesteaders had come into the area, clearing the land for farming and building canals to divert irrigation water to their farms from nearby creeks and the Portneuf River. They named their village Downey after a railroad executive who was instrumental in building the Downey Railroad Depot. (*See The Region, Federal Lands – Private Ownership and Preservation Laws; and Agriculture and Irrigation.*)

In that same year, W.A. Hyde, an entrepreneur looking for a place to start a business, visited Downey and assessed it as "a good location, splendid conditions and advantages." He stayed and established the W.A. Hyde Co. Mercantile store. It was the town's first building. Hyde then began building what would become the city's first house.

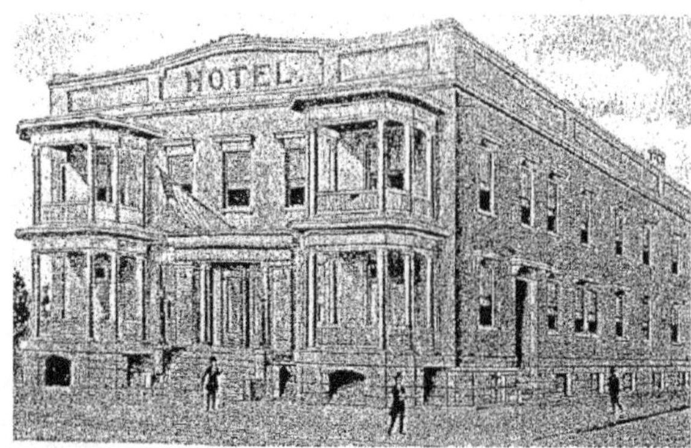

Oxford Hotel, Downey.

By 1895 a blacksmith shop, a hotel and a butcher shop had opened. In addition, the residents elected Hyde's brother, George T., as justice of the peace and made application for a post office.

About five years later, W.A. Hyde sold his business to his brother George and moved to Pocatello. In that same year, John S. Hyde, another relative, arrived and joined George in the business.

During 1900 a group of investors installed a small telephone system. Not having telephone wire, they used what became one of the icons of the West – barbed wire strung on insulators attached to farm fence posts. When the line workers came to a gate or street, they merely put up a couple of high poles, ran wire over the top and connected to the barbed wire fence on the other side.

In 1905 George and John Hyde acquired land around the settlement, laid out a town site and offered lots for sale. They donated a 10-acre tract for a public park with the stipulation that it remain a public park forever. They also donated half a city block to The Church of Jesus Christ of Latter-day Saints (Church) for a building site. In 1985 the Church built a new facility at a different location. Church leaders tore down the old building and donated the land for a city park – Woodland Park, named after a police officer killed in the line of duty. (*See The Region, Pioneer Settlements*.)

In 1906 the citizens established the first public school with John Hyde, Lars Johnson and John Criddle as trustees.

Early view of Downey, circa 1906.

George and John Hyde built a two-story brick building known as Hyde Block around 1910. The building included an amusement hall, business offices and a post office with a printing press in the basement.

In the same year, Downey State Bank was established, and a new irrigation system to irrigate the lots in town was completed.

Incorporation

On October 15, 1912, the Bannock County Commission approved the incorporation of Downey as a village. In 1967 the legislature passed municipal law making all incorporated communities cities.

Turning Points

Railroad The railroad spurred the establishment of the city and development of the valley's agricultural economy. It not only provided efficient transportation to move agricultural commodities to distant markets but also greatly increased the speed of transporting passengers and the mail. The railroad was undoubtedly one factor leading to W.A. Hyde saying the sagebrush-covered setting was "a good location (with) splendid conditions and

Tom Boam blacksmith, 1906.

advantages."

The railroad was a magnet for growth. During the decade following incorporation, the city constructed sidewalks, electric lighting became available, the Methodist congregation built a church, Globe Grain Milling constructed a flourmill and the school district built Downey High School. (*See The Region, Railroads*.)

Great Depression, World Wars and Camp for Conscientious Objectors Downey, like other cities, felt the economic ebb and flow of World War I, the Great Depression and World War II. During World War II, the military converted a 1939 Civilian Conservation Corps camp a half mile east of town into a Civilian Public Service Camp – Camp Downey – for conscientious objectors. The 27-acre site had 21 buildings that housed up to 150 and was operated by the Mennonite Central Committee. Detainees worked on the farms to offset the manpower shortage caused by military drafts and enlistments.

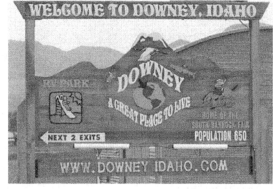

Farm Technological Innovation and Consolidation During the 1980s and 1990s, technological innovation increased farm productivity with less labor. Smaller farms were absorbed by larger, more efficient operations, further reducing the demand for labor. With no other business to provide jobs, the city's young people go elsewhere for education and employment.

Education In a bid to improve educational quality for their children in the 1950s, Marsh Valley citizens voted to consolidate their school districts. In February 1958 Downey High School students began attending the new Marsh Valley High School about 12 miles north in Arimo. Years later, voters approved building a new Downey Elementary School. The old school is now a senior citizen center.

Downey Today

Amenities and Attractions The city has three municipal parks on 12 acres that offer picnic areas, ball fields, tennis courts and playground equipment.

On the first weekend in August, the city hosts the South Bannock County Fair, which features exhibits, livestock shows, a parade and a rodeo.

Pool at Downata Hot Springs.

A few miles south of town is

Downata Hot Springs, a resort with thermal springs that burst from the ground at 113 degrees Fahrenheit. The resort features a large naturally-heated swimming pool and water slides, camping sites and a bed and breakfast. It is a favorite location for weekend camping, family reunions and parties.

Near the resort is a 700-acre marshy wetland, fishery and bird refuge. The water in the refuge comes from thermal and cold-water springs and small creeks.

Marsh at Downata Hot Springs.

The marshland is home to many species of birds – including sand hill cranes, geese, ducks, blue heron and white-faced ibis. Underneath the marshland is an 80-foot-thick layer of peat moss.

South of Downey is the geologically significant Red Rock Pass. For millennia most of Utah and parts of Idaho and Nevada were covered by Lake Bonneville – a lake nearly the same size as, but deeper than, Lake Michigan.

At that time, there was a natural dam at the base of the lake at what is now Red Rock Pass. The dam caused the lake to fill to several hundred feet deep. About 14,500 years ago, the dam breached causing a flood of massive proportions.

City offices.

The floodwater generally followed the natural drainage of the Snake River west and north to the Pacific Ocean. When the flood reached Portneuf Narrows, 45 miles northwest of Downey, the floodwaters were 400 feet high. (*See The Region, Distinctive Geographic and Geological Features – Prehistoric Lake Bonneville*.)

The city's proximity to the mountains and streams of the Caribou National Forest provides excellent opportunities for outdoor recreation. In the warmer months, activities include camping, hiking, biking, hunting, fishing and ATV riding. In the winter, snowmobiling is popular. Downhill skiing is available at Pebble Creek Ski Area, about 40 miles north.

Economy and Major Employers Agriculture is the dominant industry in the area. About 240,000 acres of farmland surround the city.

Approximately 30 businesses are located within the city. Residents say Downey has enough businesses to make life comfortable. Retail businesses include grocery and convenience stores, gas stations, a bank, a health clinic, a dental office, a lumberyard, day care centers and an adult care center. Tri-State Recycling is the largest non-retail business in town.

Education The Marsh Valley School District serves a broad geographical area. Downey Elementary serves students from kindergarten to sixth grade. Students in grades 7 to 12 are bused about 12 miles north to Marsh Valley Middle and High Schools in Arimo.

Downey's north entrance.

The nearest institution of higher learning is Idaho State University in Pocatello.

Health Care A health clinic and an adult care center are located in downtown Downey. The closest hospital is in Malad, about 20 miles south of the city.

Transportation The city is on State Highway 91 about five miles south of the highway's intersection with Interstate 15.

Downey's Hyde Memorial Airport has a 3,550-foot lighted runway that accommodates small private and charter aircraft. The closest commercial airline services are at Pocatello Regional Airport.

Downey water tower.

Utilities and Services Private companies provide telephone, electrical and satellite services. The City provides water, garbage and sewer services. Downey has its own volunteer fire department and contracts with Bannock County for police protection.

Vision for 2050

In 2050 Downey will still be a quiet, peaceful rural community, much as it is today but with a few important changes. The city will be a little larger with some light clean industries to provide jobs for a slightly larger population.

Many downtown buildings are more than 100 years old. Private interests will have restored or replaced these buildings.

There will be more entertainment facilities – including restaurants, a public swimming pool and an athletic park for youth.

The city will have a larger fully equipped station to house fire, police and emergency medical vehicles and equipment.

Overall, we see a bright future for Downey in the year 2050 – we are just sorry we will not likely be around to see it.

Oxford Peak south of Downey.

Mayors

1923** Joakim F. Hartvigsen *
1925 John Devere Morgan *
1934 Lorin Criddle *
1935 Hal S. Garretson *
1937 Kenneth W. Hamilton *
1941 Burton M. Almond *
1944 George Salvesen *
1947 Elvin Christiansen *
1954 Willis A. Barfuss *
1966 Arnold Jr. Naef *
1967 Keith Hyde
1968 Clarence Brown
1972 Merl Bloxham
1976 Vern Bloxham
1980 Frank Howe
1984 Jack Day
1988 Steve Simpson
1992 Ila Mae Cunningham
2000 Daniel K. Christensen
2001 Eugene Webb
2002 Ralph C. Riser, Jr.
2008 Dennis Phillips

* Village Chairman

** Records from 1912 to 1923 are not available

Inkom in winter.

Inkom

Statistical Data

Population: 863 *
Elevation: 4,547 feet
Precipitation: 10 inches **
Average Snowfall: 30 inches **
County: Bannock

Temperature Range – Fahrenheit: **
Spring: 26 to 67
Summer: 45 to 86
Fall: 24 to 75
Winter: 16 to 37

* U.S. Census Bureau Estimates July 2015
**Historical averages

Inkom is at the lower end of Marsh Valley tucked amid juniper and sagebrush-covered hills and outcroppings of lava rock. The Caribou-Targhee National Forest surrounds most of the city. The Portneuf River meanders through the valley, passing near the southern border of the city as it flows toward Pocatello, 15 miles northwest.

City residents have unencumbered views of the nearby mountains. The Portneuf Mountains with the 9,271-foot-high Bonneville Peak and Pebble Creek Ski Area are six miles southeast. The Bannock Mountain range with its 8,700-foot Scout Mountain is 12 miles southwest.

Pre-Incorporation Years

North of Inkom is a historic American Indian meeting place and burial site called Ingakom, from which "Inkom" derives its name.

In 1824 Peter Skene Ogden, an employee of the Hudson's Bay Company, led a successful beaver-trapping expedition to the Snake River country. During this trip, one of Ogden's French trappers named Portneuf lost his life to hostile Indians while working a tributary to the Snake River near what is now Pocatello. Ogden named the stream the "Portneuf River" after his departed colleague. The name survived and also became the name of the river valley; the mountain range on the east; and the "Portneuf Narrows," the narrow gap between mountains to the west that figured prominently in the Lake Bonneville Flood. (*See Distinctive Geographic and Geological Features – Prehistoric Lake Bonneville.*)

Boston fur trader Nathaniel Wyeth built the Fort Hall Trading Post on the Snake River northwest of what is now Pocatello in 1834. The Hudson's Bay Company acquired it in 1837. For decades, Fort Hall was a prominent Oregon Trail landmark and layover for pioneer travelers. (*See The Region, Early Trappers/Explorers*.)

Sorrell Home in Inkom, 1899. Indian Rock is on the right. The women in dark dresses are missionaries.

Prospectors discovered gold in southwestern Montana in 1862. Many supplies to the gold fields came from Utah over a wagon trail called the Gold Road, which passed near what is now Inkom. (*See The Region, Mining – The Gold Road, Precursor to Settlement of Eastern Idaho.*)

In 1865 a deadly stage hold up occurred on the Gold Road about four miles southeast of what is now Inkom. When the Ben Holladay Stage stopped at a line of boulders placed across the road by four thieves, the stagecoach's two lead horses were shot and killed by the thieves to prevent escape.

The robbery turned more deadly when one of the bandits panicked, firing several shots through the stagecoach. He killed four of the passengers and wounded another.

The stage driver and a passenger escaped by fleeing into the nearby brush and trees. The bandits, who the survivors recognized, got away with two strongboxes of gold valued then at $86,000.

Vigilantes later captured and executed three of the felons but did not recover the gold. Robbers Roost Creek and Canyon, three miles south of the crime, is a testament to the early dangers of traveling the Gold Road.

The Shoshone-Bannock Indians signed the Fort Bridger Treaty in 1868. The agreement created the then 1.8 million acre Fort Hall Indian Reservation. Under the terms of the treaty, the Shoshone-Bannock Tribes agreed to live on the reservation and the U.S. government agreed to provide food and supplies to supplement their loss of food sources.

The government, however, failed to keep its part of the agreement. The hungry Indians returned to their historic hunting grounds to find settlers, many of whom were living on the Camas Prairie near what is now Fairfield where the Indians historically gathered Camas roots for their winter's food – some of the settlers had hogs feeding on the roots, digging them out of the ground with their snouts.

The desperate Indians were incensed, and in 1878 about 200 warriors left the reservation, killing settlers, destroying property and taking provisions. The U.S. Army was soon in hot pursuit of the Indians with skirmishes in Idaho, Oregon, then back into Idaho until the Indians were defeated. These series of skirmishes over several months are called the Bannock War. (*See The Region, American Indians – The Bannock War*.)

Inkom School, 1910.

The Utah and Northern Railway Company constructed a narrow-gauge rail line from Franklin to Pocatello in 1878 – reaching the mines in Garrison, Montana, in 1882. Near the future city of Inkom, the railroad made a 90-degree bend along the edge of the marshland and prehistoric lava flows. For several years, they called the location "Big Bend."

Congress passed the Dawes Severalty Act in 1887, which, in general, allotted 160 acres of land to each Indian head of household. Any reservation land not allocated was termed surplus and made available for settlement to non-Indians – generally under provisions of the 1862 Homestead Act. (*See The Region, American Indians – Dawes Severalty Act.*)

In 1889 the Shoshone-Bannock Indians were forced to cede, by Act of Congress, the southern part of the reservation to the federal government – the part that included what are now Downey and Arimo. In 1900 Congress passed another law, ratified by President Theodore Roosevelt in 1902, that again reduced the remaining size of the reservation – this time by more than half and included the land around what is now McCammon, Inkom and Pocatello.

Rabbit Rock.

The railroad built the Inkom Train Depot in 1902, the same year President Roosevelt ratified the law making hundreds of thousands of acres of former Fort Hall Indian Reservation land open for settlement.

On June 16, 1902, thousands of people lined up in Pocatello ready to race their wagons, buggies and horses to their pre-selected homestead sites. The Pocatello Tribune reported, " ... there is a feeling of tension noticeable everywhere." With the blow of the noon railroad whistle the land-rush was on; homesteaders raced out on horseback to stake claims and then made a dash to Blackfoot to get them filed.

Inkom train depot, 1902.

In October 1902 the settlers opened Inkom's first school. Two years later, one of the settlers living on Rapid Creek opened a general store, hotel and the Inkom Post Office in the building that also served as his home.

A.J. Damron donated land for the cemetery in 1906, and by 1907 Inkom had a grocery store, a post office, a general store, a hotel, a barber, a livery, a lumber company and a shoemaker. The town also had a constable and a justice of the peace.

H. A. Without and Theodore H. Gathe filed their Inkom townsite plat with the county on December 12, 1912. They sold lots for $100 each, advertizing, "Get choice location, secure your lot now, only $5.00 down, balance $1.25 per week, no interest." Within three years, two new grocery stores opened.

Inkom Store and Post Office, 1904.

J. Simmons and J.B. Maxfield discovered a major deposit of high-grade limestone and silica suitable for the production of Portland Cement in 1928 and immediately acquired the 160-acre site. The following year, they sold the property to the Oregon Portland Cement Company which built cement kilns and manufacturing facilities near Inkom.

Incorporation

On July 8, 1946, Inkom became an incorporated village. In 1967 Inkom became an incorporated city in accordance with a change in state law.

Turning Points

Railroad The city owes its origins to the railroad line from Utah to the Montana goldfields. The railroad not only served the miners, but it also opened distant markets to agricultural commodities produced in Inkom and other Eastern Idaho communities. When the railroad came through what is now Inkom in 1878, it cut through reservation land. It would take 24 years before homesteaders were allowed to settle. However, it was the immediate availability of railroad transportation along with fertile land and water that attracted many settlers to the Portneuf Valley.

Cement Plant. For many years, the cement plant was Inkom's largest employer. Ash Grove Cement Company acquired the plant in 1983. It was then in continuous production until the downturn in 2008 and 2009 forced the company to lay off two-thirds of its workforce. This had a significant adverse effect on the city's economy.

Inkom Today

Amenities and Attractions Inkom has four city parks on 25 acres. Skyline Park was Inkom's first city park and is complete with a Veterans' Memorial. It also contains public restrooms, covered pavilion with running water, picnic benches, a volleyball court, a basketball court, horseshoe pits, children's swings and toys. Glen Peck Park, a three-acre tract, has a baseball field and open area. State Park and Helmandollar Park offer picnic areas and open spaces. City residents often rent park facilities for private gatherings.

In 1963 the Chesterfield Dam broke, flooding Inkom.

Stuart Sports Complex has 12.6 acres of soccer and baseball fields, a practice field for football, a covered shelter and restrooms. It also has a recently installed memorial called "Ring of Freedom" with a U.S. flag, a flag for each branch of the military and a POW flag.

Pebble Creek Ski Area is five miles southeast of Inkom. The resort has three chairlifts operating on the east slope of Mt. Bonneville. The resort has 1,100 acres and 54 ski runs. The vertical drop from the top of the lifts is 2,200 feet.

Lava Hot Springs, a 178-acre public park and resort managed by the Lava Hot Springs Foundation of the Idaho Department of Parks and Recreation, is 20 miles southeast in the city of Lava Hot Springs.

The heavily vegetated riparian habitat along Marsh Creek, Rapid Creek and the Portneuf River provides an excellent environment for a variety of wildlife. Outdoor enthusiasts are attracted to these waterways and the Caribou-Targhee National Forest for a variety of activities including camping, hiking, fishing, hunting and ATV riding in the warmer months and skiing and snowmobiling in the winter.

Economy and Major Employers Ash Grove Cement Company, headquartered in Overland Park, Kansas, operates with about 22 employees. The cement plant is still one of the city's major employers.

Many of the Pebble Creek Ski Area employees live in Inkom. This resort has about 30 full-time and 20 seasonal employees.

Many residents commute to work and shop in Pocatello. The Inkom downtown business community provides basic services including a grocery store, a bank, a credit union, a cafe, a convenience store, an auto repair, a day care, personal care services and two bars. Trucking and grain elevator businesses serve the nearby agricultural community.

Education Marsh Valley School District provides public elementary and secondary education. Kindergarten through sixth grade students attend school at Inkom Elementary. Students in grades 7 and 8 attend Marsh Valley Middle School and grades 9 through 12 attend Marsh Valley High School 17 miles south in Arimo.

Inkom, 1948.

The nearest institution of higher learning is Idaho State University in Pocatello.

Health Care Portneuf Medical Center in Pocatello provides most of the city's medical care needs.

Transportation Inkom is located just off Interstate 15. U.S. Highway 30 intersects the city. The Idaho Department of Transportation operates a port of entry at Inkom.

Railroad freight services are available in Pocatello.

The nearest air service is Pocatello Regional Airport, 25 miles from Inkom.

Utilities and Services Private companies provide natural gas, electricity, telephone, cable and satellite services. The City has its own volunteer fire department, quick response unit, police department and water and sewer services. The City contracts with Bannock County Landfill to provide solid waste services.

Vision for 2050

By 2050 the boundaries between Inkom and Pocatello will have drawn to within a few miles. However, coordinating land use policies with Bannock County will allow a physical and visual separation between the two cities. The zoning of privately-owned land separating Inkom and Pocatello along Portneuf Road and Old Highway 91 will continue to be agricultural, with many more five- to ten-acre mini-farms.

Many Inkom residents already commute to Pocatello to work. This trend will increase, as more people will be attracted to Inkom's affordable housing and quiet rural lifestyle.

Commercial development will grow along U.S. Highway 30. City leaders will seek to manage this growth to ensure Inkom has an attractive city center that provides daily conveniences. However, residents will continue to travel to Pocatello for many of their shopping needs.

Inkom, mid-1970s.

To accommodate commercial and residential growth, the city's area of impact and incorporated boundaries will increase. The plans to clean up and beautify the city, consistent with the needs and values of the citizens, will be complete. The city's water system will be improved with a new water well, tank and updated lines. The City will also be upgrading the sewer system within the next few years. Open space will be protected, new parks added and existing parks improved as part of the city's comprehensive park and open space system.

The City will protect geologically unstable areas from unsuitable or environmentally disruptive land use activities. The City will protect areas designated as significant wildlife habitat. Zoning will prevent development in designated floodways, and development in the flood fringe areas will be limited. The city's heritage and historic sites and buildings, such as the Old Scout Cabin, the Community Bible Church and the Ingakom and other rock outcroppings in and near town will be preserved and protected.

Inkom, today.

Mayors

1946 Parley B. Reese *
1947 Louis Hargraves *
1949 Frank Ball *
1950 Ernest Gardner *
1951 Louis Hargraves *
1954 Ross Fowler *
1957 Raymond Larsen *
1967 Raymond A. Larsen
1970 Claude Stuart
1976 Wayne Hargraves
1976 Ron Helmandollar
1986 Dale Bowman
1994 Paul Lish
2002 Ernest Moser
2006 Sheldon Ward
2006 Joel Jolley
* Village Chairman

Lava Hot Springs, circa 1990.

Lava Hot Springs

Statistical Data

Population: 406 *
Elevation: 5,072 feet
Precipitation: 15 inches **
Average Snowfall: 66 inches **
County: Bannock
Website: www.lavahotspringscity.com

Temperature Range – Fahrenheit: **
Spring: 26 to 67
Summer: 45 to 86
Fall: 24 to 75
Winter: 16 to 37

* U.S. Census Bureau Estimates July 2015
**Historical averages

Lava Hot Springs is a year-round destination resort community built around artesian flows of odor-free 102 to 140 degree Fahrenheit geothermal mineral water. Each day over three million gallons of water bubble up in the 178-acre state-owned resort complex before flowing into the Portneuf River that runs through the city. The Lava Hot Springs Foundation of the Idaho Department of Parks and Recreation manages the complex, including an Olympic-size swimming pool, water slides, hot baths and smaller pools. Privately-owned hospitality and other businesses are located nearby.

Many people assert that the warm mineral water has therapeutic attributes that provide refreshment and relief from soft tissue and joint pain. Historically, the

Shoshone-Bannock Indians would bathe in the springs for spiritual comfort as well as relief from bodily aches and pains. Later, trappers/explorers, Oregon Trail immigrants and settlers stopped to refresh themselves in the pools of clear, flowing hot water.

The city lies 35 miles southeast of Pocatello on the sloping flood plain of the Portneuf River Canyon. The Caribou National Forest, interspersed with farm and ranch land, surrounds the city. The Portneuf Mountain Range, rising to 9,271 feet, lies to the west and northwest. The Fish Creek Mountain Range with its 6,200-foot-high Mt. Moh outlines the city's eastern sky.

Main Street, 1914.

Pre-Incorporation Years

The Bannock and Shoshone Tribes referred to the hot mineral springs as "Po-Ha-Ba." Interpreted, the term means the land of healing waters. They used the waters for both physical and spiritual purposes and designated the area as neutral ground shared in peace by all tribes.

In 1812 trapper/explorer Joseph Miller led a party past the hot springs while exploring the Portneuf River. Years later, Hudson's Bay Company trappers/traders came into the area. One of these trappers – Bob Dempsey of Antrim, Ireland – built a one-room cabin west of the confluence of Dempsey Creek and the Portneuf River. By 1861 the fur business played out and the Hudson's Bay Company withdrew. Dempsey moved to Montana.

In 1841 the first immigrants to Oregon passed through Idaho. Two years later, Captain John C. Fremont, a topographical engineer, led a surveying expedition that mapped much of the West. Benoni M. Hudspeth was a member of Fremont's expedition. Oregon Trail immigrants used Fremont's maps in establishing the Oregon Trail and certain cutoffs from the main trail.

In 1849 a party of 250 immigrants led by Hudspeth blazed a shortcut southwest from Soda Springs to connect with the California and main Oregon Trails near the City of Rocks. The Hudspeth Cutoff passed by the hot springs and Bob Dempsey's cabin.

The cutoff shaved 25 miles off the main route and gave travelers an opportunity to bathe and relax at the hot springs, which they called "Dempsey's bathtub." Soon, most of the California and Oregon immigrants were using the Hudspeth Cutoff.

In 1863 the U.S. Superintendent of Indian Affairs entered into treaties with the Bannock and Shoshone Tribes that led to the 1867 creation of the Fort Hall Indian Reservation. The reservation boundaries included all of the land around the hot springs. The agreement allowed easements on reservation land for telegraph, stagecoach and railroad corridors and stations.

Mud baths, 1909.

In 1884 the Oregon Short Line Railroad – now Union Pacific – completed its rail line between Granger, Wyoming, and Huntington, Oregon. The rail line passed through the Portneuf Valley and what is now the city of Lava Hot Springs. The hot springs location became a railroad flag stop.

An increasing number of railroad passengers wanted to stop and refresh at the hot springs. Because of its increasing popularity, the federal government purchased the springs and 178 acres of reservation land from the Fort Hall Indians.

In 1887 in an attempt to open reservation land for settlement and assimilate American Indians into the white mainstream, Congress passed the General Allotment Act – also known as the Dawes Severalty Act.

Lava Hot Springs, 1914.

Under the Act, American Indians received a specified acreage allotment of reservation land, generally 160 acres per head of household. Any lands not allotted became "surplus" and available for non-Indian settlement under the 1862 Homestead Act or other federal programs. The Indian Reorganization Act of 1934 largely superseded the General Allotment Act. The new law restored remaining "surplus" land to tribal ownership to be held in trust. (*See Eastern Idaho, General Allotment Act and Redistribution of Indian Reservation Lands.*)

John Hall, an English emigrant and entrepreneur, observed the increasing popularity of the hot springs and in 1890 filed a homestead claim on land near the federal hot springs land.

In 1902 the federal government ceded its 178 acres to the State of Idaho for public use. Three years later, the railroad built a depot and Lava Hot Springs became a routine stop.

In 1911 the state appointed its first superintendent over the 178 acres and appropriated $500 for construction of a one-room enclosure over a spring-fed pool. In the same year, John Hall saw a business opportunity and platted his homestead property with the town name of "Hall City." A town of merchants and hospitality business owners and workers serving the tourist traffic soon developed. The businesses and post office that had built up around Dempsey's old cabin site about a mile downriver moved to the new town.

Incorporation

On July 24, 1915, Bannock County Commissioners approved incorporation of the village. The citizens seeking to promote the resort amenities were obviously not satisfied with the platted Hall City name, so they incorporated the village with the name "Lava Hot Springs."

Turning Points

Hudspeth Cutoff. Benoni M. Hudspeth's 1849 Oregon Trail cutoff established the hot springs as an attractive rest stop for thousands of travelers going to Oregon and California.

Lava Hot Springs Hot Pools, today.

Railroad When the Oregon Short Line Railroad built its rail line through the Portneuf Valley in 1883 and in 1905 built a train depot at Lava Hot Springs, it put the community on its map as a destination resort.

Lava Hot Springs Foundation. The federal acquisition of the springs and land from the Indians and subsequent grant of the property to Idaho insured protection of the site as an Idaho treasure.

Development of the site began slowly. In 1918 in response to the increasing popularity of the site, however, the State Legislature appropriated funds to construct an indoor Natatorium – destroyed by fire in 1982 – with mud baths and indoor and outdoor swimming pools. The Legislature also created the Lava Hot Springs Foundation to manage this largely self-sustaining operation under the Department of Parks and Recreation.

The Foundation has continued to expand its facilities. The resort now offers a broad variety of water sports, slides and a swimming pool complex supported by private hospitality, retail and service businesses.

Lava Hot Springs Today

Amenities and Attractions The city's greatest attraction is its famous Hot Springs. The Lava Hot Springs Resort complex has indoor and outdoor pools, including an award-winning Olympic AAU World Class Swimming Pool with a 33-foot-high diving tower overlooking clear, warm water that is 17 feet deep.

It is a picturesque village with a historic hotel dating from 1917 and a business district, including buildings from the 1920s. Clean air, beautiful sunsets and a pollution-free environment are some of the city's most important attributes.

Tubing the river, Lava Hot Springs.

Thousands of visitors come each year. In 2006 for example, 145,000 visitors came into the resort – 84,000 of them using the Olympic Swimming Pool with its waterslides and hydrotube.

The South Bannock County Historical Center Museum registered over 14,000 visitors traveling from other parts of the U.S. – primarily Utah – and nine foreign countries.

Attracted by the diverse number of family-oriented outdoor activities, an increasing number of families are scheduling reunions in the city. The youth especially enjoy the diving boards and water slides at the complex as well as tubing through town on the Portneuf River.

There are 200 lodging rooms and 400 campsites in or near the city. Both public and private campgrounds are available. One private campground offers non-license trout fishing in their private ponds.

Local ranches offer guided horseback riding tours and wagon rides. People ride up Mount Moh to see spectacular vistas as well as wagon ruts made a century and a half ago by thousands of Oregon Trail pioneers and gold rush miners.

The State of Idaho has 17 acres of parkland available for reservation. It includes picnic facilities, pavilions, barbeque pits, playgrounds and restrooms. The Lava Lions Club, in cooperation with other agencies, sponsors a challenging hiking and biking trail.

The city has a 9-hole golf course. Hiking, camping, hunting, cross-country skiing, snowshoeing and snowmobiling are also available on nearby ranches and public lands. Many people fish the Portneuf River. There is a privately-owned airpark, "Sky Park," with a grass runway just outside town. Downhill skiing is available at Pebble Creek Ski Resort at Mount Bonneville.

The pace of everyday life in Lava Hot Springs is leisurely. Residents fondly call their city Lava. Mule deer sometimes cross the city's streets to reach the river. Volunteerism is common. The American Legion hosts community dinners and outdoor breakfasts; the Lava Lions and Lionesses host Bingo. An active corps of volunteers staffs the Senior Center, South Bannock County Historical Center and Museum and Fire Department.

Economy and Major Employers The Lava Hot Springs Foundation has 60 employees and is the city's largest employer. Shawn's Market, with 15 employees, is the city's second largest employer.

Other businesses include 19 lodging or camping locations, eight restaurants, 11 retail shops and five businesses that offer family entertainment such as river rafting and horseback trail rides.

Olympic-sized pool, Lava Hot Springs.

Some residents have chosen to live in the city and commute to Pocatello for work.

Education The Marsh Valley School District serves the communities of south Bannock County and provides most of the city's K-12 education. Lava Elementary provides education for the city's K-6 students. Students in grades 7-12 are bused 12 miles to Marsh Valley Middle and High Schools in Arimo.

Health Care A medical clinic, dental office and assisted-living home are located in the city. The nearest hospital is the 27-bed Caribou Memorial Hospital located 26 miles east in Soda Springs.

Transportation U.S. Highway 30 intersects the city. Federal Interstate 15 is 12 miles west.

Light private and charter aircraft use the city's airport and its 3,500-foot runway located two miles west of town. The closest commercial airport is the Pocatello Regional Airport, located west of Pocatello, 44 miles from Lava Hot Springs.

Utilities and Services Private companies provide electricity, telephone, gas and satellite services. The City provides water and sewer services and fire protection. The Bannock County Sheriff's Office provides police protection. A private business provides solid waste services.

Vision for 2050

For the past several decades, the population of Lava Hot Springs has remained somewhat constant. However, historical population trends are beginning to change.

More families, including retirees, are looking for affordable housing near more populated areas. An increasing number of these families are choosing to live in beautiful and peaceful Lava Hot Springs and commute to jobs in Pocatello, Soda Springs and Grace. New construction is already underway upstream on the Portneuf River.

The Lava Hot Springs Foundation is continuing to add attractions to its complex. This will increase tourism, which, in turn, will expand business activity in the city.

While not presently in the city, county lands at Sunnyside will attract large-lot residential subdivisions. The area around Fish Creek and Dempsey Creek will continue to develop commercially with vacation entertainment businesses.

Improved public transportation systems will develop between Pocatello, Lava Hot Springs, Grace and Soda Springs. These improved bus routes will further encourage rural living and commuting to work and shop.

Mayors

1915 John Hall *
1917 P.J. Schwarz *
1922 John Hendrick *
1923 A.M. Boyce *
1923 Joe Bell *
1924 Alma Porter *
1924 John H. Roberts *
1925 A.W. Miller *
1935 Leon Fife *
1937 Myron Comish *
1938 George D. Elrod *
1939 A.W. Miller *
1943 Nolan J. Nelson *
1945 F.W. Dalton *
1945 Nolan J. Nelson *
1945 Roy Judd *
1947 Jack Ramsey *
1949 Roy Judd *
1951 Harold E. Thomas *
1955 Roy Judd *
1963 C.A. Smith *
1967 Leno D. Seppi
1975 Mark E. Campbell
1978 Dean Ware
1984 Karen Keller
1985 Leno D. Seppi
1985 Bruce E. Hansen
1986 Newton J. Lowe
1996 Mark E. Campbell
1996 Bruce E. Hansen
1999 Raymond Bailey
2008 Marshall Burgin
2016 T. Paul Davids
* Village Chairman

McCammon

Statistical Data

Population: 797 *
Elevation: 4,783 feet
Precipitation: 13 inches **
Average Snowfall: 40 inches **
County: Bannock
Temperature Range – Fahrenheit: **
Spring: 26 to 67
Summer: 45 to 86
Fall: 24 to 75
Winter: 16 to 37
* U.S. Census Bureau Estimates July 2015
**Historical averages

McCammon is a historic railroad town located at the upper end of Marsh Valley. The Caribou-Targhee National Forest borders the city on the east and west. Immediately east of the city, across the Portneuf River, is the Portneuf Mountain Range. A few miles across the valley to the west is the Bannock Range.

Pocatello is 17 miles northwest, and Lava Hot Springs is 12 miles east.

Pre-Incorporation Years

Until around 1810 when the first European and American explorers/trappers came into the region, American Indians – primarily of the Shoshone and Bannock Tribes – hunted and fished in the Marsh Valley area.

From 1825 to 1826 Peter Skeen Ogden led a beaver-trapping expedition along the Snake River and its tributaries. Indians killed one of the trappers, a French-Canadian named Portneuf. The river, valley and mountain range now bear his name.

In 1834 the British Hudson's Bay Company established its Fort Hall trading post near what is now Pocatello. In 1841 the first immigrants to Oregon's Willamette Valley passed through Idaho. They and many that followed stopped to rest and resupply at Fort Hall. In 1843 Captain John C. Fremont, a topographical engineer, led a surveying expedition that mapped much of the West. Oregon Trail immigrants used Fremont's maps in establishing the Oregon Trail and evaluating certain cutoffs from the main trail.

In 1849 a party of 250 immigrants led by Benoni M. Hudspeth, a former member of Fremont's expedition, blazed a shortcut off the Oregon Trail to connect with the California Trail at the City of Rocks, located 15 miles southeast of what are now Oakley, the City of Rocks National Reserve and Idaho's Castle Rocks State Park.

Rather than proceeding north on the main trail from Soda Springs to Fort Hall, Hudspeth led his party southwest through what is now Lava Hot Springs, skirted the south side of what is now McCammon and continued southwest to the City of Rocks. Hudspeth's Cutoff shaved 25 miles off the northern route and gave travelers an opportunity to bathe and relax at the hot springs. Soon, most immigrants traveling overland to California were using the Hudspeth Cutoff.

In 1863 prospectors discovered placer gold in what is now western Montana, then part of Idaho Territory. To accommodate the stagecoach and freight wagon traffic coming from northern Utah to the Montana gold fields, the Idaho Legislature approved private construction of a toll road and set the toll rates on a road then called the "Idaho Gold Road." The road was essentially a dirt path with major obstructions removed or filled to make it passable.

The road generally paralleled what is now I-15 to Idaho Falls where it turned north, crossing the Continental Divide at Monida Pass then on to the Montana boomtowns of Virginia City, Butte and Garrison, a distance of 466 miles between Ogden, Utah, and Garrison. Hauling freight to the Montana gold mines was often more profitable than prospecting. Freighters sold food and goods delivered to the minefields for several times their original cost.

Ben Holladay opened a stagecoach service in 1864 with stagecoach stations spaced about a day's journey apart to provide passengers and freight wagon crews with a safe place to get food and rest for the night.

The faster moving stagecoaches hauled passengers and mail. The ponderous freight wagons were about 16 feet long; 14 feet tall, including the low canvas covering; and about four feet wide. The heavy wooden spoke wheels that stood up to seven feet tall in back had a half-inch-thick and four-inch-wide iron band around their perimeters. Two or more of these freight wagons were often connected one behind the other.

From 14 to 24 mules pulled the heavy wagons whose pull-weight was generally equivalent to the aggregate weight of the mules – origin of the axiom "pull your own weight." Replicas of these wagons are featured at the "Wagon Days Festival" held each Labor Day in Ketchum.

One freighter, "Fast Freight Bill," hauled salt from Corrine, Utah, to Virginia City, Montana. When he passed through the valley, he sold saltlicks – blocks of salt – to the ranchers for their livestock.

In 1864 William Murphy built a toll bridge across the Portneuf River at what is now McCammon – then called Port Neuf – and, later, bought the rights to the toll road on which the stagecoaches and wagons ran. In 1870 Murphy was involved in a brawl outside a bar in Malad and was shot and killed. After his death, Murphy's wife, Catherine, married Murphy's manager, Henry O. Harkness.

In 1865 a deadly stage hold up occurred on the Gold Road about seven miles north of what is now McCammon. Four thieves held up the Ben Holladay Overland Stage. When the stage stopped at a line of boulders placed across the road by the thieves, the bandits shot and killed the stagecoach's two lead horses to prevent escape. The robbery turned more deadly when one of the thieves panicked, firing several shots through the stagecoach. He killed four of the passengers and wounded another, the stage driver and a passenger escaped by fleeing into the nearby brush and trees. The bandits, who the survivors recognized, got away with over two strongboxes of gold valued then at $86,000.

Vigilantes later captured and executed three of the felons but did not recover the gold. Robbers Roost Creek is located in a canyon five miles north of McCammon – a testament to the early dangers of traveling the Gold Road.

In 1868 the Shoshone-Bannock Indians signed the Fort Bridger Treaty. The agreement created the then 1.8 million-acre Fort Hall Indian Reservation. Under the terms of the treaty, the Shoshone-Bannock agreed to live on the reservation, and the U.S. Government agreed to provide food and supplies to supplement their loss of food sources.

The U.S. Government failed to keep its part of the agreement by not providing food and supplies. The hungry Indians returned to their historic fall Camas root-gathering grounds on the Camas Prairie near what is now Fairfield. They harvested and stored the Camas roots for winter food – generally prepared by crushing them and making a cake that they baked. However, when they arrived, they found settlers living on the Prairie. Many of the settlers had hogs, which fed on the Camas roots, digging them from the ground with their snouts.

The desperate Indians were incensed, and in 1878 about 200 warriors left the reservation, killing settlers, destroying property and taking provisions. The U.S. Army pursued the break-away Indians into Oregon and back to Idaho in a series of running skirmishes termed the Bannock War. Following the war, the defeated Shoshone-Bannock Indians ceded the southern part of the reservation, including McCammon, to the federal government.

Henry O. Harkness.

Following business failures and mergers of predecessor railroads, the successor railroad – the Utah and Northern Railroad Company (UNR), owned primarily by certain principals of the Union Pacific Railroad – built a narrow-gauge rail line from Franklin, Idaho. The line, completed in 1878, generally paralleled the Gold Road. However, UNR had to bypass Port Neuf – now McCammon – because railroad officials could not make a deal with Harkness for needed land.

The narrow-gauge railroad – 3 feet wide – made the long-haul stagecoach and freight wagon business to the gold fields obsolete. However, the narrow-gauge railroad also became obsolete a few years later when standard-gauge railroad tracks – 4 feet 8 " inches – became required by law for new construction.

In 1881 the Oregon Short Line Railroad began construction of a standard-gauge rail line that began at Granger, Wyoming; angled in a northwesterly direction through Pocatello, Shoshone and Nampa; and connected with the rail line in Huntington, Oregon. The rail line – completed November 17, 1884 – provided the necessary link to connect the commerce centers of Omaha, Nebraska, with Portland, Oregon. In 1882 the OSL built a standard-gauge rail line from Pocatello to Port Neuf. This line laid new rail bed, shortening the old route and establishing a depot at Port Neuf, which they renamed McCammon after J.H. McCammon, a railroad official.

Harkness Opera House & Dance Hall.

Incorporation

On January 15, 1908, McCammon became an incorporated village. In 1910 the U.S. Census reported a population of 321.

Turning Points

Railroad McCammon is a city created and named by the railroad. Henry O. Harkness's intransigence in dealing with the UNR forced the light-rail railroad to go around the future city. However, it was not a factor a few years later when the OSL constructed its standard-gauge rail on a new more direct route through Marsh Valley to Pocatello. Then OSL established McCammon as an important depot and agricultural shipping point – a position it held for several decades.

Harkness Hotel.

McCammon Today

Amenities and Attractions Lava Hot Springs Resort, located 11 miles east in the city of Lava Hot Springs, is a historic hot springs frequented by Native Americans and Oregon Trail pioneers. Today, it is a year-round destination resort community built around artesian flows of odor-free, 102 to 140 degree Fahrenheit geothermal mineral water. Each day over three million gallons of water bubble up in the 178-acre state-owned resort complex before flowing into the Portneuf River. The Lava Hot Springs Foundation of the Idaho Department of Parks and Recreation manages the complex, which includes an Olympic-size swimming pool, water slides, hot baths and smaller pools. Privately-owned hospitality and other businesses are located nearby.

The nearby national forest and public lands offer a wide variety of outdoor recreation including hunting, fishing, camping, ATV riding in the summer and snowmobiling in the winter. Downhill skiing is available 10 miles north at Pebble Creek Ski Resort at the 9,271-foot-high Mount Bonneville.

McCammon train station.

Perhaps the most significant amenity enjoyed by McCammon residents is living in a quiet rural environment while being within a half hour drive from the regional commerce center of Pocatello with its shopping malls, hospital, airport and Idaho State University.

School bus blocking a road in McCammon.

Economy and Major Employers Marsh Valley School Distrcit is the city's largest public employer.

The city's business district consists of a convenience store and a few small businesses and retail establishments.

Many residents have employment in Pocatello or Lava Hot Springs and commute to work. Most of the city's residents travel to Pocatello to do their shopping.

Education The Marsh Valley School District covers an area of approximately 1,100 square miles and provides substantially all of the valley's elementary and secondary education.

In 1955 the school patrons throughout Marsh Valley – including the cities of Downey, Arimo, McCammon, Lava Hot Springs and Inkom – voted to consolidate their school systems into a single school district. With a single school district, they were able to provide better educational facilities and curriculum at less cost.

The city's pre-school through 6th grade students attend Mountain View Elementary in McCammon. The older students attend school at Marsh Valley High School and Middle School in Arimo.

The closest institution of higher learning is Idaho State University in Pocatello.

McCammon Post Office.

Health Care Health care and ambulance service are available at a general medical clinic in Lava Hot Springs. The Bannock Regional Medical Center, Portneuf Regional Medical Center and Portneuf Valley Hospital – all in Pocatello – provide full-service medical care.

Transportation U.S. Highway 30 intersects the city before merging into Interstate 15 on the north end of town.

The closest commercial airport is Pocatello Regional Airport.

Utilities and Services Private companies provide electric, telephone and satellite services. The City provides domestic water. A Volunteer Fire Department provides fire protection, and the County Sheriff's Office provides law enforcement services. Residents and businesses are on individual septic systems.

Vision for 2050

Train passing McCammon.

In 1960 McCammon had a population of 557. In 2000 the population increased to 814 where it has since stabilized. Recent historical trends will likely continue for several years before resuming a moderate rate of growth.

By 2050 the city's population will likely be less than 1,200 with residents continuing to enjoy a peaceful, rural environment within a short drive of Pocatello and the excellent urban shopping, employment and higher education opportunities available there.

Mayors

1967 Merle Hall
1971 Hugh Swim
1972 Glade Rowe
1973 Fielding Harris
1978 Cloyde Murdock
1979 Chester Wright
1984 Bill Howell
1984 Ken Bullock
1990 Martell Gunter
2002 Ken Bullock
* Village Chairman Unknown

Pocatello.

Pocatello

Statistical Data

Population: 54,292 *
Elevation: 4,464 feet
Precipitation: 11 inches **
Average Snowfall: 37 inches **
County: Bannock
Website: www.pocatello.us

Temperature Range – Fahrenheit: **
Spring: 27 to 68
Summer: 46 to 87
Fall: 25 to 76
Winter: 16 to 39
* U.S. Census Bureau Estimates July 2015
**Historical averages

Pocatello is located at the mouth of the Portneuf River Canyon as it opens up into the broad Snake River Plain. On the east, the Pocatello Mountain Range overlooks the city. The Caribou-Targhee National Forest lies south of the city.

The Fort Hall Indian Reservation, much of which is leased to farmers, lies on both the east and west sides of the city. The Portneuf River passes through the city before flowing into the American Falls Reservoir six miles northwest. Pocatello's northern border abuts the city of Chubbuck and U.S. Interstate 86.

Pre-Incorporation Years

The Portneuf River Canyon and Valley were carved 14,500 years ago when the prehistoric Lake Bonneville broke through its natural dam at Red Rock Pass about 50 miles south of the city. The massive flood lasted eight weeks and ran up to 400 feet deep as it cut through the Portneuf Narrows and flowed into the Snake River on its course to the Columbia River and the Pacific Ocean. (*See The Region, Distinctive Geographic and Geological Features – Prehistoric Lake Bonneville.*)

For centuries the nomadic Shoshone and Bannock Indians, along with some northern plain Gros Ventre and Blackfoot Indians, lived in the region as hunter/gatherer tribes. (*See The Region, American Indians.*)

European and American trappers/explorers began coming into the region around 1810. (*See The Region, Trappers/Explorers.*)

In 1825 to 1826 Peter Skeen Ogden led a beaver-trapping expedition along the Snake River and its tributaries. On this trip, Indians killed one of his French-Canadian trappers named Portneuf. The stream where he lost his life; the Portneuf River; and, later, the valley and a mountain range were named in his honor.

For several years, British and American fur-trading companies sponsored a type of traveling general store they called a rendezvous where they brought trade goods to a mountain location to exchange goods for furs. Several hundred trappers and Indians traveled hundreds of miles to attend these rendezvous. In 1829 and 1832 they held trade rendezvous in the beaver-rich Teton Valley near what is now Driggs. They named the location Pierre's Hole after one of the trappers/traders.

Nathaniel J. Wyeth was one of the traders at Pierre's Hole. In 1834 following disappointing business deals, Wyeth began construction of a trading post on the Snake River about 11 miles north of what is now Pocatello. He named the outpost Fort Hall after Henry Hall, a wealthy Bostonian who financed Wyeth's enterprise. Wyeth flew a hand-made American flag over the fort.

Wyeth was in competition with the British Hudson's Bay Company which, in the same year, established a trading post near what is now Parma at the confluence of the Snake River and a tree-lined river that flowed from the east. A year later, the outpost's manager, French-Canadian Francois Payette, named the tree-lined river "Boise," the French word for "wooded," and the trading post "Fort Boise."

In the winter of 1836 to 1837 Wyeth sold Fort Hall to the Hudson's Bay Company, retired the American colors and returned to Boston. The Hudson's Bay Company replaced the American flag with the Union Jack. At that time, the Pacific

Northwest was known as "Oregon Country" for which England and the United States both claimed ownership.

In 1841 the first immigrants to Oregon's Willamette Valley passed through Idaho. They, and many who followed, stopped to rest and resupply at Fort Hall and Fort Boise.

In 1843 Captain John C. Fremont, a topographical engineer, led a military surveying expedition that mapped much of the West. His party stopped at Fort Hall. Congress published Fremont's maps. Overland immigrants traveling to Oregon called the route the "Oregon Trail" and used Fremont's maps extensively. Early overland travelers headed to California broke off the Oregon Trail near Fort Hall. *(See The Region, Oregon and California Trails.)*

Junction.

In 1846 the United States and England signed a treaty fixing most of the border between Canada and the United States at the 49th parallel.

In 1849 following the 1848 discovery of gold in California, a party of 250 immigrants heading to California and led by Benoni M. Hudspeth, a former member of Fremont's expedition, cut off from the main Oregon Trail west of Soda Springs. Hudspeth led his party through what is now Lava Hot Springs, skirted the south side of what is now McCammon and continued southwest to the City of Rocks – now City of Rocks National Reserve and Idaho's Castle Rocks State Park – located 15 miles southeast of Oakley.

The Hudspeth Cutoff shaved 25 miles off the northern route that passed through Fort Hall. The cutoff was also attractive because it gave travelers the opportunity to bathe and relax in the hot spring water believed to have therapeutic attributes and provide relief from soft tissue and joint pain. Soon, most immigrants traveling overland to California were using the Hudspeth Cutoff. In 1855 Fort Hall operations ceased. Snake River flooding subsequently destroyed the original fort.

In 1863 prospectors discovered placer gold in what is now western Montana, then part of Idaho Territory. To accommodate the stagecoach and freight wagon traffic coming from northern Utah to the Montana gold fields, the Territorial Legislature approved private construction of a toll road called the "Idaho Gold Road." The road was essentially a dirt path with major obstructions removed or filled to make it passable.

The road generally paralleled present-day I-15 through Marsh Valley and Pocatello to Idaho Falls where it turned north, crossing the Continental Divide at Monida Pass then on to the Montana boomtowns of Virginia City, Butte and Garrison – a distance between Ogden, Utah, and Garrison of 466 miles.

Hauling freight to the Montana gold mines was often more profitable than prospecting. Freighters sold food and goods to the miners for several times their original cost.

Ben Holladay opened a stagecoach service in 1864 with stagecoach stations spaced about a day's journey apart to provide passengers and freight wagon crews with a safe place to get food and rest for the night. One of these stations was at what is now Pocatello.

The faster moving stagecoaches hauled passengers and mail. The ponderous slow-moving freight wagons were up to 16 feet long; 14 feet tall, including the low canvas covering; and about four feet wide. The rear heavy wooden spoke wheels stood up to seven feet tall. The wheels had a half-inch-thick and four-inch-wide iron band around their perimeter. Multiple freight wagons were often connected one behind the other.

Shoshone Indian Chief Pocatello, after whom the city was named. Left, statue in park. Right, sketch.

Up to 24 mules pulled the heavy wagons whose pull-weight was generally equivalent to the aggregate weight of the mules – origin of the axiom "pull your own weight." Replicas of these wagons are featured at the "Wagon Days Festival" held each Labor Day in Ketchum.

In 1868 the Shoshone-Bannock Indians signed the Fort Bridger Treaty. The agreement created the then 1.8 million-acre Fort Hall Indian Reservation. Under the terms of the treaty, the Shoshone-Bannock agreed to live on the reservation, and the U.S.

Fort Hall Replica.

Government agreed to provide food and supplies to replace their loss of food sources.

However, the U.S. Government failed to live up to its part of the treaty. The hungry Indians tried to cope by returning to their historic encampments to hunt and gather food. Historically, they harvested and stored Camas roots for winter food and generally prepared them by crushing the bulbs and making a cake which they baked. Upon returning to their historic fall Camas root-gathering grounds on the Camas Prairie near what is now Fairfield, they found settlers living on the land, many with hogs feeding on the Camas roots which they dug from the ground with their snouts.

Teepees at sunset.

The desperate Indians were incensed and in 1878 about 200 warriors left the reservation and traveled northwest to hopefully join forces with other Indians. En route, they killed settlers, destroyed property and took provisions. The U.S. Army pursued the break-away Indians into Oregon and back into Idaho in a series of running skirmishes termed the Bannock War. Following the war, the defeated Shoshone-Bannock Indians ceded the southern part of the reservation below what is now Pocatello to the federal government.

In 1869 railroad interests completed the first continental railroad at Promontory Point near Corinne, Utah. In 1874 the Utah-Northern Railroad Company (UNRC) built a narrow-gauge rail line from Salt Lake City to Franklin, Idaho – later extended to Preston. In 1878 principals with Union Pacific formed the Utah & Northern Railway Company that, in turn, acquired the UNRC at a receivers sale and moved to complete the rail line, which generally followed the Gold Road from Franklin to the Montana gold fields.

As the railroad line came out of the Portneuf River Canyon, it ran across what is now the Idaho State University campus before heading north along the Snake River to Eagle Rock – now Idaho Falls. About 75 miles of rail line ran across reservation land. Because the railroad did not compensate the Indians for the right-of-way, it was a festering issue with the Indians – not resolved until a decade later.

The narrow-gauge railroad – 3 feet wide – made the long-haul stagecoach and freight wagon business to the gold fields obsolete. The narrow-gauge railroad was replaced a few years later when standard-gauge railroad tracks – 4 feet 8 " inches – became law for new construction.

In 1881 the Oregon Short Line Railroad (OSL) began construction of a standard-gauge line that began at Granger, Wyoming; angled in a northwesterly direction through Pocatello, Shoshone and Caldwell; and connected with the railhead in Huntington, Oregon. The rail line – completed November 17, 1884 – created another intercontinental railroad, connecting the commerce centers of Omaha, Nebraska, and Portland, Oregon.

In 1882 the OSL railroad reached what is now Pocatello which, at that time, was largely a sagebrush-covered plain. OSL purchased 772 acres of reservation land for $6,000, 40 acres of which they assigned to the terminal near the junction of the OSL and UNR railroad lines – the site of present-day Pocatello.

Union Pacific Train Station.

Except for a hotel and freight depot which OSL built at the junction for the convenience of railroad passengers and the abandoned stagecoach and freight wagon station there were no visible structures in the area.

OSL called the location "Pocatello Junction" named out of respect for a prominent Shoshone Indian Chief. The name Pocatello is likely an anglicized pronunciation of the actual name of the chief, as the Shoshone language does not contain an "L" sound. In 1859 Col. Fredrick W. Lander referenced (spelled) the chief's name "Po-ca-ta-ro." In the OSL treaty negotiations with the Indians, the railroad junction was named and spelled "Pocatilla."

The 40 acres set aside for terminal grounds soon proved inadequate because OSL designated Pocatello Junction would become a terminal – significantly increasing the importance of the community.

OSL built homes for employees but not sufficient in number to house all of the workers. Many workers built permanent homes or set up shacks and tents on reservation land. Federal Indian Agents periodically responded by tearing down structures that had encroached onto reservation property. However, the rapidly expanding population made enforcement problematic. Even the federal magistrate lived illegally on reservation land, but held court in a boxcar on OSL right-of-way property.

In 1887 two events exacerbated the problem. The Secretary of Interior issued an order for Bureau of Indian Affairs agents to clear the reservation land of all structures. At the same time, heavy winds severely damaged the railroad's buildings at Eagle Rock. Railroad officials determined that Pocatello was a better location for their regional operation and literally moved most of their Eagle Rock facilities to Pocatello. Hundreds of the railroad's Eagle Rock employees also moved; but with no other land available, they made their homes on reservation land.

In this crisis, 41 persons representing the 1,500 residents living at Pocatello Junction petitioned the Secretary of Interior to grant an exception to his order and let the structures and people remain on reservation land until Congress could make other arrangements. Their petition stated that the people needed their permanent structures to protect them "from the awful cold of the Idaho winter."

The Secretary granted their petition, and in May 1887 the federal government signed a treaty with the Indians wherein the federal government purchased additional right-of-way for the railroad and about 2,000 acres for a townsite.

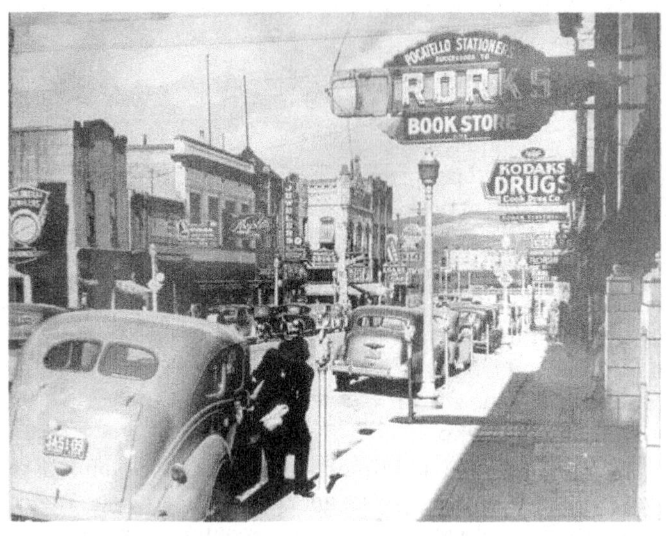

Also in 1887 Congress passed the General Allotment (Dawes) Act. The Act provided that Indians receive personal title to a specified amount of reservation land. For example, each Indian head of household received personal title to 160 acres. Any reservation land not so allotted was termed surplus and made available for settlement by non-Indians. Several years later, implementation of the Act would have a profound effect in further reducing the geographic size of the Fort Hall Indian Reservation as well as reservations throughout the country. *(See American Indians – Dawes Severalty Act.)*

In 1889 federal surveyors platted the townsite of Pocatello. The railroad and Portneuf River bisected the valley on a southeasterly to northwesterly axis. The townsite plat was "drawn" over the valley, apparently without adequate consideration given to the physical features of the river and the western foothills. The river ran through some lots and other lots extended up steep hillsides.

The plat provided streets every 300 feet in a block pattern, with alleys running down the center of each block.

The railroad tracks, which had few safe at-grade crossings, became a cultural dividing line with the more affluent homes and businesses on the west side of the tracks and the less affluent on the east. Immigrants of many nationalities who came to work for the railroad settled on the east side of the tracks making it a multicultural ethnic community. Years later, crossing the tracks became safe with viaducts constructed on Center and Halliday Streets. Construction of alternate routes across the railroad yards and tracks further enabled Pocatello's cultural integration and growth.

With the townsite platted, federal agents publicized the sale of the lots at public auction. However, such a sale was problematic as many of the town's population of around 3,000 already had homes and businesses on some of the newly platted land. The auction put them at risk of losing their improvements or having to pay for them twice. A citizens committee formed to resolve the matter recommended that when such lots came up for auction, a committee representative would announce the owner of the improvements on the lot and request that no one bid against the owner. This approach proved successful in every case.

Immediately after the drawing, Pocatello entered a period of rapid construction of new homes and businesses – giving the town a bright new face.

Panoramic view of Pocatello.

Incorporation

The city of Pocatello was declared a village on April 29, 1889, by the Bingham County Commissioners. Village status continued until 1893, at which time the State Legislature declared Pocatello a city of the second class, created Bannock County and named Pocatello as the county seat.

By 1920 Pocatello's population was 15,000 and it became a city of the first class.

Turning Points

County Seat On March 6, 1893, the legislature split off Bannock County from Bingham County with Pocatello as the county seat. Establishing Pocatello as the seat of county government increased the city's prestige and was a stable source of new jobs.

Municipal Water System Early in the city's history, Pocatello residents got most of their water from the Portneuf River. The community's first gravity-fed water supply came from a reservoir built on the west bench circa 1892 and fed by Gibson Jack and Mink Creeks. James A. Murray owned the system and sold the water to the city.

However, Murray was reluctant to spend the money needed to maintain the system. Water quality became an issue. City leaders sought to purchase Murray's water system but were unwilling to pay his price. Deteriorating water quality and a break out of typhoid fever brought things to a head. In 1916 following considerable conflict and litigation that reached the Idaho Supreme Court, Pocatello acquired ownership of the water system.

Railroad Since the time trains began passing through Pocatello in 1879, the city's growth and development have been inextricably tied to the railroad. From the early days of the Oregon Short Line to today's Union Pacific, the railroad has had a large presence in Pocatello and continues to be among its top 10 employers. Pocatello is one of the few remaining railroad terminal cities in Idaho.

Idaho State University Idaho State University is an integral part of Pocatello's heritage, culture and social fabric. It was founded in 1901 as the Academy of Idaho. In 1915 its name was changed to the Idaho Technical Institute and in 1927 to the University of Idaho-Southern Branch. In 1947 experiencing a surge in enrollment as returning soldiers used the GI Bill to finance their education, it became accredited as Idaho State College. In 1951 the legislature closed Albion State Normal School and transferred its academic programs to Idaho State College. In 1963 the school received university accreditation and became Idaho State University.

Interstate 86 and 15 In the late 1960s construction of the Interstate freeway system had a profound effect in defining the city's northern boundary with Chubbuck and the decision of developers to locate a regional retail shopping mall and numerous other businesses just off the freeway's junction.

The freeway also had the positive economic effect of bringing commerce into the city as well as inducing the growth of hospitality businesses just off the I-15 interchanges on the eastern side of the city.

Naval Ordnance Plant In 1942 at the beginning of World War II, the U.S. Navy constructed a naval ordnance plant in Pocatello for the purpose of relining the bore of heavy naval guns used by the Pacific Fleet. The Navy built the buildings with brick exteriors, heavy concrete floors and overhead cranes. Workers received $1.70 an hour, nearly three times the prevailing union wage that existed prior to the war. Many Pocatello men and women not serving in the military worked at the plant.

When the Navy shut down operations following the war, the loss of jobs had a major adverse effect on the city's economy. However, the subsequent conversion of the abandoned plant into an industrial park has attracted several businesses with many new jobs added. Ten businesses are presently housed in this industrial complex.

Pocatello Regional Airport The Pocatello Regional Airport is a former United States Army Air Force base completed in December 1942. During World War II, the base served as a training post for heavy bombers and fighter aircraft including B-24s and B-17s and a fighter squadron from Mexico. The base consisted of 325 buildings, some of which are still in use, and three runways. In 1949 the military sold the base to the City of Pocatello.

Fertilizer Manufacturing Two fertilizer plants – the J. R. Simplot Company Don Plant in Pocatello and the FMC Corporation plant in Power County, just across the Bannock County line – began operations in the 1940s and soon became two of Pocatello's major employers. The plants processed phosphate ore extracted from area mines and produced a variety of commercial fertilizers. FMC closed its operations in the late 1990s. Simplot remains one of the community's top employers.

Semiconductors In 1970 AMI Semiconductors moved its corporate headquarters and began the manufacture of semiconductors and integrated circuits in Pocatello. It soon became the city's largest employer. AMI was acquired by ON Semiconductor (ON) of Phoenix in 2008. Under ON management the plant had a reduction in labor force. However, in 2010 ON announced an expansion of its production lines at its Pocatello plant.

Annexation of Alameda In 1962 Pocatello annexed unincorporated Alameda, a community whose southern boundary abutted Pocatello along Oak Street. With the annexation, Pocatello's population grew from 28,534 in 1960 to 40,036 in 1970. The combined communities were able to improve needed municipal services and accommodate the rapid residential and business growth occurring in the northern part of town.

Garrett Freight Lines In 1913 Clarence Garrett and his brother and cousin started a commercial trucking business in Pocatello that grew into a major regional freight line with over 2,700 vehicles and nearly 3,000 employees spread across its service area.

As the company expanded, many company officers wanted Clarence to move the company headquarters and shop to a large centrally-located city. Clarence refused saying, "This (Pocatello) is where we started and this is where Garrett will stay."

In 1978 the shareholders sold the company. Following successive changes in ownership they moved the operation out of the city and discontinued the Garrett name – thus ending an important era in Pocatello's history.

Pocatello's "Smile Ordinance" In 1948 after an exceptionally long and severe winter that took its toll on the spirit of Pocatello residents, then Mayor George Phillips passed a tongue-in-cheek ordinance making it illegal to not smile on the streets of Pocatello.

In 1987 the Idaho State Journal newspaper in Pocatello wrote a story about the ordinance and the American Bankers Association (ABA), who had a campaign to get Congress to modernize federal banking statutes, gave the ordinance national attention as an example of outdated laws.

On December 10, 1987, in response to an invitation from Pocatello Mayor Richard Finlayson, representatives of the ABA visited the city and declared Pocatello the "U.S. Smile Capital." Even though the ordinance has since been rescinded, it still has the desired effect as people pass on the city's streets.

Pocatello Today

Amenities and Attractions Pocatello has over 25 parks, most of which have picnic tables and playground equipment. City parks also have facilities for both adult and youth team sports, including soccer, baseball, flag football and softball fields as well as volleyball and tennis courts. Pocatello is an Idaho Heritage City and routinely receives the Arbor Day Foundation annual award of "Tree City USA."

Ross Park, the largest park, includes the Pocatello Zoo that features native animals and the Aquatic Center that includes a tot pool, lazy river and water slide along with a full-size pool. The Bannock County Historical Museum has a replica of historic Fort Hall outpost on the Oregon Trail and Pocatello Junction on display in Upper Ross Park as well as stories of early Indian and pioneer life in Southeastern Idaho.

The Community Recreation Center offers year-round swimming, a weight room and a variety of fitness classes.

Nearby summer recreation.

There are two 18-hole public golf courses in the city. Highland is a 6,372-yard, par 72 course, and Riverside is a 6,097-yard, par 71 course. Juniper Hills is a private country club that has a 6,097-yard, par 71 course along with a dining room, indoor and outdoor tennis courts, swimming pool and lounge.

The Portneuf Greenway Foundation is in the process of building a walking and biking trail through the valley. The Greenway now has over 13 miles of trail winding along the Portneuf River through the city to public trailheads.

Information and exhibits on the natural history of the area are presented at the Idaho Museum of Natural History, located on the Idaho State University campus.

The century-old architecture of many of the buildings in Pocatello's historic Downtown and Warehouse Districts give a nostalgic feel for the bygone days of old Pocatello.

Pocatello offers a wide variety of places to worship. Religious services are held in over 105 churches, including Roman Catholic, The Church of Jesus Christ of Latter-day Saints, Methodist, Presbyterian, Baptist, Jewish and Greek Orthodox Catholic.

Also in the city are year-round swimming and tennis facilities, horse and auto racing and athletic clubs that offer a wide variety of recreational and fitness programs. In addition, there are movie theaters, bowling alleys, a roller – skating rink and a trap-shooting range.

ISU offers many cultural and other events open to the public in facilities such as the Stephens Performing Arts Center and the Holt Arena. The Idaho State Civic Symphony and Theatre ISU run a series of concerts and performances each year. ISU's Holt Arena, the first covered football stadium on a college campus, has a seating capacity of 12,000 and is the site of NCAA events as well as the Simplot Games, a February high school track and field event, Monster Truck shows, rock concerts, commercial fairs, rodeos and local high school football games.

Nearby winter recreation.

On each Labor Day weekend Saturday the Idaho State Journal sponsors the USAT&F certified Pocatello Marathon, "Running the Gap."

Each fall ISU sponsors "Pocatello Pump," a wall-climbing event that brings in competitors from throughout the Northwest.

Exhibits at ISU's Idaho Museum of Natural History include Indian relics and displays of the natural and cultural history of Idaho.

The Caribou-Targhee National Forest provides opportunities for hiking, biking, fishing, hunting, ATV riding and snowmobiling.

The 150-square-mile Hell's Half-Acre lava field, a National Natural Landmark, is located 30 miles north of the city.

The nearby 65,000-acre American Falls Reservoir with its over 200 species of birds, the national forest and other public lands offers a wide variety of outdoor recreation including hiking, hunting, fishing, boating, camping, ATV riding and water skiing and, in the winter, snowmobiling and cross-country skiing.

The City Creek Management Area, a City-owned 3,000-acre watershed and recreation area that abuts federally managed lands, is accessible on the west side of the city.

In the summer, the hiking and mountain biking trails in the surrounding foothills are popular. About 20 minutes south, downhill skiing and snowboarding are available on the slopes of the 9,271-foot-high Mount Bonneville and the Pebble Creek Ski Area and Resort. Cross-country skiing is available about 15 minutes south in the Mink Creek Recreation Area.

Pocatello has also received recognition from national publications for its business-friendly approach to starting and operating a business and its attractiveness for raising a family. For example, Kiplinger described Pocatello as a great place for families, citing the community's affordable cost of living, safe neighborhoods, solid public schools and robust employment growth with plenty of outdoor activities.

Other activities include the Idaho High School Rodeo finals in June at the Bannock County Fairgrounds; Biggest Show in Idaho fireworks display every 4th of July; Portneuf Greenway Riverfest held in June/July; North and South Bannock County Fairs; Bannock County Bluegrass Festival in August at the Bannock County Fairgrounds; ISU Mountain West Marching Band competition in October; annual Mayor's Awards for the Arts Celebration titled "Art for Food" in October; Old Town Night Lights Parade the Friday after Thanksgiving; 1st Friday Artwalk in Old Town Pocatello; ISU Chrome in the Dome event; Community Environmental Fair in April; Pocatello Downs Flat Horse Track Racing at the Bannock County Fairgrounds; Idaho Endurance Festival in May; Pocatello Iris Festival in June; Idaho Cycling Enthusiasts Race Series; Annual Idaho Music & Wildflower Festival in June at Pebble Creek Ski Resort; USA Wrestling Clinic, with Olympians, in June; POW*MIA Awareness Rally & Motorcycle Rodeo in July/August; Pocatello Triathlon in August; Southeast Idaho Senior Games & Triathlon in August; Pocatello Art Center Sagebrush Art Festival in September; Festival of Trees in December; and the Nutcracker Ballet in December.

Economy and Major Employers The city's major employers and approximate employee numbers in 2010 are Idaho State University – 3,300; Pocatello/Chubbuck School District #25 – 1,700; Portneuf Medical Center – 1,200; ON Semiconductor – 800; Heinz Frozen Food Company – 750; and Convergys Business Services – 700. Rounding out the largest employers are Pocatello City Government, Union Pacific Railroad, Varsity Contractors, Wal-Mart, Bannock County Government, Teleperformance USA and Farmers Insurance Group.

Education The Pocatello/Chubbuck School District #25 serves about 12,000 students with four high schools, three traditional and one alternative; three middle schools; and 13 elementary schools. Two charter schools and four private schools are also located in the city.

Pocatello is home to Idaho State University (ISU) which has an enrollment approaching 15,000. ISU also has satellite campuses in Meridian, Idaho Falls and Twin Falls and Outreach Centers in American Falls, Blackfoot, Montpelier, Preston and Soda Springs.

Health Care The Portneuf Medical Center, presently a 135-bed facility and soon to expand to 187 beds, provides most of the medical care needed in the city and region.

Transportation Pocatello is located at the intersection of I-15 and I-86. U.S. Highways 30 and 91 intersect the city.

Commercial air service is available at Pocatello Regional Airport. Union Pacific Railroad provides transportation for freight. Pocatello Regional Transit provides public bus service throughout the city and region.

Utilities and Services Private companies provide electricity, telephone, gas, cable and satellite services. The City provides water, sanitation, library and EMS services and police and fire protection.

Vision for 2050

In 2050 Pocatello will continue to be a regional center for education, health care, technological innovation, business development and the arts. The city's population will likely double in size with downtown infill developments, additional residential neighborhoods, new and improved parks and attractive open space and trails. We believe future city leaders will continue to plan strategically and implement those plans on a disciplined basis; insuring a continuance of the thoughtful and careful management of city resources that preceded them.

The City will continue to initiate involvement with community, education and business leaders to achieve our common purposes of encouraging desirable business development; improving transportation infrastructure and systems; protecting our clean air, water and open space; building quality neighborhoods and schools; and taking a leadership role in cooperating with local and state governments in resolving matters of mutual concern.

Mayors

1891 D. Swinehart *
1893 Ed Stein
1894 A.B. Bean
1895 W.F. Kasiska
1897 W.T. Reeves
1898 A.B. Bean
1899 J.B. Bistline
1900 Martin Rice
1901 Theo Turner
1902 O.B. Steeley
1904 D. Swinehart
1905 W.A. Cleare
1907 C.E.M. Loux
1909 D.W. Church
1911 J.M. Bistline
1913 Theo Turner
1915 George Williams
1917 A.B. Bean
1919 R. Whitaker
1921 Jesse R.S. Budge
1923 C. Ben Ross
1930 Ivan Gasser
1931 Theo C. Coffin
1933 Elmer V. Smith
1933 Chas. A. Brown
1935 Robert M. Terrell
1943 C.C. "Dinty" Moore
1947 George Phillips
1949 W.W. Halsey
1969 Don Brennan
1970 Luvern C. Johnson
1973 "Bill" Roskelley
1975 C.G. Billmeyer, Jr.
1976 Les Purce
1977 Donna Boe
1978 Grant Anderson
1979 Ione Horrocks
1981 John Evans
1983 L. Ed Brown
1985 Dean Funk
1986 Richard S. Finlayson
1990 Peter J. Angstadt
1998 Gregory R. Anderson
2002 Roger W. Chase
2010 Brian C. Blad

* Village Chairman

Bear Lake.

BEAR LAKE COUNTY

- Bloomington
- Georgetown
- Montpelier
- Paris (*County Seat*)
- St. Charles

Bloomington viewed from above.

Bloomington

Statistical Data

Population: 209 *
Elevation: 5,946 feet
Precipitation: 10 inches **
Average Snowfall: 60 inches **
County: Bear Lake

Temperature Range – Fahrenheit: **
Spring: 17 to 61
Summer: 47 to 79
Fall: 20 to 68
Winter: 6 to 32
* U.S. Census Bureau Estimates July 2015
**Historical averages

Bloomington lies in the Bear Lake Valley between the eastern foothills of the Caribou-Targhee National Forest on the west and the 19,000-acre Bear Lake National Wildlife Refuge (BLWR) on the east. The BLWR comprises most of the wetlands bordering the north shore of the stunningly blue 5.9-million-acre Bear Lake. The Wyoming border is 18 miles due east. The Utah border is 13 miles south.

Pioneers built the city at the base of the 9,575-foot-high Paris Peak of the Wasatch Mountains where Bloomington Canyon opens up into an alluvial fan sloping to the BLWR marshlands.

Pre-Incorporation Years

When the first settlers came into the Bear Lake Valley, Shoshone and Bannock Indians frequented the valley for their summer encampments, particularly the south lake area.

In 1862 Brigham Young, President of the Church of Jesus Christ of Latter-day Saints (Church), received favorable reports as to the valley's settlement potential. Young was anxious to locate arable land in the Intermountain West where the swelling flow of church converts into the Salt Lake Valley could settle.

Charles C. Rich – a member of the Church's ruling Quorum of Twelve Apostles, who would later lead the Bear Lake area settlements – wrote that the country possessed an abundance of water for irrigation, favorable locations for towns, good soil, abundant grass hay, plenty of fish and game and a climate favorable for hardy grains and vegetables. He felt it was well worth an attempt at colonization.

1962 photo of the old Bloomington Chapel, which is no longer standing.

The Church's Indian policy was that of peace and providing food and other help to the Indians. Young negotiated with area Shoshone and Bannock tribal chiefs to allow settlement. The chiefs agreed that Church immigrants could settle on the north end of the lake but not on their traditional encampment lands on the lake's south end.

On August 23, 1863, Young asked for an advance party of several families and workers from Cache Valley to follow Charles C. Rich and to build a wagon road across the mountains from Franklin to the north of the lake, 46 miles. There, they were to construct housing and animal shelters for those who would spend the winter. The following month, the advance party completed its assignment and established the community of Paris.

The Big Tree was located up Bloomington Canyon. It was hit by lightning and no longer stands.

The following spring, 700 additional settlers joined the original pioneers. In May 1864 Brigham Young visited Bear Lake Valley and advised the settlers to cultivate small farms, build good roads and treat the Indians well.

Under Rich's direction, the settlers started several new communities. In addition to Paris, they founded other communities including what are now the cities of Bloomington, Georgetown, Montpelier and St. Charles. (*See Eastern Idaho, Pioneer Settlements – Bear Lake Area.*)

The first pioneers settling in the future town of Bloomington arrived April 18,

1864.

Charles Rich and his son Joseph, both of whom had experience surveying other church settlements, surveyed the new town as they did for the other Bear Lake settlements. They used the North Star to lay out the townships on a north-south and east-west axis in 10-acre blocks separated by streets six rods wide (96 feet). They subdivided each 10-acre block into one-acre home sites.

Charles Rich named the settlement "Bloomington" as a tribute to the industry and enterprise of the pioneers. In the absence of a municipal government, the settlers looked to the Church to provide organizational structure.

Bloomington Lake.

David B. Dille, the presiding elder of the Bloomington settlers, numbered the blocks and placed the numbers in a hat. Each family drew to determine the order of the drawing then drew again for the lot they would own. That draw was, in essence, the family's title to their land. Formal title would come later when territorial law and the application of the 1862 Homestead Act finally reached these frontier communities.

The John Dunn family built the first log home in Bloomington. By the end of the summer, about 41 families had built one-room houses in the new community.

Initially, even though the soil was fertile and irrigation water abundant, it was hard to farm in this high-mountain community. During the first few years, the settlers were plagued with crop failures, heavy frosts and multitudes of grasshoppers. Many pioneers became discouraged and moved away. Gradually, those who remained learned to farm in the shorter growing season and were able to prosper.

The settlers believed it was their religious duty to educate their children. However, because students and teachers had to work on the family farm, the school year was from October through March.

In 1864 they built one of the first public buildings that also served as a school. It was a 16-by-20-foot log structure with a sod-covered roof. The room had rough slab benches and a large fireplace for heat. A canvas wagon cover divided the hall into two classrooms, one side for beginning students and one for those more advanced.

Subsequently, they held school in other public buildings until in 1894 they built a new elementary school on the site of the original school. In 1901 students who progressed past the eighth grade level traveled to Paris to attend the Fielding Academy. In 1918 school patrons built a new brick schoolhouse.

In the winter, mail delivery was particularly difficult. Edward M. Patterson was the mail carrier. During the winter of 1866 to 1867 he made thirteen trips over the mountains to Franklin on snowshoes for $1 per letter.

Around 1870 community leaders built a brick store operated much like a co-op.

In 1871 the Deseret Telegraph brought single-line telecommunication service from Franklin through Bloomington Canyon to Paris.

Monument outside City Hall and City Recreational Hall.

The inability to identify the Idaho/Utah boundary would later become an issue for the new Bear Lake Valley pioneers. While it was known that the 42nd Parallel marked the boundary, no one was sure where it was. In 1872 the federal government surveyed the actual boundary. Up to that time, most settlers believed they were in Utah Territory and established business and government relationships accordingly. When the survey was completed, it crossed at the center of Bear Lake. Settlers living on the north end found they now had over 200 miles added to their trips to their "new" seat of state government in Boise. (*See Eastern Idaho – Idaho/Utah Boundary Resolution*.)

In 1880 a toll road was completed to the southwest through Logan Canyon. This was an easier route to Cache Valley and greatly improved communication and transportation with the more populated communities around Logan, Utah.

In 1884 the Oregon Short Line completed a rail line that connected rail lines in Granger, Wyoming, and Hermiston, Oregon, essentially connecting Omaha with Portland. The line passed through Montpelier. A few years later, the railroad built a 10-mile branch line from Montpelier to Paris. Although the railroad did not reach Bloomington, it greatly improved transportation and communication to the community.

On March 27, 1901, Bell Telephone brought service to the valley.

The first church buildings built by the settlers were multi-purpose log buildings used both for religious and public purposes. In 1894 they built a large wood-frame church that was one of the largest in the valley. However, in 1916 the building caught fire and burned. They built a new church in 1917. In 1923 they built a large public facility that is now the City Hall.

Local performing arts talent provided plays and concerts. Some of the community's early pioneer actors and the Bloomington Brass Band became popular throughout the valley and made important contributions to the valley's culture.

Annual pioneer holidays included Independence Day each July 4, Pioneer Day each July 24 (the day the pioneers first came into the Salt Lake Valley), Washington's Birthday and May Day. These celebrations generally featured parades, baseball games, races and dances.

City recreational hall.

Incorporation

Around 1910 Oliver C. Dunford, a community educator, recommended to community leaders that they form a municipal government to manage civil matters as other Bear Lake Valley towns had done.

On April 11, 1910, Bloomington became an incorporated village.

On October 18, 1919, village trustees sought to construct a municipal water system. However, the village was too young to get funding support and the effort failed. The village's first water system was constructed in 1936.

In 1921 the village trustees obtained support to begin constructing cement sidewalks. In 1931 the Village Board approved an ordinance prohibiting bicycles on sidewalks. In 1932 the final strip of sidewalk was laid.

The legal status of the village changed to a city as part of the 1967 law making all incorporated municipalities cities.

Turning Points

Church Settlement Brigham Young's decision to direct Bear Lake Valley settlement was pivotal in establishing the city of Bloomington.

School Consolidation In 1967 all of the Bear Lake County schools were consolidated with the elementary school in Bloomington closing. While this consolidation improved

City park.

the delivery of education to community children, the town lost an important icon to its identity.

Church of Jesus Christ of Latter-day Saints' Building Consolidation In 1976 the Bloomington Ward of the Church consolidated with church members living on the south side of Paris. The newly configured congregation retained the name "Bloomington Ward," but the membership began meeting in a new church building in Paris. While the Church membership ceased meeting in Bloomington, the consolidation provided a boon to the community as the City acquired the old church facility and converted it to the City Hall and community center.

Bloomington Today

Amenities and Attractions The grounds around the Bloomington City Hall include a park with a fire pit, a picnic shelter with benches, a baseball diamond, a tennis court, a basketball court, horseshoe pits, playground equipment and lawn. The Hall can also be reserved and rented for day-use activities.

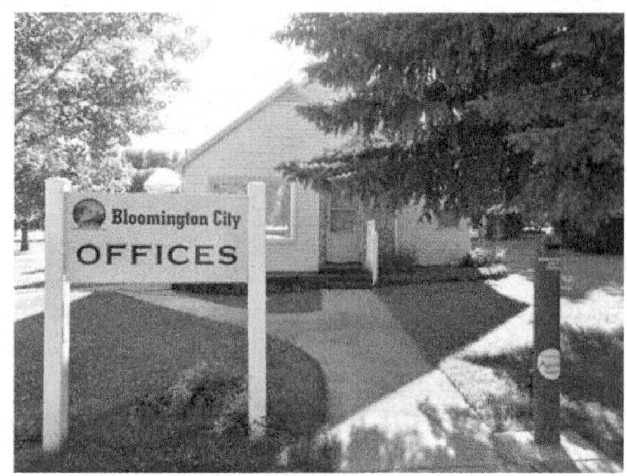

Scenic Bloomington Canyon offers camping, fishing and hiking. Public restroom and camping facilities are located nearby at "Harry's Hollow."

Up Bloomington Canyon, Bloomington Lake is a popular spot for fishing. The U.S. Forest Service maintains the road and facility that includes a parking lot with picnic tables and restrooms.

The crystal-clear, 8-mile-wide and 20-mile-long Bear Lake has outstanding beaches and offers motor and sail boating and water skiing as well as fishing for trout; whitefish; and Bonneville Cisco, one of three species of white fish of the Salmon family indigenous to Bear Lake.

Through the wind and wave action, a narrow sand bar has formed separating Bear Lake from the marsh area to the north. This sand bar, known as the North Beach Unit of Bear Lake State Park, consists of approximately 1.7 miles of sandy beach and is a very popular location for swimming, boating and picnicking. The East Bench Unit of the State Park lies six miles to the south of the North Bench Unit on the east side of the lake.

The BLWR offers roads, walking trails, canoe trails, restroom facilities and a kiosk to enhance bird watching activities.

There are many Forest Service Campgrounds in St. Charles, Paris, Emigration Canyon and Georgetown. Minnetonka Cave is located in St. Charles Canyon and the Paris Ice Cave is in the Paris Canyon north and west of the Paris Canyon Campground.

The Highline Trail runs along Wasatch Mountain ridges and is popular for hiking enthusiasts. The trail is accessible at the top of Bloomington Canyon and many other mountain canyons.

Snowmobiling is a popular sport. There are 300 miles of groomed mountain trails near Bloomington.

The Oregon Trail Center, a museum in Montpelier, celebrates the rich pioneer heritage and legacy of the Oregon Trail and the valley.

Economy and Major Employers Bloomington is a small, quiet, rural, agricultural community. In fact, some farming still takes place within the city limits. Most city residents travel to other communities for work as well as to shop and do their business. There are two small construction businesses with offices in the city.

Education Bear Lake School District provides public education services. For elementary students the district provides bus transportation to Paris. Middle and high school students have bus transportation to their schools in Montpelier.

Bloomington Post Office.

Health Care Bear Lake Memorial Hospital, located 12 miles north in Montpelier, is the closest medical facility.

Transportation U. S. Highway 89 passes through Bloomington and along the scenic west side of Bear Lake.

During the summer months, a county-sponsored free bus travels from Montpelier to Rendezvous Beach at the south end of the lake near Garden City, Utah. This bus makes morning, noon and evening runs to the tourist businesses and beaches on the west side of Bear Lake. Many tourist industry workers in Bear Lake Valley use

Barn built in 1918.

the bus to commute to work.

The Bear Lake County Airport near Paris has two lighted runways and provides service for light aircraft. United Parcel Services and Federal Express provide daily air-freight services.

Utilities and Services Private companies provide electricity, telephone, Internet and satellite services. The City provides water and sewer.

The County Sheriff's Department and the volunteer County Jeep Patrol, deputized primarily during peak tourist times, provide police protection. The County provides ambulance, EMT and solid waste services. The volunteer Paris-Bloomington Fire District provides fire protection.

Vision for 2050

Bloomington is a farming and ranching community. In 1940 when agriculture businesses were more labor intensive, the city had a population of 418. In recent decades, the population has generally held at just over 200.

By 2050 Bloomington agriculture will likely continue as an economic base for the community. However, two phenomena will likely change the economy of the city. There will likely be an increase in part-time residents buying vacation homes so they can enjoy the climate of this mile-high city and surrounding forest and lake. In addition, the workforce for the popular tourist attractions around the lake will find more affordable housing in Bloomington where they can catch free bus transportation to work.

Mayors

1910 Edward J. Haddock *
1913 Oliver C. Dunford *
1915 Joseph P. Patterson *
1917 Alma Findlay Sr. *
1919 Edward J. Haddock *
1921 Fred Huckvale *
1923 T. Jefferson Dunford *
1927 Asa Madsen *
1929 Nelse L. Krouge *
1931 George Ward *
1933 A. Victor Reese *
1939 Alma Findlay Jr. *
1941 William H. Bateman *
1942 DeLorn A. Nelson *
1947 Asa Madsen *
1949 William C. Piggott *
1955 Norman (Ben) Bateman *
1957 Thomas A. (Bus) Painter *
1959 Arden Bunderson *
1964 John Findlay *
1966 Verden D. Thornock
1968 Thomas A. (Bus) Painter
1972 Thomas T. Piggott
1976 Robert L. Taylor
1980 John N. Findlay
1983 Wayne J. Lloyd
1987 Mary A. Bateman
1996 Roy A. Bunderson
2004 Wayne J. Lloyd
2008 Roy A. Bunderson
2012 Joe W. Dunford
2014 David Madsen

* Village Chairman

Georgetown

Statistical Data

Population: 470 *
Elevation: 5,900 feet
Precipitation: 18 inches **
Average Snowfall: 36 to 48 inches **
County: Bear Lake
Website: http://georgetown.id.gov

Temperature Range – Fahrenheit: **
Spring: 18 to 64
Summer: 42 to 85
Fall: 18 to 73
Winter: 8 to 35
* U.S. Census Bureau Estimates July 2015
**Historical averages

Georgetown is a small farming community on the north end of Bear Lake Valley. The Caribou-Targhee National Forest borders the valley on the east and west. About eight miles east, Meade Peak, in the Pruess Mountain Range, rises to 9,957 feet. Approximately 10 miles west, Sherman Peak, in the Bear River Range, rises to 9,682 feet.

The Bear River flows about one mile west. The city of Montpelier is 11 miles south.

Pre-Incorporation Years

In the early 1800s trappers and explorers came into the area. At the time, Shoshone and Bannock Indians were the principal inhabitants of the valley. They primarily made their summer encampments on the south shores of Bear Lake near a place in what is now Utah called Rendezvous Beach. (*See The Region, American Indians.*)

Pioneers heading to Oregon and California Territories drove their wagon trains through the valley beginning in 1841. Many of these immigrants generally followed the route of what is now U.S. Highway 30. They left wagon ruts that are still visible in and around Georgetown. (*See The Region, Oregon and California Trails.*)

In 1862 Brigham Young, president of The Church of Jesus Christ of Latter-day Saints, received favorable reports about the Bear Lake Valley's settlement potential. Young was anxious to locate arable land in the Intermountain West where the swelling numbers of Church converts entering the Salt Lake Valley could settle.

Georgetown's first sawmill.

Charles C. Rich, a member of the Church's ruling Quorum of Twelve Apostles who would later lead the Bear Lake area settlements, wrote that the country possessed an abundance of water for irrigation. There were favorable locations for towns, good soil, abundant grass, plenty of fish and game and a climate favorable for hardy grains and vegetables. He felt it was well worth an attempt at colonization.

The Church's Indian policy was that of peace and providing food and other assistance for the Indians. Young negotiated with area Shoshone and Bannock tribal chiefs to allow settlement. The chiefs agreed that Church immigrants could settle on the north end of the lake but not on their traditional encampment lands at the lake's south end.

On August 23, 1863, Young asked for an advance party of 50 men from Cache Valley to follow Charles C. Rich and build a wagon road across the mountains from Franklin to the valley on the north end of Bear Lake, a distance of about 46 miles. They were also to build houses and animal shelters for those who would spend the winter. The following

The Georgrtown Garage, the Home of the Spit and Whistle Club.

month, the advance party completed its assignment and established Paris, the first community in the valley.

The following spring, 700 additional settlers joined the original pioneers. Under Rich's direction, the settlers started new communities where they began cultivating small farms. (*See The Region, Pioneer Settlements – Bear Lake.*)

Surveyors platted the future city of Georgetown at a location where two creeks flowed from the eastern mountains into the Bear River. Consistent with the surveys of other Church settlements, they laid out the town in 10-acre blocks separated by streets that were six rods, or 96 feet, wide and subdivided into one-acre home sites.

Georgetown 4th of July Celebration Rodeo.

However, rather than laying out the township on a north-south and east-west axis like most settlements, they platted the 10-acre blocks on either side of the street that proceeded east of the Bear River on the Oregon Trail in a north by northwest direction to what is now Soda Springs.

In May 1864 Brigham Young, accompanied by other Church leaders and families, visited the new Bear Lake Valley settlements. Charles C. Rich took the opportunity to ask Young for his advice to the settlers including the names for certain of the new communities. Young advised the settlers to build good homes, farms and roads and treat the Indians well.

Some of the (Georgetown) settlers had started calling their new community "Twin Creeks." Young suggested they name the town Georgetown after Church leader George Q. Cannon, who was part of the visiting party. It was also a name used in the East honoring George Washington. The settlers accepted his suggestion.

Georgetown Reservoir dam built 1903 to provide electricity to the area.

Georgetown's early settlers built log cabin homes, animal shelters and corrals. They diverted irrigation and domestic water from streams, dug food cellars, gathered wood for fuel and harvested grass hay as feed for their animals during the winter. They supplemented their food with wild game, trout, berries and plums that were plentiful in the area. They dried the fruit and preserved the meat by drying it or placing it in crocks of brine. They plowed the ground and planted gardens, orchards and fields of grain and alfalfa hay.

U.S. postal authorities approved the town post office on August 16, 1871. At that time, most people believed the town was located south of the 42nd parallel in Utah Territory. However, the federal survey completed in 1872 put the line through the center of Bear Lake with the northern half located in Idaho Territory. (*See The Region, Idaho/Utah Boundary Resolution*.)

Georgetown Mining Renovation.

The first school classes in Georgetown were held in private homes. In 1872 they built the first public building on donated land – a 20-by-30 one-room log hall that served as a church meeting house; recreation center; and school, providing education for grades one through eight.

Soon after settlement began, entrepreneurs began building small water-powered and steam-driven sawmills using logs brought down from the nearby forested canyons.

The settlers formed the Georgetown Irrigation Company in 1878 and constructed an extensive system of flood irrigation to water their crops and gardens. (*See The Region, Federal Land Use Laws*.)

Georgetown school patrons used sawn lumber to build a 50-by-50-foot two-story elementary school in 1890.

The Fighting Eagles basketball squad of 1950. Back row L to R: Jerry Smith, Leland Hayes, Wade Smith, Berdean Hayes, Leonard Hayes, Denton Bartschi, Marvin Smith, Larry Wilcox, Farris J. Peterson; Coach.

Early community celebrations included Independence Day and Pioneer Day – July 24, the day the first pioneers entered the Great Salt Lake Valley. These celebrations were always festive and by 1890 included music by the community brass band. There was also a rodeo, ball games, entertainment and lots of food.

In 1894 local members of The Church of Jesus Christ

of Latter-day Saints built their first chapel. The church's women's organization, the Relief Society, continued to use the old one-room log building for its meetings and activities.

A hydro-electric plant was built in 1903 near the base of the main canyon, furnishing the first electricity to Georgetown, Bennington and eastern Montpelier. The plant received water from the Georgetown Reservoir through a large wooden pipe connected to a dam located two miles further up the Bear River Canyon. Georgetown built an electric light system around 1905. Utah Power and Light purchased the hydro-electric plant around 1918.

Incorporation

On April 14, 1908, Georgetown became an incorporated village. In 1967 it became an incorporated city in accordance with the requirements of a new state law.

Turning Points

Church Settlement Brigham Young's decision to direct the settlement of Bear Lake Valley was pivotal to establishing the city of Georgetown.

Georgetown High School Marching Band, 1947.

Irrigation Agriculture underpinned Georgetown's economy; irrigation sharply increased farm productivity. Flood irrigation was used for farming and gardening until 1975 when the currently used gravity-flow sprinkling system was established.

Because of sprinkler irrigation technology, farmland that previously could only be farmed using dry-farm methods now received water. Irrigation transformed Georgetown into a beautiful agricultural oasis.

Hydro-Electric Plant In 1985 the Georgetown Irrigation Company built a hydro-electric plant on Georgetown Creek, half a mile east of the city. The plant provides year-round income for the irrigation company.

Railroad The Oregon Short Line Railroad began construction of a rail line connecting the rail heads at Granger, Wyoming, and Huntington, Oregon, in 1881. The line was completed three years later. It passed two miles west of Georgetown as it crossed Southern Idaho providing the critical link needed for transportation between the industrial centers of Omaha, Nebraska, and Portland, Oregon.

The railroad built a depot near Georgetown where steam-engines stopped to take on water. The stop also provided passenger and freight transportation services for Georgetown residents as well as improved mail delivery and jobs. In the mid-1900s diesel-powered trains and motor vehicles eliminated the need for the train stop.

Phosphate Mining In the early 1900s prospectors discovered a large phosphate deposit a few miles east of town in Right Hand Canyon, and the Utah Fertilizer Chemical Company began developing the mine in 1908. Central Farmers acquired the property in 1947 and built a processing plant, which became a major employer for city residents. However, in the 1960s El Paso Corporation acquired the property, dismantled the plant and moved the ore processing to its plant in Soda Springs. (*See The Region, Mining – Soda Springs and Pocatello – Phosphate.*)

Georgetown City Park.

Education Providing quality education was of paramount importance to Georgetown citizens. The wood-frame building built in 1890 served grades one through eight until 1913, when they built a new three-story brick building and added high school classes to the curriculum. The program received accreditation in 1926 and held its first high school graduation in 1928. Shortly thereafter, they built a gymnasium to accommodate the "Georgetown Eagles" basketball team.

In 1967 Bear Lake County residents voted to consolidate all public schools into the Bear Lake County School District with district offices in Paris. The school district built a new county-wide high school in Montpelier in 1982 and moved the middle school to the old Montpelier high school building. The school district operates elementary schools in certain cities, including Georgetown.

Georgetown Today

Amenities and Attractions The city maintains a park that includes a children's playground, covered pavilion and picnic facilities.

Georgetown south to north on main highway.

During the middle of July, the city holds its annual "Twin Creeks Day" celebration that includes bicycle and walking events, an early breakfast, lunch, an evening meal and a dance. Games, entertainment and an auction are held with the Daughters of the Utah Pioneers serving hot donuts.

Oregon Trail immigrants cut a wide swath as they passed through the Bear Lake Valley. In the Georgetown area, wagon ruts are visible one block east of U.S. Highway 30 and to the Bear River on the west.

There are spectacular outdoor recreation options in the nearby mountains, forests, lake and streams. Fishing, hunting, camping, hiking, biking and ATV riding are prominent summer activities, while Nordic skiing and snowmobiling are winter favorites. Many people come from long distances to enjoy these activities.

Georgetown in the distance.

Summit View, an improved campground and recreation area located seven miles north of town and once known as Tolo Pass for a Shoshone Indian killed there by a bear, is a prominent camping location.

Economy and Major Employers Georgetown Elementary School and the surrounding farms are major employers for the city. Most residents travel to nearby cities for work.

Education The Bear Lake County School District operates an elementary school in Georgetown. It buses older students to its middle and high schools in Montpelier.

Georgetown in winter.

The closest Idaho institution of higher learning is Idaho State University, 62 miles northwest in Pocatello.

Health Care The closest hospital is Bear Lake Memorial Hospital in Montpelier. County volunteer EMTs provide ambulance service.

Transportation U.S. Highway 30 runs through Georgetown and connects with Interstate 15 approximately 50 miles northwest at McCammon.

Air transportation for light private and charter aircraft is available at Bear Lake

County Airport in Montpelier. Pocatello Regional Airport is the closest commercial service.

Rail service for freight is available 17 miles north in Soda Springs.

Utilities and Services Private companies provide electricity, telephone, gas and Internet services. The City provides water, sewer, solid waste and police protection. It also provides fire protection with support from the station in Montpelier.

Vision for 2050

Since 1960 Georgetown's population has stayed about the same. New residents generally move into the area to enjoy a peaceful rural life style of mini-farms surrounded by large farms, mountains and forests.

There is potential for moderate growth in the future. By 2050 the development impact of Bear Lake resorts could significantly influence the city's growth. In addition, young families and retirees are finding the quiet community, located within commuting distance of jobs and services in larger cities, desirable.

To serve the city's residents and in anticipation of moderate growth, community leaders have initiated a plan to upgrade the city's water and sewer services as well and a comprehensive plan for the community.

While the city has no active promotional campaigns to attract new residents, it has sponsored the "Horizon's Vision Committee" (HVC) to create Big Hairy Audacious Goals (BHAG) vision for the future. When HVC delivers its reports, it will likely establish goals targeted around school, business opportunities and general community appearance.

Mayors

1908 Henry Hoff *
1909 Willard Stoddard *
1911 Hans Sorenson *
1913 Chris Sorenson *
1925 F.W. Bacon *
1928 Albert Bacon *
1929 E.E. Pinckney *
1933 L.D. Robison *
1935 R.B. Dunford *
1935 O.B. Solum *
1936 Frank Bartschi *
1937 Lewis Munk *
1940 Bartell Johnson *
1941 Frank Bartschi *
1943 L.D. Robison *
1949 E.OL. Solum *
1955 M. Floyd Clark *
1955 W.W. Hayes *
1959 Rex Bartschi *
1968 W.W. Hayes
1970 Newell Passey
1973 Leon Sorenson
1974 Leland Hayes
1992 Albert Johnson
1994 Joey DeClark
2002 Albert Johnson
2010 Robert Van Cleave

* Village Chairman

Aerial view of Montpelier. Photography by David C. Chamberlain of "DCConline Photography".

Montpelier

Statistical Data

Population: 2,536 *
Elevation: 5,964 feet
Precipitation: 14 inches **
Average Snowfall: 67 inches **
County: Bear Lake
Website: www.montpelier.id.gov

Temperature Range – Fahrenheit: **
Spring: 18 to 64
Summer: 42 to 85
Fall: 18 to 73
Winter: 8 to 35
* U.S. Census Bureau Estimates July 2015
**Historical averages

Montpelier lies in Bear Lake Valley 10 miles north of the 5.9-million-acre, stunningly sky-blue Bear Lake. The Bear River, the outlet to Bear Lake and agricultural life – blood line for the southeastern corner of Idaho and northern Utah, flows about one mile west of the city. It proceeds north to Soda Springs before turning west, then south, past Grace and on to Utah.

The Caribou-Targhee National Forest extends on both sides of the Valley. Southeast of the city, the Bear Lake Plateau rises to nearly 7,900 feet. The Preuss Mountains, rising to nearly 10,000 feet, lie up Montpelier Canyon about seven miles east. Approximately ten miles west is the Bear River Range of the Wasatch Mountains, with peaks rising to nearly 10,000 feet.

The Utah border is 22 miles south. The Idaho/Wyoming border is 13 miles due east.

Pre-Incorporation Years

Around 1810 the first European and American explorers/trappers began traveling into what is now Southern Idaho, trapping beaver and seeking to trade with the nomadic American Indians. One of these frontiersmen, Donald Mackenzie, led a party into the Bear Lake Valley in 1818. He named the Bear River.

The Shoshone and Bannock Tribes were the principle tribes living in what is now Southern Idaho. However, the Gros Ventre and Blackfoot Indians of the Northern Plains made periodic excursions into the area.

For several years, British and American fur-trading companies sponsored rendezvous in various locations including Bear Lake Valley. They, like a traveling general store, brought trade goods to these mountain locations to barter for furs. Several hundred trappers and Indians came great distances to attend these often raucous rendezvous.

Exhibit at the National Oregon/California Trail Center in Montpelier.

In 1829 and 1832 they held rendezvous in Teton Valley near what is now Driggs, 95 miles north of what is now Montpelier. They named the location Pierre's Hole after one of the trappers/traders.

Nathaniel J. Wyeth was one of the merchants trading at Pierre's Hole. Following disappointing business deals, Wyeth traveled west across the Preuss Mountains and entered the Bear River Valley above what is now Montpelier. He was en route to build his Fort Hall Trading Post near what is now Pocatello.

Osborne Russell, who had joined Wyeth and his trappers, wrote his observations when he first saw Bear Lake Valley on July 2, 1834. He said they "fell onto a stream called Bear River which emptied into the Big Salt Lake. This is beautiful country. The river which is about 20 yards wide runs through large fertile bottoms bordered by rolling ridges which gradually ascend on each side to the high ranges of dark and lofty mountains upon whose tops the snow remains nearly year round ... "

In 1841 the first immigrants to Oregon's Willamette Valley passed through what is now Montpelier before turning north along the Bear River to Soda Springs. For nearly two decades, most Oregon Trail immigrants heading to Oregon and California passed through what is now Montpelier. (*See Eastern Idaho – Oregon and California Trails*.)

In 1862 Brigham Young, President of the Church of Jesus Christ of Latter-day Saints (Church) headquartered in Salt Lake City, received favorable reports as to the valley's settlement potential. Young was anxious to locate arable land in the Intermountain West where the swelling flow of Church converts from Europe and America could successfully settle.

Rail yard in Montpelier.

Charles C. Rich, a member of the Church's ruling Quorum of Twelve Apostles, wrote that the (Bear River Valley) country possessed an abundance of water for irrigation; there were favorable locations for towns; good soil, abundant grass hay, plenty of fish and game; and a climate favorable for hardy grains and vegetables. He felt it was well worth an attempt at colonization.

The federal Preemption Act of 1841"squatters' rights" allowed a person to claim up to 160 acres of un-surveyed federal land and, later, pay a small fee per acre to the federal government for clear title. The Homestead Act of 1862 allowed conversion of 160 acres to a settler who improved the property and lived on the land for five years. (*See Eastern Idaho – Federal Land Use Laws*.)

The Church's Indian policy was that of peace and providing food and other help to the Indians. Young negotiated with area Shoshone and Bannock tribal chiefs about Bear Lake Valley settlement. The chiefs agreed that Church immigrants could settle on the north end of the lake but not on the lake's south shore where they held their traditional encampments – a place now known in Utah as Rendezvous Beach.

On August 23, 1863, Young asked for an advance party of several families and workers from Cache Valley, Utah, to follow Charles C. Rich and build a wagon road – 46 miles – across the mountains from what is now Preston to the north end of Bear Lake Valley. On September 18, the party left with nine wagons. They took eight days blazing a trail, removing trees and rock and filling ravines sufficient to make the road passable by horse-drawn wagons. A second group of settlers followed in October.

When the party arrived at what is now Paris, they stopped and built twenty cabins of aspen logs with pole roofs covered with sod for the settlers who would remain there for the winter. In addition, they built animal shelters and corrals and cut sufficient meadow hay to last the winter.

Aerial view of Montpelier. Photography by David C. Chamberlain of "DCConline Photography".

When spring arrived and the snows melted sufficiently to allow passage over the new mountain road, 700 additional settlers came into the valley – 15 families of which chose to travel 10 miles northeast of Paris to start a new community. In addition to Paris, the settlers established seven other settlements. (*See Eastern Idaho, Church Settlements.*)

In May 1864 Brigham Young, accompanied by other Church leaders and families, visited the new Bear Lake Valley settlements. Charles C. Rich took the opportunity of Young's visit to ask for his advice to the settlers for naming certain of the new communities. For the 15 families who settled north of Paris, he suggested they name their mountain-surrounded community Montpelier, the capitol of his home state of Vermont.

One of the first things settlers did was to build temporary shelters – many were "dugouts," rooms dug into a hill with dirt walls on three sides and covered with brush and grass. Some slept in their wagons.

Charles Rich and his son Joseph, both of whom had experience surveying other Church settlements, surveyed most of the new Bear Lake settlements. As was common in settlements started by Church members, they used the North Star to lay out the townships on a north-south and east-west axis in 10-acre blocks separated by streets six rods wide – 96 feet. They subdivided each 10-acre block designated residential into one-acre home sites.

Moving out from the center of town, they platted five and 20-acre lots. The settlers drew for their lots.

Even though they had their own land, the pioneers worked as a community for the common interests of all. They cut trees to build a community corral on one of the city lots. Each night they herded all of the livestock into the corral, and the men would take turns standing guard against predators. After building their shelters, the settlers prepared and, later, planted a community garden and built a log meetinghouse for public gatherings and church services. They worked together to divert water from streams and construct canals and ditches to irrigate their land.

They augmented the food supplies they brought and, later, raised in their gardens with wild game and native plants and fruits such as dandelions, pigweeds, thistles, fir greens, sego lily roots, chokecherries, serviceberries and native currants.

As soon as they were settled, they moved out of their dugouts and wagons and built their first houses of logs hauled down from the mountains. The homes usually had one room with a single window covered with oilcloth and a slab door with leather hinges held shut with wooden pegs. Pioneers slept in bunk beds on mattresses filled with pine needles or dry grass. At one end of the room was a fireplace for warmth, light and cooking.

They dug food cellars to keep their food cool in the summer, but not allow it to freeze in the winter; gathered wood for fuel; and harvested and stored grass hay for their livestock. They dried fruit and preserved the meat by drying it or placing it in crocks of salt brine. They plowed the ground and planted crops that would mature in the high-mountain climate, such as grain and alfalfa hay.

They used a commercial system proved effective in other Church settlements. They formed an organized barter system. Under the Church concept of tithing, each person donated 10 percent of their increase and labor to the Lord. Local Church leaders managed a "tithing house" which served like a central bank with goods and labor as "currency." (*See Eastern Idaho – Pioneer Settlements*.)

The settlers thought they lived in Utah Territory. In fact, their leader, Charles C. Rich, served in the Utah Territorial Legislature.

However, in 1872 the federal government performed a land survey of the 42nd parallel, the dividing line between Idaho and Utah Territories. The survey proved the settlers, as well as the two territorial governments, were wrong. The boundary went a mile south of Franklin in Cache Valley and through the center of Bear Lake with the northern half, including Montpelier, located in Idaho Territory and the southern half in Utah. The practical effect of correcting the error was to significantly change Idaho's official 1870 Census numbers and cause Bear Lake Valley citizens to travel more than twice the distance to do their territorial business. (*See East Idaho, Idaho/Utah Boundary Resolution*.)

In 1881 the Oregon Short Line Railroad (OSL) began building a connection between the railheads at Granger, Wyoming, and Huntington, Oregon – a distance of 472 miles. The rail line angled from Granger in a northwesterly direction through Montpelier, Soda Springs, Pocatello and Caldwell before connecting with the rail line in Huntington.

In 1882 when the construction crews reached Montpelier, OSL built a depot, repair shops, roundhouse and freight division point with stockyards where they unloaded livestock for feed and water.

Many of the railroad employees, and those that came with them, were of a temperament opposite in life-style to those of the more conservative settlers. For a time, this created a culturally divided community with each side viewing the other with suspicion. However, the mutual economic benefits coming from the railroad and other factors served to persuade residents to overlook differences and work together to build the community.

OSL completed the railroad to Huntington on November 17, 1884. It created another continental railroad. Railroad interests completed the first continental railroad in 1869 at Promontory Point near Corinne, Utah. The rail line opened Montpelier and all of Southern Idaho to the commerce centers of Omaha, Nebraska, and Portland, Oregon.

In 1890 when Idaho became a state, Montpelier was the ninth largest city.

Incorporation

On July 13, 1891, Montpelier became an incorporated village.

City Hall

Turning Points

Church Settlement Brigham Young's decision to direct Church settlement of Bear Lake Valley was pivotal in the establishment of Montpelier and the settlement of the Idaho side of Bear River Valley.

Railroad The railroad not only had the effect of significantly increasing the population and employment base of Montpelier, it also brought rapid transportation of freight, passengers and mail to the heretofore remote community.

Montpelier Today

Amenities and Attractions Bear Lake State Park, comprising 966 acres, has two locations on the east side of the lake. The North Beach Unit, located at the top of the lake, offers a 2-mile-long beach. The East Beach Unit has a 1.5-mile-long beach. Both facilities have ramps for boaters and water skiers. The lake is 20 miles long and up to 8 miles wide.

Anglers can fish for native cutthroat and lake trout. In the winter, anglers come with nets to catch Bonneville cisco – one of three species of white fish of the Salmon family indigenous to Bear Lake. The cisco live in the deep cool water until they rise in schools each January to spawn over the limited rocky areas of the lake.

The 19,000-acre Bear Lake National Wildlife Refuge starts a few miles south of Montpelier and comprises most of the wetlands bordering the north shore of Bear Lake. This refuge provides habitat for various species of duck, goose, Sandhill Cranes, Trumpeter Swan and White-Faced Ibis.

The Idaho Department of Fish and Game manages the Montpelier Wildlife Management Area (WMA) near the city of Montpelier. It comprises 2,100 acres of mule deer and elk habitat. The Georgetown Summit WMA is located north of Montpelier and provides 3,349 acres of elk and mule deer habitat.

Bear Lake Middle School.

Oregon Trail immigrants cut a wide swath as they passed through the Bear Lake Valley. Wagon ruts are still visible on some parts of the trail. The National Oregon/California Trail Center in Montpelier is an interpretive center providing a history of life on the Oregon Trail.

The city's most spectacular amenities are the outdoor recreation options available in the nearby public lands. Fishing, hunting, camping, hiking, biking and ATV riding are prominent summer activities, while Nordic skiing and snowmobiling are winter favorites. Many people come from long distances to enjoy these activities.

Economy and Major Employers Bear Lake County School District has about 200 employees and is the city's largest employer. With about 150 employees, Bear Lake Regional Hospital is the second largest employer. Several smaller businesses and government agencies have from 20 to 60 employees. The city's downtown area provides most of the other jobs.

Education In 1967 Bear Lake County residents voted to consolidate all public schools into the Bear Lake County School District with district offices in Paris. In 1982 the school district built a new county-wide high school in Montpelier and moved the middle school to the former Montpelier high school building. In addition to Montpelier, the school district operates elementary schools in certain other Bear River Valley cities.

The closest institution of higher learning is Utah State University, 68 miles southwest in Logan, Utah. Idaho State University is 90 miles northwest in Pocatello.

Health Care Bear Lake Memorial Hospital in Montpelier provides most of the city's healthcare.

Transportation U.S. Highway 30 intersects Montpelier and connects with Interstate 15 approximately 63 miles northwest at McCammon.

Air transportation for light private and charter aircraft is available at Bear Lake County Airport in Montpelier. Pocatello Regional Airport is the closest commercial service.

Rail service for freight is available in the city.

Utilities and Services Private companies provide electricity, telephone, gas and Internet services. The City provides water and sewer services and fire and police protection.

Vision for 2050

In 1960 Montpelier had a population of 3,146. In 2000 the population dropped to 2,785. Since 2000 the population has declined by nearly two percent a year.

City and community leaders are committed to reversing this adverse trend.

While these dynamic times preclude predicting the future with any degree of certainty, we believe that our initiatives will be successful and job growth will return. By 2050 Montpelier's population will exceed historic highs as people come to enjoy the quiet natural beauty of our historic community, the rugged mountain ranges in the Caribou-Targhee National Forest and the sky-blue Bear Lake.

Paris City Hall.

Paris

Statistical Data

Population: 508 *
Elevation: 5,968 feet
Precipitation: 14 inches **
Average Snowfall: 67 inches **
County: Bear Lake
Temperature Range – Fahrenheit: **
Spring: 18 to 64
Summer: 42 to 85
Fall: 18 to 73
Winter: 8 to 35

* U.S. Census Bureau Estimates July 2015
**Historical averages

Paris lies on the western side of the more than mile-high Bear Lake Valley. Fertile fields of wheat, barley and alfalfa hay surround the city. Eight miles south is the stunning, turquoise-blue, 5.9-million-acre Bear Lake. The Bear River, into which the outlet to Bear Lake flows and the source of irrigation water for the farms in the southeastern corner of Idaho and northern Utah, flows about eight miles east of the city.

The 19,000-acre Bear Lake National Wildlife Refuge, comprising most of the wetlands and lake-outlet bordering the north shore of Bear Lake, starts a few miles southeast of the city. On the west of the city is the Caribou-Targhee National Forest with its Wasatch and Bear River Mountain Ranges rising to nearly 10,000 feet.

Montpelier is eight miles northeast. The Utah border is about 16 miles south and the Idaho/Wyoming border is 19 miles due east.

Pre-Incorporation Years

When the first European and American explorers/trappers began traveling into what is now Southern Idaho trapping beaver and seeking to trade with the nomadic American Indians, the Shoshone and Bannock Tribes were the principle tribes living in what is now Southern Idaho. The Gros Ventre and Blackfoot Indians of the northern plains also made periodic excursions into the area.

Paris in the early days.

In 1818 Donald Mackenzie led a party of trappers into the Bear Lake Valley and named the Bear River.

For several years, British and American fur-trading companies sponsored rendezvous in various area locations including Bear Lake Valley. The rendezvous were like a traveling general store, where trading companies brought trade goods to mountain locations to barter for furs. Several hundred trappers and Indians came great distances to the rendezvous to barter with the trading companies as well as with each other.

On July 2, 1834, Nathaniel J. Wyeth, one of the rendezvous merchants who concluded the rendezvous system was becoming less effective, led a party of trappers into the Bear River Valley. He believed permanent trading posts would work better and was en route to build his Fort Hall trading post near what is now Pocatello.

Sleights cabin, built the first fall (1863) Paris was settled.

Osborne Russell, who was traveling with Wyeth and his trappers, wrote his observations when he first saw Bear Lake Valley. He said they "fell onto a stream called Bear River which emptied into the Big Salt Lake. This is beautiful country. The river which is about 20 yards wide runs through large fertile bottoms bordered by rolling ridges which gradually ascend on each side to the high ranges of dark and lofty mountains upon whose tops the snow remains nearly year round ... "

Paris Peak.

The first immigrants traveling overland to Oregon Country's Willamette Valley began passing through Bear Lake Valley in 1841. The route, later called the Oregon Trail, passed through what is now Montpelier and continued north along the Bear River to Soda Springs before turning west. For nearly two decades, most Oregon Trail immigrants heading to Oregon and California followed this route. (*See Eastern Idaho – Oregon and California Trails*.)

In 1862 Brigham Young, President of the Church of Jesus Christ of Latter-day Saints (Church) headquartered in Salt Lake City, received favorable reports regarding the valley's settlement potential. Young was anxious to locate arable land in the Intermountain West where the swelling numbers of Church converts from Europe and America could successfully settle.

Tabernacle under construction.

Charles C. Rich, a member of the Church's ruling Quorum of Twelve Apostles, wrote that the Bear Lake Valley country possessed an abundance of water for irrigation; there were favorable locations for towns, good soil, abundant grass hay, plenty of fish and game; and a climate favorable for hardy grains and vegetables. He felt it was well worth an attempt at colonization.

The federal Preemption Act of 1841"squatters' rights"allowed a person to claim up to 160 acres of un-surveyed federal land and, later, pay a small fee per acre to the federal government for clear title. The Homestead Act of 1862 allowed conversion of 160 acres to a settler who improved the property and lived on the land for five years. (*See Eastern Idaho – Federal Land Use Laws*.)

The Church's Indian policy was that of peace and providing food and other help to the Indians. Young negotiated with area Shoshone and Bannock tribal chiefs about Bear Lake Valley settlement. The chiefs agreed that Church immigrants could settle on the north end of the lake but not on the lake's south shore, where they held their traditional encampments – a place in what is now Utah that includes a location called Rendezvous Beach.

On August 23, 1863, Young asked for an advance party of several families and single men from Cache Valley, Utah, to follow Charles C. Rich and build a wagon road – 46 miles – across the mountains from what is now Preston to the north end of Bear Lake Valley. On September 18, the party left with nine wagons. They took eight days blazing a trail consisting of removing trees and rock and filling ravines sufficient to make the road passable by horse-drawn wagons.

Fielding Academy before it burned down.

When the party came down out of the mountains into the Bear Lake Valley, they chose a favorable location on a level plain adjacent to creeks with crystal-clear water flowing down from the mountains into the lake's north shore wetlands and Bear Lake Outlet. One of the men, Fredrick Perris, surveyed the town and then returned to Cache Valley. Those who remained to settle the new community named their town after Perris but spelled it the same as the famous city in France.

Perris platted the town under the direction of Charles Rich who, along with his son, would later survey the other townsites. They used the surveying methodology commonly used for towns started by the Church. They used the North Star to lay out the township on a north-south and east-west axis in 10-acre blocks separated by six-rod-wide – 96 feet – streets. They subdivided each 10-acre block designated residential into one-acre home sites. Moving out from the center of town, they platted farm lots. The settlers drew for their lots.

Old Dance Pavilion where the dances were held.

Before winter set in, they built twenty cabins of aspen logs with pole roofs covered with sod for the settlers who would remain. A second group of settlers arrived in October. In addition, they built animal shelters and corrals and cut sufficient meadow hay to last the winter.

When spring arrived and the snows melted sufficiently to allow passage over the new mountain road, 700 additional settlers came into the valley. In addition to

Paris, the central city for the valley, the pioneers established seven other settlements that extended over an area about 12 miles north, 10 miles south and eight miles west of Paris. (*See Eastern Idaho, Church Settlements.*)

In May 1864 Brigham Young, accompanied by other Church leaders and family members, visited the new Bear Lake Valley settlements. Charles Rich took the opportunity of Young's visit to ask him to give advice to the settlers, including the names of some of the new communities. Two of the communities for which Young suggested names were Georgetown and Montpelier.

One of the earliest photos of the Bear Lake County Courthouse.

Even though they had their own land, the pioneers worked as a community for the common interests of all. When they first arrived, they cut trees to build a community corral on one of the city lots. Each night they herded all of the livestock into the corral, and the men would take turns standing guard against predators. After building their shelters, the settlers prepared and, later, planted a community garden and built a log meetinghouse for public gatherings and church services. They worked together to divert water from streams and construct canals and ditches to irrigate their land.

Historic Paris Tabernacle today.

They augmented the food supplies they brought and, later, raised in their gardens with wild game and native plants and fruits such as dandelions, pigweeds, thistles, fir greens, sego lily roots, chokecherries, serviceberries and native currants.

They, dug root cellars to keep their food cool during the summer but not allow it to freeze in the winter, gathered wood for fuel and harvested and stored grass hay for their livestock. They dried fruit, preserved the meat by drying it or placing it in crocks of salt brine and built ice houses – blocks of ice placed in sawdust. Ice stored in this manner took several months to fully melt. They plowed the ground and planted crops that would mature in the high-mountain climate, such as grain and alfalfa hay.

They used an organized barter system that had proven effective in other early Church settlements. Under the Church concept of tithing, each person donated 10 percent of their increase and labor to the Lord. Local Church leaders managed a "tithing house" which served like a central bank with goods and labor as "currency" wherein needed public and private infrastructure was built, the economy grew and the needs of the poor were met with dignity. (*See Eastern Idaho – Pioneer Settlements*.)

Many of the Bear Lake Valley families were from Switzerland and had an affinity for dairying. Community leaders saw the compatibility of the dairy industry and the crops suited for the high-mountain climate. They encouraged the settlers to pool their resources; expand pasturelands; build a creamery and cheese factory, with pasteurizing and cream separating equipment freighted in from the East; and build a tannery and leather-working shop. About 125 families became investors and participants in the new and successful enterprise, selling their production locally and in the Utah market.

In 1863 when Idaho became a territory and the town of Paris was founded, the law was clear that the boundary between Idaho and Utah territories was the 42nd Parallel – the historic dividing line between Spanish, later Mexico, and English land claims. However, in 1863 no one knew where the actual boundary line was.

Bear Lake County Courthouse today.

For nearly a decade, most of the north Bear Lake Valley and north Cache Valley settlers thought they lived in Utah Territory. In fact, Bear Lake Valley's Charles C. Rich served in the Utah Territorial Legislature.

In 1872 when the federal government finally surveyed the boundary line, the settlers and governments of the two territories discovered the boundary went a mile south of Franklin in Cache Valley and through the center of Bear Lake with the northern half of the lake located in Idaho Territory and the southern half in Utah.

The practical effect of correcting the error in Idaho was to significantly change Idaho's 1870 Census numbers – a 19 percent change, from 14,999 to 17,804 – and cause north Bear Lake and Cache Valley citizens to travel more than twice the distance to do their territorial business. (*See Eastern Idaho, Idaho/Utah Boundary Resolution*.)

On November 17, 1884, the Oregon Short Line Railroad (OSL) completed a railroad connection between the railheads at Granger, Wyoming, and Huntington, Oregon – a distance of 472 miles. The rail line angled from Granger in a northwesterly direction through Montpelier, Soda Springs, Pocatello and Caldwell before connecting with the rail line in Huntington. The railroad reached Montpelier in 1882. There, OSL made Montpelier a freight division point with a depot, roundhouse, shops and stockyards needed to offload livestock for feeding and watering before reloading them onto the railcars.

Even though the railroad did not pass through Paris, residents benefited directly from railroad services. The railroad had a major positive impact on the economies of the city and valley.

Between 1884 and 1889 local Church member artisans constructed the Church's imposing Paris Tabernacle of Romanesque design, a house of worship in which Church leaders periodically held valley-wide conferences.

The tabernacle has a six-story bell tower and a 127-by-73-foot footprint. Swiss stonemasons cut red sandstone from a quarry located 18 miles away. They hauled timbers from the nearby mountains and skilled woodworkers shaped the interior detail, a remarkable achievement for this pioneer community.

Incorporation

On January 5, 1875, the Territorial Legislature created Bear Lake County with Paris as the county seat. On July 14, 1897, Paris became an incorporated village.

Turning Points

Church Settlement Brigham Young's decision to direct Church settlement of Bear Lake Valley was pivotal in the establishment of Paris and the settlement of the Idaho side of the Bear River Valley.

The local newspaper once was published in this house.

Dairy Industry The settlers successfully established a new, vertically integrated agricultural business that had no middlemen but rather managed production, processing, quality control and delivery of the products to the end retail and wholesale customers. The industry underpinned the valley's economy for decades.

County Seat As the county seat of government, the city received increased political influence and a relatively small but stable base of employment.

Railroad Even though the railroad did not pass through Paris, residents benefited directly from railroad services. The railroad brought rapid transportation of freight, passengers and mail to the heretofore remote Bear Lake Valley.

Paris Today

Amenities and Attractions The Paris 4th of July celebration attracts people from throughout the valley. It begins with a 9-mile Fun Run that starts in

Montpelier and ends with a chuck-wagon breakfast at the finish line in Paris. The all-day event includes a parade, a pageant in the historic tabernacle and a youth rodeo held at the fairgrounds.

Bear Lake State Park, comprising 966 acres, has two locations on the east side of the lake. The North Beach Unit, located at the top of the lake, offers a 2-mile-long beach. The East Beach Unit has a 1.5-mile-long beach. Both facilities have ramps for boaters and water skiers. The lake is 20 miles long and up to 8 miles wide.

The 19,000-acre Bear Lake National Wildlife Refuge starts a few miles southeast of the city and comprises most of the wetlands bordering the lake's north shore. This refuge provides habitat for various species of duck, goose, Sandhill Crane, Trumpeter Swan and White-Faced Ibis.

The Idaho Department of Fish and Game manages the Montpelier Wildlife Management Area (WMA) located east of Paris. It comprises 2,100 acres of mule deer and elk habitat. The Georgetown Summit WMA is located north of Paris and provides 3,349 acres of elk and mule deer habitat.

Oregon Trail immigrants cut a wide swath as they passed through the Bear Lake Valley. Wagon ruts are still visible on some parts of the trail. The National Oregon/California Trail Center in Montpelier is an interpretive center providing a history of life on the Oregon Trail.

The city's most spectacular amenities are the outdoor recreation options available in the nearby public lands. Fishing, hunting, camping, hiking, biking and ATV riding are prominent summer activities, while Nordic skiing and snowmobiling are winter favorites. In the winter, anglers come with nets to catch Bonneville cisco – one of three species of white fish of the Salmon family indigenous to Bear Lake. The cisco live in the deep cool water until they rise in schools each January to spawn over the limited rocky areas of the lake. Many people come from long distances to enjoy these activities.

Economy and Major Employers The city has no large employers. The city's downtown consists of a few convenience stores and shops, an elementary school and the tabernacle. Most of the city's residents travel to Montpelier to shop.

Education In 1967 Bear Lake County residents voted to consolidate all public schools into the Bear Lake County School District with district offices in Paris. In 1982 the school district built a new county-wide high school in Montpelier and moved the middle school to the former Montpelier high school building. In addition to Paris, the school district operates elementary schools in the valley.

The closest institution of higher learning is Utah State University, 75 miles southwest in Logan, Utah. Idaho State University is 80 miles northwest in Pocatello.

Health Care Bear Lake Memorial Hospital in Montpelier provides most of the city's healthcare.

Transportation U.S. Highway 89 intersects Paris. The highway connects with U.S. Highway 30, the Bear Lake-Caribou Scenic Byway, at Montpelier and with Interstate 15 approximately 70 miles northwest at McCammon.

Air transportation for light private and charter aircraft is available at Bear Lake County Airport in Montpelier. Pocatello Regional Airport provides the closest commercial service.

Utilities and Services Private companies provide electricity, telephone and Internet services. The City provides water and sewer services and fire and police protection.

Vision for 2050

Between 1960 and 2000 Paris's population dropped 23 percent – 746 in 1960 and 575 in 2000. Since 2000 the population has continued to decrease. These population trends are likely to continue into the foreseeable future.

Mayors

1897 William L. Rich *
1908 W.W. Richards *
1911 Amasa M. Rich *
1915 F.T. Shepherd *
1919 A.T. Pendrey *
1921 H. Edward Sutton *
1923 James L. Dunford *
1927 A.W. Shepherd *
1931 Fred J. Price *
1933 A.W. Shepherd *
1935 Dan C. Rich *
1939 R.O. Clayton *
1941 Seymour G. Sleight *
1943 Van Ness D. Wallentine *
1951 Weldon Grandy *
1958 Cyril S. Budge *
1959 James R. Hawkes *
1966 Smith Gertch
1970 Russel Athay
1981 Lloyd J. Passey
1986 Tim A. Toland
1998 David H. Matthews
2010 Brent Lewis
2011 Dana Jacobsen
2012 Brent Lewis
* Village Chairman

St. Charles City Hall.

St. Charles

Statistical Data

Population: 135 *
Elevation: 5,944 feet
Precipitation: 18 inches **
Average Snowfall: 95 inches **
County: Bear Lake
Website: www.stcharlesidaho.org

Temperature Range – Fahrenheit: **
Spring: 17 to 61
Summer: 47 to 79
Fall: 20 to 68
Winter: 6 to 32
* U.S. Census Bureau Estimates July 2015
**Historical averages

St. Charles is a charming rural community overlooking the northwestern shores of the beautiful and spectacularly blue Bear Lake. The Idaho/Utah border lies eight miles south.

The Cache National Forest and the Wasatch Mountain Range, with peaks rising to over 9,500 feet, outline the city's western sky. To the north lies the fertile high-mountain meadows and wetlands of Bear Lake Valley. Across the six-mile-wide Bear Lake is the Bear Lake Plateau, rising to over 7,878 feet. Eighteen miles due west of St. Charles is the Idaho/Wyoming border.

The ambience of rustic homes built between the lake and the western side of Cache National Forest compliments the city's leisurely pace of life.

The residents cherish their rural lifestyle and the unlimited outdoor recreational opportunities of hiking, camping, hunting and fishing in the nearby streams and lake. Ranching, farming and recreation underpin the city's economy. In the summer, tourists come to the lake for water sports and fishing. In the fall, hunters come for deer and elk.

Pre-Incorporation Years

In 1862 Brigham Young, President of the Church of Jesus Christ of Latter-day Saints (Church of Jesus Christ or Church), asked surveyor James S. Martineau to explore and evaluate the Bear Lake Valley as a place for possible settlement.

St. Charles farmers stacking hay. Left to right: John Brewer, Will Clark, John Michaelson.

Apparently, Martineau gave a positive report because Young picked sites for settlement and negotiated with Chiefs Washakie and Tagi of the Shoshone and Bannock Indian Tribes, respectively, to allow Church settlement around the north part of Bear Lake. The southern lakeshore was a traditional gathering place for Native Americans. The Church had a long-standing policy of befriending the Indians.

In August 1863 Young asked for 50 men from Cache Valley to go with Church Apostle Charles C. Rich to the Bear Lake Valley, build facilities so several families could stay for the winter and prepare for several hundred more Church members to come the next year to settle in the valley.

On September 18, the party left with nine wagons. They took eight days in building a 46-mile wagon road through the mountains east of what is now Preston in the north of Bear Lake Valley. A second group of settlers followed in October. When the party arrived at what is now Paris, they stopped and built twenty cabins of aspen logs with pole roofs covered with sod for the settlers who would remain for the winter. In addition, they cut meadow hay to feed their animals during the winter.

When spring arrived and the snows melted sufficiently to allow passage over the new mountain road, 700 additional settlers came into the valley. These settlers established nine more settlements including St. Charles – founded May 1, 1864, and named after their leader Charles C. Rich. (*See Eastern Idaho, Church*

Settlements.)

When they arrived, the land was covered with sagebrush and dry grass that had been frozen the preceding winter. Willows and brush grew near the lake and in the lower ravines and canyons. Groves of quaking aspen grew in the foothills. Pine forests covered the upper mountains.

One of the first things the new settlers did was survey the land. The town was platted in ten-acre blocks. Each ten-acre block was divided into one-acre lots. Moving out from the center of town, five- and 20-acre lots were surveyed and platted. Land was distributed among the settlers at a public drawing.

Almost immediately, they cut trees to build a community corral on one of the city lots. Each night, all of the livestock were herded into the corral and the men would take turns standing guard.

Each family also began building a temporary shelter. Many of the first homes were "dugouts," one-room living quarters dug into the hillside. The walls were dirt and sod. The roof was willows and saplings thatched with grass and sod. Other homes were made of aspen logs brought down from the foothills.

The houses usually had one room, with a single window covered with oilcloth and a slab door with leather hinges held shut with wooden pegs. Pioneers slept in bunk beds on mattresses filled with pine needles or dry grass. At one end of the room was a fireplace for light and cooking.

After building their shelters, the settlers planted a community garden and built a log meeting house for public gatherings and church services. Until their gardens were established, the settlers ate native plants and fruits such as dandelions, pigweeds, thistles, fir greens, sego lily roots, chokecherries, serviceberries and native currants.

Initially, school was held in the home of one of the settlers. Later that fall, a two-room school was built. One room was used for the school; the other was the teacher's living quarters.

The first sawmill was a slow, labor intensive but effective system. They dug a six-foot-deep pit about 14 feet long and six feet wide. Logs were laid lengthways. Holding either end of a long lumberman's saw, one man standing in the pit and another above would cut the log into boards.

In a few years, one of the settlers hauled in circular saws and equipment and built a water-powered sawmill on Big Creek Canyon. With this new source of lumber, more permanent homes, buildings and furniture were constructed.

During the summer, boys and girls would herd the livestock as they grazed in the foothills above town.

The new settlers were unfamiliar with the climate and land and thus made many mistakes. The winters were longer than expected so they didn't put up enough grass hay for the animals. Additionally, their gardens and crops were buffeted by early and late frosts and grasshoppers.

Fortunately, wildlife was plentiful. They were successful in bagging elk, deer, rabbits, wild geese and ducks, sage chickens, willow grouse and pine grouse. They caught fish from the lake and streams.

Scarlet fever and other diseases plagued the settlers and took many lives.

Gutzon Borglum.

This memorial, located on church property, was removed and the center stone was mounted for display on City property. A new memorial is under construction next to City Hall.

Women either had or developed skills as seamstresses. They would card, spin and weave their own wool and make their own clothing and quilts. Shoes were about the only things they didn't make themselves.

Official land surveys and boundaries in those early years were not clear. Initially, St. Charles was thought to be in Utah Territory. In fact it was made the first county seat of Richland County, Utah. It was not until 1872 that official surveys identified the location of the Idaho/Utah border and disclosed that St. Charles was in Idaho.

Incorporation

On January 5, 1875, the Idaho Territorial Legislature established Bear Lake County with Paris as the county seat. On September 30, 1938, the Bear Lake

County Commissioners approved St. Charles as an incorporated village.

Turning Points

Church Settlement Brigham Young's decision to direct Church settlement of Bear Lake Valley was pivotal in the establishment of the town of St. Charles as well as the other valley communities.

Economy Rather than experiencing major defining events, the St. Charles economy was somewhat self contained. To the extent the settlers produced more commodities from their farm, ranch, flourmill and sawmill businesses than they could market within the valley, they transported them to Utah for sale.

By 1920 the town had two well-equipped general stores, a barbershop, a confectionary, three lumber mills, one flourmill, a garage and repair shop, a Sego Milk Creamery, a butcher shop, a blacksmith shop, a new Church of Jesus Christ chapel and a school to house 135 schoolchildren. The voters approved the sale of bonds to finance construction of the school.

Employment opportunities increased when St. Charles Roller Mill found buyers in Tennessee for its "Sweet Sixteen" flour and Utah Power and Light built a hydro facility on the Bear River to supply reserve electricity.

The growing community added to its attractions by forming a drama group that produced several plays. It also had its own baseball team that competed in an area league.

The baseball team received such recognition that they made a baseball game part of every celebration or holiday event. The baseball players were often recognized by the physical injuries they sustained playing the game.

The ballplayers wore a small leather glove similar to today's work glove. The thin glove was particularly hard on the catcher. He sometimes ended up with sprained, bruised or broken fingers or thumbs which often healed crooked.

Usually the town constable attended the game and intervened to stop disputes from getting out of hand. Pie, ice cream and popcorn balls were sold for refreshments.

During the winter of 1950 the city hosted the valley's first cutter races on the lakeshore.

Through the years since the 1950s the town has decreased in population and commercial enterprises. With increased ease of travel, less business was profitable in the city, and more shopping was done out of town. The county schools consolidated and local students attended school in Paris. By the 1980s a Maverick gas station, Bundy's Drive In and the old post office/general store were the only businesses left operating in town. More homes were being sold as summer homes, and recreation was becoming more a part of the city.

St. Charles Today

Amenities and Attractions In the center of town is a monument dedicated to Gutzon Borglum, the sculptor who created Mount Rushmore and many other works. Borglum's parents, Danish emigrants, were traveling West and built a cabin in St. Charles to survive the winter. His father dug a one-room house half into the ground, finishing it with logs and a sod roof. The log cabin remains in St. Charles today. To commemorate Borglum's birthplace and acclaimed accomplishments, a landscaped stone plaza and monument are being constructed adjacent to the city hall and U.S. Highway 89. A seven-foot-tall bronze statue depicting Borglum and his son Lincoln will be the focus of the plaza. Lincoln oversaw the completion of Mount Rushmore after Borglum's death in 1941.

Since pioneer days, the Church served most of the social and cultural needs of the community. Church buildings are the focal points for many of these activities. The historic sandstone church built in 1911 served the community until they built a new church in 1984.

Bear Lake State Park, comprising 966 acres, has two locations on the east side of the lake. The North Beach Unit, located at the top of the lake, offers a 2-mile-long beach. The East Beach Unit, across the lake from St. Charles, has a 1.5-mile-long beach. Both facilities have boat ramps for boaters and water skiers. The lake is 20 miles long and up to 8 miles wide, with half of the lake in Idaho and half in Utah.

Anglers can fish for native cutthroat and lake trout. In the winter, anglers come with nets to catch Bonneville cisco – one of three species of white fish of the Salmon family indigenous to Bear Lake. The cisco live in the deep cool water until they rise in schools each January to spawn over the limited rocky areas of the lake.

The Bear Lake National Wildlife Refuge starts about three miles northeast of St. Charles. This 19,000-acre refuge provides habitat for various species of duck, geese, Sandhill Cranes, Trumpeter Swan and White-faced Ibis.

The Idaho Department of Fish and Game manage two wildlife areas (WMA) near St. Charles. The Montpelier WMA is located near the city of Montpelier and comprises 2,100 acres of mule deer and elk habitat. The Georgetown Summit WMA is located about 33 miles northeast of St. Charles and provides elk and mule deer habitat on 3,349 acres.

The Minnetonka Cave is located about 10 miles west of the city in St. Charles Canyon. The tour of the half-mile-long limestone cave takes visitors through many large rooms with many interesting formations. Every summer thousands of visitors find the beauties of this natural wonder an enjoyable experience.

Economy and Major Employers The city has a post office, an antique store, a grocery store with a restaurant, a gas station, a bike shop, a hamburger drive-in, an RV park and rental cabins.

St. Charles' population has declined from a high of 577 in 1917. With the closure of sawmills and the flourmill and farm and ranch consolidation, most high school graduates and young families have left the city to find employment in larger communities.

Today, retired residents account for over half of the city's population. Most working residents travel to neighboring cities for employment.

Education Bear Lake County School District, headquartered in Montpelier, provides most of the elementary and secondary education. Elementary students K-6 attend school 8 miles north in Paris. Middle and high school students attend school in Montpelier, 16 miles away.

The closest institution of higher learning is Utah State University, 48 miles southwest in Logan, Utah. The closest Idaho institution of higher learning is Idaho State University, 74 miles northwest in Pocatello.

Health Care The closest hospital is Bear Lake Memorial Hospital in Montpelier.

Transportation U.S. Highway 89 intersects the city.

The closest airport is Bear Lake County Airport in Paris. The airport has two runways – one 5,730 feet long and the second 4,590 feet. Commercial airline carriers are available at the Pocatello Regional Airport.

Utilities and Services Private companies provide electricity, telephone and satellite services. The City provides water and sewer services. The County Sheriff provides police protection under contract with the City. The volunteer Bear Lake County Fire District, with a fire truck housed in the St. Charles City Hall, provides fire protection.

Vision for 2050

In 1960 St. Charles had a population of 300. In the intervening five decades, the city has lost over half of its population.

Bear Lake is receiving increased attention as a destination for outdoor recreation and an outstanding location for a second home. To capture the stunning view of the brilliantly blue Bear Lake, developers have constructed numerous second homes in resorts high in the wooded foothills above the lake's western shore above St. Charles and the unincorporated town of Fish Haven, five miles south.

As this type of development continues, they will attract people who work in the developments and the businesses that come to serve the tourists.

Should this growth occur, environmental law might require new or improved municipal systems for the city. In that case, city and community leaders will adopt impact fee and other ordinances that insure that growth pays for growth. Importantly, regardless of the changes the next four decades bring, city leaders will work to insure the beauty of the city's location is protected; the city's heritage honored; and the quiet, peaceful environment respected.

Mayors

1938 Landon Pugmire *
1957 Ralph Booth *
1961 Gilbert (Red) Arnell
1964 L. Burdett Pugmire
1980 L. Junior Pugmire
1984 Leslie J. Hill
1996 Jess Johnson
2000 Leslie J. Hill
2004 Alan Michaelson
* Village Chairman

Building at Atomic City. Courtesy of Billie Martin and Karin Richard.

BINGHAM COUNTY

- Aberdeen
- Atomic City
- Basalt
- Blackfoot (*County Seat*)
- Firth
- Shelley

Aberdeen today.

Aberdeen

Statistical Data

Population: 1,951 *
Elevation: 4,404 feet
Precipitation: 9 inches **
Average Snowfall: 21 inches **
County: Bingham
Website: www.aberdeenidaho.us

Temperature Range – Fahrenheit: **
Spring: 24 to 67
Summer: 45 to 85
Fall: 21 to 75
Winter: 12 to 44
* U.S. Census Bureau Estimates July 2015
**Historical averages

Aberdeen is an agricultural center located three miles from the western shore of American Falls Reservoir and 12 miles upstream from American Falls Dam.

Fertile farmland, a picturesque golf course and Hazard Creek border the northern entrance to the city on Idaho Highway 39. At the southern entrance, the road passes through productive farms before curving around a lush park developed by the Aberdeen Women's Club.

Pre-Incorporation Years

In prehistoric times, the region was a lake bed now named the ancestral American Falls Lake. Archaeologists have found Pleistocene fossils of ancient mammals in the sediments.

When Oregon Trail immigrants came through the area, the land was a broad sagebrush-covered plain. The Snake River ran placidly through the plain until it dropped 50 feet at the 800-foot-wide, 200-foot-long American Falls rapids located 12 miles south of the present city of Aberdeen.

In 1894 the U.S. Congress passed the Carey Act that ceded up to 1 million acres of arid federal land to any Western state that instituted programs to build privately-owned irrigation systems to make the land arable. (*See The Region, Federal Land*

Use Laws.)

In 1904 a group of entrepreneurs formed the American Falls Canal and Power Company and received approval to construct an irrigation system. The company developed a large tract of land that encompasses what is now the city of Aberdeen. Although the record is not specific, it is believed the company formed the Aberdeen Townsite Company, which platted the town and began selling lots. When they staked the plat, the first store built in Aberdeen, the Hamilton Mercantile, wound up in the middle of the street and had to move.

One of the principals of the American Falls Canal and Power Company was Frederick A. Sweet. In researching how Aberdeen got its name, John Heer, editor of the Aberdeen Times, wrote to Sweet who responded on July 30, 1932, "At the time the town was organized, I ... was instrumental in floating the Bond issue to refinance the American Falls Canal and Power Company. A number of businessmen and bankers of Rockford, Illinois, were helping in the purchase of the bonds. Partly in their honor (they were of Scotch descent) and partly because we all liked the name, we called the town Aberdeen."

Aberdeen business district, 1909.

In the summer of 1905 Reb Randall traveled from Newton, Kansas, to visit his brother in American Falls. Randall was a minister in the Mennonite faith, a sect of Anabaptist Christians who immigrated to America to avoid persecution.

When Randall returned to Newton, he gave a positive report about a new irrigation project north of American Falls. George Bartel and three other members of the Newton Mennonite community took a train to American Falls to make a detailed evaluation. They were so impressed they sold their property in Newton and, in February 1906, moved their families to Aberdeen. Over 30 Mennonite families followed them.

First Aberdeen school.

These Mennonite settlers made up a large percentage of those who filed homestead claims in 1906. In 1909 the Mennonites built an attractive church with a bell tower. By 1910 the Mennonite congregation approved construction of a hospital in American Falls.

The town already had several businesses including a bank and telephone service in 1909. In addition, the railroad line from Blackfoot to Aberdeen was completed.

At this time, Aberdeen did not have an official village government. The Aberdeen Commercial Club, an organization formed by land reclamation and other officials, governed.

In 1911 the University of Idaho's Agricultural Experiment Station in Moscow embarked on a program to establish a network of branch stations across the state to provide research to help improve farm production.

First Mennonite Church, 1910.

Aberdeen was selected for one of the stations because it was centrally located in the rapidly developing farm belt of the Snake River Plain, had both irrigated and dry-land farming and local interests offered a cash incentive.

In May 1911 the University entered into an agreement with the Aberdeen Commercial Club to build a branch experiment station at Aberdeen. Under the agreement, the Commercial Club raised $4,500 for the station and the University leased a tract of land at the northeast corner of the town site.

First Mennonite Church, today, in Aberdeen on the corner of Washington and Fourth West.

In 1911 the Aberdeen Times was also established, and in 1913 the Aberdeen School District was organized.

Incorporation

On November 6, 1913, Bingham County Commissioners approved incorporation of Aberdeen as a village. On February 18, 1941, the Village Board announced that the population of the village had exceeded 1,000 and was now qualified to be designated an Idaho city. City elections soon followed.

Turning Points

Irrigation The advent of irrigation in 1904 marked the first significant turning point for Aberdeen. Passage of the Carey Act and state enabling legislation allowed land developers and farmers to convert sagebrush into productive farms, the underpinning of Aberdeen's economy.

Shortly after passage of the Carey Act, entrepreneurs received approval to build the Aberdeen-Springfield Canal, which diverted Snake River water from nearly 50 miles upriver near Firth to the Aberdeen area in 1895.

Seven years later, another entrepreneurial group formed the American Falls Canal and Power Company to provide irrigation water to Blackfoot, American Falls and Aberdeen farms. It also constructed a hydroelectric power plant – long since abandoned – on the American Falls.

In the same year, Congress passed the Newlands Act, creating the predecessor to the Bureau of Reclamation (Reclamation), and promoted irrigation and land reclamation projects throughout the West.

Aberdeen Residential Section, circa 1914.

One of Reclamation's first projects was a complex system of dams, canals and pumping systems on the Snake River called the Minidoka Project. When completed, the Minidoka Project included the hydroelectric Minidoka Dam, Jackson Lake located 300 miles east in Wyoming and the hydroelectric American Falls Dam and Reservoir.

University of Idaho Agriculture Research and Extension Center The 1911 decision by the University of Idaho to build its Agriculture Research and Extension Center at Aberdeen added significantly to the city's prestige and stabilized the city's economy. The Center's state-of-the-art research has inseparably linked the city with some of the finest scientific research dealing with agricultural crops and crop storage techniques in the world.

It is the repository for the National Small Grains Collection of wheat, oat and barley seed – nearly 6,000 known varieties. Any plant breeder in the world can access information from this collection.

Farmer Innovation and Inventions It is noteworthy that certain Aberdeen farmers are responsible for inventions or innovations that changed agriculture. In the 1930s and 1940s, Isaac Nelson developed and patented a conveyer for moving potatoes in potato cellars, a potato harvester that employed an elevator and a self-unloading potato truck bed.

Clifford Wride was the first to bring irrigation water to the desert without taking it out of the river. In 1948 he paid Idaho Power to run a power line to his property where he planned to drill for water despite the general belief that drilling for water in the desert was a waste of time. Wride believed otherwise. When he turned the power on, a huge stream of water gushed from the electric pump. It was the first well drilled into the massive Snake River Plain Aquifer. Wride's innovation was the forerunner for thousands of wells that now pump out of the Aquifer.

With the prospect of receiving irrigation water in pressured pipes, a family named Knudsen helped improve the irrigation wheel lines invented by the Jensen Brothers of California.

American Falls Dam and Reservoir The construction of the American Falls Dam and Reservoir in 1927 marked the fourth major turning point for the city. It placed the city within three miles of one of the largest lakes and prominent fisheries in Idaho and within 12 miles of a major hydroelectric dam. However, the reservoir presented other problems as it added a 15-mile commute for Aberdeen residents traveling to Pocatello. Residents now generally drive south to American Falls, then east to Pocatello on Interstate 86.

Food Processing In 1975 the J.R. Simplot Company built a frozen French fry potato processing plant in the city that employed 350. Today, technological innovation has allowed the company to improve productivity with significantly fewer employees.

Aberdeen Plant Research Center.

Aberdeen Today

Amenities and Attractions Aberdeen has two city parks and a library. City resident Clint Krebiel has an extensive privately-owned museum with several thousand artifacts. His private collection includes farm equipment and commercial and household items. Krebiel opens his museum to the public each year for "Aberdeen Days" as well as by appointment.

Aberdeen Days is an event sponsored by the Aberdeen Chamber of Commerce. It occurs annually on the next to last weekend in June. It is a three-day event featuring sidewalk sales, melodrama performances, food and other booths.

Once every fifth year, there is an All-High Reunion at the high school. Saturday is the big day with a "free pancake and fixin's breakfast" in the City Park. The reunion has attracted up to 2,300 people. The event includes a parade, fish fry and two performances of a melodrama.

Every second year, there is a celebration of Pioneer Day on the Saturday nearest July 24. This event features a flag raising ceremony, parade, races, games, food booths and live entertainment.

On the first Monday in December, the Chamber of Commerce sponsors a Parade of Lights that concludes with refreshments and socializing at City Hall, the library and other designated locations.

The city is home to the historic and internationally recognized "Aberdeen Research and Extension Center," the University of Idaho's 440-acre facility. Research at the Center has resulted in new and improved varieties of cereal grains, potatoes and other crops; control of plant diseases and pests; more effective use of fertilizers; and better farming practices for both irrigated and dry-land farms. Each year the Center receives visitors from throughout the world.

Three miles west of the city is the 65,000-acre and 24-mile-long American Falls Reservoir, a lake created by the American Falls Hydroelectric Dam on the Snake River. (*See Eastern Idaho: The Snake River and the Snake River Aquifer, Idaho's Economic Life Blood.*)

There are over 200 species of birds around the reservoir. Sportsman's Park, located on the lake shore, is just two miles from the city and is a popular place for picnicking; camping; boating; water skiing; and, in the winter, ice fishing.

Approximately 15 miles north is the southern boundary of the U.S. Department of Energy's Idaho National Laboratory's (INL) 570,000-acre site and National Environmental Research Park. (*See Eastern Idaho, The Region, Idaho National Laboratory – Eastern Idaho's Largest Employer.*)

Fifteen miles west is the southern portion of the 750,000-acre Craters of the Moon National Monument and Preserve that includes the Great Rift National Natural Landmark. Lava flows cover most of the preserve, sometimes isolating pockets of land that have remained undisturbed for centuries. The lava flows at Craters of the Moon are more recent, flowing up through the great rift about 15,000 years ago.

There are several volcanic craters in the preserve. The highest, located near Aberdeen, is Mosby Butte. It is 15 miles northwest of the city at an elevation of 5,498 feet.

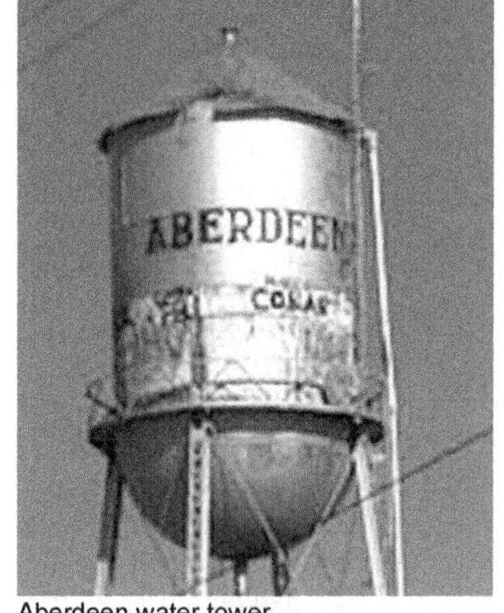

Aberdeen water tower.

The volcanic ash produced in these prehistoric volcanic eruptions form the critical component in southern Idaho's soils that produce potatoes of exceptionally high quality.

This vast preserve is open to hiking and camping. However, only the most experienced hikers, with scheduled re-supply camps of particularly water, should venture across these rugged, fissured and fractured ancient lava flows. (*See Eastern Idaho, The Region, Distinctive Geographic and Geologic Features – Craters of the Moon National Monument and Preserve.*)

About 25 miles south of the city is the 990-acre Massacre Rock State Park where several Oregon Trail immigrants and American Indians fought and lost their lives.

The park includes a unique natural feature of many huge, smooth boulders that tumbled for miles when old Lake Bonneville breached its natural dam at Red Rock Pass near Downey. This massive flood occurred 14,500 years ago. It drained most of this vast lake and cut deep gorges where the Snake River now flows. (*See Eastern Idaho, The Region, Distinctive Geographic and Geologic Features – Prehistoric Lake Bonneville.*)

Economy and Major Employers Agricultural and food processing industries are the city's economic foundation.

The J.R. Simplot Company Food Division produces frozen potato products such as French fries and employs over 200. Pleasant Valley Potato, Inc., employs 130; Duffin Potato 60 and Idaho Select's fresh pack potato operation 70. The Aberdeen Research and Extension Center has 80 full-time employees. During the summer, that number doubles with seasonal workers.

Aberdeen's retail district includes banks; service stations; restaurants; stores selling hardware, lumber, prescription drugs, groceries, women's clothing and health supplements; a beauty salon; a florist; a bar; and a motorcycle and all-terrain vehicle dealer.

In addition to the City Hall and police station, the downtown area has medical clinics, an American Legion Hall and a senior citizens center.

Education The Aberdeen School District provides substantially all of the elementary and secondary education in the area. The school campus includes a high school, a new middle school, an elementary school and a cafeteria.

The Migrant Council provides a school for Hispanic children up to 5 years old. The school begins at 5 to 6 a.m. each morning, provides meals and introduces the children to the English language. Approximately 60 children attend the school.

The closest institution of higher learning is Idaho State University 38 miles east in Pocatello.

Health Care Primary medical care is available in two clinics located in the city. The closest hospital services are 15 miles south at Harms Medical Hospital in American Falls or the Portneuf Regional Medical Centers in Pocatello.

Aberdeen City Hall.

Transportation State Highway 39 passes through the city. Interstate 86 can be accessed 15 miles south.

Union Pacific Railroad provides freight service to the city. Private and light charter aircraft use the Aberdeen Municipal Airport's 3,650-foot runway located just outside the city. The Pocatello Regional Airport, located 18 miles east, provides service for commercial aircraft.

Utilities and Services Private carriers provide electricity and natural gas. The City provides law enforcement; fire protection; and domestic water, sewer and solid waste services.

Vision for 2050

Other than the 1990s when the city's population grew by over 400, or 30 percent, Aberdeen's population has been stable. Over the next four decades the city's population will likely follow the historical pattern of modest growth.

By 2050 agricultural and food processing will still underpin the city's economy. However, technological innovation will continue to improve their productivity with fewer employees, while growth in other businesses will continue to offset these job losses.

The increasing ability of people to live in a more rural community yet conduct their business in metropolitan areas through technology will attract new residents, particularly retirees drawn by Aberdeen's favorable business climate, amenities and attractions.

The City will have upgraded its Waste Water Treatment Plant and added another well to its domestic water system, upgrading the systems to meet the needs of current residents plus several hundred new ones.

In cooperation with the County, the City will have resolved the problem of solid waste disposal.

The City will have completed the new pedestrian and bicycle path called the Aberdeen Gem Train and will provide bus services especially needed by seniors and the handicapped. The City will have also made needed improvements to its drainage system, roads and sidewalks.

Aberdeen's citizens will continue to show great community spirit. All city services including water and sewers, school facilities, emergency services, parks and library will equal or exceed the need.

The city's streets, homes and businesses will continue to be well maintained with a distinctive Main Street collection of vibrant businesses and institutions; a clean, peaceful and friendly place to live and raise a family.

Mayors

1913-1941 Unknown *
1941 Clifford Wride
1943 Sam Nealey
1945 Andy Hansen
1947 James Chapman
1954 Festus Monsen
1957 Clifford Wride
1966 Theodore Wren
1974 Clifford Wride
1981 Maurine Driscoll
1990 Larry Walters
1995 A. Morgan Anderson
2016 Larry Barrett

* Village Chairman

Atomic City Texaco station.

Atomic City

Statistical Data

Population: 29 *
Elevation: 5,015 feet
Precipitation: 9 inches **
Average Snowfall: 30 inches **
County: Bingham
Temperature Range – Fahrenheit: **
Spring: 21 to 66
Summer: 43 to 87
Fall: 16 to 75
Winter: 4 to 34
* U.S. Census Bureau Estimates July 2015
**Historical averages

All Atomic City pictures courtesy of Billie Martin and Karin Richard.

Atomic City lies on the eastern side of the Idaho National Laboratory's 570,000-acre reservation about midway between Arco and Blackfoot.

Vast acreages of desert landscape and prehistoric lava flows surround the city. The 7,517-foot-high Big Southern Butte and landmark lies 10 miles southwest.

Pre-Incorporation Years

In 1862 Tim Goodale, a trader acquainted with the American Indian and fur trader trails north of the Snake River, led a group of Oregon Trail immigrants on a shortcut beginning at Fort Hall and rejoining the main trail east of Boise near Mayfield.

The trail passed a few miles south of what is now Atomic City and north of Big Southern Butte. Goodale's Cutoff became one of the more heavily traveled routes on the Oregon Trail.

In the early 1870s prospectors discovered gold on the Yankee Fork of the Salmon River southwest of Challis. For several years, the Blackfoot-Challis stage and freight wagon road passed near what is now Atomic City.

Historically, the present site of Atomic City was not a particularly noteworthy location. Most activity centered several miles southwest at Big Southern Butte where people periodically sought to utilize Big Southern Butte as an observation station, to prospect for metals or to enjoy its natural resources.

Around 1940 a lonely service station was the only modern facility on the desert road connecting the cities of Arco and Blackfoot. The owner strategically located his service station about midway between the two cities to provide an important service to travelers whose vehicles had mechanical, radiator, tire or fuel problems, common occurrences with the vehicles of that day.

At that time, the U.S. Navy operated a proving ground and gunnery range several miles north and west of the service station.

In 1949 the U. S. Atomic Energy Commission – now the U.S. Department of Energy – created the National Reactor Training Station – now the Idaho National Laboratory (INL) – and authorized construction of laboratory and test facilities on the Navy proving grounds – now part of INL's 570,000-acre reservation.

Among the first to be constructed were nuclear reactor facilities several miles northwest of the service station. (*See Idaho National Laboratories – Eastern Idaho's Largest Employer.*)

To accommodate the large amount of traffic to and from the site, the federal government made improvements to U.S. Highway 26, making the road a straight drive across the desert between the junction of U.S. Highway 20 to Arco and Blackfoot. The improved road bypassed the service station by about a mile but provided access using the old road, Taber Road.

Thousands of construction workers came to the INL site to build the test reactors and facilities. Many found homes in nearby cities and commuted to work.

Other workers chose the service station site and set up temporary quarters because it was the closest place where water, gas and other services were available.

A collection of trailer houses and tents soon sprang up and, before long, over a thousand people lived near the service station.

This boomtown growth prompted an almost immediate need for a municipal organization to manage the common needs of the community. Prior to applying to the Bingham County Commissioners for incorporation, residents debated what to name their new town.

Initially, they named the city "Fury" because everyone was in a fury to get the town built. On reflection, most residents rejected that name and began calling the new community "Midway" because it was halfway between Blackfoot and Arco. However, when it came time to file the incorporation application, residents agreed on naming their town "Atomic City." They felt the name was appropriately distinctive and would be an attraction for INL employees who wanted to live nearer to their work.

Incorporation

On August 4, 1950, Atomic City became an incorporated village.

Turning Points

Atomic Energy and Construction Workers The U. S. Atomic Energy Commission's decision to construct its nuclear laboratory and test facilities on what is now the INL reservation provided the basis for construction workers to found Atomic City.

So long as the construction activity continued, the city prospered. When the construction projects were completed, the jobs dried up and the workers moved away. By 1960 the population had declined to 161. A few years later, the population dropped to around 25 where it has remained until the present time. Today, many of the city's residents are retired.

Atomic City is the only boomtown in Idaho that owes its brief period of growth and prosperity to construction workers and atomic energy.

Atomic City Today

Amenities and Attractions The city's quiet rural setting is perhaps its most valuable attribute. For those who prefer living away from urban areas but close enough to access the amenities of larger cities, Atomic City is a perfect place.

The vast high-desert surroundings are primarily public land open to hiking, camping and hunting.

Prehistoric volcanic buttes dot the landscape. The largest of the buttes is the 7,517-foot-high Big Southern Butte. It lies 10 miles west of the city. The butte is a National Natural Landmark, an ecological island supporting vegetation including aspen and lodge pole pine. Harsh weather often shrouds this massive four-mile diameter butte. At the top, winds of 80 miles an hour and several feet of snow are common.

Boating and fishing are available at American Falls Reservoir. The closest boat dock on the reservoir is at Aberdeen, 35 miles south.

Sixteen miles northwest is Experimental Breeder Reactor 1 (EBR 1), a National Historic Landmark and visitors center. On December 20, 1951, ERB 1 produced the world's first usable electricity generated with nuclear power. Scientists demonstrated this historic event by lighting four electric light bulbs.

Economy and Major Employers Atomic City has a convenience store/post office and a bar. Most residents drive to nearby cities to shop.

Education Elementary and secondary students ride the bus 34 miles to attend school in Blackfoot. The closest institution of higher learning is Eastern Idaho Technical College and University Place in Idaho Falls, 52 miles east.

Health Care The nearest hospital is Lost Rivers Hospital 27 miles north in Arco.

Transportation Atomic City is located 1.3 miles west of U.S. Highway 26. Blackfoot and Interstate 15 are located 29 miles southeast.

Two landing strips are available near Atomic City and Big Southern Butte. The nearest commercial air service is Idaho Falls Regional Airport.

Utilities and Services Private companies provide electricity, telephone and satellite services. The City provides water. The homes and businesses have individual septic systems. The Bingham County Sheriff's Office provides police protection.

Vision for 2050

The city's population of around 25 has remained somewhat constant for nearly five decades. Any significant change will likely be due to external influences such as the possible development of molybdenum mines at Big Southern Butte or spill-over growth in nearby cities. In 2007 the city completed a new well and water system. The water system has the capacity for significant future growth.

Mayors

** Unknown

** Lynn Staten

2006 Lee Mangum

2010 Kelli Isaacs

** Date Unknown

Basalt Post Office.

Basalt

Statistical Data

Population: 389 *
Elevation: 4,587 feet
Precipitation: 10 inches **
Average Snowfall: 30 inches **
County: Bingham

Temperature Range – Fahrenheit: **
Spring: 25 to 68
Summer: 46 to 86
Fall: 23 to 75
Winter: 13 to 37

* U.S. Census Bureau Estimates July 2015
**Historical averages

The city of Basalt is named for the nearby black basalt rock formations that lie along the Snake River. The city is located on the southeastern side of the fertile Snake River Plain about 20 miles southwest of Idaho Falls. Basalt's sister city of Firth lies about a mile southwest. The Snake River flows less than a mile west of the city.

The Blackfoot Mountain Range of the Caribou-Targhee National Forest begins three miles east and the Fort Hall Indian Reservation lies a few miles southwest.

Pre-Incorporation Years

In May 1863 prospectors found gold near what is now Virginia City in southwestern Montana. Virginia City was part of Idaho Territory until Montana

Territory was created on May 26, 1864.

The ensuing gold rush brought a steady flow of traffic between Utah and Virginia City on a wagon road named the "Gold Road." People on horses, stagecoaches and freight wagons passed through what is now Basalt and Firth on the Gold Road that crossed the Snake River and turned north at Eagle Rock – now Idaho Falls.

In 1862 Congress passed the Homestead Act and in 1877 the Desert Land Act. The Homestead Act allowed conversion of up to 160 acres of federal land to private ownership to those filers who improved and lived on the land for five years. The Desert Land Act allowed settlers to file for up to 640 acres, with the condition that they bring the land under irrigation within three years. (*See Eastern Idaho, Federal Land Use Laws*.)

In 1878 the Utah and Northern Railroad Company (U&N) began laying railroad track from Utah to Montana, generally following the Gold Road. By the end of the next year, they had extended the railroad through what is now Firth, Basalt and Idaho Falls to Spencer, about 15 miles south of the Montana border at Monida Pass. The railroad reached the Montana gold fields the following year.

From sagebrush and desolation (above) to an irrigated landscape.

One of the construction workers building the railroad was John R. Poole of Ogden, Utah. When Poole returned to Ogden, he praised the farmland potential of the Upper Snake River Plain. Many families living in northern Utah were recent converts to the Church of Jesus Christ of Latter-day Saints (Church) – coming from the Eastern United States and emigrants from foreign countries – looking for good farmland to settle.

Poole's fellow railroad workers, returning to Utah, confirmed Poole's account and, within a short time, several groups of northern Utah families were making preparations to travel north to settle in Eastern Idaho. (*See Eastern Idaho, Pioneer Settlements – Upper Snake River Plain*.)

In 1882 Church leaders asked 54-year-old Thomas E. Ricks to be an ecclesiastical leader (Bishop – later Stake President) of the immigrant settlers going to what is now the Rexburg area. By that time, Church members had over three decades of experience in Utah Territory building small irrigation water conveyances needed to turn arid sagebrush-covered land into productive farms.

Ricks accepted the call, and, by the end of the year, Church records listed 815 members living in Ricks' geographical jurisdiction, initially called the Bannock Stake. By the end of 1884, the number of members over the age of eight had increased to 1,420. (Children are not baptized into the Church of Jesus Christ of Latter-day Saints until they are eight years old – all members of the Church must be baptized.)

First Sunday School in Basalt, circa 1885.

Almost immediately after farm settlement began, plans to divert irrigation water from the rivers and streams and build canals and irrigation ditches began. The farmers benefiting from a canal formed a canal company. The canal companies borrowed money from area banks to construct their canals. The banks filled a dual role – they not only loaned money but also helped resolve arguments over water rights.

Looking east, showing the "Old Basalt" water tank, windmill, narrow gauge railroad, and the Inglestroms' home.

Once the canal companies designed the course for the canal, workers – mostly the farmers themselves – dug the water conveyances with picks, crowbars, shovels, horse-drawn Fresno scrapers and chains to move the rock. Occasionally, they used blasting powder.

Basalt Post Office, 1915-20.

It was in this environment that in 1885, a few families coming up from Utah settled on a fertile stretch of land adjacent to the Snake River called Cedar Point. Geographically, Cedar Point was part of the Lewisville Ward in the Bannock Stake. The Cedar Point settlement grew rapidly and on August 19, 1888, the Church reorganized the Cedar Point Branch into a ward that they named Basalt after the area's landscape and the large amount of basalt rock formations lining the Snake River.

Incorporation

By 1900 community leaders started to lay plans to become an incorporated village. As part of that effort, certain of them platted a town on the higher ground overlooking the historic pioneer settlement of Cedar Point.

Their plat consisted of about a dozen ten-acre blocks configured on a north-south, east-west axis and subdivided into one-acre lots. By 1906, the number of citizens in the surveyed community exceeded 200, the minimum number of citizens required to become an incorporated village. On April 11, 1906, they successfully incorporated their village with the name of Basalt.

Turning Points

Railroad The coming of the railroad in 1879 was one of the attractions that caused the early settlers of Basalt to start establishing homesteads six years later. With the railroad, area farmers were able to receive equipment and supplies and transport their production to market faster and easier.

Potato Processing Plant Idaho Supreme Potatoes, Inc., with headquarters in Firth, operates a fresh pack and specialty potato processing plant in Basalt. The plant began operations around 1975 and has about 250 employees.

A shed built by Walter Crofts. Note the dirt roof, similar to the roofs the first settlers used on their homes.

Basalt Today

Amenities and Attractions The city's greatest attraction is its location. City residents are able to enjoy numerous outdoor activities in the nearby mountains, the Snake River, streams and reservoirs as well as the vast tracts of public land on the Snake River Plain. In addition, they are close to a wide variety of urban attractions and amenities in the larger cities located nearby.

Economy and Major Employers Many city residents work at Idaho Supreme Products. Others commute to Idaho Falls, Shelley or Blackfoot for employment. The nearest commercial center for shopping is Idaho Falls.

Education The Firth School District provides K-12 education for Basalt children who attend school in Firth. The closest institutions of higher learning are University Place and Eastern Idaho Technical College, 14 miles northeast in Idaho Falls.

Basalt School was built and ready about 1920. The building burned in a fire in 1958.

Health Care The closest hospital is Bingham Memorial Hospital in Blackfoot.

Transportation U.S. Highway 91 intersects the city. Interstate 15 is located four miles west across the Snake River. The closest airport is in Idaho Falls. The

Union Pacific Railroad provides service for Basalt freight customers.

Utilities and Services Private companies provide electricity, telephone, natural gas and satellite services. The City provides water, sewer and garbage services. The County provides police protection under contract with the City.

Vision for 2050

Since 1980 Basalt's population has held at around 400. Historical trends are likely to continue.

By 2050 Basalt will be, as it is today, a peaceful rural community strategically located near larger population centers and the urban amenities they offer as well as being surrounded by a patchwork of fertile agricultural fields and, further away, vast acreages of public lands.

Pictures in this chapter arefrom the 1985 Basalt Centennial book and used with permission.

Mayors

1907 Charles Criddle *
** J.H. Berg *
** M.L. Lockyer *
** N.C. Thompson *
** J.L. Johnson *
** Charles Criddle *
** J.C. Sorenson *
** H.A. Johnson *
** F.J. Herman *
** E.B. Freemen *
** C.E. White *
** Volney Bailer *
** Lorin F. Freeman *
** Austin Brown *
** Leo Harper *
** Ross Berg *
** Jesse Wiseman, Jr. *
** Charles Lyon *
** Dennis Speas *
** Frank Coil *
1967 Forrest Stringham
1968 Jesse Wiseman
1972 William Messick
1976 Dennis Speas
1980 LeLand Zundel
1984 Michael Young
1992 Dennis Hjelm
1996 Larry Russell
2016 Larry Wagoner

* Village Chairman
** Dates Unknown

Oregon Short Line depot built in 1913 is now the home of the Idaho Potato Museum in Blackfoot.

Blackfoot

Statistical Data

Population: 11,814 *
Elevation: 4,498 feet
Precipitation: 11 inches **
Average Snowfall:31 inches **
County: Bingham
Website: www.cityofblackfoot.org

Temperature Range – Fahrenheit: **
Spring: 25 to 68
Summer: 45 to 85
Fall: 23 to 75
Winter: 14 to 38
* U.S. Census Bureau Estimates July 2015
**Historical averages

Blackfoot lies on the northeastern side of the fertile Snake River Plain between Idaho Falls and Pocatello. The Snake River flows near the city's western boundary. The Blackfoot River is on the southeastern edge of the city. The 544,000-acre Fort Hall Indian Reservation begins a few miles to the east and south of the city.

The Blackfoot Mountain Range, with peaks rising to nearly 7,500 feet, lies 25 miles to the east. To the north, west and south are vast acreages of highly productive farmland. Fields of potatoes, corn, wheat, barley, alfalfa, beans and sugar beets form a beautiful patchwork of color across the Snake River Plain.

Pre-Incorporation Years

In 1841 the first travelers on what would become the Oregon Trail trekked through vast acres of sagebrush as they followed the Snake River past what is now Blackfoot. At that time, tribes of Native American Indians, primarily Shoshone and Bannock, routinely passed through the area en route to their various seasonal encampments.

Many Native American Indians – angered by the increased flow of immigrants and settlers, broken treaties and resulting decline in the wild game and other food sources on which they relied – attacked some settlements. The "Indian Wars," really skirmishes, continued until August 1878.

In the early 1860s prospectors discovered gold near Virginia City in western Montana. A freight wagon and stagecoach road, called the "Gold Road," developed between Utah and the Montana gold fields.

In 1866 two homesteading families, Fredrick and Finetta Stevens and a Mr. Warren, were among the first to settle in the area. They chose locations near the Blackfoot River.

Warren sought to offer some protection to the scattered settlers in the event of an attack by marauding Indians. In such event, settlers could flee to his home, which he built similar to a fort with small gaps or windows in the walls, from which settlers could fire their rifles.

The first steam-powered Merry-Go-Round comes to Eastern Idaho State Fair in 1906.

Stevens operated "Stevens Stage Stop" on the Gold Road until 1872 when they discontinued the business. By that time, settlement in the area had significantly increased. Stevens and a friend, Major Danilson who was a Civil War officer, opened a general store further north in the present location of Blackfoot.

In 1878 the Utah and Northern Railroad took over construction of the railroad to Montana from a predecessor railroad. Because of Danilson's influence, the railroad placed a gentle curve in the railroad bed to run behind the Stevens-Danilson General Store. They arranged for the railroad to use the general store as a train depot until the railroad built its own facility.

The Blackfoot railroad terminal became the principal supply depot to the developing gold mines discovered two years earlier about 130 miles northwest on the Yankee Fork River near Challis. Freight wagons and stagecoaches departed from the Blackfoot train depot to the Custer County mines almost daily.

It was during this time that two homesteaders, Watson N. Shilling and W.C. Lewis, platted the future town of Blackfoot on their land.

In 1882 the U.S. Congress passed the Edmunds Anti-Polygamy Act specifically to limit the growing political power in the West of members of the Church of Jesus Christ of Latter-day Saints (also known as Mormons and LDS). Around that time, Fred T. Dubois, a graduate of Yale University, accepted a position at the Fort Hall Indian Agency. Dubois lived in Blackfoot. In 1882 he accepted an appointment as U.S. Marshal.

Intersection of Main and Pacific, circa 1913.

Dubois had a prominent career in Idaho Republican politics including influencing Idaho statehood and using his position to arrest alleged polygamists and advance the Republican cause by helping create a voters' test oath in Idaho's Constitution. The test oath disenfranchised Mormon citizens – primarily Democrats (constituting) about one-fifth of Idaho's population and who professed a belief in LDS Church doctrines on marriage, whether polygamists or not – from voting or serving on juries. In 1890 the Church of Jesus Christ of Latter-day Saints issued a manifesto prohibiting the practice of polygamy. The courts later ruled the test oath unconstitutional. Idaho voters later removed the test oath from Idaho's constitution.

Dubois and his two daughters are buried in the Blackfoot Grove City Cemetery.

On January 13, 1885, the Idaho Territorial Legislature established Bingham County with the county seat as the unincorporated community of Blackfoot. In that same year, the Territorial Legislature

Main Street today.

approved construction of the Idaho Insane Asylum – now, State Hospital South – at Blackfoot.

By 1887 the federal government sited the U.S. Land Office for Idaho's Southern District and the U.S. Third Judicial District Court at Blackfoot. The town had a livery stable, bank, retail and general merchandise stores, two brick churches, a public school and seven saloons.

In addition, Western Union had 242 miles of telegraph lines in the geographically large county of Bingham. The legislature would later split off four counties from Bingham – Freemont in 1893, Bonneville in 1911, Power in 1913 and Butte in 1917.

In April 1901 the Salmon River Railroad Company – later the Oregon Short Line Railroad – began constructing an 86-mile rail line from Blackfoot to the copper mines in Mackay and a 29-mile line to farms at Aberdeen.

Fishing.

Incorporation

On January 16, 1901, a majority of the town's taxpayers signed a petition calling for the incorporation of Blackfoot as a village. Later that year, the county commissioners approved the application.

Among the first actions of the new village trustees was to issue franchises to Rocky Mountain Bell Telephone Company and Blackfoot Power and Light Company, opening the way for residential telephone and electric service.

On June 26, 1907, the village trustees passed a resolution to change the legal status of the village to a city, recorded at the Bingham County Courthouse March 24, 1909. The 1910 U.S. Census reported that Blackfoot had a population of 2,203.

First automated potato seed cutter developed by Milestone, 1961.

Turning Points

Railroad Blackfoot owes its origins to the Utah and Northern Railroad (later the Oregon Short Line) that built a depot in Blackfoot in 1878. However, the discovery of gold in what is now western Montana brought the railroad. Later discoveries of gold in the Yankee Fork and copper at Mackay would augment the city's transportation hub economy for over three decades. During that time, a growing agriculture economy would gradually take over from the mining industry as the principal user of the railroad services in Blackfoot.

Irrigation In 1902 the American Falls Canal and Power Company provided irrigation water to Blackfoot, American Falls and Aberdeen farms. (*See Eastern Idaho – The Snake River and the Snake River Aquifer, Idaho's Economic Life Blood.*)

Potatoes Demand for fresh-packed potatoes developed in the early 1900s. Innovation in processing potatoes came with the advent of World War II in 1941 when the Army Quartermaster Corps encouraged Jack Simplot to expand his dried onion powder and flakes operation to include dehydrated potatoes for the military.

Original Spudnik scooper, 1958.

Blackfoot farmers were attracted to the Army's demand for potatoes in a major way. Potatoes became the major commodity produced by Blackfoot area farmers. Entrepreneurs responded by developing innovative methods and equipment to handle and process potatoes. Potatoes soon became the dominant commodity produced in Bingham County. Blackfoot became known as the "Potato Capitol of the World."

Eastern Idaho State Fair grounds entrance.

Blackfoot is home to the Idaho Potato Museum, which is located in the historic old Oregon Short Line Railroad Depot. The museum provides information on potato history, the growing and harvesting process, nutrition, trivia, educational potato facts and the development of the potato industry.

Now, Basic American Foods and Nonpareil, two of the city's largest potato processors, each have over 750 employees Spudnik Equipment Company and Milestone, Inc., are two of the city's largest specialized potato handling equipment manufacturers.

Idaho National Laboratories In 1949 the Atomic Energy Commission, now the U.S. Department of Energy, sited its National Reactor Training Station on a 570,000-acre reservation northwest of the city. INL also has facilities in Idaho Falls. From 1942 to 1947 the Navy operated a gunnery range on the reservation. Since 1942 these federal installations have provided employment to a significant number of Blackfoot residents. (*See Eastern Idaho – Idaho National Laboratories – Eastern Idaho's Largest Employer.*)

Nonpareil's corporate headquarters.

Blackfoot Today

Amenities and Attractions Blackfoot has 10 miles of greenbelt and over 100 acres devoted to several municipal parks that include a small lake, a soccer complex, a disc golf course, a skateboard park and lighted tennis courts.

The citizens of Blackfoot and surrounding communities enjoy an 18-hole municipal golf course and an Olympic size swimming pool with a seven-field baseball and sports complex under construction.

The Shilling House, named for its location on North Shilling Street, has been a place of hospitality and good food for over 117 years. Built in 1890 and purchased by the Henscheid family in 1964, the historic Italianate style dwelling serves as a location for public events, fine dining, and special occasions.

The Eastern Idaho State Fair continues to be the most significant and best attended civic event in Blackfoot and Bingham County. Beginning Labor Day weekend, the fair's 90 acres of facilities, events, displays and exhibits attract over 200,000 visitors annually.

The Idaho Potato Expo (Idaho Potato Museum) is located in downtown Blackfoot and is open to the public year round.

In addition to the railroad depot, the city has several other historic buildings. These buildings include St. Paul's Episcopal Church (1890); the lava rock Bingham County Historical Museum (1905); the semi-circular, courthouse annex and community center, formerly the 1,500-seat Church of Jesus Christ of Latter-Day Saints Tabernacle (1921); and the elaborately decorated Nuart Theatre (1930).

The city's location between the Snake and Blackfoot Rivers and its near proximity to reservoirs, mountains and vast tracts of public lands provide residents with a wide variety of outdoor activities including boating, biking, hiking, hunting and fishing.

Economy and Major Employers Taken together, food-processing businesses comprise the city's largest private employer.

Stan's Restaurant and Lounge.

The largest public employers are INL, Blackfoot School District and State Hospital South.

The city's vibrant downtown, with numerous financial, retail and service businesses, is also a major source of employment.

Education The Blackfoot and Snake River School Districts provide elementary and secondary education in the city. The Blackfoot School District has an enrollment of approximately 4,000 and includes a high school, alternative high school, middle school, eight elementary schools and a school specializing in early childhood and special education.

Spudnik offices and manufacturing facilities.

The Snake River School District has a high school, a junior high school, a middle school and three elementary schools.

The nearest institutions of higher learning are Idaho State University in Pocatello and, in Idaho Falls, Eastern Idaho Technical College and the Center for Higher Education.

Health Care The Bingham Memorial Hospital and two medical clinics – Blackfoot Medical and Mountain River – provide most of the medical care in the city.

Transportation Federal Interstate I-15 passes on the western edge of Blackfoot. U.S. Highways 91 and 26 intersect the city. Idaho Highway 39 connects the city with the western farming communities.

Small private and charter aircraft use the 4,300-foot-long runway at McCarley Field, located a mile north of town. Large commercial airline service is available at Pocatello Regional Airport.

Utilities and Services Public companies provide electric, telephone, gas, cable and satellite services. The City provides water and sewer services as well as fire and police protection.

Vision for 2050

For three decades, the population of Blackfoot has ranged from 10,000 to 11,000. In recent years, the population has grown about one percent annually. Should this trend continue, which is likely, Blackfoot's population in 2050 will likely not exceed 15,000.

The city's existing infrastructure is maintained at a level to accommodate moderate growth. Accordingly, no major change to the city's strategic plan is required at this time.

Tabernacle.

In 2050 Blackfoot will continue to offer a peaceful and friendly hometown environment to its citizens. The beautiful natural resources that surround the city will largely remain the same, thus providing a stable rural lifestyle enjoyed by city residents. The business community will still be progressive and energetic.

The city will continue to honor its rural heritage. In addition, the leaders of this historic community will pattern its economic planning and development decisions after the same imagination and risk as did those who came before.

Mayors

1909 Robert N. West
1911 L.M. Capps
1913 Robert N. West
1915 E.T. Peck
1917 A.B. Stephens
1919 N.J. Thorstenberg
1921 E.T. Peck
1931 Edward Thoreson
1935 J.H. Andersen
1941 Merrill C. Boyle
1942 Earl J. Miller
1945 J. Cecil Sandberg
1947 Einar M. Nelson
1949 Merrill C. Boyle
1949 Frank Smith
1951 Earl J. Miller
1958 L.R. Jeppesen
1959 Elvin A. Lindquist

1964 Louis F. Haller
1965 Gareth Ogden
1970 Delwin C. Daniels
1978 Arthur C. Bergener
1980 Howard Packham
1982 Delwin C. Daniels
1986 C. Dean Hill
1994 R. Scott Reese
2005 Mike Virtue
2014 Paul M. Loomis
* Village Chairman

The Grange Welcome to Firth Sign, Spring 2005.

Firth

Statistical Data

Population: 471 *
Elevation: 4,570 feet
Precipitation: 10 inches **
Average Snowfall: 30 inches **
County: Bingham
Temperature Range – Fahrenheit: **
Spring: 25 to 68
Summer: 45 to 85
Fall: 23 to 75
Winter: 14 to 38
* U.S. Census Bureau Estimates July 2015
**Historical averages

Firth lies near the eastern banks of the Snake River about midway between Blackfoot and Idaho Falls and about a mile from Firth's sister city of Basalt. Fields of potatoes, corn, alfalfa hay and grain surround the city, forming a checkerboard of texture and color.

The Blackfoot Mountain Range, rising to over 7,000 feet, silhouettes the eastern sky. To the west across the Snake River is Hells Half Acre Lava Field, a 125-square-mile Natural National Landmark. The Fort Hall Indian Reservation lies a few miles southwest.

Pre-Incorporation Years

In May 1863 prospectors found gold near what is now Virginia City in southwestern Montana. (Virginia City was part of Idaho Territory until Montana Territory was created on May 26, 1864.)

The ensuing gold rush brought a steady flow of traffic between Utah and Virginia City on a wagon road named the "Gold Road." People on horses, stagecoaches and freight wagons passed through what is now Firth on the Gold Road which crossed the Snake River and turned north at Eagle Rock – now Idaho Falls.

In 1862 Congress passed the Homestead Act and in 1877 the Desert Land Act. The Homestead Act allowed conversion of up to 160 acres of federal land to private ownership to those filers who improved and lived on the land for five years. The Desert Land Act allowed settlers to file for up to 640 acres, with the condition that they bring the land under irrigation within three years. (*See Eastern Idaho, Federal Land Use Laws.*)

Homestead of Lorenzo Firth, photo circa 1894.

In 1878 the Utah and Northern Railroad Company (U&N) began laying railroad track from Utah to Montana, generally following the Gold Road. By the end of the next year, they had extended the railroad through what are now Firth, Basalt, Idaho Falls and Spencer – about 15 miles south of the Montana border at Monida Pass. The railroad reached the Montana gold fields the following year.

One of the construction workers building the railroad was John R. Poole of Ogden, Utah. When Poole returned to Ogden, he praised the farmland potential of the Upper Snake River Plain. Many families living in northern Utah were recent converts to the Church of Jesus Christ of Latter-day Saints (Church), coming from the Eastern United States and emigrants from foreign countries, looking for good farmland to settle.

Poole's fellow railroad workers returning to Utah confirmed Poole's account and, within a short time, several groups of northern Utah families were making preparations to travel north to settle in Eastern Idaho. (*See Eastern Idaho, Pioneer Settlements – Upper Snake River Plain.*)

Homestead of William M. Dye, photo circa 1898.

In 1882 Church leaders asked 54-year-old Thomas E. Ricks to be an ecclesiastical leader (Bishop and later Stake President) of the immigrant settlers going to what is now the Rexburg area. By that time, Church members had over three decades of experience in Utah Territory building small irrigation water conveyances needed to turn arid sagebrush-covered land into productive farms.

Ricks accepted the call, and, by the end of the year, Church records listed 815 members living in Ricks' geographical jurisdiction, which included what is now Firth and was initially called the Bannock Stake. By the end of 1884, the number of members over the age of eight had increased to 1,420. (Children in the Church of Jesus Christ of Latter-day Saints are not baptized until they are eight years old. All members of the Church must be baptized.)

Almost immediately after farm settlement started, plans to divert irrigation water from the rivers and streams and build canals and irrigation ditches began. The farmers benefiting from a canal formed a canal company. The canal companies borrowed money from area banks to construct their canals. The banks filled a dual role – they not only loaned money but also helped resolve arguments over water rights.

Barn raising - Lorenzo Firth barn - circa 1915.

Once the canal companies designed the course for the canal, workers – mostly the farmers themselves – dug the water conveyances with picks, crowbars, shovels, horse-drawn Fresno scrapers and chains to move the rock. Occasionally, they used blasting powder.

In 1885 English emigrants Lorenzo J. Firth, Joseph H. Dye and his older brothers and their families homesteaded along a fertile stretch of land adjacent to the Snake River and the railroad track. The Dyes' homestead was on a plain called Cedar Point – later to become an ecclesiastical branch and, later, a ward of The Church of Jesus Christ of Latter-day Saints named Basalt after the area's landscape and the basalt rock formations lining the Snake River.

Lorenzo Firth, at his finished barn.

Lorenzo's homestead was less than a mile southwest. A few years later, railroad officials were looking for a place to build a station house and water tower where the steam engines could stop to take on water. Lorenzo saw the benefits of having a train stop so close to his and his friend's farms, so he offered to donate some of his land next to the railroad tracks to the railroad.

In 1903 railroad officials named the rail stop and mail drop location "Firth" in honor of Lorenzo's donation. Lorenzo platted a town site next to the railroad station, and in 1905 U.S. postal authorities opened the Firth Post Office.

The early residents of Firth who were members of The Church were members of the Basalt branch and, later, ward. By June 15, 1924, membership in the Basalt Ward had grown so large that Church leadership split the geographical boundaries of the Basalt Ward, creating two wards, a smaller Basalt Ward and a new Firth Ward.

Firth Depot, built in the early 1920s.

Incorporation

On May 25, 1929, the residents of Firth successfully petitioned the county commission to become an incorporated village.

Turning Points

Railroad The coming of the railroad in 1879 was one of the attractions that caused the early settlers of Firth and Basalt to start establishing homesteads six years later. With the railroad, area farmers were able to receive equipment and supplies and transport their production to market faster and easier.

Hauling wheat from Morgans Bridge, circa 1917.

The railroad was also the catalyst that led to the formation of Firth as a community. By naming its mail drop and station after Lorenzo Firth, the railroad, in effect, established the name of the city. From that time forward, all mail addresses for residents and businesses in the area would bear the name of Firth.

Andrus and Nelson's General Store, circa 1910s.

Potato Processing. Idaho Supreme Potatoes, Inc., has its headquarters in Firth. However, it's fresh-pack and specialty potato processing plant is in Basalt. The plant began operations around 1975 and has about 250 employees.

Firth Today

Amenities and Attractions Firth residents have the better of two worlds. The nearby public lands, mountains, Snake River, streams and reservoirs provide opportunities to enjoy a wide variety of outdoor activities including fishing, hunting, boating, riding ATVs and snowmobiles. In addition, they are close to a wide variety of urban attractions and amenities in the nearby larger cities.

Road into Firth, 2005.

Economy and Major Employers The Firth School District is the city's largest employer. Many city residents work at Idaho Supreme Potatoes, Inc. Other residents commute to Idaho Falls, Shelley or Blackfoot for employment.

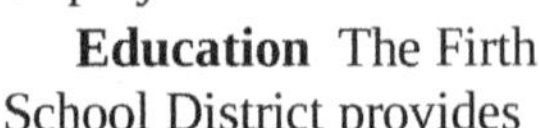

Education The Firth School District provides substantially all K-12 education. The district operates an elementary school, a middle school and a high school in the city. The district also serves children in the surrounding area, including Basalt.

The closest institutions of higher education are University Place and Eastern Idaho Technical College in Idaho Falls and BYU-Idaho 43 miles northeast in Rexburg. Idaho State University is 36 miles south in Pocatello.

Health Care The closest hospital is Bingham Memorial Hospital in Blackfoot. More specialized medical care is available at the 323-bed Eastern Idaho Regional Medical Center in Idaho Falls. Mountain View Hospital, a 20-bed acute care facility, free-standing clinics, same day surgery centers and home health care providers are also available in Idaho Falls.

Transportation U.S. Highway 91 intersects the city. Interstate 15 is five miles west. Commercial air transportation is available at Fanning Field in Idaho Falls.

Utilities and Services Private companies provide electricity, telephone, cable, natural gas and satellite services. The City provides water and sewer services and fire and police protection. The County provides solid waste and EMS services.

Vision for 2050

In 1980 Firth's population was 460. In the ensuing three decades, the population has remained somewhat constant. These trends will likely continue.

By 2050 Firth will continue to be a friendly hometown with its roots founded in agriculture and providing quality education for area children – a peaceful and quiet place to raise a family.

Mr. Potato Head, Miss Russet and the Idaho Spud at Spud Days, Shelley, circa 2004.

Shelley

Statistical Data

Population: 4,382 *
Elevation: 4,629 feet
Precipitation: 10 inches **
Average Snowfall: 30 inches **
County: Bingham
Website: www.ci.shelley.id.us
Temperature Range – Fahrenheit: **
Spring: 32 to 57
Summer: 51 to 86
Fall: 31 to 60
Winter: 11 to 25
* U.S. Census Bureau Estimates July 2015
**Historical averages

Shelley is a charming farm community 10 miles southwest of Idaho Falls and 17 miles northeast of Blackfoot. It sits on a rise east of a horseshoe bend in the Snake River between two fertile flood plains. One lies along the river and the other runs along Sand Creek at the base of the foothills and mountains to the east.

The city's proximity to Idaho Falls gives residents a small-town atmosphere close to a regional hospital, shopping, cultural events and other amenities offered by the larger city.

As a practical matter, being a small town near to Idaho Falls has become an attraction in itself. An increasing number of people are choosing to live in Shelley and commute to Idaho Falls and other cities for work. Many new residents are moving into newly annexed residential subdivisions.

Pre-Incorporation Years

John F. Shelley and two other men traveled through Eastern Idaho in 1885 looking for a place to settle. Shelley had interest in starting a new town.

As they passed through what is now the city of Shelley, they were impressed with the wild flowers and vegetation. However, they did not stop but continued on their journey for 10 miles northeast. John Shelley looked at land near Iona where he filed on a 160-acre homestead; however, he could not get the "wild flower" land to the south out of his mind. After his wife, Theodocia Chipman Shelley, joined him, they decided to move from Iona to the location that had so impressed John. (*See The Region, Pioneer Settlements – Upper Snake River Plain.*)

Shelley family, 1896.

That idea, however, presented a problem. John had already used his homestead right. The problem was resolved when they discovered that Theodocia was eligible to file for the "Shelley" property in her own name – which she did. In getting settled in their new homestead, they ordered lumber delivered by rail. When the goods arrived, they saw the railroad manifest specified the lumber was to be delivered to "Shelley." (*See The Region, Railroads.*)

John F. Shelley

John and Theodocia had planned to call the town Shelco, but the destination name on the railroad's manifest undermined that plan. The railroad knew where Shelley was and all future freight shipments would go to that location. Any change in name would be problematic and could result in the ordered goods being delivered to the wrong place. To avoid confusion, John and Theodocia decided to leave well enough alone and accept the railroad's designation of Shelley as the name of their new town.

After they had built and settled in their home, John and Theodocia completed platting the town site. Seven years after John first saw the wild flowers on the fertile floodplain, Ole P. Jensen built the town's first blacksmith shop in 1892, homesteaders were filing their claims and small businesses were opening stores and shops.

Shelley community, 1904-5

On December 14, 1892, John and Theodocia officially filed the town plat under

John's signature with the Bingham County recorder in Blackfoot.

In the early years, their home doubled as the town's post office. When they built the Shelley Mercantile Store, the post office moved to the store.

In 1901 a fire of unknown origin destroyed most of the town – except the Mercantile Store. However, the owners of the destroyed shops and buildings started rebuilding almost immediately, and, within a few months, the town was getting back to normal.

In the spring of 1902, three families – John E. Kelley, Joseph Holland, and Alfred H. Hanson – purchased or homesteaded land a mile north of town. The city would later begin growing north.

Incorporation

Inside the Shelley Post Office, 1930.

On April 12, 1904, in response to a petition signed by most of the taxpayers in the community, the Bingham County Board of Commissioners approved the incorporation of Shelley as a village. There was no census at the time of incorporation, but the 1910 U.S. Census reported the town's population was 537.

On February 2, 1921, the city changed its legal status to an incorporated city.

Turning Points

Early pioneer school house.

Development of an Agriculture-Based Economy. Two federal laws were instrumental in the growth of the city and the agricultural economy that sustained it. The Homestead Act of 1862 that allowed individuals to own 160 acres of federal land if they lived on it for five years and improved it and The Desert Land Act passed five years later that granted settlers 640 acres if they brought the land under irrigation within three years. (*See The Region, Federal Lands – Private Ownership and Preservation Laws*.)

Potato Production and Marketing. Irrigated agriculture provided the foundation of Shelley's economic growth, which paralleled the national demand for fresh-pack and processed potatoes. Eastern Idaho's volcanic ash-based soils are unusually well suited for growing potatoes of exceptional quality. (*See The Region, Agriculture and Irrigation and Famous Potatoes*.)

A major turning point occurred in 1957 when the J.R. Simplot Company built a potato-processing plant in Shelley. Ownership of the plant changed hands three times with each new owner expanding the size of the operation. Basic American Foods now owns and operates the plant. At first, potato processing was very labor intensive. Today, technology has improved the plant's productivity with certain processes necessitating a small fraction of the employees previously required.

Effect of Idaho Falls on Local Business. When Simplot built his processing plant, Idaho Falls was developing as a regional shopping center, the era of motor vehicles had arrived and travel costs were low.

Early spud balloon float.

Shelley had a growing population but more residents were traveling to Idaho Falls to do their shopping and business, siphoning customers from local retailers. Many residents also had jobs in Idaho Falls and commuted to work.

This became problematic in 1955 when many Shelley retailers began closing their doors. Some downtown buildings deteriorated to the extent that they had to be demolished.

Shelley State Street about 1910, before the Hitching Posts were removed.

Urban Renewal. Shelley approved an urban renewal project in 2005 through which the facades of many buildings were redone and interiors remodeled. Additionally, new business buildings have been constructed on most of the vacant commercial lots. In fact, the demand for commercial lots became so great that property in the central part of the city was rezoned commercial.

Today Main Street is a vibrant, attractive and interesting place to shop and do business.

Shelley Today

Amenities and Attractions The city has four city parks covering 16 acres. Amenities include a skateboard park, a tennis court, a handball court, four baseball diamonds, two basketball courts, one outdoor pool, playground equipment, portable volleyball standards, an outdoor stage and picnic shelters.

To underscore the importance of the potato industry, each autumn since 1927 the city celebrates “Spud Days” with a parade, potato eating contests and other events. The event has received national and international attention drawing crews from ABC’s Good Morning America, the Food Channel, Country Magazine and broadcasters from Sweden and Germany, even the Matchbox – toy carmaker has recognized the annual event.

A full range of outdoor recreation activities is available in or near Shelley including boating, water skiing and fishing at Palisades Reservoir, 55 miles southeast, and Ririe Lake, 15 miles west. Hunting, fishing, snow skiing, snowmobiling, horseback riding, camping and picnicking are available in the nearby Caribou National Forest and several mountain ranges.

Shelley today.

Economy and Major Employers Farming and the businesses that support agriculture have long underpinned Shelley’s economy. Fresh-packed and processed potatoes are the primary agricultural commodities and products.

The city’s largest employer is a potato processor, Basic American Foods, with a payroll of 450. The Shelley School District has over 260 employees, and GPOD Fresh Pac potatoes employs 130.

Even though residents still travel to Idaho Falls for major purchases, the city has a vibrant downtown that provides basic goods and services including a supermarket, a post office, a medical clinic and surgical center, a dental office, florists, a video rental shop, several restaurants, banks and a credit union.

Education The Shelley School District provides substantially all primary and secondary education. The district has three elementary schools, a middle school and a high school.

The closest institutions of higher education are University Place, the Idaho Falls Center for Higher Education, 11 miles northeast; Eastern Idaho Technical College in Idaho Falls; Brigham Young University-Idaho in Rexburg, 35 miles north; and Idaho State University in Pocatello, 45 miles south.

Health Care A full range of medical care is available at the 323-bed Eastern Idaho Regional Medical Center in Idaho Falls – a full service hospital serving communities as far away as Montana and Wyoming.

Mountain View Hospital, a 20-bed acute-care facility, free-standing clinics, same day surgery centers and home health care providers are also available in Idaho Falls.

Transportation U.S. Highway 91 intersects the city. Interstate 15 is five miles west. Commercial air transportation is available at Fanning Field in Idaho Falls 12 miles northeast. Rail service is available for freight only.

Utilities and Services Private companies provide electricity, natural gas, telephone, cable and satellite services. The City provides water, municipal wastewater treatment services, sanitation removal and police and fire protection. The County provides solid waste and emergency medical services.

Groundwater protection and treatment of wastewater is a major problem for a fast-growing community. To deal with this important issue, the City – in partnership with the City of Ammon and Bingham and Bonneville Counties – has built a regional wastewater treatment facility capable of handling 8 million gallons of effluent a day. The facility serves the other communities on a contract basis. It is a cooperative model for other forward-thinking local governments as they consider their long-term strategic plan to provide better municipal services at less cost.

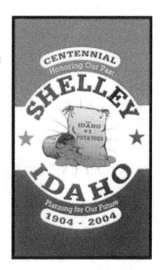

Vision for 2050

In 1960 Shelley's population was 2,612. Since 1994 the population has remained around 4,000.

Future population growth is largely subject to the economic growth in Idaho Falls and other cities. However, regardless of what occurs, city leaders and citizens are committed to retaining Shelley's small hometown charm and atmosphere.

Mayors

1904 N.C. Mickelson, W.R. Jones and H.A. Harrington made up the Village Board.
1909 Dr. Edwin Cutler *
1911 Soren Yorgensen *
1917 H.E. McMillan *
1919 Soren Yorgensen *
1921 T.J. Bennett
1925 N.S. Sage
1927 T.J. Bennett
1931 H.J. Dyer
1935 Randall L. Anderson
1937 T.J. Bennett
1939 Ted R. Isenberg
1940 Oliver Dawson
1949 J. Bert Holland
1953 Carl H. Scobie
1955 Max J. Hansen
1958 Gerald S. Johnson
1959 Arnfred Christensen
1964 Gene Bendixsen
1970 E. Douglas Kirkham
1978 L. Eugene Christensen
1994 Hever J. Hansen
2002 Eric R. Christensen
2014 Stacy Pascoe
* Village Chairman

Planting a tree for Arbor Day in Iona.

BONNEVILLE COUNTY

- Ammon
- Idaho Falls (*County Seat*)
- Iona
- Irwin
- Swan Valley
- Ucon

Ammon City Building, August 25, 2005.

Ammon

Statistical Data

Population: 14,685 *
Elevation: 4,713 feet
Precipitation: 10 inches **
Average Snowfall: 35 inches **
County: Bonneville
Website: www.ci.ammon.id.us
Temperature Range – Fahrenheit: **
Spring: 31 to 56
Summer: 48 to 82
Fall: 31 to 58
Winter: 13 to 30
* U.S. Census Bureau Estimates July 2015
**Historical averages

Ammon is located in the Upper Snake River Valley. Its western boundary abuts the city of Idaho Falls. The nearby foothills and mountains of the rugged Caribou Mountain Range rise to nearly 10,000 feet to outline the city's eastern skies.

The Blackfoot Mountain Range, rising over 7,000 feet, begins 10 miles south of the city.

Ammon is one of Idaho's fastest growing communities and Idaho's 15th largest city. It is growing at double-digit rates due to the availability of open space for affordable residential housing, the city's hometown lifestyle and its proximity to the urban amenities and job market in Idaho Falls.

Pre-Incorporation Years

In 1879 John R. Poole of Ogden, Utah, returning home from working on the construction of the Utah and Northern Railroad (U&N) from Utah to the Montana gold fields, praised the farmland potential of the Upper Snake River Plain.

Leaders of The Church of Jesus Christ of Latter-day Saints (nicknamed Mormons – see The Region, Pioneer Settlements) encouraged those looking for fertile homestead land to consider the region for settlement. On December 26, 1882, Church President John Taylor wrote, "Go into the Snake River Country, found settlements, care for the Indians ... and cooperate in making improvements ..."

Many families living in northern Utah were recent immigrant converts to the Church. Some of them had also worked with Poole for the railroad and had seen the land of the Upper Snake River Plain for themselves. They needed no persuasion.

The railroad had built its roundhouse at Eagle Rock, now Idaho Falls. By 1882 the area around Idaho Falls was bustling with economic activity.

This log building was the first school, church, recreation hall in Ammon. It was built on the original townsite, Central Block.

Around 1883 many pioneer families began homesteading the land surrounding Idaho Falls. A number of families settled along Little Sand Creek. Those settling to the north named their community Iona. Those settling further south near what is now Ammon called their community South or Lower Iona.

Early settlers described the sagebrush that covered the land as taller than a man mounted on a horse. Homesteading required enormous physical effort. Cutting the tall sagebrush and pulling its roots out of the ground was hard and tedious, albeit the large sagebrush trunks were beneficial for firewood.

As the homesteaders cleared their land and planted crops, hoards of jackrabbits came out of the hills devouring anything green. These millions of jackrabbits threatened the very food source and livelihood of the settlers. (*See The Region, Pioneer Settlements – Fighting the Jackrabbit Menace*.)

Aerial view of Hillview Village, showing Avocet Drive, Bittern Drive,Curlew Drive and Dove Drive. Two more streets were built to the west. Idaho Falls is in the background. Circa 1958, 1959, 1960.

Adequate water for domestic use was another major problem. In the beginning, settlers got their water from Little Sand Creek. However, that was often problematic because in the spring, the creek often flooded. In the late summer, it often dried up. When water was scarce, settlers hauled water from the Snake River. In winter, they melted snow. They stored their domestic water in barrels usually kept in their kitchens. Within a few years, many of the settlers had dug or drilled hand-pump wells.

An efficient irrigation system was an integral step in successfully developing the region's agricultural base. Practically every family became part of the community effort to build diversion dams on the Snake River and a complex system of irrigation canals, ditches and head gates.

Drilling of the well in the Trailwood Village subdivision, looking northeast toward Idaho Falls.

The new settlers of South Iona were primarily, if not all, members of The Church of Jesus Christ of Latter-day Saints (Church). A basic tenet of the Church is the separation of church and state. However, in the case of South Iona and many other early Church settlements, the organizational structure of the Church conveniently became the governmental structure of the community. Matters of common interest were often addressed at their church meetings.

The homesteaders' 160-acre farms spread out over a large area. Initially, the people came together in homes for school, recreation and church meetings. (*See The Region, Pioneer Settlements – Irrigation – Early Farming Practices and Federal Land Use Laws.*)

Road construction circa 1991 during the project to improve and widenAmmon Road between Sunnyside Road and East 17th Street. The bottom of the picture is near East 17th and looks south toward the foothills. This was before the City Building was built next to the church.

On February 12, 1893, the Church membership became large enough to create a separate ward presided over by a lay bishop. Church leaders named the ward Ammon after a prominent Book of Mormon figure. With the creation of the Ammon Ward, settlers began calling their community Ammon.

On January 23, 1899, William F. and Lucinda E. Owen filed the plat of the Ammon townsite at the county seat in Blackfoot – 160 acres were donated for the town by their relative, James C. Owen.

The first public building in the new town was a large log structure that served as both a school and a church. It was built by residents who worked cooperatively to haul logs from the nearby mountains and construct the facility.

Around 1898 the residents replaced the log structure with a larger frame building which served as the village school, church and recreation facility they affectionately called "Old Hall." It had a basement, a large stage and a furnace. Curtains divided the classrooms when public school and Sunday school were in session and retracted when there were large gatherings.

Incorporation

On October 10, 1905, the Bingham County Commission approved the incorporation of Ammon as a village.

On February 7, 1911, the Idaho Legislature split off the northern and eastern parts of Bingham County to form Bonneville County with Idaho Falls as the county seat. Ammon became part of Bonneville County.

On March 7, 1961, Ammon became a city of the second class and retained that designation until the Idaho Legislature changed the municipal law in 1967 that dropped all "village and class" designations.

On January 2, 2003, the city council approved an ordinance providing for a city administrator appointed by the city council.

Turning Points

Land Reclamation Laws. Passage of federal laws and programs that allowed conversion of arable public land to private ownership, construction of irrigation systems and grazing rights on public land had a profound effect on the development of Ammon.

Aerial view of Ammon, June 1992.

These programs fostered agricultural development and beneficial use of publicly-owned natural resources. (*See The Region, Federal Land Use Laws.*)

Electricity. Electrical power came to Idaho Falls in 1912 and subsequently extended to Ammon, greatly improving the quality of life for Ammon residents and businesses.

Domestic Water Systems. Ammon drilled its first domestic municipal well in 1946. Eight wells now serve the city. Some of the wells reach several hundred feet into the crystal-clear water of the Snake River Plain Aquifer.

Idaho National Laboratory. The most significant turning point for the city came in 1949 when the Atomic Energy Commission, now the U.S. Department of Energy, sited its National Reactor Training Station near Idaho Falls. INL continues to be the largest employer in the region and underpins the city's economy. (*See The Region, Idaho National Laboratory – Eastern Idaho's Largest Employer.*)

City Growth and Planning. In the late 1950s the city agreed to annex an area called Hillview. This annexation almost doubled the city land area and promoted a sharp increase in residential and retail construction. This development started a trend of residential and commercial development. In 2005 the county assessor reported that Ammon had 55 residential subdivisions.

New development also exposed the need for better city planning. On September

15, 1971, the city organized its planning and zoning commission and the city council reviewed all policy manuals dealing with land development. In March 2004 the council approved a manual of codified city ordinances that not only streamlined City management procedures but also made working with the City more user-friendly.

Dams and Irrigation Systems. The construction of Ririe Dam in 1977 finally put an end to the periodic flooding of Willow and Little Sand Creeks that sometimes devastated the area.

Property Tax Relief. The rapid development that escalated property values resulted in the city approving a sweeping 1978 budget that cut property taxes 33 percent and instituted a system of user fees. This financial accountability system has been operating for nearly three decades and is credited with meeting needs while providing budget stability and greater equity in paying for municipal costs.

Eastern Idaho Regional Medical Center. Eastern Idaho Regional Medical Center opened its 323-bed facility in Idaho Falls in 1986. A full range of state-of-the-art medical care was now available within a few minutes' drive from Ammon.

Municipal Sewer System. In 1976 the city laid sewer lines that connected to the Idaho Falls sewer system which still treats Ammon's wastewater under a contract.

Ammon has joined certain other neighboring municipalities in evaluating the feasibility of constructing a regional wastewater treatment facility. In 2005 Ammon voters approved a revenue bond to finance most of Ammon's share of the cost. The bond is contingent on the stakeholders meeting their financial and other commitments.

Ammon Today

Amenities and Attractions The city has 62 acres devoted to nine parks. The 18-acre McCowin Park, the city's largest, has a swimming pool, picnic shelter, playground equipment, tennis courts, horseshoe pits, walking path and ball fields.

The amenities of the other parks include shelters, playground equipment, Tot Park and facilities for sports and picnics.

The city has encouraged extensive tree plantings. Trees that compliment the landscape design of each park line the streets. In 2002 Ammon received the Tree City USA Award sponsored by the National Arbor Day Foundation.

The community comes together on an August Saturday at McCowin Park to celebrate the annual "Ammon Days." It starts with a community breakfast and continues throughout the day with booths, activities and lots of fun.

The legal boundaries between Ammon and Idaho Falls blend so smoothly that they are transparent to all but the knowledgeable observer. Many residents travel the short distance to Idaho Falls for the amenities offered there. However, Ammon's dramatic growth is bringing significant change and many urban amenities of its own. New city parks and a growing downtown business district are satisfying an increasing number of public needs.

Within an hour's drive, opportunities abound for boating, rafting, canoeing, hunting, fishing, camping, snow and water skiing, snowmobiling and ice fishing. Downhill skiing is available 26 miles northeast at Kelly Canyon.

The 3-million-acre Caribou-Targhee National Forest begins about 20 miles east and extends across Southeastern Idaho to the Montana, Utah and Wyoming borders, offering a variety of amenities for outdoor enthusiasts.

The 270-foot-high Palisades hydroelectric dam and reservoir lies 50 miles east of Ammon and 11 miles west of the Wyoming border on the South Fork of the Snake River. This 16,000-acre reservoir provides irrigation water and, with 70 miles of shoreline, is a popular recreation area for camping, fishing, boating and water skiing.

About 13 miles east of Ammon is the 253-foot-high Ririe Dam, which backs up a 360-acre lake providing flood control and irrigation. The lake's 32-mile shoreline includes four recreation areas. Blacktail Park, the largest recreation area is easily accessed by driving a few miles east up Iona Hill.

Part of Ririe Lake is included in the Idaho Department of Fish and Game's Tex Creek Wildlife Management Area which encompasses more than 31,000 acres of wildlife habitat offering visitors the chance to view migratory birds, elk, mule deer and moose.

Economy and Major Employers The major employers for Ammon and Idaho Falls are INL; Bonneville and Idaho Falls Public School Districts; Eastern Idaho Regional Medical Center; and Melaleuca, a wellness-product manufacturer and distributor. Many residents are also employed by the growing number of retail and service sector businesses.

Education The Bonneville School District operates a high school, middle school and five elementary schools in the city. White Pine Charter School provides education for kindergarten to eighth grade students. Snake River Montessori, a private school, offers education for pre-school through sixth grade.

Eastern Idaho Technical College in Idaho Falls offers associate degrees or certificates in several professional and technical disciplines as well as short-term customized training and general community education courses.

At University Place in Idaho Falls, Idaho State University and the University of Idaho offer more than 50 baccalaureates, masters and doctoral degree programs, two-year general education programs and specialized courses.

Brigham Young University-Idaho is located in Rexburg 27 miles northeast of Ammon.

Health Care A full range of medical care is available at the Eastern Idaho Regional Medical Center. The center is a full-service hospital, serving communities as far away as Montana and Wyoming.

Mountain View Hospital, a 20-bed acute care facility; free-standing clinics; same-day surgery centers; and home health care providers are also available in

Idaho Falls.

Transportation Interstate 15 and U.S. Highways 20, 26 and 91 are within a few miles of the city. The Targhee Regional Public Transportation Authority (TRPTA) provides public transportation throughout Ammon and the Idaho Falls area. Commercial airline service is available at Fanning Field in Idaho Falls. Rail service for freight is available in Idaho Falls.

Utilities and Services Private companies provide electricity, telephone, natural gas, cable and satellite service.

The City provides water, fire protection, road maintenance and construction. Ammon owns all of its wells and water and sewer lines but contracts with Idaho Falls for sewage treatment. The library district, located in Idaho Falls, serves Ammon and all of the residents in Bonneville County. The City provides solid waste pick up and Bonneville County operates the sanitary landfill. The Bonneville County Sheriff's Office provides police protection under contract with the City.

Vision for 2050

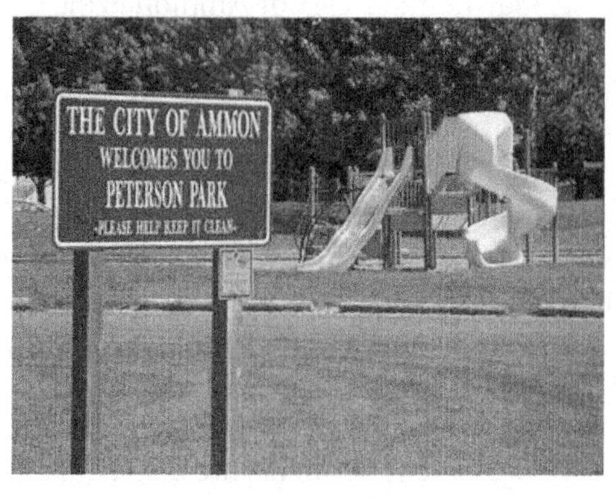

By 2025 Ammon will have a population of 25,000 and by 2050 the population will likely exceed 50,000. This growth will take place on the eastern and southern sides of the city.

A paramount consideration in strategically planning for this growth is preserving our sense of community, neighborhood feel and closeness. We believe these objectives are attainable by promoting community-based activities and celebrations that bring the community together such as Ammon Days.

By 2050 the Regional Sewer System and Water Expansion Projects currently under way will be operating effectively. Ammon will have its own post office and a growing park system that will include neighborhood parks that provide abundant open green space throughout the city. Community leaders are dedicated to strategically planning the city's future so that current and future citizens will continue to be proud of this beautiful and vibrant city.

Mayors

1905-1946 Unknown *
1946 Roy Southwick *
? Wallace Wadsworth *
1953 Reed Molen *
1955 Clifford Judy *
1957 Reed Molen *
1965 Mel Richardson *
1967 Mel Richardson
1969 Thomas D. Kershaw
1970 Keith C. Turnbow
1975 George Wehman
1983 Russell N. Swensen
1987 Gerald B. "Jerry" Mitchell
1988 C. Bruce Ard
2009 Steven W. Fuhriman
2014 Dana Kirkham
* Village Chairman

The falls at Idaho Falls.

Idaho Falls

Statistical Data

Population: 58,691 *
Elevation: 4,744 feet
Precipitation: 10 inches **
Average Snowfall: 30 inches **
County: Bonneville
Website: www.idahofallsidaho.gov

Temperature Range – Fahrenheit: **
Spring: 31 to 77
Summer: 41 to 86
Fall: 12 to 60
Winter: 10 to 44
* U.S. Census Bureau Estimates July 2015
**Historical averages

The Snake River is the defining feature of Idaho Falls. Flowing south through the middle of the city, it produces the waterfalls from which the city derived its name.

A greenbelt runs along both sides of the river for six miles offering stunning views of the falls and a series of rapids. The waterfalls and the river provide a beautiful backdrop to 95 acres of city parkland interspersed along the pathway.

The city lies on the Upper Snake River Plain surrounded by a patchwork of fertile farmland. Vast acreages of public lands with prehistoric lava flows lie to the west. The Caribou-Targhee National Forest is to the east.

Pre-Incorporation Years

For centuries, the Shoshone, Bannock and Northern Piute Indian Tribes traversed the high-desert, sagebrush-covered region. (*See Eastern Idaho, The*

Region, American Indians.)

Beginning in 1810 trappers and explorers began coming into the region followed in the 1830s and early 1840s by Christian missionaries en route to their missions to the Indians in Northern Idaho, Washington and Oregon. (*See Eastern Idaho, The Region, Early Trappers/Explorers and American Indians – Early Christian Missionaries.*)

In 1841 the first immigrant wagon train passed through the Upper Snake River Plain on its way to the Oregon coast. Soon thereafter, thousands of pioneers began passing through the area on the Oregon and California Trails and their various cutoffs, generally passing 40 miles to the south through Fort Hall near what is now Pocatello. (*See Eastern Idaho, The Region, Oregon and California Trails.*)

On July 28, 1862, prospectors made the gold discovery at Grasshopper Creek in southwestern Montana that started the boomtown of Bannack, then part of Idaho Territory. The following year, they made another discovery 80 miles east at Alder Gulch that started the boomtown of Virginia City. These and the ensuing gold discoveries in Montana started a large and steady flow of traffic to the gold fields. Many traveled from Utah through Eastern Idaho, fording the Snake River at an Indian crossing several miles upriver from what is now Idaho Falls.

Bridge over the Snake River.

On August 2, 1862, prospectors discovered gold in the Boise Basin. However, the gold rush participants coming up from Utah passed about 200 miles west of what is now Idaho Falls.

In 1864 stagecoach service began along the trail between Utah and Montana called the "Gold Road." (*See Eastern Idaho, The Region, The Gold Road – Precursor to Settlement of Eastern Idaho.*)

An entrepreneur named Harry Rickets sought to cash in on the Montana gold rush by building a toll ferry across the Snake River near the historic Indian crossing and a large rock formation in the center of the river where American Bald Eagles nested. Rickets named his business "Eagle Rock Ferry."

However, the ferry had limitations. It could only operate from late spring through fall because the river froze in the winter and when it thawed was often not safe to cross until after the spring runoff.

In 1864 entrepreneurs James M. Taylor, Robert Anderson and a few other men had a plan to offer year-round service by building a toll bridge across the narrow river canyon near what is now the center of today's Idaho Falls. They formed the Oneida Road, Bridge and Ferry Company and convinced the Idaho Territorial Legislature meeting in Lewiston to grant them a license to build the toll bridge.

They located their bridge where the river cuts a narrow gorge in the basalt cliff formations called Black Rock Canyon where the narrowest point is 83 feet.

They traveled 80 miles to get large logs long enough to bridge the canyon. They opened the bridge in 1866 under the name "Taylor's Crossing." The legislature specified the toll at 50 cents for a man and his horse and $4 for a wagon and two horses or two oxen.

Taylor's Crossing became the main route for the Gold Road, putting Rickets on the verge of going out of business. Believing he could provide a more affordable service than the toll bridge, Rickets moved his ferry near the bridge, kept the Eagle Rock Ferry name and reopened for business.

Residents of the town that grew up around the bridge and ferry were so impressed with the ferry's name; they began to call their community Eagle Rock.

In 1865 a stage station opened in a two-room log cabin. A year later, postal authorities approved a post office housed in a combination store and bank operated by postmaster Robert Anderson. By 1886 the town had its first hotel, an adobe structure called the "Burgess House."

The growing Eagle Rock community attracted large groups of farmers and settlers to the area, many of them emigrants from Utah. Their farm production was shipped over the Gold Road for sale to the miners.

As the town grew, community leaders and residents platted streets, cleared sagebrush and built boardwalks on either side of the main streets.

The Eagle Rock Water Works Company offered 35 shares at $100 each to capitalize the 50-foot-deep community well.

In 1885 they established a volunteer fire company that, 22 years later, acquired a horse-drawn fire engine.

For several years, Eagle Rock citizens read the Blackfoot Register newspaper. The publisher William E. Wheeler moved his newspaper to Eagle Rock in 1884. In 1890 a new newspaper, The Times, began publishing, followed by the Idaho Falls Post in 1905. The newspapers later combined into the Idaho Falls Post Register, which is still published today.

The first telephone service came in 1898. The Snake River Valley Telephone Company secured a 21-year franchise from the town board. By 1900 there were 28 telephones in Idaho Falls with service beginning to extend to nearby communities.

Settlement of the surrounding farmland generally followed passage of the Homestead Act of 1862 and the Desert Land Act in 1877. The Homestead Act converted 160 acres of federal land to private ownership to those who lived on the land for five years and improved it. The Desert Land Act allowed settlers to file for up to 640 acres with the condition that they bring the land under irrigation within three years. (*See Eastern Idaho, The Region, Federal Land Use Laws.*)

The Woolworth Company.

Almost immediately after farm settlement commenced, plans were developed to divert irrigation water from the rivers and streams into canals and irrigation ditches. The farmers benefiting from the water formed canal companies which borrowed money from area banks to build their canals. The banks filled a dual role. They not only loaned money but also helped resolve arguments over water rights.

Once the canal companies designed the courses, workers – mostly the farmers themselves – dug the canals and ditches with picks, crowbars, shovels, horse-drawn Fresno scrapers and chains to move the dirt and rock. Occasionally, they used blasting powder to break up and dislodge the volcanic rock.

Organized recreation and cultural and performing arts events were important to these early Idaho Falls settlers. They held dances and masquerade balls, literary recitals, musical and dramatic presentations and parades.

They also built a roller skating rink and put up a community Christmas tree decorated with candy, Chinese lanterns, flags and presents for every child in town.

In 1883 Eagle Rock musicians boasted "four organs, five pianos, one cornet band of twelve pieces (and several) violins and accordions." On occasion, the circus came to town, advertised with parades of animals including camels and elephants walking the main streets.

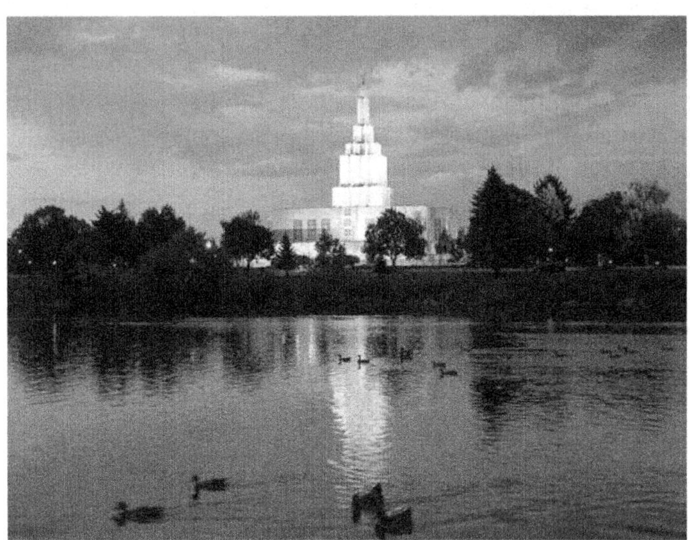

Church of Jesus Christ of Latter-day Saints Idaho Falls Idaho Temple.

As families settled in the new community, they brought their religions with them. The First Baptist Church built its first house of worship in 1884, The Church of Jesus Christ of Latter-day Saints in 1886, Trinity Methodist Church in 1886, First Presbyterian Church in 1891, Holy Rosary Roman Catholic Church in 1891 and St. John's Episcopal Church in 1895. During the next 20 years, St. John's Evangelical Lutheran Church, First Christian Church, Alliance Covenant Church, Christian Science Church and the Salvation Army all established congregations.

One of the major deficiencies in the new settlement was the lack of good medical care. In 1890 the nearest medical doctor was in Malad, Idaho, 100 miles south – a four-day ride by horse and buggy on rough dirt roads. Many people died because of lack of medical assistance, especially during periodic diphtheria epidemics and the smallpox epidemic of 1876 to 1877.

In 1879 the Utah and Northern Railroad (UNR), based in Ogden, Utah, established its Idaho headquarters in Eagle Rock. The company built a new rail bridge 50 yards south of Taylor's Crossing. By December 1881 rail service was available between the railroad depots in Ogden, Utah, and Butte, Montana. Farmers in the Eagle Rock area sent potatoes, grain, fruit and livestock north to Montana and south to the Ogden rail hub for shipment east. The Eagle Rock population had grown to 670. UNR later merged into the Oregon Short Line and Union Pacific systems.

In 1884 the Oregon Short Line Railroad completed a rail line between Granger, Wyoming, and Huntington, Oregon, which angled across southern Idaho in a northwesterly direction to Pocatello, bypassing Eagle Rock, then on to Soda Springs and Caldwell, providing a railroad link between the commercial centers of Portland and Omaha. (*See Eastern Idaho, The Region, Railroads*.)

Museum of Idaho.

Education was of prime importance to the early settlers. Initially, they held school in homes or in churches. Funding was difficult. In 1882 the newspaper reported, " … the election for voting for or against the levying of a tax to build a school house was close … , there being a majority of one in favor." In 1894 the school patrons formed an Independent School District and added a high school component to the Central School Building on Elm Street.

To improve the community's quality of life, the women in Eagle Rock established the Village Improvement Society to support cultural, religious and social endeavors. There were 40 members, paying dues of 50 cents each.

Their first project was the construction of 50 wooden trash barrels that citizens were encouraged to use instead of throwing trash into the streets and common areas. They tackled the problem of free-roaming cows through town by insisting that the owners keep their animals penned up. They also established a school lunch program and organized planting 20,000 ash, elm and birch tree saplings brought in by train from Iowa. Even back then, vandalism was an occasional problem. Soon after planting, 13 trees were broken off at the four-foot level.

In 1885 community leaders decided it was time to form a municipal organization to manage the affairs that were of common interest. Without officially incorporating with the county, they elected Eagle Rock's first governing board of trustees with Nathan H. Clark as chairman.

In 1886 a fierce windstorm destroyed the Eagle Rock roundhouse where the railroad maintenance operations were located. By then Pocatello was becoming a prominent rail hub. The railroad chose to rebuild in Pocatello rather than Eagle Rock. In some cases, shop buildings were loaded onto flatbed train cars and moved to Pocatello.

Incorporation

The loss of the railroad roundhouse was devastating. Within a few months, Eagle Rock's population dropped from around 2,000 to 400.

Community leaders showed their resiliency by assessing their condition and re-evaluating their options for growth. Their first step was to change their image. By referendum, they changed the name of their community from Eagle Rock to Idaho Falls and in 1890 incorporated as a village.

Even though the railroad moved the roundhouse, it left the passenger and freight businesses. City leaders worked with the railroad to upgrade those facilities.

A.V. Scott, one of the community leaders, was a real estate entrepreneur. He published a promotional booklet written by newspaper publisher William Wheeler called Boomers. Their efforts paid off. By 1890 four years after the roundhouse was lost, the population of Idaho Falls had risen to 1,558.

Snake River Landing.

In that same year, the first medical doctors opened offices in town. In 1906 they opened their first hospital.

On April 6, 1900, Idaho Falls changed its legal status from a village governed by a board of trustees to a city governed by a mayor and city council.

The city's first elected treasurer was Emma Hurst. One of the first women to hold elected office after Idaho adopted woman's suffrage. In 1896 Idaho voters amended the territorial constitution giving women the right to vote. Idaho was the fourth state in the nation to do so behind Wyoming in 1869, Colorado in 1893 and Utah in 1869 and 1895 – the federal Edmunds-Tucker Act of 1887 overturned Utah Territory's 1869 suffrage law.

Turning Points

The Railroad Roundhouse The establishment of the railroad roundhouse and terminal facilities at Eagle Rock had a major positive effect on the community when it came and a devastating effect when it left. When the railroad made Eagle Rock its terminal location in 1879, it brought hundreds of new jobs and families. However, the town's status as a terminal only lasted 7 years. When fierce winds destroyed the roundhouse, the railroad moved the operation to Pocatello taking 80 percent of Eagle Rock's population and economy with it.

Development of Agricultural-Based Industries More subtle, yet profound in its long-term effect on agriculture was the passage of federal laws and programs permitting private ownership of public lands for farming, supporting irrigation systems and managing the use of public lands for grazing livestock. The laws allowed thousands of farm and ranch families to earn respectable livelihoods and build vibrant communities. (*See Eastern Idaho, The Region, Federal Land Use Laws.*)

With the formation of the Idaho Falls Dry Farm Association in 1905, several thousand acres of land were cleared of sagebrush a few miles north of Idaho Falls near Osgood and dry land winter wheat planted. About nine years later, they installed an electric irrigation pumping station and canals. They renamed the association the Osgood Land and Livestock Company. In 1919 the Utah-Idaho Sugar Company purchased much of the land to support its sugar factory located just east of Idaho Falls in Lincoln. The sugar factory brought another cash crop to area farmers and provided another option for crop rotation and winter jobs at the factory processing the sugar beets.

County Seat On February 7, 1911, the legislature created Bonneville County. The voters made Idaho Falls the county seat, providing a stable employment base and attracting businesses that needed to be close to county government.

The Idaho National Laboratory The most significant turning point for the city occurred in 1949 when the Atomic Energy Commission (AEC), now U.S. Department of Energy, sited its National Reactor Training Station near Idaho Falls. The initial work at the station included prototype research and development of nuclear reactors.

On December 20, 1951, Experimental Breeder Reactor Number 1 (EBR-1) produced electricity, lighting four light bulbs. Three years later on July 17, 1955, EBR-1 supplied the world's first nuclear-generated electricity for commercial purposes by lighting the city of Arco for two hours.

The selection of Idaho Falls as the location for the National Reactor Training Station followed a meeting between a delegation of Idaho Falls executives and Atomic Energy Commission officials in Washington, D.C. The delegation argued that the vast and remote federal desert land would make an excellent test site. They pointed out that the site would be over a massive aquifer of clear cold water and within 45 miles of the Idaho Falls Airport. AEC officials agreed and selected Idaho Falls.

Idaho Falls Temple In 1945 The Church of Jesus Christ of Latter-day Saints – nicknamed Mormon for their belief that the Book of Mormon, Another Testament of Jesus Christ, is a companion to the Holy Bible and both are major cannons of scripture – built the Idaho Falls Temple, the first of the church's temples in Idaho.

This 160-foot-tall 92,177-square-foot white-cast stone building became a city landmark serving church members throughout southern Idaho. Over 100,000 members visited the temple each year to perform sacred ordinances for either themselves or their ancestral dead. These travelers had a significant positive effect on the city's retail and hospitality businesses.

With the subsequent construction of temples in Boise, Twin Falls and Rexburg, church members coming from those areas to Idaho Falls has declined significantly.

Eastern Idaho Regional Medical Center

In 1986 the Eastern Idaho Regional Medical Center opened its 323-bed facility replacing two smaller hospitals making Idaho Falls the primary health care center for a region that included parts of western Wyoming and southwestern Montana.

The hospital has attracted hundreds of other health providers and medical-related businesses to the city.

Regional Retail Center Idaho Falls is also a regional retail center which increased dramatically in 1984 with the completion of a 596,204-square-foot shopping mall. This mall has attracted many other retailers and now draws shoppers from throughout the Upper Snake River Plain and communities in Wyoming and Montana.

Idaho Falls Today

Amenities and Attractions In addition to the river and waterfalls, the city has 29 parks covering over 1,200 acres, a zoo, an aquatic center and three golf courses.

Lioness at Tautphaus Park.

Three non-profit organizations operate major cultural facilities. The Museum of Idaho features local history and scheduled national traveling exhibits. The Willard Arts Center and Colonial Theater complex has an art gallery, a children's art gallery and a theater that schedules a variety of indoor and outdoor plays, concerts and festivals. The Eagle Rock Art Museum features local and regional artists as well as major traveling exhibitions.

The city has over 100 places of worship representing numerous Christian denominations. Prominent and historical church buildings include the Idaho Falls Temple of The Church of Jesus Christ of Latter-day Saints, the First Presbyterian Church, Roman Catholic Holy Rosary Church and the Trinity United Methodist Church.

The 400-acre motorized raceway park operated by the Lions Club has a popular recreation center. The park, named "Noise Park," offers a variety of stock car and Go Kart races.

Within an hour's drive, opportunities abound for boating, rafting, canoeing, hunting, fishing, camping, snow and water skiing, snowmobiling and ice fishing.

The Caribou-Targhee National Forest and the Big Hole Mountain Range begin just 35 miles northeast of the city. Forty-five miles to the southeast are mountain ranges whose highest peaks rise to nearly 10,000 feet. On the eastern edge of the Caribou Mountain Range is Palisades Reservoir with its 70 miles of limited access shoreline.

A few miles east of the city are the 1,560-acre Lake Ririe and its tributaries and the 31,000-acre Tex Creek Wildlife Management Area. This wildlife area provides habitat for upland and migratory birds and winter range for thousands of migratory elk, mule deer and moose. The Idaho Fish and Game Department manages the area and oversees public visits.

Downhill skiing is available 26 miles northeast at Kelly Canyon. Targhee Ski Resort lies 90 miles away across the Wyoming border from Driggs.

Yellowstone and Grand Teton National Parks are 80 miles east in Wyoming.

Seventy-five miles to the west is the visitors' center for the 750,000-acre Craters of the Moon National Monument and Preserve. The preserve includes Idaho's Great Rift, the source of the lava flow that created that unique landscape. (*See Eastern Idaho, The Region, Distinctive Geographic and Geological Features – Craters of the Moon National Monument and Preserve.*)

Economy and Major Employers Founded as a transportation depot with an agricultural base, the city's economy is now more diverse. The city is the commercial, retail and medical center for most of the region including parts of western Wyoming and southwestern Montana.

Zebra at Tautphaus Park.

Agriculture and food processing continue to be important. However, technological innovation and farm consolidation have allowed these industries to be more productive with substantially fewer employees. (*See Eastern Idaho, The Region, The Region's Economic Base – Historically and Today.*)

High-technology, education, medical services, retail, financial, service and light-manufacturing businesses provide most of the jobs for the city's residents.

The city's largest employer is the contractor that runs the U.S. Department of Energy's Idaho National Laboratory (INL). Approximately 7,500 scientists, technicians and support personnel work at INL of which 60 percent live in Idaho Falls.

INL facilities include a research campus in Idaho Falls and a much larger research lab complex on a 570,000-acre reservation – often called the site – 45 miles west of the city.

Today INL is the nation's premier nuclear research facility. Its charge includes research, design and development of the next generation nuclear power plant and an enhanced portfolio of non-nuclear fuels, bio and renewable energy, hydropower, fuel reforming and related alternative and renewable energy research needed for the nation's energy and security programs. (*See Eastern Idaho, The Region, Idaho National Laboratory – Eastern Idaho's Largest Employer.*)

The next two largest private employers are Melaleuca, a food supplement and beauty products company headquartered in Idaho Falls, and the Eastern Idaho

Regional Medical Center. Each employs over 1,300.

Other large private employers with several hundred employees each include Center Partners, a call center; Wal-Mart; and Albertsons.

The largest public employers are the Idaho Falls and Bonneville School Districts that, combined, employ over 2,500. The City employs approximately 750 and Bonneville County about 450.

Education The Idaho Falls and Bonneville School Districts and four private schools provide elementary and secondary education. University Place, a specialized higher educational and research facility located next to the INL research facilities, offers specialized courses from Idaho's universities.

Eastern Idaho Technical College with an enrollment of 800 is located within the city limits and offers associate degrees and certificates in a variety of professional and technical fields.

Twenty-five miles north is Brigham Young University-Idaho in Rexburg. Fifty miles south is Idaho State University in Pocatello.

Health Care Idaho Falls is home to the Eastern Idaho Regional Medical Center, the principal medical facility in the region.

There are over 300 medical-related businesses including a wide variety of clinics and ancillary services located in the city.

Transportation Most modes of transportation are available in or near the city. Interstate 15 and U.S. Highways 20, 26 and 91 pass through the city. Union Pacific Railroad provides freight service. Five major airlines and several charter airlines use the 9,000-foot runway at Fanning Field, the Idaho Falls Regional Airport. A public transportation system operates buses throughout the city.

Utilities and Services The city has relatively inexpensive electrical energy. City-owned hydroelectric power plants produce about a third of the electrical power consumed in the city. The balance is purchased under contract or on the open market. The City's Electrical Division also provides fiber optic service.

The City provides water, wastewater, law enforcement, fire protection and emergency medical services.

The County provides solid waste management. Private carriers provide gas, telephone, wireless, cable and satellite services. Several radio and television stations are located in the city.

Vision for 2050

By 2050 the Idaho Falls city limits will extend to the county line on the north and south. Development will also increase to the west. The neighboring cities of Ammon and Iona will continue to grow on the city's eastern border.

In recent years, the city's population has grown about 1 percent annually. However, Idaho Falls is a dynamic community with several potentially high-growth employers, some of which, such as INL, are magnets for other high-tech businesses.

In addition, the nation's quest to become less dependent on foreign oil is bringing major changes supporting nuclear research and development. This will likely have a major effect on the population and economy of the city.

At a minimum, by 2050 Idaho Falls will have a population exceeding 100,000. Given the dynamics at INL and other factors attracting growth businesses to the city, the population may double that number.

The realization of what the future portends places pressure on city leaders to be prepared. The city has developed and continues to update its strategic plan and seeks to project the long-term consequences of each planning, zoning and land-use decision that comes before the mayor and city council.

By 2050 public schools will continue to be the primary providers of elementary and secondary education. However, there will be important changes in higher education programs offered in the city. University Place will have 10,000 students involved in programs offered through Idaho State University, the University of Idaho and Boise State University. Eastern Idaho Technical College will be a community college. All of these institutions will have collaborative programs that link to the research activities of INL.

The city's role as a regional retail and medical center will be of greater importance to the citizens of the region.

From a recreational and social standpoint, by 2050 there will be increased opportunities including major progress on the Snake River Greenbelt paths from Blackfoot to Ashton.

Mayors

1895 Nathan H. Clark *
1895 Robert Anderson *
1897 Thomas B. Shannon *
1898 Joseph A. Clark *
1900 Joseph A. Clark
1902 A.T. Shane
1903 Bowen Curley
1906 E.P. Coltman
1910 Louis Elg
1911 Bowen Curley
1913 Barzilla Clark
1915 George W. Edgington
1917 Henry W. Kiefer
1918 Ralph A. Louis
1919 W.A. Bradbury
1921 Ralph A. Louis
1927 Barzilla W. Clark
1936 R.V. Ewart
1937 Chase A. Clark
1940 E.W. Fanning
1949 Thomas L. Sutton
1951 E.W. Fanning
1956 John R. Rogers
1959 William J. O' Bryant
1964 S. Eddie Pedersen
1978 Thomas Campbell
1993 Linda M. Milam
2006 Jared D. Fuhriman
2014 Rebecca L. Noah Casper

* Village Chairman

Iona

Statistical Data

Population: 1,953 *
Elevation: 4,782 feet
Precipitation: 12 inches **
Average Snowfall: 23 inches **
County: Bonneville
Website: www.cityofiona.org

Temperature Range – Fahrenheit: **
Spring: 58 to 77
Summer: 55 to 86
Fall: 32 to 61
Winter: 30 to 47
* U.S. Census Bureau Estimates July 2015
**Historical averages

Iona is a small but growing community seven miles east of Idaho Falls. However, that distance is gradually narrowing as residential and mini-farm subdivisions have replaced many of the area's larger farms. Most residents work in Idaho Falls.

East of the city are the northern foothills of the Caribou Range that lies within the Caribou-Targhee National Forest. Many homes now dot these foothills.

To the west, sunsets often set the sky ablaze with color. Even with urban growth, the valley is still a vista of open space and beautiful farmland.

Pre-Incorporation Years

In the early 1800s fur trappers and explorers joined American Indians as inhabitants of the Upper Snake River Valley. Tall sagebrush and desert grasses and plants interspersed with occasional juniper trees covered most of the valley. Willows and cottonwood trees lined the tributaries to the Snake River. (*See The Region, Distinctive Geographic and Geologic Features*.)

In the late 1800s several key events converged to bring about settlement of the valley. Following the California Gold Rush, prospectors scoured the western mountains for gold. In the early 1860s they discovered gold in the western mountains of Montana. One of the primary supply roads to the Montana gold fields – called the "Gold Road" – passed from Utah through Eagle Rock, now Idaho Falls, just a few miles west of Iona before heading north to the gold fields. (*See The Region, Mining – The Gold Road – Precursor to Settlement of Eastern Idaho.*)

Covered wagon.

By 1881 the Utah and Northern Railroad, which later merged with the Oregon Short Line Railroad, laid track that generally followed the path of the Gold Road.

Many of the railroad construction workers were men whose families lived in Utah. They were impressed that sagebrush in the Snake River Valley grew as tall as young trees – a pleasing sight because it was a sign of deep, fertile soil.

When these men returned to their families in Utah, many of them made plans to return to Idaho and make their homes on the upper Snake River Plain.

Denning log cabin.

On the day after Christmas in 1882, John W. Taylor, the leader of The Church of Jesus Christ of Latter-day Saints (nicknamed Mormons – see The Region, Pioneer Settlements) (Church), wrote a letter to William B. Preston regarding settlement opportunities in Southeastern Idaho. "Go into the Snake River Country, found settlements, care for the Indians, stand upon an equal footing and cooperate in making improvements. Gain influence among all men [and women], strengthen the cords of the stakes of Zion" he counseled.

The next year, Thomas E. Ricks led several hundred Church settlers 25 miles past what is now Iona to found Rexburg and other nearby communities.

In that same year, Rufus and Wiley Norton, James Stewart and Joseph Mulliner Sr. filed their homestead claims on land along the west side of Sand Creek, near what is now Iona. It was not long before other settlers joined them.

As soon as the homesteaders filed on their land, they began the arduous task of building a temporary shelter, clearing and plowing the land, planting crops and finding ways to irrigate them. Settlers with wagons often lived in them and built lean-to shelters on the side. Others made willow huts or built dugouts cut into a hillside. For dugouts, the front consisted of stacked rock, logs or sod built around a single entrance. Dugout roofs were often willow branches covered with thatch or sod.

Two of the early settlers, James E. and Elvira C. Crompton Steele, are noteworthy examples of those who settled Iona.

Cowboys of Iona.

Steele first came to the Sand Creek area in March 1885. The creek was running full, and the vegetation was lush. He built a small cabin near the creek and traveled to Oxford to file his homestead claim. He then returned to Utah to dispose of his property there.

When Steele returned to his cabin on June 1, he was shocked to find everything, including the creek, had dried up. He said the land "looked desolate and unproductive."

He was very discouraged and had no interest in unloading his wagon or clearing the sagebrush to work his land. He was thinking of going back to Utah. After several days, Steele was sitting on the ground leaning against the wagon tongue when he fell asleep. As he slept, he said he "saw this country in a most beautiful, flourishing condition ... the sagebrush disappeared and in its place I saw farms everywhere."

Iona brass band.

When he awoke, Steele said he was "ready to unload (and) ... never wanted to go back."

Homesteaders lived on their own farms but worked cooperatively on large projects and came together for weekly church meetings. Community decisions and conflicts were often resolved when the settlers came together at these meetings. In some cases, the church authority arbitrated conflicts.

In the early years, the doctors would make house calls. Many women traveled to Salt Lake City to receive training as midwives.

In May 1886 Church President John W. Taylor visited each of the church units in the Upper Snake River Valley. He arrived at what is now Iona to assess the condition of the church members and organize a ward presided over by a lay bishop whom he would call and ordain.

At that time, the community had no name. President Taylor suggested they name the ward Iona, which he said meant "The Beautiful." The ward members approved and through common usage it also became the formal name of the town.

Iona's first sandstone church and school.

In the fall of 1886 James Steele paid 25 cents an acre for 160 acres that he platted for the future townsite of Iona. As with traditional Church settlements, his plat divided the property into 10-acre blocks subdivided into eight lots with six-rod-wide (99 feet) streets running between the blocks. The County surveyed the plat, and on October 24, 1891, the townsite committee recorded the plat at the Bingham County Courthouse in Blackfoot.

In 1887 Iona residents built a facility to house church and public meetings and hold school. With donated labor, sandstone from a nearby quarry and $1,500 in cash contributions, they built a 24-by-40-foot hall. This historic multiple-use facility is now the Stanger Memorial Art Gallery.

Charles Welcome Rockwood and his wife Anna took it upon themselves to beautify the city. They started a private nursery and planted sapling trees. In 1901 they gave the trees to residents who would plant them in their yards and care for them.

Anna Rockwood and Elvira Steele also developed a beautification plan that called for planting trees around Iona Square, the town's central park. Until irrigation water became available to the square they carried water to the trees by hand. Many of these trees still stand.

James E. Steele home.

Music, performing arts, dance and competitive sports were an important part of life in Iona. The Iona Brass Band started in 1895, and a drama company preformed in the Cloward Theater. The town had its own men's baseball and women's basketball teams.

The Herbert Brothers selected a building lot in a grove of trees and built a multi-purpose hall with a stage at one end. Chairs were set up for melodrama performances and taken down to accommodate dances and basketball. This hall had a pot-bellied stove for heat, which, after several years, led to its ruin. One cold night, the hall caught fire and burned down.

Iona Main Street.

Parents apparently wanted assistance in managing their school-age children. At nine o' clock each evening, the bell in the school tower rang. Anyone on the streets younger than 16 was escorted home by the town marshal.

To address the problem of stray livestock in the streets, they built a "stray corral" where unattended livestock were placed. Owners had to pay a fine or see their animals sold at auction.

Two of the major community celebrations were Independence Day and Pioneer Day – July 24th when the first pioneers entered the Salt Lake Valley in 1847. They had parades in the streets and at Iona Square; there were baseball games, horse-pulling contests, children's games, races, rodeos, fireworks and good things to eat.

Iona's first store.

The Fourth of July celebrations started with the "shooting of the anvil," where explosives were set off between two big anvils to control the blast. The explosion signaled it was time for everyone to come to Iona Square for the day's celebration.

Incorporation

Iona became an incorporated village on April 10, 1905. In 1910 the village reported a population of 353.

Turning Points

Irrigation Shortly after the first settlers arrived, they began building irrigation diversion dams on the Snake River and its tributaries and constructing extensive canal systems. (*See The Region, Pioneer Settlements – Irrigation – Early Farming Practices and Federal Land Use Laws.*)

With irrigation, the land became more productive and made it possible for farmers to grow an increased variety of crops.

Telephone and Electricity In October 1905 William Henry Price had the first rural telephone for miles around. The first telephone in Iona was in the general store, the Iona Merc. Until the telephone company provided home service, everyone in town would go to the Merc to make their telephone calls.

Lincoln Sugar Factory.

The first reliable electric lights came eight years later in 1913.

Railroad The community's greatest economic boost came in 1914 when the east belt of the Oregon Short Line Railroad came through Iona. With the availability of rail transportation to move commodities to distant markets, agriculture flourished.

Agriculture Until the end of the twentieth century, agriculture and food processing dominated the city's economy.

The area's volcanic-based soils were particularly suited for producing potatoes of exceptional quality. Potatoes continue to be an economic mainstay of Eastern Idaho farmers.

Annual Lion's Club July 4 breakfast.

In addition, a sugar factory built in 1903 in Lincoln – a mile southwest of Iona – gave farmers the attractive cash-crop rotation option of raising sugar beets. The sugar factory also provided seasonal employment each winter in processing the beets into sugar. This factory was a boon to the city's economy until it closed in 1978.

Technological innovation has allowed farmers and food processors to improve productivity with fewer employees. These changes along with the increased skill level required of workers have changed the economy of the area's agricultural sector. Many outlying farms are undergoing consolidation while farms located closer to the city have become ranchettes or residential subdivisions.

Iona Today

Amenities and Attractions Residents take pride in their city and continually support inclusive activities that bring the community together.

The city's central park, "Iona Square," is a popular amenity. This 10-acre park is the location for many community events.

Each April, there is a children's Easter Egg Hunt. As part of its July 24 Pioneer Day celebrations, the City sponsors "Iona Days." This historic festival offers a series of events that involve the greater Iona community and includes melodrama, breakfasts, art exhibits, competitive races, crafts and a car show. Traditionally, the concluding event is a community dinner and talent show sponsored by local congregations of The Church of Jesus Christ of Latter-day Saints.

Iona City Building, built in 1887, it was an LDS church, then a school and now houses city hall, the community center and the public library.

With federal, state and private grants, the City has made improvements including planting trees and constructing walking and bike paths around the park and major streets.

For these accomplishments, the city has received numerous awards, including the 2003 and 2004 Tree City USA Award, the 2004 Idaho Heritage City Award and the Idaho Gem City Award.

In the winter, the hills above Iona and beyond offer many miles of exceptional snowmobiling. During the balance of the year, the same area is open to mountain biking, hiking, fishing and hunting.

Just a few miles east is the 31,000-acre Tex Creek Wildlife Management Area. This area includes parts of Ririe Lake – an irrigation and flood control reservoir created by Ririe Dam that collects water from tributary streams and provides habitat for upland and migratory birds and winter range for thousands of migratory elk, mule deer and moose. The Idaho Fish and Game Department manages the area and oversees public visits and viewing of the animals.

The 1,560-acre Ririe Lake is a favorite for fishing, boating and camping. However, by late summer, irrigation demands draw down the lake. Juniper Park Campground is located near the dam at the north end of the lake, and Blacktail Park and boat dock is at the south end of the lake.

Other prominent recreation areas include Palisades Reservoir, 50 miles southeast, and Grand Targhee Ski Resort, just across the Wyoming border near Driggs.

Street in Iona.

Economy and Major Employers Most of Iona's workforce is employed by the Idaho National Laboratory (INL) in Idaho Falls or at the INL site 27 miles west in the desert. Others work for health care providers, education, retail or other service businesses or institutions.

Iona's business district is limited to several small retail shops and stores, a post office, an art gallery, a museum, a library, a community center and city hall. Most residents travel to the retail shopping malls in Idaho Falls for their shopping needs.

Flags and people lined the road to the Iona Cemetery to honor the Allcott family whose son, Pfc. Jacob Allcott, was killed in Iraq.

Education The Bonneville School District provides most of the kindergarten through high school education. Iona Elementary School, which has received Idaho's Excellence in Education Award, is located in the city. Rocky Mountain Middle School and Bonneville High School are located a mile west of the city.

The closest institutions of higher learning are the Eastern Idaho Technical College and the Idaho Center for Higher Education University Place in Idaho Falls. University Place is a campus where Idaho State University, the University of Idaho and Brigham Young University-Idaho (BYU-Idaho) offer courses and student services.

Health Care Residents travel seven miles to the medical centers and clinics in Idaho Falls for their health care needs.

Transportation U.S. Highway 26 passes within two miles of the city. Interstate 15 is located seven miles west. The nearest airport is just a few miles away in Idaho Falls. Railroad service for freight is also available in Idaho Falls.

Utilities and Services Private companies provide electricity, telephone, satellite and natural gas services. In 2005 private interests built wind turbines south of the city to augment local generation of electrical power.

The City provides water, fire protection, law enforcement services and cemetery services.

Wind turbines, circa 2005.

In 1978 the communities of Iona, Cloverdale, Lincoln and Ammon took an innovative action to insure they each had adequate wastewater treatment capability to accommodate future growth. They combined resources to form the Bonneville Sewer District. Everyone in the district was required to pay their share of the cost, whether they hooked up or not.

Vision for 2050

Over the past several years, the population of Iona has increased about 1 percent annually. Most of this growth has come from increasing employment opportunities in Idaho Falls and families choosing the quiet, more affordable rural environment of Iona. The city's actions to develop an abundant supply of clean water and its beautification initiatives are important factors in attracting these new families.

Big Hill.

In future years, Congress will place greater emphasis on using nuclear energy to reduce national dependence on foreign oil. Research at INL, as the nation's premier nuclear research facility, will grow dramatically to develop the next generation of nuclear-power plants.

Should these events occur, by 2050 Iona's population could grow over tenfold to 15,000. Many of these new INL and support business employees and their families will be attracted to Iona's beautiful surroundings and its culture as a church-going community with high moral values and a willingness to serve each other.

To accommodate this growth, the city boundaries will extend from Crowley Road, 45th East, north to the Ririe Highway, U.S. Highway 26, and from Lincoln Road east to the top of Iona Foothills and then north to the Ririe Highway.

Iona will have a public swimming pool and a new city hall. The Square will still be a prominent amenity used extensively for community and family events and celebrations.

Mayors

** James E. Steele *
** Thomas A. Nixon *
** Melvin Hardy Rushton *
** A.L. Owens *
** Clifford N. Scoresby *
** L.B. Wilde *
** Sheldon Cutler *
** D.F. Conrad *
** Orville Barnes *
** Harold Steele *
1967 Harold Steele
** Willis A. Storer
** Karen Hansen
1997 Craig Rockwood
2005 Brad Andersen
* Village Chairman
** Dates Unknown

Irwin

Statistical Data

Population: 221 *
Elevation: 5,325 feet
Precipitation: 14 inches **
Average Snowfall: 53 inches **
County: Bonneville

Temperature Range – Fahrenheit: **
Spring: 23 to 64
Summer: 42 to 84
Fall: 21 to 73
Winter: 12 to 36
* U.S. Census Bureau Estimates July 3015
**Historical averages

Irwin is located in picturesque Swan Valley below the beautiful 16,100-acre Palisades Reservoir on the Snake River. The city is nestled between two mountain ranges that are part of the Caribou-Targhee National Forest.

The Snake River Range lies on the western edge of the city and flows along the west side of the city. The Caribou Range lies to the west. The reservoir and mountains provide a stunning setting for the city.

Pre-Incorporation Years

For generations, Bannack and Shoshone Native American Indian Tribes migrated through the area.

In 1879 cattlemen began to settle in the Swan Valley, named for thousands of nesting Trumpeter swans that migrated to the valley each year.

Two families, the Ross and Higham brothers, ran over 1,000 head of cattle. They settled on the eastern side of the Snake River where their cattle grazed for free on the lush meadows and hillsides.

However, crossing the river was treacherous. In 1885 the Higham Brothers built a ferry.

Within a few years, sheep ranchers from Nevada and Utah brought their sheep herds to the valley for summer grazing. Cattlemen had no use for sheep. Sheep competed for the limited supply of grass. When sheep grazed, they ate the grass down to the crown of the roots, thus largely preventing further grazing until the next season.

In a desperate move to stop the sheep from crossing the river, the cattle ranchers destroyed the Higham Ferry. Sheep have a natural aversion to swimming because the water saturates the wool and can cause them to drown.

The conflicts between the cattlemen and the sheep men were generally resolved beginning in 1905 when the federal government adopted a grazing policy of federal lands. The policy restricted the number of animal units in any given location by requiring grazing permits and fees. In 1934 Congress further strengthened the policy with passage of the Taylor Grazing Act.

In 1951 the U.S. Bureau of Reclamation began constructing the 270-foot-high and 2,100-foot-wide earth-fill Palisades Dam, seven miles southeast of Irwin. They completed the dam in 1957.

Incorporation

On July 4, 1957, Irwin became an incorporated village.

Turning Points

Agriculture Livestock ranching and farming brought settlers to Swan Valley and was the economic foundation for creating the community of Irwin.

Palisades Dam. Construction of Palisades Dam changed life in different ways. First, it substantially reduced the risk of spring flooding. Second, as an increasing number of motorists came to take advantage of the lake's recreational opportunities, traffic through the city increased. The increased traffic flow through Irwin is providing opportunities for tourism and hospitality businesses to develop.

Irwin Today

Amenities and Attractions Irwin has one city park. The park is three acres in size and includes open areas for community gatherings, reunions, picnics and ballgames.

Each July and September at his ranch in Irwin, one of the city's community leaders, Daryl Ricks, hosts a professionally managed rodeo, called the Swan Valley Rodeo.

The city's most significant amenity is its location. Irwin lies in a beautiful outdoor paradise. The area offers many opportunities to float, fish, camp, hunt, hike, trail ride, cross-country ski, snowmobile, snowshoe and generally enjoy the great outdoors.

As part of the Yellowstone ecosystem, the area is home to some of the largest elk and Rocky Mountain Bighorn sheep herds in the country. White tail and mule deer, moose, bear, mountain lions and mountain goats also abound. The South Fork of the Snake River is one of the premier dry-fly fisheries in North America. Bird enthusiasts enjoy watching the Trumpeter swans, sandhill cranes and many others species of birds.

Jackson Hole, home of the Grand Teton National Park and the world-famous Grand Teton Mountain Range, and the adjoining Yellowstone National Park are a short drive over majestic mountain passes.

Many river rafters board rafts at Irwin to float down the South Fork of the Snake River through an imposing canyon where towering spruce, pine and fir trees provide perches for bald eagles.

The picturesque Palisades Reservoir with evergreen forests lining the shore extends southeast through mountain canyons into Wyoming. The lake is a popular fishing and boating destination. Due to fluctuating water levels in the reservoir, the best fishing occurs during spring, fall and winter seasons. Cutthroat trout, both wild and stocked; brown trout; Kokanee; and mackinaw are abundant in the reservoir. Ice fishing on Palisades Reservoir can be some of the best fishing of the year. Not only are winter trout great to eat, but the beauty of the area is enhanced by the snow and ice. Access to the reservoir is best on the side nearest Irwin.

Fishing lodge.

A few miles to the east of Irwin are Upper and Lower Palisades Lakes. These small lakes formed by landslides in the mountains near Irwin are popular with hikers, campers and sportsmen who enjoy the trails that follow the creeks up to the lakes.

Idaho Highway 26 through Irwin and along the reservoir is one of Idaho's most scenic routes.

For skiing enthusiasts, there are several nearby resorts. Kelly Canyon Ski Area is 34 miles northwest. Grand Targhee Ski Resort is 40 miles north just across the Idaho/Wyoming border. Jackson Hole, Wyoming, is 49 miles away.

Economy and Major Employers The largest private employers include a lodge that also provides a backcountry outfitting and guide service, a convenience store and restaurant. These businesses have, in total, about 20 employees. The U.S. Bureau of Reclamation and the Idaho Department of Transportation with fewer than 10 employees each are the largest public employers. Some residents commute to Idaho Falls for employment.

Education Swan Valley School District provides elementary and secondary education to Irwin students. The district offices and an elementary school that teaches students in multiple-grade classrooms for grades K-8 are located in the city. High school students ride buses or drive to either Idaho Falls (45 miles) or Ririe (40 miles) for their education.

The nearest institutions of higher learning are Idaho Falls Center for Higher Education and Eastern Idaho Technical College, both in Idaho Falls.

Health Care The nearest hospital is Teton Valley Hospital, 24 miles northeast in Driggs.

Transportation Idaho Highway 26 runs through Irwin. The Teton Scenic Byway begins 4 miles north of Irwin in the city of Swan Valley. The byway extends 69 miles north, providing panoramic views of the Snake River Valley, the Western slope of the Tetons and Fall River.

Utilities and Services Private companies provide telephone, electric and satellite services. The homes and businesses are on individual water and septic systems. A volunteer fire department provides fire protection. The City has a full-time police officer.

Vision for 2050

Over the past decade, Irwin's population has moved moderately higher from its low of 108 in 1990. This trend of slow growth will likely continue. By 2050 the city's population will likely return to its 1960 population of 330.

This growth will not require a significant change in City services. The city will retain its rural peaceful charm in one of the most beautiful regions of Idaho.

Swan Valley.

Swan Valley

Statistical Data

Population: 215 *
Elevation: 5,276 feet
Precipitation: 14 inches **
Average Snowfall: 53 inches **
County: Bonneville

Temperature Range – Fahrenheit: **
Spring: 23 to 64
Summer: 42 to 84
Fall: 21 to 73
Winter: 12 to 36
* U.S. Census Bureau Estimates July 2015
**Historical averages

The city of Swan Valley and the valley that bears the same name are in the Caribou-Targhee National Forest a mile east of the South Fork of the Snake River. The river is an exceptional cutthroat and brown trout fly-fishing stream that attracts anglers from throughout the region.

The Snake River Mountain Range, with peaks rising to over 10,000 feet, lies on the western edge of the city. The Caribou Range, with peaks rising to over 9,000 feet, is to the west and southwest.

Fertile irrigated farmland, interspersed by forestland, surrounds the city and fills the narrow valley. The beautiful 16,100-acre Palisades Reservoir, created by the Palisades Dam on the South Fork of the Snake River, is 10 miles southeast of the city.

Idaho Falls is located 45 miles northwest. The Idaho/Wyoming border is 15 miles due east. Jackson Hole, Wyoming, is 47 miles away.

Pre-Incorporation Years

For generations, nomadic American Indians – primarily of the Shoshone and

Bannock Tribes – migrated through Swan Valley to their seasonal encampments.

In 1879 cattlemen began to settle in the valley, which they named "Swan Valley" after the Whistling Swans that came each year to nest in the valley marshes.

Two of these families, the Ross and Higham brothers grazed over 1,000 head of cattle on meadowlands east of the Snake River.

However, crossing the river was treacherous. In 1885 the Higham brothers built a ferry.

The Snake River near Swan Valley.

Within a few years, sheep ranchers from Nevada and Utah brought their sheep herds to the valley for summer grazing, moving their animals across the river on the ferry. Cattlemen fiercely resisted the introduction of sheep onto the public grazing lands. They contended that the sheep ate the grass closer to the ground, leaving little grass for cattle.

In a desperate move to isolate the eastern meadowlands from the sheep, the cattlemen destroyed the Higham Ferry. Even though crossing the river was treacherous, cattle would ford the river but sheep would not. Sheep have a natural aversion to swimming because the water saturates their wool and can cause them to sink and drown.

While strained, the conflicts between the cattlemen and the sheep men did not result in bloodshed as it did in some parts of Idaho, such as around Oakley.

In 1905 Congress intervened by adopting a grazing policy for federal rangelands. The policy restricted the number of animal units in any given location by requiring grazing permits and fees. In 1934 Congress further strengthened the policy with the passage of the Taylor Grazing Act. (*See Eastern Idaho, Conflict – Cattlemen and Sheepmen.*)

In 1957 the U.S. Bureau of Reclamation completed construction of the earthen 270-foot-high and 2,100-foot-wide Palisades Dam.

Incorporation

Swan Valley first became an incorporated village, and in 1967 with a change in Idaho law, became a city.

Turning Points

Agriculture Livestock ranching and farming brought settlers to the valley and was the economic foundation for founding the city of Swan Valley.

Palisades Dam. Construction of Palisades Dam and Reservoir has had a major impact on the city as it substantially reduced the risk of spring flooding and attracts thousands of outdoor enthusiasts. They come to enjoy the natural beauty of the area and the diversity of recreation opportunities. Tourism and outdoor recreation industries now underpin the city's economy.

Swan Valley Today

Amenities and Attractions The city is home to the historic Snake River Ranger Station, the U.S. Forest Service area headquarters that began in 1908, was expanded by the Civilian Conservation Corps in the 1930s and is now listed on the National Register of Historic Places.

Fire Station #2 in Swan Valley.

The city's most significant amenity is its beautiful mountain location near crystal-clear streams and reservoirs. The area offers many opportunities to float, fish, camp, hunt, hike, trail ride, cross-country ski, snowmobile, snowshoe and generally enjoy the great outdoors.

As part of the Yellowstone ecosystem, the area is home to some of the largest elk and Rocky Mountain Bighorn sheep herds in the country. White tail and mule deer, moose, bear, mountain lions and mountain goats also abound. The South Fork of the Snake River is one of the premier dry-fly fisheries in North America. Bird enthusiasts enjoy watching the swans, sandhill cranes and other species of birds.

Jackson Hole, Wyoming – home of the Grand Teton National Park and the world-famous east slope of the Grand Teton Mountain Range – and the adjoining Yellowstone National Park are a short drive over majestic mountain passes.

Many river rafters board rafts at Swan Valley to float down the South Fork of the Snake River through an imposing canyon where towering spruce, pine and fir trees provide perches for bald eagles.

The picturesque Palisades Reservoir, with evergreen forests lining the shore, extends southeast through mountain canyons into Wyoming. The lake is a popular fishing and boating destination. Cutthroat, Brown and Mackinaw Trout and Kokanee Salmon are abundant in the reservoir. Ice fishing on the reservoir is popular, not only for catching fish but also for witnessing the spectacular beauty of the snow-covered landscape.

A few miles southeast of the city are the Upper and Lower Palisades Lakes. These small lakes, formed by landslides in the mountains, are popular with hikers, campers and sportsmen who follow the trails and creeks up to the lakes.

For skiing enthusiasts, there are several nearby resorts. Kelly Canyon Ski Area is 30 miles northwest. Grand Targhee Ski Resort is 36 miles north, just across the Idaho/Wyoming border.

Economy and Major Employers The city's largest businesses provide guided fly-fishing and hospitality services, followed by a restaurant and convenience store. Some residents commute to Idaho Falls for employment.

Education Swan Valley School District provides elementary and secondary education for the city's children. The district offices and an elementary school, where students are taught in multiple-grade classrooms for grades K-8, are located four miles southeast in Irwin. Most high school students ride buses or drive 28 miles to schools in Ririe.

The nearest institutions of higher learning are Idaho Falls Center for Higher Education and Eastern Idaho Technical College, both in Idaho Falls.

Health Care The nearest hospital is Teton Valley Hospital, 30 miles northeast in Driggs.

Transportation U.S. Highway 26 to Wyoming on the southeast and Idaho Falls on the northwest intersects the city. Idaho Highway 31 – the Teton Scenic Byway – begins in the city of Swan Valley and extends 69 miles north through Driggs and the western slope of the Grand Teton Mountain Range to Ashton.

The closest commercial airport is in Idaho Falls.

Utilities and Services Private companies provide telephone, electric and satellite services. The homes and businesses are on individual water and septic systems. A volunteer fire department provides fire protection. The City has a full-time police officer.

Vision for 2050

In 1960 Swan Valley had a population of 217. By 1990 the population had fallen to 141. At the 2000 Census the population had rebounded to 213 and has grown slowly thereafter. Recent historical trends will likely continue. By 2050 Swan Valley's population should exceed 400.

Ucon City Hall.

Ucon

Statistical Data

Population: 1,128 *
Elevation: 1,070 feet
Precipitation: 10 inches **
Average Snowfall: 30 inches **
County: Bonneville
Website: www.cityofucon.us

Temperature Range – Fahrenheit: **
Spring: 25 to 68
Summer: 46 to 86
Fall: 23 to 75
Winter: 13 to 37
* U.S. Census Bureau Estimates July 2015
**Historical averages

Ucon lies a few miles northeast of Idaho Falls on U.S. Highway 20. The city's agricultural origins are rapidly giving way to residential and mini-farm subdivisions that are filling in between the two communities. Most of the city's workforce commutes to Idaho Falls for employment.

The city's population is increasing as families choose to raise their children in the quiet rural environment of Ucon, within an easy commute of the larger city.

Pre-Incorporation Years

Soon after the 1860 to 1862 discovery of gold in what is now western Montana, prospectors, miners and freighters rushed to the Montana gold fields. The primary route – called the Gold Road – came up from Utah, crossed the Snake River at Eagle Rock – now Idaho Falls – and proceeded north into Montana.

In the late 1870s the Utah and Northern Railroad Company began construction of a rail line that generally followed the Gold Road route. In April 1879 the railroad reached Idaho Falls. By December 1881 it had reached Butte, Montana.

Many of those who worked building the railroad were from northern Utah. As they returned home, many spoke with glowing terms of the farming potential of the Upper Snake River Plain.

Leaders of The Church of Jesus Christ of Latter-day Saints (Church of Jesus Christ) encouraged immigrants coming into Utah to consider homesteading in the fertile Upper Snake River Plain.

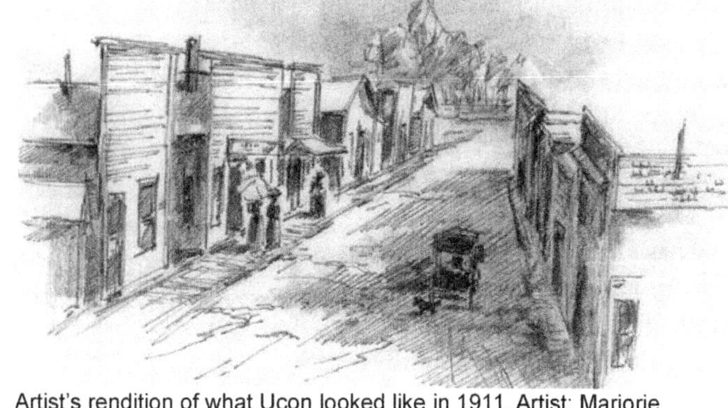

Artist's rendition of what Ucon looked like in 1911. Artist: Marjorie Clearwater. Used with permission.

Hundreds of families followed this advice and joined settlers coming from other parts of the country looking for homesteading opportunities.

In 1884 Amos and George Robinson filed homestead claims near what is now Ucon. Tall sagebrush covered the land. It was an arduous task to clear the land and prepare it for planting. The Snake River flowed four miles to the west and Willow Creek was three miles southeast. The land they chose to homestead was strategically located for diverting upstream water to irrigate their lower-elevation farms.

Within a short time, many other homesteaders followed the Robinsons and a community started to develop. Initially, the settlers named their community Willow Creek. In 1901 postal authorities notified the local postmaster and community leaders that the name of their town would have to change. The name Willow Creek, Idaho, was already in use.

Two story red brick schoolhouse, constructed in 1906. The rock church, Church of Jesus Christ of Latter-day Saints, in the background was constructed in 1904.

The community formed a town-naming committee. Unable to reach agreement, the committee decided to put each letter of the alphabet in a jar and draw three letters that would become the town's new name. They drew the letters A-K-O, thus establishing "Ako" as the community's new name.

In 1898 the Oregon Short Line Railroad built a branch line northeast from Idaho Falls to Yellowstone National Park. The railroad passed on the west side of Ako. At that time, the business district was forming to the east. Within the next few years, the business community moved west to be near the train depot, water tower, icehouse, coal shed, tool shed, stockyard and four houses.

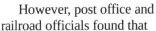

Elva Depot, built in 1904.

The growth of the community encouraged construction of other buildings. In 1904 the Church of Jesus Christ built a rock church. In 1906 the school district issued a $4,000 bond to construct a two-story red brick schoolhouse.

In 1907 the Simmons and Woolf Company built a mercantile store and community attraction for its broad range of products and customer service. The store carried products ranging from horse harnesses to fabric, food and clothes. Clerks wrapped customer's purchases in brown paper tied with a string with a piece of candy tucked inside the package. Tragically, the store could not survive the Great Depression, and in 1937 it closed its doors.

In 1907 the Ako Railroad Depot began telegraph service. However, railroad officials were not pleased with calling their train depot Ako. They, along with the postal authorities, expressed dissatisfaction.

Simmons and Woolf Company, 1907 to 1937.

The community leaders formed a new committee that also could not reach agreement. They again resorted to the "letters in a bottle" procedure. This time they came up with the name "Elva." From 1908 to 1911 the community went by that name.

However, post office and railroad officials found that Elva would not work because it was too easily confused with Elba, another Idaho town.

In 1911 community leaders formed a town-naming committee for the third time. The new committee used the previous name selection methodology and drew from a jar four letters that spelled U-C-O-N. Postal and railroad officials accepted the

Ucon name and the community immediately made application to become an incorporated city.

Incorporation

On February 11, 1911, the Idaho Legislature created Bonneville County. On May 9, 1911, the newly appointed county commissioners made Ucon an incorporated village. The community had two hotels, three mercantile stores, two movie theaters, two restaurants, a post office, city building, potato warehouses and the train depot.

Turning Points

Railroad The 1898 construction of the railroad and subsequent building of a train depot in Ucon was a major turning point for the city. It established the economic basis for the new city. It provided the means for shipping agricultural commodities to distant markets and created a new center of commerce.

Arthur Miskin and invention.

Around 1914 the railroad began adding branch lines to surrounding communities. Consequently, the Ucon Depot declined in importance and substantially all of the businesses either moved or closed. On June 24, 1960, the railroad closed the Ucon Depot.

Because of the city's close proximity to Idaho Falls, most residents retained their homes in Ucon and commuted to work in the larger city.

Ucon Today

Amenities and Attractions Ten miles southeast of the city is the 31,000-acre Tex Creek Wildlife Management Area. This Area – which includes parts of 1,560-acre Ririe Lake, an irrigation and flood control reservoir created by Ririe Dam and a favorite fishing, boating and camping amenity – collects water from tributary streams; provides habitat for upland and migratory birds; and winter range for thousands of migratory elk, mule deer and moose. Idaho Fish and Game manages the area and oversees public visits and viewing of the animals.

Twenty miles west of the city is the U.S. Department of Energy's Idaho

National Laboratory's (INL) 570,000 – acre reservation, the nation's second largest National Environmental Research Park. The INL reservation is mostly undeveloped and is home to 269 species of wild mammals, birds and reptiles and more than 400 species of plants.

Economy and Major Employers The city's business community largely consists of a few retail convenience stores, shops, service businesses and three larger businesses – MISKIN Scraper Works, Inc; Snake River Plains Potato Company; and C&S Trucking Company.

MISKIN produces a wide range of heavy equipment used worldwide in leveling, shaping and deep-tilling land. The company is a Ucon and Idaho legend. In 1917 Arthur Miskin, a farmer turned inventor and entrepreneur, founded the company.

As a farmer in the early 1900s, Mr. Miskin experienced major problems leveling his land to prepare it for flood irrigation. For several years, he experimented with his different inventions. Then in 1917 he began building and selling his patented scraper. Miskin's continued innovations have resulted in a product line that has found broad acceptance in the earth-moving business.

Education The Bonneville School District, with district offices in Idaho Falls, provides most of the K-12 education to Ucon school children. The city's elementary students attend Ucon Elementary. Middle and high school students attend school in Idaho Falls.

Signposts.

The closest institutions of higher learning are Eastern Idaho Technical College and University Place, supported by the University of Idaho and Idaho State University, in Idaho Falls. The closest University is Brigham Young University-Idaho located 23 miles northeast in Rexburg.

Health Care A full range of medical care is available at the 323-bed Eastern Idaho Regional Medical Center in Idaho Falls. The medical center is a full-service hospital, serving communities as far away as Montana and Wyoming.

Mountain View Hospital, a 20-bed acute care facility; free-standing clinics; same day-surgery centers; and home-health-care providers are also available in Idaho Falls.

Transportation U.S. Highway 20 passes the west edge of the city. Federal

Interstate 15 lies five miles west of town.

Idaho Falls Regional Airport provides air service.

Utilities and Services Private companies provide electricity, telephone, gas, satellite and cable services. The City provides water and sewer services and police and fire protection. The County provides solid waste services.

Vision for 2050

Ucon's population growth is primarily a function of increased job opportunities in Idaho Falls and at INL. In recent years, the city's population has grown over two percent. Should recent trends continue, by 2050 the city's population could more than double. Developers are already seeking annexation of their new subdivisions.

By 2050 the boundaries between Ucon and Idaho Falls will become transparent as development between the two cities continues.

Population growth, environmental requirements and the needs of existing residents will require improvements to municipal systems and parks. The cost of these improvements will be paid through either existing revenue streams, impact fees, grants or bonds approved by the voters.

Mayors

1911 Peter J. Nelson
1912 Nathan Groom
1919 Robert Andrus
1921 Josiah Godfrey
1923 John D. Anderson
1931 Firel Casper
1935 Robert Andrus
1935 Arthur Miskin
1937 Samuel A. Hill
1939 John D. Anderson
1941 Walter Cramer
1943 George Clift
1945 Jesse Brown
1946 Froyd Woolf
1951 Jesse Brown
1955 Lloy Prater
1959 Isaac Robinon
1961 Norman Brighton
1961 Ellis Rice
1964 Dale Clayton
1966 Bud Strupp
1979 Jay Radford
1983 Raymond Hill
1987 Jay Radford
1996 Bruand Cox
1997 Jay Radford
2002 Ron Wallace
2006 David Blain

Painting of Moore by Mildred Freckleton. Used with permission.

BUTTE COUNTY

- Arco (*County Seat*)
- Butte
- Moore

"Number Hill," the mountain east of the City of Arco. Beginning with the graduating class of 1920, every graduating class of Arco High School and, later, Butte County High School has painted their class number on the cliffs above the city.

Arco

Statistical Data

Population: 896 *
Elevation: 5,325 feet
Precipitation: 10 inches **
Average Snowfall: 29 inches **
County: Butte

Temperature Range – Fahrenheit: **
Spring: 21 to 67
Summer: 43 to 85
Fall: 18 to 74
Winter: 5 to 36

* U.S. Census Bureau Estimates July 2015
**Historical Averages

Arco is a city of contrasts. Geologically, it is located where the high mountain peaks of the Challis National Forest and Lost River Mountain Range end and the more recent lava flows of the massive Snake River Plain begin. Technologically, it is both a pioneer town and the first city in the world lit by atomic energy.

The city is located in the Big Lost River Valley. The Big Lost River flows just west of the city and then disappears into the porous basalt Snake River Plain Aquifer that extends over a 20,000-square-mile area and is more than 10,000 feet deep. (*See The Region, Distinctive Geologic and Geographic Areas – The Snake River and the Snake River Aquifer.*)

Lava flows, high mountains and buttes frame Arco and the valley. Idaho's tallest mountain, the 12,662-foot Borah Peak, lies 45 miles northwest. Idaho Fall is 67 miles east.

Surrounding the city are irrigated crops; rangeland; native meadows and high-desert brush, trees and grasses.

Pre-Incorporation Years

The first recorded history of the Lost River Country is in 1823 when Antoine

Godin's French fur traders tried to follow the Big Lost River from the mountains across the desert to the Snake River. They called it the "Lost River" because when it reaches the porous lava formations of the Snake River Plain and Aquifer, it sinks into oblivion. Located 20 miles east, across the Lost River Mountain Range, is the Little Lost River.

Permanent settlement began in 1878. Ranchers and farmers moved into the area, filed homestead claims, diverted water from the streams for irrigation and began to produce food for the silver, copper and gold miners and prospectors working the area.

Earliest available photo of Arco at its present location as Blackfoot-Mackay Short Line built through the Big Lost River Valley. Circa 1902.

A stagecoach station between the mines of the Wood River Valley and the smelters in Montana marked the future site of Arco. In 1884 prospectors discovered silver 18 miles west of Arco. They named their find the Horn Silver Mine, and the boomtown that grew up around the mine Era.

In 1901 the Oregon Short Line Railroad built a line from Blackfoot to Mackay. Arco became a train stop and the commercial hub of the area. New businesses opened, and nearby businesses – including the stage station – moved to the new site. Buildings in Era were dismantled and moved to the growing community. Unfortunately, the records of who platted the city have been lost.

Because Arco was located near the intersection of the railroad and stage line, the residents wanted to name their community "Junction" and applied to U. S. Postal authorities for a post office.

Parade down Arco's Main Street, 1912.

Postal authorities denied the application, stating that the name Junction was already overused. However, the U.S. Postmaster General Charles Emory Smith personally offered an alternative. At that time, German physicist and radio pioneer Georg von Arco was visiting Washington. Perhaps wanting to impress the foreign visitor, Smith offered "Arco" as the name for the new community. The petitioners accepted.

Given the subsequent relationship of Arco with nuclear-generated electricity and the concept of an electrical arc, it would be hard for a first-class advertising agency to come up with a more fitting name for the city.

The city's official newspaper, The Arco Advertiser, began publication in March 1909 and has been publishing continuously ever since.

In September 1909, investors proposed construction of Mackay Dam, a project, to irrigate 90,000 acres of which over 75 percent was west and south of Arco. With 570 registrations, it was the area's most successful land dispersal under the Carey Act. (*See The Region, Federal Land Use Laws.*)

However, the project was oversold. After disputes and lawsuits were settled, there was only enough water to irrigate 15,000 acres.

View from mountain east of the Village of Arco, Circa 1920.

Incorporation

On November 24, 1909, Arco became an incorporated village. On February 6, 1917, the Idaho Legislature approved creation of Butte County with Arco as the county seat.

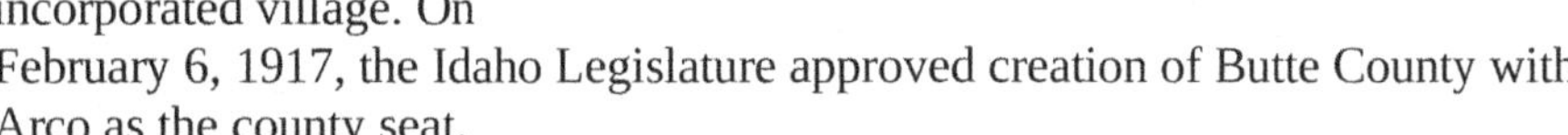

In 1951 Arco became an incorporated city. At that time, city leaders generated revenue by selling its electrical-power-generation facility to Utah Power & Light for $115,000 plus 2 percent of the facility's gross revenue for 25 years.

Turning Points

Railroad Arco owes its existence to the Oregon Short Line's 1901 construction of its rail line from Blackfoot to Mackay with a depot at the junction with the stage line. The railroad made obsolete the north-south freight wagon and stagecoach service and became a transportation hub for horse-drawn conveyances traveling to and from other directions.

American Astronauts training at the Craters of the Moon before their successful flight to the moon. The Craters was chosen for their geological training site due to the belief that the terrain on the Moon and the Craters were similar.

Irrigation Even though Mackay Reservoir failed to meet early water-storage expectations, it was sufficient to increase the productivity of a large portion of the valley's farmland and provide stability to the area's cyclical mining activity.

World Wars. After establishing a strong economic foundation in the early years, Arco experienced periods of roller-coaster prosperity and adversity during the 30 years marked by World War I, the Great Depression, World War II and mine closures.

Following World War I, many returning veterans looking for new opportunities chose to settle in the Big Lost River Valley. They swelled the population and strengthened the economic base of the city.

Idaho National Laboratory. Beginning with the establishment of the Navy gunnery range that operated from 1942 to 1947 and followed by the creation of INL, federal programs have offered good paying jobs for many Arco residents.

INL began in 1949 when the Atomic Energy Commission established the National Reactor Testing Station, the predecessor to INL on a 570,000-acre site west of Arco. Employment from INL became a stabilizing force for the Arco labor pool as mines were playing out and farms were becoming less labor intensive.

One of the favorite visitors' sites at the Craters of the Moon is the location of these three volcano spatter cones, which have well developed, paved hiking trails and safety guards around the volcanic vents at their summits.

On July 17, 1955, Arco became the first city in the world lighted by atomic energy. Electricity generated by Boiling Water Reactor No. 3, known as BORAX-III, at Experimental Breeder Reactor No. 1, or EBR-1, produced 2,000 kilowatts of electrical power for about two hours. This power replaced the normal electrical transmission to Arco. EBR-1, the world's first nuclear reactor to produce usable amounts of electricity, is now a Registered National Historic Landmark and museum located 20 miles southeast of Arco.

Researchers at INL also developed the first U.S. Navy propulsion systems for nuclear-powered submarines, and INL provided the training facilities for thousands of submarine sailors. (*See The Region, Idaho National Laboratory – Eastern Idaho's Largest Employer*.)

Tourism. The designation of the lava flows west of Arco as Craters of the Moon National Monument in 1924 brought national recognition to this exceptional terrain, creating a tourist attraction and outdoor laboratory for students who come to experience the unusual features of this national treasure. These visitors provide diversity and stimulus to Arco's economy.

INL and its nearby EBR-1 Registered National Historic Landmark and museum are other important tourist attractions for Arco.

Arco Today

Amenities and Attractions Arco has four public parks, the largest of which is Bottolfsen Park named after C.A. Bottolfsen, a native son who served as Idaho's governor from 1939 to 1941 and again from 1943 to 1945. The parks have a variety of attractions including picnic and children's playground areas and ball fields. The city also has a library and a mile-long greenbelt.

The Idaho Science Center Museum, a nuclear history park and museum for the "Submarine in the Desert," is currently under development. The museum commemorates the role Arco played in the nation's research and development of atomic power. The 24-foot-high, 70-ton sail, or fairwater tower, of the atomic submarine Hawkbill stands at the entrance.

Hawkbill Fairwater Tower Monument.

Each year on the weekend of July 17, Arco celebrates "Atomic Days." Festivities include a Saturday morning parade followed by breakfast in the park, mud volleyball, running and walking marathons, sidewalk sales and a barbeque. There is a rodeo on Friday and Saturday evenings. In addition, the city hosts a baseball tournament with teams coming from as far away as Utah.

The 750,000-acre Craters of the Moon National Monument and Preserve begins 18 miles southwest. The preserve includes Idaho's Great Rift, the source of the lava flow that created this unique landscape. (*See The Region, Craters of the Moon National Monument and Preserve.*)

Pickle's Place, home of the Atomic Burger.

About nine miles north is the 10,773-foot-high King Mountain. The Craters of the Moon Preserve and the area around King Mountain provide hiking and camping in the summer and cross-country skiing in the winter. Hang gliders also use King Mountain for their sport.

Natural Rock Bridge, a unique natural feature, is eight miles due north. Big Southern Butte, another unique natural feature, lies 15 miles southeast.

A variety of outdoor activities is available around Arco. Anglers enjoy the many high-mountain lakes, and there is excellent hunting for deer, elk and antelope. The area has several all-terrain vehicle trails. Rock hounds find exciting specimens of agate, jasper, crystals and various other rocks in nearby areas open to the public.

Economy and Major Employers Approximately 120 residents commute 30 miles to the INL site for work. The Lost Rivers Hospital and the Butte County School District each employ about 100. Butte County has 70 employees.

Arco is the county seat of Butte County and a retail shopping center for the area. Nearly 40 percent of the county's population lives in Arco. Two banks, a credit union and a variety of retail and service businesses that support tourism and the residents on the surrounding farms and ranches provide an increasing employment base for the city.

Education Butte County High School, Middle School and Arco Elementary provide elementary and secondary education.

The Idaho Virtual Academy, a statewide distance learning charter school, provides services to Arco students. Although the school originated in Arco, it is now headquartered in Sun Valley.

The Arco Recreation Hall, built in the 1930s as a WPA project, houses the Arco City Office and the gymnasium which fills the rest of the building. The sign in neon lights above the door proclaims Arco becoming the "First City in the World to be Lit by Atomic Power," which occurred on July 17,1955. Elevation 5,320 feet.

The nearest institutions of higher learning are the Idaho Falls Center for Higher Education, a facility where Idaho universities offer their programs, and Eastern Idaho Technical College.

Health Care Private clinics and the 17-bed Lost Rivers District Hospital provide medical services. A senior citizens center provides services for the elderly.

Transportation U.S. Highways 20/26 and 93 intersect near the center of town. Interstate access is available 57 miles south in Blackfoot or in Idaho Falls.

Private aircraft use the nearby 6,600-foot runway at Arco-Butte County Airport two miles south of town. Commercial air service is available in Idaho Falls.

Utilities and Services Electric and telephone services are provided by private carriers. The City provides water, sewer and solid waste collection. The Butte County Sheriff's Office provides law enforcement. The City has a volunteer fire and emergency medical services department with cross-agency support agreements with INL, Lost River Fire District, the Idaho Department of Fish & Game and the U.S. Forest Service.

Vision for 2050

Arco's population has remained around 1,000 for decades but should begin growing moderately because of INL and increased tourism. The city's existing infrastructure is adequate to accommodate this moderate growth.

Increased tourism is due to the city's location at the junction of U.S. Highways 20/26 and 93. It is a gateway to the Sun Valley Resort, scenic Stanley Basin and the Salmon River. In addition, Craters of the Moon National Monument and Preserve, EBR-1 and the area's excellent outdoor attractions will continue to bring increasing numbers of tourists.

Growth will come as INL expands its research, including the next generation of nuclear-powered electrical plants. More INL employees will also choose to live in Arco, where there is affordable housing and a peaceful hometown environment to raise their families. While tourism will become an increasing economic driver for the city, Arco will retain its small-town charm.

Mayors

1909 Unknown *
1913 J.E. Smith *
1917 C.E. Pieper *
1920 Ephraim Kidman *
1922 W.E. Brown *
1924 Alma J. Packer *
1930 W.W. Brown *
1933 H.W. Bauchner *
1939 Hugh Wetherington *
1940 Dave Daniels *
1945 Frank L. Brown *
1945 Frank S. Monson *
1949 W.S. Marvel *
1951 Ralph Ellison
1957 Kenneth J. Sims
Unknown Chic Jones
1958 Oscar Johnson
1960 Bert Harword
1961 Cecil Donnelly
1964 Paul Wetherington
1968 Howard Gibson
1970 Ralph Mefford
1976 Chic Jones
1977 William L. Scouten
1979 Chic Jones
1988 Dale Andreason
1988 Richard Scott
1990 Billy McMurtrey
1994 Chic Jones
1998 Jacques Marcotte
2002 Carol Jardine
2008 Ross Langseth
* Village Chairman

Butte City-area farm using sprinkler irrigation. All Butte City pictures courtesy UntraveledRoad - www.UntraveledRoad.com.

Butte City

Statistical Data

Population: 67 *
Elevation: 4,824 feet
Precipitation: 10 inches **
Average Snowfall: 29 inches **
County: Butte

Temperature Range – Fahrenheit: **
Spring: 21 to 67
Summer: 43 to 85
Fall: 18 to 74
Winter: 5 to 36

* U.S. Census Bureau Estimates July 2015
**Historical averages

Butte City lies at the base of the sagebrush-covered Arco Hills. These hills are at the southern end of the Salmon-Challis National Forest. The city of Arco is two miles northwest.

The Big Lost River flows about a mile to the southwest before it later disappears into the porous basalt to become part of the 20,000-square-mile aquifer that slowly flows through porous basalt up to 10,000 feet deep under the Snake River Plain.

High mountains and buttes that lie north of the city rise to over 7,500 feet. Idaho's tallest mountain, the 12,662-foot-high Borah Peak, lies 47 miles northwest.

To the immediate south and west of the city are irrigated crops and rangeland. Outside the farmland lie vast tracks of public lands covered with high-desert brush, trees, grasses and ancient lava flows.

Pre-Incorporation Years

In 1823 Antoine Godin's French fur traders tried to follow the Big Lost River from the mountains across the desert to the Snake River. They called the river "Lost River" because when it reaches the porous lava formations of the Snake River Aquifer, it sinks into oblivion.

Permanent settlement began in 1878. Ranchers and farmers moved into the area, filed homestead claims, diverted water from the streams for irrigation and began to produce food for the silver, copper and gold miners and prospectors working the area.

About 1884 prospectors discovered silver about 20 miles west of Butte City. They named their find the Horn Silver Mine and named the boomtown that grew up around the mine Era.

In 1901 the Oregon Short Line Railroad built a line from Blackfoot to Mackay. Nearby Arco became a train stop and the commercial hub of the area.

Incorporation

On June 9, 1953, Butte City became an incorporated village. In November 1967 it became an incorporated city as required by a new state law requiring all incorporated municipalities to adopt the city form of government.

Turning Points

Silver The discovery of silver at Era brought prospectors to the area.

Butte City Today

Amenities and Attractions Butte City residents generally use the amenities provided in Arco.

The U.S. Department of Energy's Idaho National Laboratory (INL) manages a 570,000-acre reservation whose western border begins just a few miles southeast of the city. (*See Eastern Idaho: Idaho National Laboratories – Eastern Idaho's Largest Employer*.)

The 750,000-acre Craters of the Moon National Monument and Preserve begins 20 miles southwest. The Preserve includes Idaho's Great Rift, the source of the lava flow that created this unique landscape. (*See Eastern Idaho – Craters of the Moon National Monument and Preserve and the Great Rift National Natural Landmark*.)

About 11 miles north is the 10,773-foot-high King Mountain, a popular location for hang-gliding enthusiasts.

The Craters of the Moon Preserve and the area around King Mountain provide hiking and camping in the summer and cross-country skiing in the winter.

Natural Rock Bridge, a unique natural feature, is 10 miles due north. Big

Southern Butte, another unique natural feature, lies about 15 miles southeast.

A variety of outdoor activities is available in the area around Butte City. Anglers enjoy the many high-mountain lakes; and there is excellent hunting for deer, elk and antelope throughout the area. The area has several all-terrain vehicle trails. Throughout the area, rockhounds find excellent hunting grounds.

Economy and Major Employers Most of the city's residents commute to INL for work or are involved with farming.

Butte City is too small to support a business community. The city's residents generally patronize the businesses in the next-door community of Arco.

Education Butte County School District provides the public education for Butte City students. All of the city's elementary, middle and high school students attend schools located in Arco.

The nearest institutions of higher learning are about 67 miles east at the Idaho Falls Center for Higher Education, a facility where Idaho universities offer their programs, and Eastern Idaho Technical College.

Health Care Private clinics and the 17-bed Lost Rivers District Hospital in Arco provide medical services. An Arco Senior Citizens Center helps provide services for the elderly.

Transportation U.S. Highways 20/26 intersect the city. Interstate access is available 55 miles south in Blackfoot or in Idaho Falls.

Private aircraft use the nearby 6,600-foot-long runway at Arco-Butte County Airport located two miles southwest of Arco. Commercial air service is available in Idaho Falls.

Utilities and Services Private companies provide electricity, telephone and satellite services. All of the residents and establishments have individual wells and septic systems.

The Butte County Sheriff's Office provides law enforcement. The Arco Volunteer Fire and EMS Department provides fire and emergency protection. The department has cross-agency support agreements with INL, Lost River Fire District, Fish & Game and the U.S. Forest Service.

Vision for 2050

In 1960 the city had a population of 104. Following a sharp decline in the 1970s, the population stabilized and for the last decade has remained at around 70.

Recent trends are likely to continue for the next few decades.

Lost River Mountains overlooking Moore.

Moore

Statistical Data

Population: 172 *
Elevation: 5,473 feet
Precipitation: 10 inches **
Average Snowfall: 29 inches **
County: Butte

Temperature Range – Fahrenheit: **
Spring: 21 to 67
Summer: 43 to 85
Fall: 18 to 74
Winter: 5 to 36
* U.S. Census Bureau Estimates July 2015
**Historical averages

Moore is in the Lost River Valley as it opens up onto the northern edge of the Snake River Plain and the prehistoric lava flows of Craters of the Moon National Monument. The White Knob Mountains – with peaks rising to over 11,000 feet – silhouette the northwestern skies. To the northeast and east are the Lost River Range and the 10,773-foot King Mountain. Both mountain ranges are in the Salmon-Challis National Forest.

The Big Lost River flows east of the city and later disappears into the ground to become part of the 20,000-square-mile Snake River Aquifer from which Southern Idaho cities and farmers pump water. The river joins other recharge sources that flow into the porous basalt aquifer that is up to two miles deep. The aquifer water flows slowly to reappear years later over a hundred miles away cascading down steep Snake River Canyon walls at Thousand Springs State Park. This cold, crystal-clear water supplies numerous trout hatcheries and replenishes the Snake River.

Idaho’s tallest mountain, the 12,662-foot Borah Peak, is 37 miles due northwest. Arco is seven miles south, and Ketchum is 58 road miles west.

Irrigated crops; rangeland; native meadows; and high-desert brush, trees and grasses cover the valley and foothills that surround the city.

Pre-Incorporation Years

Historically, the Shoshone and Bannock Tribes were the principal tribes living in the Lost River Valley. The Gros Ventre and Blackfoot Indians of the Northern Plains also made periodic excursions into the area. (*See The Region, American Indians.*)

Beginning around 1810 the first European and American explorers and trappers began traveling into Southern Idaho, trapping beaver and seeking to trade with the nomadic American Indians. (*See The Region, Trappers/Explorers.*)

In the early 1820s fur trappers worked the 135 miles of the Big Lost River that flows near Moore as they traveled south to the Snake River and beyond. Both the Big Lost River and the smaller Little Lost River, 20 miles east across the Lost River Range, end in marshlands above the porous lava formations of the Snake River Aquifer where they sink into oblivion – hence their names, "lost" rivers.

Prospectors discovered copper in 1879 a few miles west of Mackay, about 18 miles north of Moore, in the White Knob Mountains and extending 20 miles west across the mountains to the Copper Basin. Many of the ore bodies were also rich in lead, zinc, silver and gold. The general area is known as the Alder Creek Mining District. The richest discoveries were on Mackay's "Mine Hill." (*See The Region, Mining – Mackay – Copper, Lead and Other.*)

About this time, ranchers and farmers moved into the Lost River Valley area. They filed homestead claims, diverted water from the streams for irrigation and began to produce food for the miners and prospectors. These homesteads dotted the landscape between Willow Creek Summit, about 30 miles upriver from Mackay, down to the stage and freight stop at Kennedy's Corner near Arco.

The stagecoach and freight wagon line between Blackfoot and the Challis and Salmon River mining camps passed through the valley and what is now Moore.

The Oregon Short Line Railroad affiliate, the Salmon River Railroad Company, completed an 86-mile railroad line from Blackfoot, through Moore to the Mackay smelter and mining operation in 1901. (*See The Region, Railroads.*)

At about this time, an entrepreneur named Moore acquired the land next to the railroad siding that would become a dock used to load farm commodities and livestock for shipment to market. He also platted the town and applied to postal authorities for a post office in which he would be postmaster. Postal authorities approved the Moore Post Office, establishing the name of the new community.

Incorporation

On May 2, 1947, Moore became an incorporated village. In conformity with a 1967 change in Idaho municipal law, Moore became an incorporated city.

Turning Points

Mining The mining and smelting operation at Mackay was the impetus for building the railroad through Moore as well as providing the principal market for locally produced agricultural commodities.

Railroad The railroad was critical to the development of Moore's economy. It not only carried farm and ranch production to market, it also provided rapid transportation for passengers, freight and mail.

Moore Today

Amenities and Attractions The city's Benjamin Pearson Park features a picnic shelter and children's playground equipment.

Each July, Moore is the site for hang-gliding competitions at nearby 10,773-foot King Mountain. Hang-glider enthusiasts from around the world recognize King Mountain as an outstanding glider launch site. They often come to Moore for their world championship competition.

At the end of June, the community sponsors an annual car and truck show.

Arco became the first city in the world lighted by atomic energy on July 17, 1955, when electricity generated by Boiling Water Reactor No. 3 (BORAX-III) at Experimental Breeder Reactor No. 1 (EBR-1) produced approximately 2,000 kilowatts of electrical power for about two hours. This power replaced the normal electrical transmission to Arco. EBR-1, 34 miles southeast of Moore, is now a Registered National Historic Landmark and museum. Also developed at the site were the first U.S. Navy propulsion systems for nuclear-powered submarines. The site facilities were used to train thousands of submariners.

The U.S. Department of Energy's Idaho National Laboratory (INL) manages a 570,000-acre reservation that begins just a few miles southeast of the city. (*See The Region, Idaho National Laboratory*.)

Painting by Mildred Freckleton; this depicts the Betty and Joe Williams home. Used with permission.

Moore residents participate in Arco's annual events. Each year on the weekend of July 17, Arco celebrates "Atomic Days." Festivities include a Saturday morning parade followed by breakfast in the park, mud volleyball, running and walking marathons, sidewalk sales and a barbeque. There is also a rodeo on Friday and Saturday evenings. In addition, the city hosts a baseball tournament with teams coming from as far away as Utah.

The 750,000-acre Craters of the Moon National Monument and Preserve is 18 miles southwest. The Preserve includes Idaho's Great Rift, the source of the lava flow that created this unique landscape. (*See The Region, Distinctive Geographic and Geologic Features – Craters of the Moon National Monument and Preserve.*)

The Craters of the Moon Preserve and the area around King Mountain provide hiking and camping in the summer and cross-country skiing in the winter.

A variety of outdoor activities are available in the area. Anglers enjoy the many high-mountain lakes, and there is excellent hunting for deer, elk and antelope. The area has several all-terrain vehicle trails. Rock hounds come great distances to prospect for rare and unusual rocks and gemstones.

Economy and Major Employers The city has no large employers. The commercial downtown district consists of a few businesses serving farms and ranches and a few convenience stores and shops. Most residents shop at Arco.

Education Butte County School District – with a high school, a middle school and elementary schools in Arco – provides education for Moore children.

The nearest institutions of higher learning are the Idaho Falls Center for Higher Education, a facility where Idaho universities offer programs, and Eastern Idaho Technical College. Brigham Young University-Idaho is 84 miles west in Rexburg.

Health Care Private clinics and the 17-bed Lost Rivers District Hospital in Arco provide medical services for city residents. There is also a senior citizens center in Arco.

Transportation U.S. Highway 93 intersects the city. Interstate 15 is accessible 65 miles south in either Blackfoot or Idaho Falls.

The 6,600-foot-long runway of Arco-Butte County Airport is 10 miles south of town and serves light private and charter aircraft. Commercial airport service is available in Idaho Falls.

Utilities and Services Private companies provide electricity, telephone and satellite services. Independent municipal districts provide sewer and water. The Butte County Sheriff's Office provides police protection under contract with the City. The Lost River Fire Department provides fire protection.

Vision for 2050

Since 1980 the city's population has remained somewhat constant at around 200. By 2050 Moore will likely continue as it is today; a quiet agricultural community desired by families seeking a peaceful, rural place to live in a high-desert valley among towering mountain ranges.

Mayors

1947 Earl Jud *
1951 Eldred L. Braithwaite *
1958 Frank (Bud) L. Garnett *
1968 Eldred L. Braithwaite
1968 Floyd M. Pate
1974 R. Dean Waddoups
1978 Jack Sollender
1986 Darrell Hope
1987 Lin Pearon
1966 Owen Loftus
2000 Doug Hymas
2002 Anne Hainline
2007 Lin Pearson
2016 Hammond Britton
* Village Chairman

Parade in Grace, 1950.

CARIBOU COUNTY

- Bancroft
- Grace
- Soda Springs (*County Seat*)

Rodeo at Bancroft.

Bancroft

Statistical Data

Population: 371 *
Elevation: 5,420 feet
Precipitation: 15 inches **
Average Snowfall: 66 inches **
County: Caribou

Temperature Range – Fahrenheit: **
Spring: 22 to 66
Summer: 42 to 85
Fall: 21 to 75
Winter: 11 to 37
* U.S. Census Bureau Estimates July 2015
**Historical averages

Bancroft lies in the upper reaches of Gem Valley about 15 miles northwest of Soda Springs, 11 miles south of the partially preserved historic pioneer ghost town of Chesterfield and 48 miles east of Pocatello.

Caribou-Targhee National Forest and Fish Creek Mountain Range outline the city's western skyline. Petticoat Peak, the highest mountain in the range, rises to 8,033 feet and lies four miles due south of the city. Across the valley about 10 miles to the northeast is the Chesterfield Mountain Range.

Pre-Incorporation Years

In 1841 the first emigrant wagon train traveled on what would become the Oregon and California Trails. Upon reaching Soda Springs, the party divided. One group of 32, led by Thomas Fitzpatrick and Father Pierre de Smet turned northwest through what is now Bancroft on their way to Oregon Country. The other group of 37, led by John Bidwell, headed west to California.

For the next few decades, thousands of Oregon Trail pioneers traveled a similar route through what is now Bancroft on their way to their next rest stop at Fort Hall, near what is now Pocatello.

In 1882 the Oregon Short Line Railroad (OSL) began constructing a rail line between Granger, Wyoming, and Huntington, Oregon. This segment of railroad, completed in 1884, provided the connecting link between Omaha, Nebraska, and Portland, Oregon. The railroad passed through what is now Bancroft.

A new town was platted next to the railroad siding that they named Bancroft, the name of an OSL railroad executive.

At that time, Chesterfield, 11 miles north, was a growing farm community with a population of around 400. Bypassed by the railroad, Chesterfield declined in influence and Bancroft flourished.

Incorporation

On October 21, 1913, Bancroft became an incorporated village.

Turning Points

Railroad The railroad was the principal economic basis for establishing Bancroft. In the early 1900s it provided needed transportation for the lime mining and processing operation and moving farm commodities to market. Freight trains still stop at Bancroft.

Tuscher Square.

Bancroft Today

Amenities and Attractions Numerous outdoor amenities are available to Bancroft residents and visiting sports enthusiasts.

The nearby mountains have large populations of big game animals, migratory birds and other wildlife. In the winter season, sportsmen enjoy snowmobiling, cross-country skiing and ice fishing.

Blackfoot Reservoir and the 2,400-acre Blackfoot River Wildlife Management Area for cutthroat trout and upland and riparian wildlife are northeast of the city. Several other smaller nearby reservoirs and streams are also excellent fisheries.

The Idaho Department of Fish and Game also manages the 3,349-acre Georgetown Summit Wildlife Management Area for elk, mule deer and sharp-tailed grouse southeast of the city.

The historic agricultural ghost town of Chesterfield has numerous preserved buildings and a museum in the restored brick church meetinghouse.

Economy and Major Employers With over 40 employees, the North Gem

School District is the city's largest employer. Chemical Lime Company has about 23 employees and is the city's second largest employer followed by several smaller businesses and retail establishments.

Education The North Gem School District provides most of the K-12 education for the nearly 200 students living in Bancroft and the surrounding area. The district operates a high school and an elementary school in a single facility in Bancroft.

Bancroft City Hall.

The closest institution of higher learning is Idaho State University in Pocatello.

Health Care The 27-bed Caribou Memorial Hospital and general clinics in Soda Springs provide most of the city's medical care. In addition, there is a 21-bed assisted-living center and a 37-bed nursing home associated with the hospital complex.

Transportation A paved road that was the old U.S. Highway 30 intersects the city. Highway 30 and Idaho Highway 34 are about nine miles southeast. Interstate 15 is about 25 miles southwest via Highway 30.

The 3,500-foot runway of Bancroft Municipal Airport provides service to light private and charter aircraft. The closest commercial airport is in Pocatello.

Railroad service is available for freight.

Utilities and Services Private companies provide telephone, electricity and satellite services. The City provides water and sewer services and fire protection. The County Sheriff provides police protection under contract with the City.

Vision for 2050

In 1960 Bancroft's population was 416. In the 1970s it swelled to around 500 before falling back to under 400. In the past decade, the population has remained somewhat constant at around 350.

The trends of recent years will likely continue. By 2050 Bancroft will continue to be a small peaceful and friendly community – a wonderful place to live and raise a family.

Main Street, Grace, March 20, 2007.

Grace

Statistical Data

Population: 905 *
Elevation: 5,540 feet
Precipitation: 14 inches **
Average Snowfall: 53 inches **
County: Caribou
Website: www.graceidaho.com (Chamber of Commerce)

Temperature Range – Fahrenheit: **
Spring: 22 to 56
Summer: 42 to 85
Fall: 21 to 75
Winter: 11 to 37
* U.S. Census Bureau Estimates July 2015
**Historical averages

The city of Grace is a quiet farming community located on the eastern edge of the 30-mile-long, 10-mile-wide Gem Valley. The valley is nestled between the mountain ranges of the Cache National Forest on the east and the Caribou National Forest and State lands on the west. The valley's elevations are irregular and range from 4,800 to 6,000 feet. The highest peaks in the nearby mountains rise to over 9,000 feet.

The Bear River meanders through the valley and flows on the western edge of the city. About two miles north, the Last Chance Dam diverts irrigation water to valley farms before proceeding to the Idaho/Utah border, 40 miles south.

The prevailing winds come from the southwest. Grace is consistently the warmest community in Caribou County. Farmers primarily grow seed potatoes, hay and grain. Homeowners have gardens and orchards that produce a variety of fruits and vegetables.

Clouds often form over the mountains, creating spectacularly beautiful sunrises and sunsets. The community is quiet and peaceful – an ideal location for raising a family.

Pre-Incorporation Years

Before white settlers came to the Gem Valley in 1889, different tribes of Indians traveled through the area. In the early 1800s fur trappers worked the Bear River and its tributaries. (*See The Region, American Indians and Early Trappers/Explorers*.)

Over the next several decades, thousands of immigrants traveling to California and Oregon would come close to what is now Grace, but none stopped to make a home in this rugged, untamed wilderness.

Main Street, Grace, 1914.

The first immigrants to the Oregon Country – then claimed by both the U.S. and England, becoming part of the U.S. in 1846 – passed north of what is now the city of Grace near Soda Springs in 1841. Eight years later, a party of 250 immigrants headed to California and led by Benoni M. Hudspeth, an experienced mountain man, left the main Oregon Trail five miles north of the city and blazed a shortcut through what is now Hot Springs then west to rejoin the main California Trail at the Raft River near what is now Malta before continuing southwest to the City of Rocks and then on through the northwestern corner of Nevada to California. (*See The Region, Oregon and California Trails*.)

In 1862 Congress passed the Homestead Act, which deeded 160 acres of public land to those who filed a claim, improved the land and lived on it for five years. In the early 1860s emigrants began moving from Utah into Eastern Idaho but not to the Gem Valley. Getting Bear River irrigation water out of the deep gorge was too problematic. (*See The Region, Federal Lands – Private Ownership and Preservation Laws*.)

A year later, General Patrick E. Conner established Fort Conner in what is now Soda Springs. The fort closed two years later but settlers from Utah continued to settle around the fort.

On May 1, 1864, Charles C. Rich, a leader in The Church of Jesus Christ of Latter-day Saints, led several hundred people from Utah to settle around Bear Lake, 40 miles southeast of Grace and build communities. (*See The Region, Pioneer Settlements*.)

Prospectors discovered gold in Montana in 1862. The gold rush that ensued created a trade and transportation route through Idaho known as the “Gold Road” which came up from Utah and passed 20 miles west of Grace through the less rugged Marsh Valley and crossed the Snake River at Eagle Rock, now Idaho Falls, 60 miles northwest of Grace.

The Utah and Northern Railroad completed a line around 1880 that generally followed the Gold Road. Many of the rail workers were from settlements in Utah. They were impressed with the farming potential of the land in the Upper Snake River Plain. When the railroad line was completed, they returned home with glowing reports and hundreds of emigrant families moved from Utah to homestead in Eastern Idaho.

The Sam Egbert and D.D. Sullivan families came from West Jordan, Utah, in 1880 to homestead in Gem Valley near what is now Grace. They brought two covered wagons on a journey that took 10 days. Soon after, other homesteading families arrived.

Main Street, Grace, 1914.

These settlers, joined by several other homesteading families, built a bridge over the Bear River in 1893. Egbert and Sullivan had homes on the north side of the bridge which became a center of commerce and trade in the valley.

A year later, Egbert and Sullivan circulated a petition for a post office. During their deliberations on what to name the post office and town, Attorney Frank Bean of the Land Office in Blackfoot suggested they use the name of his wife – Grace. They liked the name and completed the application. The postal authorities agreed, and the new Grace Post Office opened in the Sullivan home.

Many of the first homesteaders filed claims near streams and meadows where fresh flowing water for irrigation was available. Later, settlers filed homestead claims on the more arid parts of the valley. They believed they could build irrigation systems to divert water from the Bear River a few miles upriver where the elevation was several hundred feet higher. Accessing the water, however, was problematic as it flowed through a deep rock canyon.

Parade in Grace, 1950.

For several years, beginning in 1895, multiple attempts to bring irrigation water ended in heartbreaking failure. One of the first was to build a wooden gravity-flow flume that brought a canal of water into the valley. However, in the first winter, heavy snow collapsed the wooden flume.

Then on March 4, 1897, John Trappett, George Stoddard and David Sullivan filed for 200 cubic feet per second of water from the Bear River under the name Last Chance Canal Company. For the claim to meet federal requirements, water had to flow in the canal by February 12, 1902.

Local farmers built the dam and canal cooperatively without outside capital. When the winter of 1901 to 1902 hit, they were still working on the canal and had a considerable distance to go.

With the February 12 deadline approaching, they developed an innovative solution to meeting the regulatory deadline. They built a flume from snow on which they splashed water that immediately turned to ice. They then ran water from the diversion dam through the Last Chance Canal. That spring they built a permanent flume. In June 1917 the Utah Power and Light Company (UPL) challenged the company's water right in court. Three years later, the court ruled in favor of the Last Chance Canal Company.

In 1908 Telluride Power Company – later acquired by UPL – built a hydroelectric dam on the Bear River with the power plant located a few miles south and about 530 feet below the dam. Water was delivered to the power plant through a large pipe.

The Oregon Short Line Railroad completed a five-mile branch line to Grace from its main line at Alexander in 1913.

Incorporation

The village of Grace incorporated on August 18, 1915. By **1916** there were four hotels, several retail stores, grain elevators, a flour mill and a printing office. On September 12, 1967, the village became an incorporated city in accordance with a change in state law.

Turning Points

Irrigation Development of the Last Chance Canal was critical to the future of the city's agriculture-based economy. Without adequate supplies of irrigation water, the area's farms could not have produced the seed potatoes for which the city of Grace has become famous.

Electrical Power Plant The 1908 construction of the hydroelectric dam with its power plant near Grace initially provided electricity solely for the mines in Bingham, Utah, and Eureka, Nevada. However, as soon as power became available, a group of community leaders in Grace organized a small public utility. They constructed a transmission line from the power plant to Grace, purchased electricity from the plant and resold it to its ratepayers. In 1929 UPL purchased this small electric utility.

The construction and operation of the utility was an important source of employment for the city. Many of the power plant employees and their families lived in company housing next to the plant.

Railroad The Oregon Short Line Railroad branch line to Grace served the growing base of agricultural commodity production, the city and the power plant, which in 1915 was the largest in the UPL system. The railroad provided the impetus for the town's next stage of growth and incorporation as a village.

Grace Today

Grace, 1971.

Amenities and Attractions The city maintains a two-acre park that includes playground facilities, a covered pavilion, picnic facilities and a ball field.

During the first week of August, the county sponsors the annual Caribou County Fair and Rodeo at its fairgrounds in Grace. This is a major production for the city. In addition to the rodeo, exhibits, events and carnival rides, the fair features a children's parade; watermelon bust; sidewalk sale; and a main parade with floats, school bands, horses and fire trucks.

Every March, the city hosts a three-day little league basketball tournament with about 16 teams competing.

The Gem Valley Performing Arts Center is located next to Grace High School. The high school uses this beautiful 520-seat facility for drama and music classes and performances. Each year, the Grace Chamber of Commerce sponsors a series of cultural events at the center.

New sewer plant, 1983.

Black Canyon lies a mile west of Grace. Visitors are taken by surprise when they first see the canyon that appears from almost nowhere as the 100-foot-deep narrow gorge cuts straight through solid lava rock. Its deep pools and gentle terraces make Black Canyon a favorite spot for anglers and kayakers. Black Canyon's whitewater has received national attention on the American Whitewater website and in the American Whitewater Journal. In 1997 the Journal printed an article about Black Canyon's whitewater entitled "Amazing Grace (Idaho) – one of the most difficult kayak runs in the country."

The Pioneer Historic Byway generally follows Idaho Highway 34. The byway connects 18 historical sites and unique natural features. It begins on the Idaho/Utah border near Franklin – Idaho's oldest town – and passes through Grace as it continues north then east on the pioneer trail to the Idaho/Wyoming border and Yellowstone National Park.

The Idaho Department of Fish and Game manages the 2,400-acre Blackfoot River Wildlife Management Area (WMA) 28 miles northeast of Grace. The WMA is open year round for bird watching, and viewing big game that congregate in the area during the winter. During hunting seasons, sportsmen hunt migratory and upland game birds as well as elk and deer in and near the WMA.

Niter Ice Cave is located three miles south of Grace. Thousands of years ago, a volcanic eruption formed a huge lava tube that became a cave. Early settlers in the area used the cave to store food and as a year-round source of ice. The cave is a favorite picnic spot and recreation site.

Boating, fishing and water skiing are available in nearby reservoirs. The six-mile-long Alexander Reservoir, formed by a hydroelectric dam on the Bear River, is seven miles northeast. The 15-mile-long Blackfoot Reservoir lies 30 miles northeast of the city. The much smaller Chesterfield Reservoir is 30 miles northwest. Two hot springs resorts are within short driving distances from the city – Lava Hot Springs 20 miles northwest and Riverdale Resort 25 miles south near Preston. Five miles north is the start of the Hudspeth Cutoff on the Oregon Trail. Visitors can still see the ruts carved by immigrant wagons as well as nearby pioneer burial sites.

The nearby national forests and public lands, streams and reservoirs offer a wide variety of outdoor experiences. In the winter, snowmobiling, skiing, sledding, snowboarding and skating are popular. The area also offers excellent fishing, camping, hunting, kayaking, water skiing, riding ATVs, mountain biking and hiking.

Grace City Hall, 2005.

Economy and Major Employers The Grace School District with 100 employees is the city's largest employer. Heritage Safe Company, a gun safe manufacturer, has about 26 employees. The city has over 35 agricultural-based businesses and an industrial park. Heritage Safe and other businesses that have built facilities in the park are diversifying the city's economy. Many residents commute to work. The majority work at the phosphate mining and manufacturing businesses in and around Soda Springs.

Education The Grace School District provides most of the city's public education. All of the district's schools are located in the city.

The closest institution of higher learning is Idaho State University, 55 miles northwest in Pocatello.

Health Care Grace has a doctor and a dentist. The nearest hospital is Caribou Memorial Hospital and Living Center in Soda Springs. The hospital has 24-hour emergency service. The city has ambulance service through the County with volunteer emergency medical technicians and drivers from the city and surrounding areas responding to the calls.

Transportation Idaho Highway 34 intersects the city. U.S. Highway 30 is five miles north. Interstate 15 is 32 miles northwest.

The closest airport is the 3,500-foot runway in Soda Springs, serving light private and charter aircraft. The closest commercial airfield is in Pocatello.

Railroad freight service is available in Soda Springs.

Utilities and Services Private companies provide electricity, telephone, gas,

Internet and satellite services. The City provides water, sewer, solid waste and fire protection. The Caribou County Sheriff's Department provides police protection.

Vision for 2050

Since 1960 Grace's population has grown 30 percent. However, by 2050 several actions and influences will likely cause Grace's population to more than double.

The city's industrial park has already attracted a number of light manufacturing and service businesses. Although the current industrial park is full, the city is looking into purchasing more property for industrial use.

Many future residents will be parents looking for a small, clean community nestled in the mountains with clean air and water and a hometown atmosphere in which to raise their children. An increasing number of seasonal residents and second homeowners will come to Grace seeking the joy that comes from living in a small quiet community near the mountains and nature – a place with moderate summer weather and other outdoor amenities including winter recreation, hunting, fishing, hiking and boating. An increasing number of residents are choosing to live in Grace and commute to larger cities for their employment. This will continue. Other residents will use technology to work at home.

Some of the new residents will be retirees who prefer living in a more peaceful setting within a short distance of services offered in nearby larger cities.

The city of Grace is currently doing an engineered water study and an engineered wastewater study, recently completing an engineered transportation plan. This work will help determine the future growth of the city.

Even though the city has no promotional campaign to attract seasonal residents, second homeowners or retirees, many of these families have moved to Grace.

Grace Elementary School has a wonderful program for children with special needs and US News and World Report has recognized Grace Senior/Junior High School as one of the "Nation's Best High Schools."

Mayors

1915 L. Sumner Pond *
1916 John Roghaar *
1921 A.R. Dawson *
1923 John Hubbard *
1927 Moroni W. Lowe *
1935 L. Sumner Pond *
1941 Moroni W. Lowe *
1942 William Stalder *
1943 J. Floyd Smart *
1946 Harold Peterson *
1947 Louis Stalker *
1949 Dr. C.C. Johnson *
1951 Harold B. Lowe *
1968 Clarence D. Simmons
1972 Harold B. Lowe
1976 Douglas A. Campbell
1979 Fred B. VanVleet
1981 Kenneth Roberts
1982 Roy Corbett
1984 Berdell C. McCurdy
1994 Kelly Holt
2002 Ronald W. Coombs
2006 Charles Titcomb
2014 Jackie Barthlome
* Village Chairman

Soda Springs geyser.

Soda Springs

Statistical Data

Population: 2,980 *
Elevation: 5,760 feet
Precipitation: 19 inches **
Average Snowfall: 44 inches **
County: Caribou
Website: www.sodaspringsid.com

Temperature Range – Fahrenheit: **
Spring: 33 to 63
Summer: 42 to 78
Fall: 17 to 43
Winter: 12 to 33
* U.S. Census July 1, 2015
**Historical averages

Soda Springs is located in the beautiful mile-high Bear River Valley, 40 miles north of the sparkling blue waters of Bear Lake. Lush open meadowlands of former years are now beautiful ranches and fertile irrigated farms. The cold, clear Bear River runs to the western edge of the city and fills two reservoirs.

The Aspen Mountain Range of the Caribou-Targhee National Forest overlooks the city from the north and east. The Wasatch Mountain Range overlooks the city on the west and south.

Soda Springs derives its name from the effervescent crystal-clear spring water that bursts from the ground. Early Oregon Trail visitors referred to the area as an "Oasis on the Oregon Trail."

Pre-Incorporation Years

American Indians called the valley of the Bear River with its hundreds of bubbling and boiling springs "Tosoiba" – the land of sparkling waters.

Oregon Trail ruts near Soda Springs.

Early explorers and trappers made it a point to visit the valley to drink water from the bubbly soda springs that they called "Beer Springs" because the effervescent water reminded them of lager beer.

One of the first explorers, Captain Benjamin L. E. Bonneville, gave the following account of an 1833 frontier rendezvous at Beer Springs. "On reaching them, the men threw themselves into a mock carouse. Every bubbling spring had its jovial knot of hard drinkers, tin cup in hand, quaffing, pledging, toasting and singing drinking songs. It was a singular and fantastic scene ... These groups of trappers, hunters and Indians, with wild costumes and wilder countenances; their boisterous gayety and reckless air, making merry around these sparkling fountains."

Dr. Marcus Whitman and his wife, Narcissa, and the Rev. Henry H. Spalding and his wife, Eliza, recorded their visit: "July 30, 1836, Went today ten miles off our route to visit Soda Springs."

In 1841 the first immigrant wagon train traveled on what would become the Oregon and California Trails. On reaching Soda Springs, the party divided. One group of 32, led by Thomas Fitzpatrick and Father Pierre de Smet, turned northwest toward what is now Oregon. The other group of 37, led by John Bidwell, headed west to California.

Fort Connor, 1863.

The California Gold Rush of 1849 brought hundreds of wagons and thousands of immigrants through the valley. Their journals and diaries reflect the excitement of visiting this historic Oregon Trail oasis. References are often made of visiting one of the springs they called "Steamboat," a particularly active spring that emitted sounds reminiscent of a steamboat.

One Oregon Trail immigrant family of seven experienced tragedy at Soda Springs in 1861 when they stopped to hunt for lost horses. The next morning three trappers saw a wagon by a creek and went to investigate. They discovered the bodies of a father, mother and their five children killed by Indians. George Goodhart, one of the trappers, wrote:

" ... I was selected to carry the message (to the wagon train of immigrants in which the family traveled). When I told them what had happened they said, "They were a family of our own train. We were waiting for them to catch up. The reason they were behind was that their horses had strayed away from the others and they had to hunt them up. They told us to go ahead; as they believed they would find the horses and catch up by night."

"They hitched onto a light wagon, and three men and two of the women got in and came back with me. We all decided that the best thing we could do was to bury them in their own wagon box, for we had no lumber to make a coffin ... We went and got the dead emigrants' horses and hitched them to their wagon, then hauled the bodies in it to the place of burial. We took them out and laid them down on the ground. Then we took off the wagon bed and placed it in the grave after it was dug."

The beautiful Idanha Hotel was built to lodge people who were traveling through by train.

Today, a wagon box headstone marks their gravesite in the Soda Springs Fairview Cemetery.

In late 1863 General Patrick E. Conner, the military commander over the Idaho/Utah/Nevada area, established a fort and the first settlement in Soda Springs. The purpose of Fort Conner was to suppress Indian raids along that stretch of the Oregon Trail and protect the U.S. mail routes.

A colony of dissenters from The Church of Jesus Christ of Latter-day Saints (nicknamed Mormons – see The Region, Pioneer Settlements) led by Joseph Morris came with Conner's soldiers to the new fort. Morris's group of settlers built several cabins in a low meadow near the fort and called their community Morristown.

Hooper Springs Park.

Several months earlier in January 1863, Conner led a brutal attack on an encampment of Northwestern Shoshone Indians near what is now Preston. The military termed the conflict the Battle of Bear River. Others have called it the Bear River Massacre. (*See The Region, American Indians – Bear River Massacre.*)

Conner would later use the fort as the location for signing a peace treaty with the Shoshone Indians. In 1865 the military abandoned Fort Connor.

In 1870 Brigham Young, President of The Church of Jesus Christ of Latter-Day Saints (Church), and William H. Hooper bought the elevated land northeast of Morristown for a settlement that, a year later, several families of Church members would settle and name "Upper Town." Because of its lowland setting, Morristown was called "Lower Town." In 1924 Lower Town would be covered with water along with Beer and Steamboat Springs when Idaho Power and Light Company completed the hydroelectric Alexander Dam.

In 1881 community leaders successfully petitioned the U.S. Land Office to combine Lower Town and Upper Town into a single community called Soda Springs.

The next year, the Oregon Short Line Railroad began building a line between Granger, Wyoming, and Huntington, Oregon, with a depot in Soda Springs. The rail line, completed in 1884, provided the connecting link between the commercial centers of Omaha, Nebraska, and Portland, Oregon, and created another transcontinental railroad.

Incorporation

On May 18, 1896, the Bannock County Commission approved incorporation of Soda Springs as a village. The petition stated that the city had more than 200 but less than 1,000 residents.

On February 18, 1921, the legal status of Soda Springs was changed to a city of the "second class."

Turning Points

Events Underpinning the Founding of Soda Springs A sequence of three seemingly unrelated events led to the founding of Soda Springs. First, the "oasis" quality of the effervescent soda springs attracted early frontiersmen and Oregon Trail immigrants. Followed by General Conner's selection of the site for Fort Conner and the near concurrent acquisition of land and settlement around the fort by pioneers coming up from Utah.

Railroad The establishment of a train depot in Soda Springs was important to the future growth of the city, but the most important role the railroad played was providing the transportation link needed to develop the high-grade phosphate rock ore deposits discovered a few decades later. With the development of the mines, community leaders and investors built the beautiful Idanha Hotel along with parks and other amenities to accommodate railroad travelers.

Idaho's Oldest and Newest County Seat The city itself claims a unique position among Idaho cities. It is both the oldest and the newest county seat in Idaho.

Idaho became a territory on March 3, 1863, and the first Territorial Legislature met nine months later in Lewiston. Its first official act was to create Owyhee County whose boundaries encompassed the lands lying south of the Snake River and west of the continental divide.

Within seven weeks, the legislature realized it had made a mistake by making Owyhee County too large. So it split off what is now Oneida, Bear Lake, Bannock,

Bingham, Bonneville, Jefferson, Madison, Fremont and Teton Counties into a new county called Oneida and made Soda Springs the county seat. It was the first county seat named in Idaho Territory.

Oneida County's first courthouse was the upstairs of the adobe brick Fort Connor. One night in 1866 advocates of Malad City as the county seat broke into the courthouse, stole the county books and records and transported them by covered wagon to Malad. The next year, the legislature made Malad City the seat of Oneida County government.

It would take over a half century and the creation of three more counties, each encompassing Soda Springs, before the city would again be designated as a county seat and the legislature ended its historic process of reducing large counties down to more manageable sizes.

The effort started in 1919 when Representative E. D. Whitman of Soda Springs proposed legislation to divide Bingham County into two counties. His bill drew little attention until he began explaining the value of the municipal hydropower-generation facility operated by the City of Soda Springs.

That got the ball rolling and on February 11, 1919, Governor D. W. Davis signed the law creating Caribou County with Soda Springs as the county seat. Caribou County was the forty-fourth and last county created in Idaho making Soda Springs the last city designated as a county seat.

Phosphate Mining and Processing Prospectors looking for precious metals discovered the vast deposits of black phosphate rock in the late 1800s. However, they mistook it for coal or perhaps copper ore and abandoned their claims.

Captive geyser.

Around 1903 Charles C. Jones, a mining engineer with Mountain Copper Company, Ltd., heard of coal deposits near Montpelier. When he investigated, he recognized the ore as phosphate and identified several deposits in the region. The deposits near Soda Springs are among the highest quality in the world.

In 1920 the Anaconda Copper Company developed an underground phosphate mine nine miles northeast of Soda Springs. Using the last syllables of the company's name, they called the company town that grew up around it Conda. The J.R. Simplot Company would eventually buy the mine. When the ore reserves played out at Conda, Simplot moved its mining operations to the phosphate deposits in the eastern extremes of Caribou County near the Wyoming border. Today Simplot operates an ore slurry line pumping station at Conda. Agrium, Inc., has a plant in the area that it calls Conda where it primarily manufactures a variety of phosphate-based commercial fertilizers.

In 1952 Monsanto Chemical Company built a phosphorous furnace plant just outside Soda Springs that produces elemental phosphorus. The open-pit phosphorus mines located about 15 miles north supply the plant. Monsanto's operation was a major economic boost to the community.

During this time, the methods used to mine phosphate ore changed from underground to strip mining. In the strip-mining process, excavators remove and stockpile the top soil, exposing the ore. After they remove the ore, they put the top soil back and plant native grasses, brush and trees.

Soda Springs Today

Amenities and Attractions The city has five municipal parks. Two parks, Hooper Springs and Octagon Springs, feature public fountains of the clear artesian soda water, for which the city was named.

People often drink the naturally effervescent water as it streams from the fountains or mix it with powdered punch, fruit juices and sweeteners to replicate flavors similar to commercial carbonated beverages.

Hooper Springs Park has a covered pavilion and springhouse with restrooms, benches, picnic areas, children's playground and a basketball court.

Octagon Springs Park has old-growth trees, a covered pavilion, restrooms and a wooden boardwalk.

Geyser Park is a prominent city landmark. Every hour on the hour, a geyser of lukewarm water and carbon dioxide gas shoots 100 feet into the air.

The geyser is not naturally occurring. In 1937 well drillers, attempting to find hot water for a swimming pool broke through a pressurized chamber at the 315-foot level releasing a geyser of water and gas.

The well now has a pressure cap and timer that releases the built-up pressure, producing the geyser. The park has a visitor center, boardwalk and picnic area. Residents have a tongue-in-cheek saying that their geyser is more faithful than Yellowstone's Old Faithful.

The 20-acre Arthur Kelly Park has a pavilion, restrooms, concession stand, two softball fields, two tennis courts, two youth fishing ponds, a playground, picnic tables and an outdoor ice rink. Perhaps the most prominent features of the park are the walking and equestrian trails that wind among the lava reefs, native juniper trees and ponds. In the winter, the City grooms the trails for cross-country skiing.

Corrigan City Park is located downtown and is the city's busiest park. Its 12 acres have two lighted tennis courts, a basketball court, a baseball diamond, a skate park, two sand volleyball courts, a little league diamond, a pavilion, two children's playground areas, an outdoor stage, restrooms, shade trees and picnic tables. The City holds most of its outdoor events in this park. The park is also the site of the Veterans Memorial and two historic artifacts – the "Dinkey Engine" and the "Conda Bus."

When Alexander Dam was under construction, the undersized "Dinkey Engine" hauled supplies to the dam. When the reservoir began to fill with water, the engine became trapped and had to be abandoned. In 1976 when the reservoir was drained for repairs, there sat the Dinkey Engine. The Union Pacific Railroad retrieved and restored the engine and donated it to the City of Soda Springs.

The Soda Springs Public Library has over 40,000 books, computers with Internet access and programs for children and those interested in writing and the arts.

The Pioneer Museum is located in a log cabin east of the Fairview Cemetery. The museum is open from Memorial Day to Labor Day and features artifacts used by early settlers including the operating table of Dr. Ellis Kackley, a physician who came to Soda Springs in 1898 and built the city's first hospital in 1927.

The Enders Hotel and Museum is both a museum and a bed and breakfast. This historic hotel, built in 1917, is located next to the Geyser Park Visitor's Center. It has 30 rooms furnished in early 1900s decor. Numerous artifacts and antiques of that period are on display throughout the hotel.

The Winter Carnival, Fishing Derby and Cross-Country Ski Race are held the third Saturday of January.

The city's July 4th celebration includes a community breakfast, parade, games, theater production and fireworks at Kelly Park. Other summer events include the Pizza's Run Car Show and the Caribou County Mud Challenge, a 4 x 4 Mud Race at Kelly Park.

The Christmas Craft Bazaar takes place the second week in November with food and entertainment. The Christmas Park Lighting Ceremony and arrival of Santa Claus for the children takes place on the Friday following Thanksgiving. The Community Christmas Concert is on the second Sunday in December.

Monsanto Chemical Company's manufacturing process has become a regional landmark and attraction. Outside Monsanto's manufacturing facility is a large mountain of grey calcium silicate slag produced when crushed phosphate rock, silica quartzite and carbon are heated in electric furnaces to 1,400 degrees centigrade.

Five times an hour, 24 hours a day, this molten slag is poured off into 600-cubic-foot cast-steel pots mounted on special trucks that haul it to the edge of the tailings pile and dump it. Where the slag is dumped, bright yellow and orange molten rock flow down the side of the slag mountain.

Visitors drive out of their way to see Monsanto's "man-made lava flow." The view is particularly spectacular at night.

Soda Springs is an outdoor paradise. The nearby lakes, river, reservoirs and streams abound with fish. The mountains have large populations of big game, migratory birds and other wildlife. In the winter, sportsmen enjoy snowmobiling and cross-country skiing. Ice fishing is a common attraction. Many residents and visitors view this area as one of the prime fishing and hunting spots in the Western United States.

Two Idaho Fish and Game wildlife management areas are located near the city. The 3,349-acre Georgetown Summit Wildlife Management Area for elk, mule deer and sharp-tailed grouse is 12 miles southeast and the 2,400-acre Blackfoot River Wildlife Management Area for cutthroat trout and upland and riparian wildlife is 18 miles northeast.

Economy and Major Employers The city's downtown has a variety of retail, financial and service businesses. Many residents also travel about 60 miles northwest to Pocatello to shop.

Originally, agricultural products suited for this high-mountain climate underpinned the city's economy. Hay, wheat, barley, potatoes, sheep and cattle were the primary commodities.

Farming and ranching are still important industries but phosphate mining and processing the ore into elemental phosphorus and commercial fertilizers are now the city's economic mainstay.

Monsanto is the city's largest employer with a payroll of about 500. Agrium, Inc., employs about 400, including contractors. The J.R. Simplot Company operates the Smoky Canyon Mine on the Idaho/Wyoming border and slurries the ore over 90 miles to Pocatello. The slurry line pumping station north of Soda Springs has about 20 employees.

Caribou Memorial Hospital employs 110. The city's largest public employers are the Soda Springs School District at 150, Caribou County at 50 and the City, itself, has about 30 employees.

Education The Soda Springs School District provides most of the elementary and secondary education. It operates a high school, alternative high school and middle, intermediate and primary schools in the city.

The closest institution of higher learning is Idaho State University in Pocatello.

Health Care The 27-bed Caribou Memorial Hospital and general clinics provide most of the city's medical care. In addition, there is a 21-bed assisted-living center and a 37-bed nursing home associated with the hospital.

Transportation Two byways intersect the city. The Pioneer Historic Byway – Idaho Highway 34 – extends about 50 miles due south to the Utah border and 30 miles due west to the Wyoming border. The Bear Lake-Caribou Scenic Byway – U.S. Highway 30 – intersects the city to the southeast. Federal Interstate 15 lies 33 miles west of town.

The city's airport with its 3,500-foot runway serves light private and charter aircraft. The closest commercial airport is in Pocatello. Railroad freight service is available in the city.

Utilities and Services Private companies provide telephone and satellite service. The City provides electricity, water and municipal wastewater services and police and fire protection. The County provides solid waste services.

The City owns two hydroelectric power plants at canals on Soda Creek. The City also purchases wholesale electrical energy from the Bonneville Power Administration.

Similar to private utilities, the City sells its electrical power to its customers at a profit but at rates that are among the lowest in the nation. It uses those profits to defray the cost of city services.

Vision for 2050

Over the past four and a half decades, the city's population has grown by about 31 percent from its 1960 base of 2,424. If this trend continues, by 2050 the city's population will exceed 4,000. However, it is probable that future growth will exceed historical trends.

Abundant water, open land, improved transportation infrastructure and technological innovations will be the catalyst for increased industrial expansion. The city's existing industrial businesses will be part of this expansion and remain in Soda Springs.

Well before 2050 the Idaho Department of Transportation will have widened U.S. Highway 30 to four lanes to accommodate the increase in commercial truck traffic traveling to I-15. The Highway 30 corridor will attract additional commercial development.

The city will experience the spill-over effect of growth occurring in many surrounding communities. Businesses involved with tourism and outdoor recreation will become an increasingly larger part of the city's economic base. Main Street Soda Springs will have many eateries and professional suites. In order to accommodate the consolidation of all the county school districts, school patrons will have approved a new high school and expansion of the middle and elementary schools.

View of Soda Springs from Rabbit Hill.

The City will have built a new library and improved its parks to accommodate an increased variety of recreation and year-round uses. Octagon Springs Park will be the new home for the Veterans Memorial. Needed improvements to City water and municipal wastewater systems will have been made to meet future needs and the regulatory requirements for wells and septic tanks. The airport will be relocated and developed to meet the increased demands of personal air travel.

The city will have a new community and fitness center to meet the growing demand of citizens making health and exercise a greater priority in their lives.

Mayors

1896 C.T. Woodall *
1903 J.D. Woodall *
1905 D.J. Lau *
1907 H. Dorrien *
1917 ** T.H. Horsley *
1919 Paul Tipton *
1921 Henry L.Finch
1929 J.W. Lauritson
1933 S.E. Matthews
1947 T.K. Gunnell
1953 A.L. Ozborn
1955 Allen H. Tigert
1964 Reed Stoddard
1966 Chris Phelps
1970 Allan H. Tigert
1974 Milton B. Gambles
1978 David Clegg
1986 Kirk L. Hansen
2014 James R. Smith

* Village Chairman

** Records unavailable from 1908 to 1916

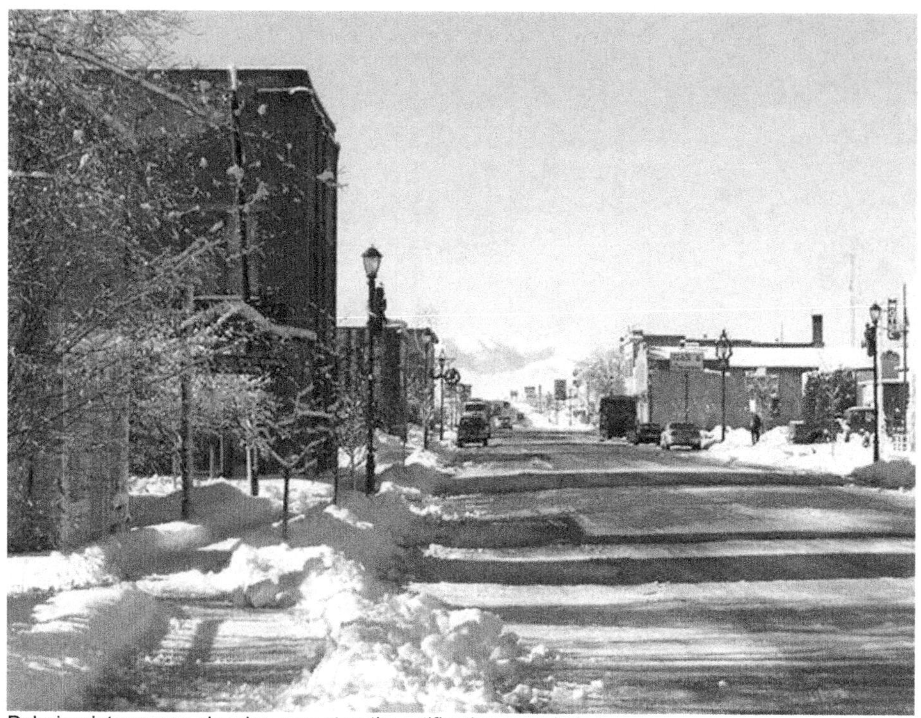
Dubois winter scene showing new streetbeautification completion.

CLARK COUNTY

- Dubois (*County Seat*)
- Spencer

Visitors touring the Dubois Civil Defense Caves.

Dubois

Statistical Data

Population: 597 *
Elevation: 5,145 feet
Precipitation: 12 inches **
Average Snowfall: 8 inches **
County: Clark

Temperature Range – Fahrenheit: **
Spring: 38 to 65
Summer: 48 to 81
Fall: 23 to 43
Winter: 15 to 33
* U.S. Census Bureau Estimates July 2015
**Historical averages

An impressive natural attribute of the city is its beautiful setting. Surrounding the city are unobstructed vistas of the upper Snake River Plain, foothills and mountains.

The city lies at the base of the Centennial Mountains and Caribou-Targhee National Forest. The 6,870-foot-high Monida Pass over the Continental Divide and the Montana border are less than 30 miles north.

In 2002 Dubois added to its peaceful setting by completing the beautification of its city entrance and downtown. Trees, lights, sidewalks and curbing now line city streets.

Dubois is the county seat for Clark County, the least populated county in Idaho. The population of Dubois represents over two-thirds of the entire county population. However, this small population belies the significance of some of the public agencies and private businesses that have operations in or near Dubois.

Pre-Incorporation Years

Prior to the railroad, Dry Creek – now Dubois – was a rest area for freighters, animals and stagecoach passengers and drivers as they traveled north to the mines in Montana.

In the late 1870s the Oregon Short Line Railroad built a rail line from Corrine, Utah, to Butte, Montana. In 1879 the line reached Dry Creek.

When laying railroad track, it was the practice of the railroad to construct rail lines in sections. The terminus of one of these sections was Dry Creek.

However, the original railroad "roundhouse" was not built at Dry Creek. It was built 16 miles south at Camas. Three years later in 1882, there was a serious drought in Camas and the railroad's well went dry.

Original site of Dubois along railroad.

Railroad officials decided that Dry Creek had a much better water supply. Accordingly, they moved the roundhouse and other buildings to Dry Creek. There they drilled a well and built a water tower, telegraph office and section house. Several men worked at the roundhouse and operated the helper engines used to get the trains over Monida Pass.

Around 1897 at the suggestion of Francis A. Pike, a principal in the Miller and Pike Company Store, the town changed its name to Dubois – after Fred T. Dubois.

Fred T. Dubois.

Fred T. Dubois was a former U.S. Marshal, Territorial Delegate to the U.S. Congress and – after Idaho became a state on July 3, 1890 – represented Idaho in the U.S. Senate.

Dubois was a leading influence in Idaho becoming the nation's 43rd state.

He also is well known for his efforts in creating; maintaining; and, as U.S. Marshall, enforcing Idaho's 1884 test oath against members of The Church of Jesus Christ of Latter-Day Saints (Mormon). The law was repealed in February 1893; however, the test oath preserved the dominance of Dubois's political party and disenfranchised Idaho Mormons from voting, holding public office and serving on juries for nine years. (*See Eastern Idaho – Politics, Polygamy and Voting Rights.*)

In the next several years, the city grew from its early railroad roundhouse location to its present location west of Beaver Creek – formerly Dry Creek.

Soon homesteaders began filing claims on potential farmland in the area. (See Southwest Idaho – Cities of the Magic Valley.) Over the next few decades, this gradual influx of new residents shifted the city's principal economic base from the railroad to agriculture and livestock.

Several Christian denominations played important roles in the city's development. In 1904 the Protestant Episcopal Church built the first church in Dubois. Its architecture is early Gothic Revival. In 1940 the Roman Catholic Church purchased the building. Around 1960 local residents purchased the church and converted it into the Heritage Hall Museum, which displays historical antiques and artifacts of the area.

In 1917 the Community Baptist congregation built their church.

Early days mail carrier from Dubois to Small.

In 1919 the Church of Jesus Christ of Latter-day Saints erected its first church north of the town site. In the early 1940s church members relocated the building near the center of town. The building was expanded and remodeled two times after moving it to the new site. In 2001 the church constructed a new building and donated the old building to the Clark County School District.

Incorporation

On November 15, 1916, the Fremont County Commissioners approved a petition making Dubois an incorporated Village, with Charles H. Oakley as Chairman. At the time, Dubois had a population of about 600.

The June 26, 1918, newspaper business directory listed approximately 30 retail businesses, a bank, two medical doctors, a dentist, veterinarian, lawyer and a school with 200 students and five teachers.

Early Dubois roundhouse.

It described the Oregon Short Line Railroad facility as having an eight-stall roundhouse that could handle five helper engines and crews. It said that the railroad's monthly payroll exceeded $20,000.

The article referenced that the town had sold $40,000 in bonds for a municipal water well and conveyance system.

It described the surrounding country as "the best dry farming land in the entire West."

Turning Points

Railroad The first key turning point occurred in 1882 when the railroad established a roundhouse at Dubois. That action established the village and set in place all that would follow.

In 1927 the railroad shut down the roundhouse operation, and many jobs were lost.

County Seat On February 1, 1919, the Legislature created Clark County with Dubois as the County Seat. At that time, the population of the village was still near 600.

Early Dubois water tank for trains with coal chute.

Even though its population has not changed appreciably over the past 86 years, the character and economic base of the city have changed dramatically.

Civilian Conservation Corps and Civil Aviation Administrative Service The Great Depression of the 1930s also caused the loss of many jobs; however, in 1938 the economy improved. The Civilian Conservation Corps (CCC) brought 195 men from Illinois and Wisconsin to build public facilities near Dubois. The CCC first constructed their barracks near what is now the location of Lindy Ross Elementary School. They then built a road and bridge across Beaver Creek to Highway 91. Some of the workers married local women and remained in Dubois to raise families.

About the same time, the Civil Aviation Administrative Service (CAA) built an airport at Dubois with flood and beacon lights. Three decades later, the Federal Aviation Administrative Service replaced the CAA and moved the operation to Idaho Falls.

Cold War The cold war with communist countries had another direct impact on Dubois. About one mile north of the city is a smooth-floor "lava tube" – 35 feet deep, 700 feet long and 60 feet wide. Around 1962 the Army Corps of Engineers licensed the cave as a shelter in the event of nuclear attack. When complete, the ventilated facility had a two week supply of water, food, medicine and electrical generating power to handle 2,200 people from Clark County and the western part of Jefferson County. The shelter is now sealed and under the direction of the Clark County Commissioners.

Dubois railroad depot.

Agriculture The advent of deep wells and sprinkler irrigation has had a profound effect on Dubois area farms. It brought the rolling hill dry-farm land under irrigation. Land that was previously devoted to winter wheat now grows alfalfa hay and potatoes.

This added diversity of agricultural commodities has encouraged new businesses and employment. For example, Larsen Farms potato processing and alfalfa hay compacting plants employ many Dubois residents.

The 1915 decision by the U.S. Department of Agriculture to build its Sheep Experiment Station near Dubois has been another stimulant to the city's economy.

Tourism Another important turning point is emerging. Dubois's natural geographical setting and location are becoming more attractive for tourists and outdoor recreation enthusiasts.

Hand sketch of present-day Heritage Hall Museum, originally the First Community Episcopalian Church.

Dubois Today

Amenities and Attractions The city has several amenities designed to be helpful to residents and visitors – including two municipal parks and the Heritage Hall Museum.

The building that houses the Heritage Hall Museum was the first church built in Dubois. It is a Gothic Revival style building and is listed on the National Historic Register. The Protestant Episcopal and Roman Catholic congregations used the building before it became a museum.

The City of Dubois donated its old city hall to the Community Library Board. The board received several grants to remodel the building. It now houses the city library and visitor's center.

Near the Interstate 15 exit, are several private businesses offering fuel, food and camping facilities.

In early April each year, the Dubois Ranger District of the Caribou-Targhee National Forest hosts "Sage Grouse Days." In April, the Greater Sage Grouse and the Columbian Short Tail Grouse congregate for mating. The Dubois Ranger District personnel coordinate and encourage visitors to come to learn of the wildlife habitat and observe the grouse during the mating rituals as they dance

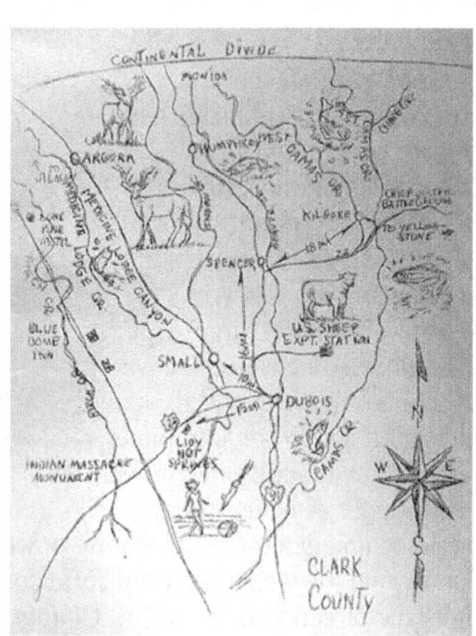

Hand-drawn map, 1960.

near their “leks.”

Economy and Major Employers Most sheep ranchers across the nation are familiar with Dubois. The 48,000-acre U.S. Sheep Experiment Station (USSES) begins six miles north of the city. The USSES operation has over 3,000 mature sheep of several breeds. After lambing season each year, the sheep population swells to 6,500. Sheep not needed for research are sold. The station has about 30 full-time research scientists, technicians and workers including two from the University of Idaho. Part-time employment swells during wool shearing and lambing seasons.

Dedication of Dubois Rest Area: Bonnie Burns, Marva McGarry, daughter of B.H. and Annie Thomas, Harry and Thelma Harn and Mayor Herb Sill. Thomas and Harn donated land for the Rest Area.

Larsen Farms is one of the largest family-owned agriculture businesses in Idaho, Colorado and Nebraska. The corporate offices of the company are in the City of Hamer, 17 miles south; however, it has significant operations near Dubois. The company has a fresh-pack warehouse and shipping facility, a potato processing plant and an alfalfa hay compacting facility within a few miles of Dubois.

The highest grade of potatoes are packaged and shipped fresh. They process lesser grades into dehydrated and other potato products.

Larsen’s hay processing terminal is a 120,000-square-foot facility that grinds and compresses top quality alfalfa hay into compressed bales for shipping across the nation. Owners of high-value animals such as racehorses are major customers.

Early steam powered train taking on water and coal at Dubois water tank.

The Dubois Leather and Shoe Shop is a niche business owned by Steve and Bev Gilger. They have developed a business of making and repairing customized tack and cowboy boots. The excellent quality of their work is in demand by “Old West” enthusiasts residing throughout the nation.

The district office of the Caribou-Targhee National Forest is located in Dubois and has been there for over half a century.

The Spencer opal mines yield exceptionally fine opals. The mines are located about 13 miles northeast of the City of Spencer. The miners and those who process the opal live in Dubois and Spencer.

Survey crew working before construction began for city beautification project.

Education Clark County has a single public school district. The schools are all located in Dubois. Students in the outlying areas are bused.

Pre-school students through first grade attend Oakley Elementary School, a former church donated to the district in 2001 by the Church of Jesus Christ of Latter-day Saints after they constructed a new building. Students in grades 2-5 attend Lindy Ross Elementary School constructed in 1972. Older students, grades 6-12, attend Clark County Junior-Senior High School built in 2002.

BYU-Idaho, located less than 50 miles away, is the closest university.

Summer in downtown Dubois.

Health Care Most residents travel 40 miles to Madison Memorial Hospital in Rexburg or 50 miles to Idaho Falls Regional Medical Center for medical service.

The Seventh District Health Department is at Dubois one day per week to give immunization shots only. There are no other medical facilities. There are volunteer emergency medical technicians and an ambulance for emergencies.

Transportation During the gold rush days of the late 1880s, the Dubois "Hole-in-the-Rock State Station" was a railroad transportation hub. It was on the main gold trail from Corrine, Utah, to Montana with a spur connecting to the mines in Salmon, Idaho.

Today situated at the intersection of Interstate 15, County Road A-2 and State Highway 22, the city is still a transportation hub.

Dubois Municipal Airport has a 4,750-foot runway and provides service for light charter and private aircraft. The nearest commercial airport is 50 miles south at Idaho Falls.

Utilities and Services Private companies provide the city's telephone and electrical services. Water and sewer are municipal systems.

Vision for 2050

By 2050 Dubois may lose its small-town atmosphere, but will be substantially larger than it is today due to influx of people moving to a less populated area from the cities south.

Dubois is strategically located for increased tourism. The Lost Gold Scenic Trail Loop, established in 2002; the Nez Perce Trail; the Fort Henry Historic Byway; Sacagawea Scenic Byway; Craters of the Moon National Monument and Yellowstone National Park are all accessible through Dubois. These attractions will continue to entice visitors seeking the frontier trails and scenic wonders of this area.

Many private businesses will have built facilities in or near Dubois to capitalize on the increased tourism traffic passing through the city on Interstate 15, State Highway 22 or Clark County Road A-2.

By 2050 Clark County Road A2 will be improved and connected to Island Park Highway 20. The Idaho Department of Transportation will also have completed the Dubois Rest Area and the overpass.

The City will have either built or entered into a public-private partnership to construct an 18-hole golf course and a Skate Park for youth.

The Clark County Library and Visitors" Center along with the popular Heritage Hall Museum will retain their historic and restored facilities. Our children and visitors must learn and remember the city's colorful heritage.

Recently, Dubois has had new homes, churches and businesses constructed. This infill will continue. Residents will either restore or replace existing vacant buildings. Open lots will either have structures built on them or will be beautified and maintained.

Photo Credits for Dubois Chapter: from Clark County Historical Society Collection (donated from various sources to the Historical Society), also Clark County Enterprise, Rexburg Standard Journal, Jefferson Star, Harry Harn, Jackie Hoopes, Dubois Forest Service, Beaver Creek and Community Baptist Churches, U.S. Postal System, Department of Highways, and Railroad.

Mayors

1917 C.H. Oakley *
1919 L.D. Reynolds *
1921 C.E. Jones *
1927 S.C. Idol *
1929 W. Garretson *
1929 H.R. Harn *
1935 H.R. Webster *
1937 Wm. E. Laird *
1941 B.H. Thomas *
1943 C.B. Waring *
1945 O.A. Rasmussen *
1949 R.D. Laird *

1955 Paul Stolt *
1947 O.A. Rasmussen *
1959 H.E. Kator *
1961 L. Youngstrom *
1963 L.E. Hodges *
1963 C.B. Waring *
1967 C.B. Waring
1972 H.P. Sill
1976 O.M. Wagoner
2000 Keith R. Tweedie
2012 Randy Mead
* Village Chairman

Spencer

Statistical Data

Population: 33 *
Elevation: 5,860 feet
Precipitation: 13 inches **
Average Snowfall: 28 inches **
County: Clark

Temperature Range – Fahrenheit: **
Spring: 22 to 65
Summer: 45 to 84
Fall: 20 to 73
Winter: 10 to 33

* U.S. Census Bureau Estimates July 2015
**Historical averages

Spencer lies at the base of the Caribou-Targhee National Forest, 15 miles south of the 6,870-foot-high Monida Pass on the Continental Divide and the headwaters of Beaver Creek.

To the southwest of the city are vast acreages of public lands managed by the BLM. To the southeast is the 48,000-acre United States Sheep Experiment Station. Rexburg, the closest urban center, is 45 miles southeast. Dubois is 15 miles south.

Situated in the broad ravine created by Beaver Creek, the land around Spencer has been for centuries a thoroughfare for travelers moving between Eastern Idaho and western Montana. It has been the path used by American Indians, gold miners, stagecoaches and freight wagons. Today, the railroad and Interstate 15 intersect the city which is also the location of the largest known opal gemstone deposit in Idaho.

Pre-Incorporation Years

For centuries, nomadic American Indians – principally of the Shoshone and Bannock Tribes – occupied the land of the Upper Snake River Plain.

In 1810 Captain Andrew Henry led the first party of explorers/trappers into the region. About 35 miles southeast of what is now Spencer – near what is now St. Anthony – they built a log stockade and shelter, which they named Fort Henry, on the Henrys Fork of the Snake River. They spent the winter at the fort and trapped for beaver. In the spring, they moved on.

In October 1811 the Wilson Price Hunt party stayed at the deserted Fort Henry for two weeks while they built canoes with which they unsuccessfully attempted to navigate the Snake River to the Columbia River and the Pacific Ocean.

In 1863 prospectors discovered placer gold in what is now western Montana – then part of Idaho Territory. Stagecoach and freight wagon traffic began moving passengers, food and supplies from northern Utah to the Montana gold fields on a pioneer wagon road named the "Gold Road."

The road generally paralleled what is now I-15, crossing the Continental Divide at Monida Pass and then on to the Montana boomtowns of Virginia City, Butte and Garrison – a distance of 466 miles between Ogden, Utah, and Garrison.

Hiram H. Spencer.

In 1789 the Utah and Northern Railroad Company built a rail line that generally paralleled the Gold Road. The railroad made the stagecoach and freight wagon road obsolete.

A few years later, the railroad company built a roundhouse, well, water tower, telegraph office and section house at what is now Dubois. Several men worked at the roundhouse and operated the helper engines used to get the trains over Monida Pass.

Fifteen miles up into the mountains, railroad officials built a station they named Spencer after Hiram H. Spencer, a local merchant and customer of the railroad. They platted the town and applied to county officials to make the town an incorporated village.

Incorporation

On July 28, 1947, Spencer became an incorporated village.

Turning Points

Railroad Spencer had its origins as a railroad town during the time trains had to stop frequently to take on water and fuel. When innovation in train engines allowed longer hauls between stops, the trains ceased their routine stops at Spencer.

Opal Mine In 1948 two deer hunters discovered the opal gemstone mine. In 1964 they sold their claim to the Stetler family. The mine is now open to the public. Visitors and rock hounds can work the mine and purchase raw opal or buy opal jewelry at the mine or two other jewelry stores in the city. The mine now underpins the city's economy.

Spencer Today

Amenities and Attractions The opal mine at Spencer is a tourist attraction. Open to the public, rock hounds and other visitors enjoy working the mine. Raw opals and opal jewelry are also available for purchase.

Every spring during their mating seasons, the Greater Sage Grouse and the Columbian Short Tail Grouse congregate in sagebrush clearings in what is termed "Leks." At these times, the male birds perform a ritualistic dance that involves fanning their spike-looking tail feathers and inflating the large air sacks around their necks.

In April, the Caribou-Targhee National Forest Dubois Ranger District hosts the annual "Sage Grouse Days" in Dubois. As part of the activities, visitors and wildlife students travel great distances to observe the large wild birds in their Leks and receive information and instruction from district personnel.

Spencer Opal Mines.

Perhaps the most

significant attraction for Spencer residents is their close proximity to public lands, rivers and lakes. The area around Spencer offers excellent fishing, hunting, camping and boating opportunities in both Idaho and Montana. Most Forest Service Roads are available for hiking and biking, some for ATV riding and, in the winter months, snowmobiling is popular.

Economy and Major Employers The city has no dominant employers. The city's commercial district consists of the mine, a cafe, a restaurant and bar and two jewelry stores.

Education Clark County School District provides K-12 education for Spencer children who ride buses to the schools in Dubois, 15 miles away.

The closest institution of higher learning is Brigham Young University-Idaho in Rexburg.

Health Care The closest hospital is Madison Memorial Hospital in Rexburg.

Transportation Interstate 15 intersects the city.

Dubois Municipal Airport has a 4,750-foot runway and provides service for light private and charter aircraft. The closest commercial airfield is Idaho Falls Regional Airport, located 63 miles south of Spencer.

Utilities and Services Private companies provide electricity, telephone and satellite services. The homes and businesses have individual wells and septic systems. Police protection is provided by the Clark County Sheriff's Office under contract with the City.

Vision for 2050

In 1960 Spencer had a population of 100. A decade later, the population fell to 45. In 1990 there were 11 residents in the city. By 2000 the population had come back to 38. The future growth of the city is a function of the broader economy and tourism. Recent historical trends will likely continue for several years. By 2050 the city's population should exceed 50.

Construction of a smelter in 1880 gave birth to Clayton. Courtesy Clayton Historical Association & Museum.

CUSTER COUNTY

- Challis (*County Seat*)
- Clayton
- Mackay
- Stanley

Aerial photo of the City of Challis.

Challis

Statistical Data

Population: 1,056 *
Elevation: 5,288 feet
Precipitation: 7 inches **
Average Snowfall: 17 inches **
County: Custer

Temperature Range – Fahrenheit: **
Spring: 26 to 67
Summer: 46 to 85
Fall: 23 to 74
Winter: 12 to 39
* U.S. Census Bureau Estimate July 2015
**Historical averages

Challis is located on the western edge of the fertile 30-square-mile Round Valley. The Salmon River flows about a mile east of the city as it passes through irrigated farm and ranch land, sagebrush-covered foothills and Black Cottonwood forests lining the riverbank. Garden Creek flows through the historic center of Challis as it makes its way to the Salmon River. Sun Valley is 14 miles due south; however, traveling on paved highways, it is 60 miles away.

The city is in the Challis National Forest in one of the most sparsely populated parts of Idaho and near some of the most rugged and scenic parts of the state. The 12,662-foot Borah Peak, Idaho's highest mountain, is 30 miles southeast. The 11,820-foot Castle Peak of the White Cloud Mountains is 30 miles south. The Frank Church-River of No Return Wilderness Area begins a few miles west of the city.

Challis is the Custer County seat. Federal agencies manage 93 percent of the county's 3.2 million acres. The diversity of the terrain is striking. Some high mountains are shafts of bare rock jutting into the sky. Lower elevations grow native plants including pine, juniper, sagebrush and a variety of grasses and woody and flowering plants.

The valley, mountains, rivers and streams are home to many species of wildlife including mule deer, white tail deer, elk, bighorn sheep, hawks, bald eagles, osprey, migratory waterfowl, trout and migratory steelhead and salmon. Wildlife watching is an everyday activity in Challis.

Mining and ranching were Challis' first industries and continue to influence the life and character of the city and its residents.

Pre-incorporation Challis.

Pre-Incorporation Years

The first non-Indians to enter Round Valley came in 1822 when Michael Bourdon, a Hudson's Bay Company fur trapper, led a party into the valley to trap beaver.

In 1824 Alexander Ross led a party of 144 men, women and children through the area.

In 1830 John Work entered Round Valley, trapping beaver and hunting buffalo. He wrote that "Banack Snake" Indians had recently camped in the valley and that buffalo had grazed the grass short.

In the early 1870s prospectors discovered placer gold in the Yankee Fork River. A gold rush ensued with numerous mining claims filed throughout the region.

One of these claims belonged to three prospectors working the Yankee Fork. In 1876 they discovered a major gold ore body. They named their find the General Custer Mine after General George Custer who had died two months earlier in the Battle of the Little Big Horn in Montana. In 1881 the Idaho Legislature created Custer County. They chose to name the county Custer because of the General Custer Mine and the prospering mining community of the same name.

After working their claim, the three prospectors concluded that they would not or could not develop the mine by themselves. They sold their mine to an English firm named Hagen and Grayson (H&G). In 1878 H&G developed the town of

Bonanza near the mine site and an ore-processing mill and town north of the mine that they called Custer. By 1911 the mines played out and Custer and Bonanza became ghost towns.

The mine owners needed large quantities of supplies and heavy mining equipment to develop the mines and support the miners. Alex Toponce, a freighter and entrepreneur, obtained a charter from the Idaho Legislature to build a toll road between Challis and Bonanza. He completed his toll road in 1879. In 1933 as part of the federal effort to put people to work during the Great Depression, the Civilian Conservation Corps (CCC) reconstructed the old toll road.

Most freight came to the mines from Corrine, Utah, over a wagon trail to the Montana gold fields known as the Gold Road. At Blackfoot, freighters turned north off the Gold Road to what is now the city of Challis.

In 1869 railroad interests completed the transcontinental railroad at Promontory, Utah.

A decade later, the Utah and Northern Railroad Company began building a railroad line that generally paralleled the Gold Road. In 1878 the railroad reached Blackfoot, which greatly speeded travel time to Challis. From Blackfoot, supplies and passengers to Challis and the mines still came on mule and horse-drawn freight wagons and stagecoaches.

Putting in the sidewalks, 1892.

The 1870s was a hectic period. Homesteaders came into Round Valley to raise cattle and crops for sale to the miners. Freighters brought their goods to a trailhead staging station where they prepared their loads for crossing the mountains into the land of the Yankee Fork.

In 1876 Alvah P. Challis and his associates saw a need to build a community that could serve the freighters, miners and homesteaders. They laid out a townsite and named it Challis. In 1881 Richard H. Browne prepared the formal plat for the town.

By 1880 the population of Challis exceeded 600 and had several buildings including three hotels and four saloons. The next year when the Legislature created Custer County, the county voters elected Challis as the county seat.

The economy remained strong for over a decade; however, after that the mines began to play out and employee layoffs ensued. In 1894 fire destroyed much of the Challis business district. Owners rebuilt many of the buildings but the decline in the mining industry was taking its toll on the community. By 1900 Challis's population had fallen to 398.

In 1907 Congress created the Challis National Forest and made its headquarters in Challis. Today the Salmon-Challis National Forest headquarters are in Salmon. Challis is currently the headquarters to the Middle Fork Ranger District, one of six ranger districts in the national forest.

This event proved helpful to the city's economy as the Forest Service hired local men and women to help build roads, ranger stations and campgrounds and control forest fires.

Incorporation

On October 16, 1907, Challis became an incorporated city.

Turning Points

Mining and Ranching The discovery of gold on the Yankee Fork River in the early 1870s and Challis's strategic location as a transportation center were the primary factors that led to the city's founding.

The light colored stones, located in the Challis High School, are from the 1922 Challis High School. The plaque to the left says, "These stones are from the old 1922 high school. The Earthquake of October 28, 1983, damaged the high school beyond repair."

Since its founding, the city's economic stability has experienced dramatic swings that parallel the boom and bust cycles of the area's mining communities. The decline in mine production at the Bonanza and Custer and Bayhorse Mines during the late 1800s and early 1900s was a major economic blow to Challis. The city's economy avoided collapse because of the economic strength of the cattle ranching, tourism and outdoor recreation industries.

Subsequent mining discoveries have also produced boom and bust turning points. For example, in 1967 prospectors discovered a large ore body of molybdenum – a hardening agent used in the production of steel – near Clayton, about 20 miles south of Challis. Mine production began in 1983, and the mine soon reached a peak employment of 400. Many of these families moved into new residential subdivisions built in Challis. However, by 2001 molybdenum prices had collapsed and the mine personnel had declined to just 20 employees. Many of their new Challis homes were sold and trucked to other towns.

Great Depression and the CCC During the Great Depression of the 1930s, one of the federal CCC projects was the reconstruction of the historic toll road between Challis and Bonanza. As in times of old, Challis became the transportation hub for the movement of construction materials and personnel to the remote CCC camps and work sites. This reconstruction project breathed economic life into the Challis economy.

Adapting to the Changing Economy While mining and cattle ranching were the city's economic drivers of the past, businesses catering to tourism and outdoor sports and recreation are taking the economic lead in the city today.

Most of the people who now use the land in this beautiful region come for relatively brief periods to camp, hike, hunt, fish, ski, ride snowmobiles or ATVs and re-live the region's rich history. As a result, an entire body of businesses has started to promote and serve this growing market.

Challis today.

Challis Today

Amenities and Attractions The 10-acre Challis Centennial Park lies adjacent to the high school. The park has a pavilion, picnic facilities, playground, amphitheater, tennis courts and ball fields. The city also has a nine-hole golf course.

Challis's cultural venues include the North Custer Historical Society Museum, Land of the Yankee Fork Interpretive Center, Mad Dog Art Gallery and events sponsored by the Challis Arts Council. Many of Challis' historic log buildings survive in the downtown business and residential district. Challis has 23 historic buildings listed on the National Register of Historic Places.

Two miles south of town at the junction of State Highway 75 and U.S. Highway 93 is the interpretative center of the Land of the Yankee Fork State Park. The interpretative center has historic exhibits of the mining history of the region, a gold panning station and audiovisual programs.

The interpretative center in located on a 21-acre site that includes campgrounds and the Challis Bison Jump – a location where mounted American Indians chased unsuspecting herds of Bison off a 59-foot cliff to be slaughtered for food, pelts and tools.

The Idaho Department of Parks and Recreation, the Salmon-Challis National

Forest and the Bureau of Land Management manage the greater park area that lies within a 90-mile loop called the Custer Motorway Scenic Drive.

The loop extends 46 miles southwest over a former toll road built in 1879 to the mining ghost towns of Custer and Bonanza. This section of the loop crosses over an 8,800-foot-high pass and has many sections that are unimproved and unsuitable for low-clearance vehicles and trailers. The loop then continues south past the Yankee Fork Gold Dredge to Sunbeam on State Highway 75, past the mining town of Clayton, and then returns north to Challis.

Today the U.S. Forest Service and Friends of Custer Society have restored many of the old buildings still standing at Custer and the few buildings left in Bonanza. Fires swept through Bonanza in the late 1800s and destroyed most of that town's buildings. Both guided and self-guided tours are available in Custer.

The Yankee Fork Gold Dredge is located on the Yankee Fork River, two miles south of Bonanza. Beginning in 1940 this 112-foot-long by 54-foot-wide and 64-foot-high dredge dug temporary dams on the river on which it floated, removing eight-yard buckets of gravel at a time as it moved across the valley floor digging and washing the gold from the gravels. By 1952 after producing about $1.1 million of gold and silver, an amount slightly under the cost of production, the dredge shut down. The owner then donated the dredge to the U.S. Forest Service leaving behind over five miles of dredge tailing mounds.

Main Street.

Annual events in Challis include the Lilac Festival, the Steelheader's Ball, Challis Rodeo, the Choral Rendezvous and the Braun Brother's Reunion outdoor concert.

Challis Hot Springs, located five miles north of the city, is a camping resort with an outdoor geothermal mineral water swimming pool with camping and RV hook-up facilities near the Salmon River.

Downhill and cross-country skiing are available at the nearby Chipmunk Ski Hill – a single surface lift facility.

In addition, the area around Challis has hundreds of miles of dirt roads and trails. In the summer anglers fish for steelhead trout and salmon in the Salmon River and its tributaries. Many others hike into one of the high-mountain lakes, such as Bayhorse and Buster. Other activities include camping, hiking, hunting, riding snowmobiles or ATVs and floating the Salmon River.

Economy and Major Employers The Challis School District has about 110 employees and is the city's largest employer. The U.S. Forest Service is second with 90 employees. Custer County has over 40 employees headquartered in the city.

Challis is the community and business center for the farms and communities within a 30-mile radius. Many residents work at two full-service grocery stores, hardware stores, restaurants, banks, bars, and other retail and service businesses.

Agriculture is an important industry for the city; however, technological innovation and consolidation has improved the industries' productivity with significantly fewer employees. Fewer families coming to town to shop has had an adverse effect on the city's economy.

Mining is also important to the city's economy. In the past decade, low metal prices and federal environmental requirements have caused many area mines to close or significantly reduce operations. However, with recent increases in metal prices, mining activity is beginning to increase.

Education The Challis School District provides most of the K-12 education. The school district comprises over 4,000 square miles. The Challis middle and high schools and one of its elementary schools are located in the city. The closest institution of higher learning is 137 miles south at the College of Southern Idaho in Twin Falls.

Health Care There is a general medical clinic in the city. The closest hospital is Steele Memorial Hospital 47 miles north in Salmon. Hospital services are also available 56 miles south at St Luke's Wood River Medical Center in Ketchum.

Transportation U.S. Highway 93 intersects the city. State Highway 75 to Stanley and Sun Valley branches off from U.S. 93 two miles south of town.

The 4,600-foot runway at Challis Airport is two miles north of town. The airport serves as the jumping off point for flights into the Frank Church-River of No Return Wilderness and other backcountry destinations. The closest commercial airfield is Friedman Memorial about 70 miles south in Hailey.

Utilities and Services Private companies provide electricity, telephone and satellite services. The City provides water and sewer services and fire and police protection. The County provides solid waste services.

Vision for 2050

If historical trends continue, by 2050 Challis' population will approximate 1,000. However, should new mining activity in the area develop or the demand for outdoor recreation and tourism increase, the city's population will exceed historical trends. The city's present municipal systems are adequate to handle existing needs and moderate growth. However, the city will undertake improvement to enhance the quality of life for its citizens and strengthen its economy.

Mayors

Unknown
???? Janette Burstedt Piva
2008 Jay Cook
2010 Mark Lupher
2016 Ike Funkhouser
* Village Chairman

Aerial view of Clayton. Courtesy of Clayton Historical Association & Museum.

Clayton

Statistical Data

Population: 7 *
Elevation: 5,489 feet
Precipitation: 7 inches **
Average Snowfall:17 inches **
County: Custer
Website: www.claytonidaho.org (historical assoc. & museum site)

Temperature Range – Fahrenheit: **
Spring: 9 to 59
Summer: 34 to 78
Fall: 13 to 68
Winter: -2 to 34
* U.S. Census Bureau Estimates, July 2015
**Historical averages

Clayton is a historic silver-lead ore-smelting town located in the Salmon-Challis National Forest. The Frank Church-River of No Return Wilderness Area begins a few miles north of the city. The 11,820-foot-high Castle Peak of the White Cloud Mountains is about 20 miles south.

The city consists of about two dozen homes and a bar set on a relatively flat bench of land near the mouth of Kinnikinnic Creek as it flows into the Salmon River. Kinnikinnic is the name of a mixture of leaves and bark, sometimes mixed with tobacco, first used by American Indians for smoking. Challis is located 25 miles north and Ketchum is 95 miles south.

Pre-Incorporation Years

In the early 1870s prospectors discovered placer gold about 20 miles due west of what is now Clayton on the Yankee Fork River. A gold rush ensued with numerous mining claims filed throughout the region.

In the late 1870s prospectors discovered numerous deposits of silver-lead ore up Kinnikinnic Creek in the mountains of the Bayhorse Mining District. However, they had no means to process the ore and extract the metals.

In 1879 J.E. Clayton and a group of Omaha investors formed the Idaho Mining and Smelting Company (IMS&C) and began plans to build a mill, smelter and general store at a townsite they named after Clayton. The company bridged the East Fork of the Salmon River and built a road east to the north-south wagon road used by freighters bringing supplies from the rail depot at Blackfoot to Challis.

Kinnikinnic Creek in fall. Courtesy of Clayton Historical Association & Museum.

The July 17, 1880, issue of Yankee Fork Herald reported conditions at that time, " ... we reached the mouth of Kinnikinnic [creek], distant from Bonanza [gold mining town on the Yankee Fork River] 30 miles. Here we found a streak of business. Everything was bustle and stir ... .Men were coming on every trail to get employment or to locate. Wages were $2.50 (a day) with board and $3.50 without. A town will be built fast as materials can be had ... .The company [IMS&C] will have a road completed to East Fork in time for the machinery ... All the idle men in Challis have been put to work at East Fork [road and bridge] and Kinnikinnic and fifty more were needed at last account."

Early Clayton from the east. Courtesy Clayton Historical Association & Museum.

On September 15, 1880, the mill started operations with a capacity of processing 30 tons of ore per day. Freighters hauled the ore from the mines in the mountains to the smelter on heavy wagons. For the first two years the smelter ran on coke shipped in from Pennsylvania. Subsequently, the company employed 48 men to harvest timber and produce 180 tons of charcoal annually to feed the smelter furnaces.

The mill closed during the winter because of the heavy snows. Clayton's population fluctuated with the annual opening and closing of the mill. Those who remained in town purchased their supplies from the IMS&C store.

Incorporation

Clayton was first incorporated as a village, and then on September 26, 1960, Clayton became an incorporated city.

Ice House. Courtesy Clayton Historical Association & Museum.

Turning Points

Mining Clayton is a town founded at the confluence of Kinnikinnic Creek and the Salmon River by the IMS&C around 1879 as the site for its silver-lead ore smelter and company store. The town's mining-based economy has endured decades of boom and bust business cycles.

In 1910 the IMS&C store closed and other stores opened. In 1921 Mark Crawford led a group of investors who leased and refurbished the old company store including the addition of hardwood floors and a stage to make it suitable for a dance hall and school functions.

The smelter and store. Courtesy Clayton Historical Association & Museum.

In the early 1920s as a means to secure a captive source of lead for manufacturing of auto batteries, Ford Motor Company began acquiring silver-lead mining claims throughout the Bayhorse Mining District. They built homes in Clayton for some of their mine employees. By 1926 Ford had acquired all of the IMS&C holdings, including the smelter and store.

A few years later, Ford closed the smelter and shipped its concentrated ore to a more efficient smelter in Tooele, Utah. During the 1930s Ford dismantled the smelter and sold metal for scrap. Around 1946 Ford sold the mine to H.F. Magnuson Company. However, the old company store remained open and served as the post office until 1950. The building is listed on the National Register of Historic Places and is now home to the city's museum.

In 1967 prospectors discovered a large ore body of molybdenum, a hardening agent used in the production of steel, on Thompson Creek about six miles west of Clayton. However, mine production did not begin until 1983 and soon reached a peak employment of 400. While many of the mineworker families lived in new residential subdivisions in Challis, the mine had a significant positive effect on Clayton's economy until 2001, when molybdenum prices reached a low point and mine operations largely ceased. However, by the end of the decade prices improved and mine operations resumed.

Highway 75 In 1935 the Idaho Transportation Department constructed Highway 75. Ford Motor Company facilitated the road by granting an easement relocating Clayton's main street through town. The highway helped the city by facilitating tourist business and providing residents with easier access to other cities in the region.

Clayton Today

Amenities and Attractions The Clayton Museum is located in the old company store and is operated by the Clayton Area Historical Association. In 2008 the museum received the Preservation Society of Idaho's Orchid Award.

Idaho Mining & Smelter Company Store Museum. Courtesy Clayton Historical Association & Museum.

Clayton's most prominent attraction is its setting near areas of exceptional natural beauty. There are hundreds of miles of dirt roads and trails near the city. In the fall and spring, anglers come to the Salmon River to fish for steelhead trout. Salmon and trout season is in the summer. Whitefish are in season year round. Many outdoor enthusiasts hike in to one of the high-mountain lakes. Other activities include camping, hiking, hunting, riding snowmobiles or ATVs and floating the Salmon River.

Clayton 1900 to 1912. Courtesy Clayton Historical Association & Museum.

Today, the U.S. Forest Service and Friends of Custer have restored many of the old buildings at the mining ghost town of Custer located up Yankee Fork River about 28 miles northwest of Clayton. Both guided and self-guided tours are available. The EPA has also given the Idaho Department of Parks and Recreation a Brownfield Cleanup Grant for the historic Bayhorse Mining District. IDPR will clean up hazardous substances and create a 574-acre interpretative historic state park.

Also on the Yankee Fork is the Gold Dredge. Beginning in 1940 this 112-foot-long by 54-foot-wide and 64-foot-high dredge dug temporary dams on the river to create a reservoir upon which it floated, removing eight-yard buckets of gravel at a time as it moved across the valley floor digging and washing the gold from the gravels. By 1952 after producing about $1.1 million of gold, an amount slightly under the cost of production, the dredge shut down. The owner donated the dredge to the U.S. Forest Service leaving behind over five miles of dredge tailing mounds.

The New State Hotel. Courtesy of Clayton Historical Association & Museum.

Economy and Major Employers The resumption of Thompson Mine operations has not yet had an effect on Clayton's population. The local bar and home-based businesses provide most of the employment within the city. Some residents commute five miles east to the Three Rivers (flagstone) Rock Quarry and to Challis for work.

Education The Challis School District provides most of the K-12 education. Clayton students age K-4 attend school in Clayton. Older children ride buses to elementary, middle and high schools in Challis. The closest institution of higher learning is Boise State University, located about 108 miles southwest in Boise.

Health Care The closest medical service is a general medical clinic in Challis. The closest hospital is Steele Memorial, 85 miles north in Salmon.

Transportation Idaho Highway 75, the Salmon River Scenic Byway, intersects the city. Challis Airport has a 4,600-foot runway that can serve light aircraft. The closest full-service airport is in Boise.

Utilities and Services Private companies provide electricity, telephone and satellite services. The homes and businesses have individual wells and septic systems. The Custer County Sheriff's Office provides police protection.

Fisher's Blacksmith Shop & Livery Stable. Note branded doors. Courtesy of Clayton Historical Association & Museum.

Vision for 2050

In 1980 Clayton's population was 43. By 1990 it had declined to 26 where it has held for about two decades. The 2010 census showed that Clayton's population had declined to seven.

Absent population growth resulting from the resumption of operations at the Thompson Mine and increased tourist traffic, recent historical population trends will likely continue for decades. By 2050 Clayton will continue to be a peaceful little town that appeals to people who prefer a quiet lifestyle near some of the most scenic parts of Idaho.

Mackay circa 2005. Photo courtesy of Judy Malkiewicz.

Mackay

Statistical Data

Population: 483 *
Elevation: 5,900 feet
Precipitation: 9.5 inches **
Average Snowfall: 36 inches **
County: Custer
Website: www.mackayidaho-city.com

Temperature Range – Fahrenheit: **
Spring: 19 to 65
Summer: 42 to 85
Fall: 18 to 73
Winter: 4 to 36
* U.S. Census Bureau Estimates July 2015
**Historical averages

Mackay lies in the Big Lost River Valley of the Salmon-Challis National Forest. The Big Lost River flows from Mackay Reservoir four miles northwest and passes along the western edge of the city.

Two mountain ranges bracket the city. The Lost River Mountain Range with peaks rising to over 12,000 feet on the northeast and the White Knob Mountains with peaks over 11,000 feet to the southwest.

Valley residents often refer to Mackay as the "Top of Idaho" because it is over a mile high and near nine of the 11 highest peaks in Idaho including the 12,662-foot-high Borah Peak, the state's tallest.

The broader community of Mackay includes families who live outside the city limits. Many residents in unincorporated communities like Darlington, Leslie, Barton Flat, Alder Creek, Old Houston and Chilly have Mackay mail addresses.

The closest cities are Challis, the county seat, 54 miles northwest; Arco, 26 miles southeast; and Blackfoot 86 miles south. Idaho Falls is 96 miles southeast.

Pre-Incorporation Years

In 1879 prospectors discovered copper in the White Knob Mountains, a few miles west of the present-day site of Mackay and extending 20 miles west to the Copper Basin. Many of the ore bodies were also rich in lead, zinc, silver and gold. The general area is termed the Alder Creek Mining District. The richest discoveries were located on Mackay's "Mine Hill." (*See Eastern Idaho, The Region, Mining – Mackay – Copper, Lead and Other*.)

Stage to Mackay at the Houston Bridge, circa 1900.

In addition to the miners and prospectors working in the mountains those days, a few homesteads dotted the landscape from Willow Creek Summit, about 30 miles upriver from Mackay, down to the stage and freight stop 25 miles south at Kennedy's Corner near Arco.

The valley had a stagecoach and freight wagon stop next to the river bridge about four miles downriver from the present site of Mackay. The name of the stagecoach stop was Houston. It had a population of about 400. The stagecoach line was the main supply route connecting Blackfoot to the Challis and Salmon River mining camps to the northwest. (*See Eastern Idaho, The Region, Mining – Challis and the Yankee Fork – Gold and Salmon Area – Gold, Silver, Cobalt and Other*.)

Pouring the cement core during the construction phase of the Mackay Reservoir, circa 1918.

The White Knob Mining Company acquired the mines on Mine Hill around 1900. The company's principal owner was John Mackay, one of the investors in the mines of the Nevada Comstock Lode.

Mackay charged the company's chief engineer, Wayne Darlington, with managing the company and the mine.

Within a year, Darlington built the mine's infrastructure and smelter, arranged to have the Oregon Short Line Railroad build a spur line from Blackfoot to the smelter and platted a company town he named "Mackay" in honor of the principal owner.

Darlington required that the deeds to the platted lots carry a restriction against alcohol. Mackay was to be a "dry" town. However, in 1903 the City passed an ordinance repealing the restriction.

Empire Copper Company Smelter complex, circa 1905.

The mine complex included a 12-mile railway system to transport ore down the mountain to the new concentrator and smelter and a domestic water system for the mill and the town fed by springs on the hill.

With the development of Mackay, the town of Houston withered away. The exodus of businesses and residents from Houston to Mackay began almost immediately. Some of Mackay's first buildings such as the church parsonage and drug store were moved from Houston. The first buildings actually erected in Mackay were a print shop, a law office and the newspaper called the Mackay Telegraph.

Providing adequate lodging facilities for mineworkers and residents was a particular problem. The company removed some pressure by building 24 homes for some workers. Tents were common until miners built their own lodgings.

Mackay depot, circa 1920.

In September 1909 investors proposed construction of Mackay Dam, a project to irrigate 90,000 acres of which over 75 percent was west and south of Arco. With 570 registrations, it was the area's most successful land dispersal under the Carey Act. (*See Eastern Idaho, The Region, Federal Land Use Laws.*)

As originally planned, the dam would be 125 feet high. People living in Mackay and below the dam, bolstered by a prominent engineer's condemnation of the dam's design, fiercely objected to the project – too much risk the dam could fail.

The developers scaled back the height of the dam to 65 feet and proceeded building the system that included extensive irrigation canals and ditches.

However, the project was oversold – too little water to irrigate too much land located too far away from the reservoir. After disputes and lawsuits were settled, there was only enough water to irrigate 15,000 acres.

Incorporation

In response to a petition signed by 250 Mackay residents, the Custer County Commission in Challis approved incorporation of Mackay as a village with Wayne Darlington as chairman on October 14, 1901.

The town grew rapidly. When the village incorporated, hotels, lodging houses, churches and schools were under construction.

Rodeo Parade, circa 1951.

Turning Points

Mining Mackay owes its existence and very name to White Knob Mining Company owners and managers. Their decision to buy and develop the mines and town and bring in the railroad caused Mackay, rather than Houston, to be the area's dominant community.

Mine production peaked between 1910 and 1930. For the next three decades, the town experienced a roller-coaster economy caused principally by fluctuations in metal prices, labor conflicts, world wars and the Great Depression. The 1920 census listed the city's population at 1,309, which rose and fell with the economy until stabilizing at around 600 in 1960.

The patented mine property had numerous owners and, at other times, was in receivership or under control of Custer County or the Internal Revenue Service.

Mackay Business Park, May 2005.

The mine produced prodigious amounts of metal over its 50-year life. When mine operations finally ceased in 1975, Mine Hill had yielded 62 million pounds of copper; 15 million pounds of lead; 5 million pounds of zinc; 2 million ounces of silver; and 42,000 ounces of gold.

Railroad While mining was Mackay's backbone, the railroad insured the new community's success. The train not only carried passengers and goods for the mine, but served the towns and surrounding farm and livestock businesses as well.

The frequency of rail shipments in and out of Mackay tracked the decline in mine production. In 1971 just four years before the mine officially closed, the railroad ceased operations and later removed the track.

Panoramic view of Mackay, circa 1903.

Idaho National Laboratory The U.S. Atomic Energy Commission located what is now INL in Idaho Falls with a research site on the high desert between Arco and Idaho Falls in 1949. (*See Eastern Idaho, The Region, Idaho National Laboratory – Eastern Idaho's Largest Employer*.)

Today, about 30 INL employees live in Mackay and ride the INL bus to work. INL is Mackay's second largest employer.

Agriculture Farming and ranching added diversity and stability to the community's economy and local sources for fresh food. Construction of Mackay Reservoir not only provided water to irrigate many farms, it became one of the more prominent fisheries in the area.

May Main Street, circa 1904.

In more recent years, technological innovation and consolidation of farms and ranches has caused increased agricultural productivity with fewer workers. This decline in the agriculture workforce has had an adverse effect on Mackay's retail businesses.

Outdoor Recreation and Tourism With the decline of the mining and the railroad businesses, tourism has emerged as the economic focus of the community. City and community leaders' campaigns to promote the area's natural and historic attributes to tourists and recreationists are paying off. More and more people are coming to enjoy the natural beauty of the surrounding national forests and to fish and hunt and tour Mackay's historic mining district.

Mackay Today

Amenities and Attractions For a small city, Mackay has impressive amenities. It has two parks that are shaded by native black cottonwood and aspen trees, a public rest area and RV waste dump, a public tourist park and free camping area and a nine-hole public golf course.

The city has a public library and community senior center and is home to the South Custer Historical Society and its Lost Rivers Museum.

Community organizations include the Masonic Lodge; American Legion; Lion's Club; and the Mackay Women's Club, which dates back to 1907.

The Mackay Community Church, the Church of Jesus Christ of Latter-day Saints and St. Barbara's Catholic Church provide worship opportunities.

Mackay Main Street, 1940s.

To build the tourist attraction of its mining history and to help preserve its mining heritage, the City developed a self-guided tour of its "Mine Hill" in 2004. It includes scenic views and numerous, interpreted mining sites and structures. The tour has received national recognition and is included in a valley-wide ATV trail system sponsored by the Idaho Department of Parks and Recreation.

During the tourist season from May to October, most recreational vehicle parks are full. Throughout the year, sports enthusiasts travel great distances to recreate near Mackay.

Anglers come to fish for trout in the Big Lost River and Mackay Reservoir. Hunters come for trophy elk, deer, antelope, mountain goat and other big game that are abundant in the area. Hikers, bikers and campers visit the mountains to explore hundreds of high-mountain lakes and trails.

The historic Mount McCaleb Cemetery, overlooking Mackay Reservoir, was once the resting place of Captain McCaleb, leader of a six-man escort for freight wagons bringing goods from Blackfoot to Challis. McCaleb's body was later moved to Salmon. Attacked by a large war party of Bannock Indians, the 14 men in the convoy fought for two days. McCaleb was the only fatality among the defenders. (*See Eastern Idaho, The Region, American Indians.*)

Annual attractions include "Idaho's Wildest Rodeo," the "White Knob Challenge" mountain bike race and the regionally famous and heavily attended "Mackay Free Barbecue" held each September.

Economy and Major Employers In addition to INL, private employers include San Felipe Ranches, Lost River Rural Electric Cooperative, several retail businesses and a bank.

Mackay School District has over 40 employees and is the city's largest public employer. The Lost River District Office of the Salmon-Challis National Forest has 15 employees.

Local farmers, ranchers, the International Moose Foundation and the Lost River Highway Department add to the employment base.

The population of the greater Mackay area has remained relatively constant for 50 years. However, the demographics of the area have changed significantly. Retired and summer-only residents have increased while the number of young families with children has declined.

To encourage tourism and new businesses, the City has joined with other area communities, including Arco, to form the Lost Rivers Economic Development Inc. The city has also built a business park that currently has three tenants.

Since the end of active mining operations on "Mine Hill" years ago, some geological and exploratory testing has taken place and goes on today. However, even with current high prices for metals, the high cost of start up, the difficulty in meeting environmental regulations and the questionable amount of remaining ore reserves make resumption of mining operations unlikely.

Education The Mackay School District covers the greater Mackay area and includes a high school, middle school and elementary schools.

The closest institution of higher learning is the Idaho Falls Center for Higher Education.

Health Care The Mackay Clinic provides out-patient care service several days per week. A volunteer EMT group equipped with two ambulances provides emergency medical services. Residents also use medical facilities at the Lost Rivers Medical Center in Arco. Those with elective and non-emergency surgical procedures travel to one of the regional medical centers at Idaho Falls, Pocatello or Sun Valley for specialized or in-patient care.

Transportation U.S. Highway 93, the only north/south highway in Eastern Idaho, passes through the city. There is a 40-mile improved and partially paved county road that crosses over the mountains on the west to connect with Sun Valley and Ketchum. Using paved highways, the distance is 110 miles.

Mackay Main Street circa 2004. Photo courtesy of Judy Malkiewicz.

Light private and charter aircraft use the 4,400-foot runway at Mackay Airport.

Utilities and Services Private companies provide electricity, telephone and satellite services. The City provides water, sewer, law enforcement and fire protection with 18 volunteer firefighters. The County provides solid waste service.

Vision for 2050

By 2050 Mackay will be far different than it is today. A growing number of small businesses, tourism and agriculture will underpin the economy. It is unlikely that mining in any form will return. The population will include retirees from across the nation. They will move to Mackey to take advantage of the charm and beauty of this small but growing high-desert community surrounded by national forests and streams.

Responding to the city's stepped-up promotional efforts, many more INL personnel and their families will choose to live more economically in Mackey and either commute or telecommute to their jobs. Summer and winter recreational opportunities will bring increasing numbers of tourists.

The increased construction of affordable housing will be supported by necessary improvements to Mackay's public infrastructure. Many of these improvements will be in cooperation or partnership with the U.S. Forest Service, BLM and economic development organizations.

Expansion will not be restricted to Mackay's city limits. It will spread through the Big Lost River Valley. Though some ranches may give way to development, the ranching and agricultural industry will continue to have a stabilizing effect on the city's economy. Through all of the projected changes and growth, the most difficult task will be to maintain the quality of life associated with the quiet, laid-back lifestyle that attracted residents to this wonderful little community in the first place. Success may well depend on the community's continued strong optimistic spirit of hope and volunteerism. The Mackay of 2050 will be a better place.

Mayors

1901 Wayne Darlington *
1902 H.B. Garletz *
1903 J.F. Hendricks *
1904 H.B. Garletz *
1905 Alex Burnett *
1907 Charles Baker *
1913 Frank Leland *
1915 J.H. Greene *
1917 N.H. Farrell *
1918 J.R. Jones *
1918 George Morgan *
1919 Les E. Dillingham *
1927 Charles Baker *
1931 O.H. Tschanz *
1937 R.T. Greene *
1941 E. Glen Pence *
1945 Fred Diers *
1949 Ivan Taylor *
1950 B.C. Jones *
1953 Ivan Taylor *
1957 Lyle Ivie *
1959 Hilmer Lindberg *
1976 Oval Caskey
1992 Garn Dye
1994 Oscar Wornek
2004 Otto Higbee
2012 Lowell Frauenholz
2016 Wayne Olsen
* Village Chairman

Stanley Post Office.

Stanley

Statistical Data

Population: 68 *
Elevation: 6,240 feet
Precipitation: 14 inches **
Average Snowfall: 72 inches **
County: Custer
Website: www.stanley.id.gov

Temperature Range – Fahrenheit: **
Spring: 9 to 59
Summer: 34 to 78
Fall: 13 to 68
Winter: -2 to 34
* U.S. Census Bureau Estimates July 2015
**Historical averages

Stanley is situated in one of the most spectacular near-pristine regions of Idaho. The Frank Church-River of No Return Wilderness and the Salmon River Mountains lie to the north. To the south and west is the Sawtooth Wilderness. To the southeast is the White Cloud Mountain Range. The nearly 800,000-acre Sawtooth National Recreation Area that encompasses parts of three national forests – Boise, Salmon-Challis and Sawtooth – surrounds the city. (*See Eastern Idaho, The Region, Distinctive Geographic and Geologic Features.*)

The city lies at the northeast base of the Sawtooth Mountain Range, sometimes referred to as America's Alps. The range includes over 33 distinctive peaks – the tallest, Thompson Peak, towers over Stanley at 10,751 feet.

There are hundreds of alpine lakes in the mountains surrounding Stanley. Redfish Lake, the most famous, lies five miles south of the city in a picturesque setting near the base of the 10,299-foot-high Mt. Heyburn.

The White Cloud Mountain Range, so named because of its many cream-colored limestone peaks, is about 10 miles southeast of Stanley. Castle Peak, the highest peak in the range, rises to 11,815 feet and is one of the most notable mountain peaks in Idaho.

The Salmon River, the "River of No Return" and longest un-dammed and free-flowing river in the lower 48 states, flows through Stanley. The river's headwaters are about 30 miles south of Stanley in the Smoky Mountains and continue 425 miles through wilderness areas and deep canyon gorges before emptying into the Snake River about 50 miles south of Lewiston.

Stanley is about 60 road miles north of Ketchum and Sun Valley and about 130 road miles northeast of Boise. Stanley is renowned to be the coldest city in Idaho and the only city in the nation where three National Scenic Byways intersect.

Pre-Incorporation Years

Beginning in 1810 European trappers/explorers first came into Southern Idaho in search of beaver along the Snake River and its tributaries and to trade with the American Indians. (*See Eastern Idaho, The Region, American Indians and Early Trappers/Explorers*.)

In 1824 Alexander Ross of the British Hudson's Bay Company led a party of trappers over Lemhi Pass, trapped the Lemhi and Salmon Rivers and eventually moved over to trap beaver in what is now the Treasure Valley.

Early days in Stanley.

Following a skirmish with the Blackfoot Insians in 1831 where he lost several men, John Work, then manager of the Hudson's Bay operation in the area, retreated to the Salmon River to continue trapping. Finding few beaver, he left the area and never returned.

Prospectors discovered placer gold in the Boise Basin in 1862. The year following, 16,000 fortune hunters flooded the area, starting boomtowns wherever they made significant discoveries and branching out for hundreds of miles from the basin in their search for the precious metal. (*See Southwestern Idaho, The Region, Mining – Boise Basin Gold*.)

John Stanley, for whom the city of Stanley was named, was the oldest member of a party of 23 prospectors who had been working the gold fields of Warren, 50 miles northeast of McCall, and were leaving in search of better prospects in the streams to the southeast.

They worked their way through Bear Valley, Cape Horn and into the Stanley Basin panning for gold. They found gold on two dry gulches, but in order to effectively work the discovery, they would have to bring water from a long distance. Because of Stanley Basin's remote location from any supplies and concern about armed conflict with Indians that were in the area, they decided to leave.

Thirteen wanted to return to Warren, and the others wanted to go on to the Boise Basin. They divided their provisions and separated. Those working their way back to Warren suffered extreme hardship in the rugged river gorges, losing one man and many horses.

Conoco station, Stanley.

John Stanley and his nine companions headed southwest to Bannock – now Idaho City. They had only traveled 15 miles on an Indian trail when they came upon a band of 60 Indians who quickly dispersed into the trees. The men were fearful that the Indians had dispersed only to have a council of war before attacking them. However, they were relieved when seven of the Indians rode out in plain sight. A young man dismounted, removed his blanket and laid his rifle on the ground, a sign he wanted one of the white men to come unarmed to parley. Frank Coffin, who was accomplished in the Chinook language, was selected to go. After Coffin explained that they were a just a band of gold prospectors headed to Boise country, the Indians let them go.

Junior Class Dog Sled Races, March 2010.

A few years later, Coffin again met the young chief on the Wood River near what is now Bellevue. The chief recognized Coffin who had since grown a moustache and reminded his white friend that he had also changed – he was no longer a papoose chief.

For the next several years, small groups of prospectors continued to come into the Stanley Basin looking for gold with limited success. Warren Callahan, a gold prospector on the way to the Montana gold fields, discovered galena outcroppings – lead and silver ore – in the Wood River Valley in 1864. However, at that time, development of hard-rock mines in remote areas was problematic. Transportation alternatives and ore-refining technology were limited and there were still hostilities with American Indians.

By 1879 circumstances had changed. There was general peace in the area as the military had suppressed incursions by members of the Shoshone and Bannock Tribes the year before. In addition, technology for refining lead-silver ore had improved and expectations were high that the Oregon Short Line would soon be available.

With that news, about 3,000 prospectors converged on the Wood River Valley and the Stanley Basin. In the Wood River Valley, they found numerous deposits of galena ore, often lying in veins up to two feet thick. The veins contained 40 to 60 percent lead and up to 100 ounces of silver per ton. In 1880 lead sold for $.05 a pound and silver $1.50 an ounce. During this time, prospectors established the mining towns of Bellevue, Hailey and Ketchum. (*See Southwestern Idaho, The Region, Mining – Wood River Valley – Silver and Lead*.)

A few years later, other prospectors found gold and galena in areas they called Seafoam and Greyhound around 30 miles north of Stanley. A like distance to the east, others made major discoveries of gold on the Yankee Fork of the Salmon River, so named by a group of prospectors who called themselves Yankees and who had come and left empty handed over a decade earlier. (*See Eastern Idaho, The Region, Mining – Challis and the Yankee Fork – Gold*.)

Pioneer Park.

Stanley's location on a thoroughfare to the mines allowed it to become a supply center for many of the prospectors and miners working in these areas and a place where ranchers and farmers could sell their livestock and commodities.

Obtaining food and other supplies to supplement the wild game bagged by the prospectors and miners was problematic. Supplies were shipped long distances by freight wagon or packhorse. The goods were expensive. A mineworker who earned $3 a day had to pay $1.50 a dozen for eggs and $8 and $7, respectively, for a hundred pounds of potatoes and flour. Cats, used to control mice, cost $5 each.

In the spring of 1880 one of the Wood River Valley miners defied the conventional wisdom that asserted that the elevations were too high for farming. He successfully planted a garden of mostly potatoes.

Many settlers filed homestead claims in the Wood River Valley and the Stanley Basin, planting wheat and other crops that grew well in the short growing season to sell to the miners. Cattle and sheep ranchers brought in their herds to graze and sold meat and dairy products. These agricultural businesses became important additions to the Stanley Basin economy, and by 1880 the trail over Galena Summit to Ketchum had become a toll road.

In the late 1880s Arthur and Della McGowan filed a homestead claim in what is now Stanley. They raised cattle, opened a store and butcher shop and began supplying the miners. A few years later, the McGowan's successfully applied for a post office they named Stanley. In 1919 Bartlett Falls acquired the land and platted the Stanley townsite.

After several years, the panning method of extracting placer gold became unproductive. Confident that there was a lot more gold in the district's gravels, miners began dredging the previously worked streambeds for placer gold in 1889. The most famous dredge, the Yankee Fork Gold Dredge built in 1940, still stands as an artifact and museum about 30 miles northeast of Stanley, 12 miles north of the hamlet of Sunbeam.

Incorporation

Two major events contributed to Stanley's June 9, 1947, incorporation as a village. Early that year, the Idaho Legislature passed law governing the sale of liquor by the drink and the licensure of establishments offering those beverages. A provision of the law required businesses selling spirits to be located within incorporated cities or villages.

In that same year, Bill Harrah, the Nevada gaming industry magnate and founder of the Harrah Hotel and Casino complexes, began buying property in Stanley with plans to build hospitality and retail facilities, adding to those already operating in the town. As an incorporated village, Stanly was able to issue licenses to sell liquor by the drink.

Turning Points

Mining Located on a thoroughfare between the larger mining areas of the Wood River Valley and the Yankee Fork as well as the Seafoam and Greyhound mining areas, Stanley's early economy and that of nearby farms and ranches was tied to mining.

Lower Stanley Lower Stanley is an unincorporated community located on the western banks of the Salmon River, a mile north and downriver from Stanley. It is near the intersection of the Nip and Tuck Road, a trail used by the early miners, and present-day Highway 75.

As the two communities grew, their relationship grew apart and a crisp rivalry developed. One of the major reasons for the differences stemmed from both communities wanting the Stanley Post Office, thereby being able to lay claim to the "Stanley" name. Generally operating out of stores, the post office moved back and forth between the two communities until postal authorities built a permanent facility in what is now Stanley in 1943. However, that action did not soften the separatist feelings that still divide the two communities.

Today, the city of Stanley has grown to be the economic center of the Stanley Basin. Lower Stanley's commercial district consists of several small retail and hospitality businesses.

Bill Harrah Harrah's acquisition of Stanley property increased until his organization owned about half of the city. Bill Harrah's biographer wrote, " ... [He took] up fishing, which took him to Idaho and the Salmon River. He discovered real pleasure in fishing for steelhead, and riding horseback to his favorite fishing hole."

Bill Harrah died in 1978 at age 66. In recent years, the Harrah Trust has sold off most of its Stanley properties.

Harrah's efforts to build Stanley's hospitality businesses had a major positive effect on the city's economy. By divesting itself of its properties, Harrah Trust has benefitted the city by allowing today's entrepreneurs an opportunity to buy property and grow their businesses in Stanley.

Tourism. The trappers and prospectors who thought the riches of Stanley Basin lay in beaver pelts and placer gold were disappointed. Today, it is clear that the most valuable natural resource of the Basin is the sheer beauty and unparalleled majesty of the Sawtooth and White Cloud Mountain Ranges, broad meadows and alpine lakes. National magazines have listed these vistas as among the most spectacular in the lower 48. Today, tourism underpins Stanley's economy.

Stanley Today

Amenities and Attractions Stanley's Pioneer Park is located seemingly at the base of the majestic Sawtooth Mountains and is available for private reservations. It features a covered picnic shelter; bathrooms; picnic tables; a baseball diamond and bleachers; rustic log soccer goals; children's playgrounds; and, during the winter, a lighted outdoor ice rink.

Recurring events that draw tourists are the Sawtooth Mountain Mama's Arts and Crafts Fair, which takes place the 3rd weekend in July; the Sawtooth Music Festival, which takes place the last weekend in July; the Sawtooth Salmon Festival, which is always the end of August, the last weekend, usually; the Stanley Fireman's Ball in September; fireworks and a parade over the 4th of July; the Sawtooth Ski Festival, the first weekend in March; the Sawtooth Valley Winterfest in February; and the Stanley Sled Dog Rendezvous in March. More information can be found at www.stanleycc.org.

The Stanley Museum, operated by the all-volunteer Historical Museum and Interpretive Association, is located between Stanley and Lower Stanley at the mouth of Valley Creek. It is open Memorial Day to Labor Day, 11 a.m. to 5 p.m. The Museum features artifacts of the Stanley/Sawtooth Country including history of the U.S. Forest Service and the histories of trapping, mining, ranching and mountaineering in this rugged place. The museum also has an oral history collection and Museum Store that features books, maps and other historical and natural history items for sale.

The nearly five-mile-long Redfish Lake is named for the now endangered sockeye salmon that once returned from the Pacific Ocean in massive numbers.

Turning red as they neared their spawning grounds, the shimmering fish near the surface gave the lake a red cast.

The north end of the lake has many developed cabins, campsites, a boat ramp, a lodge and restaurants. The Redfish Lake Lodge sponsors the "Music from Stanley" each Sunday during the summer.

The three National Byways that intersect at Stanley are the Sawtooth, the Ponderosa Pine and the Salmon River. The Sawtooth begins in Shoshone and proceeds north through the cities of the Wood River Valley – Belleview, Hailey and Ketchum – before ending at Stanley. The Ponderosa Pine begins in Boise and passes through Idaho City before ending in Stanley. The Salmon River starts on the Continental Divide at Lost Trail Pass – where Lewis and Clark's Indian guide lost the trail west to the Pacific Ocean – and passes through the cities of Salmon and Challis before ending at Stanley.

Stanley is a summer Mecca for outdoor enthusiasts. Hikers and bikers can enjoy hundreds of miles of backcountry trails and Forest Service roads. Many of the trails are open to ATVs.

In the winter, the extensive trails offer a variety of options for snowshoeing, skiing and snowmobiling. For those who choose to spend time in the snowy mountains, yurts can be rented from the Forest Service.

Anglers come from all over the nation to enjoy outstanding fishing on the numerous rivers and creeks and hundreds of alpine lakes. Others make part of their visit a raft trip down the Salmon River, camping and hiking in the mountains or climbing some of the area's high mountains.

About 12 road miles east is the unincorporated community of Sunbeam. Proceeding north of Sunbeam on an improved road are the gold mining ghost towns of Custer and Bonanza and the Yankee Fork Gold Dredge. Those who want to proceed further, with a high-clearance vehicle, can cross the 8,800-foot-high pass to Challis and drive the former toll road built in 1879 between Challis and the mines.

The Yankee Fork Gold Dredge is a relic of bygone days. In 1940 entrepreneurs built the 112-foot-long, 54-foot-wide and 64-foot-high Gold Dredge to pick up any gold not recovered using less sophisticated methods. The dredge dug temporary dams on the Yankee Fork River, creating the reservoir on which it floated. Using a massive conveyer-type belt of several eight-yard buckets, it dug up the gravels and washed the gold from them in a built-in sluice as it floated across the valley floor. By 1952 after producing about $1.1 million of gold, an amount slightly under the cost of production, the dredge shut down. The owner then donated the dredge to the U.S. Forest Service, leaving behind over five miles of tailing mounds produced by the dredge. Under current law, if allowed at all, the land would have to be restored to its original condition.

Economy and Major Employers There are a variety of hospitality businesses offering lodging including motels, cabins and ranch resorts. These businesses provide most of the city's employment. The largest public employer, the U.S. Forest Service, has about 20 employees.

Education Challis School District provides elementary and secondary education. Students K-8 attend elementary school in Stanley. Junior and senior high school students attend in Challis.

Health Care Stanley has a medical clinic. The closest hospital is St. Luke's Medical Center-Wood River in Ketchum.

Transportation The north-south Idaho Highway 75 intersects the city. South of Stanley, Highway 75 is the Sawtooth Scenic Byway, and north of Stanley the highway is the Salmon River Scenic Byway. Idaho Highway 21 from Boise is the Ponderosa Pine Scenic Byway. It intersects the city and ends at its junction with Highway 75.

Utilities and Services Private companies provide electricity, telephone and satellite services. The City provides police and fire protection. The city's homes and businesses have individual wells and septic systems.

Vision for 2050

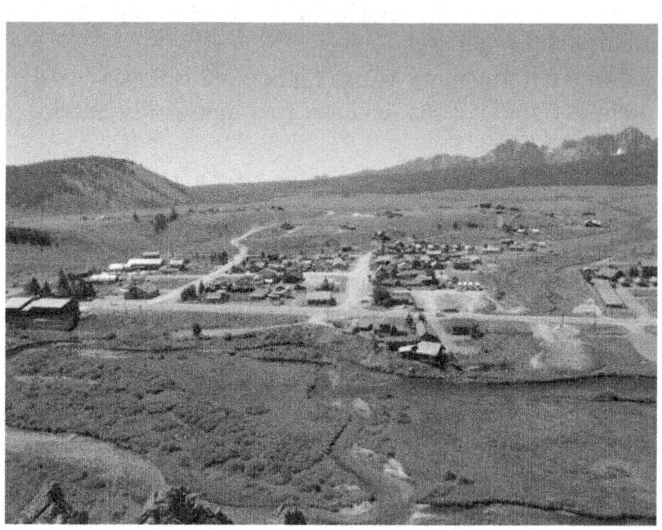

Stanley's population has three classifications – two of which are cyclical. The tourist element swells each summer to a peak of several thousand and then subsides as the weather turns cold. As the tourist cycle begins, hospitality businesses add part-time workers commensurate with need. The permanent residents are primarily owners, managers and caretakers of the hospitality businesses. They stay the winter to care for the property and provide service to the sharply reduced number of tourists, travelers and visitors passing through town.

Most private property owners around Stanley have entered into the federal "Scenic Easement" program wherein they receive cash in exchange for the development rights to the property. Property owners can still graze livestock and farm the land, but cannot develop their real estate. While this reduces real estate development and controls population, it preserves the natural beauty of the land.

In 1960 Stanley had a permanent population of 35. Subsequently, the tourist business swelled and investors began to build more and larger businesses to serve the tourists. In 1980 the population increased to 99 and has since stabilized.

However, conditions are changing. More tourists are coming to enjoy the Basin's winter sports, including snowmobiling. The number of full-time residents will increase as hospitality businesses adjust to meet this year-round demand.

Historical population trends will likely continue for several years and then slowly increase commensurate with the growth in the hospitality industry.

By 2050 residents of Lower Stanley will likely see the opportunity to combine their efforts and resources with Stanley in promoting economic development. In addition, increased costs of building infrastructure to protect the environment will also encourage the communities to come together for their common good.

Mayors

1947-1968 Unavailable *
1968 JesseWall
1969 Glen Brewer
1970 Stan Iwakiri
1972 Stella Critchfield
1972 Clarence Cole
1973 Larry McCoy
1974 Jack Kirch
1976 Gerald Nicholson
1984 Lloyd (Bud) James
1989 Launna Gunderson
1993 John Kirch
1996 Khema (Bunny) Danner
1999 Hilda Floyd
2000 Paul Frantellizzi
2002 Bob Downing
2003 Paul Frantellissi
2006 Hannah Stauts
2010 Herb Mumford
* Village Chairman

A beautiful Oxford sunset.

FRANKLIN COUNTY

- Clifton
- Dayton
- Franklin
- Oxford
- Preston (*County Seat*)
- Weston

Overlooking Clifton.

Clifton

Statistical Data

Population: 283 *
Elevation: 4,852 feet
Precipitation: 14 inches **
Average Snowfall: 32 inches **
County: Franklin

Temperature Range – Fahrenheit: **
Spring: 26 to 67
Summer: 46 to 87
Fall: 23 to 76
Winter: 12 to 37
* U.S. Census Bureau Estimates July 2015
**Historical averages

Clifton lies on the northeastern edge of the fertile 50-mile-long Cache Valley. The northern third of the valley is in Idaho and the lower two-thirds are in Utah. The Caribou-Targhee National Forest with its Bannock Mountain Range, rising to over 8,000 feet, lie west of the city.

To the east, fertile farms, irrigation canals, streams, reservoirs and wetlands stretch for about 15 miles across the valley before meeting the mountains of the Bear River Range, also in the Caribou-Targhee National Forest. This range has peaks rising to over 9,000 feet.

Preston is about 14 miles southeast. Malad lies across the Bannock Mountains about 20 miles west. The Idaho/Utah border is about 13 miles due south.

Pre-Incorporation Years

Pioneer settlement of the southern part of Cache Valley began in 1850, three years after the first migration of members of The Church of Jesus Christ of Latter-day Saints (Church or Church of Jesus Christ) into the valley of the Great Salt Lake.

The Cache Valley settlements moved progressively north. In 1860 the farming community of Franklin was established.

In 1862 the federal government established a military fort in the foothills overlooking Salt Lake City under the command of Colonel Patrick E. Connor. The fort was to protect the overland mail, emigrants headed West, settlers and an increasing number of gold prospectors in the regions to the north.

Cliffs near Clifton.

On January 29, 1863, following an Indian attack in what is now western Montana where one prospector was killed, Connor led his army in an attack against a large body of Shoshone encamped on the Bear River about six miles east of what is now Clifton. Initially, the dug-in Shoshone warriors were winning the battle, until Conner directed his cavalry in flanking movements that overran the Indians. The army killed nearly 400, including women and children, with half that number escaping or being taken prisoner. Twenty-two of Connor's soldiers lost their lives with about 130 wounded or disabled by frostbite. (*See Eastern Idaho, American Indians – Bear River Massacre*.)

In July 1864 Ezra T. Benson, a member of the Church's Quorum of Twelve Apostles, called an exploring party of seven men to locate, select and plat townsites north of Franklin. They established several new communities including what are now the Idaho cities of Clifton, Dayton, Oxford, Preston and Weston.

Settlement of Clifton began in 1865. The settlers were members of the Church traveling up from Utah Territory seeking arable land on which to establish their homes and farms. (*See Eastern Idaho, Pioneer Settlements – Cache Valley*.) They originally named the community Rushville because of the nearby bulrushes growing around the headwaters of Deep Creek.

In 1865 settlers in Bear Lake Valley, located across the Bear River Mountain Range about 35 miles due west of what is now Clifton, decided to establish homesteads south of St. Charles contrary to the settlement agreements Church leaders had reached with the Shoshone and Bannock Indians. The Shoshone destroyed these farms and sent the encroaching settlers fleeing back to St. Charles for safety.

In 1866 the Indians also threatened the north Cache Valley settlers causing them to abandon their farms and homes and move to the relative safety of Franklin. In 1867 these settlers felt it was safe to return to their homes and continue building their settlements.

In 1869 the township was surveyed and the name changed to Clifton after a high cleft of rock lying west of the settlement.

Alpaca near Clifton.

In 1872 the federal government surveyed the 42nd parallel. Prior to that time, most of the northern Cache Valley settlers managed their business affairs as though they were part of Utah Territory. Following the official survey, many of the northern Cache Valley settlers were disappointed when they found that they lived in Idaho. They now had to travel approximately 300 miles north to do their State business in Boise rather than traveling about 110 miles south to Salt Lake City. (*See Eastern Idaho, Idaho/Utah Boundary Resolution*.)

In 1890 the Oregon Short Line Railroad built a rail line through Clifton en route to the Montana gold fields. Area residents now had an efficient way to transport freight and agriculture commodities as well as providing efficient passenger and mail services.

Incorporation

In June 1915 Clifton became an incorporated village. It became a city in 1967 when the change in state law gave city legal status to all incorporated municipalities.

Turning Points

Idaho/Utah Boundary Resolution The 1872 federal survey of the 42nd parallel made clear that Clifton was in Idaho Territory as opposed to Utah Territory where many hoped they would be. While that knowledge had little effect on people's day-to-day activities, it had an important effect on how the city and its residents dealt with matters affecting territorial law and politics.

Railroad The coming of the railroad in 1890 had a major impact on the city's economy as well as improving the quality of life for its citizens.

Clifton Today

Amenities and Attractions The nearby Caribou-Targhee National Forest and Bannock Mountain Range offer city residents a wide variety of outdoor activities. Hiking, biking, ATV riding, hunting and fishing are popular outdoor sports.

A marker commemorating the Bear River Massacre, the bloodiest battle in

Idaho history, is located near Clifton on a gravel road just off U. S. Highway 91.

Residents also enjoy the amenities of nearby larger cities in Idaho and Utah.

Economy and Major Employers Most residents commute to nearby larger communities for employment. The city's retail district is limited, consisting of a few retail shops. Most residents travel to Preston to do their shopping.

The agriculture community that once underpinned the city's economy has undergone major consolidation. Farms have become larger and more productive with substantially fewer employees. Principal crops include grains, alfalfa, beans and potatoes.

Wheat field near Clifton.

Education The West Side School District provides primary and secondary education for all of the communities in western Franklin County. Clifton students attend school in Dayton. The closest institution of higher learning is Utah State University about 38 miles south in Logan, Utah.

Health Care The 21-bed Franklin County Medical Center in Preston is the nearest hospital.

Transportation County road D1 intersects Clifton and connects the city with Oxford on the north and Dayton, and Weston on the south. State Highway 36 intersects D1 just south of Dayton. Highway 36 intersects U.S. Highway 91 in Preston. The 3,400-foot runway at Preston Airport provides service for small private and charter aircraft. Pocatello Regional Airport lies about 63 miles northwest. Ogden-Hinkley Airport is located about 70 miles south in Utah.

Railroad freight service is available in Preston.

Utilities and Services Private companies provide electricity, telephone and satellite services. The City provides domestic water. The city's homes and businesses are on individual septic systems. The County Sheriff's Office provides police protection under contract with the City.

Vision for 2050

Since 1980 Clifton's population has ranged between 208 and 267. These historical trends will likely continue.

In 2050 Clifton will continue to be a small rural community – a quiet, friendly and peaceful place to raise a family.

Mayors

Unknown

** David Weatherspoon

2006 John Gailey

* Village Chairman

Dayton in the autumn.

Dayton

Statistical Data

Population: 462 *
Elevation: 4,818 feet
Precipitation: 16 inches **
Average Snowfall: 51 inches **
County: Franklin
Temperature Range – Fahrenheit: **

Spring: 26 to 67
Summer: 46 to 87
Fall: 23 to 76
Winter: 12 to 37

* U.S. Census Bureau Extimates, July 2015
**Historical averages

Dayton is a small farming community located on the northwestern edge of the 50-mile-long, 20-mile-wide Cache Valley – the northern third of which is in Idaho and the southern two-thirds in Utah.

The Bannock Mountains on the west and the Bear River Mountains on the east bracket the northern part of the valley. Both ranges rise to nearly 9,000 feet and are now part of the Caribou-Targhee National Forest. The Bear River and its numerous tributaries create meadows and marshes in the central part of the valley.

Dayton is eight miles due north of the Idaho/Utah border on rising foothills about seven miles west of the city of Preston, the Franklin County seat.

Pre-Incorporation Years

For centuries, tribes of nomadic American Indians – primarily of the Northern or Northwestern Shoshone Tribes – frequented the Cache Valley. (*See The Region, American Indians*.)

Settlement of Cache Valley began following the arrival of thousands of members of the Church of Jesus Christ of Latter-day Saints (Church) – nicknamed Mormons, Latter Day Saints or LDS – into the Salt Lake Valley beginning in 1847.

The first of these emigrants were refugees driven from their Illinois homes by mobs. Thousands of converts to the faith from European countries soon joined them and began colonizing the Intermountain West. (*See The Region, Pioneer Settlements*.)

Cache Valley settlements started on the southern end of the valley in Utah and moved progressively north across the 42nd parallel – the historic dividing line between English and Spanish claims to the West and marked the southern boundary of the Oregon Territory created by Congress in 1848, the Washington Territory in 1859 and the Idaho Territory in 1863. (*See The Region: Federal Lands – Private Ownership and Preservation Laws; and Idaho Territory – Change in Idaho Territorial Boundaries, Suffrage and Statehood*.)

Original plaque giving a brief account of the settling of Dayton.

Church leaders counseled that it was cheaper to feed Indians than fight them and usually entered into treaties with various Indian bands with typically generous gifts of food for the Indians passing through their communities. However, many Indians became increasingly unhappy with the settlers taking over the area, cultivating farms and grazing herds of livestock on land where the Indians previously roamed and hunted. Their feelings were further inflamed as passing immigrant groups and miners were abusive and sometimes killed the Indians. Settlers moving into northern Cache Valley were always on guard against hostilities with the Indians.

Robb "Little Owl" Martin plays a flute during a memorial program at the site of the Bear River Massacre on January 29, 2011.

The first Cache Valley settlers unknowingly crossed the 42nd parallel into Idaho and started the community of Franklin in 1860, making it Idaho's oldest town. (*See The Region, Idaho/Utah Boundary Resolution*.)

In 1862 the federal government dispatched Colonel Patrick E. Connor and 700 California volunteers to establish Camp Douglas in the eastern hills overlooking Salt Lake City.

That same year, Shoshone-Bannock Indians attacked a group of gold miners in what is now western Montana, killing one of the miners. A surviving miner asked for federal help. A federal court issued an order calling for the arrest of the accused Chiefs Bear Hunter, Sandpitch and Sagwitch. Utah Territory Chief Justice John F. Kenny asked Conner to assist the U.S. Marshal in serving the warrant. Learning that a large band of Northwestern Shoshone under the three chiefs was camped on the Bear River several miles north of Franklin – about five miles northeast of what is now Dayton – Colonel Connor marched his garrison in sub-zero weather to make the arrests.

On January 29, 1863, Connor directed his troops to attack the Indians, resulting in more Indian casualties than any other conflict between the U.S. Army and Indians. (*See The Region, American Indians – Bear River Massacre*.)

Dayton stockyards.

Eighteen months later, Ezra T. Benson, a member of the Church's Quorum of Twelve Apostles, called an exploring party of seven men to locate, select and plat townsites north of Franklin. They identified several new communities including what would become the present-day cities of Clifton, Dayton, Weston and Oxford. Some of the Indians threatened the settlers spreading north of Franklin in 1866. In response to this threat, the settlers in northern Cache Valley abandoned their farms and homes and fled to the relative safety in the more settled areas around Franklin.

Dayton Elementary School which was built in 1914 and used until 1959.

By 1867 the concern about Indian raids had subsided and the settlers returned to their homes. The military removed many of the Indians to the Fort Hall Indian Reservation, established that year by treaty. Albeit 11 years later, a break-away band of about 200 warriors, angry about their circumstances and unfulfilled promises made by the U.S. government, left the reservation and launched attacks upon settlers far to the northwest of Preston. After a series of skirmishes that the military called the Bannock War, the U.S. Army and volunteers successfully suppressed further conflicts with the Shoshone and Bannock Indians in Idaho. (*See Native American Indians – The Bannock War*.)

The first homesteaders came to what is now Dayton in 1867. Joseph Chadwick and his family built a log structure near Five Mile Creek and the wagon road. Part of the building served as the Chadwick home. One room was a mercantile store where Chadwick sold supplies to freighters and stagecoach passengers passing through as well as permanent settlers. Concerned about attack from Indians, the communities of Oxford; Stockton; and Rushville – which is now Clifton – banded together to build a fort in the Oxford town square for protection. (*See The Region, Federal Lands – Private Ownership and Preservation Laws*.)

Chadwick and the other settlers named the wagon stop "Five Mile" because upon arriving at the Chadwick store a traveler had five miles to go to reach the town of Clifton to the north or Weston to the south. Later, because of the Chadwick store, people began informally calling the community "Chadville." However, adoption of a formal name for the community remained unresolved.

Church leaders called William B. Preston – a native of Virginia and founding father of Logan, Utah – to be the ecclesiastical head of the northern Cache Valley communities. On one of Preston's periodic visits to what is now Dayton, the question of what to name the town came up. Preston mused that they could name the town Dayton because when he came into town from other communities, he always arrived during the day. The residents liked the suggestion and in 1881 after years of common use, the community formally adopted the name of "Dayton."

Dayton water project.

The first railroad constructed in Idaho reached Franklin on May 2, 1874. The Utah Northern Railway Company (UNRC) had received approval from Congress to build a line from Utah to the Montana Territory goldfields by way of Bear River Valley and Soda Springs. However, the under-capitalized company had to stop construction at Franklin – later extending a spur to Preston. On October 4, 1877, investors affiliated with the Union Pacific Railroad acquired UNRC and formed the Utah and Northern Railroad Company (U&N) to complete the rail line.

However, the U&N determined that the UNRC route was technically too difficult to build and obtained approval for a new route several miles west of Franklin – a route that more closely followed the wagon supply road to Montana. The U&N line proceeded north near the western Bear River Valley communities, including Dayton; then on to Pocatello and Eagle Rock – now Idaho Falls – and across Monida Pass into Montana. The rail line reached Pocatello in August 1878 and Monida Pass about 21 months later. At the turn of the century, the railroad built a station and stockyards at Dayton. (*See The Region, Mining – The Gold Road – Precursor to Settlement of Eastern Idaho; and Railroads*.)

Trying to get water to irrigate their crops was a major problem. The settlers built flood irrigation systems from the creeks flowing down from the western Bannock

Mountains and through the valley. However, there was still inadequate water to irrigate all of the farms.

In 1900 several farmers from Dayton, Clifton and Weston decided to form the Oneida Canal Company; sell bonds; and build an irrigation system that would bring water from Mink Creek, 30 miles east, to irrigate the land on the west side of the valley. They implemented the plan and filed on Mink Creek water rights. They estimated they could build the 30-mile canal system, an inverted siphon across the Bear River and several storage reservoirs along the way in five years at a cost of $282,000 – delivering sufficient water to irrigate 33,000 acres.

Ten years later, after experiencing huge construction delays and cost overruns and being heavily in debt, there was only enough water to irrigate 4,000 acres.

West Side High School.

Amalgamated Sugar Company (ASC) operated factories in Lewiston and Cornish, Utah, around 20 miles south of the Oneida Irrigation District service area. It was in the company's best interest for the irrigation company to succeed so farmers could plant thousands of acres of sugar beets.

ASC put forth a plan in 1916 to essentially dissolve the Oneida Irrigation District, assume certain bonded indebtedness and move the irrigation district's net assets into a new company – Twin Lakes Canal Company. The new company would sell stock and move forward with a much less ambitious irrigation plan, which included completion of Twin Lakes Reservoir east of Clifton and irrigating from 13,000 to 20,000 acres. The farmers and bondholders agreed to the proposal, but they continued to experience years of delay. When they finally completed the revised plan, the cost had ballooned to $1,540,000, but the Twin Lakes Canal Company was at last delivering water to the farmers. The sight of the first water rushing down the canal from the reservoir was electrifying for the settlers. On the night they released water from Twin Lakes Reservoir into the canal, settlers waited expectantly about five miles downstream. When they saw the churning water racing down the canal, Stephan Callan – community and Church leader – stood on the bank yelling, "Here she comes! Here she comes!"

Dayton's first schoolhouse was a log cabin purchased from the town of Weston in 1881. Within a year, there were 20 families in Dayton. They replaced the cabin with a two-room frame building that was not only a schoolhouse, but also a community hall used for public and religious gatherings until 1909. Then the community built the Lincoln School between Dayton and Weston on land donated by Joseph Coburn. It served students in the towns as well as the outlying areas.

A two-story brick school was built on the north end of Dayton in 1914. It had a gym and a lunchroom in the basement. The women in nearby homes cooked large pots of soup. The students, grades one through eight, brought their own dishes and spoons, which they cleaned and kept in their desks.

Incorporation

On July 13, 1914, Dayton became an incorporated village. In accordance with the 1967 change in state law, the town changed its legal status to an incorporated city.

Turning Points

Irrigation Agriculture underpinned Dayton's early economy. It turned high-desert fields into a checkerboard of productive farms. Today, the Twin Lakes Canal Company and its predecessor, the Oneida Canal Company, have emerged from an early history of inordinate problems into an efficient and financially sound business, providing irrigation water through a complex system of reservoirs, canals and siphons with additional water pumped from the Bear River.

Railroad The Oregon Short Line Railroad built a line through Dayton in 1878 and a railroad station and stockyards in 1906. The railroad was an important part of Dayton, providing passenger and mail service and transportation for freight, coal and livestock. This had a major positive effect on the area's agricultural economy. Farmers had close access to railroad transportation to distant markets for their commodities. The railroad closed the station and razed the structures in 1964.

Village Incorporation and Domestic Water System In 1915 the year following incorporation, the village built a 65,000-gallon water storage tank to receive water from nearby springs, a pressurized water system for domestic and firefighting use. However, the springs eventually proved inadequate and difficult to maintain.

In 1935 the citizens concluded that they needed a larger and better source of water. They identified excellent springs higher up in the mountains west of the city but gaining access to the water was problematic. It was located on the opposite side of a low mountain. They considered two options – building an electrical pumping station at the head of the springs to pipe the water over the mountain to the city or building an engineered 600-foot-long tunnel through the mountain separating the springs from the city. They chose the tunnel. However, the engineer's bid for the tunnel was too high. Drawing upon their pioneer spirit, the men of Dayton said, "We will do it ourselves." In 1936 the federal Works Progress Administration (WPA), renamed the Works Projects Administration in 1939, approved funding for the tunnel. They completed the tunnel in the summer of 1937. The citizens then laid pipes through the tunnel connecting the higher elevation catch basin constructed at the springs to the storage tank below.

Over the years, the community has upgraded the water system several times. Today, the city has 350,000- and 150,000-gallon storage tanks. The city's water comes from three springs and two wells.

West Side School District Patrons of the Dayton School, serving grades one through eight, condemned the school building in 1957, and students began attending elementary schools in Weston and Clifton.

The West Side School District is a 1945 consolidation of schools in Oxford, which at the time was School District #202 – including Clifton, Dayton, Linrose and Weston.

One factor affecting the consolidation was that the Weston High School had just burned down. School patrons in the area needed to select a site for the new high school. In a special election on August 1, 1945, Dayton citizens voted to sell a large village park to the school district for the new school.

In 1949 they built the West Side High School in Dayton. The facility included school and district offices, 23 classrooms, a kitchen, cafeteria, media center, an industrial arts area, gymnasium, baseball diamond and a football stadium. Subsequently, in addition to major renovations to keep the facility up to code, the district added a gymnasium, a softball field, a fine arts building, new district offices, an auditorium and a modern rubberized track that encircles the football field.

The district bused grade school students to Weston and Clifton until it built the Harold B. Lee Elementary School in Dayton in 1989.

Harold B. Lee Elementary School.

Dayton Today

Amenities and Attractions Dayton has a 2.8-acre park that has a pavilion, picnic areas, volleyball fields, horseshoe pits and children's playgrounds. A tennis court is located at the high school.

The nearby Caribou-Targhee National Forest and the Bannock and Bear River Mountain Ranges offer city residents a wide variety of outdoor activities. Hiking, biking, ATV riding, hunting and fishing are popular outdoor sports.

Residents also enjoy the many amenities of larger cities located nearby in Idaho and Utah.

Economy and Major Employers West Side School District is the city's principal employer. Most residents commute to nearby larger communities for employment. The city's retail district is limited to a few businesses. Most residents travel to Preston to do their shopping.

The agricultural community that once underpinned the city's economy has undergone major consolidation. Farms have become larger and more productive with substantially fewer employees. Principal crops include grains, alfalfa, beans and potatoes. Three dairy farms operate in the area.

Education The West Side School District provides primary and secondary education for all of the communities in western Franklin County. The district has an enrollment approximating 500 and operates an elementary, middle and high school in the city.

The closest institution of higher learning is Utah State University about 33 miles south in Logan. Idaho State University is in Pocatello, about 70 miles north.

Health Care The 21-bed Franklin County Medical Center in Preston is the nearest hospital.

Transportation County Road D1 intersects Dayton and connects the city with Oxford, Clifton, Weston and the Utah state line on a north-south route. At Weston, D1 intersects Idaho Highway 36, which extends west, intersecting Interstate 15 near Malad.

The 3,400-foot Preston Airport, six miles east, provides service for small private and charter aircraft. Larger commercial aircraft are available at Pocatello Regional Airport or Ogden-Hinckley Airport, about 80 miles south in Utah.

Railroad freight service is available in Preston.

Utilities and Services Private companies provide electricity, telephone and satellite services. The City provides domestic water. Homes and businesses have individual septic systems. The County Sheriff's Office provides police protection. The Franklin County Fire District provides fire protection with a satellite fire station in Dayton.

Dayton City Park.

Vision for 2050

Dayton's population has grown from 212 in 1960 to 444 in 2000 and has since remained somewhat constant. In the next 40 years, the city's population will likely increase less than 1 percent annually. Should that projection hold, by 2050 Dayton would have a population approaching 600.

The city can manage this growth within existing systems and will likely continue to be a bedroom community for commuters who work in nearby larger cities, with residents shopping in those cities.

To address the need for improved roads in town, the City is planning to install curbs, gutters and sidewalks within a one-half-mile radius of the schools to provide safe walking routes for the children.

There is a reasonable likelihood that by 2050 a public transportation system will be operating, carrying valley residents in Idaho to the larger cities in the region.

The City owns additional land suitable for recreational development.

Most of the new construction in the city will come from more cost effective subdivision development as opposed to individual home construction.

Mayors

1914 Joseph Hansen *
1917 J.P. Schow *
1919 S.J. Callan *
1925 Robert Jones *
1927 A.F. Dalley *
1931 V.D. Smart *
1933 Charles Jones *
1935 LeRoy Archibald *
1937 M.L. Phillips *
1941 Albert Moser *
1945 LaVor E. Jensen *
1947 Joseph Hansen *
1959 V.D. Smart *
1964 Walter Beutler *
1967 Walter Beutler
1976 Earl Ward
1980 Eugene Griffith
1988 Paul Winward
1996 Tarrel Shepherd
2000 Wesley Beutler
2004 Richard Reeder
2008 Dee Virile Christensen
2014 Aaron M. Beutler

* Village Chairman

** No records are available between March 1921 and June 1925.

Aerial view of Franklin.

Franklin

Statistical Data

Population: 741 *
Elevation: 4,501 feet
Precipitation: 16 inches **
Average Snowfall: 51 inches **
County: Franklin
Website: http://franklinidaho.org

Temperature Range – Fahrenheit: **
Spring: 26 to 67
Summer: 46 to 87
Fall: 23 to 76
Winter: 12 to 37
* U.S. Census Bureau Estimates July 2015
**Historical averages

Franklin, Idaho's oldest city, lies on the northeastern side of the fertile Cache Valley. The Cub River flows northwest of the city and circles to the west, where it then flows southward into Utah.

The Bear River Mountain Range, rising to over 9,000 feet, punctuates the city's eastern skyline. About 10 miles west, the Bannock Mountain Range rises to over 8,000 feet. Both the Bear River and Bannock Mountain Ranges are in the Caribou-Targhee National Forest.

The northern third of the 40-mile-long Cache Valley is in Idaho and the rest in Utah. The Idaho/Utah border is a mile south of the city. The U.S. Census Bureau includes all of Franklin County in the Logan, Utah, Metropolitan Statistical Area.

Pre-Incorporation Years

For centuries, nomadic tribes of principally Shoshone and Bannock Indians migrated through the Cache Valley. (*See The Region, American Indians*.)

Beginning around 1818 the first European trappers came to the valley. Because the area had many natural caves where they could hide their beaver pelts and supplies, the trappers named the valley "Cache" for the French word "cacher" meaning to hide.

Several mountain men and trappers worked the valley. Jim Bridger called it Willow Valley because of the abundance of willow trees that bordered the valley's many streams. Others described the valley as rich and fertile, abounding in game but with cold and devastating winters. Trappers worked the streams until the mid-1840s when most of the beaver were trapped out. (*See The Region, Trappers/Explorers*.)

Settlement of Cache Valley began in 1850. These settlers were members of The Church of Jesus Christ of Latter-day Saints (Church), also known as Mormons, Latter-Day Saints or LDS – refugees driven from their homes in western Illinois in the dead of winter. (*See The Region, Pioneer Settlements*.)

Old mill.

They crossed the Great Plains into the heretofore unsettled Great Basin. The main body of around 15,000 began arriving in the Great Salt Lake Valley in 1847. At that time, the Great Basin was part of Mexico. It became U.S. Territory in 1848 following the war between the United States and Mexico, a war in which the U.S. Army intercepted the Mormon's westward trek and inducted about 500 men to fight in the war along with 34 women – wives of soldiers, many with children – who filled support duties such as laundresses.

Tent city.

The unit, called the "Mormon Battalion," made a grueling march from Council Bluffs, Iowa, to San Diego, California – one of the longest military marches in U.S history (2,000 miles) – before the army discharged them to join their families, who were settling in the Great Basin. Many settled in Cache Valley, including cities in what is now Franklin County.

Captain Jefferson Hunt was in command of the company in the Mormon Battalion which made the first known gesture of peace between Mexico and the U.S. in what was called "The Exchange at the Presidio," commemorated by statues and a memorial in Tucson, Arizona. He is buried in a family cemetery at Red Rock Pass near Oxford, Idaho.

Thousands of new converts coming from Europe and the United States followed the original migration of Church members and added momentum to the new agricultural settlements springing up throughout the Intermountain West. (*See The Region, Federal Lands, Private Ownership and Preservation Laws.*)

Fur farm.

In Cache Valley, settlements began in the southern part of the valley and moved progressively north. Beginning in 1859 the flow of settlers into the valley increased significantly.

On April 14, 1860, the Thomas Smart family from England led a group of 13 families to the confluence of Worm Creek and the Cub River in the northern part of Cache Valley. Others soon joined them. Three months later, James Henry Martineau surveyed the town of Franklin.

Brigham Young visited the new settlement in June 1860. He named the town Franklin after Franklin D. Richards, a member of the Church's Quorum of Twelve Apostles, and appointed Preston Thomas, a proven leader, as its bishop. Thomas received the sustaining vote from the settlers and served as the community's ecclesiastical and municipal leader without pay.

By the end of the year, there were 61 families in Franklin. The settlers built a public square and a community of log-cabin houses in a fort-like configuration with the cabin doors facing the interior. Within the interior the settlers built a bowery for church and public meetings, a community well and a corral to hold their livestock at night. Immediately outside the public square, each family selected, by lottery, a 10-acre farm parcel.

Marlow Woodward poultry farm.

During the week, they used the bowery for a schoolhouse for about 70 students. They spread straw on the floor as insulation from the cold ground.

Several miles northwest of Franklin, between Worm Creek and the Bear River, there was a meadowland called Worm Creek Bottoms with native grasses and meandering streams reminiscent of a worm trail.

Many Franklin residents established squatter claims in Worm Creek Bottoms where they cut winter hay and grazed their livestock.

Franklin surveyor James Martineau, who also surveyed several other Cache Valley towns, wrote in his journal, "The Cache Valley immigration of 1859-60 was something of a population boom for the area with over 2,500 settlers coming into the valley."

Old Doney home.

Maintaining good relationships with the Indians was important to these frontier settlers. Church leader Brigham Young counseled that it was better to feed the Indians than fight them. Settlers generally sought to befriend the Indians and provide food and supplies when requested, even when they had limited quantities for themselves. In 1860 Church leaders received approval from Shoshone tribal leader Chief Kettemere to establish settlements in the northern end of Cache Valley.

This policy of co-existence worked reasonably well with most of the Indians and settlers. However, not all Indians agreed with Chief Kettemere. Already angry about the large numbers of prospectors and travelers coming into the region, they took some of their resentment out on the settlers and continued to raid outlying farms and rustle livestock. The settlers formed local militias they called Minute Men that could come on short notice to protect against Indian raids.

Old jail.

By the 1860s a complex set of circumstances, prejudices and events occurring in the broader region would, on January 29, 1863, come to a head at a terrible battle when soldiers led by Colonel Patrick Edward Connor attacked a large band of Shoshone Indians encamped several miles north of Franklin. Later called the Bear River Massacre, it was one of the bloodiest killings of Indians in U.S. history.

As the battle ended, some of the unscrupulous members of Connor's troops, technically following their orders to not shoot women and children, went through the village killing the wounded and committing unspeakable atrocities.

When the carnage was over around 250 Indians were killed, including women and children. Twenty-four soldiers lost their lives. About 160 women and children were spared and allowed to take food and trek north to find their people. Several Indian warriors escaped.

Franklin residents opened their homes to the wounded on both sides and to children orphaned or needing assistance. Two days later, the settlers assembled 18 horse-drawn sleds and transported the dead and wounded soldiers back to barracks at Camp Douglas near Salt Lake City. Conner was promoted to brigadier general.

Oldest Idaho town marker.

The military named the conflict the "Battle of Bear River." Non-military historians called it the "Bear River Massacre."

The site, four miles north of Preston, is marked by a stone monument erected by the Daughters of Utah Pioneers. It was designated a National Historic Landmark in 1990. The Western Shoshone Indians acquired property at the site in 2008 and plan to build a memorial. (*See The Region, American Indians – Bear River Massacre.*)

Ezra T. Benson, a member of the Church's Quorum of Twelve Apostles, called an exploring party of seven men in 1864 to locate, select and plat townsites north and west of Franklin. They established several new communities in what is now Franklin County including what are now the cities of Clifton, Dayton, Weston and Oxford. (*See The Region, Pioneer Settlements – Cache Valley.*)

In 1866 some Indians threatened the settlers spreading north of Franklin. In response, the settlers abandoned their farms and fled to the relative safety of the more settled areas around Franklin.

That same year, the Shoshone and Bannock Indians signed a treaty to move to the Fort Hall Indian Reservation, the northern Cache Valley settlers moved back to their homes and the Franklin settlers built a schoolhouse of sandstone. The next year, the Deseret Telegraph Company extended its lines to Franklin.

Princess Theatre.

A break-away band of about 200 Bannock warriors, angry about their circumstances and unfulfilled treaty promises made by the U.S. government, left the reservation in 1878 and launched attacks on settlers hundreds of miles northwest of Franklin. After a series of skirmishes that the military called the Bannock War, the Army successfully suppressed further conflicts with the Shoshone and Bannock Indians in Idaho. (*See The Region, American Indians – The*

Bannock War.)

As more settlers moved into the northern end of the valley, their livestock began grazing on the open range. To protect their unfenced property and better manage their livestock, Franklin residents built cabins in the "bottoms" and stayed the summer. Gradually, these Franklin settlers moved to their Worm Creek Bottom property and built permanent homes, naming their settlemont Worm Creek. In 1881 they renamed their community "Preston" in honor of their former leader, Preston Thomas.

Old Whitehead home.

The location of the boundary between Idaho and Utah Territories – the 42nd parallel – became a pivotal issue for northern Cache Valley residents in 1872. As Congress created or modified territories or created states in the Northwest, it continued to use, on paper, the historic 42nd parallel as a dividing line. However, Congress did not perform an actual land survey of the line until 1872.

The lack of an official survey was problematic. Residents of Franklin and other northern Cache Valley and Bear Lake settlers believed they were in Utah Territory and managed their business and governmental affairs accordingly.

When the federal government completed the survey in 1872, it marked the 42nd parallel a mile south of Franklin. Because Franklin's founding predated any other town in Idaho, the survey established Franklin as Idaho's oldest community.

Relic hall now.

Settlers living above the 42nd parallel were disappointed to find they were in Idaho Territory. It placed them in a less hospitable political environment and caused them to travel approximately 300 miles northwest to the territorial capital in Boise to do their territorial and political business rather than traveling a little over 100 miles south to the Utah territorial capital in Salt Lake City. (*See The Region, Idaho/Utah Boundary Resolution.*)

The first railroad constructed in Idaho Territory, the Utah Northern Railroad line, reached Franklin on May 2, 1874. The plan was for the railroad to proceed from Utah Territory through Franklin then through the Bear River Valley and Soda Springs to Montana. However, when the railroad reached Franklin it stopped because the owners had financial problems and had to sell. For a brief time, Franklin became the railroad terminus and a major transportation center.

Several hundred freight wagons and stagecoaches moved goods and passengers between Franklin and the Montana gold fields.

The railroad's new owners extended the line to Preston and then abandoned further construction on the previously planned route. Instead, they built a new rail line that entered Idaho Territory about eight miles west of Franklin. This line moved northwest through Marsh Valley, Pocatello and Eagle Rock – now Idaho Falls – then on to Montana.

Franklin Cemetery.

Until 1890 the Church of Jesus Christ of Latter-day Saints' doctrine included acceptance of plural marriage under certain circumstances as was done in ancient Israel. In the 1880s most members of the Church supported the Democratic Party and represented about a fourth of Idaho Territory's population. However, Republicans controlled the governor's office and the legislature. Many Republican politicos worried that if Church members voted as a block, it could shift the balance of power in state and local governments to the Democrats – an event that could also prevent approval of Idaho becoming a state by the Republican-controlled U.S. Congress.

Those seeking to limit the Church's political influence saw polygamy as its Achilles heel, and, even though most adult male members of the Church were monogamists, they successfully used polygamy as a lightning rod to inflame political and public opinion against the Church.

In 1885 the Idaho Territorial Legislature passed a Test Oath Law that stripped the civil rights to vote, hold office or serve on juries from monogamous men who were members of an organization that approved of polygamy, bigamy or celestial (eternal) marriage. The Test Oath had no practical effect on polygamous men as they were felons and had already lost their civil rights.

In Franklin, as well as many Eastern Idaho cities, the Test Oath resulted in a huge power shift from the majority to the minority of citizens with all the potential mischief such undemocratic actions could produce.

At that time, Idaho law also denied suffrage rights to women, certain ethnic groups, adults under guardianship and felons. (*See The Region, Idaho Territory – Change in Idaho Territorial Boundaries 1863 to 1890, Suffrage and Statehood.*)

Ball diamond and bleachers.

Church leaders issued a manifesto on October 6, 1890, ceasing further practice of plural marriage in compliance with federal law. The Idaho Legislature repealed the Test Oath on February 1, 1895, and many members of the Church became Republicans. (*See The Region – Politics, Polygamy and Civil Rights.*)

Incorporation

Prior to the 1872 federal survey, Cache County commissioners in Utah Territory had recognized Franklin as an incorporated municipality. On January 30, 1897, Franklin became an incorporated Idaho village. It became a city in 1967 in accordance with a change in Idaho municipal law.

Turning Points

Idaho/Utah Boundary Resolution The 1872 federal survey of the 42nd parallel made clear that Franklin, Preston and other northern Cache Valley communities were in Idaho Territory as opposed to Utah Territory. While that knowledge had little effect on people's day-to-day activities, it had an important effect on how the city and its residents dealt with matters affecting territorial law and politics.

Park.

Railroad The coming of the railroad in 1872 had a major impact on the city's economy and improved the quality of life for its citizens. Even though railroad officials chose another route to Montana, the railroad continued to provide service to Franklin and Preston.

Franklin Today

Amenities and Attractions The city's Pioneer Park, the town's original central square, features a fireplace, picnic tables, a fountain and a monument honoring the founders of Franklin. Next to the park is Relic Hall, a museum built of logs in 1937 during the Great Depression, and other historic buildings relating to Franklin's early history. Artifacts and mementos of the town's past and rich pioneer heritage are exhibited in the Hall.

Franklin has several historic homes and businesses built in the late 1800s using sandstone quarried nearby by masons, who emigrated from England.

On the last Saturday of June, the community celebrates Idaho Day, honoring its pioneer founders. The celebration features a parade, a flag-raising, a picnic in the park, concessions and a Dutch oven supper.

The nearby Caribou-Targhee National Forest and Bear River Mountain Range offer city residents a wide variety of outdoor activities. Hiking, biking, ATV riding, hunting, fishing, boating, rafting and snowmobiling are popular outdoor sports.

A marker commemorating the Bear River Massacre is about 12 miles north of Franklin on a gravel road just off U. S. Highway 91.

Residents enjoy the numerous urban shopping and other urban amenities available in the nearby larger cities of Idaho and Utah.

Economy and Major Employers Many residents commute to nearby cities for employment. The city's commercial area includes a convenience store and restaurants. Agricultural businesses still dominate the surrounding area. However, the agricultural community that once underpinned the city's economy has undergone major consolidation. Farms have become larger and more productive with substantially fewer employees, requiring the workforce to seek employment elsewhere. Today, the principal farm crops include grains, alfalfa, beans and potatoes.

Education The Preston School District provides primary and secondary public education for Franklin students. The district operates a high school, a junior high school and two elementary schools in Preston. Franklin children ride buses to Preston for school.

The closest institution of higher learning is Utah State University about 20 miles south in Logan. Idaho State University is about 70 miles north in Pocatello.

Health Care The 21-bed Franklin County Medical Center in Preston provides most of the medical services needed in the area.

Transportation North-south U.S. Highway 91 extends through the western part of the city.

The 3,400-foot runway at Preston Airport provides service for small private and charter aircraft. Pocatello Regional Airport is the closest commercial airport in Idaho. Ogden-Hinkley Airport is about 70 miles south in Utah.

Railroad freight service is available in the city.

Utilities and Services Private companies provide electricity, telephone and satellite services. The City provides water and sewer services and mosquito abatement. The Franklin County Sheriff's Office provides police protection and the

Franklin County Fire District provides fire protection. Weekly solid waste pick up is supplied by Franklin County.

Vision for 2050

In 1960 Franklin's population was 446. Since that time, the city has experienced moderate population growth. During the past decade, the city's population has stabilized at around 650.

Recent population trends will likely continue for several years. "Legacy Ranch," a housing development located south of the original city limits, has been annexed into the city and provides "bedroom" accommodations for the adjoining larger cities including Preston; Pocatello; and Logan, Utah.

As economic conditions improve, Franklin's population will likely return to moderate growth as young families with employment in Logan choose to live in the small, peaceful and affordable community of Franklin and commute to work.

Mayors

1897 James Herd *
1899 J.B. Scarborough *
1901 B.P. Porter *
1902 J.B. Scarborough *
1909 Hyrum Hatch *
1911 James Robinson *
1913 S.C. Parkinson *
1915 A.B. Nash *
1917 E.P. Monson *
1918 L.L. Hatch *
1919 P.G. Whitehead *
1921 L.L. Hatch *
1921 P.G. Whitehead *
1925 J.B. Scarborough *
1927 Uriah Wilkinson
1931 Abe Whitehead
1947 Ivan Geary *
1947 Sheldon Doney *
1949 William Robinson *
1951 Dee Kingsford *
1953 Ben Porter *
1955 W.P. Waddoups *
1957 Dennis Lowe *
1966 Harley Lowe *
1967 Harley Lowe
1972 Floyd Robinson
1980 Brent Atkinson
1988 Louis Mendoza
2004 Robert U. Wilkinson
2008 Wayne Priestley
2012 Jeremy Kimpton
2014 J. Todd Hawkes

* Village Chairman

Oxford Peak.

Oxford

Statistical Data

Population: 48 *
Elevation: 4,803 feet
Precipitation: 14 inches **
Average Snowfall: 32 inches **
County: Franklin

Temperature Range – Fahrenheit: **
Spring: 26 to 67
Summer: 46 to 87
Fall: 23 to 76
Winter: 12 to 37
* U.S. Census Bureau Estimates July 2015
**Historical averages

Oxford is a small farming community located at the far north end of the fertile 50-mile-long Cache Valley. The northern third of the valley is in Idaho and the lower two-thirds are in Utah. The Caribou-Targhee National Forest with its Bannock Mountain Range rising to over 8,000 feet lies west of the city.

To the east, fertile farms, irrigation canals, streams, reservoirs and wetlands stretch for about 10 miles across the valley to the Oneida Narrows Reservoir, the Bear River Mountain Range and Caribou-Targhee National Forest.

Preston is about 20 miles southeast. The Idaho/Utah border is about 18 miles due south.

Pre-Incorporation Years

Pioneer settlement of the southern part of Cache Valley began in 1850, three years after the first migration of members of The Church of Jesus Christ of Latter-day Saints (Church or Church of Jesus Christ) into the valley of the Great Salt Lake.

The Cache Valley settlements moved progressively north. In 1860 they established the farming community of Franklin.

In July 1864 Ezra T. Benson, a member of the Church's Quorum of Twelve Apostles, called an exploring party of seven men to locate, select and plat townsites north of Franklin. They established several new communities including what are

Boice family homestead in Oxford.

now the Idaho cities of Clifton, Dayton, Oxford, Preston and Weston.

Settlement of Oxford – a community named for Oxford Slough, a low area used by settlers to ford Deep Creek – began in 1865. The settlers were members of the Church traveling up from Utah Territory seeking arable land on which to establish their homes and farms. (*See Eastern Idaho, Pioneer Settlements – Cache Valley.*)

In 1865 settlers in Bear Lake Valley, located across the Bear River Mountain Range about 35 miles due west of what is now Oxford decided to establish homesteads south of St. Charles contrary to agreements Church leaders had reached with the Shoshone and Bannock Indians. The Shoshone destroyed these farms and sent the encroaching settlers fleeing back to St. Charles for safety.

In 1866 the Indians also threatened the north Cache Valley settlers, causing them to abandon their farms and homes and move to the relative safety of Franklin. In 1867 these settlers felt it was safe to return to their homes and continue building their settlements.

In 1872 the federal government surveyed the 42nd Parallel dividing Idaho and Utah Territories. Prior to that time, most of the northern Cache Valley settlers managed their business affairs as though they were part of Utah Territory. Following the official survey, many of the northern Cache Valley settlers were disappointed when they found that they lived in Idaho. They now had to travel approximately 300 miles north to do their territorial business in Boise rather than traveling about 110 miles south to Salt Lake City. (*See Eastern Idaho, Idaho/Utah*

Boundary Resolution.)

In 1890 the Oregon Short Line Railroad built a rail line through Weston, Dayton, Clifton and Oxford en route to the Montana gold fields. The railroad provided area residents with an efficient way to transport their freight and agriculture commodities as well as providing efficient passenger and mail services.

Incorporation

Oxford first became an incorporated village, and its status changed to a city in 1967 when the change in state law gave city legal status to all incorporated municipalities.

Turning Points

Idaho/Utah Boundary Resolution The 1872 federal survey of the 42nd parallel made clear that Oxford was in Idaho Territory as opposed to Utah Territory where many hoped they would be. While that knowledge had little effect on people's day-to-day activities, it had an important effect on how the city and its residents dealt with matters affecting territorial law and politics.

Railroad The coming of the railroad in 1890 had a major impact on the city's economy as well as improving the quality of life for its citizens.

Oxford Today

Amenities and Attractions The nearby Caribou-Targhee National Forest and Bannock Mountain Range offer city residents a wide variety of outdoor activities. Hiking, biking, ATV riding, hunting and fishing are popular outdoor sports.

A marker commemorating the Bear River Massacre, the bloodiest battle in Idaho history, is located near Oxford on a gravel road just off U. S. Highway 91. (*See Eastern Idaho, American Indians – Bear River Massacre*.)

About six miles north is Red Rock Pass, where 14,500 years ago the prehistoric Lake Bonneville – a lake the size of Lake Michigan – breached sending flood waters across the Snake River Plain and cutting deep Canyons through which the Snake River presently flows. The Great Salt Lake and other low-lying lakes in Utah are remnants of this prehistoric freshwater lake. (*See Eastern Idaho, Major Geologic Features – Prehistoric Lake Bonneville.*)

Economy and Major Employers Most residents commute to nearby larger communities for employment. The city's retail district is limited, consisting of a few retail shops. Most residents travel to Preston to do their shopping.

The agriculture community that once underpinned the city's economy has undergone major consolidation. Farms have become larger and more productive with substantially fewer employees. Principal crops include grains, alfalfa, beans and potatoes.

Education The West Side School District, with offices in Dayton, provides primary and secondary public education for all of the communities in western Franklin County. Oxford students attend school in Dayton.

The closest institution of higher learning is Utah State University about 38 miles south in Logan, Utah.

Health Care The 21-bed Franklin County Medical Center in Preston is the nearest hospital.

Transportation County Road D1 connects Oxford with Clifton, Dayton, and Weston on the south. State Highway 36 intersects D1 just south of Dayton. Highway 36 intersects U.S. Highway 91 in Preston.

The 3,400-foot runway at Preston Airport provides service for small private and charter aircraft. Pocatello Regional Airport lies about 63 miles northwest. Ogden-Hinkley Airport is located about 70 miles south in Utah.

Railroad freight service is available in Preston.

Utilities and Services Private companies provide electricity, telephone and satellite services. The City provides domestic water. The city's homes and businesses are on individual septic systems. The County Sheriff's Office provides police protection under contract with the City.

Vision for 2050

Since 1980 Oxford's population has stayed around 52 to 53. These historical population trends will likely continue.

In 2050 Oxford will still be a quiet, friendly and peaceful place to raise a family.

Preston

Statistical Data

Population: 5,217 *
Elevation: 4,716 feet
Precipitation: 16 inches **
Average Snowfall: 51 inches **
County: Franklin
Website: www.prestonidaho.net

Temperature Range – Fahrenheit: **
Spring: 26 to 67
Summer: 46 to 87
Fall: 23 to 76
Winter: 12 to 37
* U.S. Census Bureau Estimates July 2015
**Historical averages

Preston lies at the north center of the 50-mile-long Cache Valley. The northern third of the valley is in Idaho and the lower two-thirds are in Utah. The Caribou-Targhee National Forest with its Bannock Mountain Range is five miles west and the Bear River Range, also in the Caribou-Targhee National Forest, is four miles east.

The Bear River flows a mile west of the city. Checkerboard patterns of farmland interspersed by juniper and brush-covered hills and public lands surround the city.

The Idaho/Utah border is four miles south. Franklin, Idaho's oldest city, is three miles south. Preston is included in the Logan, Utah, metropolitan statistical area.

Pre-Incorporation Years

Pioneer settlement of the southern part of Cache Valley began in 1850, three years after the first migration of members of The Church of Jesus Christ of Latter-day Saints (Church or Church of Jesus Christ) into the valley of the Great Salt Lake.

Settlement of the northern third of the valley began in 1860 following agreement with the Shoshone Tribe of Native Americans to whom the settlers provided gifts of food and supplies. The first families began settling at the confluence of Worm Creek and the Cub River. In June 1860 Brigham Young, leader of the Church, visited the new settlement. He named the town Franklin after Franklin D. Richards, a member of the Church's Twelve Apostles, and appointed Preston Thomas, a proven leader, as Bishop – unpaid ecclesiastical leader – of the new community.

By the end of the year, there were 61 families in Franklin. The settlers built a fort-like community with their log-cabin houses clustered around a square, the doors facing toward the center. Immediately outside the square, each family owned a 10-acre farm lot.

The land northwest of Franklin included a meadowland between Worm Creek and the Bear River. The meadowland, called Worm Creek Bottoms, had native grasses and streams, reminiscent of a worm trail, meandering through the meadow.

Many Franklin residents established squatter claims in Worm Creek Bottoms where they cut winter hay and grazed their livestock. (*See Eastern Idaho, Federal Land Use Laws.*)

In 1862 the federal government established a military fort in the foothills overlooking Salt Lake City under the command of Colonel Patrick E. Connor. The fort was to protect the overland mail, immigrants headed West, settlers and an increasing number of gold prospectors in the regions to the north.

On January 29, 1863, following an Indian attack in what is now western Montana where one prospector was killed, Connor directed his army in a frontal attack against a large body of Northwestern Shoshone encamped on the Bear River about two and a half miles north of what is now Preston.

Initially, the dug-in Shoshone warriors were winning the battle, until Conner directed his cavalry in flanking movements that over ran the Indian encampment. Implementing Connor's extermination order, the Army killed nearly 400 – including women and children – with half that number escaping or being taken prisoner. The Indians killed twenty-two of Connor's soldiers. About 130 soldiers were wounded or disabled by frostbite. (*See Eastern Idaho, American Indians – Bear River Massacre.*)

In July 1864 Ezra T. Benson, a member of the Church's Quorum of Twelve Apostles, called an exploring party of seven men to locate, select and plat townsites north of Franklin. They established several new communities including the cities of Clifton, Dayton, Weston and Oxford. (*See Eastern Idaho, Pioneer Settlements – Cache Valley.*)

In 1866 some of the Indians threatened the settlers spreading north of Franklin. In response to this threat, the north Cache Valley settlers abandoned their farms and homes and fled to the relative safety of the more settled areas around Franklin.

By 1867 the concern about Indian raids subsided and the settlers returned to their homes. Many of the Shoshone and Bannock Indians moved to the Fort Hall Indian Reservation established that year by treaty. Albeit in 1878 a break-away band of about 200 Bannock warriors, angry about their circumstances and unfulfilled promises made by the U.S. government, left the reservation and launched attacks upon settlers far to the northwest of Preston. After a series of skirmishes called the Bannock War, the military successfully suppressed further conflicts with the Shoshone Bannock Indians in Idaho. (*See Eastern Idaho, American Indians – The Bannock War*.)

As more settlers moved into the area, their livestock that were grazing on the open range began grazing in Worm Creek Bottoms. Franklin residents who had squatters' rights in the Bottoms built cabins where they stayed the summer to protect their property and herd their livestock. Gradually, they left Franklin and built permanent homes on their Worm Creek Bottom property. They named their settlement Worm Creek.

In 1872 the federal government surveyed the 42nd Parallel through the Western U.S. Prior to that time most of the northern Cache Valley settlers managed their business affairs as though they were part of Utah Territory. Following the official survey, many of the northern Cache Valley settlers were disappointed when they found that they lived in Idaho Territory. They now had to travel approximately 300 miles north to the territorial capital of Boise to do their territorial and political business rather than traveling 110 or so miles south to Salt Lake City. (*See Eastern Idaho, Idaho/Utah Boundary Resolution*.)

In 1881 the residents of Worm Creek changed the name of their community to Preston in honor of Preston Thomas, the Church's first Bishop in Franklin who died in 1877.

Until October 6, 1890, the Church of Jesus Christ's doctrine endorsed the practice of plural marriage under certain circumstances. Eastern Idaho's rapid population growth gave the Church an increasing political power base. In the 1880s most members of the Church supported the Democratic Party and represented about a fourth of the territory's population; however, Republicans controlled the governor's office and the Legislature. Many Republican politicos worried that if the Church members voted as a block, it could shift the balance of power in state and local governments to the Democrats.

Those seeking to limit the Church's influence saw polygamy as its Achilles heel. Tolerant of informal extramarital relationships common in society (non – practicing monogamists); these politicos expressed outrage at the Church's formal approval of plural marriage. They successfully used polygamy as a lightning rod to inflame political and public opinion against the Church and its members.

In 1885 the Idaho Territorial Legislature passed anti-polygamy and Test Oath Laws. Under the Test Oath, any man practicing polygamy or professing membership in an organization that approved of polygamy, even though they did not practice polygamy themselves (most church members were monogamists), were stripped of their civil rights to vote, hold office or serve on juries. At that time, Idaho law also denied suffrage rights to women, certain ethnic groups, adults under guardianship and felons.

In Preston and many Eastern Idaho cities, the Test Oath resulted in a huge power shift from the majority to the minority of citizens with all the potential mischief such undemocratic actions could produce.

On February 1, 1895, the Idaho Legislature repealed the Test Oath and many members of the Church became Republicans. (*See Eastern Idaho, Politics, Polygamy and Civil Rights*.)

In 1890 the Oregon Short Line Railroad built a rail line through Clifton en route to the Montana gold fields. Area residents now had an efficient way to transport freight and agriculture commodities as well as efficient passenger and mail services.

Incorporation

On July 25, 1900, Preston became an incorporated village. It became a city in 1967 when the change in state law gave city legal status to all incorporated municipalities.

Turning Points

Idaho/Utah Boundary Resolution. The 1872 federal survey of the 42nd parallel made clear that Franklin, Preston and other north Cache Valley communities were in Idaho Territory as opposed to Utah Territory. While that knowledge had little effect on people's day-to-day activities, it had an important effect on how the city and its residents dealt with matters affecting territorial law and politics.

Railroad The coming of the railroad in 1890 had a major impact on the city's economy as well as improving the quality of life for its citizens.

County Seat. On January 30, 1913, the Idaho Legislature created Franklin County with Preston as the county seat. This designation added to the prestige and stable employment base of the city.

Preston Today

Amenities and Attractions The nearby Caribou-Targhee National Forest and Bannock Mountain Range offer city residents a wide variety of outdoor activities. Hiking, biking, ATV riding, hunting and fishing are popular outdoor sports.

A marker commemorating the Bear River Massacre, the bloodiest battle in Idaho history, is located two and a half miles north of Preston on a gravel road just off U.S. Highway 91.

Residents also enjoy the amenities of nearby larger cities in both Idaho and Utah.

Economy and Major Employers With over 230 employees, Preston School District is the city's largest employer. The Franklin Medical Center has 150 employees and is the second largest employer. Two small manufacturing businesses, downtown retail establishments and government offices employ most of the other citizens. Many residents travel to Logan to work and shop.

The agriculture community that once underpinned the city's economy has undergone major consolidation. Farms have become larger and more productive with substantially fewer employees. Principal crops include grains, alfalfa, beans and potatoes.

Education The Preston School District provides primary and secondary public education for area students. The district operates a high school, junior high school and two elementary schools in the city.

The closest institution of higher learning is Utah State University about 27 miles south in Logan.

Health Care The 21-bed Franklin County Medical Center in Preston provides most of the medical services needed in the area.

Transportation North-south U.S. Highway 91 and east-west Idaho Highways 34 and 36 intersect the city.

The 3,400-foot runway at Preston Airport provides service for small private and charter aircraft. Pocatello Regional Airport lies about 70 miles northwest. Ogden-Hinkley Airport is located about 70 miles south in Utah.

Railroad freight service is available in the city.

Utilities and Services Private companies provide electricity, telephone and satellite services. The City provides water and sewer as well as police and fire protection.

Vision for 2050

In 1960 Preston's population was 3,640. In the past decade, the city's population has grown at about two percent annually.

Historical growth trends of one to two percent annually will likely continue. In that event, by 2050 Preston will have a population approaching 8,000. The city's existing infrastructure is adequate to accommodate this moderate growth with routine improvements and needed increases in capacity paid through existing revenue streams or bond issues approved by the voters.

Mayors

1913 L.N. Larsen *
1915 Nephi Larson *
1919 J.S. Marron *
1921 George E. Crockett *
1925 L.E. Hansen *
1935 T.R. Bowden *
1939 J. Clifford Forsgren *
1943 Edwin A. Crockett *
1947 Ernest Eberhard, Jr. *
1951 Rulon Dunn *
1955 Sherwin Webb *
1964 R.G. Cranney *
1966 O.R. Cutler
1970 Glen Gamble
1974 Lyle Shipley
1978 Wayne D. Bell
1982 Richard A. Bowman
1983 Reed Benchley
1984 J.D. Williams
1988 J. Walter Ross
1996 Jay B. Heusser
2004 Neal P. Larson
2008 F. Lee Hendrickson
2016 Mark Beckstead
* Village Chairman

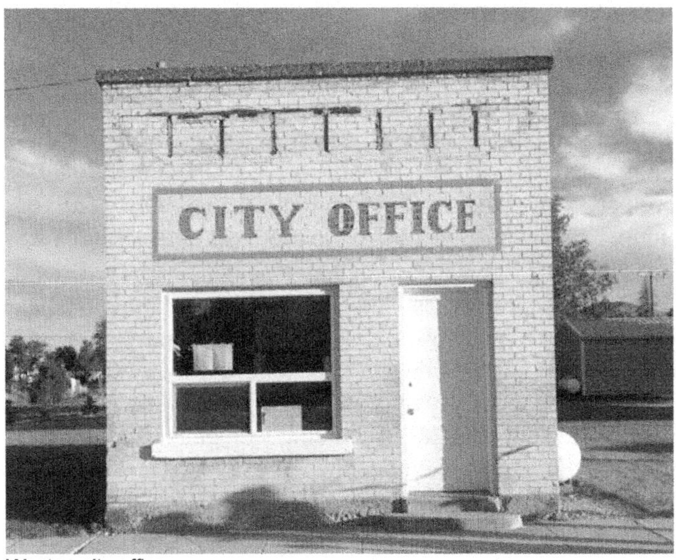

Weston city office.

Weston

Statistical Data

Population: 448 *
Elevation: 4,744 feet
Precipitation: 14 inches **
Average Snowfall: 32 inches **
County: Franklin

Temperature Range – Fahrenheit: **
Spring: 26 to 67
Summer: 46 to 87
Fall: 23 to 76
Winter: 12 to 37
* U.S. Census Bureau Estimates July 2015
**Historical averages

Weston lies on the eastern edge of the fertile 50-mile-long Cache Valley. The northern third of the valley is in Idaho and the lower two-thirds are in Utah. The Caribou-Targhee National Forest – with its Bannock Mountain Range rising to over 8,000 feet – lies west of the city.

To the east, fertile farms, irrigation canals, streams, reservoirs and wetlands stretch for about 15 miles across the valley before meeting the mountains of the Bear River Range, also in the Caribou-Targhee National Forest. This range has peaks rising to over 9,000 feet.

Franklin is about 14 miles east. The Idaho/Utah border is about six miles due south.

Pre-Incorporation Years

Pioneer settlement of the southern part of Cache Valley began in 1850, three years after the first migration of members of The Church of Jesus Christ of Latter-day Saints (Church or Church of Jesus Christ) into the valley of the Great Salt Lake.

The Cache Valley settlements moved progressively north. In 1860 they established the farming community of Franklin.

In 1862 the federal government established a military fort in the foothills overlooking Salt Lake City under the command of Colonel Patrick E. Connor. The fort was to protect the overland mail, immigrants headed West, settlers and an increasing number of gold prospectors in the regions to the north.

On January 29, 1863, following an Indian attack in what is now western Montana where one prospector was killed, Connor led his army in an attack against a large body of Shoshone encamped on the Bear River approximately 15 miles northeast of Weston. Initially, the dug-in Shoshone warriors were winning the battle, until Conner directed his cavalry in flanking movements that over ran the Indians. The army killed nearly 400 – including women and children – with half that number escaping or being taken prisoner. Twenty-two of Connor's soldiers were killed and about 130 were wounded or disabled by frostbite. (*See Eastern Idaho, American Indians – Bear River Massacre.*)

Old Weston grade school bell tower now holds a place of honor in the park.

In July 1864 Ezra T. Benson, a member of the Church's Quorum of Twelve Apostles, called an exploring party of seven men to locate, select and plat townsites north and west of Franklin. They established several new communities including what are now the cities of Weston, Clifton, Dayton, Oxford and Preston.

Settlement of Weston began in 1865. The settlers were members of the Church traveling up from Utah Territory, seeking arable land on which to establish their homes and farms. (*See Eastern Idaho, Pioneer Settlements – Cache Valley.*) They named their town Weston because it was located on the west side of the valley and it was the maiden name of one of the settlers, Ann Weston Maughan.

Lars Fredrickson wrote about the initial settlement of the town in his diary. He said, "They all dug a hole in the ground and put a roof on [homes called dugouts] ... with an open fireplace and a chimney ... They planted some crops mostly wheat ... (They then began building a dam on Weston Creek for irrigation) ... The men put in willows ... and sod ... They made a rack of two poles (woven together to form a stretcher) with small willows so it could hold dirt ... then a man at each end to carry the load ...

"The creek was full of beavers; so as soon as the beavers understood there was going to be a dam built, they would work at night adding willows ... plastered with mud ... in about four weeks they had the water out and getting their grain irrigated ... "

In 1865 settlers in Bear Lake Valley, located across the Bear River Mountain Range about 35 miles due west of what is now Weston, had an incident that affected the settlers on north Cache Valley. Some of those settlers decided to establish homesteads south of St. Charles, contrary to the settlement agreements Church leaders had reached with the Shoshone and Bannock Indians. The Shoshone destroyed their farms and sent the encroaching settlers fleeing back to St. Charles for safety.

In 1866 the Indians, apparently heartened by their success in the South Bear Lake area, threatened the settlers spreading north of Franklin. The north Cache Valley settlers abandoned their farms and homes and fled to the relative safety in the more settled areas around Franklin. By 1867 the threats had subsided, and the settlers returned to their homes. By the following year, most of the Shoshone and Bannock Indians were living on the Fort Hall Indian Reservation. (*See Eastern Idaho, American Indians – The Bannock War.*)

In 1867 when settlers returned to the Weston area, many chose to locate on the land to the south and west of their original settlement. They settled on the west side of the Bear River in the "south fields" area and on March 26, 1868, J.H. Martineau surveyed and later platted the town of Weston.

In 1867 John Maughan, the appointed religious leader of the Weston settlers, built a log cabin on his property that served as the community's first schoolhouse in which there were five students. In the same year, James Mack built a flour mill on Weston Creek.

The settlers' communication with the outside generally came through Franklin. Travel on the rough wagon road connecting the two communities was arduous. In 1868 the settlers built a bridge across the Bear River to Franklin, greatly reducing the difficulty of the trip. During those years, mail service from Logan came twice a week.

In 1868 they also hauled logs from Clifton Basin and erected a large building on the public square that served as a church meetinghouse, public school and amusement hall.

In 1872 the federal government surveyed the 42nd Parallel through the Western United States. Prior to that time, most of the northern Cache Valley settlers managed their business affairs as though they were part of Utah Territory. Following the official survey, many of the northern Cache Valley settlers were disappointed when they found that they lived in Idaho Territory. They now had to travel approximately 300 miles northwest to the territorial capital of Boise to do their territorial and political business, rather than traveling 110 or so miles south to Salt Lake City. (*See Eastern Idaho, Idaho/Utah Boundary Resolution*.)

In 1890 the Oregon Short Line Railroad built a rail line through Clifton en route to the Montana gold fields. Area residents now had an efficient way to transport freight and agriculture commodities as well as efficient passenger and mail services.

Incorporation

On January 1, 1903, Weston became an incorporated village. It became a city in 1967 when the change in state law changed the legal status of incorporated municipalities to that of a city.

Turning Points

Idaho/Utah Boundary Resolution. The 1872 federal survey of the 42nd parallel made clear that Weston and the other north Cache Valley communities were in Idaho Territory as opposed to Utah Territory where many hoped they would be. While that knowledge had little effect on people's day-to-day activities, it had an important effect on how the city and its residents dealt with matters affecting territorial law and politics.

Grandstand in Weston City Park.

Railroad The coming of the railroad in 1890 had a major impact on the city's economy as well as improving the quality of life for its citizens.

Weston Today

Amenities and Attractions Weston has a wonderful city park with a large old-time grandstand, a ball field, tennis courts, a pavilion, restrooms and a children's playground. It is great for family reunions.

Each July 24 the city celebrates its Mormon pioneer heritage with a parade, food and games at the city park.

The nearby Caribou-Targhee National Forest and Bannock Mountain Range offer city residents a wide variety of outdoor activities. Hiking, biking, ATV riding, hunting and fishing are popular outdoor sports.

Weston City Park tennis courts.

A marker commemorating the Bear River Massacre, the bloodiest battle in Idaho history, is located five miles north of Preston on a gravel road just off U.S. Highway 91. Preston is 10 miles east of Weston.

Residents also enjoy the amenities of nearby larger cities in both Idaho and Utah.

Economy and Major Employers Most residents commute to nearby larger communities for employment. The city's retail district is limited, consisting of a few retail shops. Most residents travel to Preston and Logan to do their shopping.

The agriculture community that once underpinned the city's economy has undergone major consolidation. Farms have become larger and more productive with substantially fewer employees. Principal crops include grains, alfalfa, beans and potatoes.

Education The West Side School District provides primary and secondary education for all of the communities in western Franklin County. Weston students attend school in Dayton. The closest institution of higher learning is Utah State University about 38 miles south in Logan.

Playground equipment in Weston City Park.

Health Care The 21-bed Franklin County Medical Center in Preston is the nearest hospital.

Transportation County road D1 and Idaho Highway 36 intersect the city. Just south of the city, county roads intersect U.S. Highway 91 at Franklin.

The 3,400-foot runway at Preston Airport provides service for small private and charter aircraft. Pocatello Regional Airport is about 63 miles northwest. Ogden-Hinkley Airport is located about 70 miles south in Utah.

Railroad freight service is available in Preston.

Utilities and Services Private companies provide electricity, telephone and satellite services. The City provides domestic water. The city's homes and businesses are on individual septic systems. The County Sheriff's Office provides police protection under contract with the City. The Franklin County Fire District provides fire protection.

Vision for 2050

In 1960 Weston's population was 284. Since 1990 the city's population has ranged from 390 to 437. The more recent historical trends will likely continue.

In 2050 Weston will continue to be a peaceful rural community near open public lands yet close to larger cities, some with regional shopping and service centers. Weston is a wonderful place to live and raise a family.

Mayors

1903-1967 Unknown *
1967 Sterling Bingham
1976 Maurice Tingey
1986 Clint Buttars
1990 Sterling Wirthlin
1994 Leo Daley
2010 Camille Larsen
2014 Layne Harris
* Village Chairman

Fly fishing.

FREMONT COUNTY

- Ashton
- Drummond
- Island Park
- Newdale
- Parker
- St. Anthony (*County Seat*)
- Teton
- Warm River

Mesa Falls and a rainbow.

Ashton

Statistical Data

Population: 1,064 *
Elevation: 5,255 feet
Precipitation: 19 inches **
Average Snowfall:91 inches **
County: Fremont
Website: www.cityofashton.com

Temperature Range – Fahrenheit: **
Spring: 29 to 73
Summer: 38 to 81
Fall: 11 to 59
Winter: 10 to 40
* U.S. Census Bureau Estimates July 2015
**Historical averages

Ashton is a historic railroad and farm-based community situated in the northeast corner of Idaho. Located nearby are some of Idaho's more fabulous scenic vistas, diversity of terrain and destination tourist attractions.

The lower reaches of the Henry's Fork of the Snake River, an internationally known fly-fishing stream, flows past the western edge of the city.

Traveling cross country, Yellowstone National Park begins 18 miles northeast. However, the park entrance at West Yellowstone, Montana, is 50 miles away.

The Grand Teton National Park entrance in Wyoming is 39 miles away. The Teton Mountains, whose highest peak rises to 13,771 feet, outline Ashton's southeastern sky.

Pre-Incorporation Years

In 1872 President Ulysses S. Grant signed the law establishing Yellowstone National Park. Ninety-six percent of the park is in Wyoming, three percent in Montana and one percent in Idaho. It was the nation's first national park.

In the 1800s emigrant pioneers, primarily from Utah, began homesteading arable land around what is now the city of Ashton.

In 1899 the St. Anthony Railroad Company began construction of a rail line from Idaho Falls to St Anthony. In 1905 the Yellowstone Park Railroad Company (later the Oregon Short Line Railroad) began constructing a rail line to the west entrance of Yellowstone National Park with a branch line extending south from Ashton to Driggs and Victor. In 1909 the rail line reached the Park.

William Ashton, Chief Engineer for the railroad, selected a new townsite. Following a common railroad practice of naming new railroad towns and facilities after its executives, William named the new town "Ashton" after himself.

Ashton train depot, now the Ashton Christian Fellowship Church.

He directed train personnel to build the depot north of town. The depot would have a four-bay engine-maintenance building that also stored engines needed to help the trains make the steep grades to West Yellowstone. Ashton named that depot Ingling after the railroad's master mechanic, William J. Ingling.

In 1904 two educators who also ran a real estate office, C.C. Moore and H.G. Fuller, purchased 640 acres of land for a townsite. Ashton directed W.J. King, the railroad surveyor, to plat the new city including the names of the streets. King platted the town on the land secured by Moore and Fuller. Moore served as Idaho's Governor from 1923 through 1926.

$15,000 was raised to build this old school in 1906.

Moore and Fuller also recruited 13 community leaders to become members of the townsite committee. They raised $15,000 to build a four-room brick school. Committee members involved in the lumber business brought in building materials needed to construct the new homes and businesses.

On February 14, 1906, the first train pulled into Ashton. A large crowd and considerable fanfare greeted the passenger train, carrying railroad and local dignitaries. The celebration concluded with a dance and party at the newly finished Miller Brothers grain elevator. However, it would take until 1908 before summer train service reached the Yellowstone Branch of the railroad.

Incorporation

On August 11, 1906, Ashton became an incorporated village. At that time, the Ashton business community included the grain elevators, several retail shops, a newspaper, medical doctor, pharmacy, barbershop and undertaker.

Turning Points

Railroad Ashton owes its origins to the railroad. The railroad not only established the city as an area business and shopping center, it brought a new employment base and facilitated economic expansion.

Truck loaded with potatoes. Gifford farm, circa 1966-67.

Farmers no longer needed to transport their production to the nearest railhead over uncertain roads using slow mule or horse-drawn freight wagons.

Tourists and visitors to Yellowstone National Park could now comfortably travel great distances in a fraction of the time.

However, by the 1950s improved roads and motor vehicles were offering attractive alternatives to railroad passenger and freight services. In 1960 the railroad shut down its passenger service to West Yellowstone. In 1990 the railroad also ceased rail service to Driggs and Victor.

Replica of one-room schoolhouse, Hess Heritage Museum.

The rail line from Idaho Falls to Ashton, now owned by the Eastern Idaho Railroad, continues to provide freight service.

Agriculture In the early 1930s most potato farmers used potatoes they saved from the previous year's crop for seed. The University of Idaho Agriculture Experimental Station scientists discovered that this practice exacerbated bacterial and viral diseases that contributed to reduced yield or crop failure. The practice also acted as an impediment to farmers experimenting with improved strains of potatoes.

Research showed that the best certified seed potatoes grow in higher elevations where the growing season is short and diseases do not have time to develop. The land around Ashton is ideal for growing seed potatoes. Ashton farmers seized on this niche business and added certified seed potatoes to their list of farm commodities produced. Ashton is now a major player in growing certified seed potatoes.

Over the past several decades, technological innovation accompanied by farm consolidation has made farms more productive with fewer employees. These innovations include pumping water from deep wells; sprinkler irrigation; development of commercial fertilizers; certified seed; improved seed varieties; better farm practices; weed control and high-tech trucks, tractors and equipment. These innovations have improved the prosperity of farmers. The declining agricultural workforce caused by these innovations has also had an adverse effect on the number of farm workers coming into the city to shop.

Ashton supports sports. Everyone in town tried to go to the state football championship game circa1989. The town was almost deserted - hence the sign.

World Wars and the Great Depression World Wars I and II, the economic depressions of the 1920s and 1930s and periodic drought had consequences that devastated many individual families and businesses. However, in general, the city and its economy survived each event a bit wiser and stronger.

New Economy Tourism and outdoor recreation industries are providing a new direction for the city's economy. Many old as well as new businesses are expanding or coming to serve an increasing number of visitors attracted by the beauty of southeastern Idaho.

Ashton street.

Ashton Today

Amenities and Attractions The city's most prominent winter attraction is Ashton's American Dog Derby, an annual dog sled race. In 1993 the Ambassador's Cup Sports Foundation restored this annual event that started in 1917. Originally, the course was a 55-mile course between West Yellowstone and Ashton. In 1921 a crowd of 10,000 witnessed the race. However, several years later it closed.

Today the event takes place each February and attracts mushers from throughout the nation. The round-trip course takes two days over a rigorous trail through the fields and forests between Ashton and Island Park.

In commemoration of this event, Ashton's North Fremont High School students made "Huskies" the school mascot.

In the snow season, generally from November through March, Ashton also serves as a snowmobile trailhead. Groomed trails lead out of Ashton to connect with several other groomed trails leading to spectacular sights throughout the region. In the summer and fall, ATV enthusiasts use these trails.

New school, opened 2004.

Each August, the city supports the Mesa Falls Marathon. The marathon passes through a variety of exceptionally beautiful terrain and is attracting an increasing number of participants each year.

Other events each year are the July 4th Independence Day Parade and an old-fashioned cattle drive down the middle of Main Street sponsored by the Cordingley family. A beef dinner served at the historic Opera House follows the cattle drive.

A one-time event occurred in 2006, the city's centennial celebration. As part of the celebration, artisans designed and manufactured a Centennial gun, coin, and other memorabilia. One local family has turned its homestead into a farm museum. The museum hosts hundreds of tourists every year.

The abandoned railroad bed to Victor and West Yellowstone is now a Rails to Trails pathway, open for pedestrian and bicycle traffic; an outstanding tourist attraction.

Three scenic byways – the Mesa Falls Scenic Byway (State Highway 47), Teton Scenic Byway (State Highway 32) and U.S. Highway 20 – intersect in the city.

Twenty miles to the north on Highway 20 is Island Park Caldera. It is 18 by 23 miles in diameter. Perhaps half a million years ago the roof of the volcano's magma chamber collapsed to form the caldera. Centuries of erosion have obscured much of the caldera rim. However, the south and west rim of a 1,200-foot scarp is still visible at Big Bend Ridge.

A few miles north of the city are the hydroelectric dam and 400-acre reservoir. The reservoir is a popular lake for fishing, boating and water skiing.

The 11,000-acre Harriman State Park is located 18 miles north of the city. The park features tours; fly-fishing; hiking; horseback riding; and viewing a variety of wildlife including Trumpeter Swan, moose, elk and Sandhill Crane.

The St. Anthony Sand Dunes lie 20 miles southwest. These dunes cover an area 35 miles long and up to five miles wide. The height of the dunes themselves range from 70 to 365 feet – a height greater than the dunes in Death Valley, California.

The spectacular Upper and Lower Mesa Falls, unique natural features, lie about 15 miles north. The surrounding public lands with its many rivers, streams and lakes are an outdoor sportsman's paradise.

Economy and Major Employers Ashton does not have a dominant employer. The North Fremont School District and the Ashton Nursing Home with about 75 employees each are the city's largest employers. Fall River Rural Electric and the U.S. Forest Service are next with 40 and 20 employees, respectively.

Farming and related businesses are no longer dominant employers; however, they are a stabilizing influence on the city's economy. Many of the farmers who still live around Ashton are descendants of the original homesteaders and grow certified seed potatoes, wheat, barley, alfalfa hay and canola.

Many Ashton residents drive to larger cities to shop. Many young people find employment in Island Park working for tourist or construction businesses.

Education Fremont County Public School District serves all of the students in the county. Schools in Ashton include Ashton Elementary, North Fremont Middle School and North Fremont High School. The closest institution of higher learning is BYU-Idaho in Rexburg, 26 miles southwest.

Health Care General outpatient services are available at the "Medical Center" in Ashton. The Ashton Nursing Home provides care for the elderly, recovering and disabled. The closest hospital is Madison Memorial Hospital in Rexburg.

Transportation U.S. Highway 20 is the primary road. It connects the city with Rexburg and Interstate 15 to the south and Yellowstone National Park to the northeast. Idaho Highway 32 connects Ashton with the cities to the south in the Teton Basin. Idaho Highway 47 is a beautiful drive through Mesa Falls.

Rail service is available for freight only between Ashton and Idaho Falls.

The closest commercial-carrier airport is Yellowstone Airport, 48 miles northeast near West Yellowstone, Montana.

Utilities and Services Private companies provide electrical, telephone and satellite services. The City provides water and sewer services as well as fire and police protection.

Vision for 2050

For the past two decades, Ashton's population has held in a narrow range averaging about 1,150. However, by 2050 this will change dramatically. Tourists and those who enjoy the outdoors are finding Ashton an attractive home base from which to explore the fabulous natural beauty of the surrounding area. By 2050 tourism and outdoor recreation industries will likely underpin the city's economy.

Many mountain bikers and joggers will come to use the "Rails to Trails" path from Ashton to Tetonia, Victor and Jackson Hole. The Scenic Byway Corridor Management Plan will be a reality, bringing visitors to town via the Mesa Falls Byway. The city will have daily mass transportation service to accommodate senior citizens and commuters.

As population growth occurs, city and community leaders will monitor the consequence of growth on land planning, transportation and municipal services. Our objective is to insure that as the city grows, Ashton retains its charm and beauty as a desirable place to work and raise a family.

Mayors

1906 H.L. Cannon *
** H.G. "Fess" Fuller
2001 Teddy Stronks

* Village Chairman
** Dates Unknown

Old grain elevator in Drummond.

Drummond

Statistical Data

Population: 15*
Elevation: 5,400 feet
Precipitation: 19 inches **
Average Snowfall: 91 inches **
County: Fremont

Temperature Range – Fahrenheit: **
Spring: 29 to 73
Summer: 38 to 81
Fall: 11 to 59
Winter: 0 to 40
* U.S. Census Bureay Estimates July 2015
**Historical averages

Drummond is surrounded by rolling hills of grain punctuated by an occasional farmhouse. The Grand Teton Mountain Range outlines the eastern sky.

The residents remaining in this once thriving community occupy nine of the city's homes. The others are owned by non-residents and used as vacation homes.

Pre-Incorporation Years

When the Oregon Short Line Railroad built its rail line through what is now Drummond around 1907, it connected several Eastern Idaho farming communities and provided the transportation needed by hundreds of farmers and ranchers to ship their commodities and livestock to distant markets. (*See Eastern Idaho, The Region, Railroads.*)

Drummond began as a railroad stop on land homesteaded by Elmo Lamont. The railroad's chief engineer at the time, Bill Ashton, said that he would name the train stop after the homesteader. However, shortly thereafter Ashton was seriously injured by a runaway team of horses and had to be replaced. Ashton's successor was a man named Drummond.

Drummond was a bald man of middle age and excellent character with a strong voice that could be heard from a long way off. It was said of him that, "Even at conversational level, his voice seemed to be pitched at someone a rod or two down the right of way."

Drummond railroad depot.

Drummond used his position as the new chief engineer to set Ashton's plan aside. He named the train stop after himself, saying he would give the name of Lamont to another community further east. He then successfully applied for the Drummond post office which opened October 31, 1911, and was involved in platting the town. The mail came by train and was then delivered to the surrounding communities by horse and wagon. In the winter the mail carrier used a dog sled.

Lloyd VanSickle delivering mail by dog sled to Squirrel, 1947-48.

Around that time Charles and Josephine Burrall owned the town's general merchandise store as well as a store in nearby Squirrel. In 1914 Josephine's brother, John Carlson, and his wife and four young sons came to Drummond to help run the stores.

A year earlier, area residents built a three-story brick schoolhouse in Drummond. The building had a coal-fired, steam-heat furnace in the basement, five classrooms, an indoor volleyball court and restrooms. However, it only included classes up to the 10th grade.

In order for the children to take the last two years of high school, they boarded with families in the towns that had high schools. Many Drummond families lived in a second home in Ashton while their children attended high school, returning to their Drummond farms when school was out.

At that time, the Presbyterian Church was the only church in town. A traveling minister came periodically to hold services for area families. Other families traveled to Ashton or combined to hold services in their homes.

Early winter days in Drummond.

However, a terrible tragedy was about to strike this peaceful community. The tentacles of the global influenza pandemic of 1918 to 1919 reached Drummond with devastating force. Two families particularly affected by the virus – generally known as the Spanish Flu – were the Burrall and Carlson families. When the epidemic was over, only Charles Burrall and his nephews, the two youngest Carlson children, survived.

Incorporation

Drummond incorporated as a village on January 10, 1917. Three months later, the citizens passed a bond to pay for a municipal well and water distribution system.

On October 14, 1919, they passed another bond to enlarge the water system. At that time, the population of the city was about 1,000. The business community consisted of two general stores, a drugstore, barbershop, pool hall, two grain elevators, a lumberyard, hotel and a bank.

Drummond school house.

The next year, Idaho Governor Charles Moore helped persuade "a trainload of people" from Missouri to homestead around Drummond, Lamont and France.

Turning Points

Railroad The railroad created the town and for decades provided the transportation system that promoted the agricultural settlement of the area. Drummond became the railroad shipping point for the area's dry-land wheat farmers. In 1938 an estimated 250,000 bushels of Drummond wheat were loaded on rail cars.

However, the country was entering an era of more efficient motor vehicles and hard-surface roads connecting communities. By the middle of the century, trucks were hauling more commodities than trains. Unable to compete, the railroad shut down and abandoned its rail line through Drummond, jobs were lost and more residents moved.

Dry-Land Wheat and Farm Consolidation Early farmers found the arid land to be most suitable for raising dry-land winter wheat. As the years, passed technological innovation in agricultural equipment, farming practices, improved plant varieties and motorized transportation encouraged farmers to invest in equipment that could cultivate more land with improved productivity and substantially fewer workers. In that environment, smaller farm operations began selling or leasing their property to larger operators. With these changes, there were fewer families and workers coming to town and retail businesses suffered.

Drummond School students, 1917 (above), 1935 (below).

Schools In 1948 Drummond became part of the Ashton school system, now Fremont County Joint School District with offices in St. Anthony. After that, students previously attending school in Drummond rode buses to their schools in Ashton. Drummond's red brick school building fell into disrepair and was eventually torn down.

Drummond Today

Amenities and Attractions The state-owned "Rails to Trails" hiking and biking path runs through town on the abandoned railroad right-of-way – one of the last remnants of Drummond's more vibrant past.

Economy and Major Employers The Village Bar is the only remaining business in Drummond. Most residents travel 10 miles northwest to Ashton for their shopping and business needs.

Education School children attend public school in Ashton.

The closest institution of higher learning is 30 miles southwest at Brigham Young University-Idaho in Rexburg.

Health Care Drummond residents travel to Ashton and the hospitals in Driggs and Rexburg for their medical and health care needs.

Transportation Drummond is 10 miles off U.S. Highway 20.

The nearest commercial airport is Fanning Field in Idaho Falls.

Utilities and Services The City provides water service. Fall River Rural Electric Cooperative provides electricity. Residents use individual septic tanks. Fremont County Sheriff's Department provides police protection. A volunteer fire department in Ashton provides fire protection.

Vision for 2050

The area's sheer beauty is the city's best attribute. By 2050 several factors will converge to bring people back to enjoy the beautiful, peaceful setting that Drummond offers.

Rough Riders Saloon in Drummond.

Rural lifestyles are becoming more in demand. Satellite and other information technologies are changing the need for people to live in a metropolitan area for employment.

Drummond's existing and functioning municipal services and utilities make it a desirable location to live in peace and quiet within an easy commute of excellent retail and educational facilities.

The "Rails to Trails" path from Ashton to Tetonia is an outstanding amenity for hiking and biking enthusiasts, who like to get out in nature. This amenity will be an important attraction for new residents.

The growth in second-home residences experienced by Teton Basin cities will eventually spill over to Drummond.

Mayors

Merle Harshbarger *
1988 Fred Niendorf
1992 Charles B. Kuehlewind
2006 Ellis Shirley
2010 Twyla Formasi

* Village Chairman – City records are skimpy or nonexistent until 1955. A minute book shows that Merle Harshbarger served as Village Chairman for an indeterminate time.

Snowmobiles at Island Park Lodge.

Island Park

Statistical Data

Population: 273 *
Elevation: 6,320 feet
Precipitation: 19 inches **
Average Snowfall: 92 inches **
Website: www.islandparkid.govoffice2.com

Temperature Range – Fahrenheit: **
Spring: 15 to 59
Summer: 38 to 79
Fall: 16 to 70
Winter: 5 to 31

* U.S. Census Bureau Estimates July 2015
**Historical averages

The city's name, Island Park, describes its beautiful geographic and geologic setting. One national and two state parks are nearby. The Old Faithful Geyser of Yellowstone National Park lies 20 miles due east across the mountains. Henry's Lake State Park is on the north. Harriman State Park is on the south and west.

The city lies in the northeast corner of Eastern Idaho in an ancient caldera, one of the largest in the world. The continental divide forms a 15-mile-wide and equally long irregular crescent north of the city as it wraps around the famous Henry's Lake fishery. The Grand Targhee National Forest surrounds the city. The nearby mountains offer several scenic vistas, pristine springs, rivers and streams.

The city boundaries are unique in Idaho. Island Park is 34.8 miles long and 500 to 5,000 feet wide. Its elevations range from 6,290 to 6,400 feet. Residents proudly boast that their city has the longest Main Street in America.

Main Street has significant open space interspersed with lodges, motels, restaurants, lounges, convenience stores, gas stations, tackle shops and recreational vehicle rental businesses.

Pre-Incorporation Years

At the time Lewis, Clark and the Corps of Discovery completed their expedition in 1806, Shoshone-Bannock and Crow Indians hunted and fished in what is now Island Park.

In 1810 Andrew Henry, employed by the Missouri Fur Company, led a group of explorers and trappers across the continental divide and found the lake that would bear his name. Impressed with the abundant wildlife, they built cabins and established a trading post on the west side of the Henry's Fork of the Snake River, a few miles south of what is now St. Anthony. They called their post Fort Henry.

Ranching, on the old highway.

Beaver trapping was excellent, but the winter was very cold. The wild game moved south, forcing the trappers to kill their horses for food. In the spring of 1811 Henry and his men abandoned the site and returned to Missouri.

For the next several decades, other fur trappers periodically came into the area. However, settlement did not begin for several decades, and then it generally occurred further south at lower elevations.

In the 1880s, however, Swiss emigrants sponsored by the Arangee Land and Cattle Company attempted to develop a colony. Unfortunately, in 1889 the company went broke. Still, many company settlers stayed in the general area as homesteaders and cattle ranchers.

Brrrrrr!

Yellowstone Park, created by the U.S. Congress in 1872, was the nation's first national park and was becoming an increasingly popular tourist attraction. Oregon Short Line Railroad officials saw an opportunity to provide transportation to the park.

In 1881 the railroad surveyed a route from Idaho Falls to Yellowstone National Park with rail line construction starting a few years later.

Around the turn of the century, the railroad reached Island Park. With it came additional homesteading. Many new settlers became "tie hacks" and harvested logs for making railroad ties. Others provided guide services for hunters, anglers and tourists brought in by the railroad.

Homesteaders broke up the land and raised hay and grain. Lettuce grew well in the cool climate and became an important crop. Some settlers became cattle ranchers, and others raised dairy cows and produced cheese.

Over the next several years, construction projects changed living standards in the area. In 1916 park officials began building hard-surface roads through Yellowstone Park. Henry's Lake Dam – completed in 1924 – provided irrigation water storage for lower Snake River Valley farmers. In 1933 the power plant on the Buffalo River – built by the Civilian Conservation Corps – introduced hydroelectric power to an area that had previously relied on gas generators. In 1935 the Island Park Dam was completed.

Incorporation

By 1947 several hospitality and retail businesses had built up along U.S. Highway 20. At that time, the Idaho Legislature passed a law governing the sale of liquor-by-the-drink and the licensure of establishments offering liquor. A provision of the law required businesses that sold alcoholic beverages to be licensed and located within incorporated cities or villages.

This requirement prompted the businesses along U.S. Highway 20 to ask the Fremont County Commission in St. Anthony to make Island Park an incorporated village. The boundaries were 34.8 miles long and included all businesses selling alcoholic beverages between Last Chance and the Montana border.

On May 16, 1947, the county commissioners incorporated the village and appointed a board of trustees to serve until the next election.

On August 18, 1949, there were 70 registered voters in the village. Harvey

Schwendiman, the village's first Chairman, garnered 57 of the 58 votes cast and held the seat for 24 years. Island Park became an incorporated city in 1967 as required by a change in state law.

Turning Points

Yellowstone National Park Congressional action in 1872 to create Yellowstone National Park was the basis for bringing rail passenger service and later a highway to Island Park. Tourists traveling to the park by automobile became customers for the retail businesses that built up along U.S. Highway 20.

Change in Idaho's Alcohol Beverage Code The 1947 change in the state's liquor law precipitated the incorporation of the village in its unique form.

Island Park Today

Amenities and Attractions In the summer, Island Park is a destination for anglers looking to catch trophy trout and families vacationing at resorts and ranches. Others may come to ride horses, hike or bike in the mountains or camp next to a stream or lake. Many come to see the bald eagles, grouse, sandhill cranes, songbirds, raptors, waterfowl, large and small mammals and wildflowers.

Fun with snow plowing.

In the winter, the area is a wonderland. The forest has over 500 miles of snowmobile trails and groomed trails for snowshoeing and Nordic skiing.

Thousands of travelers from all over the world come every year to enjoy this picturesque area. Many have second homes and come more frequently.

Numerous hospitality businesses – including lodges, restaurants, resorts, motels, lounges, ATV and snowmobile rental and other retail businesses – line the city's elongated Main Street. However, just off that narrow commercial corridor is a broad expanse of beautiful scenery and open spaces.

Island Park cemetery.

The 11,000-acre Harriman State Park and Wildlife Refuge is a haven for a variety of waterfowl, elk, deer and moose.

Eight miles of the famous fly-fishing Henry's Fork of the Snake River flows through the park. The park also has over 20 miles of trails for hiking, biking, horseback riding and cross-country skiing. Some of the historic Railroad Ranch buildings are available for tours and lodging.

Henry's Lake State Park offers campfire and Junior Ranger programs. There are 44 sites for camping and several camping cabins next to the 6,000-acre lake. Anglers fish for cutthroat, brook and rainbow trout.

Elk Creek Lake.

Mesa Falls Scenic Byway starts six miles south on State Highway 47. The Mesa Falls Recreation Area has a visitor's center in the historic lodge near Upper Mesa Falls. Both Upper and Lower Mesa Falls have trails and picnic areas.

The northern end of the city is 14 miles from the west entrance to Yellowstone National Park.

Island Park Caldera, in which the city is located, is approximately 18 miles wide and 23 miles long. Perhaps half a million years ago, the roof of the volcano's magma chamber collapsed to form the caldera. Centuries of erosion have obscured much of the caldera rim. However, the south and west rim of a 1,200-foot scarp is still visible at Big Bend Ridge.

Colors of fall.

The Island Park Dam is located a mile west of the city. The dam, built in 1937 at the head of Box Canyon, forms the 8,400-acre Island Park Reservoir. The dam provides hydroelectricity and irrigation water for the lower Snake River Plain. The reservoir is popular for camping, fishing and water skiing.

The St. Anthony Sand Dunes are 50 miles southwest. These dunes cover an area 35 miles long and up to five miles wide. The height of the dunes themselves ranges from 70 to 365 feet – a height greater than the dunes in Death Valley, California.

Other locations with unique natural features include Big Springs located northeast of the city. Big Springs has a continuous flow of 92,000 gallons of water a minute and is the primary water source for the Henry's Fork of the Snake River.

The flow of spring water from Big Springs to Mack's Inn is on the National Water Trail. Big Springs is also home to the Johnny Sack Cabin and Waterwheel. This 1935 vintage home is on the National Register of Historic Places with examples of Johnny Sack's artful methods of using bark in the construction of furniture.

Four historic byways are near the city – Fort Henry Historic Byway, Lost Gold Trails Loop, Nez Perce Historic Trail and Mesa Falls Scenic Byway.

The Nature Conservancy (TNC) owns the 1,600-acre Flat Ranch. The ranch has a visitors" center where TNC hosts educational programs about the area's natural resources. In addition, several ranches near Henry's Lake are under conservation easements that prohibit development.

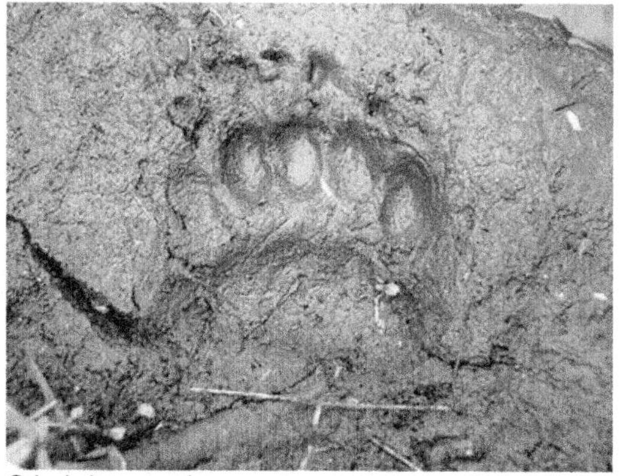
Grizzly bear track.

Island Park is a destination for geology buffs and "rock hounds." Because the city lies in an ancient volcanic caldera, there are many areas of exposed volcanic rock. Garnet Hill, located near Henry's Lake, is a favorite spot to find garnet gemstones, especially after spring runoff.

Economy and Major Employers The hospitality and real estate industries underpin the city's economy. Several resorts and lodges, with fewer than two dozen employees each, provide a variety of accommodations for tourists including restaurants, cabin and condominium rentals and RV parking. They provide supervised float and horseback trips and fly-fishing guide services. In the winter, they rent snowmobiles and winter gear and conduct guided tours.

There are working cattle ranches nearby that have accommodations for tourists. Patrons of these ranches can watch the cowboys do their jobs, participate in cattle drives, ride horses, fish or just relax.

Many visitors are fly-fishing enthusiasts who come to fish on the famous Henry's Fork of the Snake River or many of the other nearby streams and lakes. For the more experienced angler, the city has specialized fishing equipment shops and expert guides.

The community's real estate professionals have an active market serving people looking for second homes and becoming part-time residents.

Education The Fremont County School District provides primary and secondary education. The school district buses Island Park students 30 miles south to Ashton.

The closest institution of higher learning is Brigham Young University-Idaho in Rexburg, 58 miles southwest.

Health Care The city has a general medical clinic and ambulance service. The closest hospital is Madison Memorial Hospital in Rexburg.

Transportation U.S. Highway 20 passes through the city and is the city's "Main Street."

Light private and charter air service is available at West Yellowstone, Montana, 20 miles east. Commercial air service is located 75 miles away at Jackson Hole, Wyoming, or 86 miles south in Idaho Falls.

Utilities and Services Private companies provide electricity, telephone and satellite services. Residences and businesses use individual wells and septic systems. A volunteer fire department provides fire protection. The Fremont County Sheriff's Department provides law enforcement. The County also provides solid waste services.

Moose.

Vision for 2050

In 1960 Island Park had a population of 53. Since then, the city's population has grown steadily until, in recent years, it has held at just under 300. This growth will continue as the city's hospitality and real estate industries promote their businesses.

Growth has also been influenced by the spillover from Yellowstone National Park with increasing numbers of visitors coming to the beautiful, less-crowded scenic locations in Idaho. The natural beauty of the Island Park area will also attract more vacation home buyers.

Island Park is prepared to manage future growth. The city's municipal services are adequate, with routine maintenance, to meet the demands of growth for many years.

The vision for the city is an integral part of the Fremont County vision. In all of the county's future growth, residents will continue to appreciate and protect the community's open spaces and natural places.

Mayors

1947 Harvey Schwendiman *
1971 Glen McKay
1994 Mayors Sherri Owens
2000 Lauri Augustin
2003 Brad Smith
2004 Tom Jewell
* Village Chairman

Aerial view of Newdale.

Newdale

Statistical Data

Population: 309 *
Elevation: 5,000 feet
Precipitation: 14 inches **
Average Snowfall: 70 inches **
County: Fremont

Temperature Range – Fahrenheit: **
Spring: 18 to 66
Summer: 41 to 83
Fall: 17 to 73
Winter: 7 to 34
* U.S. Census Bureau Estimates July 2015
**Historical averages

Newdale is an agricultural community 11 miles northeast of Rexburg. It is beautifully located on a gentle slope overlooking the Snake River Valley. Immense fields of waving grain and acres of potatoes, beets, alfalfa hay and seed peas surround the city. The Teton River flows three miles to the north.

The Targhee National Forest and the Big Hole Mountain Range, rising to over 9,000 feet, begin 10 miles southeast of the city.

The Idaho/Wyoming border is 30 miles due west of the city. The famed Yellowstone National Park and the Grand Teton Mountain Range and Jackson Hole lie on the Wyoming side of the border. The roads from Newdale to these resort areas wind for miles over high mountain passes and through some of the most spectacular natural scenery in the nation.

Pre-Incorporation Years

The first settlement in the region began in 1883. Then, leaders of the Church of Jesus Christ of Latter-day Saints (The Church or Church of Jesus Christ) directed the 54-year-old Thomas E. Ricks to lead a large body of immigrant settlers traveling to homestead in Eastern Idaho. Ricks, a Kentuckian, joined the Church in 1844. He crossed the Great Plains to Salt Lake City in 1848 and was a proven leader. The district under Ricks' ecclesiastical jurisdiction centered in Rexburg and grew to include several other communities.

Farm near Newdale.

In 1906 settlers diverted water from Canyon Creek into the Canyon Creek Canal they constructed. The canal delivered gravity-flow irrigation water to the lower elevations of tall sagebrush and native grass-covered land. Farmers built irrigation ditches and soon they transformed the high-desert into an agricultural oasis. Around 1910 farmers built the Enterprise Canal to irrigate additional acreage.

The Oregon Short Line Railroad wanted to build a branch line that formed a loop from Idaho Falls to the farms and agricultural businesses developing east of Rexburg.

Teton-Newdale Cemetery; note monument to the ill-fated Willie Handcart Company in the foreground.

On June 27, 1914, two area property owners and entrepreneurs – Fred and Samuel Schwendiman – sold a corridor of land to the Oregon Short Line Railroad. Railroad representatives selected the Schwendiman site as the location of its train depot, which they named Newdale. The Schwendiman brothers platted the town, which they also named Newdale. On December 3, 1914, they filed Articles of Incorporation creating the Newdale Investment Co. that immediately began to sell lots. In 1915 the railroad built its depot and settlers began to flock to the new community.

In January 1916 the town borrowed $15,000 to drill a well and construct an elevated storage tank and waterworks. Around the same time, Utah Power and

Light extended its electrical lines into town and other entrepreneurs provided telephone service.

Substantially all of the settlers in and around the village were members of The Church of Jesus Christ. On December 17, 1916, the Church organized the Newdale Ward (congregation).

Incorporation

On January 24, 1917, Newdale became an incorporated village with signs posted on the roads outside the city stating “Newdale, Watch it Grow.” Grow it did – by 1921 the new village had a national bank, several general stores, a lumberyard, a drug store, a hardware store, implement yards, several warehouses, a barbershop, commission houses, a hotel, a blacksmith, a carpenter shop, a livery stable and even an opera house.

Green Canyon Hot Springs near Newdale.

Turning Points

Irrigation and the Railroad Irrigation transformed the rich soil around Newdale into highly productive farmland. This, in turn, was the basis for the railroad coming to town which, in-turn, helped propel the economic and population growth of the community.

Community Schools and Facilities In July 1918 school patrons in the town formed a new school district. In order to meet school and community needs, in December 1919 the citizens constructed an eight-room brick facility with wood stoves in each room and an auditorium. The building had no plumbing. However, there were out houses, a ball diamond, a playground and swings.

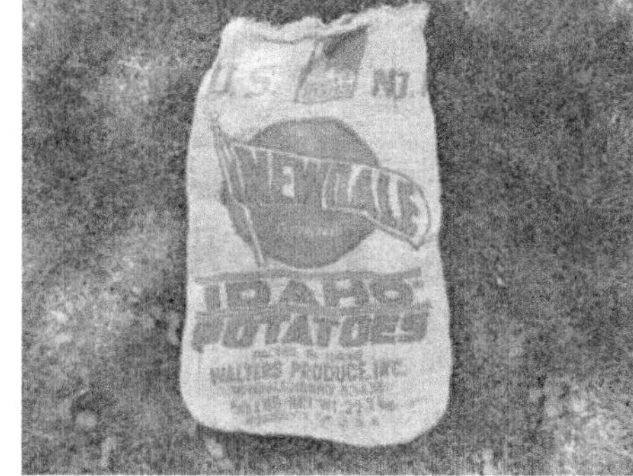

They used the facilities for school needs and community and church events. Sam Schwendiman Park now stands at the location of the old Newdale School and playgrounds.

World War I and the Growth of Agriculture During the First World War, Newdale was an important grain shipping center. For example, during the 1918 to 1919 crop-storage years, the railroad moved 403 railroad cars of wheat from Newdale. In addition, the railroad moved nearly 200 cars of other farm commodities and livestock. This was a period of economic prosperity for the city.

The Great Depression During the Great Depression of the 1930s, many families lost their homes. Farmers sold or lost their farms and moved away. This decline in population also worked a hardship on the schools. In 1948 the Newdale School consolidated with the Sugar-Salem School District and closed.

Teton Dam On June 5, 1976, the Teton Dam, located three miles north of the city, failed and caused major damage and loss of life in communities caught in the flood. Newdale, located on higher ground, did not sustain any physical damage. However, the loss of the dam precluded economic growth that could have come from the recreation and tourist business that the reservoir would foster.

Newdale Today

Amenities and Attractions Newdale has a municipal park named after the city's founder, Sam Schwendiman.

Teton Dam disaster.

Green Canyon Hot Springs is located several miles southeast. Hot geothermal spring water flows through the resort's indoor and outdoor swimming pools.

The city of Rexburg is a regional shopping and medical center and home to Brighma Young University-Idaho (BYU-Idaho). Many Newdale residents travel to Rexburg to enjoy the many museums, festivals and activities offered by the university and the city.

Economy and Major Employers Agricultural-based businesses underpin the city's economy. Walter's Produce, a potato-processing warehouse, and General Mills, a grain distribution center, are the two major businesses still operating in Newdale.

Most of the smaller farms of the past are now under the management of large farming operations. Technological innovation and the effect of economies of scale have caused massive consolidation of farm operations. Newdale area farms and food-processing businesses are now much more productive with a fraction of the previously required labor force.

Similar phenomena have happened in the food-processing industry.

Education Fremont County School District provides most of the city's K-12 education. Primary grade students are bused three miles west to attend Trenton Elementary. High school students attend school seven miles northwest in St Anthony.

The closest institution of higher learning is BYU-Idaho.

Health Care The closest hospital is Madison Memorial Hospital in Rexburg.

Transportation State Highway 33 intersects the city. Interstate 15 lies 30 miles to the west. U.S. Highway 20 lies 10 miles west.

The 4,200-foot runway at Rexburg-Madison County Airport provides air service for private and charter aircraft. The closest commercial airport is 42 miles away in

Idaho Falls.

Rail freight service is available in Rexburg.

Utilities and Services Public companies provide electricity, telephone and satellite services.

Vision for 2050

For the past few decades, Newdale's population has remained somewhat constant at around 350. However, there is reason to expect that historical trends will not continue into 2050. At some point, the dramatic population growth of Rexburg will spill over to Newdale. People will be attracted to the city's peaceful and affordable environment for parents to come and raise their families while commuting a short distance to work and shop.

The city and community leaders plan strategically. Should significant growth occur, the city will improve or expand municipal systems with existing revenues, impact fees, grants or bonds approved by the voters.

Mayors

1917 George W. Bean *
1917 Joseph Fleishman *
1919 Edwin M. Stocks *
1923 Roy Graham *
1938 Harvey Schwendiman *
1945 LaVell Schwendiman *
1950 Lou W. Klingler *
1960 Grant Klingler *
1962 Jay Robinson *
1964 Rex Howard *
1968 Jay Robinson
1972 Norman Ross
1974 John Guy Roberts
1975 Layne Harris
1986 Wayne Hansen
1988 Floyd Simper
1992 Shayne Hansen
2012 Ferron Martineau

* Village Chairman

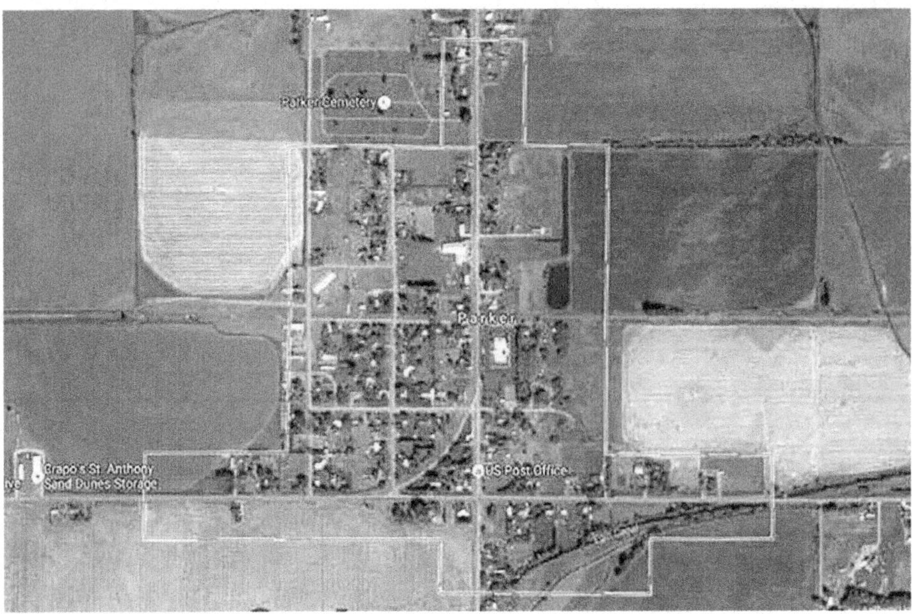

Aerial view of Parker.

Parker

Statistical Data

Population: 298 *
Elevation: 4,924 feet
Precipitation: 14.2 inches **
Average Snowfall: 46 inches **
County: Fremont

Temperature Range – Fahrenheit: **
Spring: 18 to 66
Summer: 41 to 83
Fall: 17 to 73
Winter: 7 to 34

* U.S. Census Bureau Estimates July 2015
**Historical averages

Parker is an agricultural community located on the Upper Snake River Valley Plain. Lush fields of potatoes, wheat, barley, alfalfa hay and corn border the city. The famous trout fly fishery – the Henry's Fork of the Snake River (Henry's Fork) – flows on the southeast corner of the city.

The St. Anthony Sand Dunes, a designated Unique Natural Feature, is two miles northwest. The dunes cover an area 35 miles long and up to five miles wide. They rise from 70 to 365 feet – a height greater than the dunes in Death Valley, California.

North and west of the city are vast tracts of high-desert plains and hills managed by the BLM. The Caribou-Targhee National Forest lies about 20 miles northeast. St. Anthony is five miles east and Rexburg is about 12 miles south.

Pre-Incorporation Years

In 1810 Captain Andrew Henry led the first party of explorers/trappers into the area of the Henry's Fork. They built a log stockade and shelter, which they namedFort Henry, on a river bench about five miles downstream from what is now St. Anthony. They spent the winter in their fort and trapped for beaver. In the spring, they moved on.

In October 1811 the Wilson Price Hunt party stayed at the deserted Fort Henry for two weeks while they built canoes on which they unwisely hoped to navigate the Snake River to the Columbia River and the Pacific Ocean. When they reached what is now Twin Falls, they had a fatal accident and loss of supplies. They determined that the river route was impossible, abandoned their canoes and completed their harrowing journey on foot.

Isaac Wardle home in Parker.

In 1863 prospectors discovered gold in what is now southwestern Montana. A stagecoach and freight wagon road, called the Gold Road, soon developed from Utah through Marsh Valley, Pocatello and Eagle Rock – now Idaho Falls – where the road crossed the Snake River and continued north over Monida Pass to Montana. Eagle Rock became a center of commerce that began to attract settlers into the Upper Snake River Plain.

In 1878 the Utah and Northern Railroad Company completed a narrow-gauge railroad that extended from Ogden, Utah, to the Montana mines on a line that generally followed the Gold Road. The railroad not only provided freight, passenger and mail transportation for the mines, it also facilitated the sale of farm commodities in distant markets and the movement of settlers coming into Eastern Idaho.

Around 1879 settlers began moving up from Utah to homestead on the fertile Upper Snake River Plain.

In 1882 leaders of The Church of Jesus Christ of Latter-day Saints (Church) asked 54-year-old Thomas E. Ricks to be an ecclesiastical leader (Bishop) of the immigrant settlers going to what is now the Rexburg area. Within a few years, the

Parker Chapel, late 1800s.

emigrants from Utah had established several settlements in Eastern Idaho. (*See Eastern Idaho, Pioneer Settlements – Upper Snake River Plain*.)

One of these settlements was Parker. In 1881 settlers in this area began constructing a 16-mile-long irrigation canal they named Egin. The settlers built the Egin Canal by hand and with horse-drawn Fresno scrapers. As they completed sections of the canal, they allowed the diverted river water to flow into the new section. In 1886 they completed the entire canal.

Settlers platted the town of Parker in 1883 – named in honor of Wyman W. Parker, the local bishop of the Church. They then successfully applied to the postal authorities for a new post office named Parker.

In 1899 the St. Anthony Railroad Company began construction of a rail line from Idaho Falls to St. Anthony – later extended to West Yellowstone. This brought railroad service to within five miles of Parker.

William Carbine home in Parker.

Incorporation

On February 13, 1905, Parker became an incorporated village.

Turning Points

Church Settlement The migration of settlers from Utah to the Upper Snake River Valley resulted in the founding of Parker and converting the sagebrush-covered plain into a fertile oasis.

Railroad The railroad from Utah to Montana built in 1878 passed about 22 miles west of Parker. It was instrumental in the development of Parker and the region.

Parker Today

Amenities and Attractions Fremont County conducts its annual fair each August at the fairgrounds in St. Anthony. The fairgrounds are also the location for the annual Pioneer Days Rodeo and fireworks show, demolition derbies and other events.

The white quartz St. Anthony Sand Dunes are popular for dune buggy, snowmobile and sand skiing enthusiasts as well as those who just want to experience an exhilarating walk on vast tracts of sand.

The 11,000-acre Harriman State Park is located 43 miles north of the city. The park features tours; fly-fishing; hiking; horseback riding; cross-country skiing; and viewing a variety of wildlife including Trumpeter Swan, moose, elk and Sandhill Crane.

The surrounding public lands – with the many rivers, streams, lakes and open space – are an outdoor sportsman's paradise.

Economy and Major Employers The city has no dominant employers. The city's commercial district consists of convenience stores and shops. Most residents travel to nearby cities to work, shop and do business.

Education The Fremont County School District provides most of the elementary and secondary education. The city's children attend school in St. Anthony.

The nearest institution of higher learning is Brigham Young University-Idaho in Rexburg.

Health Care The nearest hospital is Madison Memorial Hospital in Rexburg.

Transportation St. Anthony's Stanford Field has a 4,500-foot runway that serves light private and charter aircraft. Facilities for larger aircraft are available 37 miles southwest at the Idaho Falls Regional Airport.

Red Road, a county road that connects with Rexburg to the south, intersects the city. U.S. Highway 20 is accessible in St. Anthony. Interstate 15 is accessible 37 miles south in Idaho Falls or 30 miles west at Sage Junction.

Utilities and Services Private companies provide electricity, telephone and satellite services. The City provides water and sewer services and fire and police protection.

Parker in winter.

Vision for 2050

In 1960 Parker had a population of 284. In 2000 the population had increased to 319. Since that time it has remained stable. Historical trends will likely continue. By 2050 Parker will continue to be a wonderful place to live for about 400 residents who enjoy a slower pace of life and living in a peaceful community close to the urban amenities of larger cities.

St. Anthony

Statistical Data

Population: 3,454 *
Elevation: 4,972 feet
Precipitation: 14.2 inches **
Average Snowfall: 46 inches **
County: Fremont
Website: www.cityofstanthony.org

Temperature Range – Fahrenheit: **
Spring: 18 to 66
Summer: 41 to 83
Fall: 17 to 73
Winter: 7 to 34
* U.S. Census Bureau Estimates July 2015
**Historical averages

St. Anthony lies on the Upper Snake River Valley Plain surrounded by farm and ranch land. The famous trout fly fishery, the Henry's Fork of the Snake River (Henry's Fork), flows through the city. Rexburg is about 12 miles southwest.

The St. Anthony Sand Dunes are seven miles west. The dunes are designated a Unique Natural Feature, covering an area 35 miles long and up to five miles wide. They rise from 70 to 365 feet – a height greater than the dunes in Death Valley, California.

Vast tracts of public lands border the fertile farmland surrounding the city. A few miles north and west are high-desert plains and hills managed by the U.S. Bureau of Land Management. The Caribou-Targhee National Forest is about 15 miles northeast.

Pre-Incorporation Years

Captain Andrew Henry led the first party of explorers/trappers into the area in 1810. They built a log stockade and shelter, which they named Fort Henry, on a river bench about five miles downstream from what is now St. Anthony. They spent the winter in the fort and trapped for beaver. In the spring, they moved on.

The Wilson Price Hunt party stayed at the deserted Fort Henry for two weeks in October 1811 while they built canoes on which they planned to navigate the Snake River to the Columbia River and the Pacific Ocean. They portaged around the Idaho and American Falls but the long stretches of treacherous waterfalls and rapids that they scouted ahead persuaded them to abandon their canoes and proceed on foot.

St. Anthony Mill & Elevator Company.

In 1879 the first white settlers in the St. Anthony area built dugouts along the riverbank about 10 miles west of what is now St. Anthony. A year later, they began construction on the 16-mile-long irrigation canal they named Egin. The settlers built the canal by hand with horse-drawn Fresno scrapers. As they completed sections of the canal, they allowed the diverted river water to flow into the new section. In 1886 they completed the entire canal.

Riverside Hotel.

Carlos H. Moon filed a homestead claim in 1887 on the north side of the river near where the Egin Ditch Co. had built an office and the Davenport Brothers a blacksmith shop.

Moon planned to build a new town on his claim. He immediately set out to find investors to help finance his enterprise. He named the community St. Anthony because the rapids on the Henry's Fork reminded him of St. Anthony Falls, Minnesota. On June 19, 1888, he formed the St. Anthony Canal, Improvement and Townsite Company. Investors paid $50 a share for their stock. On July 12, 1888, the company drove the first survey stake for the new town and began selling lots. Business lots sold for $300 to $400 and residential lots $15 to $100.

Postal authorities approved a post office for the new community on October 3, 1888, with Moon as postmaster. Moon first operated the post office out of his home and, later, his store.

On May 11, 1899, the St. Anthony Railroad Company incorporated and began building a 39-mile main line from Idaho Falls to St. Anthony. In September, the railroad tie contractor – Thompson Mercantile of St. Anthony – floated 25,000 ties down the Snake River and distributed them along the surveyed route. The railroad reached St. Anthony in the spring of 1900 and built a depot about a half-mile south of the river. A new business district sprang up around the depot.

By 1890 city businesses had grown to include two private schools and the Fremont County News, the area's first newspaper.

Phillip Oakden built the community's first hotel, the 10-room Pioneer Hotel, in 1892. He later built and operated the larger Idaho Hotel on West Main Street. W.M. Hopkins and Sons opened a two-story mercantile store with the upper floor used as an opera house. Because newsprint was unavailable in the winter of 1893, the Fremont County News printed on brown wrapping paper furnished by Hopkins' store.

St. Anthony, panoramic view.

Moon built a toll bridge over the Henry's Fork just west of the current bridge, and the village trustees on November 1, 1895, filed a plat extending the village to the south side of the river.

The legislature created Fremont County in 1893 and, over the objections of Rexburg area residents, made St. Anthony the county seat. At that time, the county comprised what are now Fremont, Clark, Teton, Madison and Jefferson Counties. Ballot attempts to move the county seat to Rexburg failed to get the two-thirds vote. Rexburg would have to wait until the legislature created Madison County in 1913 to become a county seat.

The County constructed its first courthouse, a small wood-frame structure on the present courthouse site. They razed the wood courthouse in 1909 and replaced it with the now historic two-story brick courthouse.

The County also built a bridge across the Snake River to connect the north and south parts of the community, essentially making Moon's toll bridge obsolete.

The first telephone line reached St. Anthony in 1897 but it was slow to attract hookups. The January 1902 telephone directory listed 34 phones, six of which were residences. Phone numbers were two digits.

John H. Allan Seed Company.

By 1898 the city's population had reached 550. The stagecoach and the mail ran daily. A second newspaper, the Fremont Republican, opened. There were two attorneys; two doctors; two hotels; stores that sold hardware and logs, furniture, drugs, millinery, confections, bakery goods and notions; two banks; two jewelers; a shoemaker; a barbershop; five saloons; two liveries; a blacksmith; a wheelwright; a grain elevator; and a feed company. Plans were under way for a flourmill and a starch factory but the flourmill would not be completed until 1905.

St. Anthony's cooler temperatures and soils are ideal for growing pea seed. The Coulter-Adams Seed Company played an important role in developing this new agricultural commodity, resulting in other pea-seed companies coming to the area during the early 1900s. For the next five decades, the pea-seed companies employed hundreds of workers during the growing and sorting seasons.

Standing on Courthouse steps circa 1927-1928. Back Row from left: Roy Callow, Day Police; Grant Powell, Night Police; Tom Patten, Deputy Sheriff. Front Row from left: Oscar Cusick, Mayor; Cap Hudson, Chief of Police; Jimmy Fredrickson, Sheriff; Pat Bailey, Deputy Sheriff.

Voters approved a bond in 1899 to finance construction of a large rock school on the north end of town. School officials planned to open school in the new building following the Christmas break. However, before school could start, an unexpected thaw flooded the schoolyard, undermining the building's foundation. With money pledged by local businesses, they carefully salvaged the building, rebuilt the foundation and restored the school to its original condition.

Incorporation

On October 13, 1899, St. Anthony became an incorporated village. Electrical power reached the city on June 30, 1902. The 1910 U.S. Census reported the village population at 1,238. In 1925 the village became an incorporated city.

Turning Points

Agriculture Agriculture underpinned St. Anthony's economy for decades. Most of the early settlers in the area were homesteaders. Initially, they raised hay, grain and livestock. In the early 1900s seed companies, attracted by the fertile land and cooler temperatures, found the area to be an excellent location for growing seed peas. By 1920 farmers were selling about a million dollars worth of seed peas annually. With construction of a sugar factory eight miles south at Sugar City in 1904, sugar beets became a prominent cash crop. Around 1940 potatoes replaced sugar beets as the dominant cash crop. The Sugar City factory closed in 1943.

WWI doughboy, statue.

Today, technological innovation and consolidation have dramatically improved farm productivity with a fraction of the labor previously required. Most farms are now run by large operators. While this phenomenon increased farm and ranch profitability, the loss of agricultural jobs has had an adverse effect on the city's economy.

St. Anthony, circa 1930.

Railroad Railroad transportation had a major positive effect on the economy of the city and the nearby farms and ranches. Principals in the St. Anthony Railroad Company formed the Yellowstone Park Railroad Company in 1905 and in 1909 completed construction of a 70-mile rail line from St. Anthony to the west entrance of Yellowstone National Park in Montana. It also built a 38-mile branch line from Ashton south to Driggs. Later, the Oregon Short Line built a seven-mile line from

Driggs to Victor.

State Correctional Programs In 1903 the State began construction of the Idaho Industrial Training School on a 650-acre farm two miles west of the city. Inmates built many of the brick buildings, the tiled swimming pool and other campus facilities. They worked at the campus brickyard and produced much of their food on the campus farm and dairy.

With 145 beds, the campus is now the largest of the Idaho Department of Juvenile Corrections three facilities and St. Anthony's second largest employer. The juvenile corrections program includes providing inmates with a high school education and professional/technical training.

Fremont County courthouse.

Natural Resources Good stands of timber and deposits of stone and clay suitable for making brick are located near St. Anthony. Initially local settlers used these building materials to meet local needs. However, the opportunity to develop a significant commercial lumber business came in the mid-1960s. Pine bark beetle infestations were killing large stands of timber in the nearby national forest. The U.S. Forest Service was offering timber contracts to remove millions of board feet of infected trees.

County leaders offered land to the Idaho Stud Mill Company to build a sawmill. The mill brought hundreds of jobs and good wages. By the late 1980s, however, access to timber on federal lands became more restricted. The mill closed with serious adverse consequences to the city's economy.

Teton Dam In the early 1970s the U.S. Bureau of Reclamation began construction of the 3,100-foot-wide and 305-foot-high Teton Dam on the Teton River a few miles southeast of St. Anthony. Construction jobs provided a major boost to the city's economy. However, on June 5, 1976, as the reservoir was filling for the first time, the dam failed, sending a tidal wave of death and destruction over much of the Snake River Plain. (*See The Region Teton Dam Disaster*.)

St. Anthony, circa 1950.

Since the city was located above the dam, it escaped physical damage. Unfortunately, the tragedy eliminated the recreational and economic opportunity that St. Anthony residents had anticipated.

St. Anthony Today

Amenities and Attractions One of the more striking features of the city is the drive along Bridge Street, the alternate business route of U.S. Highway 20. Flowerbeds and planters filled with a variety of flowers line both sides of the street, creating a beautiful array of color through the center of town. At night in the main business district, light poles reminiscent of a bygone era cast a soft glow on the street below.

St. Anthony sand bar.

The city has 15 parks on over 17 acres – Clyde Keefer Memorial Park, Veterans Memorial Park, American Legion/Daughters of Utah Pioneers Park, South Side Park, Harry Worrell Park, St. Anthony Sand Bar, Boys Town Park, Boyd Yancey Memorial Park, Ralph Litton Park, St. Anthony Baseball Diamonds, Jaycee Park, Skater's Haven Skate Park, Cedar View Park, Henry's Fork Greenway North and Henry's Fork Greenway South.

Clyde Keefer Memorial Park is on the south side of the Henry's Fork. The park has a life-size bronze statue of a WWI "Idaho Doughboy" standing on a tall base of native lava rock overlooking the river. The statue, sculpted by the prominent Western artist Aavard Fairbanks and erected in 1923, is a memorial to Fremont County residents who fought in the war. The park also has monuments to Vietnam War veterans, POWs and MIAs as well as a large covered shelter with several picnic tables.

The American Legion/Daughters of the Utah Pioneers Park, generally called Pioneer Park, lies immediately across the river from Clyde Keefer Park. This park has two monuments. One commemorates Fort Henry, built five miles south in 1810 by Captain Andrew Henry. The other memorializes the Fremont County pioneers of 1879 to 1890 and the first house of worship built in the Upper Snake River Valley in June 1882 at Egin, about 5 miles southwest, by members of The Church

Skate park.

of Jesus Christ of Latter-day Saints. This landscaped park has a large flowerbed that spells out "IDAHO" in white flowers.

Boyd Yancey Memorial Park, formerly Fort Henry "Horsey" Park, is a children's park that has picnic facilities and a large concrete area used for such activities as rollerblading, skate boarding and basketball.

St. Anthony Sand Bar is a swimming and children's playground park on the Henry's Fork.

City airport, Stanford Field.

The St. Anthony Baseball Diamonds has two baseball fields with bleachers – one lighted.

Henry's Fork Greenway offers two improved trails that border the Henry's Fork for two and a half miles. In the warmer months, walkers, joggers, skaters and even cyclists use the wildlife-viewing trails. In the winter, the trails are groomed for cross-country skiing and snowshoeing.

On the last weekend of May just prior to the start of Idaho's general fishing season, the community sponsors the "Free Fisherman's Breakfast" at Clyde Keefer Park. The breakfast of pancakes, sausage and hash browns has become a prominent regional event for thousands of residents and anglers who come to the Henry's Fork to ply their fly-fishing skills.

Each August at the fairgrounds, located on the south edge of town, the County sponsors the Fremont County Fair. The fairgrounds are also the location for the annual Pioneer Days Rodeo and fireworks show, demolition derbies and other events.

Each April, the community sponsors the Cowboy Poets Festival at the city's historic Roxy Performing Arts Theater. Other historic buildings include the Fremont County Courthouse completed in 1910 and now listed on the National Register of Historic Places, the Roman Catholic Church built in 1904 and The Church of Jesus Christ of Latter-day Saints Yellowstone Stake Tabernacle started in 1909 and completed in 1916.

Aerial view of St. Anthony.

The Tabernacle, an imposing edifice, was made available for community functions when not in use by the church. The Tabernacle had to be destroyed to make way for the rerouting of Highway 20 through St. Anthony.

The white quartz St. Anthony Sand Dunes are popular for dune-buggy, snowmobile and sand-skiing enthusiasts as well as those who just want to experience an exhilarating walk on vast tracts of sand.

The 11,000-acre Harriman State Park is 43 miles north of the city. The park features tours; fly-fishing; hiking; horseback riding; cross-country skiing; and viewing a variety of wildlife including Trumpeter Swan, moose, elk and Sandhill Crane.

The spectacular Upper and Lower Mesa Falls, Unique Natural Features, are about 33 miles north.

The surrounding public lands with many rivers, streams, lakes and open space are an outdoor sportsman's paradise.

Economy and Major Employers With over 340 employees, the Fremont County School District is the city's largest employer. The Idaho Department of Juvenlie Corrections has over 150 employees and is the city's second largest employer. Other large public employers include Fremont County with 55 employees and the Idaho Department of Corrections Adult Work Camp with 36.

Agriculture-related businesses continue to be a major source of private emplooyment. In 2006 the City opened an industrial park that should attract other private employers.

Many city residents commute to other area cities for employment. The downtown retail and service businesses provide most of the city's other jobs.

Education The Fremont County School District provides most of the elementary and secondary education.

The nearest institution of higher learning is Brigham Young University – Idaho in Rexburg.

Health Care A medical clinic and assisted-living center are located in the city. The nearest hospital is Madison Memorial Hospital in Rexburg.

Transportation U.S. Highway 20 intersects the city. State Highway 33, extending south to Driggs and Victor, begins seven miles south of the city.

The city's airport, Stanford Field, has a 4,500-foot runway and is available for light private and charter service. Facilities for larger aircraft are available 42 miles southwest at the Idaho Falls Regional Airport.

Utilities and Services Private companies provide electricity, telephone, natural gas, cable and satellite services. The City provides garbage collection, water and sewer services and fire and police protection.

Vision for 2050

For decades, St. Anthony's population has remained at around 3,000. By 2050 that could change as the city considers additional annexations. New homes are cropping up inside the city limits, and developers are planning new subdivisions within the city's area of impact.

City leaders are working hard to encourage the moderate growth that insures St.

Anthony remains a vibrant community. Infrastructure improvements in recent years include a major upgrade of sewer lines and the treatment plant. A 2005 comprehensive water study identified improvements needed in the coming years.

The City has helped fund a transportation study that includes a pavement management plan for upgrading city streets. An active Parks and Recreation Commission is developing a master parks plan, promoting tree plantings and updating playground equipment.

The City is promoting economic development. The industrial park next to the airport will bring in new businesses. Within the next several years, the greenway paths that now border the north and south sides of the Henry's Fork will have a connection across the river.

City and community leaders and volunteers will work to build a stronger sense of community in St. Anthony. This will include making the Free Fisherman's Breakfast, the Pioneer Days celebration, SummerFest and performing arts held in the historic Roxy Theater even more popular and exciting events.

We see St. Anthony's downtown being revitalized and extended to include small businesses in nearby residential areas. Population growth will come as our town's potential residents discover the scenic beauty that exists here.

Our 2050 vision of St. Anthony is one of hope, enthusiasm, planning and commitment. St. Anthony will continue to be a clean, caring, safe and vital place to work, live and raise a family.

Mayors

1905 James G. Gwinn *
1909 W.L. Miller *
1913 I.E. Houghton *
1915 James Smith *
1917 F.M. Snell *
1919 W.D. Yager *
1921 James Smith *
1923 R.L. Maxwell *
1925 James G. Gwinn
1929 O.H. Cusik
1931 Gilbert Charles Orme
1933 J.O. Johnson
1937 A.G. Miller
1939 E.M. Jergensen
1941 J.O. Johnson
1943 E.P. Coburn
1945 E. Glenn Cameron
1947 C. William Oliver
1949 Bill Frome
1953 Clyde Keefer
1959 Harry Lewies
1961 Clyde Keefer
1964 W.H. Bell
1968 Duwayne Allgood
1970 M.J. Rose
1978 Neils O. Thueson
1982 M.J. Rose
1990 Boyd Yancey
1994 Roy Parker
1997 Charles Sorenson
2002 Bill Beck
2008 Garth Rose
2010 Neils Thueson

* Village Chairman

Teton Mountain range.

Teton

Statistical Data

Population: 712 *
Elevation: 4,949 feet
Precipitation: 11 inches **
Average Snowfall: 54 inches **
County: Fremont
Website: www.cityofteton.com

Temperature Range – Fahrenheit: **
Spring: 20 to 70
Summer: 30 to 90
Fall: 15 to 80
Winter: 10 to 30
* U.S. Census Bureau Estimates July 2015
**Historical averages

Teton lies on a long and relatively flat alluvial plain that gently slopes downward from east to west. Farmland – with fields of potatoes, wheat, barley and hay – surrounds most of the city.

The Teton River flows north and west of town. The famed Grand Teton Mountain Range is 30 miles east on the Idaho/Wyoming border. The mountain range, whose highest peak rises to 13,771 feet, forms a beautiful silhouette in the eastern and southeastern sky.

Pre-Incorporation Years

The events that led up to the founding of Teton started in 1879, following completion of the Utah and Northern Railroad from Utah to the Montana gold fields. Many of the railroad construction workers were from northern Utah. As they returned home, one of the railroad workers – John R. Poole, of Ogden – was the first to praise the farmland potential of the Upper Snake River Plain. The reports of the returning construction workers prompted several groups of families to leave Utah to homestead in Eastern Idaho.

In 1882 leaders of the Church of Jesus Christ of Latter-day Saints (Church of Jesus Christ or Church) asked 54-year-old Thomas E. Ricks to be the Bishop of the immigrant settlers going to the Rexburg area. Ricks, a Kentuckian, joined the Church in 1844; crossed the Great Plains to Salt Lake City in 1848; and was a proven leader.

The district that was under Ricks' ecclesiastical jurisdiction included several new communities in an area called the Bannock Ward, later to become a stake (diocese) with Ricks as president.

The settlement of the future city of Teton was started in the early spring of 1883 by eleven men who had traveled up from Cache Valley, Utah. When they arrived in what is now Rexburg, they camped just east of town. They contacted Ricks about their desire to find suitable land for homesteading. Three days later, Ricks, guided them nine miles northeast to a slightly higher elevation near the Teton River.

Main Street.

When they arrived at the location Ricks identified, they said that they saw fertile soil with plenty of water and a fine view of the Teton peaks. They decided this was where they would settle. These men were Henry Sorensen, John Anderson, Niles Peter Anderson, Fred Gardner, John W. Gardner, James Francis Graham, Joseph Graham, Charles W. Bird, Freeman Bird, George Gittens, and John Tom Gittens.

Within a week, these settlers made their homestead claims and arranged for Andrew S. Anderson, the surveyor sent by the Church to assist Ricks, to come and survey the best place to build a diversion dam and irrigation canal. On April 30, 1883, Anderson responded and, with the help of the settlers, surveyed the future course of the Teton Canal.

The following day, May 1, 1883, Anderson, together with Ricks and the eleven settlers, platted the town site. The men decided to name the new village Teton because it was next to the Teton River and had an excellent view of the Teton Mountain Range.

With the prospect of receiving irrigation water delivered through the Teton Canal, many other families came to settle and join in the cooperative effort to build the canal for a share of the water.

Shortly after they platted the village, a town began to take shape. The Teton Mercantile Company was the first commercial structure. A post office, a blacksmith shop, a saloon and the Teton Flour Mill – which still stands today – soon followed.

As the community grew, the settlers built additional canals. The system of irrigation canals and ditches built by these early settlers are still the fundamental structure of today's surface irrigation system.

Incorporation

On February 19, 1901, Teton had a population of about 200. On that date, accompanied by an application signed by 74 residents, the Fremont County Commissioners made Teton an incorporated village. They appointed the board of trustees to serve until the next election.

Turning Points

Thomas E. Ricks Ricks was a consummate public servant. He had first-hand knowledge of the region and willingly left his personal responsibilities to assist the others without remuneration. He provided the leadership that organized the community as well as the irrigation systems that would make the settlement successful. That early spring day in 1883 when the 11 settlers asked Thomas E. Ricks for advice was pivotal to the founding of Teton.

Teton Dam and Flood On June 5, 1976, the newly constructed Teton Dam located in a mountain gorge north of the city ruptured sending an 80-billion-gallon tidal wave of water down the valley.

Teton's higher elevation allowed the city to escape most of the devastation experienced by the cities and farms downriver. However, rising floodwaters still caused significant damage to many structures such as the town's sawmill where the floods weakened the footings to the point that made the sawmill unusable.

A major adverse effect of the flood on the city was less physical damage than it was the loss of economic opportunity. Prior to the flood, businesses that would benefit from recreational and other innovative opportunities associated with the dam and the large reservoir it created were flourishing. After the flood, the city's commercial and industrial vibrancy faded. The Tabernacle Civic Center in Rexburg houses the Teton Flood Museum. (*See Eastern Idaho – Teton Dam.*)

Teton Today

Amenities and Attractions One of the city's most prominent attractions is its near proximity to Rexburg and Brigham Young University-Idaho (BYU-Idaho) that is located there. Teton residents are able to enjoy the benefits of a peaceful small-town atmosphere yet live nine miles from the regional shopping and medical center of Rexburg and the cultural and educational opportunities offered at the university.

The university sponsors many public concerts, plays and recitals as well as opening many of its athletic facilities to the public. The university's influence underpins the economy and enhances the cultural and social well being of Teton and area residents.

Teton is also convenient for outdoor enthusiasts. Sightseeing, camping, hunting, fishing, mountain biking, ATV riding, skiing and snowmobiling are available within a short drive from the city.

About 40 miles southeast, State Highway 33 passes through the Teton Basin where it parallels the western side of the Grand Teton Mountain Range for about 20 miles before crossing into Jackson Hole, Wyoming. Jackson Hole is 67 miles southeast of Teton.

Teton Flour Mill in Winter. Photographed by Talsan Schulzke.

Yellowstone National Park lies about 35 miles due east. However, following Highway 20, the entrance to the park at West Yellowstone, Montana, is 68 miles distant.

The Targhee National Forest begins 15 miles southeast of Teton.

The St. Anthony Sand Dunes is a 175-square-mile area where the wind has created sand dunes that range from 75 to 365 feet high. The sand dunes lie 20 miles northwest of Teton and are popular for motor-sport and family recreation. A few miles north of the sand dunes are the Civil Defense Caves, large underground caverns that are actually lava tubes formed by prehistoric volcanic activity.

Economy and Major Employers The city's downtown commercial area consists of several small retail stores, shops and small businesses. They are located along Main Street – State Highway 33 – and near the intersection of Main and Center Streets.

Many of the city's workforce commute to Rexburg for work.

Education Teton Elementary School (grades K-5) is part of Fremont County School District and located in the city. Middle and high school students attend schools in either Sugar City (Sugar-Salem School District) or the Fremont County School District schools in St. Anthony.

Those seeking advanced degrees can live at home and attend BYU-Idaho.

Health Care The closest hospital is the 50-bed Madison Memorial Hospital in Rexburg.

Transportation State Highway 33 passes through the city. Four miles west, Highway 33 intersects U.S. Highway 20. Interstate 15 is located 30 miles west.

Railroad freight service is available in Rexburg. The Rexburg-Madison County

Airport – 4,200-foot runway – provides service for light private and charter aircraft. The closest commercial airport is Fanning Field in Idaho Falls, 40 miles southwest.

Utilities and Services Private companies provide electricity, telephone and satellite services. The City provides water and sewer services.

Vision for 2050

Since 1980 Teton's population has remained somewhat constant at around 600. However, as Rexburg continues to experience growth, there will be an increasing number of families that work in Rexburg but come to Teton for more affordable housing and to enjoy the quiet, peaceful atmosphere of the small town.

Should such growth develop, it is expected to occur gradually. The city's municipal services and infrastructure have the capacity to accommodate moderate growth. However, improvements will be necessary within the next several years to meet the needs of existing residents and meet environmental regulations. The City will pay the cost of those improvements through existing revenues, grants, impact fees or bonds approved by the voters.

Mayors

1901 John Donaldson *
** Erastus Jensen
** W.M. Baird
** James W. Siddoway
** Jacob Johnson
** Rudolph Naef
** Ben Gillette
** John Eames
** Robert Logan
** F.H. Siddoway
** John Briggs
** Ern Quirl
** C.V. Rackham
** S.E. Moss
** S.H. Moss
** Melvin Johnson
** J.E. Clark
** Artell Bright
** John Bean
** Reed Tucker
** Ray Baker
** Ted Hikida
** Horace Thomson
** Dave Johnson
** James Siddoway
** Merlin Bean
** Byron Ward
** Garner Simmons
** Phil Baker
** Bryon Parker
2008 Phil Sutherin
* Village Chairman
** Dates Unknown

Aerial view of Warm River.

Warm River

Statistical Data

Population: 3*
Elevation: 5,295 feet
Precipitation: 19 inches **
Average Snowfall: 91 inches **
County: Fremont

Temperature Range – Fahrenheit: **
Spring: 29 to 73
Summer: 38 to 81
Fall: 11 to 59
Winter: 10 to 40
* U.S. Census Bureau Estimates July 2015
**Historical averages

The city of Warm River lies in the Caribou-Targhee National Forest on the banks of the 50-degree fast-flowing Warm River and just a few miles east of the river's confluence with Ashton Reservoir and the famous trout fishery, the Henry's Fork of the Snake River. Idaho Highway 42, the Mesa Falls Scenic Byway, borders the city.

Mesa Falls and Lower Mesa Falls – designated Unique Natural Features – are on the Henry's Fork six miles north of the city on Highway 42.

With a 2010 Census population of 3, Warm River is the smallest city in Idaho. Its mailing address is a P.O. Box in Ashton, eight miles southwest.

Pre-Incorporation Years

In the early 1800s before the first European and American explorers and trappers began traveling into what is now Eastern Idaho, nomadic Native American Indians – principally of the Shoshone and Bannock Tribes – made summer encampments in the land of the Henry's Fork. The Gros Ventre and Blackfoot Indians of the northern plains also made periodic excursions into the area.

In 1810 Captain Andrew Henry led the first party of explorers/trappers into the area. On a bench of the river about five miles south of what is now St. Anthony, they built a log stockade and shelter, which they named Fort Henry. They spent the winter in their fort and trapped for beaver. In the spring, they moved on.

Cabin on the river at night.

In October 1811 the Wilson Price Hunt party stayed at the deserted Fort Henry for two weeks while they built canoes on which they hoped to navigate the Snake River to the Columbia River and the Pacific Ocean. When they reached what is now Twin Falls, they had a fatal accident and loss of supplies. They determined that the river route was impossible, abandoned their canoes and completed their harrowing journey on foot, as they had unwisely released their horses.

Settlement of what is now Eastern Idaho began in the late 1800s, following the discovery of gold in southwestern Montana in the early 1860s and construction of the railroad from Utah to Montana two decades later. Substantially all of this settlement activity occurred south of Warm River. (*See Pioneer Settlements – Upper Snake River Plain.*)

The first Warm River settlers were emigrants from England, homesteaders who came in 1896 and staked their claims at the bottom of the Warm River Canyon.

Entrepreneurs constructed a sawmill near the site of what is now the City of Warm River in 1906. A year later, the railroad line from St. Anthony to the western entrance of Yellowstone National Park reached Warm River. The railroad built a 60-foot turntable at its Warm River siding to turn around locomotives used to push trains over the 6,934-foot-high Reas Pass – Continental Divide – several miles east of Island Park. The station had a 50,000 gallon water tower for servicing the steam engines and stockyards used by the railroad's agricultural customers.

The sawmill would eventually employ 24 and would produce around 20,000 board feet of lumber a day. The rest of the town was also bustling. It had a post office; hospitality businesses including a resort, dancehall, cafe and bar; a school;

and a church. The school served elementary students with two teachers and up to 45 students in first to eighth grades. High school students attended school in Ashton, generally living with extended family or friends. The Church of Jesus Christ of Latter-day Saints started the town's first church congregation – the Warm River Ward – in 1909. Church membership peaked a few years later as people moved away. It had a membership of 23 families – 103 people – in 1914.

The first significant improvement to the road through Warm River that would become Idaho Highway 47 started when contracts were let in 1920 to reconstruct the dugway going down into Warm River Canyon and construct a new bridge across the river.

During the 1930s the Idaho Department of Fish and Game built a fish hatchery east of Mesa Falls on the Warm River, part of a 1938 federally funded Civilian Conservation Corps (CCC) project. The CCC provided local people with employment by building forest roads and fish hatchery facilities.

Three Rivers Ranch.

The railroad continued to play a major role in the Warm River economy until 1946 when it moved its operation to Ashton.

The fish hatchery closed during the 1950s. The hatchery property is now the Warm River Cabin Campground with the hatchery manager's house beautifully preserved with wooden bunks and available for public rental.

Incorporation

Warm River became an incorporated village on June 9, 1947. Likely in response to a 1947 Idaho law requiring businesses that sold liquor-by-the-drink to have liquor licenses and be located in incorporated municipalities. By incorporating, the city allowed the hospitality businesses in town to continue to sell liquor.

Turning Points

Bridge at Three Rivers Ranch.

Sawmill The lumber company at Warm River was an important employer in the city until the mid-1960s when the mill was disassembled and the equipment sold.

Railroad The St. Anthony Railroad Company completed a rail line from Idaho Falls to St. Anthony in

1900. Principals in the railroad company and other investors formed the Yellowstone Park Railroad Company five years later and completed a 70-mile rail line from St. Anthony to the west entrance of Yellowstone National Park in Montana in 1909.

The railroad reached Warm River in 1907 where it built a 60-foot turntable and other facilities, facilitating the growth of the community's sawmill and agriculture businesses and adding another important employer to the town's economy until the train moved its personnel to Ashton in 1946.

State Fish Hatchery The Idaho Department of Fish and Game fish hatchery – built during the 1930s – was important to the town's economy until it closed in the 1950s.

Idaho Highway 47 and U.S. Highway 20 The road to Warm River would eventually become Idaho Highway 47 – built by the Idaho Transportation Department to principally provide access to the fish hatchery, sawmill and the scenic attractions of Mesa Falls and Lower Mesa Falls. The tourist traffic was a boon to Warm River retail and hospitality businesses. However, that all changed when U.S. Highway 20 to Island Park and Yellowstone National Park was completed about eight miles west of Warm River. By 1957 vehicle traffic on Idaho Highway 47 through Warm River had dropped dramatically, and businesses began to close.

Warm River Today

Amenities and Attractions The city's principal attraction is its location, natural beauty and fabulous fishing on the Warm River and other nearby streams.

Harriman State Park is located about 25 miles northwest of the city and 18 miles north of Ashton. This 11,000-acre, 6,120-foot-high wildlife refuge offers a variety of activities including rental cabins, camping and horseback riding. The Mesa Falls Scenic Byway – Idaho Highway 47 – runs through the city.

With such nearby attractions as Mesa Falls, Harriman State Park and Warm River Cabin Campground, the city is located in some of the most beautiful natural surroundings in Idaho. It is a paradise for outdoor enthusiasts.

Economy and Major Employers Outdoor recreation is the town's principal business. Three Rivers Ranch, a commercial resort with a lodge and several cabins, offers guided fly-fishing and fishing trips with meals prepared and served at the lodge. The Forest Service's Warm River Cabin Campground includes a cabin available for rent and places for tent and other camping.

Education Any children in Warm River attend school in Ashton. The closest institution of higher learning is Brigham Young University-Idaho, 35 miles southwest in Rexburg.

Health Care The closest hospital is Madison Memorial in Rexburg.

Transportation Idaho Highway 47 passes on the northwest side of the city. It connects with U.S. Highway 20 at Ashton and again 25 miles north of Warm River near Harriman State Park.

Utilities and Services Private companies provide electricity, telephone and satellite services. The homes have individual wells and septic systems. The Fremont County Sheriff provides police protection.

Vision for 2050

In 1960 the U.S. Census reported the city's population at 20, in 1980 two. A few years later, the population increased to about 10 and then dropped to three in the 2010 U.S. Census. The city's population will likely continue to be very small for decades to come.

Mayors

1947 Berta Lewies

? Lonnie Allen

Sunset over the Mud Lake Valley.

JEFFERSON COUNTY

- Hamer
- Lewisville
- Menan
- Mud Lake
- Rigby (*County Seat*)
- Ririe
- Roberts

Aerial view of Hamer.

Hamer

Statistical Data

Population: 51 *
Elevation: 4,800 feet
Precipitation: 10 inches **
Average Snowfall: 30 inches **
County: Jefferson

Temperature Range – Fahrenheit: **
Spring: 20 to 69
Summer: 44 to 87
Fall: 16 to 76
Winter: 4 to 35
* U.S. Census Bureau Estimates July 2015
**Historical averages

Hamer is a small farming community located about 35 miles north of Idaho Falls on Interstate 15. Vast acreages of public lands, interspersed with large farms and ranches surround the city.

The lakes, streams and wetlands of the 10,578-acre Camas National Wildlife Refuge and the adjoining 8,853-acre Idaho Department of Fish and Game's Mud Lake Wildlife Management Area are located to the immediate west of the city.

Pre-Incorporation Years

For millennia, Native American Indians came to the area that now comprises the Camas National Wildlife Refuge and the Mud Lake Wildlife Management Area to hunt and fish.

In 1863 prospectors discovered placer gold in what is now western Montana. A stagecoach and freight wagon trail soon developed from Utah to the Montana gold fields. The trail, called the Gold Road, crossed the Snake River at Idaho Falls and continued about 85 miles north to Monida Pass and on into Montana.

The stagecoach company built relay stations every 12-15 miles where travelers could rest and eat. One of these relay stations, named Sandhole Station, would become the city of Hamer.

A few years after completion of the transcontinental railroad at Promontory Summit in northern Utah in 1869, the Utah and Northern Railroad – later merged into the Oregon Short Line Railroad – began constructing a rail line from Corrine, Utah, to Butte, Montana. The rail line generally followed the Gold Road. In 1879, the rail line reached Sandhole Station.

The railroad built its roundhouse and depot five miles north of Sandhole Station at Camas. Three years later in 1882, there was a serious drought and the railroad's Camas well went dry.

Railroad officials found that Dry Creek, later named Dubois and located 16 miles north of Camas, had a much better water supply. They moved their roundhouse and other buildings to Dubois. There they drilled a well and built a watertower, telegraph office and section house. Several men worked at the roundhouse and operated the helper engines used to get the trains over the 6,824-foot-high Monida Pass.

As a general practice, the railroad built train stops about every 20 miles. With the abandonment of the Camas location, Sandhole Station, located about 20 miles south of Dubois, became a train stop.

Sam Turman, a long-time Hamer resident, said the railroad steam engines would stop at Sandhole Station for water and load locally produced cattle and sheep for market.

Old Highway 91 through Hamer.

Sam Turman's grandfather, James Ross Turman, came to the area as an employee of the railroad. He worked leveling railroad track beds with a Fresno (horse-drawn) scraper. James liked the location so much he filed a homestead claim at Sandhole Station near the railroad track. In 1908 he constructed a general store out of lava rock. Sam Turman said, "The store had everything from pickles and candy in barrels, big rounds of cheese, horseshoes, neck yokes and anything a farmer or rancher would need. The upstairs had rooms that were rented out to school teachers or sheep herders."

James then applied to the postal authorities for a post office operated out of his store. His application specified the post office name of Hamer, named after Col. Thomas R. Hamer – a resident of St Anthony, Spanish-American War veteran and Idaho Territorial Congressman in the U.S. House of Representatives.

Incorporation

Hamer was first incorporated as a village. Its status changed to a city with a change in legislation in 1967.

Turning Points

Montana Gold Rush The city owes its existence to the 1863 discovery of gold in Montana. It was the transportation demand of the Montana mining interests that led to the establishment of the Sandhole Stage Stop and Railroad Train Station at what is now Hamer.

The railroad, in turn, brought its employee James Ross Turman, who chose to stay and became the city's founder.

Hamer Store.

Homestead Act of 1862 The Homestead Act was critical to the development of Hamer and the farms and ranches around the city. Most of these farms and ranches, as well as the siting of Hamer itself, are due to this Act of Congress that converted arable public land throughout the West to private development.

Hamer Today

Amenities and Attractions The city's small population obscures its importance to the area's far-flung farm and ranch families. The city is the center for events that bring the greater community together. The city has a post office, an elementary school that houses the public library and a Church of Jesus Christ of Latter-day Saints meeting house and grounds that often are used for community events. Its retail businesses consist of a tire and parts store, scale house and a bar.

Annual community events include an Independence Day celebration each July and a Christmas program put on by the students at the school.

Two service organizations, the Hamer Lions Club and the Hamer Friends of the Library support the community.

The Camas National Wildlife Refuge and the Mud Lake Wildlife Management Area are prominent attractions. A broad array of migratory and native birds and animals thrive among the diverse habitats of the area. Ducks, geese, Trumpeter swans, songbirds, raptors, moose, elk, deer and pronghorn antelope inhabit these wildlife preserves. Both the Refuge and Management Area have facilities to accommodate the increasing numbers of people coming to watch the birds and view the big game that come out of the mountains each winter.

Hamer has continual winds, clean air and spectacular sunrises and sunsets. Over the centuries, the winds produced the St. Anthony Sand Dunes. These sand dunes begin about 10 miles northeast of the city and cover an area 35 miles long and up to five miles wide. The height of the dunes themselves range from 70 to 365 feet – a height greater than the dunes in Death Valley, California.

In the winter, the winds often produce high sweeping snowdrifts that turn the landscape into a beautiful winter wonderland; a paradise for cross-country skiers and snowmobilers.

Economy and Major Employers Several large farms in the area produce potatoes, alfalfa hay and malt barley. In addition, there are several family-owed and operated ranches. Most ranchers keep their animals on their ranches through late fall and winter calving. In the spring after the calving season, they herd the cattle to the public grazing lands in Jefferson and Clark Counties.

Hamer has a limited economic base. The farm and ranch families drive to larger communities to do most of their shopping and business.

However, Hamer serves an important role for bringing these farm and ranch families and many of their employees together as a distinct community with shared interests.

Education The West Jefferson County School District, headquartered 18 miles away in the unincorporated town of Terreton, provides substantially all of the K-12 education. Hamer Elementary has about 75 students and provides education for grades K-4. All other students are bused to Terreton to attend elementary, junior high school and high school.

The closest institution of higher learning is Brigham Young University-Idaho, located 30 miles to the southeast in Rexburg.

Health Care The closest hospitals are in Rexburg and Idaho Falls.

Transportation Hamer is near Interstate 15. The closest commercial airport is in Idaho Falls.

Utilities and Services Private companies provide electricity, telephone and satellite services. The city's homes and businesses have individual wells and septic tanks. The Jefferson County Sheriff's Office provides police protection. The city has a Quick Response Unit attached to the City of Mud Lake Ambulance Service located 20 miles southwest.

Vision for 2050

The population of Hamer has remained constant for more than a decade. The historical population trends will likely continue. By 2050 the city will still be performing its principal role of providing a central location for the elementary education, postal and church needs of the rural area's far-flung farm and ranch families.

Lewisville Post Office.

Lewisville

Statistical Data

Population: 476*
Elevation: 4,800 feet
Precipitation: 12 inches **
Average Snowfall: 45 inches **
County: Jefferson

Temperature Range – Fahrenheit: **
Spring: 25 to 67
Summer: 46 to 86
Fall: 22 to 59
Winter: 11 to 34
* U.S. Census Bureau Estimates July 2015
**Historical averages

Lewisville lies on the Upper Snake River Plain five miles south of the apex of an over 100,000-acre peninsula created by the Snake River. The river flows northwest from

Palisades Reservoir to the mouth of Henry's Fork at Menan Buttes, makes an irregular 90-degree turn west for about seven miles, before making another 90-degree turn south to Idaho Falls. Early settlers called this fertile range with its vast tracts of grass and sagebrush-covered land, meandering creeks and marshes the "Island."

Today, fields of potatoes, alfalfa hay, wheat, corn and barley form a checkerboard of color and texture around the city. Rexburg, home of Brigham Young University-Idaho (BYU-Idaho), is 13 miles northeast. Idaho Falls, headquarters of Idaho National Laboratories (INL), is 16 miles south.

Pre-Incorporation Years

In 1810 the first white men – European and American explorers/trappers – came into the Upper Snake River Plain. Before that, American Indians – principally of the Shoshone and Bannock Tribes – were the exclusive inhabitants of the area.

Osborne Russell was one of the first European and American explorers/trappers to pass through the Market Lake area located about six miles northwest of what is now Lewisville.

In his journal, *Journal of a Trapper – Nine Years in the Rocky Mountains, 1834-1843,* Russell referenced the lake and surrounding marshland. He said he saw American Indians, buffalo, antelope, beaver, elk, moose, deer, mink, muskrat, weasel, waterfowl and grouse. Early trappers named the area "Market Place" because of the wide variety of game available for harvest.

Lewisville church dedication, 1890.

In August 1841 the first overland migration of settlers to Oregon Country began. They passed 50 miles south at Fort Hall. During the next three decades, tens of thousands more settlers would follow on the Oregon Trail.

In 1863 prospectors found placer gold at Virginia City, in what is now southwestern Montana. Horse-and-mule-drawn stagecoaches and freight wagons carried people and supplies from Utah to the Montana gold fields over a wagon road called the "Gold Road." One of the stage stops, Market Lake Stage Station, was near what is now Roberts, seven miles west of Lewisville.

Glicchrist Store, 1898.

In 1878 the Utah and Northern Railroad began construction of a rail line that generally followed the path of the Gold Road. It went north from Idaho Falls through what are now Roberts and Dubois, across the Continental Divide at Monida Pass and into Montana. The railroad construction crews included many men recruited from the rapidly growing settlements in northern Utah – converts to The Church of Jesus Christ of Latter-day Saints (the Church) from Europe and the Eastern United States.

In February 1879 one of the construction workers returning home – John R. Poole of Ogden, Utah – went hunting on the Island and met Israel Heal. Heal was one of several pioneers who in 1867 had begun settling around the Snake River near what are now Menan and Lewisville. Heal ran a large herd of cattle on the Island. Poole asked Heal what he thought about homesteaders settling the Island. Heal said, "I don't believe God intended that a few men should have all this great country to raise horses and cows in." President Abraham Lincoln signed the

Homestead Act in 1862. (*See Eastern Idaho, Federal Land-Use Laws.*)

Poole returned to Utah where increasing numbers of Church convert emigrants from Europe and the Eastern United States were coming. He extolled the farming potential of the Island and urged those looking for a place to settle to visit. Uniformly impressed, these pioneers came, staked their 160-acre homestead claims and brought their families to settle the new land.

Lewisville Amusement Hall.

Initially, these homesteaders settled in locations most favorable for irrigated farming. Their communities tended to be spread out. Some of these settlements did not have a community core until they built a multi-purpose public hall, which they used for school, church and community gatherings.

The first community in the area was Menan, an Indian word meaning "island." It had been variously known as "Heal's Island," "Poole's Island" and "Cedar Buttes." Lewisville, located two miles south of Menan, was arguably the second community established on the Island.

As more Church members moved from Utah to Eastern Idaho, Church leaders asked 54-year-old Thomas E. Ricks to be the Bishop of the immigrant settlers going to the Upper Snake River Plain. Ricks, a Kentuckian, joined the Church in 1844 and in 1848 was part of the Mormon exodus from Illinois to Salt Lake City. Ricks' ecclesiastical jurisdiction soon expanded to include several new communities, including Menan and Lewisville. Then called the Bannock Ward, Ricks' ecclesiastical jurisdiction later became the Bannock Stake (diocese), comprising several geographical designations called "wards."

Lewisville Grade School.

The railroad played an important role in transporting these settlers to the Upper Snake River Plain. In one year – 1882 to 1884 – Bannock Ward membership – children under eight years of age are not included in the membership count – increased from 815 to 1,420. Within a decade, several thousand Church members had settled in the Upper Snake River Plain.

After establishing their homestead claims, settlers immediately began building shelters and clearing and leveling the land, banding together to build irrigation canals and ditches and diverting water from the Snake River and creeks into the canals and ditches they used to irrigate their farms. Over the succeeding few years, their complex system of irrigation canals and ditches turned the dry sagebrush-covered land into a fertile agricultural oasis.

Incorporation

On January 11, 1904, Lewisville became an incorporated village.

Turning Points

Railroad Even though seven miles distant, construction of the Utah and Northern Railroad line to the Montana gold fields had a profound effect in the founding and future prosperity of Lewisville and the entire area.

Lewisville fire station.

The railroad was what brought former railroad employee John R. Poole to discover the fertile land for himself and, in turn, influence many other families to settle on the Island.

The railroad later provided transportation critical to the success of the city. It not only allowed convenient transportation of passengers and rapid movement of mail and freight within seven miles of the city, but area farmers and ranchers could efficiently ship their commodities to market.

Lewisville Today

LDS Church.

Amenities and Attractions The city is close to beautiful scenery and outdoor activities. The Caribou-Targhee National Forest is within an hour's drive to the north, east and southeast of the city. Vast tracts of public lands managed by the BLM begin five miles northwest. In addition to camping, hiking, hunting, fishing, snowmobiling and ATV riding, downhill skiing is available 28 miles east at Kelly Canyon Ski Area. The ski resort is 6,600 feet at the summit and has 26 runs.

State and federal agencies have established several wildlife management areas (WMA). The 5,071-acre Market Lake WMA is located about nine miles northwest. The 10,578-acre Camas National Wildlife Refuge and the 8,853-acre Mud Lake WMA are a few miles west of Hamer, 23 miles northwest of Lewisville. The small, but important, 71-acre Gem State WMA is near Lewisville. The 5,619-foot-high Menan Buttes are located about five miles north of the city.

The city's close proximity to the much larger cities of Idaho Falls and Rexburg is an important amenity. Lewisville residents are able to live in a smaller town yet within a short drive of the educational, cultural, shopping and entertainment opportunities available in those cities.

Economy and Major Employers The city's commerce district consists of a few small businesses and a convenience store. Most residents commute to other cities to work, shop and do their business.

Education Jefferson County School District serves Lewisville's elementary and secondary students. Elementary age children attend school in Menan. Middle and high school students travel seven miles southeast to Rigby. The closest institutions of higher learning are Brigham Young University-Idaho in Rexburg and Eastern Idaho Technical College and University Place in Idaho Falls.

Lewisville library.

Health Care A health clinic and private medical practitioners provide health care in Rigby. The nearest hospital is Madison Memorial Hospital in Rexburg.

Transportation State Highway 48 borders the city on the west. Interstate 15 is accessible at Roberts. U.S. Highway 20 is five miles east. The Rigby-Jefferson County Airport in Rigby has a 3,500-foot runway that provides service for light private and charter aircraft. The closest commercial airport is the Idaho Falls Regional Airport.

Utilities and Services Private companies provide electricity, telephone and satellite services. The City provides water and sewer services as well as police and fire protection.

Vision for 2050

Lewisville's population of around 500 has remained somewhat constant for nearly 40 years. These historical trends will likely continue to 2050.

Mayors

1904 Richard F. Jardine *
1904 Welby H. Walker
1907 Samuel G. Marler
1908 John Walker
1911 Wallace Fife
1915 Frank H. Goody
1917 William P. Walker
1919 Warren L. Shurtleff
1929 Edward B. Hunter
1933 Arthur J. Goody, Jr.
1935 Thomas J. Jackson
1939 Wallace Ball
1943 Joseph A. Jardine
1947 Parley J. Harker
1951 A. Vernon Ball
1957 Neal Erickson
1961 Elmer F. Ellsworth
1974 Marc E. Burrows
1967 Gale W. Clement
1980 James Dee Young
1988 Lynn L. Anderson
1996 Kenneth Walker
1996 Lynn L. Anderson
1998 Christopher Moore
2004 Barbara Blair
2010 Curtis Thomas
2014 George A. Judd

* Village Chairman

Menan with buttes in the background.

Menan

Statistical Data

Population: 747 *
Elevation: 4,806 feet
Precipitation: 12 inches **
Average Snowfall: 45 inches **
County: Jefferson

Temperature Range – Fahrenheit: **
Spring: 25 to 67
Summer: 46 to 86
Fall: 22 to 74
Winter: 11 to 34
* U.S. Census Bureau Estimates July 2015
**Historical averages

Menan lies on the Snake River Plain near the apex of an over 100,000-acre peninsula created by the Snake River. The river flows northwest from Palisades Reservoir to the mouth of Henry's Fork at Menan Buttes, makes an irregular 90-degree turn west for about seven miles, before making another 90-degree turn south to Idaho Falls. Early settlers referred to this fertile irregular shaped horseshoe with its meandering creeks and marshes as the "Island."

Today, lush fields of potatoes, alfalfa hay, wheat, corn and barley have replaced the creek-fed meadows and tracts of sagebrush-covered land that once characterized the peninsula.

Rexburg is about 13 miles northeast. Idaho Falls is 18 miles south.

Pre-Incorporation Years

In 1810 prior to the time explorers/trappers began coming into the region, American Indians – principally of the Shoshone and Bannock Tribes – were the exclusive inhabitants of the area.

Osborne Russell was one of the first European and American explorers/trappers to pass through the Market Lake area located about six miles northwest of Menan.

In his journal, Journal of a Trapper – Nine Years in the Rocky Mountains, 1834-1843, Russell referenced the lake and surrounding marshland. He said he saw American Indians, buffalo, antelope, beaver, elk, moose, deer, mink, muskrat, weasel, waterfowl and grouse. Early trappers named the area "Market Place" because of the wide variety of game available for harvest.

In August 1841 Father Pierre de Smet, the Roman Catholic missionary and explorer who established several church missions in the West, was a member of the first overland migration of settlers to Oregon Country. They passed 50 miles to the south at Fort Hall. During the next three decades, tens of thousands more settlers would follow on the route called the Oregon Trail.

In 1863 prospectors found placer gold at Virginia City, in what is now southwestern Montana. Horse-and-mule-drawn stagecoaches and freight wagons carried people and supplies from Utah to the Montana gold fields over a wagon road called the "Gold Road." One of the stage stops, Market Lake Stage Station, was near what is now Roberts, seven miles west of Menan.

Old Annis Church Building on the Lorenzo-Menan Highway, later renovated and now used as the Sereno Event Center.

In 1878 the Utah and Northern Railroad began construction of a rail line that generally followed the path of the Gold Road. It went north from Idaho Falls through what are now Roberts and Dubois, across the Continental Divide at Monida Pass and into Montana. The railroad construction crews included many men recruited from the rapidly growing settlements in northern Utah – converts to The Church of Jesus Christ of Latter-day Saints (the Church) from Europe and the Eastern U.S.

In February 1879 one of the construction workers returning home – John R. Poole of Ogden, Utah – went hunting on the island and met Israel Heal. Heal was one of several pioneers that in 1867 had begun settling around the Snake River near what is now Menan. Heal ran a large herd of cattle on the Island. Poole asked Heal what he thought about homesteaders settling the island. Heal said, "I don't believe God intended that a few men should have all this great country to raise horses and cows in." President Abraham Lincoln signed the Homestead Act in 1862. (*See Eastern Idaho, Federal Land-Use Laws.*)

Poole returned to Utah, which was receiving an increasing number of Church convert emigrants from Europe and the Eastern United States. He extolled the farming potential of the Island and urged those looking for a place to settle to visit the Island. Uniformly impressed, these pioneers came, staked their homestead claims and brought their families to settle the new land.

Initially, these homesteaders staked their 160-acre homestead claims in locations where the contour and elevation of the land was most favorable for irrigated farming. Thus, initially, their communities tended to be spread out.

They named their community Menan, an Indian word meaning “island.” Previously the area had been variously known as “Heal’s Island,” “Poole’s Island” and “Cedar Buttes.”

As more Church members moved from Utah to Eastern Idaho, they asked 54-year-old Thomas E. Ricks to be the Bishop of the immigrant settlers going to the Upper Snake River Plain. Ricks, a Kentuckian, joined the Church in 1844, and in 1848 was part of the Mormon exodus from Illinois to Salt Lake City. His ecclesiastical jurisdiction soon expanded to include several new communities, including Menan, then called Bannock Ward – later to become the Bannock Stake (diocese) that comprised several geographical designations called “wards.” The railroad played an important role in transporting these settlers to the Upper Snake River Plain. In one year – 1882 to 1884 – Bannock Ward membership – children under eight years old are not included in the membership count – increased from 815 to 1,420. Within a decade, several thousand Church members had settled in the Upper Snake River Plain.

Clements home in Menan.

After establishing their homestead claims, settlers immediately began building shelters and clearing and leveling the land, banding together to build irrigation canals and ditches and diverting water from the Snake River and creeks into the canals and ditches they used to irrigate their farms. Over the succeeding few years, their complex system of irrigation canals and ditches turned the dry sagebrush-covered land into a fertile agricultural oasis.

Incorporation

In 1907 Menan became an incorporated village.

Turning Points

Railroad Even though seven miles away, construction of the Utah and Northern Railroad line to the Montana gold fields had a profound effect in the founding and future prosperity of Menan.

The railroad was what brought former railroad employee John R. Poole to discover the fertile land for himself and, in turn, influence many other families to settle on the Island.

The railroad later provided transportation critical to the success of the city. It not only allowed convenient transportation of passengers and rapid movement of mail and freight within seven miles of the city, but area farmers and ranchers could efficiently ship their commodities to market.

Menan Today

Amenities and Attractions The city is close to beautiful scenery and outdoor activities. The Caribou-Targhee National Forest is within an hour's drive to the north, east and southeast of the city. Vast tracts of public lands managed by the BLM begin five miles northwest. In addition to camping, hiking, hunting, fishing, snowmobiling and ATV riding, downhill skiing is available 30 miles east at Kelly Canyon Ski Area. The ski resort is 6,600 feet at the summit and has 26 runs.

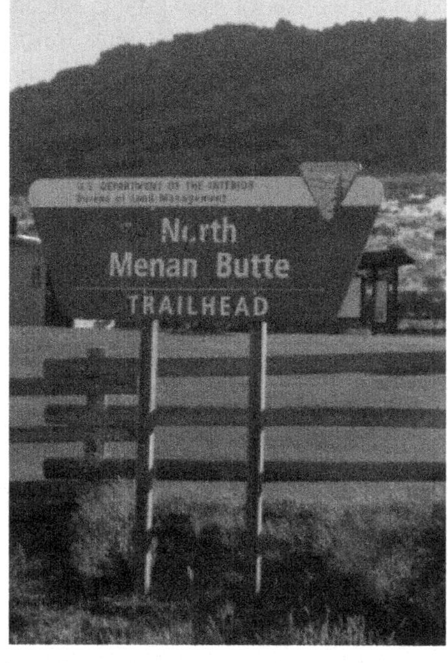

State and federal agencies have established several wildlife management areas (WMA). The 5,071-acre Market Lake WMA is located about seven miles northwest. The 10,578-acre Camas National Wildlife Refuge and the 8,853-acre Mud Lake WMA are a few miles west of Hamer, 22 miles northwest of Menan. The small but important 71-acre Gem State WMA is near Menan. The 5,619-foot-high Menan Buttes – two of the largest volcanic "tuff" cones in the world – are located about three miles north of the city.

The city's close proximity to the much larger cities of Idaho Falls and Rexburg are important amenities. Menan residents are able to live in a smaller town yet within a short drive to the educational, cultural, shopping and entertainment opportunities available in those cities.

Economy and Major Employers Jefferson County School District is the city's largest employer.

The city's commerce district consists of a few small businesses and a convenience store. Many residents commute to Rexburg and Idaho Falls to work, shop and do business.

Education Jefferson County School District provides public schooling for elementary and secondary students in Menan. There is an elementary school and alternative high school in the city. Middle and high school children attend school nine miles southeast in Rigby.

The closest institutions of higher learning are Brigham Young University-Idaho in Rexburg and Eastern Idaho Technical College and University Place in Idaho Falls.

Health Care A health clinic and private medical practitioners provide health care in Rigby. The nearest hospital is Madison Memorial Hospital in Rexburg.

Transportation State Highway 48 borders the city on the west. Interstate 15 can be accessed at Roberts. U.S. Highway 20 is six miles east.

The Rigby-Jefferson County Airport in Rigby has a 3,500-foot runway that provides service for light private and charter aircraft. The closest commercial airport is the Idaho Falls Regional Airport.

Utilities and Services Private companies provide electricity, telephone and satellite services. The City provides water and sewer services as well as police and fire protection.

Vision for 2050

In 1960 Menan had a population of 496. Over the intervening 48 years, the city's population increased on average less than one percent annually. Historical trends will likely continue. In 2050 Menan's population will be less than 1,000.

Field of alfalfa near the City of Mud Lake.

Mud Lake

Statistical Data

Population: 369 *
Elevation: 4,790 feet
Precipitation: 10 inches **
Average Snowfall: 30 inches **
County: Jefferson

Temperature Range – Fahrenheit: **
Spring: 20 to 69
Summer: 44 to 87
Fall: 16 to 76
Winter: 4 to 35
* U.S. Census Bureau Estimates July 2015
**Historical averages

The city of Mud Lake is located a few miles southwest of the 10,578-acre Camas National Wildlife Refuge and the adjoining 8,853-acre Idaho Department of Fish and Game's Mud Lake Wildlife Management Area (WMA). The WMA includes streams, wetlands and the six-mile-wide and up to two-and-a-half-mile-long Mud Lake.

The city lies near the base of a broad, up to 15-mile-deep and 40-mile-long crescent of irrigated farmland in a vast dry high desert. The crescent extends from above Hamer, located 14 miles due northeast of the city of Mud Lake; wraps around the south side of the WMA past the city of Mud Lake; and then proceeds northwest to above the unincorporated community of Monteview.

Idaho Falls lies about 35 miles southeast of Mud Lake City. Rexburg is about 36 miles west. The substantially larger in population but unincorporated community of Terreton is two miles west.

Pre-Incorporation Years

Until around 1810 when the first European and American explorers/trappers came into the region, American Indians – primarily of the Shoshone and Bannock Tribes – hunted and fished the area that now comprises the WMA.

In 1863 prospectors discovered placer gold in what is now western Montana. A stagecoach and freight wagon trail soon developed from Utah to the Montana gold fields. The trail, called the Gold Road, crossed the Snake River at Idaho Falls and continued north to Monida Pass and on into Montana.

The stagecoach company built relay stations every 12 to 15 miles, where travelers could rest and eat. One of these relay stations, named Sandhole Station, would become the city of Hamer.

Mown field of alfalfa near Mud Lake.

A few years after completion of the transcontinental railroad at Promontory Summit in northern Utah in 1869, the Utah and Northern Railroad – later merged into the Oregon Short Line Railroad – began constructing a rail line from Corrine, Utah, to Butte, Montana. The rail line generally followed the Gold Road. In 1879 the rail line reached Sandhole Station.

The railroad built its roundhouse and depot five miles north of Sandhole Station at Camas. Three years later in 1882, there was a serious drought and the railroad's Camas well went dry.

Railroad officials found that Dry Creek – later named Dubois and located 16 miles north of Camas – had plenty of water. They moved their roundhouse and other buildings to Dubois. There they drilled a well and built a water tower, telegraph office and section house. Several men worked at the roundhouse and operated the helper engines used to get the trains over the 6,824-foot-high Monida Pass.

As a general practice, the railroad built train stops about every 20 miles. With the abandonment of the Camas location, Sandhole Station became a train stop.

Sam Turman – a long-time Hamer resident whose grandfather founded Hamer – said the railroad steam engines would stop at Sandhole Station for water and load locally produced cattle and sheep for market.

Many of these cattle and sheep grazed in the meadows and on the adjoining grass and sagebrush-covered land surrounding the large shallow lake. Each summer the streams feeding the lake declined in volume and the lakeshores receded leaving exposed lake-bottom and a long muddy circumference around the lake. Local ranchers thus named the shallow body of water "Mud Lake."

Incorporation

Mud Lake was incorporated as a village. In 1967 with a change in Idaho state law, Mud Lake became a city.

Turning Points

Homestead Act The Homestead Act of 1862 was critical to the development of Mud Lake and the farms and ranches around the city. (*See Eastern Idaho – Federal Land Use Laws.*)

Railroad The railroad stopping at Hamer was close enough to the community of Mud Lake that it not only allowed convenient transportation of passengers and rapid movement of mail and freight, but it allowed area ranchers and farmers to efficiently ship their livestock and commodities to market.

Mud Lake Today

Amenities and Attractions The WMA is a prominent attraction for wildlife observation and recreation. A broad array of migratory and native birds and animals thrive among the diverse habitats of the WMA. Ducks, geese, Trumpeter swans, songbirds, raptors, moose, elk, deer and pronghorn antelope inhabit these wildlife preserves. Both the refuge and management area have facilities to accommodate the increasing numbers of people coming to watch the birds and view the big game that come out of the mountains each winter.

Mud Lake Bank of Commerce.

Mud Lake has continual winds, clean air and spectacular sunrises and sunsets. Over the centuries, the winds produced the St. Anthony Sand Dunes. These sand dunes begin about 24 miles due northeast of the city and cover an area 35 miles long and up to five miles wide. The height of the dunes themselves range from 70 to 365 feet – a height greater than the dunes in Death Valley, California.

In the winter, the winds often produce high sweeping snowdrifts that turn the landscape into a beautiful winter wonderland – a paradise for cross-country skiers and snowmobiles.

Economy and Major Employers Agriculture underpins the city's economy. Several large farms in the area produce potatoes, alfalfa hay and malt barley. In addition, there are several family-owned and operated ranches. Most ranchers keep their animals on their ranches through late fall and winter calving. In the spring, after the calving season, they herd the cattle to the public grazing lands in Jefferson and Clark Counties.

Mud Lake has a limited economic base. The city's commercial businesses consist of a few farm and ranch supply and convenience stores. Residents and farm and ranch families drive to larger communities to do most of their shopping and business.

However, Mud Lake, along with Terreton, serves an important role for bringing area farm and ranch families and many of their employees together as a distinct community with shared interests.

Black birds on Mud Lake.

Education The West Jefferson County School District, headquartered in Terreton, provides substantially all of the K-12 education for the city's children. Mud Lake students attend elementary, junior high school and high school in Terreton.

The closest institutions of higher learning are Eastern Idaho Technical College and University Place in Idaho Falls and Brigham Young University-Idaho in Rexburg.

Health Care The closest hospitals are in Rexburg and Idaho Falls.

Transportation Idaho Highway 28-33 intersects the city. Interstate 15 is 14 miles west.

Mud Lake West Jefferson County Airport is located three miles west of town. It provides service for light private and charter aircraft. The closest commercial airport is in Idaho Falls.

Utilities and Services Private companies provide electricity, telephone and satellite services. The city's homes and businesses have individual wells and septic tanks. The Jefferson County Sheriff's Office provides police protection. A Quick Response Unit is attached to the City of Mud Lake.

Vision for 2050

For the past few decades, Mud Lake's population has ranged between 200 and 300. Historical trends will likely continue. By 2050 Mud Lake will continue to be a small peaceful community of fewer than 400 residents.

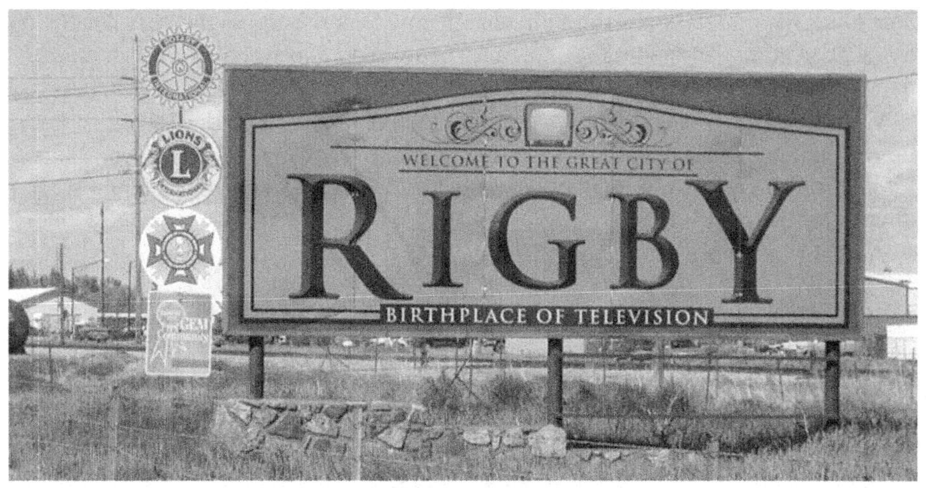

Rigby

Statistical Data

Population: 4,037 *
Elevation: 4,850 feet
Precipitation: 9 inches **
Average Snowfall: 32 inches **
County: Jefferson
Website: www.cityofrigby.com

Temperature Range – Fahrenheit: **
Spring: 22 to 66
Summer: 45 to 84
Fall: 20 to 74
Winter: 10 to 34
* U.S. Census Bureau Estimates July 2015
**Historical averages

Rigby is a historic farming community on the Upper Snake River Plain. Fields of mostly potatoes, alfalfa hay, wheat, corn and barley surrounded the city. The Snake River flows just a few miles to the east and north. The Caribou-Targhee National Forest and Kelley Mountain Ski Resort lie about 21 miles east.

The city is on U.S. Highway 20 between Idaho Falls, 15 miles southwest, and Rexburg, 13 miles northeast.

Pre-Incorporation Years

In 1810 Andrew Henry led a party of trappers/explorers into Eastern Idaho and established a post at what is now Henry's Lake, about 75 miles northeast of Rigby. At that time, tall sagebrush covered the land around what is now Rigby. American Indians migrated through the area as they traveled to their seasonal encampments.

In 1863 prospectors discovered gold in Virginia City, Montana. Freighters and stagecoach companies built a wagon road – called the Gold Road – from Utah to the Montana goldfields.

In 1879 the Utah and Northern Railroad built a rail line from Utah to the

Montana gold fields generally following the trail of the Gold Road. The rail line went north from Idaho Falls through what is now Dubois, across the continental divide at Monida Pass and into Montana. The railroad construction crews included many men recruited from the rapidly growing settlements in northern Utah.

When one of the construction workers – John R. Poole of Ogden, Utah – returned home, he extolled the farmland potential of the Upper Snake River Plain. As other railroad construction workers returned home, they confirmed Poole's glowing assessment.

At that time, the population of Utah was swelling. A stream of immigrant converts to the Church of Jesus Christ of Latter-day Saints (Church) – also known as Mormons – fueled the rapid population growth. When news of the settlement potential of the Upper Snake River Plain reached northern Utah, several families began preparing to homestead in Eastern Idaho. The railroad played an important role in transporting these settlers to the Upper Snake River Plain.

A Rigby street scene. Courtesy Rexburg Historical Society.

In 1882 Church leaders asked 54-year-old Thomas E. Ricks to be the Bishop of the immigrant settlers going to the Rexburg area. Ricks, a Kentuckian, joined the Church in 1844 and in 1848 was part of the Mormon exodus from Illinois to Salt Lake City, Utah.

In January 1883 Ricks led the first party of settlers to what is now Rexburg. One of Ricks" counselors was William F. Rigby, an emigrant convert from Saddleworth, England. Rigby immediately went to work building sawmills in Beaver Canyon to provide lumber to the growing number of settlers.

Ricks named the ecclesiastical jurisdiction, consisting of several new communities, Bannock Ward – later to become a stake (diocese). By the end of 1883 Church records listed 815 members living in the Bannock Ward. By the end of 1884 the number had increased to 1,420.

Main Street. Courtesy Keith Hammond.

As the settlers arrived, they immediately went about establishing homestead claims, building shelters and clearing and leveling the land – banding together to build irrigation canals and ditches and diverting Snake River water into the canals to irrigate their farms. Over the succeeding few years, their complex system of irrigation canals and ditches turned dry sagebrush-covered land into a fertile agricultural oasis.

The first settlers to file homestead claims around what is now Rigby came in 1884. They named their community Rigby after William F. Rigby. Characteristic of Mormon settlements, they surveyed the town on a north-south axis with eight-rod-wide – 132 feet – streets. They marked Main Street by pulling a railroad tie behind a team of horses to break down the sagebrush.

Rigby High School, circa 1920s.

Some of the more public-minded settlers donated a total of $20 to buy a lot on which they constructed the first public building – an assembly hall large enough to hold church services. However, the seller of the property apparently did not have clear title.

A real estate schemer and opportunist, Jack Robinson, discovered the legal omission and filed on the property. When the settlers arrived a few days later to hold a scheduled meeting, they were surprised to see their personal property set outside the building with Robinson armed with a pistol. He told them he had properly filed a claim and the property was his. The settlers consulted authorities and learned there was little they could do but buy Robinson's claim. They paid him $250. Presumably, Robinson got out of town.

Waiting their turn to unload, near Rigby Depot, 1911. Courtesy Keith Hammond.

One of Ricks' first priorities was to see to the education of the children. He formed a board of education with leaders that included himself and William Rigby. In 1888 that board created the Bannock Stake Academy, the forerunner to Brigham Young University-Idaho.

In 1889 the community applied for and received a post office named Rigby.

In May 1899 entrepreneurs formed the St. Anthony Railroad Company and built a railroad from Idaho Falls, through Rigby, to St. Anthony. They would later build lateral branches connecting several nearby communities. By 1909 the line would extend to Yellowstone National Park. This rail line was of major importance to Rigby because, previously, the nearest rail depot was the Utah and Northern Railroad, about 15 miles west at Roberts. Now Rigby had direct access to railroad transportation.

Incorporation

On June 14, 1903, Rigby – with a population of over 200 – became an incorporated village.

Turning Points

Utah and Northern Railroad Employees from Utah The glowing reports of the farming potential of the Upper Snake River Plain from railroad construction employees returning home to Utah set in motion a series of events that led to the settlement of Rigby and many other communities in Eastern Idaho.

Broulim's Market.

The encouragement to settle in Eastern Idaho came from the highest office of the Mormon Church. On December 26, 1882, John Taylor – then president of the Church of Jesus Christ of Latter-day Saints – wrote to church members looking for a place to settle, "Go to the Snake River Country, found settlements, care for the Indians, stand upon an equal footing and cooperate in making improvements ... "

Irrigation The settlers that came from Utah to Eastern Idaho brought considerable practical knowledge and experience regarding successful irrigation practices. Utah settlers had been developing these irrigation practices for over three decades. This knowledge and skill allowed the settlers in the Rigby and Upper Snake River Valley areas to move quickly to engineer the complex system of irrigation canals and diversion dams needed to irrigate their farms. Irrigation made possible or dramatically improved crop yields. More importantly, it allowed farmers broader diversification in rotation to and selection of crops with the highest cash value.

Jefferson County museum.

St. Anthony Railroad Company For the period 1883 to 1899, the Utah and Northern Railroad was the principal railroad in the region. However, it bypassed Rigby several miles to the west. In 1899 the St. Anthony Railroad Company brought rail service directly through Rigby. The railroad built a passenger and mail depot and loading dock for livestock, grain, coal, lumber and other commodities.

Rigby Today

Amenities and Attractions Rigby has four city parks covering 48 acres with a fifth planned for development. The Northwest Park is a soccer park. Central Park is in the center of town. It has two Little League baseball fields, picnic shelters, restrooms, children's playground facilities, basketball and tennis courts, horseshoe pits and a WWII anti-aircraft gun. Veterans Memorial Park memorializes all military service men and women who lived in the area that is now Jefferson County. Along with picnic facilities, it has a WWII army tank on display. Rigby South Rodeo Park has a rodeo arena, grandstand and bleachers, racetrack, restrooms and concession areas. It also has picnic areas, children playgrounds, skateboarding, basketball and volleyball courts, a climbing rock for children, three athletic fields and a walking path.

Jefferson County Courthouse.

The city has two golf courses, the 18-hole Jefferson Hills Golf Course and the 9-hole Cedar Park Golf Course.

The city and community offer several annual events. Each May the Jefferson County high school and middle school rodeo athletes compete at South Rodeo Park. The County sponsors the Jefferson County Stampede each June followed by the county fair on the second week of August. The Jefferson County Sheriff's Posse puts on their performances each September. Each December owners hook up their fast horses to sleek sleighs for the traditional cutter races.

Rigby Rodeo Grounds.

Rigby Lake, also known as Jefferson County Lake, is located a mile outside the city. Lake amenities include boat docks, picnic shelters and campsites.

The Jefferson County Historical Museum has 14,000 square feet of artifacts and exhibits. One of the more prominent exhibits is devoted to a native son, Philo T. Farnsworth – the inventor of television. (*See Eastern Idaho, Invention of Electronic Television.*)

In 1921 as a 14-year-old student at Rigby High School, Philo conceived the idea of electronic television while tilling a potato field. Going back and forth with a horse-drawn harrow, he realized that an electron beam could scan images the same way. He illustrated his mathematical formula at school. On September 7, 1922, Farnsworth proved his theory. Farnsworth's patents showed he was the first to form and manipulate an electron beam in the production of television images. However, RCA, a major U.S. electronics company, filed its own patents and challenged Farnsworth in court. In a protracted court case, the court evaluated the documentation of prior art and found in favor of Farnsworth.

Rigby's proximity to the much larger cities of Idaho Falls and Rexburg is an important amenity. Rigby residents are able to live in a smaller town yet are within a short drive to the educational, cultural, shopping and entertainment opportunities

Park in Rigby.

available in those cities.

The city is also close to beautiful scenery and outdoor activities. The Caribou-Targhee National Forest is within an hour's drive north, east and southeast of the city. In addition to camping, hiking, hunting, fishing, snowmobiling and ATV riding, downhill skiing is available at Kelly Canyon Ski Area. The ski resort is 6,600 feet at the summit and has 26 runs, four ski lifts and two rope tows.

In addition to the vast acreages of Forest Service and BLM lands in the area, state and federal agencies have established several wildlife management areas (WMA). Those near Rigby include the 5,071-acre Market Lake WMA, located about 15 miles northwest above Roberts. The 10,578-acre Camas National Wildlife Refuge and the 8,853-acre Mud Lake WMA are a few miles west of Hamer. The small, but important, 71-acre Gem State WMA near Menan and the 5,619-foot-high Menan Buttes – two of the largest volcanic tuff cones in the world – are located about 8 miles north of the city.

Economy and Major Employers Over 300 city residents commute to work at the Idaho National Laboratory (INL) in Idaho Falls or at the INL site 60 miles west.

INL is the city's largest employer.

The Jefferson School District and the County have 625 and 148 employees, respectively, who work within the city.

Two potato warehouses – Rigby Produce and Taylor's Produce – along with Broulim's Food Stores each have about 80 employees. Most other residents involved in the workforce commute to Idaho Falls or Rexburg for work or are employed in the many retail, service, agricultural or other small business or governmental entities that operate in the city.

Education Jefferson County School District provides public schooling for elementary and secondary students in Rigby. There are two elementary schools, two middle schools and a high school in the city.

The closest institutions of higher learning are Brigham Young University-Idaho in Rexburg and Eastern Idaho Technical College and University Place in Idaho Falls.

Health Care A health clinic and private medical practitioners provide health care in the city. The nearest hospital is Madison Memorial Hospital in Rexburg. Other hospitals are available in Idaho Falls.

Transportation U.S. Highway 20 and Idaho Highway 48 intersect the city. Interstate 15 lies 15 miles south in Idaho Falls.

The Rigby-Jefferson County Airport with a 3,500-foot runway provides service for light private and charter aircraft. The closest airport with large commercial carriers is the Idaho Falls Regional Airport.

Utilities and Services Private companies provide natural gas, electricity, telephone and satellite. The City provides water and sewer services as well as police and fire protection.

Veterans War Memorial.

Vision for 2050

The U.S. Census reported Rigby's population in 1980 and 1990 at around 2,600. In the succeeding 16-plus years, the city's population grew by 610, well over one percent a year. We expect growth will continue as more families come to Rigby for affordable housing and enjoyment of the city's peaceful rural setting.

By 2050 Rigby's population will likely exceed 6,000. Many residents will commute to other cities for employment. Existing businesses will expand and new businesses come to serve the growing population in the city's area of impact. Many residents will continue to travel to nearby cities for shopping and other services.

This growth will require expansion of city services. However, the city will manage the cost of these services within existing revenue sources and impact fees assessed on new development.

Mayors

1903 E.S. Mathias *
1907 A. Cordon *
1909 J.H. Steele *
1911 George E. Hill *
1917 Frank Hardesty *
1919 Dan McCarty *
1921 Bash L. Bennett *
1925 George A. Cordon *
1927 Ira S. Taylor *
1933 A.P. Smith *
1935 Bash L. Bennett *
1945 Charlie Broulim *
1947 C.L. "Berry" Jones *
1949 Raymond Ball *
1953 C.L. "Berry" Jones *
1957 Raymond Ball *
1959 A.B. Eckersell *
1966 R.W. DaBell
1970 G. Keith Madsen
1978 Ralph G. Peterson
1982 Claude Tremelling
1986 Keith Scott
1994 Nile H. Hall
1998 Keith Scott
2002 John Anderson
2006 Art Goody
2007 Ryan Brown
2010 Keith Smith
2014 Jason Richardson
* Village Chairman

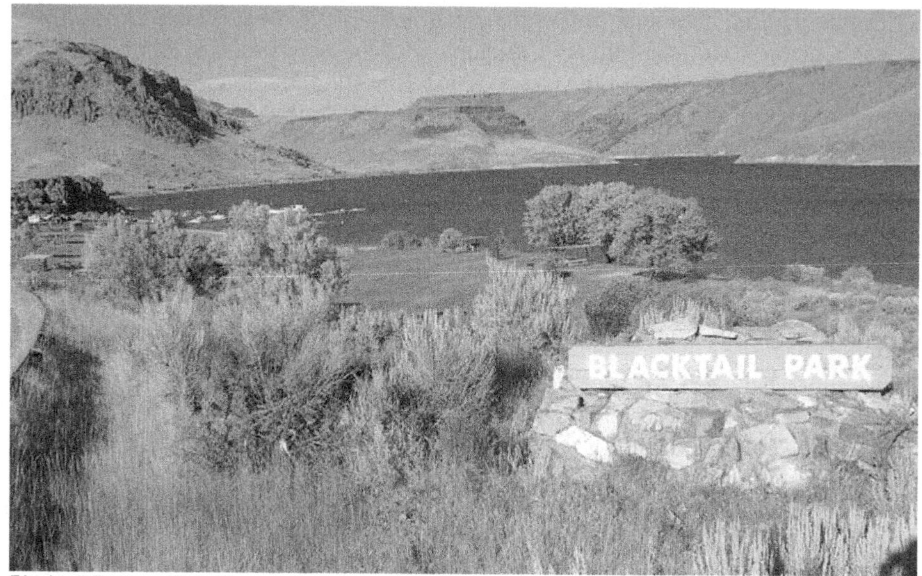

Blacktail Park on Ririe Reservoir.

Ririe

Statistical Data

Population: 636 *
Elevation: 4,962 feet
Precipitation: 9 inches **
Average Snowfall: 32 inches **
County: Jefferson and Bonneville

Temperature Range – Fahrenheit: **
Spring: 22 to 66
Summer: 45 to 84
Fall: 20 to 74
Winter: 10 to 34

* U.S. Census Bureau Estimates July 2015
**Historical averages

Ririe lies on the eastern edge of the upper Snake River Plain. Fields of potatoes, wheat, barley, alfalfa hay and corn form a mosaic of shapes, color and texture around the city.

The Caribou-Targhee National Forest and the foothills of the Caribou Mountain Range begin a few miles southeast of the city. Four miles south is the 1,560-acre Ririe Lake and the 31,000-acre Tex Creek Wildlife Management Area. The Snake River flows two miles to the north.

The 6,600-foot-high Kelly Mountain and the Kelly Canyon Ski Resort are located 10 miles east of town. Rexburg is 12 miles north, Idaho Falls 15 miles southwest.

Pre-Incorporation Years

Before the first explorers/trappers began traveling into what is now Eastern Idaho, nomadic American Indians – principally of the Shoshone and Bannock Tribes – occupied the land of the Upper Snake River Plain. The Gros Ventre and Blackfoot Indians of the northern plains also made periodic excursions into the area.

In 1810 Captain Andrew Henry led the first party of explorers/trappers into the region. About 20 miles north of what is now Ririe, his party built a log stockade and shelter that they named Fort Henry. They spent the winter at the fort and trapped for beaver. In the spring, they moved on.

Thomas Morgan Ferry near Ririe, circa 1906.

In October 1811 the Wilson Price Hunt party stayed at the deserted Fort Henry for two weeks while they built canoes with which they unwisely hoped to navigate the Snake River to the Columbia River and the Pacific Ocean. When the canoes reached the treacherous rapids near what is now Twin Falls, they had a fatal accident and loss of supplies. They determined the river route impossible, abandoned their canoes and completed their harrowing journey on foot.

In 1841 the first immigrants to Oregon's Willamette Valley passed through Soda Springs, about 60 miles south of what is now Ririe.

Lovell homestead, the first buildings in Ririe townsite.

In 1843 Captain John C. Fremont, a topographical engineer, led a surveying expedition that mapped much of the West. Oregon Trail immigrants used Fremont's maps, published by Congress, in establishing the Oregon Trail and certain cutoffs from the main trail.

In 1863 prospectors discovered placer gold in what is now western Montana –

then part of Idaho Territory. Stagecoach and freight wagon traffic began moving passengers, food and supplies from northern Utah to the Montana gold fields on a pioneer wagon road they named the "Idaho Gold Road."

The road generally paralleled what is now I-15, crossing the Continental Divide at Monida Pass and then on to the Montana boomtowns of Virginia City, Butte and Garrison – a distance of 466 miles between Ogden, Utah, and Garrison, Montana.

In 1878 the Utah and Northern Railroad Company built a rail line that generally paralleled the Gold Road. The railroad made long-haul stagecoach and freight wagon businesses obsolete.

Many of the railroad construction workers were men from Utah. They were impressed with the Upper Snake River Plain soil that produced sagebrush as tall as a man riding a horse.

When these men returned to their families in Utah, many made plans to return and settle in Eastern Idaho.

Working in the Conant Dugway near Ririe with a Fresno Scraper.

In 1881 the Oregon Short Line Railroad (OSL) began constructing a rail line that began at Granger, Wyoming; angled in a northwesterly direction through Soda Springs, Pocatello, Shoshone and Caldwell; before connecting to the rail line in Huntington, Oregon. The rail line, completed November 17, 1884, provided the necessary link to connect Southern Idaho with the commerce centers of Omaha, Nebraska, and Portland, Oregon.

At that time, the population of Utah was swelling with a stream of immigrant converts to the Church of Jesus Christ of Latter-day Saints (Church) (also known as Mormons). When news of the settlement potential of the Upper Snake River Plain reached northern Utah, several more families began preparing to go there. The railroad played an important role in transporting these homesteaders.

In 1882 Church leaders asked 54-year-old Thomas E. Ricks to be the ecclesiastical leader (Bishop) of the immigrant settlers going to the Rexburg area. Ricks, a Kentuckian, joined the Church in 1844 and in 1848 was part of the Mormon exodus from Illinois to Salt Lake City, Utah.

In January 1883 Ricks led the first party of settlers to the Rexburg area. One of Ricks' counselors was William F. Rigby, an emigrant convert from Saddleworth, England. Rigby immediately went to work building sawmills to provide lumber for the growing number of settlers.

Ricks named his new ecclesiastical jurisdiction, consisting of several new communities, Bannock Ward – later to become a stake (diocese) with several wards, each led by a bishop. By the end of 1883 Church records listed 815 members over the age of eight living in the Bannock Ward. By the end of 1884 the number had increased to 1,420.

As the settlers arrived, they immediately built shelters, filed their homestead claims, cleared and leveled the land for irrigation, banded together to build irrigation canals and ditches and diverted Snake River water into the canals. Over the succeeding few years, their complex system of irrigation canals and ditches provided water to area farms. They converted dry sagebrush-covered land into a fertile agricultural oasis.

David Ririe.

In 1888 David Ririe – a young single man who had moved from Utah – filed a homestead claim near what is now Ririe, built a cabin and began developing his farm.

Three years later, the Joseph Lovell family established a homestead on adjacent land. However, that winter Joseph died, leaving his family destitute. David helped the widow Lovell and her children establish their home and farm. Both farms were successful. David married Leah Ann, one of the Lovell daughters, and built a large stone home. This historic home still stands and is on the National Register of Historic Places.

Ririe Main Street, 1918.

Over the succeeding years, more families settled in the general area. They called their community Shelton. In 1899 railroad interests built a rail line from Idaho Falls, through Rexburg, to St Anthony. In 1914 railroad interests built a second rail line from Idaho Falls to St Anthony. However, this line passed near Shelton and extended into the farm areas located several miles east of the St. Anthony railroad built in 1899.

David Ririe played an important role in getting landowners to sell or grant rights-of-way to the railroad. When the railroad came, officials platted a town and built a station at Shelton. However, they named the Depot and town "Ririe" in recognition of David's assistance. A year later, postal authorities approved the Ririe Post Office. Shelton residents and businesses immediately changed their mailing addresses to Ririe.

Incorporation

On January 20, 1917, Ririe became an incorporated village.

Turning Points

Irrigation Shortly after the first settlers arrived, they began building irrigation diversion dams on the Snake River and its tributaries and constructing extensive canal systems. (*See Eastern Idaho – Irrigation.*)

With irrigation, the land became substantially more productive and increased the varieties of crops farmers could raise.

Railroad Ririe owes its origins to the railroad in two ways. The railroad to Montana, constructed in 1878, brought the workers, who returned to their families in Utah carrying the news of the excellent farming potential of the Upper Snake River Plain.

Thirty-six years later, the town of Ririe was born when railroad officials, building a new rail line, established and named the town of Ririe with a train depot and post office.

With the close availability of rail transportation for moving farm commodities and livestock to market, the agriculture industry around Ririe flourished.

Ririe Sunday School, circa 1919.

Agriculture Agriculture and food processing have underpinned the city's economy for most of the past century. The area's volcanic-based soils are particularly suited for producing potatoes of exceptional quality. From 1903 to 1978 a sugar factory operated in Lincoln, 11 miles southwest of Ririe. While the factory operated, sugar beets gave farmers the attractive cash-crop rotation option.

Technological innovations have allowed farmers and food processors to improve productivity with fewer employees. These changes and the increased skill level required of workers have changed the economies of the agriculture industry and the city. Many outlying farms are undergoing consolidation and the need for fewer employees.

Ririe Today

Amenities and Attractions BYU-Idaho sponsors many public concerts, plays and recitals as well as opening many of its athletic facilities to the public. The University's influence enhances the cultural and social wellbeing of Ririe citizens.

The Tex Creek Wildlife Management Area includes parts of Ririe Lake – an irrigation and flood control reservoir created by Ririe Dam – and collects water from tributary streams, provides habitat for upland and migratory birds and winter range for thousands of migratory elk, mule deer and moose. Idaho Fish and Game manages the Area and oversees public visits and viewing of the animals.

Ririe Lake is a favorite for fishing, boating and camping. However, by late summer, irrigation demands draw down the lake. One park, Juniper Park Campground, is located near the dam at the north end of the lake. Blacktail Park and Boat Dock is at the south end of the lake.

About 36 miles southeast is the picturesque 270-foot-high Palisades Dam and Reservoir on the Snake River. Evergreen forests line the reservoir's shoreline, extending over 15 miles southeast into Wyoming.

Ririe residents enjoy the city's close proximity to public lands, rivers and lakes. Many take advantage of the area's excellent fishing, hunting, camping and boating opportunities. In the warmer months, there are extensive hiking and biking trails, some open to ATV riding. In the winter, there are snowmobiling, Nordic skiing and ice fishing on Palisades Reservoir.

Economy and Major Employers Idaho Pacific Corporation, a potato processor, has about 130 employees and is the city's largest private employer. With about 100 employees, Ririe School District is the city's largest public employer. Many of Ririe's workforce travel to Idaho Falls for employment and to its regional retail shopping malls for most of their shopping needs.

Education The Ririe School District has responsibility for educating the children living in the city and the surrounding farm areas. The district has elementary, middle and high schools in the city.

The closest institution of higher learning is BYU-Idaho in Rexburg.

Health Care The closest hospital is Madison Memorial Hospital in Rexburg.

Transportation Idaho Highway 48 intersects the city. The east-west County Line Road, the border between Jefferson and Bonneville Counties, intersects the southern edge of the city. U.S. Highway 26 lies a mile south of the city. Interstate 15 can be accessed in Idaho Falls.

Utilities and Services Private companies provide electricity, telephone, satellite and natural gas services. The City provides water and sewer services and fire and police protection.

Vision for 2050

In 1960 Ririe had a population of 560. For the past 50 years, the city's population has remained somewhat stable at around 600, except in the 1990s when it exceeded 700.

Historical trends will likely continue for several years. As general economic conditions improve, the city will grow at less than one percent annually as it did in the 1990s. By 2050 Ririe's population will likely approximate 800.

Mustang Events Center, Roberts.

Roberts

Statistical Data

Population: 576 *
Elevation: 4,775 feet
Precipitation: 9 inches **
Average Snowfall: 33 inches **
County: Jefferson
Website: www.robertsid.govoffice2.com

Temperature Range – Fahrenheit: **
Spring: 25 to 67
Summer: 46 to 86
Fall: 22 to 74
Winter: 11 to 34
* U.S. Census Bureau Estimates July 2015
**Historical averages

Roberts is a quiet suburb 17 miles north of Idaho Falls. Fields of potatoes, alfalfa hay and grain surround the city. Interstate 15 borders the city on the west. The Snake River lies to the immediate east.

The 5,071-acre Market Lake Wildlife Management Area, with its 1,700 acres of marshes and wetland meadows, lies to the city's immediate north. Above the lake are vast acreages of public lands managed by the BLM. Idaho National Laboratory's (INL) 570,000-acre reservation begins about eight miles west.

Pre-Incorporation Years

Early school wagons.

Osborne Russell was one of the first European or American explorers/trappers to pass through the Market Lake area. In his journal, published after his death, titled Journal of a Trapper – Nine Years in the Rocky Mountains, 1834-1843, Russell referenced the lake and surrounding swampland. He said he saw American Indians, buffalo, antelope, beaver, elk, moose, deer, mink, muskrat, weasel, waterfowl and grouse. Early trappers named the area "Market Place" because of the wide variety of game available for harvest.

In August 1841 Father Pierre de Smet, the Roman Catholic missionary and explorer who established several church missions in the West, passed through the area on his way to Fort Hall, 75 miles south. Trappers with the British Hudson's Bay Company also worked the general area.

Lt. John Mullan was assigned to a military detachment in 1852 under the direction of General Isaac I. Stevens. Mullan was a new graduate of West Point and the officer who, eight years later, would become famous for building the first wagon road across the rugged mountains of northwestern Montana and Northern Idaho.

First school in Roberts.

Stevens' orders were to map a western route for a new railroad line. He assigned Lt. Mullan to explore a possible route from Camp Stevens on the Bitterroot River in Montana to Salt Lake City, Utah. In December 1852 Lt. Mullan and Gabriel, a Flathead Indian interpreter and guide, crossed over the Continental Divide at Monida Pass and continued south toward the Snake River. When they reached the area of Market Place; however, the Snake River had flooded – creating a large lake.

Gabriel was surprised. He told Lt. Mullan he was there only "two snows" ago. At that time, it was a beautiful grassy basin alive with buffalo and antelope.

In 1863 prospectors found placer gold at Virginia City, in what is now southwestern Montana. Three years later, prospectors discovered gold near Salmon, Idaho. For the next 20 years, horse-and-mule-drawn stagecoaches and freightwagons carried people and supplies to the gold fields. One of the stage stops, Market Lake Stage Station, was near what is now Roberts.

At that same time, three men – Thomas Lauder and two brothers, John Newton and William J. Adams – purchased a freight outfit in Corinne, Utah, and went into the freighting business. They loaded their wagon with liquor and flour and started for the goldfields. As they came to Market Lake Stage Station, they saw hundreds of acres of wild hay waving in the wind.

Early Market Lake.

The men were so impressed, they decided that John and Thomas would take the freight to the goldfields and William would ride his horse back to the claims office in Oxford, Idaho, and file their homestead claims. After William filed and staked the claims, he rode back to Corrine where he telegraphed his wife. He told her to sell their belongings and come to the natural hay country of Market Lake where they would start their life anew.

On October 8, 1868, the three families arrived at Market Lake Stage Station and started to develop their homesteads on the meadow.

William's wife was the first white woman to settle in the area. On December 13, 1870, she gave birth to her first child in a dry irrigation "head gate."

John built a log house from drift logs washed upon the banks of the Snake River. He later added a room that became the Market Lake Post Office, Trading Post and Saloon.

Trappers came to Market Lake to trade beaver pelts for tobacco and flour. Flour sold for a dollar a pound. Indians camping along the Market Lake slough east of town or on the lake bottom also came to the settlement to trade. John won and held their friendship, always giving them a choice beef and the pick of the horses.

Market Lake train depot.

In the winter of 1871 the Indians suffered from a smallpox epidemic. John befriended and cared for them; however, many died. Those who survived were grateful for John's efforts in caring for them. They called him "Medicine John."

It was around this time that Gilmer Saulbury won the contract to carry the mail. He hired Thomas Lauder to drive the mail stage. He also hired William Adams to manage the Market Lake Station and furnish hay and wood to the Sand Hole – now Hamer – and Camas Creek Stations.

In 1879 the railroad reached Market Lake. Railroad officials dug a well and built a depot and a water tower for the steam-driven engines. The railroad enhanced the town's position as the trading and shipping point for the farms and ranches in the area.

Market Lake bridge, looking east, 1904.

In 1889 the town's first newspaper, the Market Lake Sentinel, began publication. In 1892 Martin Patrie built a hotel and assisted in platting the town. The citizens built a schoolhouse of brick. Other entrepreneurs built the Bank of Market Lake.

In the same year, homesteaders using picks, shovels and horse-drawn Fresno scrapers completed the Butte & Market Lake Canal into which they diverted Snake River water. The irrigation water dramatically increased the productivity of the farmland and the prosperity of the farmers.

Incorporation

Bank of Roberts.

On January 20, 1910, town leaders circulated a petition to incorporate the town as a village. The petition also changed the name of the community to Roberts after H. A. Roberts, an Oregon Short Line official who they hoped would add some shops to the railroad's business presence in the town.

The County approved the application and name change; however, the new railroad shops did not come. Nevertheless, the town still grew. By 1920 the population of Roberts had doubled to approximately 400.

Turning Points

Stagecoach Station Establishment of the Market Lake Stage Station in the 1860s was instrumental to the founding of Roberts and the economic base from which the community grew.

Railroad While the stage station formed the genesis of the community, the railroad lifted it to the next level and provided the impetus for naming the city Roberts.

Teton Dam – Failure and Flood On June 5, 1976, the newly constructed Teton Dam on the Teton River ruptured sending a tidal wave of 80 billion gallons of water down the valley. Roberts was in the path of the flood. The flood either destroyed or significantly damaged all of the structures in the city as well as the crops and animals on the surrounding farms.

The U.S. Bureau of Reclamation (BOR) constructed the dam and accepted responsibility for the dam failure. While the destruction from the flood was devastating, BOR paid damages. The subsequent clean up and rebuilding had a major positive effect on the city's economy. (*See Eastern Idaho, Teton Dam.*)

Roberts Today

Amenities and Attractions The city has a public library and a city park.

Each July, the City hosts Market Lak eDay, the community's founders day. The event includes a Lion's Club breakfast; a parade; a vendor's fair with food, entertainment and merchandise; and, in the evening, a street dance, a bon fire and fireworks.

Two miles north of Roberts is the Market Lake Wildlife Management Area operated by the Idaho Department of Fish and Game. This wildlife management area is home to a variety of waterfowl, shorebirds and wild animals. The 10,578-acre Camas National Wildlife Refuge is located 15 miles north near Hamer. To the west of the wildlife refuge is the Idaho Department of Fish and Game's Mud Lake Wildlife Management Area. This wildlife management area comprises 8,853 acres of wetlands, encompassing all of Mud Lake.

Old Roberts High School, now the Mustang Events Center.

A broad array of migratory and native birds and animals thrive among the diverse habitats of the area. Ducks, geese, Trumpeter swans, songbirds, raptors, moose, elk, deer and pronghorn antelope inhabit these wildlife preserves. Both the wildlife refuge and management areas have facilities to accommodate the increasing numbers of people coming to watch the birds and view the big game that come out of the mountains each winter.

Market Lake Day.

The St. Anthony Sand Dunes – dunes that range from 70 to 375 feet high – begin 25 miles northeast of the city.

Economy and Major Employers Six potato-processing and fresh-pack businesses are located within seven miles of Roberts and are the city's largest employers.

Several residents ride buses to the INL site, located 45 miles west of town, or commute to Idaho Falls for employment. (*See Eastern Idaho, Idaho National Laboratories – Eastern Idaho's Largest Employer.*)

Some residents work at downtown businesses, including a grain elevator and stores selling groceries, fuel, auto repair, restaurants and a tavern. Many residents travel to the large retail stores in Idaho Falls to do their shopping.

At the Mustang Events Center.

Education Jefferson County School District provides most of the K-12 education. K-5 students attend Roberts Elementary. The older students ride buses to the school district's middle, junior and high schools located 15 miles west in Rigby.

The closest institutions of higher learning are in Idaho Falls – the Idaho Falls Center for Higher Education and the Eastern Idaho Technical College.

Health Care A general medical clinic is available in Rigby. The closest hospitals are the regional medical center and specialized hospitals in Idaho Falls.

Transportation Federal Interstate 15 has an interchange on the southwest side of the city. State Highway 48 starts in Roberts and connects the city with the communities to the east.

Railroad service is available for freight.

The Rigby-Jefferson County airport – 3,500-foot runway – in Rigby is available for light private and charter aircraft. The closest commercial airport is in Idaho Falls.

Utilities and Services Private companies provide electricity, telephone and satellite services. The City provides water and sewer services. Jefferson County provides police services. The City's fire and EMS departments are staffed by volunteers.

Vision for 2050

In the past five decades, Roberts' population has grown over 60 percent. Most of this growth has occurred in the past two decades when the growth rate has exceeded one percent annually. We expect recent population trends to increase. By 2050 the city's population will more than double.

This population growth will come from an increasing number of families choosing to take advantage of Roberts' affordable housing and peaceful, rural environment close to their employment in Idaho Falls and the expectede xpanding job market at INL.

There will also be an increased population of retired persons. Many retirees will be people who already live in or near the city and choose to stay as they reach their retirement years.

The area's food-processing businesses and farms will continue to be important sources of jobs for city residents. However, technological innovation and consolidation will continue to allow these businesses to improve productivity with fewer employees. A more educated workforce will replace the job loss in agriculture-based businesses.

Mustangs and riders.

As this growth occurs, city leaders will make the required improvements to its infrastructure – paid with existing revenue streams, grants, system-impact and hook-up fees and/or bonds approved by the voters.

Developers of subdivisions down gradient from the city's municipal wastewater systems will construct lift stations to pump the effluent. The City will also widen principal corridor streets.

Mayors

1910 Wm. (Leige) Whitlatch *
1911 Charles L. Neyman *
1912 B.L. Bennett *
1913 Charles Harwood *
1915 George French *
1917 Roy R. Skinner *
** Lewis Ledbina *
1930 John Burwell *
1931 Lee Hand *
1933 Ed Ledvina *
1936 Harold Jackson *
** Loftus Surerus *
1956 Rollo Dutson *
1958 Earl French *
1959 Harold Larson *
1964 J.C. Sorensen *
1966 Harold Larson *
1968 Betty Lang
1972 McKean O. Laird
1977 Albert R. Furrows
1978 Jay Lamb
1982 McLean O. Laird
1984 Loren R. Lounsbury
1994 Sally Lounsbury
1995 Ben Poston
2004 Gary Mitchell
2012 Robert (BJ) Berlin
* Village Chairman
** Dates Unknown

A moose in the backyard of a Leadore resident—within the city limits.

LEMHI COUNTY

- Leadore
- Salmon (*County Seat*)

Leadore

Statistical Data

Population: 102 *
Elevation: 5,980 feet
Precipitation: 9 inches **
Average Snowfall: 19 inches **
County: Lemhi

Temperature Range – Fahrenheit: **
Spring: 17 to 63
Summer: 38 to 83
Fall: 14 to 71
Winter: -2 to 36
* U.S. Census Bureau Estimates July 2015
**Historical averages

Leadore lies in the Lemhi Valley 48 miles southeast of the city of Salmon. The mountain ranges on either side of Leadore are part of the Salmon-Challis National Forest. The Lemhi Mountain Range, with peaks rising to nearly 11,000 feet, begins 10 miles west. The Continental Divide and Beaverhead Mountains of the Bitterroot Mountain Range, with peaks rising to over 8,000 feet, begin a few miles east.

The Lemhi River, which merges with the Salmon River at the city of Salmon, flows on the eastern side of Leadore.

Vast tracts of public lands, interspersed with large fields of hay and grain, surround the city. In the warmer months, ranchers graze thousands of head of cattle on the open range. In the winter, farm production provides winter feed for the livestock.

Pre-Incorporation Years

The land of the Salmon and Lemhi Rivers has long been a place for American Indian encampments, particularly during the salmon runs. The Shoshone Indians were the primary inhabitants with Bannock and Nez Perce frequently living in the valleys during their seasonal encampments and food gathering migrations. (*See The*

Region, American Indians.)

Lewis, Clark and the Corps of Discovery, including Sacajawea and Clark's black slave York, were the first known Euro-Americans to enter what is now Idaho.

They first crossed the Continental Divide in 1805, crossing over the 7,373-foot-high Lemhi Pass on the Idaho/Montana border, 21 miles due north of what is now Leadore. (*See The Region, Lewis and Clark.*)

Donald Mackenzie of the North West Company of Montreal opened a fur trading route through the valleys in 1822. Within 20 years, the fur trappers had largely trapped out the beaver populations and moved on. (*See The Region, Trappers/Explorers.*)

From May 1855 to March 1858 The Church of Jesus Christ of Latter-day Saints (Church) established and operated its Salmon River Mission about 20 miles northwest of what is now Leadore. They called the location "Fort Limhi" after a Book of Mormon figure. (*See The Region, Pioneer Settlements.*)

Leadore train depot.

The name was subsequently misspelled "Lemhi." Future settlers as well as Indians came to use the misspelled word extensively. In addition to Lemhi Pass, Lemhi is the name given to a river, a valley, a mountain range and a county. The area's Shoshone Indians also used the name "Lemhi Shoshone" to differentiate themselves from other Shoshone bands.

Initially, the mission enjoyed success with the missionaries making friends with each of the different tribes of Indians – Bannock, Nez Perce and Shoshone – who came to catch and dry salmon. However, the missionaries were ill-prepared to deal with long-standing mistrust and intertribal conflicts. Even though the missionaries tried to help members of each tribe, leaders of the Bannock Tribe asserted that the missionaries were in league with the Nez Perce. The Bannocks enlisted support from the Shoshone, and about 200 warriors attacked the men herding livestock in the nearby meadows. They killed three of the missionaries and stole 235 head of cattle and 31 horses.

Within a few weeks, the Shoshone tribal leaders came to the fort to express regret and seek peace. They returned 36 head of cattle and said the Bannock had taken the rest. Unwilling to put any more people at risk trying to maintain such a small remote outpost, Church leaders in Salt Lake City, Utah, closed the mission. (*See The Region, American Indians and Early Christian Missionaries.*)

Prospectors, many of whom were southern sympathizers, found placer gold in

July 1866 in the mountains about 20 miles west of Salmon. They called the location Leesburg after Confederate General Robert E. Lee. A gold rush ensued, and, by fall, Salmon had become a tent city.

The population exploded to 2,000. Freighters brought supplies to the miners from Lewiston, Idaho; Montana; and Utah. Supplies from Lewiston came by pack mules and horses over 200 miles of rugged mountain trails. The supplies from Montana came a shorter distance but over very rugged terrain. The freighters coming from Utah traveled the Montana "Gold Road" from Corrine, Utah, until reaching Eagle Rock – now Idaho Falls. Then they turned northwest to Salmon. The Utah supply link was the longest route – 300 miles – but better suited for the giant freight wagons pulled by up to 20 mules. (*See The Region, Mining – The Gold Road – Precursor to Settlement of Eastern Idaho.*)

A view down Main Street.

On the road to Salmon two miles north of what is now Leadore was a stage stop named Junction City – a transportation hub at the crossroads of the Bannock Pass Road north to Montana, the old Emigration Road southeast to Utah and the River Roadway northwest to Salmon. Junction City grew so rapidly that the Territorial Legislature considered making it the county seat when it created Lemhi County in 1869.

Some ranchers feeding cattle with their wagon and work horses.

The Salmon gold rush resulted in prospectors scouring the surrounding mountains in the Salmon area. They not only found more gold but silver-lead ore, tungsten, tin, copper and cobalt as well. (*See The Region, Mining – Salmon Area – Gold, Silver, Cobalt and Other*.)

On April 29, 1910, the Gilmore and Pittsburgh Railroad (G&P) completed a 118-mile railroad line from Armstead, Montana, to Salmon. The railroad crossed the Continental Divide at the 7,681-foot Bannock Pass, 10 miles northeast of Leadore.

When G&P first began surveying for the line, area residents thought it would go through Junction City. However, Mrs. A.M. Stephenson, who owned the land that G&P wanted to purchase for the depot in Junction City, asked too much.

G&P broke off negotiations with Stephenson and in 1908 moved the rail line to the west side of the valley where it built its depot named Leadore after the lead ore mined in the area.

The town of Leadore became the new three-way transportation junction where the main rail line coming down from Montana connected with the northern line going to its terminus at Salmon and the 19-mile southern spur ending at the lead-silver mines and Gilmore, now a ghost town. The railroad loaded ore on its freight cars at both Salmon and Gilmore and shipped it to the smelters in Montana.

Old Leadore garage and post office.

The early growth of Leadore was fueled by Junction City businesses literally putting their buildings on skids and moving them to the new transportation hub.

One of these buildings was Gorham Pool Hall. It arrived in Leadore in 1911 and was converted to the community's schoolhouse. Construction of a new two-story school was completed in 1913. The first graduation took place in May 1918. With most of the population and businesses moving to Leadore, the once thriving town of Junction City withered.

Leadore flourished until the Great Depression of the early 1930s. At its peak, the thriving community had a bank, a newspaper, bars, a barber shop, several mercantile shops, a butcher shop, an implement company, a grange hall and an American Legion Hall.

Incorporation

On May 28, 1947, Leadore became an incorporated village. In compliance with new state law, on September 13, 1967, Leadore became an incorporated city.

Leadore Community Center building.

Turning Points

Railroad By constructing its junction at Leadore, the railroad provided the jobs that underpinned the town's economy and established it as a regional center of commerce. The Leadore Depot burned down in the 1970s.

Agriculture While the railroad established the city, cattle ranching provided a sustaining economic influence. Around 1940 when the mines played out, the railroad had to close leaving cattle ranching as the area's principal commercial industry.

Leadore Today

Amenities and Attractions Leadore has a city park with camping sites and a rodeo arena. The city also has two cemeteries – Yearian and McRea.

A view of Leadore from the McRea Cemetery. Courtesy of Glen Lackey.

Each 4th of July beginning at 7 a.m., the emergency medical technicians serve a breakfast of pancakes, sausages, scrambled eggs, rhubarb syrup, hot cocoa, milk, tea and coffee. Breakfast is followed by a parade at noon and a Rodeo Play Day at 1 p.m. at the rodeo arena.

Each May, the community comes together for the Fireman's Hamburger Feed fundraiser and, in October, the Fireman's Ball.

The city built a replica of the historic Leadore Depot in 2001 on the original depot's foundation and footings. The facility is the city's community center.

The two hearts up by Gun Sight Peak. Courtesy Mev Peterson.

The city's principal attraction is its beautiful wilderness setting. The Lemhi River, which begins at the bridge on Idaho Highway 29 where five creeks or springs join, and the public lands that surround the city provide unlimited opportunities for rafting; kayaking; canoeing; fishing; horseback riding; ATV riding; hiking; backpacking; mountain climbing; mountain biking; camping; and, in the winter, snowmobiling and cross-country skiing.

Nearby attractions include segments of the Nez Perce Trail and the brick dome charcoal kilns managed by the U.S. Forest Service. The charcoal kilns are several miles south of the city. Historically they provided charcoal for the mine smelters across the valley in the unincorporated historic mining community of Nicholia.

The Nez Perce Trail is part of the National Trails System and marks the path of the non-treaty Nez Perce as they fled east from the pursuing U.S. Army in the Nez Perce War of 1877. The Nez Perce came from the north into Leadore on a trail that followed what is now Idaho Highway 29 and then Idaho Highway 28 south before turning east to Dubois and on to Montana. (*See Northern Idaho, The Region, American Indians – Nez Perce War.*)

Economy and Major Employers With about 40 employees, the South Lemhi School District is the city's largest employer. The Leadore Ranger District of the Salmon-Challis National Forest has about 14 employees and is the city's second largest employer. Several ranches and small businesses are also sources of employment. The business district includes two gas stations/convenience stores, one bar/cafe, a post office, two motels, one laundromat, a library and two churches.

Most residents travel to the Lemhi County seat of Salmon to shop and do business.

Education The South Lemhi School District provides primary and secondary education for the city's children and those living on nearby ranches. The district also has a one-room kindergarten through sixth grade elementary school 25 miles north in the unincorporated town of Tendoy.

The closest Idaho institution of higher learning is Brigham Young University-Idaho, 120 miles southeast in Rexburg. The University of Montana-Western in Dillon, Montana, is 73 miles away.

Health Care The closest hospital is Steele Memorial Hospital in Salmon.

Transportation North-south Idaho Highway 28 intersects the city. Idaho Highway 29 northeast to Bannock Pass on the Idaho/Montana border begins in Leadore. The Leadore airport has a 3,500-foot airstrip that provides service for light private and charter aircraft. The Lemhi County Airport near Salmon has a 5,150-foot runway and offers service for larger aircraft. The closest commercial airport is near Idaho Falls or Missoula, Montana.

Utilities and Services Private companies provide electricity, telephone and satellite services. Leadore homes and businesses have individual wells and septic systems. A volunteer fire department and Leadore EMTs provide fire protection and emergency services. The County Sheriff's Office provides police protection under contract with the City.

Vision for 2050

In 1960 Leadore had a population of 141. In 1990 the population had declined to 74. Since 2000 the city's population has stabilized at around 90. Should these recent trends continue, by 2050 Leadore's population will be around 150.

Mayors

* Roland Davidson
* Orian Lindskog
* Jack Weigand
* Gary Dennis
1978 LaVinna Stroud
1980 Steve Stokes
* Gary Anderson
1994 LaVinna Stroud
1998 Terri Proulx
2002 Mike Ries
2010 Courtney Howell
2013 John Warren
* Information Not Available

Aerial photo of Salmon City. Photo courtesy City of Salmon.

Salmon

Statistical Data

Population: 3,033 *
Elevation: 4,000 feet
Precipitation: 9.48 inches **
Average Snowfall: 20 to 27 inches **
County: Lemhi
Website: www.city of salmon.com

Temperature Range – Fahrenheit: **
Spring: 30 to 60
Summer: 60 to 107
Fall: 40 to 75
Winter: 0 to 30
* U.S. Census Bureau Estimates July 2015
**Historical averages

Salmon is an urban oasis in the heart of a vast wilderness in the Salmon-Challis National Forest and near the confluence of the pristine Salmon and Lemhi Rivers. The wild and scenic Salmon River bisects the city just before it makes a gradual 90 degree turn west to cut through the 2.5 million-acre Frank Church-River of No Return Wilderness and 180 miles of Salmon River Canyon that is more than one mile deep.

The city is named after the Salmon River which, in turn, is named after the anadromous red sockeye salmon that historically migrated in massive numbers to spawn in the river and its tributaries. It is called the River of No Return because in the early days, boats bringing in supplies could only make a one-way trip down river and then were dismantled as the boat could not return upriver because the rapids were too fast and treacherous.

The western foot of the Continental Divide and the Idaho/Montana border are 10 miles west. Idaho Falls is 161 miles southeast and Missoula, Montana, 117 miles north.

Pre-Incorporation Years

The Salmon and Lemhi River valleys were historic American Indian seasonal encampments, particularly during the salmon runs. The Shoshone Indians were the primary inhabitants of the region except during the seasonal food-gathering migrations when they were frequently joined by members of the Bannock and Nez Perce Tribes. (*See Eastern Idaho, The Region, American Indians.*)

Lemhi Shoshone teepees, about 2 miles north of Salmon City. Courtesy Lemhi County Historical Museum.

In 1805 Meriwether Lewis, William Clark and their Corps of Discovery – including Sacajawea, her infant child, her husband Charbonneau and Clark's black slave York – were the first known white and black men to enter what is now Idaho.

They entered by crossing the Continental Divide over the 7,373-foot-high Lemhi Pass on the Idaho/Montana border, 30 miles southeast of what is now Salmon. In his book Undaunted Courage, Steven E. Ambrose wrote that the site is still largely pristine and one of the few locations that have not significantly changed since Lewis and Clark first saw it in 1805. (*See Eastern Idaho, The Region, Lewis and Clark.*)

When Lewis and Clark entered Lemhi Valley they hoped to find a tribe of Shoshone Indians to trade for horses and directions to the Columbia River and the Pacific Ocean. When they reached the valley, they had the good fortune of meeting a tribe whose chief, Cameahwait, was Sacajawea's brother.

Statue of Sacajawea at the Sacajawea Cultural, Educational and Interpretive Center. Sculptor: Agnes Vincen "Rusty" Talbot. Courtesy Cheryl Jones.

With the support of the Shoshone, the Corps of Discovery found that the Salmon River was too treacherous to navigate, and the trail over the mountains to the Columbia River was farther north. They immediately turned north and trekked through what is now Salmon and into Montana, re-entering Idaho over 100 miles north over the Bitterroot Mountain's 5,233-foot Lolo Pass. (*See Northern Idaho, The Region, Lewis and Clark.*)

In 1822 Donald McKenzie of the Northwest Company of Montreal opened a fur-trading route through the valleys. Beaver trapping continued for over 20 years before fading out.

From May 1855 to March 1858 The Church of Jesus Christ of Latter-day Saints operated its Salmon River Mission about 20 miles south of what is now Salmon. They called the location "Fort Limhi" after a figure referenced in the Book of Mormon, one of the church's sacred books of scripture.

Two members of the Lemhi Shoshone (or Agai-Dika), circa 1905. On the left, the son of Chief Tendoy. Courtesy Lemhi County Historical Museum.

The name was subsequently misspelled "Lemhi." Future settlers as well as Indians came to use the misspelled word extensively. In addition to Lemhi Pass, Lemhi is the name given to a river, a valley, a mountain range and a county. The area's Shoshone Indians also used the name "Lemhi Shoshone" to differentiate themselves from those in Fort Hall.

The mission started with 27 men. Several families followed. The missionaries constructed cabins, dug a well, built a fort and an irrigation system, planted crops, helped the Indians with food production and preservation and achieved some success in teaching them Christian principles. They also began shipping large quantities of dried salmon to Utah.

The Shoshone and Bannock Tribes were enemies with the Nez Perce. During the winter of 1857 to 1858, the tribes conducted raids and each accused the other of stealing large numbers of horses. The missionaries sought to befriend each of the tribes and promote peace. However, the Bannock tribe and some Shoshone became angry. They felt the missionaries were in league with the Nez Perce.

Lemhi County Miners. Courtesy Rose and Bill Bolton.

About 200 Shoshone and Bannock Indians attacked the outskirts of the fort on February 25, 1858, stealing 235 head of cattle and 31 horses. They killed three of the missionaries and wounded several others. Within a few weeks, the Shoshone came to the fort to express regret and seek peace. They ultimately returned 36 cattle and said the Bannock had taken the rest.

The raid illustrated the vulnerabilities of the small remote outpost. Mission leaders sent word of the attack to Brigham Young. Young sent a contingent of 150 armed men and supplies with instructions to close the mission and bring the missionaries and their families back to Utah. As the missionaries abandoned the mission, they left 1,000 bushels of wheat with the Indians who had accepted their teachings. (*See Eastern Idaho, The Region, American Indians – Early Christian Missionaries.*)

Eight years later during the summer of 1866, prospectors discovered placer gold in the mountains about 20 miles west of Salmon. The prospectors were Southern sympathizers and named their mining community Leesburg after Confederate General Robert E. Lee. Word of the discovery quickly got out and a gold rush ensued. By fall Salmon had become a tent city.

Packers on Main Street in Salmon City, circa 1875. Courtesy Lemhi County Historical Museum.

The November 24, 1866, issue of The Montana Post reported, “A town has been laid off on the opposite (west) side of the Salmon River ... The situation is beautiful, and I am of opinion that ere long it will be a thriving little village.”

During 1866 entrepreneurs built a wooden toll bridge over the Salmon River that allowed foot traffic and pack animals to move between the east and west sections of the community.

The next year, the town’s population had exploded to 2,000. Freighters brought supplies to the miners from Lewiston, Idaho; Montana; and Utah. Supplies from Lewiston came by pack mules and horses over 200 miles of rugged mountain trails. The supplies from Montana came a much shorter distance but over very rugged terrain. The freighters coming from Utah traveled the Montana “Gold Road” from Corrine, Utah, until it reached Eagle Rock, now Idaho Falls, and then turned northwest to Salmon. The 300-mile-long Utah supply link was the longest route but better suited for the heavy freight wagons needed to supply the growing community.

Leesburg, the first mining town in Lemhi County, circa 1890. Courtesy of Lemhi County Historical Society.

The Salmon gold rush resulted in prospectors scouring the surrounding mountains. They not only found more gold, but silver, tungsten, tin, copper and cobalt. These discoveries sustained the Salmon economy for several decades. (*See Eastern Idaho, The Region, Mining – The Gold Road – Precursor to Settlement of Eastern Idaho and Salmon Area – Gold, Silver, Cobalt and Other*.)

The year following discovery of gold at Leesburg, a man named Van Dreff surveyed the Salmon townsite on the east side of the river and built his home on his newly platted Main Street. Many residents living on the west side of the river agreed that Van Dreff's location was more suited for development and moved their homes and businesses to Van Dreff's town site.

Less than two years later on January 9, 1869, the Idaho Territorial Legislature created Lemhi County, the ninth county in Idaho Territory, and designated the unincorporated "Salmon City" as the county seat. Colonel George L. Shoup became chairman of the county commission.

A view of the old bridge in Salmon City, circa 1905, standing on the east side of town. Courtesy Lemhi County Historical Museum.

Shoup built the "Pioneer Mercantile" store on Main Street a year later. This log building housed the general store and bank and was a gathering place for religious groups and the local Masonic chapter. Shoup later became territorial governor. He was serving in that position on July 3, 1890, when Idaho became a state. He became Idaho's first governor and, two years later, successfully ran for the U.S. Senate.

Cattle and sheep ranchers began grazing their herds in the area around 1870. Several years later, agriculture would provide valuable diversification to the local economy.

Cows on Carmen Creek, circa 1915. Courtesy of Rose and Bill Bolton.

However, at that time mining was still king and transporting ore to the processing mills was a major problem. Initially, the miners used freight wagons. Then in 1906 they acquired a steam-traction engine, a heavy tractor-type piece of equipment "that could pull four ore cars" over the wagon roads, but it only made 12 runs before it wore out.

Finally on April 29, 1910, the Gilmore and Pittsburgh Railroad completed its 118-mile line from Armstead,

Montana, to Salmon, crossing the Continental Divide over the 7,681-foot Bannock Pass. At Leadore, Idaho, the line split with one line going 45 miles north to its terminus at Salmon and the other proceeding 19 miles south to the lead-silver mines at Gilmore.

With the railroad carrying the Salmon and Gilmore mine production to the Montana smelters, mine production surged.

Incorporation

On October 10, 1892, Salmon became an incorporated village, 23 years after becoming the county seat. Less than three months earlier, the Idaho Hydraulic Gold Miner editorialized on July 30, 1892, that there was no location " ... for a city more desirable as a business and healthful location than the ground upon which Salmon City now stands. Surrounded with two ... fertile valleys ... mountains loaded with ... precious mineral, two ... swift running rivers ... [and] a climate (in the mountain regions) that cannot be excelled ... "

The city changed its legal status to an incorporated city in 1911. A year earlier, the U.S. Census reported Salmon's population at 1,434.

The open pit operation at Cobalt. The open pit was the final portion of the 1950s operations at the Blackbird Mine, 1957 to 1959. Courtesy Richard Benedict.

Turning Points

Mining Salmon owes its origin to the 1866 discovery of gold at Leesburg. Other discoveries of gold, silver, tungsten, tin, copper and cobalt supported mining operations that economically sustained the community for over 70 years.

Boom and bust mining economy became a way of life in Salmon. As old mines played out, new mines developed. Overlying this was unpredictable metal prices that were sometimes prone to sharp fluctuations due to events taking place nationally or in the world.

The Gilmore and Pittsburgh Train, 1910 to 1939.

In the late 1930s events leading to World War II revived Salmon's ailing economy. The Nazi occupation of North Africa in 1940 blocked U.S access to the African cobalt mines. This posed a serious problem because America needed cobalt to produce hardened steel, alloys and magnets. In order to quickly develop and process Salmon's cobalt ore reserves, the federal government worked with the mine owners to develop the mines and process the ore. At peak production, 1,500 people lived in the mining community of Cobalt 20 miles southwest of Salmon. Others settled in Salmon. Until they closed in 1960, the cobalt mines put the city on a solid economic footing.

Five years later, a copper mine opened south of the city, providing another five years of prosperity before it too closed.

In 1994 Meridian Gold, Inc., reworked the Leesburg mines, eventually employing over 500 before closing in 2000.

Railroad The principal reason the railroad came to Salmon was to serve the mining industry. However, the trains no sooner started arriving in 1910 than the local agriculture, livestock and wood products businesses began using the service.

Still it was mining that kept railroad service to Salmon alive. Two decades later when the mining business began to decline, so also did railroad service. The 1930 U.S. Census reported that only 14 percent of the city's population was involved in mining. In 1939 the predictable occurred, the railroad announced it would close.

The final run into Salmon came in 1940. The train literally backed up to the terminal and, as the engine slowly pulled the rail cars out of town making its way to Gilmore, crews followed, dismantling the track and loading the rails on the train's flatbeds.

Main Street, 1914. Courtesy Lemhi County Historical Museum.

Sawmills Salmon's first wood products businesses principally served the needs of mining. Heavy timbers were needed to shore up mine shafts and lumber to build mine buildings. The miners and the greater community at large also needed lumber for homes, farms and businesses. By 1920 several local sawmills were producing a combined two million board feet annually.

During World War II, annual production approached five million board feet.

Lumber that could be consumed locally was exported. During the 1960s and 1970s the timber industry often had the largest payroll in the county.

Federal Environmental Law and Policies In the early 1970s federal environmental law, wilderness designations and litigation by various environmental groups had the effect of limiting access to federal land for mining and timber. (*See Eastern Idaho, The Region, Mining and Forest Products – the decline of Two of Idaho's Signature Industries.*)

County Seat Establishing Salmon as the Lemhi County seat of government in 1869 added to the city's prestige and provided a small but stable source of employment.

Salmon River Bridge, built 1926. Courtesy Hope Benedict.

Transportation Infrastructure Construction of a steel suspension bridge in 1905 to replace the wooden toll bridge over the Salmon River was a boon to the city. By 1926 better roads, more traffic and the advent of gasoline-powered cars and trucks prompted state transportation officials to build a steel reinforced concrete bridge over the river. That bridge, since upgraded, is now part of U.S. Highway 93.

Fires Fire destroyed major parts of the city in 1897, then again in 1931 and, lastly, in 1962. The community and property owners faced each disaster with resiliency, rebuilding after each fire.

Stage at the side of the Shenon Hotel (also called the Shenon House and the Shenon Block),circa 1900. Phil and Minnie McKinney Shenon built this hotel in 1895. Courtesy Rose and Bill Bolton.

Public Utilities Telephone, electricity, water and sewer systems were generally not available until after 1900. These services often started with groups of people creating a small utility to serve a specific purpose or group of customers. Later, economies of scale persuaded these small operators to sell or to consolidate with larger businesses.

The transmission quality of the small telephone systems formed to provide service between the city and the various mines was not consistent. When the railroad came in 1910, it added better quality telephone service to its right-of-way. In 1916 most of the individual telephone operations consolidated into the Lemhi Telephone

Company.

Electricity was not available in Salmon until around 1890. In 1928 several small hydroelectric companies consolidated with Idaho Power.

In the early 1900s the city developed municipal water and sewer services.

Federal Employees With more than 90 percent of the land in the region under federal control, the increased numbers of federal employees needed to manage the vast tracts of public land has had a stabilizing effect on the city's economy. The U.S. Forest Service and Bureau of Land Management are now the city's largest employers.

Salmon Today

Amenities and Attractions The city's principal amenity and attraction is its beautiful wilderness setting with the Salmon River flowing through town. The public lands that surround the city provide unlimited opportunities for whitewater rafting, kayaking and canoeing, fishing, horseback riding, hiking, backpacking, mountain biking, camping and cross-country skiing. Downhill skiing on groomed trails is also available at Powder Mountain Ski Resort, 45 miles north at Conner, Montana.

The city has four parks that include an ice-skating and hockey rink, swimming pool, tennis courts, a nine-hole golf course and a number of athletic fields for baseball, softball and soccer.

The Salmon Arts Council is the primary sponsor of cultural events including plays and concerts, often with guest artists. Performing arts facilities include the Meriwether Theater and an outdoor amphitheater. The Sacajawea Cultural, Educational and Interpretative Center and the Lemhi County Museum have other historical displays. Art galleries display the talents of local artists.

Sixteen Christian denominations have congregations in the city, including The Church of Jesus Christ of Latter-day Saints, Episcopal, Faith Bible Chapel, Methodist, Roman Catholic, Salmon Valley Baptist, Seventh-day Adventist and Shepherd Valley Lutheran.

Economy and Major Employers The city has a vibrant full-service business district. There are motels; a supermarket; and convenience, automobile, department, gift, antique, hardware and building supply stores.

Haying, circa 1915. Courtesy Rose and Bill Bolton.

With a combined employment of over 200, the U.S. Forest Service and Bureau of Land Management are the city's largest employers. The Salmon School District has well over a hundred employees.

Education The Salmon School District provides most of the elementary and secondary education within the city and surrounding area. The school district has elementary, middle, high and alternative schools. A charter and private school also operate in the city.

The Salmon Innovation Center provides support for new businesses and continuing education programs.

Salmon National Forest Fire Crew, 1937. Courtesy Salmon National Forest.

Higher education degrees are available from several universities using their Internet-based programs. The City library provides computers with Internet access. The closest institution of higher learning is the University of Montana-Missoula, 134 miles north. The closest Idaho institution of higher learning is Brigham Young University-Idaho, 157 miles southeast in Rexburg.

Health Care The 13-bed Steele Memorial Hospital in Salmon provides general medical care. It is staffed by general practitioners and visiting specialists. The city also has a medical clinic, three dental centers, a chiropractic office, a senior citizen center, nursing home and assisted-living facilities.

Transportation Highway 93 intersects the city. It connects to Missoula on the north and Blackfoot to the south. State Highway 28 begins in the city and parallels the Continental Divide for about 75 miles in a southeasterly direction before intersecting with other roads that connect with several Eastern Idaho cities.

Lemhi County Airport near Salmon has a 5,150-foot runway and offers service for light charter and private aircraft. The closest commercial airport is near Missoula.

Utilities and Services Private companies provide electricity, telephone and satellite service. The City provides water and sewer services and fire protection. The Lemhi County Sheriff's Office provides police protection under contract with the City. The County provides solid waste services.

Vision for 2050

Salmon is located in one of the most beautiful and geologically diverse parts of the state and the nation. Living in Salmon offers a distinct back-to-nature quality of life. Innovative technologies are allowing options on how to conduct business and where people live.

Recreation-based industries such as white water rafting, winter sports and anadromous steelhead trout fishing are bringing an increasing number of tourists and outdoor adventurers to Salmon. Over the next four decades, this will increase. Tourism will be a major industry in the city.

By 2050 many Salmon residents will be using technology to do business around the world. Federal land management and public school employees will continue to be the city's largest public employers.

The City's investment in the Innovation Center, created to help fledgling industries get established and create jobs, will be paying off. There will be a growing body of light manufacturing and service businesses in the city.

For the past several decades, Salmon's population has been in the 3,000 range. Job growth from existing and new business activity should cause the city's population to begin growing at a moderate rate of 1 to 2 percent annually. As the city grows, existing revenue sources and growth impact fees will be adequate to pay for needed improvements to the city's infrastructure.

Mayors

1903 William Peterson *
1905 E.K. Abbott *
1905 George H. Monk *
1906 John Kadletz *
1906 Thomas J. Atkins *
1907 William Patterson *
1909 Frank C. Miller *
1911 Emerson Hill
1913 William Peterson
1915 Thomas Atkins
1917 L.E. Glennon
1921 George K. Brown
1923 Charles F. Hanmer, M.D.
1941 Fred L. Viel
1947 Gerald Butler
1957 L.N. Gwartney
1959 Sherman Furey, Jr.
1961 William J. Cannon
1974 Don Vial
1977 William J. Cannon
1982 Bill Miller
1984 Neal James
1986 Jack Nelson
1990 Pat Hauff
1996 Stanley B. Davis
2008 John Miller
2010 Leo Marshall

* Village Chairman (records prior to 1903 destroyed by fire)

Rexburg LDS Temple.

MADISON COUNTY

- Rexburg (*County Seat*)
- Sugar City

Historic Carousel in Porter Park.

Rexburg

Statistical Data

Population: 27,094 *
Elevation: 4,865 feet
Precipitation: 13.77 inches **
Average Snowfall: 66 inches **
County: Madison
Website: www.rexburg.org

Temperature Range – Fahrenheit: **
Spring: 22 to 66
Summer: 45 to 84
Fall: 20 to 74
Winter: 10 to 34
* U.S. Census Bureau Estimates July 2015
** Historical averages

Rexburg lies in the Upper Snake River Plain. A patchwork of irrigated farmland surrounds the city. The South Fork of the Teton River flows on the city's northern edge.

Beautiful and diverse public lands lie in almost every direction. The southwest corner of Yellowstone National Park is about 40 miles due northeast. The St. Anthony Sand Dunes, a Unique Natural Feature, lies 12 miles north. The lower reaches of the Henry's Fork of the Snake River are five miles to the west. The Caribou-Targhee National Forest begins about 15 miles southeast.

Rexburg is home to Brigham Young University-Idaho (BYU-Idaho). Early settlers founded the university's predecessor just five years after they arrived. In the early years, residents of Rexburg nurtured the school. Today, the university's operation and the businesses it influences underpin the city's economy.

Pre-Incorporation Years

When the Lewis and Clark expedition first crossed into Idaho in 1805, tall sagebrush and grass covered the land where Rexburg now stands. American Indians migrated through the area to their seasonal encampments.

Trappers and explorers passed through but generally did not stop. However, one trapper – Richard Leigh, often referred to as "Beaver Dick" – made it his home. In 1876 his Indian wife and children died from smallpox. Their graves are preserved just west of Rexburg.

Beaver Dick and his first family. He had two families with different Indian wives.

The events leading up to the founding of Rexburg started in 1879. John R. Poole of Ogden, Utah, had been working on the Utah and Northern (U&N) rail line from Utah to the Montana gold fields. While hunting on the Snake River Flood Plain 20 miles southwest of Rexburg, he came upon a group of cattle ranchers from Virginia. One rancher, Israel Heal, ran his herd on a large island created by two channels of the river. Interested in homesteading, Poole asked Heal for his opinion. Heal said, "I don't believe God intended that [just] a few men should have all this great country [to themselves] to raise horses and cows in."

When Poole returned to Ogden, he praised the farmland potential of the area. Many families living in northern Utah were recent converts to the Church of Jesus Christ of Latter-day Saints (the Church or Church of Jesus Christ). Many had emigrated from European countries to the United States and traveled west to Utah. Some of the men had also worked for the U&N and had seen the land of the Upper Snake River Plain for themselves, and they needed no convincing. Several groups of families began preparations to travel north to homestead in Eastern Idaho.

Pioneer home in Rexburg, corner of 1st South and Center Street.

In 1882 Church leaders asked 54-year-old Thomas E. Ricks to be an ecclesiastical leader (Bishop) of the immigrant settlers going to what is now the Rexburg area. Ricks, a Kentuckian, had joined the Church in 1844, crossed the Great Plains to Salt Lake City in 1848 and was a proven leader.

In January 1883 Ricks led the first party of settlers to what is now Rexburg. The land, located between two large rivers with a smaller one close by, was ideal. Game was plentiful, the soil fertile, grass for the animals abundant and there was plenty of water for irrigation.

Two months later, Andrew S. Anderson – on assignment by Church leaders – arrived to survey the new town. The settlers first wanted to name their town "Ricksburg" after their leader. Perhaps due to Ricks' modesty, they agreed to name the town Rexburg on the assertion Rex was the German stem word for Ricks.

Steam engine used on Rexburg Bench.

As settlers kept coming, the district under Ricks' ecclesiastical jurisdiction – called the Bannock Ward – soon included several new communities. "Bishop Ricks" assisted people in the new communities in many ways including providing advice, organization and building town sites. Ricks also helped organize the settlers for surveying and building diversion dams and irrigation canals.

By the end of the year, church records listed 815 members living in the Bannock Ward. By the end of 1884 the number had increased to 1,420. As the number of Bannock Ward members grew, church leaders created independent wards and branches in each community. The geographical area of the Bannock Ward became a stake (diocese) with Ricks as stake president.

In describing the land around Rexburg, some of the recorded phrases were "buffalo grass as high as the saddle stirrups on a horse," "five head of horses [needed] to pull a one-bottom plow through the sod," "mosquitoes so thick ... [I could] hardly endure them" and "Mosquito Flats."

Twenty-two horse driven harvester.

Homesteaders found their efficiency improved by pooling their labor. For example, they could build a one-room log home in a day if several men worked together and the logs were available.

On October 24, 1883, William F. Rigby brought in the first sawmill. He had been using the mill on the Montana border for making railroad ties. When the rail line was finished, he dismantled his sawmill, put it on wagons and moved it to Rexburg.

By the end of 1883 Ricks started the Rexburg Cooperative (general) Store and brought consumer goods into the area. Soon a furniture and hardware store, bank and post office opened.

In 1884 Ricks bought a new steam-powered flourmill at the delivered cost of $2,300. Settlers from all around the area came to Rexburg to barter some of their wheat to have the balance made into flour – a practice that lasted for decades.

First mill for grinding wheat.

In 1886 Henry Flamm, the town's first mayor, opened a general store that sold goods on credit. Under Flamm's credit policy, patrons did not pay their bills until they harvested their crops.

Politically, the last two decades of the nineteenth century were troubled times for the Church of Jesus Christ in Rexburg and elsewhere. The religion's rapid growth gave the Church an increasing political power base. Around 1885 most members of the Church in Idaho supported the Democratic Party; however, Republicans controlled the Legislature in Idaho. Many Republican politicos worried that if the Church members voted as a block, it could shift the balance of power in state and local governments.

The Church of Jesus Christ's doctrine endorsed the practice of plural marriage under certain circumstances. Those seeking to limit the Church's influence saw polygamy as the Church's Achilles heel. They successfully used polygamy as a lightning rod to inflame political and public opinion against the Church and its members.

Rexburg winter, 1890s.

In 1882 Congress passed the Edmunds Act declaring polygamy a felony. In 1885 the Idaho Territorial Legislature passed anti-polygamy and Test Oath laws. In 1890 provisions of those laws became part of Idaho's constitution. Under the Test Oath, any man practicing polygamy or professing membership in the Church of

Jesus Christ, even if not practicing polygamy – most members were monogamists – were denied the right to vote, hold office or serve on juries. Idaho's law and constitution also denied voting rights to women, certain ethnic groups and adults under guardianship. All of Idaho's original suffrage restrictions have since been repealed.

Since most Rexburg residents were members of the Church of Jesus Christ, the voting prohibition law shifted political control to a relative few people in the city. In exerting their power, they voted to change the name of Rexburg to "Kaintuck," in honor of Harvey W. "Kentucky" Smith who had defended the Idaho Test Oath before the U.S. Supreme Court.

Early delivery truck.

In 1890 Wilford Woodruff, President of the Church of Jesus Christ of Latter-day Saints, issued the "Manifesto" prohibiting the further practice of plural marriages by Church members (polygamy) upon punishment of excommunication.

On February 1, 1895, the Idaho Legislature repealed the Test Oath and many members of the Church became Republicans. (*See Eastern Idaho, Politics, Polygamy and Civil Rights*.)

The Church taught that men and women should get as much education as possible and use that education for the betterment of themselves, their families and society. Consequently, education was an important aspect of pioneer life in Rexburg.

Ricks College campus, 1960.

Idaho public education was slow in coming to the outlying areas. Rexburg families taught school in private homes until they could build schoolhouses. On November 12, 1888, local Church leaders created the Bannock Stake Academy – equivalent to a high school. Within a few years, all stakes in Idaho established private "academies."

Church authorities established local boards of education to direct these private schools. Some families paid their children's tuition with agricultural products or by hauling and chopping wood needed to heat the schools. As the public school system became established, it was an easy transition to convert the academies into public schools.

In 1903 Bannock Academy was renamed Ricks Academy. Ricks Academy continued to develop higher education courses. It became Ricks College, the predecessor to BYU-Idaho.

Madison County Courthouse.

Lack of trained medical personnel and knowledge of sound sanitation and health practices presented a formidable challenge to the pioneers. In the absence of physicians and nurses, home remedies, coupled with the prayers of loved ones, sustained those who were ill. Many testified of witnessing miracles. However, when epidemics passed through, the effect could be devastating. In 1886 a diphtheria epidemic killed 68 area residents.

In 1893 Hannah Sorenson organized the Rexburg Hygiene and Physiological Reform Society. The work of the society, including giving seminars in obstetrics and hygiene, played an important role in improving the health of the community.

Incorporation

In 1893 the Rexburg business district was flourishing. The town had a blacksmith and harness shops, livery stable, several general and specialty stores and shops, three hotels, an undertaker, an architect, an implement house, a meat market and a saloon.

Rexburg tabernacle.

On July 11, 1893, the Fremont County Commissioners incorporated the Village of Rexburg.

Turning Points

Brigham Young University-Idaho. On June 21, 2000, Gordon B. Hinckley, President of the Church of Jesus Christ of Latter-day Saints, announced that on August 10, 2001, Ricks College would become a four-year university and would have its name changed to Brigham Young University-Idaho. That announcement set in motion a series of events that has forever changed the city's economy and culture. Since the date of that announcement, the city's population has grown over 60 percent.

It is noteworthy that this dramatic growth came without a significant increase in crime. Many citizens attribute the low crime rate to the University's honor code that requires student integrity; morality; graciousness in personal behavior, dress and grooming standards; application of Christian ideals in everyday living; and abstinence from mind-altering or addictive substances.

Circumstances were not always bright for the school. During the Great Depression, financial exigency threatened the school with closure. In 1937 school trustees offered the school to the State. However, the Idaho Legislature failed to pass enabling legislation.

Therefore, local residents embarked on a fundraising campaign to keep the school open. The Church of Jesus Christ also lent financial and administrative support. Later, the Church made the school part of its educational system.

Railroad In 1899 the St. Anthony Railroad Company began a 39-mile rail line from Idaho Falls to St. Anthony with branch lines connecting other cities in between. On November 22, 1899, the rail line reached the depot grounds in Rexburg. The railroad played an important role in facilitating commerce for the city's business and nearby agricultural communities.

New bio-filter tower, exterior.

Agricultural Markets and Products. For nearly a century, Rexburg's economy relied on the labor-intensive requirements of hundreds of family farms and food-processing businesses. In recent decades, there has been a technological transformation in the agriculture and food-processing industries. With regard to farming, large operators either acquired or leased most of the smaller family farms. These larger operations are much more productive and efficient with a fraction of the workers. A similar transformation has happened in the food-processing industry.

Leading up to that transformation were agriculture-based turning points that affected the city's economy. In 1904 the sugar beet factory – constructed a few miles north in Sugar City – created an opportunity for farmers to plant a new profitable cash crop. In 1941 when World War II started, the military needed massive quantities of dried and processed potatoes. Farmers changed from growing sugar beets to potatoes. Agriculture's overall gross receipts did not suffer, but in

1942 the sugar beet factory closed.

Municipal Services. Around 1907 the city established its first municipal water system, a 50-foot surface well blasted through lava rock. Around 1913 the city graveled its streets and laid ten miles of paved sidewalks. Several years later, the city paved its streets. In 1919 the city constructed its first municipal sewer system.

County Seat. The Legislature created Madison County on February 18, 1913, with Rexburg as the county seat. This action not only brought a relatively small but stable employment base to the city, it significantly advanced the city's prestige and political influence.

Impact of Entrepreneurial Businesses. In the late 1900s two entrepreneurial businesses gave the city national recognition as well as providing a large number of jobs – Diet Center, a U.S. and Canadian weight-loss franchisor, and Artco, a national wholesale printer and direct seller of wedding accessories and photo cards.

Out-of-state businesses have since acquired these companies. However, Artco operations have remained in Rexburg.

Teton Dam Failure. On June 5, 1976, the newly constructed Teton Dam, located in a mountain gorge above the city, failed with the result of sending an 80-billion-gallon tidal wave down the valley. It flooded approximately two-thirds of the city, destroying or seriously damaging most affected structures.

Ricks College, on the bench overlooking the lower part of the city, escaped damage. The college used its facilities to house and care for flood refugees.

The U.S. Bureau of Reclamation constructed the dam, accepted responsibility for the dam's failure and paid damages. The subsequent clean up and rebuilding had a major positive effect on the city's economy. (*See Eastern Idaho, Teton Dam.*)

Porter Park path.

Rexburg Today

Amenities and Attractions The city has seven city parks. Included in these parks is Porter Park, the city's largest. This 85-acre park is located in downtown Rexburg. The park offersseveral picnic and children's playground areas as well as ball fields, a jogging path and a historic carousel. Another park, Nature Park, is located on the North Fork of the Teton River. It has a jogging path, picnic and playground facilities and fishing ponds. Smith Park, on the east side of the city, has a gazebo, picnic and playground areas, ball fields and an antique steam engine. BYU-Idaho Gardens is a park used by landscape and horticulture students and offers a diversity of landscaping ideas.

Several privately financed or theme parks include Clair Boyle Skate Board Park, Evergreen Kiwanis Park, Eagle Park, Rotary Park and Louisiana Pacific Park (under development). Yellowstone Bear World, a drive-through wildlife park, is located five miles south.

The city has three golf courses open to the public. Rexburg's 18-hole Teton Lakes Golf Course has received wide-spread recognition for its beauty and design. A similar course is under construction near Teton Lakes. The city's oldest course, located by the airport, has nine holes.

Each summer, many retirees – "Sunbirds" – leave their winter homes in the Sunbelt states for Rexburg's dry and cooler climate. To welcome these summer visitors, the university offers public symposiums and cultural, historical, academic, drama, dance, and music events and programs. Many tourists make Rexburg their base camp for day trips to see the famous resorts of West Yellowstone, Jackson Hole and Sun Valley.

The city sponsors or supports several events including the Idaho International Dance and Music Festival; the Teton Dam Marathon; the RUSH triathlon; the Madison County Fair; the Storytelling Festival; and, in the winter, the Snow Fest and Street Lighting Festival.

The Upper Valley Orchestra performs weekly concerts during the summer evenings. The Cantabile Singers, Carousel Chorus and high school orchestra have frequent performances.

Recently the City purchased a historic movie theater for use in promoting the performing arts.

Historic and religious landmarks with manicured grounds and flower gardens include the Tabernacle Civic Center, housing a 1,000-seat auditorium and the Teton Flood Museum; the BYU-Idaho campus; the Aviation Museum; and the Church of Jesus Christ of Latter-day Saints Temple grounds.

Main Street at night.

The Temple, dedicated in February 2008, is one of four Church Temples in Idaho. Its imposing size near the BYU-Idaho campus makes it a prominent landmark. Prior to the temple's dedication, it opened for public viewing. Different from other church buildings that are open to the public, worthy Church members use temples to perform sacred ordinances. Temples close on Sundays.

Economy and Major Employers With over 1,100 employees, BYU-Idaho is the city's largest employer. The change to a four-year university in 2001 caused a boom in construction, both on and off campus. On campus, the University has, and is adding, many new school buildings and expanding or upgrading others. Off campus, new apartment buildings and residential subdivisions proliferate. Retail and other businesses have and are expanding their facilities.

The second largest employers, Artco Printing and Madison School District, have about 500 employees each. In addition, the city has several public and private entities with fewer than 500 employees. The city's downtown business district – with several financial, hospitality, retail and service businesses – provides a significant number of jobs.

Education The Madison School District provides most of the city's elementary and secondary education. The district operates three elementary schools in Rexburg and four in the county. It also operates a middle school, a junior high school, a high school and an alternative high school. In addition, several private schools offer a variety of choices from elementary through high school.

BYU-Idaho serves over 13,000 students on a campus that exceeds 400 acres. About 20 percent of the University students are married, some with children and/or working spouses. About 40 percent come from Idaho, the balance come from other states and nations.

Health Care The 50-bed Madison Memorial Hospital and many physicians and clinics located in the city provide most of the area's health care needs.

Transportation U.S. Highway 20 and State Highway 33 intersect the city. Interstate 15 is about 10 miles west on Highway 33. The 4,200-foot Rexburg-Madison County Airport serves light charter and private aircraft. Commercial airline service is available at Fanning Field, 31 miles southwest in Idaho Falls.

Typical of many cities founded by Church of Jesus Christ pioneers, Rexburg has ten-acre blocks divided into four sub-lots each. Streets run on a north-south, east-west grid with Main Street eight rods – 132 feet – wide and side streets six rods – 99 feet – wide. It is as though streets were designed for today's traffic needs.

Utilities and Services Private companies provide electricity, telephone, natural gas and satellite services. The City provides water, sewer and drainage services as well as fire and police protection.

Vision for 2050

Primarily due to the establishment of BYU-Idaho, the city's population has grown at unprecedented rates. However, the effects of change in the school's status from a two-year college to a university are now showing moderation.

While over the past several years the city's population has grown at an average rate of ten percent annually, over the next four decades, we believe that annual average rate will decline to less than three percent. However, by 2050 the city's population could still more than double.

City services have now largely adjusted to the recent population surge. The maintenance and improvements needed for existing systems should not require significant change for several years. We anticipate that growth-related revenues will pay the cost of any needed expansion of municipal systems and services required by growth.

Mayors

1893-1902 Unknown *
1903 Henry Flamm
1904 Eli McIntire
1905 John L. Jacobs
1906 H. Dewsnup
1907 James W. Webster
1909 Thomas E. Ricks
1911 Robert G. Archibald
1915 Fred S. Parkinson
1917 Nathan Ricks
1919 John L. Ballif, Jr.
1921 Robert G. Archibald
1923 Richard H. Smith
1923 L.Y. Rigby
1927 Peter Mickelsen
1929 Arthur Porter
1935 Harlo B. Rigby
1937 D. William Stowell
1943 Joseph B. Demott
1949 Joseph M. Parkinson
1951 Wayne N. Smart
1953 J. Fred Smith
1958 Alex E. Archibald
1959 Gilbert Larsen
1966 A.H. "Whitey" Brock
1970 Henry Shirley
1974 John C. Porter
1990 Nile L. Boyle
1993 Bruce Sutherland
2004 Shawn Larsen
2010 Richard Woodland
2016 Jerry Merrill

* Village Chairman

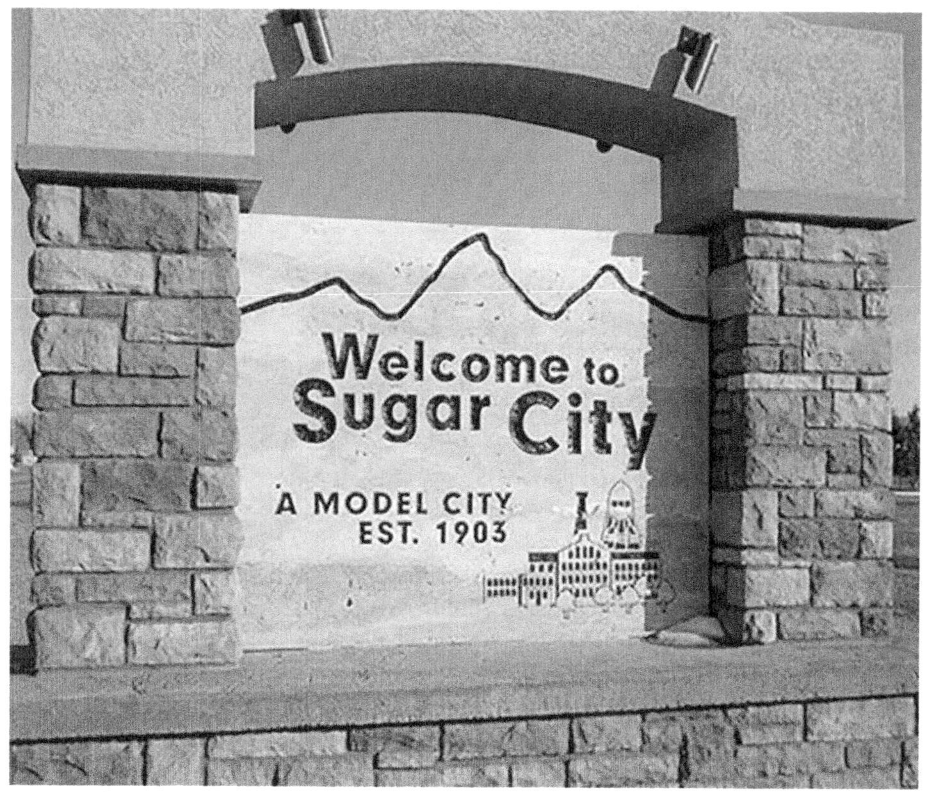

Sugar City

Statistical Data

Population: 1,367 *
Elevation: 4,892 feet
Precipitation: 14 inches **
Average Snowfall: 60 inches **
County: Madison
Website: www.sugarcityidaho.gov

Temperature Range – Fahrenheit: **
Spring: 20 to 70
Summer: 30 to 90
Fall: 15 to 80
Winter: 10 to 30

* U.S. Census Bureau Estimates July 2015
** Historical averages

Sugar City lies on the Upper Snake River Plain. Fertile farmland of potatoes, wheat, barley, corn and alfalfa hay surrounds the city. Within 10 miles north and west, are vast tracts of brush and lava covered public land managed by the BLM. The Caribou-Targhee National Forest begins about 10 miles southeast. Rexburg is three miles southwest.

In June 1976 the city experienced near total destruction by flood, yet three years later emerged stronger and more beautiful than before. (*See Eastern Idaho, Teton*

Dam Collapse and Flood.)

Irrigation and the conversion of the arable sagebrush-covered Upper Snake River Plain into an agricultural oasis came long before the founding of Sugar City.

Pre-Incorporation Years

The first non-Native Americans that passed through the Upper Snake River Plain were a party of trappers/explorers led by Andrew Henry. They came around 1811 and built a winter camp six miles north of what is now Sugar City next to a now famous trout fishery, the Henry's Fork of the Snake River.

Historic Sugar City home.

For the next few decades, trappers continued to come into the area in search of beaver pelts. In 1841 the first overland migration of settlers headed to the Oregon Coast passed about 70 miles south – the Oregon Trail. In 1863 prospectors discovered gold in what is now western Montana. A major supply route to the mines – known as the "Gold Road" – passed about 25 miles west of what is now Sugar City.

In 1879 the Utah and Northern Railroad completed a rail line from Utah, through the Upper Snake River Plain, to the Montana gold fields. Many of the railroad construction workers were from northern Utah. With the railroad line completed, the construction workers returned home. One of these workers, John R. Poole of Ogden, was outspoken in his praise of the farmland potential of the Upper Snake River Plain with its soils that produced tall sagebrush and had many rivers and streams. Other returning workers confirmed Poole's assessment.

Downtown Sugar City.

At that time, Utah was experiencing a heavy influx of immigrant converts to the Church of Jesus Christ of Latter-day Saints (Church of Jesus Christ or Church). These families were looking for promising locations to settle. The reports of the returning railroad construction crews persuaded hundreds of Utah's families to load their wagons and travel over a hundred miles north to settle in Eastern Idaho's Upper Snake River Plain.

In 1882 leaders of the Church asked 54-year-old Thomas E. Ricks to be the

Bishop of the immigrant settlers headed for what is now the Rexburg area. Ricks – a Kentuckian who joined the Church in 1844 and crossed the Great Plains to Salt Lake City in 1848 – was a proven leader.

The district that was under Ricks' ecclesiastical jurisdiction would soon include thousands of settlers and several new communities collectively called the Bannock Ward, later to become a stake (diocese) that oversaw several wards with Ricks as president.

By the time of Sugar City's founding twenty years later, settlers of the Upper Snake River Plain had turned their homesteads into productive irrigated farms with gravity-flow water diverted from the area's rivers and streams through complex systems of canals and ditches – farmland highly suited for growing sugar beets.

Around 1890 the St. Anthony Railroad Company constructed a branch line from Idaho Falls to St. Anthony.

In August 1903 a venture between principals in several Utah sugar factories and American Sugar Refining Company of New York purchased the land on which Sugar Citynow stands. In 1907 the venture became the Utah-Idaho Sugar Company or U&I Sugar. These principals formed the "Sugar City Townsite Company."

The townsite company platted the town of Sugar City and sold building lots. They positioned the sugar factory, completed in 1904, on the northeast corner of town. The railroad built a train depot and sidings to accommodate the sugar factory's needs.

The townsite company platted the town site with a ten-acre park in the center. Streets were graded and lined with boardwalks and shade trees. They stipulated that all homes were to be 30 feet from a sidewalk and to be "respectable." The townsite charter disallowed sale of intoxicating liquors, gambling and prostitution.

Harold Harris Building.

One of the first public buildings constructed was a two-story building named the "Townsite Building." On the lower floor were a department store, drug store, telephone exchange and post office. On the upper floor were an elaborately decorated opera house and dance hall and offices for the local newspaper, the Sugar City Times, and the chamber of commerce.

When used as an opera house, the facility had seating capacity for 800. When used for dancing the highly polished maple floor could accommodate 200 couples. They held dances each Friday night. The facility became one of the most popular dancehalls in the region. The Opera Company provided most of the performing arts entertainment in the city.

The downtown business district soon had a mercantile; furniture, hardware and lumber stores; a meat market; a bank; a pharmacy; two barbershops; and a flourmill that operated 24 hours a day.

In 1904 entrepreneurs formed a city baseball team and built a 500-seat grandstand. They also built a one-half-mile-long horse-racing track.

In 1904 patrons built the first school in Sugar City. Within five years, the city had three schools.

Incorporation

On January 8, 1906, Sugar City became an incorporated village. By 1910 the village had a population of 391.

Turning Points

Early Settlement. The large influx of emigrants from Utah into the Upper Snake River Plain in the late 1800s created the agricultural framework the sugar factory needed.

Sugar Factory. Sugar City was a town founded solely on the production of sugar. In the early 1900s it was the largest sugar factory in Idaho. The plant operated until 1942. During its 38 years of operation, it processed 2.1 million tons of sugar beets, yielding over 8.1 million 100-pound bags of sugar – 405,000 tons.

Heritage Park.

The sugar factory was a boon to the local economy. Sugar beets not only provided a profitable cash crop for farmers, they produced work for youth – thinning, weeding and topping beets – a food source for livestock – beet pulp, molasses and beet tops – and seasonal (winter) work at the factory for about 200 area residents.

The sugar factory brought regional recognition to the city. Management gave local residents prizes for the best-kept yards, gardens and homes.

During the Great Depression, Sugar City suffered. The bank closed – many people lost their life savings. However, the sugar factory kept producing.

By 1941 conditions changed. The World War II military had begun purchasing large quantities of dried potatoes, a staple in the G.I. diet. Area farmers began rotating their crops from sugar beets to the higher-value potatoes.

At the same time, U&I Sugar found it could improve profitability by consolidating its processing plants into larger more efficient operations. When U&I Sugar closed and dismantled its Sugar City factory, it transported the local sugar beet harvest to its Idaho Falls factory.

Closure of the factory had a devastating effect on the Sugar City community. Many retail stores closed. Residents, who could not find work within commuting distance from their homes, moved. In 1929 the town's population reached about 1,200. Following the plant closure, the population fell 50 percent.

Teton Dam. On June 5, 1976, the newly constructed Teton Dam, located on the Teton River northwest of Sugar City, broke and buried the city in a sea of raging dirty water. The flood left behind a scene of mud and destruction. In parts of the city, a person could stand on one side of town and see the other side because the flood leveled most of the structures in between. School buildings and the Church of Jesus Christ facilities escaped structural damage.

During the next two months, residents and volunteers, some traveling from communities hundreds of miles away, removed the mud and debris. They cleaned the schools and church for occupancy. By September, school was back in session.

A few people began to rebuild that fall; others waited until later. By 1980 scores of new homes stood on beautiful landscaped yards where just three years before there was stinking mud, broken houses and piles of debris. (*See Eastern Idaho, Teton Dam Collapse and Flood.*)

Sugar City Today

Amenities and Attractions Sugar City has three municipal parks. Each park encourages an active lifestyle. Park facilities include a double tennis court, two lighted baseball fields and a hill where children climb.

Another park has an interchangeable baseball/softball field, a sand pile, a children's playground and a sheltered picnic area with covered barbecue pits. The downtown area is quiet and inviting with numerous trees and benches bordering Main Street.

Heritage Park is the location of annual community activities including the children's Easter Egg Hunt, the Arber Day observance and the Pioneer Day Breakfast. Other annual community events are homecoming at Sugar-Salem High School and the Christmas tree lighting.

One of the city's most prominent attractions is its proximity to Rexburg and Brigham Young University-Idaho (BYU-Idaho). The university sponsors many public concerts, plays and recitals as well as opening many of its athletic facilities to the public. The university's influence underpins the economy and enhances the cultural and social wellbeing of Sugar City. The university employs many of the city's residents.

Sugar City residents are able to enjoy the benefits of a peaceful small-town atmosphere, yet live next door to the regional shopping and medical center of Rexburg and the cultural and educational opportunities offered at the university.

Yellowstone National Park lies about 40 miles due east. However, following U.S. Highway 20, the entrance to the park at West Yellowstone, Montana, is 80 miles north.

The Targhee National Forest begins about 13 miles southeast of Sugar City.

The St. Anthony Sand Dunes is a 175-square-mile area where the wind has created sand dunes that range from 75 to 365 feet high. The sand dunes lie 10 miles northwest of Sugar City and are popular for motor-sport and family recreation. A few miles north of the sand dunes are the Civil Defense caves, large underground caverns that are actually lava tubes formed by prehistoric volcanic activity.

Sugar City's close proximity to vast acreages of public land make it convenient for outdoor enthusiasts to camp; hunt; fish; ski; and ride mountain bikes, ATVs and snowmobiles.

Economy and Major Employers NorSun of Idaho, Inc., a potato processor with over 250 employees, is the city's largest private employer. With 200 employees, Sugar-Salem School District is the city's largest public employer. Two smaller food-processing companies also have operations in the city. The city's retail businesses consist of a convenience, grocery and hardware store; post office; potato warehouses and other businesses. Most residents travel to Rexburg or other nearby communities to do their shopping.

Education The Sugar-Salem School District provides most of the city's elementary and secondary education. The district operates an elementary school, grades PK to 3; intermediate school, grades 4-6; junior high school, grades 7-8; high school, grades 9-12; and an alternative high school.

The closest institute of higher learning is Brigham Young University-Idaho in Rexburg.

Health Care Most residents travel to Madison Memorial Hospital in Rexburg for their health care needs.

Transportation U.S. Highway 20 and Idaho Highway 33 intersect the city. Interstate 15 is about 30 miles west. The closest airport service for light private and charter aircraft is Rexburg-Madison County Airport in Rexburg. Idaho Falls Regional Airport provides services for large commercial aircraft.

Railroad service is available for freight.

Utilities and Services Private companies provide electricity, telephone, satellite, cable and natural gas. The City provides water, sewer, trash removal and street maintenance services. The City of Rexburg provides wastewater treatment under contract with Sugar City. The Madison County Fire Protection District has a fire station in the city and provides fire protection. The Madison County Sheriff's Office provides police protection.

Vision for 2050

In 1960 the city's population was 584. In 1980 four years after the flood, the population increased to 1,022. Since that time, the Sugar City population has increased an average of 1.8 percent per year.

These growth trends will likely continue. By 2050 the city's population should more than double. In anticipation of this growth, the City has established design and review standards and annexed 350 acres of development property. The City will soon open a 27-lot business park north of Center Street between Highway 20 and the railroad. In addition, the City has approved a private 50-acre business and retail development west of Highway 20.

The wastewater treatment services agreement with Rexburg provides sufficient capacity to meet the city's growth needs for many years. Expansion of other municipal services, parks and infrastructure will be paid by existing revenue sources, growth impact fees or bonds approved by the voters.

Throughout the city's history, town residents have dealt with major catastrophe. Whether loss of the town's principal employer or leveled by flood, the city has emerged stronger than before. These tragedies have built character in the people. Whatever the future holds, Sugar City residents will continue to support strong family values, quality education and a strong work ethic.

Mayors

1906 Thomas Austin *
1907 Alfred Ricks *
1919 J.W. Phillips *
1923 Alfred Ricks, Sr. *
1927 J. Morgan Smith *
1929 Charles O. Hamilton *
1931 Leffel A. Bean *
1947 J. Kenneth Thatcher *
1952 John Wilding *
1957 Emery Thomas *
1961 LaMar Barrus *
1968 Glenn W. Dalling
1972 Lawrence Grover
1976 Lyle H. Moon
1988 Rondo Barrus
1992 Albert W. Burton
1996 Roy P. Hill
2000 Lawrence E. Nielsen
2004 Glenn W. Dalling
2016 David Ogden
* Village Chairman

Evans Co-op Block, 2005, downtown Malad.

ONEIDA COUNTY

- Malad (*County Seat*)

Malad City Industrial Park.

Malad

Statistical Data

Population: 2,017 *
Elevation: 4,520 feet
Precipitation: 14 inches **
Average Snowfall: 32 inches **
County: Oneida
Website: www.maladidaho.org

Temperature Range – Fahrenheit: **
Spring: 22 to 68
Summer: 42 to 88
Fall: 20 to 77
Winter: 10 to 38
* U.S. Census Bureau Estimates July 2015
**Historical averages

Malad is located in a high-desert valley 13 miles north of the Idaho/Utah border. The Caribou National Forest and Bannock Mountain Range wrap around the north and east sides of the city. The 9,095-foot-high, 10-mile-distant Elkhorn Peak outlines the northern sky. The Malad River flows about two miles west of the city.

The Pleasantview Hills and the Samaria Mountains frame the valley on the west and southwest. Seventeen miles west, just over the Pleasantview Hills, is the 47,000-acre Curlew National Grassland.

Malad is the county seat of Oneida County and the retail and medical service center for the area. Approximately 50 percent of the county's population resides in the city.

Pre-Incorporation Years

For centuries, nomadic American Indians, primarily of the Shoshone and Bannock tribes, exclusively migrated through what is now the Malad Valley.

Beginning in 1811 trappers/explorers began working the Snake and other rivers in what are now Western and Eastern Idaho. From 1816 to 1832 Donald McKenzie, a trapper/explorer working for the North West Company, organized annual "Snake Country" fur trapping and trading expeditions.

During one of these expeditions, some of McKenzie's French-Canadians who were trapping beaver along what is now the Malad River came down with a sickness they attributed to drinking river water. These French-speaking trappers gave the river a name they thought suitable for causing their malady, the "Riviere aux Malades," or the Malad River. This phenomenon also occurred in 1819. French-Canadians trapping beaver on the four-mile-long river that flows through what is now Malad Gorge-Thousand Springs State Park located a few miles north of Hagerman also named that river "Malades" or Malad for the same reason.

Main Street prior to 1942.

Trappers/explorers Alexander Ross, in 1824, and John Work, in 1830, experienced the same illness. However, Work did a better job of identifying the cause of the sickness. He determined the problem was eating the tail of beaver whose diet included poisonous water hemlock, which grew along the riverbanks, for which the beaver had developed immunity.

In 1843 Captain John C. Fremont started his official mapping exploration that aided in establishing the main Oregon Trail. That year Fremont's 39-member detachment passed through the Malad Valley.

The Malad Valley was also a corridor for other migrations. Immigrants going to California branched off the Oregon Trail and passed through the upper valley.

In 1855 Brigham Young, head of the Church of Jesus Christ of Latter-day Saints (Church), asked an advance group of 27 men to travel north from Utah to start the Salmon River Mission – Fort Lemhi, near what is now Salmon. The Malad Valley was the corridor used by the men and their families and other settlers who followed. They used the route again in 1858 when a rescue party of 150 armed men and the entire colony abandoned the mission and returned to Utah Territory.

In the early 1860s with the discovery of gold in Montana and the Boise Basin, the stagecoach and freight wagon route – called the "Gold Road" and used to transport goods and passengers from Utah to the gold fields – passed through the Malad Valley.

In 1863 A.W. Vanderwood opened a mail station at Mt. Springs on the east side of the Malad River. In 1864 Henry Peck and his family built a cabin next to Deep Creek, at the location of what is now Malad. About a dozen settlers followed Peck in filing homestead claims, building shelters and clearing their land.

In 1865 several Church converts from Wales settled in the valley. Several other Welsh emigrant families soon joined the Welsh colony. To accommodate the diversity of language, the settlers wrote minutes of early town meetings in both English and Welsh.

Settlers of other faiths soon followed, and Malad began to be a more religiously diverse community but with shared Christian values.

In 1864 the Idaho Territorial Legislature created Oneida County – named after Lake Oneida in New York – with Soda Springs as the county seat. Soda Springs was the site of a military post built to suppress Indian raids along the Oregon Trail. In 1866 Colonel P.E. Connor, the fort's commandant, signed a peace treaty with the Shoshone Indians and abandoned the fort.

Evans Coop Block, 1905.

By 1866 Malad, influenced by its strategic location on the Gold Road, had become the largest and fastest growing town in Oneida County. In that year, the Idaho Legislature approved moving the county seat from Soda Springs to Malad.

Incorporation

In 1866 concurrent with becoming the county seat of Oneida County, Malad became an incorporated village. Several decades later, even though the village population grew sufficiently to qualify becoming a city, village leaders were slow to act.

An edition of the local 1940 newspaper, The Idaho Enterprise, reported "Malad Village is the only town in the state with a population over 1,000 that does not have a city form of government."

On March 13, 1941, the county commissioners approved changing the legal status of Malad to an incorporated city. In the first city election of officers, two political groups – the Taxpayers and Citizens parties – emerged and coalesced into two competing platforms and slates of candidates.

The Taxpayers Party platform favored keeping taxpayer interests at the forefront, avoiding unnecessary taxation, supporting business, draining and oiling the streets, constructing sidewalks and gutters, letting the volunteer fire department personnel choose their own officers and cooperating with other government agencies and the Chamber of Commerce. Their slogan was "Pay as we go."

On the other hand, the Citizens Party platform favored the addition of parks and recreational facilities, development of civic pride, improving sewage facilities and sanitary conditions, establishment of a community incinerator to reduce fire hazards, enlarging and irrigating the cemetery plants and grass and developing policies (ordinances) supporting home ownership. Their slogan was "Every family a homeowner." The Citizens Ticket won with 707 of the 1,111 votes cast.

Turning Points

Railroad In 1906 the Oregon Short Line Railroad completed its branch line from Ogden to Malad. The railroad was a big economic boost to the city. It provided direct transport of large quantities of locally produced agricultural commodities to major markets. Rail freight service continues to be important to the city's economy. In 2005 the railroad built a rail spur to the Malad Industrial Park.

Roads and Motor Vehicles With the advent of improved motor vehicles, the need for better roads became increasingly important to Malad's economy. However, good roads were slow in coming.

In 1918 Clarence Garrett – president of the then emerging regional trucking company, Garrett Freightlines – was transporting four tons of furniture between Pocatello and Salt Lake City. Garrett said that his truck "got stuck" on a hill near Malad on a road that was nothing more than a trail. He said he traded gas for help getting his rig out of the mud.

However, the roads gradually improved, over the next several years federal and state highway departments paved the federal highway between Pocatello and Salt Lake City. The highway ran through Malad, providing an important source of business for local merchants.

In 1952 federal and state highway authorities relocated the highway about a mile to the east of the city. The corridor they used would later become Interstate 15. While a boon to the motoring public, completion of the highway and, later, I-15 had an immediate adverse effect on Malad's downtown retail economy. Traffic that used to stop now bypassed the city.

Flooded creek bed in 1980.

However, city and community leaders are finding opportunities to use the freeway exits to Malad at Idaho Highways 36 and 38 to promote economic activity. Retail businesses that provide food and services for I-15 travelers are developing facilities near the intersection of Highway 38. The city is also promoting area attractions for freeway travelers to visit.

Industrial Park Around 1974 city leaders were successful in getting regulatory approval and a federal grant to build an industrial park. The park has resulted in increased job opportunities and a more diversified employment base.

Today, the industrial park is full and adding a new phase. While highly controversial when it was first proposed, the park now has broad public approval.

City Improvements In 1980 the City constructed a 27-mile spiral-weld steel pipe mainline for a pressurized underground residential and agricultural irrigation system. The magazine Better Roads reported, " ... the $4 million Deep Creek Irrigation Line is the nation's largest and possibly [the] most efficient Rural

Conservation and Development Project."

In 1995 the city installed new sidewalks, street gutters, planters and lighting in the downtown business district.

Malad Today

Amenities and Attractions Malad has four parks. City Park offers picnic areas, children's playgrounds, athletic fields and is the location of most community events.

A bronze memorial of a WWI soldier standing before a brick wall is located in a small city park. Engraved on the wall are the names of the service men and women from Oneida County who lost their lives defending their country.

Veterans' Memorial-a bronze statue of a WWI soldier stolidly guards a solid brick wall that houses the names of the servicemen and women from Oneida County.

The City supports or sponsors several traditional events. The Easter Egg Hunt in the park, the Classic Car show of restored and hot-rod automobiles and the Malad High School Rodeo take place in the spring.

Each summer around June 30, the community sponsors the "Welsh Heritage Festival" at City Park. The festival keeps alive the Welsh heritage of those who immigrated to the Malad area in the late 1800s. The event includes cultural games; crafts; food booths; and the "eisteddfod" celebration of traditional Welsh music, language and dancing. Over 2,000 people attend this annual event.

Malad celebrates Independence Day with an early morning Cannonade that reminds people that the "Early Bird Breakfast in the Park" is starting. There is a colorful parade down Main Street followed by traditional old-time events including "The Wild West Shoot Out," live productions put on by the Malad Valley Theater Guild, ball games, foot races, food booths, music, dancing, an afternoon auction, bed races – contestants race beds through town for prizes – and a fireworks display.

Other summer events include the Oneida County Fair, the demolition derby and a truck-pulling contest.

In the fall and winter, there are the Halloween Costume Contest, the Parade of Homes – best-decorated homes for Christmas – and the Fireman's Ball.

Throughout the year, the Iron Door Playhouse presents several live productions of musicals, cowboy poetry, plays and melodramas. The name of the playhouse stems from a legend that in the 1800s a band of robbers hid, yet undiscovered, gold coins beneath an old iron door somewhere in the Samaria Mountains.

The city has several historic buildings, one of which houses the Oneida County Pioneer Museum. Another is Evans Co-op – Idaho's oldest department store, opened in 1865.

The surrounding mountains, streams and seven small reservoirs stocked with trout provide opportunities for a variety of outdoor sports. Fly-fishing on float tubes on the reservoirs or nearby streams is popular. The mournful calls made by the many coyote in the area are common. In the winter, the reservoirs are favorites for ice fishing. Deer and elk hunting are also popular sports.

Several hundred thousand acres of nearby public lands have extensive trails for hiking, biking, equestrian and ATV riding in the warmer months and, in the winter, cross-country skiing and snowmobiling.

Malad's First Set of City Officials. One cannot discuss commitment and loyalty without honoring H. Ward Thomas, who is the third from the right. This loyal city stalwart served as the Malad City Treasurer for 58 years, under all eleven mayors. A special recognition was given to Mr. Thomas upon his retirement in 1998. Malad lost a dedicated civil servant when Mr. Thomas passed away on May 6, 1999.

During the spring and early summer, a strange phenomenon takes place in the Samaria Mountains – thundering noises echo through the mountains. Geologists speculate that as the winter snows melt, moisture seeps into geothermal heated crevices and caves and creates the rumblings heard throughout the valley.

Economy and Major Employers Thousands of acres of dry and irrigated farmland and ranches surrounded the city. However, the small farms that once underpinned the city's economy have changed. Technological innovation and economies of scale have fostered consolidation of smaller farms into larger operations that produce more with much less labor.

Today, the city's largest public employers are the Oneida County School District with 150 employees, the Oneida County Hospital with 100 employees and Oneida County with 42 employees.

The largest private employer is Hess Pumice, industrial abrasives, with 85 employees. The balance of the city's employers is made up of several small manufacturing, financial, retail and service businesses. Many businesses, including Hess Pumice, are located in the railroad accessable Malad City Industrial Park.

Education The Malad County School District provides substantially all of the elementary and secondary education.

The closest institution of higher learning is Idaho State University in Pocatello, 57 miles north. Utah State University is 60 miles southeast in Logan.

Health Care The 11-bed Oneida County Hospital, a long-term care facility and a few medical clinics provide most of the community's health care needs.

Transportation The city's eastern boundary borders Interstate 15. State

Highway 38 connects the city with several small Oneida County communities to the west. State Highway 36 begins two miles north of the city and connects with the cities in Franklin County.

The 4,950-foot runway at Malad City Airport serves light private and charter aircraft. The closest commercial airport is Pocatello Regional Airport, 54 miles north.

Rail freight service is available in the city.

Utilities and Services Private companies provide electricity, telephone and satellite services. The City provides water and sewer services and fire protection. The County Sheriff's Office provides police protection under a contract with the City. The County provides solid waste services.

Idlewild at the Welsh Heritage Festival, 2005.

Vision for 2050

Over the past five decades, Malad's population has plateaued at around 2,000. Looking to the future, the city will grow moderately as more businesses come to the expanded Malad City Industrial Park and the I-15 exits. By 2050 the city's population will exceed 3,000.

Within the next decade, Malad will have a new county jail, hospital and nursing home facility. Malad Elementary School students will attend a totally renovated or new facility. The water and sewer systems will meet certification standards and have the capacity to meet the needs imposed by projected population and industrial growth. The City and other sponsors of the Malad Welsh Heritage Festival will have developed it into a regional event that will draw several thousand people annually. The expanded festival will be extremely beneficial to the economy and to the community.

The civic pride exhibited in the city's first election in 1940 has continued. In the face of natural disasters and world conflict that challenge the city's wellbeing, city residents will continue to take the steps needed to improve their infrastructure and protect their way of life.

Mayors

1866-1941 Unknown *
1941 Dr. O.H. Maybe
1945 Guy Benson
1947 Edward G. Williams
1950 R. LeRoy Thomas
1955 Claude Kent
1961 John V. Evans
1967 Glen B. Williams
1976 J. Marvin Hess
1980 Seth Thomas
1984 Terrill E. Schwartz
1996 E. Spence Horsley
2015 Joan Hawkins
* Village Chairman

Field of mown hay near Rockland.

POWER COUNTY

- American Falls (*County Seat*)
- Rockland

American Falls today.

American Falls

Statistical Data

Population: 4,314 *
Elevation: 4,415 feet
Precipitation: 10 inches **
Average Snowfall:30 inches **
County: Power
Website: www.cityofamericanfalls.com

Temperature Range – Fahrenheit: **
Spring: 29 to 69
Summer: 49 to 86
Fall: 27 to 75
Winter: 18 to 39
* U.S. Census Bureau Estimates July 2015
** Historical averages

American Falls is located on a gentle stretch of foothill land that commands a magnificent view of the beautiful American Falls Dam and Reservoir and the meandering Snake River below the dam. On the opposite side of the city is Interstate 86.

The Fort Hall Indian Reservation begins about five miles east of the city. The city of Pocatello lies 23 miles northeast.

Pre-Incorporation Years

Until about 14,500 years ago, prehistoric Lake Bonneville covered much of what is now Idaho south of Downey as well as northwestern Utah and eastern Nevada. Around that time, the lake breached its natural dam at Red Rock Pass, a few miles south of Downey. The upper 350 feet of the ancient lake flooded north until it reached the Snake River where it turned west and north, flooding what is now American Falls and, later, cutting huge canyons as it flowed on to the Pacific Ocean. The Great Salt Lake is a remnant of that ancient fresh-water lake.

The flood ripped giant boulders from mountainsides, smoothing them as they rolled and tumbled in the raging waters, depositing them wherever the force of the flood subsided. Massacre Rocks State Park, nine miles west of American Falls, is the site where many of these huge boulders stand as reminders of the ancient Lake Bonneville flood.

In October 1811 Wilson Price Hunt began the first expedition of Euro-Americans through what is now American Falls. Funded by John Jacob Astor, founder of a fur-trading empire, they set out by canoe on the upper Snake River to find a water route to the mouth of the Columbia River and Fort Astoria on the Pacific coast. They likely camped at the head of the falls (American Falls) for the night before portaging the next day. At that time, the falls were a series of rapids that dropped 50 feet over a stretch of white water 800 feet wide and 200 feet long.

American Falls old town looking southeast from grain elevator.

Unfortunately, on October 28 the company met disaster several miles downriver at Caldron Linn a treacherous stretch of the river near what is now Burley. There, one man was lost along with supplies and a canoe. After scouting ahead and finding even more difficult rapids and waterfalls, they abandoned river travel and set out on foot for their coastal destination.

Eighteen years later, all but one member of a small band of trappers employed by the American Fur Company lost their lives when their boat broke up in the falls. The falls were given the name "American Falls" in honor of those trappers.

American Falls old town.

Fur trapper and entrepreneur Nathaniel Wyeth established a trading post near the confluence of the Portneuf and Snake Rivers 11 miles north of what is now Pocatello in July 1834. He named the post Fort Hall after his principal investor, Henry Hall, and flew the American flag over the fort. For many years, most of the travelers headed west stopped at Fort Hall and passed by what is now American Falls.

On August 3, 1836, a party including Presbyterian missionaries Dr. Marcus and Narcissa Whitman – who started an ill-fated, turned deadly, mission among the

Cayuse Indians in eastern Oregon – and Henry and Eliza Spalding – who started a successful mission with the Nez Perce in Northern Idaho – arrived at Fort Hall. Narcissa and Eliza were the first white women to cross the Rocky Mountains. They left the fort on August 4th, and, on the following day, Narcissa recorded that the party "passed the American Falls in the Snake River ... the roar of the water is heard at a considerable distance." She noted that the Snake River Valley was "very grateful to the eye."

Wyeth sold the fort to the British Hudson's Bay Company in 1837. At that time, Hudson's dominated the fur trade in Idaho. The Union Jack flew over Fort Hall until the Treaty of 1846 between the U.S. and England, which fixed the dividing line between Canada and the U.S. at the 49th parallel.

The first overland migration of pioneers to Oregon's Willamette Valley crossed Idaho in 1841. Two years later, Captain John C. Fremont's 39-man mapping expedition followed about the same route as the first migration. Several months later, Congress published Fremont's journal and maps, which became widely used by travelers on the Oregon Trail. Fort Hall and Fort Boise were landmarks on those maps, and for many years the trading posts were welcome rest stops for the travelers.

American Falls before the dam.

The Oregon Trail was used by people headed West until 1869 when the transcontinental railroad was completed at Promontory Point in Utah Territory. Tens of thousands of people passed through Fort Hall and often recorded the beauty and roar of the American Falls.

Of all the Oregon Trail immigrants passing by American Falls, only the wagon trains that passed through on August 9, 1862, are commemorated at Massacre Rocks State Park.

Kosanke & Co and Thornhill, American Falls.

Two of the wagon trains, Adams and Smart, were attacked by Indians northeast of the rocks, and several people were killed. Men from these and other wagon trains pursued the attackers with the result of additional immigrants killed. The number of Indian deaths is not known. The grave sites of some of those killed lie at the southern end of the

Rocks.The site became a state park in 1967.

Register Rock, next to Rock Creek a few miles southwest of Massacre Rocks State Park, was a noted landmark and campsite for Oregon Trail immigrants. Hundreds of immigrants wrote their names, dates and messages on the huge boulder with whatever medium they had – pencil, paint, wagon grease or chisel.

During the 1870s settlement around American Falls consisted primarily of cattle and sheep ranching. A few homesteaders were staking claims and diverting water from nearby streams to irrigate their farms.

Leader Hardware Company.

In addition to farming, a limited amount of gold prospecting was taking place along the sandbars of the Snake River. One of the more successful area prospectors was John Calder. He discovered flour or fine gold in the 1870s downriver from American Falls at a place he called Bonanza Bar.

In 1881 the Oregon Short Line Railroad began building a 542-mile line connecting the main Union Pacific Railroad at Granger, Wyoming, to the Oregon Railway and Navigation Company line at Huntington, Oregon – a critical link creating another transcontinental railroad.

When the railroad reached American Falls in early 1882, it stopped to build a 790-foot-long bridge across the river – a formidable task that included building three 180-foot-long heavy wooden trusses and a 250-foot-long steel span. The wooden trusses were replaced with steel in 1894.

The railroad set up a camp and established a post office on the west side of the Snake River. The camp included around 3,000 people and thousands of draft and other animals. Gambling, drinking, fighting, brothels, robbery and other vices were prevalent. The contractors hired guards to protect the payroll.

Moving of American Falls, circa 1925. J.O. Cotant is driving the steam engine, which is a 1910 Rummley 36 horsepower with a double cylinder. Courtesy John Cotant.

The story goes that two camp contractors, Carlyle and Corrigan served notice on Tex and Johnson, the leaders of the camp's principal criminal element, demanding that they leave the country. When they declined to do so, the contractors had Tex and Johnson arrested and hung them from the American Falls Bridge. They buried the bodies on a nearby hill and ordered the saloons to close, prohibiting them from reopening within two miles of camp.

Not long after the first train crossed the bridge on June 10, 1882, the company closed the camp and moved on, building the rail line to the next stop at Shoshone. Before they left American Falls, they built a water tank for the steam locomotives and a train depot that would become the core of the town and a boon to the emerging agricultural economy.

Around 1887 the town of American Falls included a hotel with a restaurant attached; a livery stable; a saloon; two stores, one made of stone and the other of logs with a sod roof; a ferry; a railroad depot; and several frame and log sod-roof homes.

Rising water from dam taking over old American Falls town site. Notice the old grain elevator sticking up out of the water in about the center of the picture.

A few years previously, a gang of cattle rustlers led by Bob Paxton and Charles Reddington operated a cattle ranch a mile west of American Falls, actually a front for their far-reaching cattle rustling operation. In the Old West, vigilante law was common and cattle rustling a capital crime.

To deal with the cattle rustlers, the ranchers in the region banded together to form a cattleman's association. However, their early efforts were frustrated. Finally, the association sent a detective, Bradley Jackson, to American Falls to deal with Paxton. He arrived by train in August 1886. When Paxton came to town a few days later, his spies told him about Jackson.

Snake River below American Falls Dam.

Paxton didn't waste any time and boldly confronted Jackson who admitted he worked for the association. In a strange turn of events, the two adversaries were inseparable for several days, drinking and eating together, carefully watching each other in a deadly standoff. The townspeople feared that if Paxton killed Jackson, the rustlers would kill them too – ostensibly to eliminate witnesses.

On September 13, 1886, the two men met at the hotel for dinner. An old miner with bushy eyebrows was also at the table. Seeking to show off his prowess with a gun, Paxton said the miner's eyebrows were too long and he was going to trim them. He went for his gun, but Jackson stood up with his gun in hand. He said to Paxton who was looking down, "Look up, Paxton, your time has come, you have lived long enough." As Paxton looked up, Jackson shot him in the forehead. Upon hearing their leader had been killed, Paxton's gang fled the country.

Jackson surrendered to the townspeople who took him into custody but allowed him to keep his gun for protection. Jackson was exonerated of any wrong doing and, later, married a local girl.

In 1894 the U.S. Congress passed the Carey Act that ceded up to 1 million acres of arid federal land to any Western state that instituted programs to build irrigation systems and convert the land into private irrigated farms.

Idaho's first Carey Act project was proposed in 1895 by the American Falls Canal and Power Company, leading to the construction of the Aberdeen-Springfield Canal which was to irrigate 80,000 acres west of the Moreland-Thomas district. The main canal is 86 miles long and has 100 miles of lateral canals.

In 1905 the three competing power plants operating at American Falls on the east, center and west side of the river were consolidated into the Southern Idaho Water Power Company which was one of the electric utilities that combined to form Idaho Power Company in 1916.

In 1902 Congress passed the Newlands Act which created the predecessor to the Bureau of Reclamation (Reclamation) and promoted irrigation and land reclamation projects throughout the West. One of Reclamation's first projects was a complex system of dams, canals and pumping systems on the Snake River called the Minidoka Project. When complete, the Minidoka Project included the American Falls Dam and Reservoir, built in 1927.

Incorporation

The original town of American Falls became an incorporated village on July 11, 1906. The town was situated on the prehistoric lakebed lowlands that in two decades would be covered by the backwaters of American Falls Dam, a reservoir that is one of the largest bodies of water in Idaho.

On American Falls reservoir.

At the time of incorporation, the town consisted principally of the original townsite which included the train depot and two developments – one built in the late 1880s along with the fair grounds, ball field and grandstands and another subdivision built in 1906 whose foundations, roads and sidewalks can still be seen when the reservoir is low.

By 1911 the population had grown to 950 with a thriving business district that included several stores, shops, hotels, banks, restaurants, a garage, churches, a newspaper and a jail.

Turning Points

Railroad The railroad was the basis for establishing the city and post office. For several decades the railroad continued as a major contributor to the area's economy, connecting the city and its agricultural economy with distant markets. Many area farmers sold their wheat and barley to the elevator companies located near the train depot which, in turn, shipped the commodities to the commercial centers of Portland, Omaha and beyond.

County Seat On January 30, 1913, the Legislature divided counties, including Blaine, to create Power County with American Falls as the county seat. Power County voters approved making it a dry county. As a result, West's Bottle and Jug, a store that was established under the alcohol ordinances of Blaine County became part of Power County and had to close.

Origin of Skaggs Grocery and Drug Stores Sometime prior to 1910, Samuel and Nancy Skaggs moved from Missouri to American Falls. In April 1915 this ordained Baptist minister opened a grocery store on the principles of buying in large quantities and selling for less – cash-only. From that first grocery store in American Falls, certain of Samuel and Nancy's six sons and posterity created and grew several grocery and drug chains that through sale, merger or partnerships with other chains forever engrained the Skaggs name with the nation's retail grocery and drug industry. Businesses in which Skaggs family members or businesses played prominent roles include Safeway, Pay Less Drug Stores, American Stores, Albertsons and Osco Drug.

American Falls Dam Two dams have been built at American Falls. The first dam and reservoir caused the entire town to move to higher ground, and the second dam replaced the first dam, which was failing.

The first American Falls Dam, completed April 20, 1927, is one of an integrated series of dams and reservoirs on the Snake River from Jackson Lake in Wyoming to Lake Walcott near Rupert. It was built by the Bureau of Reclamation as part of its huge Minidoka Project. American Falls is the project's largest reservoir.

The most difficult part of building the 94-foot-high and 5,277-foot-long composite concrete and earthen dam was not its construction and financing, which was provided by the federal government, but resolving the problems that the 23-mile-long reservoir would have on people and businesses. The reservoir would flood 56,000 acres including the original city, farms and Indian reservation lands as well as railroad track and power plants. Water rights issues also had to be resolved and just compensation for losses determined.

The new city was platted on higher ground and had a park in the center of town; commerce lots would be on one side of the square faced by government buildings on the other. Churches were to be situated on the other two sides of the park, and homes were platted out from there.

The alignment of the streets was not without controversy. The platted streets did not follow the normal north-south, east-west axis but were laid out diagonally, parallel to the reservoir shore. Residents complained, "How will we ever teach our children which direction is north or south?" The city planners responded that the city was laid out so that the sun could shine in every window.

All told, 344 residences; 46 businesses; three hotels; one school; six churches; one hospital; six grain elevators; one flour mill; and numerous sheds, chicken coops and garages were moved onto the higher ground of the newly platted city. Family members often rode in their homes while in transit.

Those moving St. John's Lutheran Church were not able to complete their work by Sunday. Undeterred, the faithful attended services in the church while it was jacked-up on wheels – an event that made national news. The last building moved was the Oregon Short Line Railroad Depot, which was placed in its new location on July 13, 1926.

The Oneida Milling and Elevator Company's grain elevator was the only structure that was not moved. Its 40-foot-deep foundation and 106-foot reinforced concrete walls still stand with its top rising above the water – a silent reminder of the remarkable history of American Falls.

Two years after completion of the dam, cracks began to appear in the concrete. Core drillings made in 1960 revealed that some of the concrete was in an advanced state of deterioration because of chemical reactions between the alkali and aggregate in the cement. As a safety measure, the water storage capacity was reduced, and in 1973 Congress authorized the funds to replace the dam.

However, two years before the new dam was built, the Teton Dam failed releasing a flood of water into the Snake River. The fear that the old American Falls Dam would not hold proved unwarranted. The concrete portion of the old dam was replaced immediately downstream of the old structure in 1978.

American Falls Today

Amenities and Attractions American Falls has five city parks comprising 160 acres – City Park, Lee Street Park, Trenner Park, Vard Meadows Park and Stebbins Park – and a 9-hole golf course.

The city's largest festival is American Falls Days, which takes place each August and includes a parade, a carnival, a talent show, a rodeo and a full day of games and booths at City Park.

Over 200 birds inhabit the reservoir and the surrounding marshlands and hills. Though almost any time of the year is a good time for bird watching, the American Falls Shorebird Festival, held each August, is a special time for visiting birdwatchers.

The Snake River and the reservoir offer many opportunities for boating, fishing and ice fishing.

The 990-acre Massacre Rocks State Park, named after the deadly 1862 conflict between Shoshone Indian warriors and Oregon Trail immigrants, is nine miles southwest of town. Oregon Trail wagon ruts are visible from highway rest areas at either end of the park.

Today, visitors call the state park beautiful, serene, restful and rich in history. The park has a museum and offers camping, hiking and fishing on the Snake River. Birdwatchers have found the park to be a prime site for observing a variety of birds throughout the year, particularly during the spring migration. The park contains about 300 species of plants – the most common of which are sagebrush, Utah juniper and rabbit brush.

Register Rock is just west of the Massacre Rock Visitor Center. Many Oregon Trail immigrants inscribed their names and dates of passage on the large rock. A scenic picnic area surrounds Register Rock.

The 3,300-acre Sterling Wildlife Management Area, located north of the city on the shores of American Falls Reservoir, provides excellent habitat for upland game and waterfowl.

About 15 miles west is the lower portion of the 750,000-acre Craters of the Moon National Monument and Preserve that includes the Great Rift National Natural Landmark.

The Sawtooth National Forest lies 25 miles south, the Fort Hall Indian Reservation begins just east of town and the Caribou-Targhee National Forest is 20 miles south of the reservation.

The American Falls Archaeological District is located in the Snake River Canyon downstream from American Falls. Some artifacts found at the digs date back 14,000 years. This archaeological district is on the National Register of Historical Places.

Economy and Major Employers Agriculture underpins the city's economy. Lamb Weston, Inc., a potato processor with nearly 480 employees, is the city's largest private employer. With 170 employees, Double L Manufacturing, a manufacturer of farm equipment, is the second largest private employer. American Falls School District has about 200 employees and is the city's largest public employer.

American Falls has a vibrant commercial center with many residents employed in the city's retail, health care, financial, government and other service businesses or activities. The local newspaper, the Power County Press, is published weekly.

Education American Falls School District provides most of the city's elementary and secondary education. The city has two elementary schools, a middle school and a new high school. The school district constructed the high school auditorium to accommodate performing arts productions. The community holds a variety of musical and theatrical events in the auditorium facility throughout the year.

The nearest institution of higher learning is Idaho State University in Pocatello.

Health Care The 10-bed Harms Memorial Hospital, three medical clinics and the Power County Nursing Home handle most of the city's health care needs.

Transportation Federal Interstate 84 borders the city on the south and east. Idaho Highway 39 intersects the city. Idaho Highway 37 proceeds south connecting the city with Rockland, the Curlew National Grassland and Oneida County.

American Falls Airport has a 4,900-foot runway. The closest airport with commercial carrier service is Pocatello Regional Airport.

Railroad service is available for freight.

Utilities and Services Private utilities provide electricity, natural gas, phone, cable and satellite services. The City provides water and sewer services as well as police and fire protection.

Vision for 2050

American Falls skate park.

The population of American Falls has more than doubled over the past 50 years since 1960 when it was 2,123. Over the past decade, the U.S. Census disclosed a population increase of 346 for an average annual increase of 0.8 percent.

Should recent historical trends continue, by 2050 the city's population will exceed 6,000. Existing municipal systems will be adequate to accommodate this moderate rate of growth with routine improvements and upgrades.

City leaders are committed to achieving the city's mission of continuing to provide a friendly, diverse and positive atmosphere for the citizens of American Falls – fostering community pride in our charming and safe hometown community – a wonderful place to live and raise a family.

Mayors

1906 John L. McKnow *
1909 W.T. Oliver *
1911 D.W. Davis *
1913 H.A. Lang *
1915 H.C. Wones *
1917 Wm. J. Hanson
1921 C.G. Spriggs
1922 Chas Johnson
1923 W.M. Davie
1927 T.C. Sparks
1933 R.W. Peterson
1935 Vard W. Meadows
1945 Dr. Newton H. Farrell
1950 H.C. Allen
1951 W.C. Loofbourrow
1953 A.J. Watts
1953 R. Phillip Peterson
1956 A.J. Watts
1961 Roland Kramer
1964 G. Howard Evans
1965 Ralph "Moon" Wheeler
1973 Emil Grischowsky
1974 Merton W. Ferguson
1978 Howard Selcho

1982 Ken Morgan
1986 Merton W. Ferguson
1990 Wayne Egan
1994 Dan Neu
1998 Deborah K. Rudeen
2002 Cecil Weisenburger
2006 Amy W. Wynn
2013 Marc Beitia
* Village Chairman

Rockland

Statistical Data

Population: 288 *
Elevation: 4,560 feet
Precipitation: 10 inches **
Average Snowfall: 30 inches **
County: Power

Temperature Range – Fahrenheit: **
Spring: 26 to 70
Summer: 47 to 90
Fall: 23 to 79
Winter: 14 to 42
* U.S. Census Bureau Estimates July 2015
** Historical averages

The city of Rockland lies in the Rockland Valley 13 miles south of American Falls and 35 miles southwest of Pocatello. Rock Creek, the town's namesake, flows through the city. The city is near the center of the valley with numerous farms with irrigated fields of wheat, barley and alfalfa hay extending to the north and south.

On the east is the Deep Creek Mountain Range, a mostly treeless range that runs south of American Falls to the unincorporated town of Holbrook in Oneida County. The second tallest mountain in this range, Bannock Peak, is located 10 miles east of Rockland and rises to 8,263 feet.

On the west of the valley, the up to 7,492-foot-high Sublett Mountains – named after William L. Sublett, a prominent trapper and fur trader who in the 1830s worked the streams of Southern Idaho – extends from the Snake River south about 50 miles to the unincorporated hamlet of Stone just north of the Idaho/Utah border.

Pre-Incorporation Years

Nomadic American Indians – principally of the Shoshone and Bannock Tribes – inhabited the area of what is now American Falls and Rockland long before the first explorers/trappers began traveling into what is now Eastern Idaho.

In 1810 Captain Andrew Henry led the first party of explorers/trappers into Eastern Idaho. They built a log stockade and shelter a few miles north of what is now Rexburg on the Henry's Fork of the Snake River. They named their post Fort Henry and spent the winter trapping beaver. In the spring, they moved on and never returned.

In October 1811 Wilson Price Hunt led a party of explorers who stayed at the deserted Fort Henry for two weeks while they built canoes with which they, unwisely, hoped to navigate the Snake River to the Columbia River and the Pacific Ocean. When they reached what is now American Falls, they portaged around the falls, which at that time was a series of rapids that dropped 50 feet over an 800-foot-wide and 200-foot-long stretch of the river. When they reached the treacherous rapids near what is now Twin Falls, they lost a man and supplies. They determined the river route impossible, abandoned their remaining canoes, stashed most of their supplies and completed their harrowing journey on foot.

In 1934 Nathaniel J. Wyeth, a fur-trading merchant, constructed a trading post, which he named Fort Hall, on the Snake River about 11 miles north of what is now Pocatello.

In 1843 Captain John C. Fremont, a topographical engineer, led a surveying expedition that mapped much of the West. He stopped at Fort Hall for supplies and traveled near what is now American Falls.

Alvin Morgan placenear Rockland, circa 1929.

Oregon Trail immigrants used Fremont's maps, published by Congress, in establishing the Oregon Trail and certain cutoffs from the main trail. (*See Eastern Idaho, Oregon and California Trails.*)

The main Oregon Trail passed about 12 miles north of Rockland on the south side of the Snake River. What is now Massacre Rocks State Park (MRSP) was part of the trail. MRSP is the location of a large clustering of giant boulders deposited 14,500 years ago when the natural Lake Bonneville dam at Red Rock Pass, a few miles south of Downey, breached. The massive flood that followed ripped giant boulders from mountainsides, smoothing them as they rolled in the raging waters and depositing them wherever the force of the flood subsided. One of these rock deposit locations was at MRSP. (*See Eastern Idaho, Major Geologic Features –*

Prehistoric Lake Bonneville.)

In August 1862 Indians hid in the MSRP boulders and ambushed a small wagon train. When it was over, 10 pioneers and an unknown number of Indians were dead.

Following the first arrivals in the Salt Lake Valley in 1847, the population of Utah continued to swell with a stream of immigrant converts to the Church of Jesus Christ of Latter-day Saints. As they came, they spread throughout the Great Basin establishing hundreds of settlements.

In 1860 Franklin became the first permanent settlement in what is now Idaho. At that time, the settlers thought they were in Utah Territory. (*See Eastern Idaho, Idaho/Utah Boundary Resolution.*)

Within five years, Church pioneers would found a half dozen more settlements north of Franklin, as well as numerous settlements across the eastern mountains in the north Bear Lake region and to the northwest into the Malad River Valley. The largest migration of settlers from Utah Territory into Eastern Idaho came in the early 1880s with the settlement of the Upper Snake River Plain. (*See Eastern Idaho, Pioneer Settlements.*)

In 1876 pioneers coming up from Utah Territory founded the town of Rockland. Three years later, Utah pioneers settled Oakley, 50 miles southwest of Rockland.

July 4, 1916.

During the 1870s many pioneers, not from Utah Territory, began settling near what is now American Falls. Ranchers moved onto the land, grazing their cattle and sheep on the meadows, plains and hillsides. Homesteaders soon followed, staking their farming claims along the Snake River and its tributaries where they could most easily divert water to irrigate their farms.

In 1879 the U.S. Army suppressed the last resistance from Native Americans in Idaho. In a series of skirmishes termed the Bannock War, the remaining Shoshone and Bannock Indians were compelled to accept living on the Fort Hall Indian Reservation. (*See Eastern Idaho, American Indians – The Bannock War.*)

In 1881 the Oregon Short Line Railroad began building a railroad line between Granger, Wyoming, and Huntington, Oregon. The railroad passed through Pocatello, American Falls, Mountain Home and Caldwell before reaching its destination at Huntington. When completed in 1884 the rail line provided access to the commercial centers of Omaha, Nebraska, and Portland, Oregon.

In 1882 when the railroad reached American Falls, railroad officials built a depot. The railroad was a major boost to the local agricultural economy, including that of the farmers and ranchers around Rockland.

Incorporation

On June 14, 1909, Rockland became an incorporated village.

Turning Points

Utah Migration Thousands of Church converts streaming into Utah were looking for arable land in the West, suitable for irrigation, where they could build communities and raise their families. When informed about the settlement potential of what is now Rockland, a colony of pioneers came up from Utah and settled.

Railroad The arrival of the railroad in American Falls in 1882 greatly improved Rockland's agricultural economy and the quality of life for its citizens. Farmers and ranchers had a ready market for their wheat, barley and livestock. Mail delivery time improved dramatically and movement of goods and traveling long distances became practical.

Rockland Today

Amenities and Attractions One of the city's major attractions is its near proximity to the American Falls Dam and Reservoir on the Snake River. The 103-foot-high and 5,277-foot-long dam creates a reservoir that covers 65,000 acres. Over 200 birds inhabit the reservoir and the surrounding marshlands and hills. Whistling swans, bald eagles, geese, ducks, pelicans and blue herons are common.

City of Rockland.

The river and the reservoir offer many opportunities for boating, fishing and ice fishing. Boat docks on the reservoir are available at Sportsman's Park near Aberdeen on the north side of the reservoir. There is a public boat dock on the west shore as well as Seagull Bay Yacht Club, a private facility. In addition, the Oregon Trail Sportsman Access is located on the lower side of the falls at the end of Falls Avenue. The Willow Bay Marina complex is located on the reservoir. It is open year round and has a 128-acre recreation area with RV hookups, cafe and store.

The 990-acre Massacre Rocks State Park is an excellent place to connect with history where Oregon Trail immigrants kept watch for Indian ambush as they wove their wagons and livestock through the many tall boulders they called "Gate of Death" and "Devil's Gate." Oregon Trail wagon ruts are visible from the highway rest areas at either end of the park.

Today, visitors call the park beautiful, serene, restful and rich in history. Between Memorial Day and Labor Day, the park staff offers outdoor campfire programs. Spectacular sunsets often greet those attending the evening campfires.

The park has a museum and offers camping, hiking and fishing on the Snake River. Birdwatchers have found the park to be a prime site for observing birds, particularly during the spring migration. The park contains about 300 species of plants – including sagebrush, Utah juniper and rabbit brush.

Register Rock is just west of the Massacre Rock Visitors Center. Many Oregon Trail immigrants inscribed their names and dates of passage on the large rock. A scenic picnic area surrounds Register Rock. Today, horse owners riding the equestrian trails can water and rest their animals in the Register Rock corral.

The 3,300-acre Sterling Wildlife Management Area (WMA) is located just east of Aberdeen on the shores of American Falls Reservoir. The WMA provides excellent habitat for upland game and waterfowl.

About 15 miles west is the lower portion of the 750,000-acre Craters of the Moon National Monument and Preserve, which includes the Great Rift National Natural Landmark. Lava flows interspersed with pockets of land that have remained undisturbed for centuries cover the preserve. The most recent lava flows pushed up through the great rift about 15,000 years ago.

The Sawtooth National Forest is popular for hikers, bikers, campers, hunters and ATV riders.

The American Falls Archaeological District is located in the Snake River Canyon downstream from American Falls. Some artifacts found at the digs date back 14,000 years. This archaeological district is on the National Register of Historical Places.

The University of Idaho's 440-acre Aberdeen Research and Extension Center lies 25 miles north of the city. Research at the Center has resulted in countless discoveries and innovations including new and improved varieties of cereal grains, potatoes and other crops; control of plant diseases and pests; use of fertilizers; and identifying best farming practices for both irrigated and dry farms. Each year the Center receives visitors from throughout the world.

Economy and Major Employers The Rockland School District is the city's largest employer. The city's business district consists of a convenience store. Most of the city's residents shop in American Falls.

Education The Rockland School District has around 140 students in grades K-12. All of the classrooms are located in one attractive public school building.

The closest institution of higher learning is Idaho State University in Pocatello.

Health Care The closest hospital is Harms Memorial Hospital in American Falls.

Transportation Idaho Highway 37 north to American Falls and south to Holbrook and Stone intersects the city. Interstate 86 is accessible in American Falls.

American Falls Airport has a 4,900-foot runway. The closest airport with commercial carrier service is Pocatello Regional Airport.

Utilities and Services Private companies provide electricity, telephone and satellite services. The City provides water and sewer services as well as police and fire protection.

Vision for 2050

In 1960 Rockland had a population of 258. The U.S. Census reported the city's 2000 population at 316 where it has held steady. Historical trends will hold.

By 2050 Rockland's population will likely not exceed 400. Residents will continue to enjoy their quiet, peaceful valley setting several miles away from the closest urban area.

Balloon Fest, Driggs.

TETON COUNTY

- Driggs (*County Seat*)
- Tetonia
- Victor

Driggs City Hall.

Driggs

Statistical Data

Population: 1,662 *
Elevation: 6,183 feet
Precipitation: 16 inches **
Average Snowfall: 63 inches **
County: Teton
Website: www.driggs.govoffice.com

Temperature Range – Fahrenheit: **
Spring: 25 to 52
Summer: 44 to 77
Fall: 27 to 57
Winter: 8 to 32
* U.S. Census Bureau Estimates July 2015
** Historical averages

Driggs lies in the Teton Valley three miles west of the Idaho/Wyoming border. On the eastern side of the valley, the mountains of the famous Grand Teton Range rise to 13,771 feet. Eight miles west, the Big Hole Mountains rise to over 9,000 feet. The mountain ranges make for spectacular sunrises and sunsets. In the mornings, the sun rising over the Grand Tetons lights up the Big Hole Mountains. The evening sunsets create a colorful glow on the Grand Tetons.

About 30 miles north is the southwest corner of Yellowstone National Park. However, using surface roads, the park entrance is about 90 miles away. Two and a half miles of the western side of Yellowstone National Park are in Idaho.

The Grand Targhee Resort is about 20 miles northeast of the city in Wyoming. The only surface road access to the resort is through Driggs.

Pre-Incorporation Years

When Lewis, Clark and their Corps of Discovery were returning from their successful expedition to the Pacific Ocean in 1806, they stopped at the Mandan Indian Villages in what is now North Dakota. There they met two frontiersmen, Joseph Dickson and Forest Hancock. Dickson and Hancock were coming up the Missouri River on their way to trap beaver on the Yellowstone River. (*See The*

Region, Lewis and Clark.)

John Colter, a member of the Lewis and Clark expedition, requested and received an honorable discharge from Lewis and Clark so that he could join Dickson and Hancock. Two years later, Colter became one of the first white men to enter the beaver-rich Teton Valley.

While camped with a village of about 800 Crow Indians on a flat between Teton and Leigh Creeks near what is now Driggs, a war party of about 1,500 Gros Ventre (Blackfoot) Indians attacked the camp. Colter's skill with a rifle was a decisive factor in repulsing the attack.

Drug store in Driggs, 1912.

Colter then traveled north and was the first white man to discover what is now Yellowstone National Park. It was during these travels that he came upon a band of Gros Ventre Indians who recognized him as the rifleman they faced earlier. They captured Colter, stripped him of his clothes and released him to run for his life with spear-wielding Indians in hot pursuit. Colter lost his pursuers and eventually found his way to a camp of white traders. He then returned to his farm in Missouri where he spent his remaining days.

Around 1818 French-Canadian trappers began arriving in the Teton Valley. One was an Iroquois Indian named Vieux Pierre. Pierre reported the beaver-rich valley to the Hudson's Bay Company, which named it "Pierre's Hole." Valleys were often called "holes." (*See The Region, Early Trappers/Explorers.*)

Drug store in Driggs, 2013.

In 1832 Pierre's Hole was the location of a prominent rendezvous for traders, trappers and Indians. At the rendezvous, trading companies exchanged tobacco, whisky, gunpowder, traps, clothing, food and supplies for furs.

At the conclusion of this rendezvous, events turned deadly when about 100 of the departing fur trappers and their Indian allies encountered a tribe of several hundred

Gros Ventre Indians. Two of the Indians traveling with the trappers killed a Gros Ventre chief who came to parley. A fierce battle ensued with numerous deaths on both sides. The battle ended with the remaining Gros Ventre men, women and children escaping quietly into the night.

The beaver were trapped out by 1840. Following the discovery of placer gold over 100 miles north in what is now western Montana in 1862, prospectors came into the Teton Valley, but had little success.

Artists Thomas and Peter Moran, noted for their paintings of the Teton Mountains, came into what is now Driggs in 1879. Thomas wrote, "The Tetons here loomed up grandly against the sky and from this point it is perhaps the finest pictorial range in the United States or even in N. America."

Farmers market.

Hiram C. Lapham – with his wife, children and brother – came from Kansas to the Teton Valley on June 1, 1882, to settle and raise cattle. Before moving to the valley, Hiram taught school for a year in Albion.

Over the next five years, settlement in the valley progressed slowly. The first dwellings were log cabins with earthen floors and roofs covered with poles, brush and sod.

In early 1883 leaders of The Church of Jesus Christ of Latter-day Saints (Church) asked Thomas E. Ricks to lead the first party of settlers from Utah to settle and build communities in the Upper Snake River Plain. Over 1,400 people had established settlements in Ricks' ecclesiastical jurisdiction by the end of 1884, and hundreds more came each year. Rexburg was about 40 miles to the west of the Teton Valley and was the nearest post office.

Driggs city park in winter.

Utah emigrants Mathoni Pratt and Thomas Wilson came into the Teton Valley in 1888 to evaluate its settlement possibilities. Though sparsely settled, they found the valley promising. However, some of the settlers sought to dissuade them from coming, asserting that the valley was " ... a rendezvous for horse thieves and outlaws."

Pratt and Wilson were unimpressed with the settlers' tongue-in-cheek description of the valley. They returned to Utah with glowing reports. Primarily through word-of-mouth, emigrant families began planning the 400-mile wagon trip from Salt Lake City. From 1888 to 1890 about 300 families moved to the valley – several with the last name of Driggs.

These settlers were primarily members of The Church of Jesus Christ of Latter-day Saints. Church leaders organized them into an ecclesiastical unit named the Aline Ward. As a result, the community was generally called Aline.

Most farms had milk cows. In 1893 Samuel Kunz established the valley's first cheese factory and encouraged farmers to increase their dairy herds. One year later, another cheese factory opened in Driggs.

At the same time B.W. Driggs petitioned postal authorities for the Aline Post Office with himself as postmaster. The petition bore the signature of many people named Driggs. Postal authorities rejected the Aline name but approved the petition with a different name – the Driggs Post Office.

Dog sled race.

Ranching and farming underpinned the Driggs economy. Following the construction of shelters, the settlers' first priorities were plowing the ground for gardens, hay, grain and other crops; building diversion dams on the streams; and digging irrigation canals and ditches. Some settlers began building water-powered sawmills on the larger streams to produce lumber for their homes and barns.

By late 1901 Henry and Elen Harper Wallace, whose son Howard was one of the first settlers, platted the Driggs townsite on their 160 acres. In preparing the plat, they named the streets Little, Wallace, Ashley, Howard and Harper after members of their family.

Music and dancing were common forms of community entertainment. Around 1915 the City donated land to E. Beesley, a noted fiddler, and Charles Carr, a local carpenter, for construction of a two-story building at the corner of Little and Main Streets with a dance hall on the upper floor. The building is now Key Bank.

For many years, the availability of professional medical care was limited. The

Church organization for women, the Relief Society, trained several women to be midwives. These women often traveled long distances in dangerous weather to serve their patients. Their pay was often food or produce.

Dr. Ora Keith, an unmarried woman, began a medical practice in Driggs in 1906. For the next decade, she made house calls, even in blizzards, with a team of horses pulling her buggy. In her honor, many people named their children Ora or Keith.

On April 15, 1909, The Teton Valley News published its first edition.

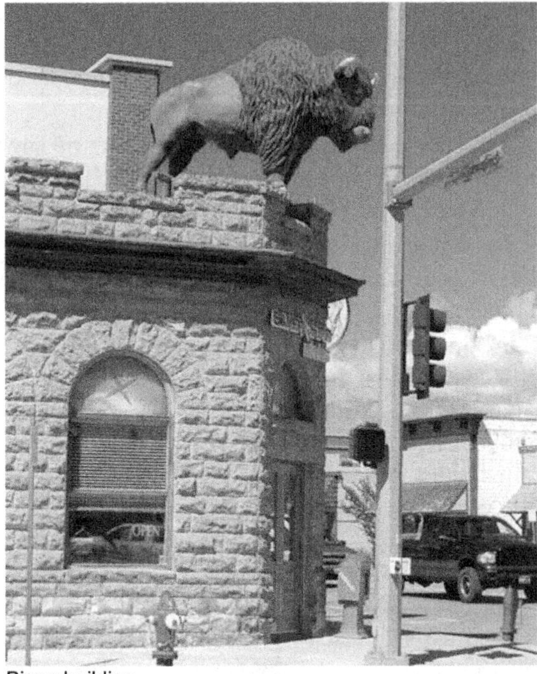

Bison building.

Incorporation

On May 23, 1910, with a town population of about 200, the Fremont County Commission approved the citizens' application to make Driggs an incorporated village. Its status changed to a city in 1967 due to a change in state municipal law.

Turning Points

Railroad The Yellowstone Park Railroad Company – later the Oregon Short Line – constructed a 38-mile line from St. Anthony to Driggs in 1912. A year later, the railroad extended the line seven miles further to Victor. The railroad not only opened the valley to more rapid transportation, but it facilitated the shipment of agricultural commodities to market. No longer would cattlemen have to drive their livestock or farmers transport their commodities 75 miles west to the railheads at Market Point – now Roberts – and, later, to St. Anthony for shipment.

The extension of the railroad to Victor also facilitated development of the limestone mine near Victor. Beginning in 1926 the mine provided limestone, a critical ingredient in the manufacture of sugar, to the sugar beet factory near Idaho Falls.

The railroad also served Jackson, Wyoming, residents. Jackson freight wagons came across the 8,429-foot-high Teton Pass to pick up goods shipped to the Victor Train Depot. In later years, Jackson and Grand Teton National Park visitors traveled to Victor where they boarded buses that carried them over the pass into Wyoming.

By the mid-1960s motor vehicles and air travel replaced the railroad, causing it to cease passenger service. In 1988 the railroad also shut down its freight service.

Agriculture For several decades, agriculture and food processing underpinned the local economy. Dairy products and cattle were major exports. In 1926 six local cheese factories and creameries exported cheese, cream and butter.

Driggs snowscape.

In recent decades, technological innovation and economies of scale in these businesses significantly improved their productivity with a much smaller workforce. Today, agriculture and food processing provide few jobs for city residents.

Teton Valley Hospital The federal Works Progress Administration built the Teton Valley Hospital in Driggs in 1939. At the dedication of the hospital on May 9, Dr. O.D. Hoffman, the hospital's first physician, explained that before the hospital opened, physicians made house calls traveling in a covered sleigh with a stove inside.

Plein air art in the park.

County Seat The Idaho Legislature created Teton County out of a division from Madison County on January 26, 1915. The next year, voters elected Driggs as the county seat. As the local seat of government, Driggs gained political prestige and several stable jobs.

The County spent $25,000 to build the courthouse at the corner of Little and Main Streets in 1924.

Grand Targhee Resort – Adapting to a Tourism-Based Economy In the early 1960s the Driggs economy was in decline. Private investors from Eastern Idaho, supported by a community effort aimed at stimulating the local economy, were instrumental in obtaining state and federal aid in building a 12-mile road east of Driggs high into the mountains of the Caribou-Targhee National Forest in Wyoming.

Investors opened the Grand Targhee Resort with two lifts and a lodge the day after Christmas in 1969. Idaho Governor Don Samuelson dedicated the facility on February 2, 1970. The resort has a base elevation of 7,408 feet; a top elevation of 10,000 feet; and an average annual snowfall of 500 inches.

Over the years, the resort has expanded. Currently it has a residential community and 2,000 acres for skiing. During the winter, the resort offers snowshoe and snowmobile tours, sleigh-ride dinners and spa services. In the summer, the resort hosts two major music festivals – the Targhee Festival and the Bluegrass Festival. Horseback riding, mountain bike races and marathons are other summer activities.

Many of the resort workers live in Driggs. The city's economic drivers have now shifted from agriculture to tourism and recreation.

Driggs Today

Amenities and Attractions The City of Driggs has over 28 acres of parks, some of which are under development.

Driggs City Park is a five-acre parcel in the heart of town. It has mature trees, shrubs, a pavilion, a Little League baseball diamond, a t-ball field, a fire pit, an outdoor basketball court, a children's playground, a winter ice skating rink and an athletic field.

Teton GeoTourism Center, Driggs.

Lion's Park is a three-acre, tree-lined park with an athletic field used principally for Little League baseball and soccer.

The eight-acre Fifth Street Park has not yet been fully developed. Amenities of this former gravel pit include a skate park with a Dreamland-designed 10-to-five-foot-deep bowl, a BMX bicycle track and a 9-hole Disc Golf Course with most of the holes located on eight acres leased to the City. Nature trails wind through the wooded portion of the park.

There are several smaller parks including neighborhood subdivision parks that offer picnic areas, pedestrian paths, children's playgrounds, basketball courts and sand volleyball.

Several community and private groups have donated use of their property to create a 2.5-mile Nordic skiing and skating track, part of which runs near the high school.

Golf is available at several nearby resorts and communities.

The city's most prominent amenity is its scenic location. The Teton River, fed by numerous mountain streams and flowing near the eastern and southern borders of the city, is an excellent trout fishery. Its rapids are also an attraction to white-water kayak and canoe enthusiasts.

Hiking, biking and horseback riding are available on hundreds of miles of national forest trails that begin a short distance from the city. Many of these trails interconnect with trails in Grand Teton National Park. The Driggs-Victor Trail is a paved path on the abandoned railroad track that once ran between the two cities.

In the winter, many of the trails used for hiking and biking in the summer become groomed Nordic skiing trails. The Grand Targhee Resort also offers backcountry skiing and snowmobile touring in the adjoining public lands.

The Teton Arts Council provides art classes and shows, music performances and live theatrical performances. The Teton Valley Foundation also brings cultural, educational and recreational events to the city.

Driggs, 2013.

Non-profit groups work to enrich the lives of local residents and protect cultural and natural values. The Teton Valley Trails and Pathways supports improvement and maintenance of local trails. Friends of the Teton River and the Teton Regional Land Trust help maintain the area's natural beauty and wildlife habitat. The Teton Valley Recreation Association facilitates organized sports.

The Driggs City Center is a popular location for community meetings and events. The Driggs Senior Center offers affordable lunches three times a week.

The Teton Valley Museum has displays and exhibits highlighting early pioneers, mountain men and American Indians. There is an antique warplane collection at the airport.

Historic buildings include the "Corner Drug," a cut-stone two-story structure built in 1906. The bottom floor was always a drug store. However, the top floor was originally used for high school classrooms and, later, a courtroom.

The two-story Key Bank building was built in 1916 with offices on the ground floor and a dance hall on the upper level.

Economy and Major Employers Most of the Driggs workforce is employed outside the city, principally at the Grand Targhee Resort. Others work in Jackson, Wyoming, and on area construction projects.

The other large employers include the Teton Valley Hospital, with about 150 workers; the Teton County School District, with over 100; Broulim's Thriftway, a grocery store, with over 60; and Teton County, with a payroll of about 50. The balance of the city's employment comes from several retail shops and stores, small manufacturing and service businesses, federal agencies and the City.

Education Teton County School District, Eastern Idaho Head Start and three private schools provide primary and secondary education. The National Outdoor Leadership School (NOLS Teton Valley) provides training courses for students 14 to 15 years old in wilderness skills, leadership and environmental ethics.

The closest institution of higher learning is Brigham Young University-Idaho in Rexburg. Eastern Idaho Technical College offers extension courses in the city.

Health Care The 13-bed Teton Valley Hospital and three clinics provide for most of the city's medical care needs.

Transportation Idaho Highway 33, connecting Driggs with Rexburg and Jackson, intersects the city.

Public transportation between Driggs and Jackson is available on START Bus, a public transportation system funded by the city of Jackson, Teton County in Wyoming and federal funds. The bus is particularly helpful for residents of Driggs and the Teton Valley who commute to Jackson for employment.

Air transportation is available for light private and charter aircraft at the 7,300-foot Driggs-Reed Memorial Airport.

Utilities and Services Private companies provide electricity, telephone, Internet, cable and satellite services. The City provides water and wastewater treatment services. The City's wastewater facility also serves other communities. Teton County administers solid waste pick up and landfill services.

The Teton County Sheriff's Office provides police protection. The Teton County Fire District and Teton County Ambulance District respond to fire and medical emergencies. The County also administers a volunteer search and rescue organization.

Vision for 2050

Over the past decade, Driggs' population has grown over 5 percent annually as opposed to the annual 3 percent rate of growth experienced in the preceding decade. This surge is largely due to the city receiving increased recognition for its spectacular scenery, outdoor recreation, tourism and the continued growth of the Grand Targhee Resort as well as resorts near Jackson Hole, Wyoming. This growth will likely continue, but at a more moderate rate.

Many residents have participated in planning the city's future through public and neighborhood meetings and responses to surveys. There is consensus that tourism will likely underpin the city's future economy. However, owners of other businesses seeking a high quality of life for themselves and their employees will also find opportunities in Driggs.

The city's pedestrian-friendly environment will attract downtown specialty shops and restaurants. Residential areas will be within walking distance of the downtown area. Walking and bicycle pathways will connect distinctive and attractive neighborhoods.

The city's park system and associated recreational activities will continue to expand and add to the city's high quality of life. The park system, along with expanded school facilities, will ensure greater opportunities for the city's youth.

Growth will require new or improved public systems. The City will pay for these improvements from user fees and approved tax structures.

City and community leaders are committed to following the City's Master Plan. In the next four decades, the city will have preserved its small-town character, natural beauty, critical environmental areas, open space and surrounding farmland. Through beautification, maintenance, restoration or demolition of unattractive structures and surroundings, Driggs will have preserved a strong sense of place – a place that is in harmony with the past.

Mayors

1919 E.C. Dalby *
1921 W.B. Stone *
1923 Ira R. Fowler *
1923 F.C. Madsen *
1931 H.L. Crandall *
1933 F.C. Madsen *
1935 J.H. Harper *
1937 E. Ralph Kearsley *
1938 V. Penfold
1949 James Hunter *
1951 Don Choules *
1957 William Ellis *
1959 Reed Christensen *
1966 Don Choules *
1969 Alvin Dalley
1994 Velma Dustin
1998 Louis B. Christensen
2010 Daniel Powers
2014 Hyrum Johnson

* Village Chairman

Main Street, Tetonia.

Tetonia

Statistical Data

Population: 272 *
Elevation: 6,060 feet
Precipitation: 14 inches **
Average Snowfall: 74 inches **
County: Teton
Website: www.tetoniaidaho.org

Temperature Range – Fahrenheit: **
Spring: 19 to 62
Summer: 41 to 79
Fall: 18 to 69
Winter: 8 to 33
* U.S. Census Bureau Estimates July 2015
** Historical averages

Tetonia lies in the upper Teton Basin (Valley) about six miles west of the Idaho/Wyoming border. The Teton River, a tributary to the Snake River, is four miles west of the city. The Grand Teton Mountain Range, rising up to 13,771 feet, forms the valley's eastern boundary. Even though the eastern slope of the Grand Teton Mountains – viewed from the Jackson Hole, Wyoming, area – is the most stunning and famous, the west slope of the mountains is also spectacular.

Eight miles southwest of the city are the Big Hole Mountains, rising to over 9,000 feet.

About 21 miles due north is the southwest corner of Yellowstone National Park. However, using surface roads, the park entrances are much more distant. Most of the park is in Wyoming; however, the western two and a half miles of the park extend into Idaho and Montana.

Fertile farms and ranches surround the city. Driggs and Victor are nine and 17 miles south, respectively. Rexburg is 40 miles west.

Pre-Incorporation Years

In 1808 two years after his discharge from the Lewis and Clark expedition, John

Colter was one of the first white men to enter the beaver-rich Teton Valley.

At this time, Coulter was camped with a village of about 800 Crow Indians on a flat between Teton and Leigh Creeks near what are now Tetonia and Driggs. A war party of about 1,500 Gros Ventre (Blackfoot) Indians attacked the camp. Colter's marksman skill with a rifle was a decisive factor in repulsing the attackers.

Colter then traveled north and was the first white man to discover what is now Yellowstone National Park. It was during these travels that he came upon a band of Gros Ventre Indians who recognized him as the rifleman they faced earlier. They captured Colter; stripped him of his clothes; and, for sport, released him to run for his life, barefoot with spear-wielding Indians in hot pursuit. Colter lost his pursuers and eventually found his way to a camp of white traders. He then returned to Missouri, content to spend his remaining days on his farm.

Around 1818 French-Canadian trappers began arriving in the Teton Valley. One of the trappers was an Iroquois Indian named Vieux Pierre. Pierre reported the potential of the beaver-rich valley – called "holes" – to the Hudson's Bay Company. They designated the valley "Pierre's Hole."

In 1832 Pierre's Hole was the location of rendezvous for traders, trappers and Indians. At the rendezvous, trading companies packed in tobacco, whisky, gunpowder, traps, clothing, food and supplies to trade for furs.

Dog sled team at Tetonia, early 1900s.

At the conclusion of one of the rendezvous, events turned deadly when about 100 of the departing fur trappers and their Indian allies encountered a tribe of several hundred Gros Ventre Indians. Two of the Indians traveling with the trappers recognized and killed a Gros Ventre chief who came to parley. A fierce battle ensued with numerous deaths on both sides. The battle ended with the Gros Ventre men, women and children escaping quietly into the night.

By 1840 the beaver had been trapped out. Few white men came into the valley until the early 1860s. Energized by the bonanza gold discoveries a hundred miles north in what is now western Montana, prospectors searched area streambeds for the precious metal. Finding none, they moved on.

In 1879 artists Thomas and Peter Moran, noted for their paintings of the Teton Mountains, came into the valley. Thomas wrote, "The Tetons here loomed up grandly against the sky and from this point it is perhaps the finest pictorial range in the United States or even in N. America."

In the early 1880s a stream of settlers, principally coming up from Utah Territory, began filing homestead claims in the Upper Snake River Plain.

On June 1, 1882, Hiram C. Lapham – with his wife, children and brother – came into the Teton Valley to establish a ranch and raise cattle. Before moving to the valley, Hiram had taught school for a year 150 miles west in Albion.

In January 1883 leaders of the Church of Jesus Christ of Latter-day Saints (the Church) asked Thomas E. Ricks to lead a large party of settlers from Utah to settle and build communities in the Upper Snake River Plain. Under Ricks' leadership, they established Rexburg and several other communities. About 1,420 people had established settlements in Ricks' ecclesiastical jurisdiction by the end of 1884, with more coming each year. Initially, the nearest post office for area settlers – including those few that had come into the Teton Valley – was Rexburg.

In 1888 Utah emigrants Mathoni Pratt and Thomas Wilson came into the Teton Valley to evaluate its settlement possibilities. They found the valley sparsely settled, but promising. They returned to Utah with glowing reports. Primarily through word-of-mouth, emigrant families began planning the 400-mile wagon trip from Salt Lake City to the Teton Valley. From 1888 to 1890 about 300 families immigrated to the valley.

Those settling on the north end of the valley named their community Tetonia, after the nearby Teton Mountain Range.

These settlers were primarily members of the Church. Church leaders organized and named the valley's first ecclesiastical unit in what is now Driggs. They named the unit the Aline Ward. Members in the outlying communities, such as Tetonia, were made branches and held church services in their own communities.

In 1894 B.W. Driggs petitioned postal authorities for a post office named Aline with Driggs as postmaster. The petition bore the signature of many people named Driggs. Postal authorities approved the post office with the name of "Driggs."

Ranching and farming underpinned the valley's economy. Following the construction of shelters, the settlers' first priorities were plowing the ground for gardens, hay, grain and other crops; building diversion dams on the streams; and irrigation canals and ditches. Some settlers began building water-powered sawmills on the larger streams to produce lumber for their homes and barns.

Most farms had milk cows. In 1893 Samuel Kunz established the valley's first cheese factory. This cheese-making facility encouraged more farmers to increase their dairy herds and build more creameries and cheese factories.

Music and dancing were common forms of community entertainment. E. Beesley, a noted fiddler, and Charles Carr, a local carpenter, built a dance hall in Driggs. Tetonia residents often traveled by buggy to the dances held in the Driggs Dance Hall.

For many years, the availability of professional medical care was limited. The Church organization for women, the Relief Society, trained several women to be midwives. These women often traveled long distances in dangerous weather to serve their patients. Their pay was often food or produce.

In 1906 Dr. Ora Keith, an unmarried woman, began a medical practice in Driggs. For the next decade, she made house calls, even in blizzards, with a team of horses pulling her buggy. In her honor, many people named their children Ora or Keith.

On April 15, 1909, the Teton Valley News, located in Driggs, published its first edition.

Incorporation

On November 18, 1910, Tetonia became an incorporated village.

Turning Points

Railroad Around 1912 the Yellowstone Park Railroad Company – later the Oregon Short Line – constructed a 38-mile railroad line from St. Anthony, through Tetonia to Driggs. In 1913 the railroad extended the line seven miles further to Victor. The railroad had a major positive effect on the valley's economy. The speed of mail delivery, passenger travel and freight delivery improved dramatically.

No longer would cattlemen have to drive their livestock or farmers transport their commodities on wagons 75 miles west to the railheads at Market Point – now Roberts – and, later, to St. Anthony for shipment.

The extension of the railroad to Victor also facilitated development of the limestone mine near Victor. Beginning in 1926 the mine provided limestone, a critical ingredient in the manufacture of sugar, to the sugar beet factory near Idaho Falls.

The railroad also served Jackson, Wyoming, residents. Jackson freight wagons came across the 8,429-foot-high Teton Pass to pick up goods shipped to the Victor Train Depot. In later years, Jackson and Grand Teton National Park visitors traveled to Victor where they boarded buses that carried them over the pass into Wyoming.

By the mid-1960s motor vehicle and air travel replaced the railroad, causing it to cease passenger service. The railroad continued to provide freight service in the valley.

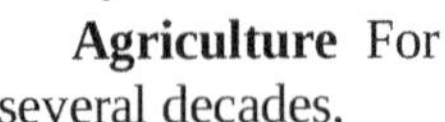

Agriculture For several decades, agriculture and food-processing businesses underpinned the local economy with cheese, cream and butter as the principal exports.

In recent decades, technological innovation and economies of scale significantly improved the productivity of agricultural-based businesses. Today, agriculture and food-processing businesses provide few jobs for valley residents.

Teton Valley Hospital On May 9, 1939, the federal Works Progress Administration built the Teton Valley Hospital in Driggs. At the dedication of the hospital, Dr. O.D. Hoffman, the hospital's first physician, explained that before the hospital opened physicians made house calls traveling in a covered sleigh with a stove inside.

Grand Targhee Resort – Adapting to a Tourism-Based Economy In the early 1960s, private investors from Eastern Idaho, supported by a community effort to stimulate the local economy, obtained state and federal aid in building a 12-mile road east of Driggs high into the mountains of the Caribou-Targhee National Forest in Wyoming.

On December 26, 1969, the investors opened the Grand Targhee Resort with two lifts and a lodge. Idaho's Governor Samuelson dedicated the facility on February 2, 1970. The resort has a base elevation of 7,408 feet, a top elevation of 10,000 feet and an average annual snowfall of 500 inches.

Over the years, the resort has expanded. Currently it has a residential community and 2,000 acres for skiing. During the winter, the resort offers snowshoe and snowmobile tours, sleigh-ride dinners and spa services. In the summer, the resort hosts two major music festivals, the annual Targhee Festival and BluegrassFestival. Horseback riding, mountain bike races and marathons are other summer activities.

While many of the resort workers live in Driggs, the facility has attracted increased traffic through Tetonia and strengthened the city's economy.

Tetonia Today

Amenities and Attractions Tetonia business interests have combined with the business interests in the cities of Driggs and Victor to form the Teton Valley Chamber of Commerce.

The city's most prominent amenity is its scenic location. The Teton River, fed by numerous mountain streams, is an excellent trout fishery. Its rapids are also an attraction to white-water kayak and canoe enthusiasts.

Hiking, biking and horseback riding is available on hundreds of miles of national forest trails that begin a short distance from the city. Many of these trails interconnect with trails in Grand Teton National Park. Bikers and hikers use the abandoned railroad track that runs through Tetonia. The portion of the trail between Driggs and Victor is paved.

In the winter, many of the trails used for hiking and biking in the summer become groomed Nordic skiing trails. The Grand Targhee Resort also offers backcountry skiing and snowmobile touring in the adjoining public lands.

Economy and Major Employers Teton County School District is the city's largest employer. Many of the city's residents commute to Jackson, Wyoming, for work.

Education Teton County School District provides elementary and secondary education. Children ages K-5 attend school at Tetonia Elementary School in

Tetonia. Older children commute to the district's middle and high schools in Driggs.

The closest institution of higher learning is Brigham Young University-Idaho in Rexburg.

Health Care The closest hospital is the 13-bed Teton Valley Hospital in Driggs.

Transportation State Highway 33 to Driggs and Jackson Hole, Wyoming, on the south and Rexburg to the west intersect the city. Highway 33 is part of the Teton Scenic Byway – starting at Swan Valley, Highway 31, and ending 69 miles later at Ashton, Highway 32.

Public transportation between Driggs and Jackson, Wyoming, is available on START Bus, a public transportation system funded by the City of Jackson and Teton County in Wyoming and federal funds. The bus is particularly helpful for residents of the Teton Valley who commute to Jackson for employment.

The closest air transportation for light private and charter aircraft is available at the 7,300-foot Driggs-Reed Memorial Airport. The closest airport for larger carriers is near Idaho Falls.

Utilities and Services Private companies provide electricity, telephone, Internet, cable and satellite services. The City provides water and wastewater treatment services. The Teton County Sheriff's Office provides police protection. The Teton County Fire District and Teton County Ambulance District respond to fire and medical emergencies.

Vision for 2050

In 1960 Tetonia had a population of 194. In 2000 the U.S. Census reported that the city had a population of 247. Since that time, the city's population has fluctuated within a plus or minus 10 percent of that number.

Historical population trends will likely continue. By 2050 the city will continue to be a small rural community of less than 400 situated in a location of spectacular natural beauty.

Mayors

1939 W.O. Hastings
1941 H.J. Willmore
1947 Russell Rammell
1951 W.C. Berry
1955 Ralph Heilson
1963 Russell Rammell
1971 Ralph Heilson
1972 Frank Hogan
1978 Sam Beard
1979 John Briggs
1980 Russell Rammell
1984 LaRae Rammell
1996 Dave Oveson
1997 Kendall Smith
2002 Joseph A. Kopplow
2004 Nancy Nead
2007 Rex Jardine
2011 Gloria Hoopes
** Records unavailable from 1910 to 1939

Victor in the valley.

Victor

Statistical Data

Population: 1,945 *
Elevation: 6,207 feet
Precipitation: 16.7 inches **
Average Snowfall: 73.7 inches **
County: Teton
Website: www.victorcityidaho.com

Temperature Range – Fahrenheit: **
Spring: 19 to 62
Summer: 41 to 79
Fall: 18 to 69
Winter: 8 to 33
* U.S. Census Bureau Estimates July 2015
** Historical averages

The City of Victor lies near the Idaho/Wyoming border at the southwestern edge of the Grand Teton National Park and the famous Teton Mountain Range in Wyoming.

Even though the view of the eastern side of the Teton Mountains is more famous, the view from the west of the 13 peaks that rise over 12,000 feet with the tallest, the Grand Teton, rising to 13,771 feet, is also stunning. People in Victor and the Teton Valley call the western side, the "quiet side of the Tetons."

The Caribou-Targhee National Forest and the Big Hole Mountain Range – rising to over 9,000 feet – lie to the west and south of the city.

When viewed just outside the city limits, the surrounding foothills of pine, fir and quaking aspen forests with the high mountains in the background take the breath away. A person should not drive in this area without stopping for a moment to behold the gorgeous portrait that nature has provided.

Pre-Incorporation Years

For centuries, Native American Indians frequented the area around what is now Victor during their summer encampments. Beginning in the early 1800s, European, Canadian and American fur trappers began coming into the area.

Some fur traders followed the practice of having annual mountain rendezvous at various locations as opposed to permanent trading posts. In 1829 and 1832 fur traders set up rendezvous in the low-lying, beaver-rich Teton Valley near what is now Driggs. They named the location Pierre's Hole, after one of the trapper-traders.

The 1832 rendezvous, one of the largest held, included several hundred mountain men, trappers and Indians. The fur companies bartered whisky, tobacco and supplies for furs.

The 1832 rendezvous turned deadly when about 100 departing fur trappers and some of their Indian allies encountered a tribe of several hundred Gros Ventre Indians, a Blackfoot Indian Tribe, traveling about eight miles south of Pierre's Hole near what is now Victor. Two of the Indians traveling with the trappers killed a Gros Ventre chief who came to parley. A fierce battle ensued with numerous deaths on both sides. The battle ended with the remaining Gros Ventre men, women and children escaping quietly into the night.

Victor Main Street.

In 1888 the first known settlers, Gideon & Alice Murphy, moved their family from Lyman, Wyoming, into the area of what is now Victor. Several other families moving up from Cache Valley, Utah, soon followed them. They were members of the Church of Jesus Christ of Latter-day Saints (Mormon) – converts and emigrants from Great Britain, Scandinavia, Switzerland and Germany. They knew the 6,200-foot-high elevation and harsh winters of the Teton Valley could be a challenge. However, they felt the beauty of the area and the availability of land, irrigation water and timber would more than compensate.

Early Victor.

Indeed, the life of the first settlers required considerable physical and emotional strength to survive. They had to build diversion dams on the creeks that were headwaters to the Teton River and dig irrigation canals and ditches by hand and horse-drawn plows and scrapers. The early log cabins of dirt floors, drafty walls, leaky roofs and leather-hinged doors required a special endurance.

On the other hand, their crops did well and animal reproduction was high. They augmented their food supply with wild game and berries on the land and fish in the streams. Berries do well at the south end of Teton Valley; fruit trees do not. For this reason alone, a child finding an orange in his or her stocking at Christmas time considered it a real treat.

For several years until a flourmill and sawmill were built, supplies, such as flour, came in on freight wagons.

The immigrants located in four communities that were in near proximity to each other. They named their settlements Trail Creek, Fox Creek, Chapin and Cedron. Together, they comprised a village and ward (ecclesiastical unit). They wanted to name their broader community Raymond – out of respect for the bishop of their ward, David Raymond Sinclair – and apply for a post office.

Stagecoach in front of Victor Post Office.

However, when they applied, U.S. postal authorities rejected the name of Raymond as it was already in use. Upon re-evaluation, community leaders selected the name of Victor – in recognition of Claud Victor, a mail carrier who devotedly carried the mail on his back through rain or snow as he traveled between Jackson Hole, Wyoming, and the south end of Teton Valley. Postal authorities approved creation of the Victor Post Office.

Incorporation

On January 2, 1896, Victor became an incorporated village. In that same year, Ben (Grandpa) Jones built Victor's first hotel. The greatest challenge for the new village was fighting fires and providing an adequate water system, streets and cemetery.

First library in Victor.

Turning Points

Agriculture The prospect of making a living as farm and ranch families attracted the first settlers to the Teton Valley. For nearly 100 years, farming and ranching were the basis of Victor's economy. However, over that period, important aspects of agriculture changed. Technological innovation and farm consolidation have allowed agricultural businesses to improve productivity with less labor.

While the reduction of farm jobs had an adverse effect on the city's economy, another phenomenon began to offset that effect. The city's scenic beauty and close proximity to the Jackson, Wyoming, area have attracted many new residents. This, in turn, has brought an increasing number of job opportunities to Victor, particularly in tourism and hospitality businesses. To accommodate these new residents, real estate developers are converting farm and ranch land into commercial and residential subdivisions.

Limestone Mining From 1926 to 1970 a business in Victor mined limestone discovered near Fox Creek. Limestone is a critical ingredient used in the manufacture of sugar. The company shipped the processed limestone by rail to the sugar beet factory near Idaho Falls. When the Idaho Falls sugar factory shut down, the mine went out of business.

Railroad In 1913 the Oregon Short Line Railroad extended its rail line seven miles from Driggs to Victor and built a depot.

Victor train depot.

The railroad had a major positive effect on the city's economy and the wellbeing of its residents. In addition to jobs, it provided convenient transportation for shipping limestone to the Idaho Falls sugar factory, moving agricultural commodities and livestock to market, providing mail and passenger service and bringing goods to the town's residents.

The railroad also had a major effect on Jackson Hole, Wyoming, residents. They often had goods shipped to the Victor Train Depot because they could get delivery faster there than from any point in Wyoming. Jackson Hole freight wagons came across the 8,429-foot-high Teton Pass to pick up goods at the Victor Train Depot and return.

In the mid-1960s the railroad ceased providing passenger service. Loss of this service had a major adverse effect on the city's economy. The passenger train, known as the "Park Train," brought visitors into Victor where they boarded buses to Jackson Hole and Grand Teton National Park and back. This trip was very popular and profitable for Victor hospitality businesses.

In the early 1970s the railroad ceased freight service to Victor. With the end of rail service, the railroad dismantled the stockyards and railroad tracks and donated the train depot to the City. Motor vehicles were in common use; however, residents considered loss of rail service as a loss to the whole community. The City has preserved the depot as a historic monument.

Victor Today

Amenities and Attractions The city has four city parks located in total on 25 acres.

The city's most significant attraction is its scenic location. The nearby Targhee National Forest allows outdoor enthusiasts to enjoy backpacking, fishing, mountain biking and hunting, while providing exquisite vistas for those who just want to take hikes and enjoy the wildlife and lush scenery.

For those who love winter activities, Victor is within 27 miles of prominent downhill ski resorts. The Grand Targhee Resort is across the state border just west of Driggs. Other ski resorts are near Teton Village and Jackson Hole, Wyoming. There are several groomed cross-country ski trails throughout Teton County, some of which start within the city limits.

Victor Pool Hall.

One prominent home-grown amenity has become a popular attraction over its four decade history. Pierre's Playhouse is a family run dinner playhouse open Thursday through Saturday from mid-June to Labor Day. It combines an all-you-can-eat Dutch-oven dinner with melodrama plays depicting life in the 1890s.

Economy and Major Employers Teton County School District is the city's largest employer. Victor's business district consists of numerous eating establishments and several small shops and boutiques.

Pillars of light scrape the night sky over Victor.

Education Teton County School District, headquartered in Driggs, provides elementary and secondary education. Elementary students attend school in Victor. Middle and high school students travel by bus to Driggs.

The closest institution of higher learning lies 47 miles northwest at BYU-Idaho in Rexburg.

Health Care Medical practitioners have offices in the city. The nearest hospital is Teton Valley Hospital in Driggs.

Transportation State Highway 33 – which connects the city with Driggs to the north and Jackson, Wyoming, to the east – intersects the city. State Highway 31 connects the city with Swan Valley and U.S. Highway 26, 13 miles to the south.

Driggs Municipal Airport, with its 9,300-foot runway is the closest air service. Railroad freight service is also available in Driggs.

Utilities and Service. Private companies provide electricity, natural gas, cable and satellite services. The City's volunteer fire department provides fire protection. The Teton County Sheriff's Office provides police protection under contract with the City.

Vision for 2050

For several decades prior to 1990, Victor's population ranged from 240 to 290. During the 1990s Victor's population began growing at accelerated rates. For the past several years, Victor's population has grown an average of over 13 percent annually. This growth is largely influenced by growth in the nearby Jackson Hole area.

Looking east toward Victor.

Victor's growth rate has been several times faster than that of its two county sister cities to the north – Driggs and Tetonia. Victor is now the largest city in the county. If current trends continue, by 2050 Victor's population could approximate 6,000.

In anticipating this growth, city leaders seek to make planning and zoning decisions that strategically evaluate their long-term effects with the costs paid by impact fees and taxes coming from growth and those benefited.

The city leaders' goal is to build on the past by respecting the city's legacy and heritage in a manner that achieves the city's slogan, "a town to come home to."

By 2050 the downtown historic district will have a distinct character with a pedestrian-friendly walking tour around Victor. There will be adequate parking for residents and tourists alike. Developers will have built an industrial park to attract small manufacturing and service businesses likely connected to outdoor recreation.

During the intervening years between now and 2050, city leaders will seek to build an infrastructure of parks, roads, public systems, community events and attractions that will allow Victor to continue as a quiet, economically stable and interesting hometown city.

Mayors

1896-1915 Unknown *
1916 J.D. Killpack
1917 V.B. Brinton
1920 C.M. Hatch
1926 E.N. Kearsley
1937 George Dewey
1949 C.F. Novasio
1950 R.O. Rytting
1960 Floyd Stratton
1975 Richard H. Whiting
1985 R. Kirk Olson
1998 Don L. Thompson
2010 Scott Fitzgerald
2012 Zachery Smith
2016 Jeff Potter
* Village Chairman

BIBLIOGRAPHY

The 2000 Comprehensive Plan: City of Eagle, Idaho. Eagle: Eagle City Council, 1999.

2005-2006 Teton Valley Visitors Guide. Idaho Falls: Canyon Media for the Teton Valley Chamber of Commerce, 2004.

The 2007-2008 Teton Valley Activity Guide. Idaho Falls: Canyon Media for the Teton Valley Chamber of Commerce, 2006.

2009 and 2010 Answer Book. Coeur d'Alene: Coeur d'Alene Press (supplemental publication), March 31, 2009, and April 28, 2010.

Abramson, Ruby. Spanning the Century: The Life of W. Averell Harriman, 1891-1986. New York: William Morrow & Co., 1992.

Aiken, Katherine G. Idaho's Bunker Hill: The Rise and Fall of a Great Mining Company, 18851981. Norman: University of Oklahoma Press, 2005.

Alt, David, and Donald W. Hyndman. Roadside Geology of Idaho. Missoula: Mountain Press Publishing Company, 1989.

---Roadside Geology of the Northern Rockies. Missoula: Mountain Press, 1972.

Anderson, Abraham C. Trails of Early Idaho. Caldwell: Caxton Printers, Ltd., 1940.

Anderson, Alfred Leonard. Detailed Geology of the Minnie Moor and Queen of the Hills Mining Property. Moscow: University of Idaho, 1950.

---, et al. Detailed Geology of Certain Areas in the Mineral Hills and Warm Springs Mining District. Moscow: University of Idaho, 1950.

---, and Warren Richard Wagner. A Geological Reconnaissance of the Hailey Gold Belt (Camas District) Blaine County, Idaho. Moscow: University of Idaho, 1946.

Arrington, Leonard J. History of Idaho. Moscow: University of Idaho Press, 1994.

Atteberry, Jennifer. "Domestic and Commercial Architecture in Caldwell." Idaho Yesterdays, Winter 1980, pp. 2-17.

Baker, Bessie's Meadows Valley High School English Class. History of Meadows Valley. 1945.

Basalt Centennial Committee, Verlyn Dye Outcelt, Chairman. Basalt Idaho Centennial. Idaho Falls, Idaho: Valley Litho., 1985.

Beal, Merrill D., and Merle W. Wells. History of Idaho. New York: Lewis Historical Publishing Company, 1959.

Beierle, Amber. "Boise's Birthday." Office of the City Historian <http://www.boisehistory.com> 2004.

Benedict, Hope A. "A Common Heritage: A Promise of Abundance: Cow Camps, Mining, and Timber Operations of Lemhi County." Salmon: Salmon National Forest, 1994.

Bingham County History. Written and compiled by the people of Bingham County, Idaho. Blackfoot: Bingham County Centennial Book Committee, 1985.

Bingham, Randy E. Burley Irrigation District History: The First 100 Years. Burley: Burley Irrigation District, nd.

Bird, Annie Laurie. Boise, the Peace Valley. Caldwell: Canyon County Historical Society, 1975, c1934.

---My Home Town. Caldwell: Caxton Printers, 1968.

---Old Fort Boise. Parma: Old Fort Boise Historical Society, 1971.

Blase, Fred W. "Political History of Idaho Territory 1863-1890." Master's Thesis, University of California, 1924.

Boone, Lalia Phipps. From A to Z in Latah County, Idaho: A Place Name Dictionary. Moscow: Latah County Historical Society, 1983.

Bottolfsen, C.A. Author and editor. Articles about the early history of the Lost River from the files of the South Custer County Historical Society.

Bourasaw, Noel V. "James Frederick Wardner Series." Skagit River Journal of History and Folklore. <http://www.skagitriverjournal.com/WA/Whatcom/FairhavenSth/Pioneers/Pre1900/Wardner/Wardner01-JamesBioPortal.html> August 2010.

Bowen, A.W. Progressive Men of Southern Idaho. Chicago: A.W. Bowen & Co., 1904.

Brainard, Wendell. Golden History Tales from Idaho's Coeur d'Alene Mining District. Ray Chapman, ed. Kellogg: Wendell Brainard, 1990.

Brock, Eugene Linda, et al. Pioneer Settlers and Pioneer Ranches of Valley County. A Valley County History Project. Grand Junction: Action Services, 2002.

Brosnan, Cornelius James. History of the State of Idaho. Idaho: Charles Scribner's Sons, 1918.

Buckway, JaNene Johnson. Wendell: Hub City of Magic Valley. Shoshone: Wendell 75th Anniversary Committee, 1984.

Burg, Thomas E. White Pine Route: The History of the Washington, Idaho and Montana Railway Company. Coeur d'Alene: Museum of North Idaho Publications, 2003.

Caldwell Centennial Calendar 1883-1983: 100 Years of Documentary in Words and Pictures.

Caldwell: Caldwell Historic Preservation Commission, 1982.

Each day of this 1983 calendar contains an historic note. It is indexed.

Caldwell Public Library. Oral History Committee. Voices from the Past. Caldwell: Caldwell Public Library.

A series of slide-tape programs about early Caldwell including businesses, music, women, architecture and irrigation.

"Caldwell Revisited 1883-1923." News Tribune. July 4, 1976. A special edition printed during the U.S. bicentennial year.

Carlson, Jimmie I. "Remaking Idaho's Capitol City: A Case Study in Urban Renewal." Masters' Thesis, Boise State University, 1996.

Carney, Ellen. Historic Soda Springs: Oasis on the Oregon Trail. Wayan: Traildust Publishing, 1998.

Carns, Iva Hollingsworth. Steamboats and Memories. Coeur d'Alene: Iva Carns, 1990.

Casner, Nick, and Valerie Kiesig. Trolley: Boise Valley's Electric Road, 1891-1928. Boise: Black Canyon Communications, 2002.

"Cavalcade Issues." Idaho Press Tribune.

The Idaho Press Tribune publishes a special series in the spring of each year, which often includes historical articles. Some have been indexed.

Chapman, Ray. Uncle Bunker. Kellogg: Chapman Publishing, 1994.

---. History of Idaho's Silver Valley: 1878-2000. Kellogg: Chapman Publishing, 2000.

---. History of Kellogg, Idaho, 1885-2002. Kellogg: Chapman Publishing, 2002.

Chedsey, Zona, and Carolyn Frei, eds. Idaho County Voices: A People's History From the Pioneers to the Present. Grangeville: Idaho County Centennial Committee, 1990.

Clanton, Dorothy M. The Georgie Oakes: The Lady of the Lake.

---Bringing the Iron Horse to the Coeur d'Alenes.

Clark, Lynda Campbell. Nampa, Idaho, 1885-1985: A Journey of Discovery. Nampa: Pacific Press, 1985.

Clements, Louis J., and Harold S. Forbush. Pioneering the Snake River Fork Country.

Rexburg: Eastern Idaho Publishers, 1972.

A Completed Century 1888-1988. Caldwell: Centennial Committee Boone Presbyterian Church, 1987.

Conley, Cort. Idaho for the Curious: A Guide. Cambridge: Beckeddy Books, 1982.

Cox, Cheryl A., and Lexie Ann French. Second Stories: Historical Narratives of Idaho Falls Women. Idaho Falls: The Graphic Experience, 1986.

Crosby, Mike. “A Common Heritage: Lemhi County, the Salmon National Forest, and the Civilian Conservation Corps.” Salmon: Salmon National Forest, 1994.

Crow, Donna Fletcher. Kathryn: Days of Struggle and Triumph. Chicago: Moody Press, 1992.

---Elizabeth: Days of Loss and Hope. Chicago: Moody Press, 1993.

---Stephanie: Days of Turmoil and Victory. Chicago: Moody Press, 1993.

Crowder, David Lester. Rexburg, Idaho: The First One Hundred Years 1883-1983. Rexburg: D.L. Crowder, 1983.

Culdesac Idaho Centennial 1903-2003: 100 Years of Memories. Culdesac: Culdesac Gem Committee, 2003.

Davis, Belinda. A Study of Irrigation and the Development of Ada County. Boise: Ada County Historical Preservation Council, 1990.

Davis, L.J. “Tearing Down Boise.” Harpers. November 1974.

Declo History Committee and Declo Alumni Association, contributors. Declo, My Town, My People. Burley: Burley Reminder, Incorporated, 1974.

DeVoto, Bernard, ed. The Journals of Lewis and Clark. Boston: Houghton Mifflin Company, 1953.

Dillion, Wilda Collier. Deaths and Burials: Boise Barracks Military Reserve, Idaho, 1863-1913.

Boise: W.C. Dillion, 2003.

Downing, James L. History of Teton City, Idaho: 1833-1900. Rexburg: Ricks College, 1971.

Driggs, B.W. History of Teton Valley, Idaho. Louis J. Clements and Harold S. Forbush, ed.

“Rexburg: Arnold Agency, 1926” revised 1970, copyright 1970 by Louis J. Clements, Rexburg: Eastern Idaho Publishing Company.

Driggs Idaho Stake: Diamond Jubilee 1901-1981. Rexburg: Ricks College Press, 1982.

Driscoll, Ann Nilsson. They Came to a Ridge. Moscow: News Review Pub. Co., 1970.

Druss, Claudia, et al, eds. Patterns of the Past: The Ada County Historic Sites Inventory. Boise: The Arrowrock Group, 2001.

Eagle Island State Park Master Plan. Boise: Beck & Baird, 2000.

Elsensohn, Sister M. Alfreda. Pioneer Days in Idaho County, Volume 2. Cottonwood: Caxton Printers, 1971.

Etulain, Richard W., and Bert W. Marley, eds. The Idaho Heritage: A Collection of Historical Essays. Pocatello: Idaho State University Press, 1974.

Fanselow, Julie. Idaho Off the Beaten Path: A Guide to Unique Places. Guilford: Globe Pequot Press, 2010.

1. ---”What a Democracy Looks Like: Kuna, Idaho: Where a Community Pulls Together to Face Growth.” Study Circle Resource Center, 2004.

Feser, Bonnie Jean Bacon. Georgetown, ID (Twin Creeks), 1869-1950. Georgetown: Bonnie Jean Bacon Feser, 2006.

Fick, Bob. “Idaho Governor Awards $2.1 Million in Community Grants.” Gem County Chamber of Commerce. OpenPotion. 7 July 2006. <www.emmettidaho.com> August 2010.

Fisher, Vardis. Idaho Encyclopedia. Federal Writers’ Project. Caldwell: Caxton Printers, Ltd. 1938.

Fisk, Dale, and Don Dopf. The P&IN to the Golden Heart of Idaho: The Story of the Pacific

& Idaho Northern Railway. Boise: Writers Press, 2001.

Flanders, Robert Bruce. Nauvoo: Kingdom on the Mississippi. Urbana: University of Illinois Press, 1965.

Fogg, P.M. A History of the Minidoka Project, Idaho, to 1912 Inclusive. Boise: Bureau of Reclamation, 1915.

Frandsen, Rebecca, and Ruth Ann Olson. The Best Trader on the Emigrant Road: The Life and Adventures of Bob Dempsey, Mountaineer. Lava Hot Springs: Greater Lava Hot Springs Chamber of Commerce, 1979.

---Lava Hot Springs. For City of Lava Hot Springs Tourist Information Center

Franzen, John G. Southeastern Idaho Cultural Resources Overview, Burley and Idaho Falls Districts: Final Report R-2196. Jackson: Commonwealth Associates, 1981. Pp 115-191.

French, Hiram T. History of Idaho: a narrative account of its historical progress, its people and its principal interests. Chicago: Lewis Publishing Co., 1914.

Fritzen, Mary Jane, ed. Idaho Falls, City of Destiny. Idaho Falls: Bonneville County Historical Society, 1991.

---Bonneville County: Its Formation and Description. Idaho Falls: Bonneville County Heritage Association, 2006.

Gentry, James R., et al. A Centennial History of Bliss, Idaho: 1883-1983. Gooding: Pilot Press, 1983.

---In the Middle and on the Edge: The Twin Falls Region of Idaho. Twin Falls: College of Southern Idaho, 2003.

Gidley, J.W. Hunting Fossils on the Old Oregon Trail. Smithsonian Institution, 1930.

Gilbert, Millie. “Emmett – Spotlight City.” Idaho Magazine. March 2005. 33-40.

Gittins, H. Leigh. Pocatello Portrait: the early years, 1878 to 1928. Moscow: The University Press of Idaho, 1983.

Gooding County History Book Committee. Gooding County Roots and Branches, 1989. Gooding: Taylor Publishing Company, 1989.

Graff, Leo W. Jr. “Fred T. Dubois-Biographical Sketch.” Idaho State University: Eli M. Oboler Library. Idaho State University. n.d. <http://www2.isu.edu/library/special/mc004b.htm> 12 Jan 2007.

Gray, Dale M. “Moved Properties in American Falls, Idaho.” National Register of Historic Places. Nomination 2005.

Groefsema, Olive. Elmore County: Its Historical Gleanings " A collection of pioneer narratives, treasured family pictures, and early clippings about the settling of Elmore County, Idaho. Caldwell: Caxton Printers, Ltd., 1949.

Hafen, LeRoy R., ed. Trappers of the Far West: Sixteen Biographical Sketches. Lincoln: University of Nebraska Press, 1965.

Hailey, Leona Cartee. “Boise in the Seventies.” Cartee Collection, Idaho State Historical Society MS 376.

Haines, Aubrey L. Historic Resource Study: Historic Sites Along the Oregon Trail. Denver: Denver Service Center, Historic Preservation Team, National Park Service, 1973.

Haines, Jr., Francis D., ed. The Snake Country Expedition 1830-1831: John Work’s Field Journal. Norman: University of Oklahoma Press, 1971.

Hall, Jory. Kuna Civil War to Chauatuqua: Thumbprints Across the Pages of History. Kuna: Thumbprints, 1997.

Hart, Alfred B. “History of Bloomington, Idaho.” compiled May 12, 1933.

Hart, Arthur A. Wings over Idaho: An Aviation History. Caldwell: Caxton Press, 1991.

Hartkopf, Frank. History of Bingham County, Idaho. Laramie: University of Wyoming, 1942.

Hartman, Hugh H. The Founding Fathers of Boise. Boise: Hugh H. Hartman, 1989.

Hawkes, Blaine. (Uncopyrighted local history book, used with permission of the author.)

Hawley, James H. History of Idaho, the Gem of the Mountains. Chicago: The S.J. Clarke Publishing Co., 1920.

Hay, O.P. "The Pleistocene of the Western Region of North America and Its Vertebrate Animals." Washington: Carnegie Institution of Washington Publication N. 322B:1-346, 1927.

Hine, Robert. Community on the American Frontier. Norman: University of Oklahoma Press, 1980.

History of Arimo: Including Arkansas, Hawkins Basin, Marsh Center, and Robin. Compiled by the Arimo Centennial History Committee for the Idaho Centennial. Arimo: Arimo Centennial History Committee, 1991.

History of the Brick Plant at Troy, Idaho. Troy: Troy Historical Society.

History of Cassia County and Burley Idaho. 1952.

History of North Idaho. or An Illustrated History of North Idaho: Embracing Nez Perce, Idaho, Kootenai and Shoshone Counties, State of Idaho. Spokane: Western Historical Publishing Company, 1903.

Holladay Engineering Company. "Wastewater System Preliminary Engineering Report " 6/1/051-12.

Holland, Wendolyn. Sun Valley: An Extraordinary History. Ketchum: The Idaho Press, 1998.

Holm, Debra Nelson, et al. Nampa's People, 1886-1986: Discovering Our Heritage. Nampa: Nampa Centennial Committee, 1986.

Horton, Alice, et al., eds. Beautiful Bonneville. Logan: Herff Jones, 1989.

House, Connie. Firestorm! Big Blowup II in North Idaho. Coeur d'Alene: Listos Publications, 1992.

Hult, Ruby El. Steamboats in the Timber. Coeur d'Alene: Caxton Printers, 1952.

---Northwest Disaster: Avalanche and Fire. Portland: Binford & Mort, 1960.

Idaho Poets and Writers Guild. These to Remember. S.L.: The Guild, 1962.

Idaho Power Company. "Early History of the Idaho Power Company." 1929.

Idaho State Historical Society. Emigrant Trails of Southern Idaho. (Idaho Cultural Resource Series Number 1). Boise: U.S. Bureau of Land Management, 1993.

---. "Goodale's Cutoff from Boise Valley to Powder River." (Reference Series Number 1048). Boise: Idaho State Historical Society, 1994.

---"Massacre Rocks." (Reference Series Number 234). Boise: Idaho State Historical Society, 1971.

---"Route of Alexander Ross, 1824." Idaho State Historical Society Reference Series, Number 86. July 1990. <http://history.idaho.gov/sites/default/files/uploads/reference-series/0086.pdf> April 2016.

---Postmarked Idaho: A List of Idaho Post Offices. Boise: Idaho State Historical Society, 1975.

---"Weldon Brinton Heyburn: May 25, 1852 " October 18, 1912. (Reference Series Number 544). Boise: Idaho State Historical Society, 1971.

---"The Beginning of the New York Canal." Idaho State Historical Society Reference Series, Number 190. March 1972.

---"Packer John's Cabin." Idaho State Historical Society Reference Series, Number 292. 1996.

---"Seven Devils." Idaho State Historical Society Reference Series, Number 116. 1981.

---"Gilmore and Pittsburgh Railroad." Idaho State Historical Society Reference Series, Number 215. 1976.

---"Salmon Falls and Thousand Springs." Idaho State Historical Society Reference Series, Number 184. 1987.

---"Oregon Trail Routes in and around Boise." Idaho State Historical Society Reference Series, Number 921. 1989.

Idaho State Transportation Department. Idaho Highway Historical Marker Guide. Boise: Idaho State Transportation Department, 2010.

Idaho Travel Council. Idaho: Official State Travel Guide. Boise: Idaho Department of Commerce, nd.

Idaho: Where the Past Comes Alive. Idaho City: Idaho City Chamber of Commerce.

Inman, Mary J. Twin Falls Centurybook: 1904-2004. Twin Falls: Hosteler Press, 2003.

International Daughters of the Utah Pioneers. Pioneer Women of Faith & Fortitude. Salt Lake City: Daughters of the Utah Pioneers, 1998.

Iona Centennial History Book 1883-1983: A Centennial History Book, Containing Historical Material and Personal Histories, Submitted by the Residents and Previous Residents of Iona, Bonneville County, Idaho. Rexburg: Ricks College Press, 1983.

Irving, Washington. Astoria or Anecdotes of an Enterprise Beyond the Rocky Mountains. Philadelphia: Carey, Lea & Blanchard, 1836.

Johnson, Stella E. History of Troy 1892-1992. Troy: Stella E. Johnson, 1992.

Jordan, Grace Edgington. The King's Pines of Idaho: A Story of the Browns of McCall. Pontiac: Kirkwood Pub. Co., 1998.

Klenck, Dee. A Jewel Between Two Rivers: the History of Fruitland, Idaho. Fruitland: Gem Publishing Company, 1990.

Kunkler, Lois Roark. "A Brief History of the Eagle High School Broncs." The Eagle Express, Jan. 13, 1995, p. 1.

Kuna Chamber of Commerce. Gateway to the Birds of Prey: Kuna, Idaho. Kuna: Economic Development Committee, Kuna Chamber of Commerce, 1999.

Layton, Stanford J., ed. Utah's Lawless Fringe: Stories of True Crime. Salt Lake City: Signature Books, 2001.

Lee, William H. "A History of Phosphate Mining in Southeast Idaho." U.S. Geological Survey, U.S. Department of Interior, Open File Report #00-425, Version 1.0. <http://geopubs.wr.usgs.gov/open-file/of))-425> September 2010.

Lemhi County History Book Committee. Centennial History of Lemhi County, Vol. I. Salmon: Lemhi County History Book Committee, 1992.

Leppert, Elaine and Lorene Thurston. Early Caldwell Through Photographs. Caldwell, Idaho: Caldwell Committee for the Idaho State Centennial, 1990.

Link, Paul Karl, and E. Chilton Phoenix. Rocks, Rails & Trails, 2nd Edition. Pocatello: Idaho Museum of Natural History, 1996.

Lohrey, Dana, et al. The Elk City Wagon Road. Centennial Edition. Grangeville: Dana Lohrey, 1995.

Longley, C.L. "Assay Office in Boise Holds Venerable Place in Story of Yellow Dust." Boise: Idaho Statesman, January 19, 1930.

Longteig, Margaret Nell, and Rheba Miller. Remember When. 1976.

Lorenzen, Marilyn. Personal knowledge and writings.

Lovell, Edith Haroldsen. Captain Bonneville's County. Idaho Falls: The Eastern Idaho Farmer, 1963.

Lowell, Helen, and Lucile Peterson. Our First Hundred Years: A Biography of Lower Boise Valley 1814-1914. Caldwell: Caxton Printers, 1976.

Lucas, F.A. The Fossil Bison of North America. Washington: Smithson.Proceed.v.21, 1899.

Lukas, J. Anthony. Big Trouble. New York: Simon and Schuster, 1997.

Lyon, Ruth B. The Village that Grew: Emmettsville, Martinsville, Emmett. Lithocraft for R.B. Lyon, 1979

MacGregor, Carol. "The Founding Community in Boise Idaho: 1882-1910. Ph.D. Diss., University of New Mexico, 1999.

Madsen, Brigham D. The Shoshoni Frontier and the Bear River Massacre. Salt Lake City,

Utah: University of Utah Press, 1985.

"Magic Valley Region Wildlife Management Areas." Idaho Fish and Game. <www.fishandgame.idaho.gov/cms/wildlife/wma/carey> April 2016.

Marker, Joe L. Eagle Rock, U.S.A. (now Idaho Falls, Idaho). Idaho Falls: Roboco Printing, 1980.

Market Lake Centennial Committee, ed. Market Lake Centennial (1867-1967). Roberts: Market Lake Centennial Committee, 1967.

McConnell, W.J. Early History of Idaho. Glendale: The Arthur H. Clark Company, 1913.

McDevitt, Thomas. Idaho's Malad Valley: A History. Pocatello: Little Red Hen, Incorporated, 2001.

McGonigal, Mary Brown. Spring of Gladness: Reminiscences of Pioneer Life in the Wood River Valley. Ketchum: McGonigal, 1976.

McLeod, Geo A. History of Alturas and Blaine Counties Idaho. Hailey: The Hailey Times, 1930.

Mendiola, Judy. "A History of Eagle, Idaho." Eagle: The Author, 1998.

Meyers, Rex. "The Implausible Gilmore and Pittsburgh." The Colorado Rail Annual, No. 15. Golden: Colorado Railroad Museum, 1981.

Miller, John B. The Trees Grew Tall. Moscow: The News Review Publishing Company, 1972.

Mills, Nellie Ireton. All Along the River: Territorial and Pioneer Days on the Payette. Montreal: Payette Radio Limited, 1963

Mini-Cassia Chamber of Commerce & Visitor Center. <http://www.minicassiachamber.com/> April 2016.

Mitchell, Victoria E. History of Selected Mines in the Alder Creek Mining District, Custer County Idaho. Special Staff Report. Moscow: Idaho Geological Survey, University of Idaho, 1997.

Monroe, Julie R. Moscow: Living and Learning on the Palouse. Charleston: Arcadia Publishing, 2003.

---et al. Rekindled Spirit. Moscow: Idaho State Historical Society, 2009

Neilsen, Judith. "A Brief History of the Washington, Idaho & Montana Railway Company." University of Idaho Special Collections & Archives, Manuscript Group 139, 1982.

Okelberry-Jones, Sharon. History of Oakley, Idaho. Unspecified Publisher, 1990.

Oppenheimer, Doug. Sun Valley: A Biography. Boise: Beatty Books, 1976.

Otness, Lillian Woodworth. A Great Good Country: A Guide to Historic Moscow and Latah County, Idaho. Moscow: Latah County Historical Society, 1983.

Parker, Karen, et al. Teton Centennial: 100 Years of Progress, 1883-1983. Teton: Teton Centennial Committee, 1983.

Petersen, Keith. Company Town: Potlatch, Idaho, and the Potlatch Lumber Company. Pullman: Washington State University Press, 1987.

Pettite, William Stibal. Memories of Market Lake, Vol. II. Roberts: William Pettite, 1977.

Pfeifer, Friedl. The Sun Valley Ski Book. New York: A.S. Barnes & Company, 1939.

Plastino, Ben J. Coming of Age: Idaho Falls and the Idaho National Engineering Laboratory 1949-1990. Ed. Diane Plastino Graves. Chelsea: Bookcrafters, 1998.

"Portrait of a Small City: Eagle, Idaho." Boise: Journal of Commerce, 1979, no paging.

Postmarked Idaho: List of Idaho Post Offices. Boise: Idaho State Historical Society, 1975.

Quinn, Larry. A History of Magic Valley. Twin Falls: Publishing West Associates, 1996.

Ransel, Sandra, and Charles Durand. Crossroads: A History of the Elmore County Area. Mountain Home: Elmore County Historical Research Team, 1985

Rasker, Ray, and Ben Alexander. Working Around the White Clouds. Bozeman: Sonoran

Institute, 2003.

Records and minutes of the various cities in Idaho.

Reed, Mary. "Latah Legacy" articles published by Latah County Historical Society

Reid, Wallace and Bates. Blackfoot Historic Homes and Buildings. 1996.

The Renaissance: a Book of Historical Nature and Especially a Record of Past Year's Events at the College of Idaho. Caldwell: Associated Body of the College of Idaho, 1908.

Rexburg Community Review. Boise: Idaho Rural Partnership, 2004.

Ricketts, Virginia. Then and Now in Southern Idaho. Jerome: Falls City Publishing, 1998.

Roberts, Edwards. Shoshone and Other Western Wonders. New York: Harper & Brothers, 1888.

Robertson, Donald B. Encyclopedia of Western Railroad History; Volume II: The Mountain States. Dallas: Taylor Publishing Co., 1991.

Rockwood, Craig, et al. Iona History Book, Vol. II. Iona: Iona Historical Committee, 2005.

Ronda, James P. Lewis and Clark among the Indians. Lincoln: University of Nebraska Press, 1984.

Route of the Oregon Trail in Idaho. Boise: Idaho Department of Highways, 1963.

Rowland, Frank P. Founding of McCall, Idaho. Caldwell: Caxton Printers, 1960.

Russell, Osborne. Journal of a Trapper: Nine Years in the Rocky Mountains, 1834-1843. Edited from original manuscript by L.A. York. Boise: Syms-York, 1914.

Salant, Priscilla, et al. Profile of Rural Idaho. Boise: Idaho Commerce & Labor, nd.

Scharnhorst, Marie H. "Genesee, 100 Years." Latah Legacy (Spring, 1989, V. 18 No. 1). Moscow: Latah County Historical Society, 1989. Pp 3-36.

Scott, Donna. A ribute to the Past, a Legacy for the Future. Miriam Booth Breckenridge, et al, eds. Twin Falls: Twin Falls County Business History, 1990.

Scott, Orland A. Pioneer Days on the Shadowy St. Joe. Coeur d'Alene: Caxton Printers Ltd, 1968.

The Settlement of the Kuna Region, 1900-1925. Caldwell, Caxton Printers, 1983.

"Seventieth Anniversary and 'Days of '83' edition." Caldwell News Tribune. May 6, 1953. An excellent special edition of the newspaper describing Caldwell's early days; the advertisements are histories of many local businesses.

Shadduck, Marvin E. The Dalton Story. Coeur d'Alene: Museum of North Idaho, 2003.

Shallat, Todd, and Johnny Hester. "Trails and Rails: Boise as a Transportation Hub." Office of the Boise City Historian. <http://www.boisehistory.com/> 2005.

Shoup, George E. History of Lemhi County. Reprint. Salmon: Salmon Public Library Association, 1992.

Sims, Robert C., and Hope Ann Benedict, eds. Idaho Governors: Historical Essays on Their Administrations. Boise: Boise State University Press, 1992.

Singletary, Robert. Kootenai Chronicles. Coeur d'Alene: Century Publishing, 1995.

Slavik, Walter K.M. "Pioneering Public Power: Minidoka Project, Idaho." The Reclamation Era. Boise: Bureau of Reclamation, 1941.

Smith, Evelyn L. A Century of Progress, Evolution to Excellence, 1889-1989: A History of the Schools of Mullan, Idaho. Mullan: Mullan Education Foundation, 1989.

Smith, Robert Wayne. The Coeur d'Alene Mining War of 1892: A Case Study of an Industrial Dispute. Corvallis: Oregon State University Press, 1961.

Smythe, Rachel. Entertaining Strangers. Salt Lake City: Amber Pen, 2005.

Solum, Romola Hansen. History of Georgetown. Lola Hoskins, researcher.

South Custer County Historical Society, Inc. photograph collection.

Spence, Clark C. For Wood River or Bust: Idaho's Silver Boom of the 1880s. Moscow: University of Idaho Press, 1999.

Stacy, Susan M. Proving the Principle: A History of the Idaho National Engineering and Environmental Laboratory, 1949-1999. Washington: United States Government Printing, 2000.

---Legacy of Light: A History of the Idaho Power Company. Boise: Idaho Power Company, 1991.

Stapilus, Randy. It Happened in Idaho. Guilford: Globe Pequot Press, 2002.

Stearns, H.T., Lynn Crandall, and Willard G. Steward. Geology and Ground-water Resources of the Snake River Plain in Southeastern Idaho: Water Supply Paper 774. Boise: U.S. Government Print Office, 1938.

Stene, Eric A. The Minidoka Project. Denver: Bureau of Reclamation History Program, 1993.

Stoll, William T., and H.W. Whicker. Silver Strike: the True Story of Silver Mining in the Coeur d'Alenes. Boston: Little, Brown, and Co., 1932.

Stoddard, Bonnie J., researcher and compiler. History of Dubois.

Strahorn, Carrie Adell. Fifteen Thousand Miles by Stage. New York: Putnam's, 1911. Two chapters tell of the establishment of Caldwell, "City Building-Caldwell, and other Towns on the Frontier" and "Pot-Pourii." The University of Nebraska published a two-volume edition in 1988.

Tacke, Kathryn. Regional Economist. "Idaho County Workforce Trends." Boise: Idaho Department of Labor, January 2010

Taking the Scenic Route: A Guide to Idaho Scenic Byways. Boise: Idaho Transportation Department, 2000.

Taylor, Dorice. Sun Valley. Sun Valley: Ex Libris Press, 1980.

Tollefson, Gene. BPA and the Struggle for Power at Cost. Portland: Bonneville Power Administration, 1987.

Toponce, Alexander. Reminiscences of Alexander Toponce. Norman: University of Oklahoma Press, 1971.

Travel the Oregon Trail in Caribou County: A Self-guided Tour of Sites Documented in Emigrant Diaries & Journals of Early Explorers. Soda Springs: Soda Springs Chamber of Commerce, 2004.

Trego, Byrd. Author, editor, and newspaper publisher. Articles about the history of the Lost River from the files of the South Custer County Historical Society.

Trent, Geneva. History of Eagle Fire Department. Eagle: Eagle Historic Preservation Commission, 1997.

Tweedy, Doug. Clearwater County Profile. Orofino: Idaho Department of Commerce and Labor, 2006.

Twin Falls Historical Society. Twin Falls County Territorial Centennial 1863-1963: A Folk History of Twin Falls County, Idaho. Twin Falls: Standard Printing Company, 1963.

Walgamott, Charles S. Reminiscences of Early Days: a Series of Historical Sketches and Happenings in the Early Days of Snake River Valley. Twin Falls: Idaho Citizen, 1926.

---Six Decades Back. Moscow: University of Idaho Press, 1936

Walker, Deward E., Jr. Indians of Idaho. Moscow: University of Idaho Press, 1978.

Walker, Lola, Lula Barnard, and Faunda Bybee. Tosoiba: Sparkling Waters. Soda Springs: Daughters of the Utah Pioneers, 1958.

Wells, Merle. Gold Camps and Silver Cities: Nineteenth Century Mining in Central and Southern Idaho, 2nd edition. Moscow: Idaho Department of Lands, Bureau of Mines and Geology, 1983.

Wells, Merle, and Arthur Hart. Boise: An Illustrated History. Sun Valley: American Historical Press, 2000.

Whitlock, Flint, and Bob Bishop. Soldiers on Skis: A Pictorial Memoir of the 10th Mountain Division. Boulder: Paladin Press, 1992.

Whitman, Narcissa Prentiss. My Journal 1836. Edited and with introduction by Lawrence L. Dodd. Fairfield: Ye Galleon Press, 1994.

Winslow, Dilla Tucker. From Sagebrush to Green Fields: A History of Greenleaf Idaho. Private Printing, 1984. (Permission to re-publish granted to the City of Greenleaf by the heirs of Dilla Tucker Winslow.)

Witherell, Jim. "History Along the Greenbelt." Boise: Ada County Centennial Committee, 1990.

Woods, Shelton, ed. Valley County Idaho Prehistory to 1920. A Valley County History Project. Grand Junction: Action Publishing, 2002.

Wright, Patricia, and Lisa B. Reitzes. Tourtellotte & Hummel of Idaho: The Standard Practice of Architecture. Logan: Utah State University Press, 1987.

Young, Virgil M. The Story of Idaho. Moscow: University of Idaho Press, 1990.

Yorgason, Blaine and Brenton. Roger and Sybil Ferguson History. Unknown.

Unpublished works:

Adkinson, Virginia, local White Bird resident and historian. Research and writings.

Asker, Bonita, local White Bird resident and historian. Research and writings.

Baker, Ronald J. "Chronology of Eagle, Idaho" Unpublished manuscript on file at Eagle Public Library Reference Dept., 2005.

Benedict, Hope Ann. "Place and Community in the Mining West: Lemhi County, Idaho, 1866-1929" Ph.D. diss., University of Oregon, 1996.

Bennett, E.H. "Genesee Timeline." Unpublished history and notes about Genesee, Idaho.

Benton, Jon. "Thirsty for a Water System."

Benton, Josh. "Telephone Troubles."

Brown, Kimberly Rice, unpublished files.

Burtenshaw, Frances D. Compiled writings of George F. Shelley, Theodocia M. Dana, and Mary S. Davis. "Eagle Public Library History." Unpublished manuscript on file at Eagle Public Library Reference Dept., 1984.

Hale, Kent. "Oakley Has Magnificent Homes." (Information sheet provided by the City.)

Hansen, Hortense. "History of the City of Shelley."

Kreiman, Marilyn. "Biography of Pear Lucile Small Lewis."

"A history of the Kuna Grange," unpublished manuscript, 2005. Compiled by Sharon Fisher, Lecturer, Kuna Grange, 2005, from information originally written by Mrs. Laura Rea (originally made available by Mrs. Ben Aylsworth of Nampa, and compiled from old record books and data collected by E. G. May and B. Mathews), Lois Dustman, and Ruth Burningham. Help also provided by Wayne and Blanche Kuhlman and Florence Chaney.

Miller, John B. Unpublished articles.

Peterson, Lynn. Research paper: History of St. Charles, Idaho.

Sleeper, Richard. "Biography of Richard Crampton Sleeper."

Smith, Elizabeth. "History of the Salmon National Forest," ca. 1970.

Strong, Sam. Unpublished recollections.

Thomason, William J. "Reubens History." 1990.

Wilde, J.P., Journal Correspondent. "Story of Georgetown."

Newspapers and Magazines:

American Falls Press. "Tragedy Brought Moral Uplift, Recollections of W.T. Oliver." February 25, 1915.

---"American Falls Townsite Jumped, Recollections of W.T. Oliver." March 11, 1915.

---"Untold Wealth Within Reach, Recollections of W.T. Oliver." March 18, 1915.

American Whitewater Journal. Issue 4, July/August 1997.

The Arco Advertiser. Bound files.

Better Roads Magazine. November 1952.

Blackfoot Magazine. By the Greater Blackfoot Area Chamber of Commerce, 2005-2006.

The Blackfoot News.

Bonner County Daily Bee. <www.bonnercountydailybee.com>

Bovill Herald. 1911-1912.

Bovill Record. 1913.

Buhl Herald. April 1941.

Burley Bulletin.

Burley Herald.

Burley Herald-Bulletin.

Caldwell Daily News.

Caldwell News.

Caldwell News Weekly.

Caldwell News Tribune.

Caldwell Press Tribune.

Caldwell Progress Bulletin.

Caldwell Times.

Caldwell Tribune.

Daily Idahonian.

Family Circle Magazine. August 2010.

Forbes Magazine. March 2008.

Gem State Rural. Sept 15, 1895-May, 1916.

Genesee News. 1888-1968.

The Harrison Searchlight. June 2005 and June 2006 issues.

Hoot Owl. On microfilm at the Salmon Public Library.

Hub City Irrigationist.

Idaho County Voices.

The Idaho Enterprise.

Idaho Farm Journal. Black Canyon Edition, September 29, 1949.

The Idaho News.

Idaho Press-Tribune.

Idaho Recorder. On microfilm at the Salmon Public Library.

Idaho State Journal. "Malad's Early History Was Replete with Color." By Mary Matthews, November 25, 1982.

Idaho Statesman.

Idaho's Yesterdays. Vol. 7 No. 4.

Inc. Magazine. 2008.

Independent Enterprise.

Irrigation Age. September 1980.

Kiplinger. 2008.

The Kooskia Mountaineer. 1927.

Latah County Press. 1944-46.

Lemhi Herald. On microfilm at the Salmon Public Library.

Lewiston Morning Tribune. "Town sprouts out of nowhere." By Jodi Walker, April 27, 2006.

Mackay Miner Newspaper. Microfilm and hard copy newspaper issues 1907-1975.

McCall Magazine.

Money Magazine. June 2010.

The Morning News.

Moscow Mirror. January 1, 1892. (Article on Vollmer first published in the Alliance Ledger.)

Mountain Home News.

Mullan News Bulletin. Summer Edition.

Mullan Progress. 1912-1918.

Mullan Tribune.

News Review. 1934.

News Tribune. Nov 16, 1966 " June 30, 1981.

North Side News. Bicentennial Edition, July 1, 1976.

---October 22, 1981.

North Side News: 75th Anniversary Edition. August 5, 1982.

Northern Idaho News. September 22, 1908.

---1908-1910.

Outdoor Life Magazine. June/July 2009.

Parma Review. "Our Yesterdays from 1910 to 1980, a historical record published December 1980 in celebration of its 70th anniversary.

Pierce city ordinances.

The Recorder Herald. July 2010.

Rupert Pioneer Record. August 22, 1907.

Sandpoint Online. <www.sandpointonline.com>

Semi-Weekly Mining News. On microfilm at the Salmon Public Library.

Snake River Echoes.

South Idaho Press. July 6, 1970. (Article by Al Dawson)

---March 11, 2004. (Article by Renee Wells)

Spokesman Review.

Star Mirror. 1934.

The Star-News.

The Times News. June 24, 1987.

Twin Falls News.

Twin Falls Weekly. 1904-1906.

United States Department of Agriculture, Issue 12-06. "Agriculture In Idaho." June 28, 2006.

US News and World Report. November 29, 2007.

The Warren Times.

Wendell Irrigationist.

Documents and Records:

1888 Polk Directory for Shoshone County.

1981-92 Polk Directory.

2000, 2008 and 2010 Census.

2005-06 Emmett Area Telephone Book.

2005-2006 Idaho Blue Book.

2006-2020 City of Driggs Comprehensive Plan. Adopted November 2, 2006, by the Driggs City Council.

A Pause for Reflection. Estes.

Ada County Historic Preservation Council 2006 Preservation Plan for Cultural and Historic Resources.

Adams County historical records.

Bloomington Comprehensive Plan. November 2008.

Boise Basin Museum.

Bonner County Historical Society.

Books of Deeds filed in Valley County Courthouse, Cascade, Idaho.

Boundary County Museum.

Bruneau-Grand View School District Records.

"Cassia County Agent Annual Report for 1923."

City of Dubois records.

City of Mountain Home records.

City of Orofino records.

City of Post Falls records.

City of Roberts Comprehensive Plan Revised. 2007.

City of Stites archives of meeting minutes and published ordinances.

City of Teton Comprehensive Plan, 2004.

City of Wendell Gem Community Update. "A Peek Into the Past." 2003-2008.

Clark County Historical Society.

Clearwater County Guide for Newcomers brochure.

Clearwater Historical Museum.

Coeur d'Alene Tribe official website. <http://www.cdatribe-nsn.gov/> 2016.

Comprehensive Plan for the cities of Juliaetta and Kendrick.

Craig Mountain Lumber Company papers, University of Idaho, September 1980.

Downtown Rexburg Revitalization Blueprint.

Elmore County Historical Foundation.

Excerpts taken from paper written by JaNene Buckway, chair, Lincoln County Centennial Committee, 1995.

Excerpts taken from Shoshone Historic Walking Tour, written by Christy Pyles, chair, Gem Community Committee and the residents of Shoshone, 1995.

Explorations and Fieldwork of the Smithsonian Institution in 1929, Publication 3060:31-36.

"Final Environmental Impact Statement." U.S.D.A. Forest Service, Salmon National Forest, June 1991.

Fremont and Clark County courthouse records.

Grand View City records.

Grand View Water and Sewer Association, Inc., records.

Historic Opera Theatre brochure, Glenns Ferry Opera Theatre.

Historic Oakley brochure.

Idaho Atlas and Gazetteer. DeLorme, 2002.

Idaho Historical Society archives and public records.

Idaho Parks and Recreation records.

Idaho State Archives/Historic Records. Collection AR202: "Bridge and Highway Contracts."

Idaho State Mining Records.

Idaho State Veterans' Cemetery: Cultural Resource "Inventory and Assessment, Ada County, Idaho." Grand View: Frontier Historical Consultants, 2002.

J.R. Simplot Company records.

Jerome Jt. School District No. 261 Physical Plant Inventory.

Jerome School District records.

Jobs Plus records.

Johnson Flying Service records, Missoula, MT.

Larsen Farms.

Latah County Courthouse Records and Documents.

Latah County Historical Society Archives.

Latah County Historical Society Research Library. Moscow, Idaho.

Lemhi County Commissioners Records.

Madison Economic Partners. 2008-2009 Community Profile. "Sugar City: Sweetest Town Around."

---Sugar City Business Park: a Great Place to Build a Business. 2009.

McCall Area Comprehensive Plan.

Meadows Valley School District records.

Minutes and Ordinances from the City of Bovill Archives.

Minute books for the City of Cambridge.

Minutes of past meetings of the Horseshoe Bend City Council.

Minutes of stockholders of Georgetown Reservoir Company held April 27, 1903.

Minutes of the Salmon City Council.

Mountain Home Economic Development records.

Mountain Home Historical Museum pamphlet.

National Weather Service.

New Meadows City and Village records.

New Meadows Master Plan & Revitalization.

North Central Idaho Travel Association. Discover North Central Idaho. 2004-2006.

Personal records and pictures of Iona Residents.

Post Falls Chamber of Commerce.

Post Falls High School documents and records.

Post Falls Historical Society files.

Post Falls School District records.

Recreation Features Report.

The Rexburg Civic Life and Community Involvement Focus Team.

Richards, Bob, Economic Development, History of Spears Mfg. Jerome Idaho: Historical timeline from Spears purchase of Tupperware Plant to 2003.

Riverbed Commerce Park records.

Salmon Historical Society records.

Sanborn Fire Insurance Maps: Caldwell. New York: Sanborn Map Company. The Caldwell Public Library has mounted photocopies of the maps for 1888, 1890, 1892, 1900, 1908, 1911 and 1921.

Sandpoint Experiment Station 1910-2004.

Scenic Payette River Historical Society records.

Sugar City 2008 Comprehensive Plan.

Teton Scenic Byway Corridor Management Plan. Teton Scenic Byway Committee, Planmakers Planning & Urban Design, 2008.

The Twin Falls North Side Land and Water Company records. August 31, 1909.

University of Idaho Library Archives.

Upper Snake River Historical Society records and archives.

U.S. Forest Service records.

Valley County Comprehensive Plan.

Village of Notus Ordinance book dated 1921-1988.

Wastewater Status Update for the City of Greenleaf. April 28, 2009.

Wikipedia. “Skaggs Family.”

Welcome to Oakley brochure.

Websites:

About the University of Idaho. <http://www.ucm.uidaho.edu/default.aspx?pid=86023> November 2005.

Ada County Development Services. “A Brief History of the Kuna Area.” (PowerPoint Presentation.) <https://adacounty.id.gov/Portals/0/HisPreServ/Doc/ABriefHistoryoftheKunaAreaforweb.pdf> May 2016.

---”Ada County Chronicles: An Overview of the Development of Ada County.” (PowerPoint Presentation.) <https://adacounty.id.gov/Portals/0/HisPreServ/Doc/AdaCountyChroniclesHandout6perpage.pdf > May 2016.

Ada County Historic Preservation Council. “A Walking Tour of Kuna’s Beginnings.” <https://adacounty.id.gov/Portals/0/HisPreServ/Doc/kuna_Walking_Tour_Brochure201 2.pdf> May 2016.

AirNav.com <http://www.airnav.com> 2005.

America’s Promise Alliance for Youth. “100 Best Communities for Youth: Meridian, Idaho.” May 2016.

Bannock Development Corporation. <www.bannockdevelopment.org> July 2010.

Bonner County History Museum. <http://www.bonnercountyhistory.org> August 2010.

Cassia County. “Cassia County History.” <http://www.cassiacounty.org/about-cassiacounty/history.htm> 2005.

Cinema Treasurers “Howells Opera House.” <http://cinematreasurers.org/theaters/4167>

City Data. <www.citydata.com>

City of Ashton. “Whistles and Smoke: Ashton’s Railroad Legacy.” <www.cityofashton.com/whistles-and-smoke> April 2016.

City of Dalton Gardens. <www.daltongardens.govoffice.com> 2005.

City of Dover. <www.doveridaho.org> 2016.

City of Eagle. “Official web site of the City of Eagle, Idaho.” <http://www.cityofeagle.org> September 2010.

City of Fairfield, Idaho. <www.fairfieldidaho.us> 2016.

City of Hayden. <www.cityofhaydenid.us> 2005.

City of Heyburn. <www.heyburnidaho.org> May 2016.

City of Kooskia. <www.kooskia.com> 2016.

The City of Lewiston: Idaho’s Only Seaport. <http://www.cityoflewiston.org/> May 2016.

City of Moscow. <http://www.ci.moscow.id.us> 2005.

---Peterson, Jon R., et al. “Growth in Moscow: A Study of Modest Population Growth and Rising Economic Prosperity.” <http://www.ci.moscow.id.us/records/City20Reports/Why_is20_Moscow_Growing_06.pdf#search=Growth%20in%20moscow%3A%20a%20study%20of%20modest%20population%20growth%20and%20rising%20economic%20prosperity> 2006.

The City of Mountain Home. <www.mountain-home.us> May 2016.

City of Pocatello. <www.pocatello.us> August 2010.

City of Rigby. <www.cityofrigby.com> 2016.

CityTownInfo.com. <http://www.citytowninfo.com> May 2016.

Community Library. <http://leadore.lili.org> May 2016.

"Dam Details: Little Wood River Dam." Bureau of Reclamation. <http://www.usbr.gov/projects/Facility.jsp?fac_Name=Little+Wood+River+Dam&groupName=General> April 2016.

Drive the Top Ten. <www.drivethetop10.com> 2005. (May 2016, no longer a viable site.)

Elk River Lodge & General Store. <www.elkriverlodge.net> 2006.

Ellersick, Steven Donald. White Pine Savages: Ellersicks in the Lumber Industry. <http://myplace.frontier.com/~sde22ssw/Eller5-sde.html> May 2016.

Epodunk. <http://epodunk.com> 2005.

Farnovision. <http://www.farnovision.com/> 2016.

Felton, Ann. "Airport Expansion, 1929." Office of the Boise City Historian. <http://www.boisestate.edu/history/cityhistorian/3workpapers_pdf/airport_expands.pdf> 2004.

Fremont County Idaho. <www.co.fremont.id/us> 2016.

Full text of History of Custer County, Idaho. <http://www.archive.org/stream/historyofcusterc00blac/historyofcusterc00blac_djvu.txt> 2016

Gem County Historical Society and Village Museum. <www.gemcountymuseum.org> August 2010.

Grand Targhee Resort. <www.grandtarghee.com> 2016.

Greater American Falls Area Chamber of Commerce <http://www.amfallschamber.com/> May 2016.

Greater Newport Area Chamber of Commerce. <http://newportareachamber.com/> 2016.

Greater Pocatello Chamber of Commerce. <www.pocatelloidaho.com> July 2010.

Greater Yellowstone Resource Guide. <http://www.free-press.biz/> 2005.

Handy, J.A. Heyburn " Its Origin and Early History. 1959. <http://heyburn.id.gov/index.asp?SEC=59AED487-1297-4A0D-B5FB6B8A80C30AB0&DE=8A62CC31-8BB8-4F3C-9E05D99AB627AC01&Type=B_PR> May 2016.

Hayden Chamber of Commerce. <www.haydenchamber.org> 2016.

Hester, Johnny. "Subdivisions of Boise." Office of the Boise City Historian. <http://www.boisestate.edu/history/cityhistorian/2atlas_subdivisions/index_subdivisions.html> 2005.

History of Kootenai County. <www.kcgov.us/community/history>

History of Latah County: Moscow. <http://users.moscow.com/lchs/history.html#moscow> November 2005.

Howell, Thomas. Snake River 4x4. "History of Warm River, Idaho." <http://www.snakeriver4x4.com/warmriver.php> 2005.

Idaho Chapter Oregon California Trail Association. <www.idahoocta.org> August 2010.

Idaho City Chamber of Commerce. <www.idahocitychamber.org> May 2016.

Idaho Community Profiles. <http://www.epodunk.com/communities_id.html> May 2016.

Idaho Department of Commerce. <http://commerce.idaho.gov/> 2016.

Idaho Fish and Game. <http://www.fishandgame.idaho.gov> 2005.

Idaho Fish and Wildlife Service. <www.fws.gov> 2016.

Idaho Rural Partnership. March 2005 Community Review. Kuna: A World of Potential. <http://www.irp.idaho.gov/Documents20and20Settings/14/Site20Documents/Site20Media/Community20Review/Kuna20Community20Review%20Report.pdf> May 2016.

Idaho State Parks. <http://www.stateparks.com/idaho_parks_and_recreation_destinations.html> May 2016.

Idaho State University. <http://www.isu.edu> 2005.

Idaho Wool Growers Association. <http://www.idahowool.org/> August 2010.

inidaho.com. "Plan Your Trip to Donnelly Idaho." <http://www.inidaho.com/City.asp?

City=Donnelly> 2016.

Jackson Hole. <http://www.jacksonhole.com/> 2006.

Kiplinger. <http://www.kiplinger.com> September 2010.

"Lake Pend Oreille History." Sandpoint Online.com: Lake Guide. <http://www.sandpointonline.com/rec/lakeguide/history.html> August 2010.

Lava Hot Springs Area History. <http://lavahotsprings.com/info/history.html> May 2016.

Los Angeles Times. "Regional Report: Vanishing Railroads." <http://articles.latimes.com/1990-06-20/news/mn-226_1_union-pacific> 2005.

Miners Inch. <http://sizes.com/units/miners_inch.htm> August 2010.

Minidoka County Idaho. "Minidoka County History." <http://www.minidoka.id.us/general/history.htm> May 2016.

Moscow Chamber of Commerce. <http://www.moscowchamber.com> March 2007.

National Park Service. <https://www.nps.gov> May 2016.

---�National Register of Historic Places. <https://www.nps.gov/nr> May 2016.

National Weather Service. <www.weather.gov> 2016.

Nez Perce Tribal Web Site. <www.nezperce.org> 2016.

Northwest Nazarene University. <www.nnu.edu> 2016.

OVAC Oakley Valley Arts Council. <http://oakleyvalleyartscouncil.org/>

Palouse Country. "Moscow's Unique Beginning." <http://the.palouse.net/Moscow/history/history_beginnings.htm> November 10, 2005. (No longer a viable site in May 2016.)

Pocatello Marathon. <www.Pocatellomarathon.com> August 2010.

Portneuf Greenway Foundation. <www.pgfweb.com> August 2010.

Portneuf Medical Center. <www.portmed.org> August 2010.

Roots Web. "Coeur d'Alene Tribe History." <http://www.rootsweb.ancestry.com/~idreserv/cdhist.html> 2016

Rupert's Wilson Theatre. www.ruperttheatre.com

Rural Northwest.com. "Kootenai History: Hayden was booming at turn of century." <http://www.ruralnorthwest.com/artman/publish/printer_4478.shtml> 2005.

Sangres. <http://www.sangres.com> August 2016.

School District #25. <www.d25.k12.id.us> August 2010.

Schwantes, Carlos. "A Brief History of the University of Idaho." <www.ucm.uidaho.edu/default.aspx?pid=86022> November 2005.

"Silver Creek Preserve." The Nature Conservancy in Idaho. <http://www.nature.org/ourinitiatives/regions/northamerica/unitedstates/idaho/placesweprotect/silver-creek-preserve.xml> April 2016.

Smith, Jerry E. A History of "Rancharrah". <http://www.jerryesmith.com/index.php/42> 2016.

Snake River Stampede. <www.snakeriverstampede.com> 2016.

Southeast Idaho – Be Here! <www.seidaho.org/grace.htm> April 2016.

South Lemhi School District. <www.leadoreschool.org> May 2016.

St. Luke's Jerome Medical Center. <https://www.stlukesonline.org/communities-andlocations/facilities/hospitals-and-medical-centers/st-lukes-jerome-medical-center> 2016.

Stanley: Trailhead to Idaho Adventure. <http://stanleycc.org/> 2016.

Star Idaho. <http://staridaho.us/> 2016.

Steppe, Kali. "Clang, Clang, Clang Went the Trollies." Office of the Boise City Historian, <http://www.boisehistory.com/> 2004.

Swan Valley Elementary School. <http://sd92.k12.id.us> 2006.

Tamarack Resort. <http://www.tamarackidaho.com> 2005.

Teton Valley Trails and Pathways. <http://tvtap.org> 2016.

Three Rivers Ranch: for the discriminating flyfisher. <http://www.threeriversranch.com> May 2016.

Time. “Electrical Engineer Philo Farnsworth.” <http://content.time.com/time/magazine/article/0,9171,990620,00.html> 2016.

Topozone. <www.topozone.com> 2016.

Troy, Idaho USA. <http://www.troyidaho.net> May 2016.

Twin Lakes Canal Company history <http://www.twinlakescanalcompany.com/history.html> 2006.

Uhlenkott, Dale “Popeye.” “Ferdinand, Idaho: Memoirs of Frank M. Bieker.” <http://idaho.idgenweb.org/PDF/Ferdinand%20Story%20Aug%2013%202004.pdf> April 2016.

Ultimate Idaho.com. <www.ultimateidaho.com> 2016.

United States Census Bureau. <http://www.census.gov/> 2016.

United States Geological Survey. <https://www.usgs.gov> 2016.

Upper Lemhi Valley Chamber of Commerce. <www.leadorechamber.com> May 2016.

U.S. Bureau of Reclamation. <www.usbr.gov> May 2016.

U.S. Forest Service. <www.fs.fed.us> May 2016.

U.S. Parks. <http://www.us-parks.com/> 2016.

Utah Power in the Gem Valley and Grace. <http://www.graceidaho.com/html/utahpower.html> April 2016.

Visit Idaho. <https://visitidaho.org/> 2016.

“The War Mothers’ Organization in Elmore County.” Elmore County, Idaho: a proud part of the ID GenWeb Project. <http://elmore.idgenweb.org/Military/Mothers.html> April 2016.

Warner, Eva. Historical Sketch of Heyburn, Idaho: The Town that Refused to Die. Written March 1970. <http://heyburn.id.gov/index.asp?SEC=59AED487-1297-4A0D-B5FB6B8A80C30AB0&DE=5E77EFFE-88FA-4D41-AD99034E9E5D0C36&Type=B_PR> May 2016.

Washington County: The Heart of Idaho. “History of the County.” <http://co.washington.id.us/about-washington-county/> May 2016.

Water Archives. <http://www.waterarchives.org> August 2016.

The Weather Channel. <https://weather.com/> May 2016.

Weather Today. <www.weathertoday.net> July 2010.

Welcome to Glenns Ferry, Idaho: A Community of Opportunity! <http://glennsferryidaho.org> April 2016.

Welcome to Grace & Gem Valley: Grace Chamber of Commerce. <http://www.graceidaho.com> April 2016.

Wendell Chamber of Commerce: Hub City of Magic Valley. <http://www.wendellchamberofcommerce.org/> May 2016.

Western Regional Climate Center data <http://www.wrcc.dri.edu/> 2016.

Wheels That Won the West. <www.wheelsthatwonthewest.com> April 2016.

Wikipedia: the Free Encyclopedia. “Teton Dam.” <http://en.wikipedia.org/wiki/Teton_Dam> December 12, 2005.

---”Fort Hall” <https://en.wikipedia.org/wiki/Fort_Hall,_Idaho> 2005.

---”Notus, Idaho.” <https://en.wikipedia.org/wiki/Notus,_Idaho> 2016.

---”Oregon Shortline Railroad.” <https://en.wikipedia.org/wiki/Oregon_Short_Line_Railroad> 2016.

---”Pend Oreille County, Washington.” <https://en.wikipedia.org/wiki/Pend_Oreille_County%2C_Washington> August 2010.

Wolf Education & Research Center. <http://wolfcenter.org/> 2016.

Interviews:

Baker, Laurie, Eagle Historical Museum.
Bath, Teri, Eagle Chamber of Commerce.
Banner, Kent.
Bentz, Laurice.
Bergmann, Sharon, City of Eagle City Clerk.
Blanchard, Tom.
Brown, David.
Buster, Dick, Environmental Protection Specialist. September 2005.
Cada, Dave.
Carnegie, Amy.
Clark, Walter E., history of Georgetown, Idaho.
Collard, Mark.
Coyner, Barbara.
Crosby, Wayne.
Dahl, Melanie.
Everett, Kelly.
Fiori, Frank A.
Fisher, Betty.
Friend Dan, City of Eagle Fire Chief.
Gibson, Mike, Business Manager, Jerome School District.
Gillerman, Dr. Virginia, Economic Geologist/Associate Research Geologist, Idaho Geological Survey.
Good, Austin. Oral History.
Goodman, Don. Oral History.
Guerber, Steve, Former Eagle City Council member.
Hart, Arthur A., historian.
Hatzenbuhler, Ron, ISU Professor.
Hays, Sam H. Oral History.
Henderson, Ray, Minerals Specialist, U.S. Forest Service. September 2005.
Hiller, John.
Hopkins, Terry, First American Title.
House, Rod, Idaho State Archives/Historic Records Center.
Hatzenbuhler, Ron, ISU Professor.
Jackson, Kathy, Reubens City Clerk.
Jatkevicius, Jim. Boise Public Library.
Kenyon, Dale.
Kesler, Kelly.
Kunau, Lex.
Lierman, Amy. Public Relations, Idaho Transportation Dept. “History of I-84 US93 and Hwy 25.” April 26, 2006.
Marshall, Ron.
Matheson, John.
Mendiola, Judy.

Merrill, Nancy, Former Eagle Mayor.

Miller, Amy.

Miller, Wendy.

Moldenhauer, Rocky and Dawn.

Moser, Lynn, Eagle Sewer District.

Ogden, Jerry.

Parrish-Manwaring, Angelyn.

Peak, Clifford.

Porath, Mrs.

Pruett, Jimmy J.

Richardson, Greg.

Rupe, Kevin.

Sales, Dorothy.

Scott, Diane, Eagle Historical Preservation Commission.

Sims, Larry, Hauser Fire Chief.

Standley, Carla, a historian writing a book about the PI&N Railroad and a general historian and researcher of Meadows Valley.

Stephens, Dick, 1964.

Stevens, Louise Powers, September 29, 1994.

Thomasen, Everta. February 26, 2007.

Trent, Geneva, Eagle Historical Museum.

Urquidi, Richard.

Utt, Edith.

Valantine, Virgil.

Wallace, Doris, EISF Manager, 2005.

Ward, Opal.

Wiggers, Gene, Chief Pocatello Project. 2008.

Made in the USA
Monee, IL
19 February 2021

60039957R00312